Lecture Notes in Computer Science 5904

Zhenjiang Hu (Ed.)

Programming Languages and Systems

7th Asian Symposium, APLAS 2009
Seoul, Korea, December 14-16, 2009
Proceedings

Springer

Volume Editor

Zhenjiang Hu
Information Systems Architecture Research Division
National Institute of Informatics (NII)
2-1-2 Hitotsubashi, Chiyoda-ku, Tokyo 101-8430, Japan
E-mail: hu@nii.ac.jp

Library of Congress Control Number: 2009939533

CR Subject Classification (1998): D.3, D.2, F.3, D.4, D.1, F.4.1

LNCS Sublibrary: SL 2 – Programming and Software Engineering

ISSN	0302-9743
ISBN-10	3-642-10671-4 Springer Berlin Heidelberg New York
ISBN-13	978-3-642-10671-2 Springer Berlin Heidelberg New York

springer.com

Printed in Germany

Typesetting: Camera-ready by author, data conversion by Scientific Publishing Services, Chennai, India
Printed on acid-free paper SPIN: 12802777 06/3180 5 4 3 2 1 0

Preface

This volume contains the proceedings of the 7th Asian Symposium on Programming Languages and Systems (APLAS 2009) held in Seoul, Korea, December 14–16, 2009. The symposium was sponsored by the Asian Association for Foundation of Software (AAFS), Research on Software Analysis for Error-free Computing (ROSAEC) Center of Seoul National University, and SIGPL of Korean Institute of Information Scientists and Engineers.

Following our call for papers, 56 full submissions from 18 countries were received. Each paper was reviewed by at least three Program Committee members with the help of external reviewers. The Program Committee meeting was conducted electronically over a period of two weeks in August 2009. As a result of active discussions, 21 papers (37.5%) were selected. I would like to thank all the members of the APLAS 2009 Program Committee for the tremendous effort they put into their reviews and deliberations, and all the external reviewers for their invaluable contributions. The submission and review process was managed using the EasyChair system.

In addition to the 21 contributed papers, the symposium also featured three invited talks by Koen Claessen (Chalmers University of Technology, Sweden), Naoki Kobayashi (Tohoku University, Japan), and Armando Solar-Lezama (Massachusetts Institute of Technology, USA).

Many people helped to promote APLAS as a high-quality forum in Asia to serve program language researchers worldwide. Following a series of well-attended workshops that were held in Shanghai (2002), Daejeon (2001) and Singapore (2000), the past formal APLAS symposiums were successfully held in Bangalore (2008), Singapore (2007), Sydney (2006), Tsukuba (2005), Taipei (2004) and Beijing (2003). Proceedings of the past formal symposiums were published by Springer as LNCS 5356, 4807, 4279, 3780, 3302 and 2895.

I am grateful to the General Chair, Kwangkeun Yi, for his invaluable support and guidance that made our symposium in Seoul possible and enjoyable. I am also indebted to the local organizers, notably Gyesik Lee and Jungsuk Kang, for their considerable effort in planning and organizing the meeting itself. I thank Kiminori Matsuzaki for serving as the Poster Session Chair. Last but not least, I would like to thank the AAFS Chairs, Atsushi Ohori and Joxan Jaffar, and the Program Chairs of the past APLAS symposiums, especially Ganesan Ramalingam, for their advice.

December 2009 Zhenjiang Hu

Organization

General Chair

Kwangkeun Yi	Seoul National University, Korea

Program Chair

Zhenjiang Hu	National Institute of Informatics, Japan

Program Committee

Manuel M.T. Chakravarty	University of New South Wales, Australia
Wei-Ngan Chin	National University of Singapore, Singapore
Nate Foster	University of Pennsylvania, USA
Ralf Hinze	University of Oxford, UK
Zhenjiang Hu	National Institute of Informatics, Japan
Ik-Soon Kim	Electronics and Telecommunications Research Institute, Korea
Julia Lawall	DIKU, Denmark
Sebastian Maneth	NICTA/University of New South Wales, Australia
Sungwoo Park	Pohang University of Science and Technology, Korea
Ganesan Ramalingam	Microsoft Research, India
Chung-chieh Shan	Rutgers University, USA
Kazushige Terui	Kyoto University, Japan
Peter Thiemann	University of Freiburg, Germany
Kazunori Ueda	Waseda University, Japan
Janis Voigtländer	Technical University of Dresden, Germany
Bow-Yaw Wang	Academia Sinica, Taiwan
Jianjun Zhao	Shanghai Jiaotong University, China

Local Arrangements Chair

Gyesik Lee	Seoul National University, Korea

Poster Session Chair

Kiminori Matsuzaki	Kochi University of Technology, Japan

External Referees

Kazuyuki Asada
Gilles Barthe
Michele Basaldella
Annette Bieniusa
Aaron Bohannon
Avik Chaudhuri
Florin Craciun
Vijay D'silva
Gabriel Ditu
Derek Dreyer
Patrick Eugster
João Paulo Fernandes
Chunfeng Gao
Cristian Gherghina
Paul Govereau
Clemens Grelck
Bhargav Gulavani
Tom Harper
Guanhua He
Aquinas Hobor
Petra Hofstedt
Hans Hüttel
Daniel James
Neil Jones
Gabriele Keller
Andrew Kennedy
Uday Khedker
Taeho Kim
Oleg Kiselyov
Naoki Kobayashi
Rafal Kolanski
Akash Lal
Martin Lange
Roman Leshchinskiy
Paul Levy
Guoqiang Li
Daniel R Licata
Yu-Seung Ma
Andreas Maletti
Matthieu Martel
Karl Mazurak
Trevor McDonell
Eric Monfroy
Kenichi Morita
Keisuke Nakano
Huu Hai Nguyen
Aditya Nori
Bruno C.D.S. Oliveira
Scott Owens
Matthew Parkinson
Ross Paterson
Frank Pfenning
Alexandre Pilkiewicz
Andrew Pitts
Corneliu Popeea
Maurizio Proietti
Alan Schmitt
Tom Schrijvers
Qiang Sun
Josef Svenningsson
Jeffrey Vaughan
Jérôme Vouillon
Meng Wang
Baltasar Trancón-y-Widemann
Simon Winwood
Hongseok Yang
Taiichi Yuasa
Ping Zhu

Table of Contents

Separation Logic

Logic and Foundation Theory

Software Security and Verification

The Twilight Zone: From Testing to Formal Specifications and Back Again

Koen Claessen

Chalmers University of Technology, Gothenburg, Sweden
koen@chalmers.se

Talk Abstract

This talk aims to shine some light on the grey area that lies in between two related but different topics: testing and formal specifications. Testing is the most widely used verification method used by software developers of all walks of life; formal specifications are an unambiguous means of stating what software should do and not do.

The red thread going through the talk is the popular property-based testing tool QuickCheck. QuickCheck uses random testing to check formal specifications that are written in a restricted executable logic, producing minimal counter examples to failing properties. Thus, using QuickCheck we generalize the act of executing a specific test case against a specific expected behavior, to the act of executing many automatically generated test cases against a general specification.

This is a very powerful method, but it also introduces a number of issues. Firstly, where does the general specification come from? Often, just formally specifying software seems equally hard as implementing it! Secondly, how should a general specification be expressed as a testable property? Thirdly, what test data should we generate?

The talk contains ongoing work in different efforts within our research group to deal with these issues: We are developing a companion tool to QuickCheck that uses random testing to automatically generate specifications from programs – a good starting point for a full formal specification of the program. We are looking at how we can systematize the path that starts from a high-level logical specification and that ends with an effective list of testable properties – this path often consists of non-trivial choices. We also have a way of calculating which particular kinds of test data polymorphic functions should be tested on.

Finally, the talk addresses some of the open questions that we do not have good answers to. In particular, we will see examples of software that is extremely hard to test effectively using methods that are known to us.

Z. Hu (Ed.): APLAS 2009, LNCS 5904, p. 1, 2009.

Types and Recursion Schemes for Higher-Order Program Verification

Naoki Kobayashi

Tohoku University

Abstract. Higher-order recursion schemes (recursion schemes, for short) are expressive grammars for describing infinite trees. The modal μ-calculus model checking problem for recursion schemes ("Given a recursion scheme G and a modal μ-calculus formula φ, does the tree generated by G satisfy φ?") has been a hot research topic in the theoretical community for recent years [1,2,3,4,5,6,7]. In 2006, it has been shown to be decidable, and n-EXPTIME complete (where n is the order of a recursion scheme) by Ong [5].

The model checking of recursion schemes has recently turned out to be a good basis for verification of higher-order functional programs, just as finite state model checking for programs with while-loops, and pushdown model checking for programs with first-order recursion. First, various program analysis/verification problems such as reachability, flow analysis, and resource usage verification (or equivalently, type-state checking) can be easily transformed into model-checking problems for recursion schemes [8]. Combined with a model checking algorithm for recursion schemes, this yields a sound, complete, and automated verification method for the simply-typed λ-calculus with recursion and finite base types such as booleans. Secondly, despite the extremely high worst-case time complexity (i.e. n-EXPTIME completeness) of the model checking problem for recursion schemes, our type-based model-checking algorithm [9] turned out to run reasonably fast for realistic programs. We have implemented a prototype model checker for recursion schemes TRecS, and are currently working to construct a software model checker for a subset of ML on top of it.

The talk will summarize our recent results [8,9,10,11] on the model checking of recursion schemes as well as its applications to higher-order program verification, and discuss future perspectives.

References

1. Knapik, T., Niwinski, D., Urzyczyn, P.: Deciding monadic theories of hyperalgebraic trees. In: Abramsky, S. (ed.) TLCA 2001. LNCS, vol. 2044, pp. 253–267. Springer, Heidelberg (2001)
2. Knapik, T., Niwinski, D., Urzyczyn, P.: Higher-order pushdown trees are easy. In: Nielsen, M., Engberg, U. (eds.) FOSSACS 2002. LNCS, vol. 2303, pp. 205–222. Springer, Heidelberg (2002)
3. Aehlig, K., de Miranda, J.G., Ong, C.-H.L.: The monadic second order theory of trees given by arbitrary level-two recursion schemes is decidable. In: Urzyczyn, P. (ed.) TLCA 2005. LNCS, vol. 3461, pp. 39–54. Springer, Heidelberg (2005)

Z. Hu (Ed.): APLAS 2009, LNCS 5904, pp. 2–3, 2009.

4. Knapik, T., Niwinski, D., Urzyczyn, P., Walukiewicz, I.: Unsafe grammars and panic automata. In: Caires, L., Italiano, G.F., Monteiro, L., Palamidessi, C., Yung, M. (eds.) ICALP 2005. LNCS, vol. 3580, pp. 1450–1461. Springer, Heidelberg (2005)
5. Ong, C.-H.L.: On model-checking trees generated by higher-order recursion schemes. In: LICS 2006, pp. 81–90. IEEE Computer Society Press, Los Alamitos (2006)
6. Aehlig, K.: A finite semantics of simply-typed lambda terms for infinite runs of automata. Logical Methods in Computer Science 3(3) (2007)
7. Hague, M., Murawski, A., Ong, C.-H.L., Serre, O.: Collapsible pushdown automata and recursion schemes. In: Proceedings of 23rd Annual IEEE Symposium on Logic in Computer Science, pp. 452–461. IEEE Computer Society, Los Alamitos (2008)
8. Kobayashi, N.: Types and higher-order recursion schemes for verification of higher-order programs. In: Proceedings of POPL 2009, pp. 416–428 (2009)
9. Kobayashi, N.: Model-checking higher-order functions. In: Proceedings of PPDP 2009. ACM Press, New York (2009)
10. Kobayashi, N., Ong, C.-H.L.: Complexity of model checking recursion schemes for fragments of the modal mu-calculus. In: Albers, S., et al. (eds.) ICALP 2009. LNCS, vol. 5556, pp. 223–234. Springer, Heidelberg (2009)
11. Kobayashi, N., Ong, C.-H.L.: A type system equivalent to the modal mu-calculus model checking of higher-order recursion schemes. In: Proceedings of LICS 2009, pp. 179–188. IEEE Computer Society Press, Los Alamitos (2009)

The Sketching Approach to Program Synthesis

Armando Solar-Lezama

Massachusetts Institute of Technology

Abstract. Sketching is a new form of localized software synthesis that aims to bridge the gap between a programmer's high-level insights about a problem and the computer's ability to manage low-level details. In sketching, the programmer uses partial programs to describe the desired implementation *strategy*, and leaves the low-level details of the implementation to an automated synthesis procedure. This paper describes the sketching approach to program synthesis, including the details of the SKETCH language and synthesizer. The paper will then describe some of the techniques that make synthesis from sketches possible, and will close with a brief discussion of open problems in programmer guided synthesis.

1 Introduction

Sketching is a new form of localized program synthesis that allows programmers to express their high-level insights about a problem by writing a *sketch*—a partial program that encodes the structure of a solution while leaving its low-level details unspecified. In addition to the sketch, programmers provide the synthesizer with either a reference implementation or a set of test routines that the synthesized code must pass. The SKETCH synthesis engine is able to derive the missing details in the sketch to produce a working implementation that satisfies the correctness criteria established by the programmer. By combining the programmers insight expressed in the sketch with the synthesizer's ability to reason exhaustively about all the low-level details of the problem, sketching allows complex algorithms to be implemented with minimal human effort.

To illustrate the use of sketching on an interesting programming problem, consider the problem of reversing a linked list. It is relatively easy to write a recursive solution to this problem, but the performance of the simple implementation is likely to be unacceptable. A more efficient implementation must use a loop instead of recursion, and must construct the new list backwards to avoid the linear storage. Sketching allows the programmer to express these insights as a partial program without having to think too much about the details of the implementation.

The sketch for this problem is shown in Figure 1. The body of reverseEfficient encodes the basic structure of the solution: allocate a new list, and perform a series of conditional pointer assignments inside a while loop. In order to define the space of possible conditionals and assignments, the sketch uses regular expression notation to define sets of expressions in lines 1 to 3. The sketch, in short, encodes

Z. Hu (Ed.): APLAS 2009, LNCS 5904, pp. 4–13, 2009.

```
#define LHS {| tmp | (l | nl).(h | t)(.next)? |}
#define LOC {| LHS | null |}
#define COMP {| LOC ( == | != ) LOC |}

list reverseEfficient(list l){
    list nl = new list();
    node tmp = null;
    bit c = COMP;
    while(c){
            repeat(??)
               if( COMP ){ LHS = LOC; }
            c = COMP;
    }
}
```

```
// test harness
void main(int n){
  if(n >= N){ n = N-1; }
  node[N] nodes = null;
  list l = newList();
  //Populate the list, and
  //write its elements
  //to the nodes array
  populateList(n, l, nodes);

  l = reverseSK(l);

  //Check that node i in
  //the reversed list is
  //equal to nodes[n-i-1]
  check(n, l, nodes);
}
```

Fig. 1. Complete sketch and specification for the linked list reversal problem

everything that can be easily said about the implementation, and constrains the search space enough to make synthesis tractable.

Together with the sketch, the programmer must provide a specification that describes the correct behavior of the reversal routine. The SKETCH synthesizer allows the user to provide specifications in the form of parameterized or non-deterministic test harnesses. Figure 1 shows the test harness for the list reversal; the synthesizer will guarantee that the harness succeeds for all values of n¡N. On a laptop, the complete synthesis process takes less than a minute for N=4.

The sketching approach to synthesis applies just as effectively to concurrent programs, where the synthesizer's ability to orchestrate low-level details is even more desirable given the difficulty that programmers have in reasoning about the effects of different thread interleavings. To illustrate the use of sketching in this domain, consider the problem of implementing a barrier. A barrier is a synchronization mechanism that forces a group of threads to stop at a particular point in the program until all threads in the group have reached this point. Figure 2 shows the specification for a barrier. The specification is given as a simple test method where N threads repeatedly call the next method of the barrier. The test uses a two dimensional array to check that no thread races past the barrier before its left and right neighbors have reached the next method.

```
struct barrier{
  int nthreads; bit sense; bit[N] localSenses;
}
void main(){
   bit[N][T] grid = 0;
   barrier b = newBarrier(N);
   fork(int thread; N){
     for(int i=0; i<T; ++i){
       grid[i][thread] = 1;
       next(b, thread);
       assert grid[i][left(thread)] && grid[i][right(thread)];
}   }  }
```

Fig. 2. Specification for a sense reversing barrier

The goal of the synthesizer is to find an implementation of the next method that doesn't allow any thread interleavings under which the assertion might fail.

The sketch for the barrier is based on the following high-level insights from [1]. First, the barrier needs to be able to count how many threads have called next; in the sketch, this is done with a READ_AND_DEC instruction which reads the value of b.count into the local variable tmpCount and then decrements it. It's tempting to believe that threads can simply wait for the count to reach zero before continuing, but that doesn't work when the barrier is called from inside a loop; such a scheme would make it possible for a thread to go one full iteration around the loop before the counter has been reset, thus allowing the thread to go through the barrier a second time. This problem is resolved by the second insight: rather than waiting on the count, the barrier should keep a global sense bit; the barrier is released by reversing the sense bit; threads that go a full iteration around the loop will find the barrier with the inverted sense and will wait until the sense is reverted again.

```
#define VALUES {| lsense | b.nthreads | tmpCount | ??|}
#define BITVALUES {| (!)?(b.sense | lsense) | ?? |}
#define COND   {| ?? | (VALUES ( == | != ) VALUES) |}

static void next(barrier b, int thread){
    bit lsense = b.localSenses[thread];
    int tmpCount;


    READ_AND_DEC( b.count, tmpCount );

    reorder{
      if(COND ){ b.count = b.nthreads; }
      if( COND ){ b.sense = BITVALUES; }
      if( COND ){WAIT( {| b.sense (== | !=) lsense |}  )}
      if( COND ){ lsense = BITVALUES; }
    }
    b.localSenses[thread] = lsense;
}
```

Fig. 3. Complete sketch and for a sense reversing barrier

In order to express these insights in a sketch, the programmer starts by defining all the different operations that the thread might need to perform after reading and decrementing the counter. The next method must at some point do all of the following: a) reset the count, b) update the global sense, c) wait on the global sense, d) update the local sense. The programmer knows that the barrier will have to perform all of these operations, but it's not clear in what order or under what conditions. The sketch in Figure 3 expresses both the insight described so far, as well as the programmer's ignorance. All the actions listed before are listed in the sketch inside a `reorder` block. The `reorder` block reflects the programmer's ignorance about the correct order for these statements, giving the synthesizer the freedom to reorder them as necessary. Each statement in the `reorder` is guarded by an `if` statement, giving the synthesizer the freedom to select under what conditions each statement should execute. On a Core Duo

L9400 1.86GHz laptop, it takes the synthesizer less than three minutes to solve the sketch in Figure 3 and model check the solution to prove it correct for the bounded case where N=3 and T=3.

2 The Core Sketch Language

The SKETCH language is divided into two parts: the core SKETCH language [5], and a set of high-level constructs implemented as syntactic sugar on top of the core. The core SKETCH language is a simple imperative language extended with a single construct: a constant integer/boolean hole denoted by the symbol ??.

From the point of view of the core SKETCH language, the role of the synthesizer is to replace each integer hole with a suitable constant so that the resulting program will be correct according to the given correctness criteria. For example, consider the simple program in Figure 4. On the left of the figure, you can see the original sketch; the specification is simply the assertion in the code, and the correctness condition is that the assertion should be satisfied for all inputs within the bound specified by the synthesizer. On the right you can see the resulting code after the synthesizer has replaced the integer hole with a suitable constant. The synthesis process is simply a search for suitable integer constants.

```
int bar(int x){
    int t = x*??;
    assert t == x+x;
    return t;
}
```

```
int bar(int x){
    int t = x*2;
    assert t == x+x;
    return t;
}
```

Fig. 4. Simple illustration of the integer hole

The single integer hole is more powerful than it appears at first sight; by composing integer holes with other language constructs, it is possible to represent many interesting families of expressions. For example, in codes that manipulate arrays, it is common for array indexes to be affine functions of the loop induction variables. If an array access sits inside a loop-nest containing the induction variables i and j, we can represent the set of possible affine functions of i and j using integer holes as i*?? + j*?? + ??. It is also possible to combine integer holes with conditionals to express complex algorithmic choices. For example, consider the problem of swapping two bit-vectors x and y without using a temporary register. The insight is that the numbers can be swapped by assigning x xor y to x and y repeatedly in a clevery way. The challenge is to find the correct sequence of assignments. The insight, therefore, involves no integer constants, but the integer hole can still be used to encode it as illustrated by Figure 5. After replacing the integer holes with concrete values, the synthesizer performs a cleanup-pass to eliminate any control flow that may have been introduced solely for the purpose of giving choices to the synthesizer, so the resulting code looks like the program on the right of figure Figure 5.

```
//    sketch                                              //    solution
int swap(ref int x, ref int y){                           int swap(ref int x, ref int y){
    if(??){ x = x ^ y; } else{ y = x ^ y; }                   y = x ^ y;
    if(??){ x = x ^ y; } else{ y = x ^ y; }                   x = x ^ y;
    if(??){ x = x ^ y; } else{ y = x ^ y; }                   y = x ^ y;
}                                                         }
```

Fig. 5. Sketching a register-free swap using the integer hole

3 Syntactic Extensions

The core SKETCH language is like the assembly language of synthesis; it is expressive enough to describe arbitrarily complex sets of choices, but it is too low level for practical programming. The SKETCH language addresses this problem by defining a number of syntactic extensions to make it easier to write sketches such as those in Figures 1 or 3. The most important of these constructs are: a) the regular expression generators, b) the `repeat` statement, and c) the `reorder` block.

Regular expression generators. These constructs (hereafter Re-generators) allow the programmer to use a regular grammar to define families of expressions from which the synthesizer can chose the correct completion for a hole. RE-generators were used extensively in the sketches shown in Figures 1 or 3.

The Re-generator construct has the form {|e|}, where e is a regular expression. The regular expression can include choice $e_1|e_2$ as well as optional expressions e?. We purposely excluded Kleene closure because it increased the search space significantly without a clear programmability benefit.

The current version of the synthesizer implements Re-generators in a fairly straightforward manner. For Re-generators that are used as r-values, the synthesizer will enumerate all the expressions that can be generated from the regular expression e and use an integer hole to select which expression to use. So for example, the VALUES generator in Figure 3 is expanded into a conditional statement like the one shown below in Figure 6.

For generators that appear in an l-value, the idea is essentially the same; we enumerate the expressions defined by the generator and we use an integer

```
// {| lsense | b.nthreads | tmpCount | ??|}
// is replaced by rv, where rv is defined
// by the following block of code.
int t1 = ??;
assert t1<4;
int rv;
if(t1==0) rv = lsense;
else if(t1==1) rv = b.nthreads;
else if(t1==2) rv = tmpCount;
else rv = ??;
```

Fig. 6. Expanding a Re-generator

hole to decide which one to assign to. The strategy of fully expanding the set is inefficient, and in some sketches leads to excessive growth in the resulting intermediate representation; surprisingly, though, this simple strategy is sufficient to efficiently synthesize complex sketches such as the ones in Figures 1 and 3.

Repeat statement. The `repeat` statement was used in the sketch in Figure 1 to express the programmer's ignorance about how many assignments should be inside the body of the loop. In general, the statement `repeat`(n) c is equivalent to writing n different copies of the statement c. The key feature of the `repeat`, and what distinguishes it from a regular `for` loop, is that if the body c contains any holes, each copy of the body can be resolved to a different statement. For example, in the case of the `repeat` in Figure 1, the `repeat` will be expanded to n potentially different assignment statements.

The implementation of the `repeat` block is also relatively simple; the repeat statement is unrolled and the body replicated in a pre-processing phase. If the repeat count n is a hole, the repeat block is unrolled into a set of nested `if` statements, with the unroll factor determined by a command line flag.

Reorder block. The `reorder` block gives the synthesizer the freedom to decide the correct ordering for a set of statements. The most compelling use of `reorder` is to provide the synthesizer with a "soup" of statements that must be assembled into a correct implementation. It is particularly useful in concurrent sketches where the order of seemingly independent statements can be crucial to the correctness of an algorithm.

In order to implement the `reorder` block, we use a representation that is exponential in the number of statements, but is still surprisingly efficient. The basic idea is as follows. Suppose that we start with a list of m statements $s_0; \ldots ; s_{m-1}$, and we want to insert a statement s_m somewhere in the list. We can encode this easily in 2*m+1 statements as shown in Figure 7.

```
i=??;
if(i=0){ s_m;} s_0;
if(i=1) {s_m;} s_1;
...
if(i=m-1){ s_m;} s_{m-1};
if(i=m){ s_m; }
```

Fig. 7. Expanding a `reorder`

The sketch synthesizer uses this construction to recursively build a representation of the `reorder`. To do this, the synthesizer starts with statement s_0 and uses the construction above to add s_1 before or after it. Then, it repeats the process to insert s_2 into the resulting sequence; the same process is repeated to insert each subsequent statement. The resulting representation has 2^i copies of s_i, and requires on the order of n^2 control bits.

The reason why this is efficient is that most reorder blocks in sketches have at most a handful of expensive statements. The SKETCH implementation initially sorts the statements so that s_0 is the most expensive and s_n is the cheapest one, so the encoding ends up with only one copy of the most expensive statement and many copies of all the smaller ones.

Together, these high-level constructs allow programmers to express their insight about the structure of an implementation and the building blocks that should be used to construct it. The constructs allow programmers to reason in terms of "soups" of statements, and sets of expressions, instead of having to manually translate their insights into the core SKETCH language. At the same time, by compiling these constructs into the core language, the synthesizer gets the benefit of a simple uniform representation that is very well adapted to the available decision procedures.

4 Solving Sketches with Counterexample Guided Inductive Synthesis

Once the high-level constructs have been compiled down to the core SKETCH language, the synthesizer must find the correct values for all the holes in the sketch. Specifically, it must find values that will avoid assertion failures under all possible inputs, or in the case of concurrent sketches, under all possible thread interleavings.

In order to solve this problem, the SKETCH synthesizer relies on Counterexample Guided Inductive Synthesis (CEGIS). The key insight behind CEGIS is that it is often possible to find a small set of carefully selected inputs such that any implementation that works correctly for those inputs will work correctly in general.

The core of the algorithm is a constraint-based inductive synthesis procedure. From a sketch, the procedure builds a set of constraints $Q(x, c)$ such that Q will be true if and only if the sketch works correctly on input x when assigning value c to the holes (in general both x and c are vectors of values). The procedure also takes in a set $E = x_0, \ldots, x_i$ of concrete inputs (or parameters to the test harness) and produces a solution that is guaranteed to work correctly for all the inputs in the set. The inductive synthesis problem is much more tractable than the general synthesis problem, because the synthesizer doesn't have to reason about the behavior of the program under all possible inputs; only under the inputs provided.

In order for inductive synthesis to produce a correct answer, the system needs to a) have a mechanism to produce good inputs to drive the inductive synthesizer, and b) be able to decide when a correct solution has been discovered. CEGIS achieves these two goals by combining the inductive synthesizer with an automated validation procedure; a model checker in the case of SKETCH. The set of test inputs is seeded with a single random input, and the inductive synthesizer is asked to produce a candidate solution. The candidate is passed to the validator to decide whether the candidate is correct. If it is, then the algorithm has converged, and the program is returned. Otherwise, the validator produces a witness; a counterexample input that shows why the candidate is incorrect. This

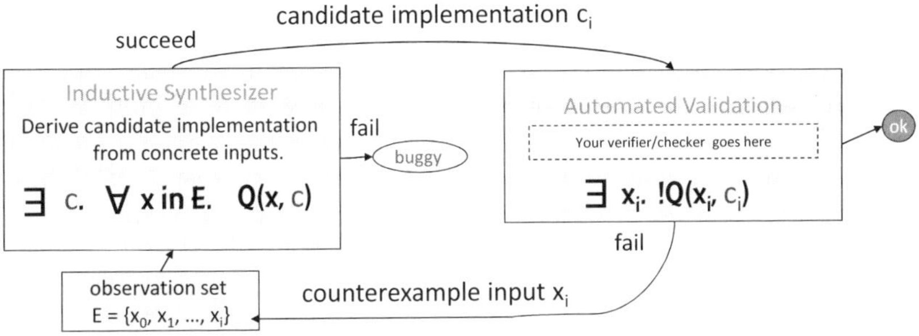

Fig. 8. Counterexample Guided Inductive Synthesis

witness is a perfect input to the inductive synthesizer, because it is guaranteed to cover an aspect of the implementation that none of the previous inputs were covering. Thus, by adding this input to the set of observations of the inductive synthesizer, the synthesis process moves forward, and a new solution is produced that is closer to the desired solution. The complete algorithm is illustrated in Figure 8.

In the case of concurrent sketches, the process is very similar; the key difference is that the validation procedure produces a trace rather than an input. This poses a challenge to the inductive synthesizer, which must use the counterexample trace to rule out not just the candidate that produced the trace, but any candidates that share the same problem. The details of how this is done can be found in [2] and [4], but the key idea is to extract from the counterexample trace precise information about the ordering of events that lead to the error. This information about the ordering of events is used to ensure that any candidate generated either avoids failure when those events are ordered in the same way, or rules out that ordering through the use of locking. Overall, the CEGIS procedure is remarkably effective at quickly producing enough good test inputs to get the inductive synthesizer to produce a correct solution.

5 Experience

A thorough evaluation of the Sketch synthesis engine for both sequential and concurrent programs can be found in [2]. Overall, we have been able to successfully synthesize the low-level details of algorithms in a variety of domains including ciphers, scientific computation, linked data-structures, as well as concurrent objects and data-structures. Despite the success of the tool, a number of important challenges remain in order to make program directed synthesis a standard tool in every programmer's toolkit.

Improving programmability. While the sketch language provides a handful of high-level constructs to help programmers express their insight without having to reason about the low-level details, the language is still too low-level for many domains. For example, for the body of the loop in the sketch from Figure 1, the programmer had to go through the very mechanical process of describing the set of memory locations that could be reached from the lists l and nl. We have found this process to be error prone, as it is easy for programmers to forget choices which turn out to be necessary to construct the solution; for example, many programmers might forget to include `null` in the set LOC. Moreover, when programmers make mistakes and their sketches cannot be solved, it can be difficult for them to find the problems, since debugging a partial program can be more difficult than debugging a concrete one.

A solution to these challenges will have to involve multiple facets, including higher level mechanisms for expressing insights so programmers make fewer errors, language constructs that allow for more interactive exploration of the space of solutions, and diagnostic mechanisms that can pinpoint errors in a sketch.

Exploiting Higher Level Insight. Another big challenge is improving the performance of synthesis by harnessing high-level insights, either about a specific program or about an entire domain. In the case of individual programs, we want to exploit high-level invariants that the programmer might know, in order to reduce the search space and make the synthesis more tractable.

In our PLDI 07 paper [3], we showed how synthesis could be made much more effective for programs in a particular domain by incorporating domain specific insight into the synthesizer. We believe such domain-specific insight can make an enormous difference. This will be particularly true in the case of parallelism. For parallel programs, reasoning about concurrency, and about the effect of all possible interleavings is extremely expensive. However, large classes of parallel programs are written in a very disciplined manner that prevents threads from non-deterministically modifying shared memory. Exploiting this discipline should allow for dramatic performance improvements in the synthesis of many concurrent programs.

Moving beyond semantic equivalence and safety. In many situations, programmers care about many other factors that go beyond functional correctness. Performance, for example, is a central consideration in many domains. Another closely related property involves statistical properties of an implementation. For example, a hash table will be correct regardless of the implementation of the hash function, but we would like the synthesizer to find an implementation that leads to a good distribution of keys. In some cases, some implementations may be preferred on purely aesthetic grounds; they are easier to read, or contain simpler control flow. The challenge is to develop synthesis strategies that can optimize on these non-functional criteria while still remaining tractable.

6 Conclusions

Sketch is part of a new breed of programmer guided synthesis tools that aim to make synthesis practical by exploiting the tremendous advances in program analysis and decision procedures over the last ten years, and combining them with the programmer's high-level insights. Another research effort in this area is the Paraglide project [7], which applies powerful domain specific algorithms to achieve programmer guided synthesis of concurrent data structures. Another notable effort in this direction is the work on proof theoretic synthesis by Srivastava et. al. which aims to use techniques from program verification to synthesize complex algorithms from sketch-like skeletons [6].

All of these tools attempt to create a synergy between the strengths of the human programmer and the power of modern analysis tools, with the ultimate goal of making it easier to design and program systems that are more reliable and efficient.

References

1. Herlihy, M., Shavit, N.: The art of multiprocessor programming. Morgan Kaufmann, San Francisco (2008)
2. Solar-Lezama, A.: Program Synthesis By Sketching. PhD thesis, EECS Dept., UC Berkeley (2008)
3. Solar-Lezama, A., Arnold, G., Tancau, L., Bodik, R., Saraswat, V., Seshia, S.: Sketching stencils. In: PLDI 2007: Proceedings of the 2007 ACM SIGPLAN conference on Programming language design and implementation, vol. 42, pp. 167–178. ACM, New York (2007)
4. Solar-Lezama, A., Jones, C., Arnold, G., Bodík, R.: Sketching concurrent datastructures. In: PLDI 2008 (2008)
5. Solar-Lezama, A., Tancau, L., Bodik, R., Saraswat, V., Seshia, S.: Combinatorial sketching for finite programs. In: ASPLOS 2006, San Jose, CA, USA. ACM Press, New York (2006)
6. Srivastava, S., Gulwani, S., Jeffrey, F.: From program verification to program synthesis. Submitted to POPL (2010)
7. Vechev, M., Yahav, E.: Deriving linearizable fine-grained concurrent objects. SIGPLAN Not. 43(6), 125–135 (2008)

Large Spurious Cycle in Global Static Analyses and Its Algorithmic Mitigation

Hakjoo Oh

School of Computer Science and Engineering
Seoul National University

Abstract. We present a simple algorithmic extension of the classical call-strings approach to mitigate substantial performance degradation caused by spurious interprocedural cycles. Spurious interprocedural cycles are, in a *realistic* setting, key reasons for why approximate call-return semantics in both context-sensitive and -insensitive static analysis can make the analysis much slower than expected.

In the traditional call-strings-based context-sensitive static analysis, because the number of distinguished contexts must be finite, multiple call-contexts are inevitably joined at the entry of a procedure and the output at the exit is propagated to multiple return-sites. We found that these multiple returns frequently create a single large cycle (we call it "butterfly cycle") covering almost all parts of the program and such a spurious cycle makes analyses very slow and inaccurate.

Our simple algorithmic technique (within the fixpoint iteration algorithm) identifies and prunes these spurious interprocedural flows. The technique's effectiveness is proven by experiments with a realistic C analyzer to reduce the analysis time by 7%-96%. Since the technique is *algorithmic*, it can be easily applicable to existing analyses without changing the underlying abstract semantics, it is orthogonal to the underlying abstract semantics' context-sensitivity, and its correctness is obvious.

1 Introduction

In a global semantic-based static analysis, it is inevitable to follow some spurious (unrealizable or invalid) return paths. Even when the underlying abstract semantics is context-sensitive, because the number of distinguished contexts must be finite, multiple call-contexts are joined at the entry of a procedure and the output at the exit are propagated to multiple return-sites. For example, in a conventional way of avoiding invalid return paths by distinguishing a finite $k \geq 0$ call-sites to each procedure, the analysis is doomed to still follow spurious paths if the input program's nested call-depth is larger than the k. Increasing the k to remove more spurious paths quickly hits a limit in practice because of the increasing analysis cost in memory and time.

In this article we present the following:

- in a realistic setting, these multiple returns often create a single large flow cycle (we call it "butterfly cycle") covering almost all parts of the program,

Z. Hu (Ed.): APLAS 2009, LNCS 5904, pp. 14–29, 2009.

- such big spurious cycles make the conventional call-strings method that distinguishes the last k call-sites [14] very slow and inaccurate,
- this performance problem can be relieved by a simple extension of the call-strings method,
- our extension is an algorithmic technique within the worklist-based fixpoint iteration routine, without redesigning the underlying abstract semantics, and
- the algorithmic technique works regardless of the underlying abstract semantics' context-sensitivity. The technique consistently saves the analysis time, without sacrificing (or with even improving) the analysis precision.

1.1 Problem: Large Performance Degradation By Inevitable, Spurious Interprocedural Cycles

Static analysis' inevitable spurious paths make spurious cycles across procedure boundaries in global analysis. For example, consider the semantic equations in Fig 1 that (context-insensitively ($k > 0$)) abstract two consecutive calls to a procedure. The system of equations says to evaluate equation (4) and (6) for every return-site after analyzing the called procedure body (equation (3)). Thus, solving the equations follows a cycle: (2) $\rightarrow$ (3) $\rightarrow$ (4) $\rightarrow$ (5) $\rightarrow$ (2) $\rightarrow \cdots$.

Such spurious cycles degrade the analysis performance both in precision and speed. Spurious cycles exacerbate the analysis imprecision because they model spurious information flow. Spurious cycles degrade the analysis speed too because solving cyclic equations repeatedly applies the equations in vain until a fixpoint is reached.

The performance degradation becomes dramatic when the involved interprocedural spurious cycles cover a large part of the input program. This is indeed the case in reality. In analyzing real C programs, we observed that the analysis follows (Section 2) a single large cycle that spans almost all parts of the input program. Such spurious cycles size can also be estimated by just measuring the strongly connected components (scc) in the "lexical"[1] control flow graphs. Table 1 shows the sizes of the largest scc in some open-source programs.[2] In most programs, such cycles cover most (80-90%) parts of the programs. Hence, globally analyzing a program is likely to compute a fixpoint of a function that describes almost all parts of the input program. Even when we do context-sensitive analysis ($k > 0$), large spurious cycles are likely to remain (Section 2).

1.2 Solution: An Algorithmic Mitigation without Redesigning Abstract Semantics

We present a simple algorithmic technique inside a worklist-based fixpoint iteration procedure that, without redesigning the abstract semantics part, can

---

[1] One node per lexical entity, ignoring function pointers.

[2] We measured the sizes of all possible cycles in the flow graphs. Note that interprocedural cycles happen because of either spurious returns or recursive calls. Because recursive calls in the test C programs are immediate or spans only a small number of procedures, large interprocedural cycles are likely to be spurious ones.

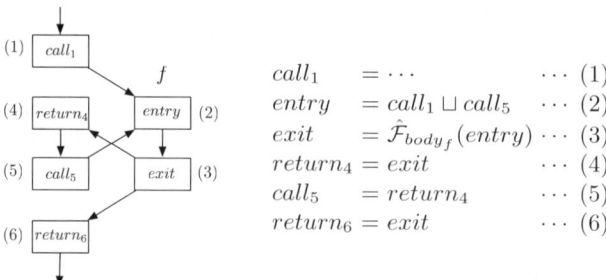

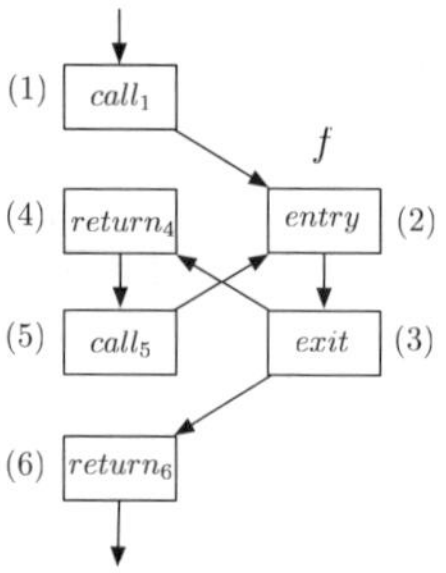

$$
\begin{aligned}
call_1 &= \cdots & \cdots (1)\\
entry &= call_1 \sqcup call_5 & \cdots (2)\\
exit &= \hat{\mathcal{F}}_{body_f}(entry) & \cdots (3)\\
return_4 &= exit & \cdots (4)\\
call_5 &= return_4 & \cdots (5)\\
return_6 &= exit & \cdots (6)
\end{aligned}
$$

Fig. 1. Spurious cycles because of abstract procedure calls and returns. The right-hand side is a system of equations and the left-hand side shows the dependences between the equations. Note a dependence cycle $(2) \to (3) \to (4) \to (5) \to (2) \to \cdots$.

effectively relieve the performance degradation caused by spurious interprocedural cycles in both context-sensitive ($k > 0$) and -insensitive ($k = 0$) analysis.

While solving flow equations, the algorithmic technique simply forces procedures to return to their corresponding called site, in order not to follow the last edge (edge $(3) \to (4)$ in Fig 1) of the "butterfly" cycles. In order to enforce this, we control the equation-solving orders so that each called procedure is analyzed exclusively for its one particular call-site. To be safe, we apply our algorithm to only non-recursive procedures.

Consider the equation system in Fig 1 again and think of a middle of the analysis (equation-solving) sequence, $\cdots \to (5) \to (2) \to (3)$, which indicates that the analysis of procedure f is invoked from (5) and is now finished. After the evaluation of (3), a classical worklist algorithm inserts all the equations, (4) and (6), that depend on (3). But, if we remember the fact that f has been invoked from (5) and the other call-site (1) has not invoked the procedure until the analysis of f finishes, we can know that continuing with (4) is useless, because the current analysis of f is only related to (5), but not to other calls like (1). So, we process only (6), pruning the spurious sequence $(3) \to (4) \to \cdots$.

We integrated the algorithm inside an industrialized abstract-interpretation-based C static analyzer [5,6] and measured performance gains derived from avoiding spurious cycles. We have saved 7%-96% of the analysis time for context-insensitive or -sensitive global analysis for open-source benchmarks.

1.3 Contributions

- We present a simple extension of the classical call-strings approach, which effectively reduces the inefficiency caused by large, inevitable, spurious interprocedural cycles.

  We prove the effectiveness of the technique by experiments with an industrial-strength C static analyzer [5,6] in globally analyzing medium-scale open-source programs.

Table 1. The sizes of the largest strongly-connected components in the "lexical" control flow graphs of real C programs. In most cases, most procedures and nodes in program belong to a single cycle.

Program	Procedures in the largest cycle	Basic-blocks in the largest cycle
spell-1.0	24/31(77%)	751/782(95%)
gzip-1.2.4a	100/135(74%)	5,988/6,271(95%)
sed-4.0.8	230/294(78%)	14,559/14,976(97%)
tar-1.13	205/222(92%)	10,194/10,800(94%)
wget-1.9	346/434(80%)	15,249/16,544(92%)
bison-1.875	410/832(49%)	12,558/18,110(69%)
proftpd-1.3.1	940/1,096(85%)	35,386/41,062(86%)

- The technique is meaningful in two ways. Firstly, the technique aims to alleviate one major reason (spurious interprocedural cycles) for substantial inefficiency in global static analysis.

  Secondly, it is purely an algorithmic technique inside the worklist-based fixpoint iteration routine. So, it can be directly applicable without changing the analysis' underlying abstract semantics, regardless of whether the semantics is context-sensitive or not. The technique's correctness is obvious enough to avoid the burden of a safety proof that would be needed if we newly designed the abstract semantics.
- We report one key reason (spurious interprocedural cycles) for why less accurate context-sensitivity actually makes the analyses very slow. Though it is well-known folklore that less precise analysis does not always have less cost [10,12], there haven't been realistic experiments about the explicit reason.

1.4 Related Work

We compare, on the basis of their applicability to general semantic-based static analyzers[3], our method with other approaches that eliminate invalid paths.

The classical call-strings approach that retains the last k call-sites [14,1,9,10] is popular in practice but its precision is not enough to mitigate large spurious cycles. This k-limiting method is widely used in practice [1,9,10] and actually it is one of very few options available for semantic-based global static analysis that uses infinite domains and non-distributive flow functions (e.g., [1,6]). The k-limiting method induces a large spurious cycle because it permits multiple returns of procedures. Our algorithm is an extension of the k-limiting method and adds extra precision that relieves the performance problem from spurious interprocedural cycles.

[3] For example, such analyzers include octagon-based analyzers (e.g.,[2]), interval-based analyzers (e.g.,[5,6]), value set analysis [1], and program analyzer generators (e.g, [9]), which usually use infinite (height) domains and non-distributive flow functions.

Another approximate call-strings method that uses full context-sensitivity for non-recursive procedures and treats recursive call cycles as gotos is practical for points-to analysis [15,16] but, the method is too costly for more general semantic-based analysis. Though these approaches are more precise than k-limiting method, it is unknown whether the BDD-based method [16] or regular-reachability [15] are also applicable in practice to general semantic-based analyzers rather than pointer analysis. Our algorithm can be useful for analyses for which these approaches hit a limit in practice and k-limiting is required.

Full call-strings approaches [14,7,8] and functional approaches [14] do not suffer from spurious cycles but are limited to restricted classes of data flow analysis problems. The original full call-strings method [14] prescribes the domain to be finite and its improved algorithms [7,8] are also limited to bit-vector problems or finite domains. Khedker et al.'s algorithm [8] supports infinite domains only for demand-driven analysis. The purely functional approach [14] requires compact representations of flow functions. The iterative (functional) approach [14] requires the domain to be finite.

Reps et al.'s algorithms [11,13] to avoid unrealizable paths are limited to analysis problems that can be expressed only in their graph reachability framework. Their algorithm cannot handle prevalent yet non-distributive analyses. For example, our analyzer that uses the interval domain with non-distributive flow functions does not fall into either their IFDS [11] or IDE [13] problems. Meanwhile, our algorithm is independent of the underlying abstract semantic functions. The regular-reachability [15], which is a restricted version of Reps et al.'s algorithm [11], also requires the analysis problem to be expressed in graph reachability problem.

Chambers et al.'s method [4] is similar to ours but entails a relatively large change to an existing worklist order. Their algorithm analyzes each procedure intraprocedurally, and at call-sites continues the analysis of the callee. It returns to analyze the nodes of the caller only after finishing the analysis of the callee. Our worklist prioritizes the callee only over the call nodes that invoke the callee, not the entire caller, which is a relatively smaller change than Chambers et al.'s method. In addition, they assume worst case results for recursive calls, but we do not degrade the analysis precision for recursive calls.

2 Performance Problems Due to Large Spurious Cycles

If a spurious cycle is created by multiple calls to a procedure f, then all the procedures that are reachable from f or that reach f via the call-graph belong to the cycle because of call and return flows. For example, consider a call-chain $\cdots f_1 \rightarrow f_2 \cdots$. If f_1 calls f_2 multiple times, creating a spurious butterfly cycle $f_1 \bowtie f_2$ between them, then fixpoint-solving the cycle involves all the nodes of procedures that reach f_1 or that are reachable from f_2. This situation is common in C programs. For example, in GNU software, the `xmalloc` procedure, which is in charge of memory allocation, is called from many other procedures, and hence generates a butterfly cycle. Then every procedure that reaches `xmalloc` via the call-graph is trapped into a fixpoint cycle.

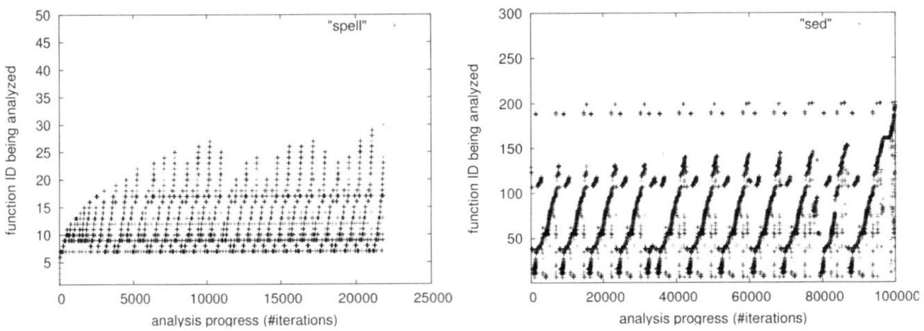

spell-1.0 (total #procs:31)
(2,213 LOC, > 30 repetitions)

sed-4.0.8 (total #procs:294)
(26,807 LOC, > 150 repetitions)

Fig. 2. Analysis localities. Because of butterfly cycles, similar patterns are repeated several times during the analysis and each pattern contains almost all parts of the programs.

In conventional context-sensitive analysis that distinguishes the last k call-sites [14], if there are call-chains of length l ($> k$) in programs, it's still possible to have a spurious cycle created during the first $l - k$ calls. This spurious cycle traps the last k procedures into a fixpoint cycle by the above reason.

One spurious cycle in a real C program can trap as many as 80-90% of basic blocks of the program into a fixpoint cycle. Fig 2 shows this phenomenon. In the figures, the x-axis represents the execution time of the analysis and the y-axis represents the procedure name, which is mapped to unique integers. During the analysis, we draw the graph by plotting the point (t, f) if the analysis' worklist algorithm visits a node of procedure f at the time t. For brevity, the graph for sed-4.0.8 is shown only up to 100,000 iterations among more than 3,000,000 total iterations. From the results, we first observe that similar patterns are repeated and each pattern contains almost all procedures in the program. And we find that there are much more repetitions in the case of a large program (sed-4.0.8, 26,807 LOC) than a small one (spell-1.0, 2,213 LOC): more than 150 repeated iterations were required to analyze sed-4.0.8 whereas spell-1.0 needed about 30 repetitions.

3 Our Algorithmic Mitigation Technique

In this section, we describe our algorithmic technique. We first describe the traditional call-strings-based analysis algorithm (section 3.1). Then we present our algorithmic extension of the classical algorithm (section 3.2).

We assume that a program is represented by a supergraph [11]. A supergraph consists of control flow graphs of procedures with interprocedural edges connecting each call-site to its callee. Each node $n \in Node$ in the graph has one of the five types :

$$entry_f \mid exit_f \mid call_f^{g,r} \mid rtn_f^c \mid cmd_f$$

The subscript f of each node represents the procedure name enclosing the node. $entry_f$ and $exit_f$ are entry and exit nodes of procedure f. A call-site in a program is represented by a call node and its corresponding return node. A call node $call_f^{g,r}$ indicates that it invokes a procedure g and its corresponding return node is r. We assume that function pointers are resolved (before the analysis). Node rtn_f^c represents a return node in f whose corresponding call node is c. Node cmd_f represents a general command statement. Edges are assembled by a function, succof, which maps each node to its successors. *CallNode* is the set of call nodes in a program.

3.1 Normal$_k$: A Normal Call-Strings-Based Analysis Algorithm

Call-strings are sequences of call nodes. To make them finite, we only consider call-strings of length at most k for some fixed integer $k \geq 0$. We write $CallNode^{\leq k} \stackrel{\text{let}}{=} \Delta$ for the set of call-strings of length $\leq k$. We write $[c_1, c_2, \cdots, c_i]$ for a call-string of call sequence $c_1, c_2, \cdots, c_i$. Given a call-string δ and a call node c, $[\delta, c]$ denotes a call-string obtained by appending c to δ. In the case of context-insensitive analysis ($k = 0$), we use $\Delta = \{\epsilon\}$, where the empty call-string ϵ means no context-information.

Fig 3.(a) shows the worklist-based fixpoint iteration algorithm that performs call-strings(Δ)-based context-sensitive (or insensitive, when $k = 0$) analysis. The algorithm computes a table $\mathcal{T} \in Node \rightarrow State$ which associates each node with its input state $State = \Delta \rightarrow Mem$, where Mem denotes abstract memory, which is a map from program variables to abstract values. That is, call-strings are tagged to the abstract memories and are used to distinguish the memories propagated along different interprocedural paths, to a limited extent (the last k call-sites). The worklist $\mathcal{W}$ consists of node and call-string pairs. The algorithm chooses a work-item $(n, \delta) \in Node \times \Delta$ from the worklist and evaluates the node n with the flow function $\hat{\mathcal{F}}$. Next work-items to be inserted into the worklist are defined by the function $\mathcal{N} \in Node \times \Delta \rightarrow 2^{Node \times \Delta}$:

$$\mathcal{N}(n, \delta) = \begin{cases} \{(r, \delta') \mid \delta = \lceil \delta', call_f^{g,r} \rceil_k \wedge \delta' \in \mathsf{dom}(\mathcal{T}(call_f^{g,r}))\} & \text{if } n = exit_g \\ \{(entry_g, \lceil \delta, n \rceil_k))\} & \text{if } n = call_f^{g,r} \\ \{(n', \delta) \mid n' \in \mathsf{succof}(n)\} & \text{otherwise} \end{cases}$$

where $\mathsf{dom}(f)$ denotes the domain of map f and $\lceil \delta, c \rceil_k$ denotes the call-string $[\delta, c]$ but possibly truncated so as to keep at most the last k call-sites.

The algorithm can follow spurious return paths if the input program's nested call-depth is larger than the k. The mapping δ' to $\lceil \delta', call_f^{g,r} \rceil_k$ is not one-to-one and $\mathcal{N}$ possibly returns many work-items at an exit node.

We call the algorithm Normal$_k$($k = 0, 1, 2, \ldots$). Normal$_0$ performs context-insensitive analysis, Normal$_1$ performs context-sensitive analysis that distinguishes the last 1 call-site, and so on.

3.2 Normal$_k$/RSS: Our Algorithm

Definition 1. *When a procedure g is called from a call node $call_f^{g,r}$ under context δ, we say that $(call_f^{g,r}, \delta)$ is the call-context for that procedure call. Since* *each call node* $call_f^{g,r}$ *has a unique return node, we interchangeably write* (r, δ) *and* $(call_f^{g,r}, \delta)$ *for the same call-context.*

Our return-site-sensitive (RSS) technique is simple. When calling a procedure at a call-site, the call-context for that call is remembered until the procedure returns. The bookkeeping cost is limited to only one memory entry per procedure. This is possible by the following strategies:

1. **Single return:** Whenever the analysis of a procedure g is started from a call node $call_f^{g,r}$ in f under call-string δ, the algorithm remembers its call-context (r, δ), consisting of the corresponding return node r and the call-string δ. And upon finishing analyzing g's body, after evaluating $exit_g$, the algorithm inserts only the remembered return node and its call-string (r, δ) into the worklist. Multiple returns are avoided. For correctness, this single return should be allowed only when other call nodes that call g are not analyzed until the analysis of g from $(call_f^{g,r}, \delta)$ completes.
2. **One call per procedure, exclusively:** We implement the single return policy by using one memory entry per procedure to remember the call-context. This is possible if we can analyze each called procedure exclusively for its one particular call-context. If a procedure is being analyzed from a call node c with a call-string δ, processing all the other calls that call the same procedure should wait until the analysis of the procedure from (c, δ) is completely finished. This one-exclusive-call-per-procedure policy is enforced by not selecting from the worklist other call nodes that (directly or transitively) call the procedures that are currently being analyzed.
3. **Recursion handling:** The algorithm gives up the single return policy for recursive procedures. This is because we cannot finish analyzing recursive procedure body without considering other calls (recursive calls) in it. Recursive procedures are handled in the same way as the normal worklist algorithm.

The algorithm does not follow spurious return paths regardless of the program's nested call-depth. While Normal_k starts losing its power when a call chain's length is larger than k, $\mathsf{Normal}_k/\mathsf{RSS}$ does not. The following example shows this difference between Normal_k and $\mathsf{Normal}_k/\mathsf{RSS}$.

Example 1. Consider a program that has the following call-chain (where $f_1 \overset{c_1,c_2}{\rightarrow} f_2$ denotes that f_1 calls f_2 at call-sites c_1 and c_2) and suppose $k = 1$:

$$f_1 \overset{c_1,c_2}{\rightarrow} f_2 \overset{c_3,c_4}{\rightarrow} f_3$$

– Normal_1: The analysis results for f_2 are distinguished by $[c_1]$ and $[c_2]$ hence no butterfly cycle happens between f_1 and f_2. Now, when f_3 is called from f_2 at c_3, we have two call-contexts $(c_3, [c_1])$ and $(c_3, [c_2])$ but analyzing f_3 proceeds with context $[c_3]$ (because $k = 1$). That is, Normal_k forgets the call-context for procedure f_3. Thus the result of analyzing f_3 must flow back to all call-contexts with return site c_3, i.e., to both the call-contexts $(c_3, [c_1])$ and $(c_3, [c_2])$.

– $\mathsf{Normal}_1/\mathsf{RSS}$: The results for f_2 and f_3 are distinguished in the same way as Normal_1. But, $\mathsf{Normal}_1/\mathsf{RSS}$ additionally remembers the call-contexts for every procedure call. If f_3 was called from c_3 under context $[c_1]$, our algorithmic technique forces Normal_k to remember the call-context $(c_3, [c_1])$ for that procedure call. And finishing analyzing f_3's body, f_3 returns only to the remembered call-context $(c_3, [c_1])$. This is possible by the one-exclusive-call-per-procedure policy.

We ensure the one-exclusive-call-per-procedure policy by prioritizing a callee over call-sites that (directly or transitively) invoke the callee. The algorithm always analyzes the nodes of the callee g first prior to any other call nodes that invoke g: before selecting a work-item as a next job, we exclude from the worklist every call node $call_f^{g,r}$ to g if the worklist contains any node of procedure h that can be reached from g along some call-chain $g \to \cdots \to h$, including the case of $g = h$. After excluding such call nodes, the algorithm chooses a work-item in the same way as a normal worklist algorithm.

Example 2. Consider a worklist $\{(call_f^{g,r_1},\delta_1),(call_g^{h,r_2}, \delta_2), (n_h, \delta_3), (call_h^{i,r_4}, \delta_4)\}$ and assume there is a path $f \to g \to h$ in the call graph. When choosing a work-item from the worklist, our algorithm first excludes all the call nodes that invoke procedures now being analyzed: $call_g^{h,r_2}$ is excluded because h's node n_h is in the worklist. Similarly, $call_f^{g,r_1}$ is excluded because there is a call-chain $g \to h$ in the call graph and h's node n_h exists. So, the algorithm chooses a work-item from $\{(n_h, \delta_3), (call_h^{i,r_4}, \delta_4)\}$. The excluded work-items $(call_f^{g,r_1}, \delta_1)$ and $(call_g^{h,r_2}, \delta_2)$ will not be selected unless there are no nodes of h in the worklist.

Fig 3(b) shows our algorithmic technique that is applied to the normal worklist algorithm of Fig 3(a). To transform Normal_k into $\mathsf{Normal}_k/\mathsf{RSS}$, only shaded lines are inserted; other parts remain the same. *ReturnSite* is a map to record a single return site information (return node and context pair) per procedure. Lines 15-16 are for remembering a single return when encountering a call-site. The algorithm checks if the current node is a call-node and its target procedure is non-recursive (the $\mathsf{recursive}$ predicate decides whether the procedure is recursive or not), and if so, it remembers its single return-site information for the callee. Lines 17-22 handle procedure returns. If the current node is an exit of a non-recursive procedure, only the remembered return for that procedure is used as a next work-item, instead of all possible next (successor, context) pairs (line 23). Prioritizing callee over call nodes is implemented by delaying call nodes to procedures now being analyzed. To do this, in line 12-13, the algorithm excludes the call nodes $\{(call_{\_}^{g,\_}, \_) \in \mathcal{W} \mid (n_h, \_) \in \mathcal{W} \wedge \mathsf{reach}(g, h) \wedge \neg\mathsf{recursive}(g)\}$ that invoke non-recursive procedures whose nodes are already contained in the current worklist. $\mathsf{reach}(g, h)$ is true if there is a path in the call graph from g to h.

Correctness and Precision. One noticeable thing is that the result of our algorithm is not a fixpoint of the given flow equation system, but still a sound approximation of the program semantics. Since the algorithm prunes some computation steps during worklist algorithm (at exit nodes of non-recursive procedures), the result of the algorithm may not be a fixpoint of the original equation

$(01):\ \delta \in Context = \Delta$
$(02):\ w \in Work = Node \times \Delta$
$(03):\ \mathcal{W} \in Worklist = 2^{Work}$
$(04):\ \mathcal{N} \in Node \times \Delta \to 2^{Node \times \Delta}$
$(05):\ State = \Delta \to Mem$
$(06):\ \mathcal{T} \in Table = Node \to State$
$(07):\ \hat{\mathcal{F}} \in Node \to Mem \to Mem$

$(09):\ FixpointIterate\ (\mathcal{W}, \mathcal{T}) =$

$(11):\ $ **repeat**

$(13):\quad (n, \delta) := \mathsf{choose}(\mathcal{W})$
$(14):\quad m := \hat{\mathcal{F}}\ n\ (\mathcal{T}(n)(\delta))$

$(23):\quad$ **for all** $(n', \delta') \in \mathcal{N}(n, \delta)$ **do**
$(24):\quad\quad$ **if** $m \not\sqsubseteq \mathcal{T}(n')(\delta')$
$(25):\quad\quad\quad \mathcal{W} := \mathcal{W} \cup \{(n', \delta')\}$
$(26):\quad\quad\quad \mathcal{T}(n')(\delta') := \mathcal{T}(n')(\delta') \sqcup m$
$(27):\ $ **until** $\mathcal{W} = \emptyset$

$(01):\ \delta \in Context = \Delta$
$(02):\ w \in Work = Node \times \Delta$
$(03):\ \mathcal{W} \in Worklist = 2^{Work}$
$(04):\ \mathcal{N} \in Node \times \Delta \to 2^{Node \times \Delta}$
$(05):\ State = \Delta \to Mem$
$(06):\ \mathcal{T} \in Table = Node \to State$
$(07):\ \hat{\mathcal{F}} \in Node \to Mem \to Mem$
$(08):\ ReturnSite \in ProcName \rightharpoonup Work$

$(09):\ FixpointIterate\ (\mathcal{W}, \mathcal{T}) =$
$(10):\ ReturnSite := \emptyset$
$(11):\ $ **repeat**
$(12):\quad \mathcal{S} := \{(call_-^{g,\cdot}, \_) \in \mathcal{W} \mid (n_h, \_) \in \mathcal{W} \wedge reach(g, h) \wedge \neg recursive(g)\}$
$(13):\quad (n, \delta) := \mathsf{choose}(\ \mathcal{W} \setminus \mathcal{S}\ )$
$(14):\quad m := \hat{\mathcal{F}}\ n\ (\mathcal{T}(n)(\delta))$
$(15):\quad$ **if** $n = call_f^{g,r} \wedge \neg recursive(g)$ **then**
$(16):\quad\quad ReturnSite(g) := (r, \delta)$
$(17):\quad$ **if** $n = exit_g \wedge \neg recursive(g)$ **then**
$(18):\quad\quad (r, \delta_r) := ReturnSite(g)$
$(19):\quad\quad$ **if** $m \not\sqsubseteq \mathcal{T}(r)(\delta_r)$
$(20):\quad\quad\quad \mathcal{W} := \mathcal{W} \cup \{(r, \delta_r)\}$
$(21):\quad\quad\quad \mathcal{T}(r)(\delta_r) := \mathcal{T}(r)(\delta_r) \sqcup m$
$(22):\quad$ **else**
$(23):\quad\quad$ **for all** $(n', \delta') \in \mathcal{N}(n, \delta)$ **do**
$(24):\quad\quad\quad$ **if** $m \not\sqsubseteq \mathcal{T}(n')(\delta')$
$(25):\quad\quad\quad\quad \mathcal{W} := \mathcal{W} \cup \{(n', \delta')\}$
$(26):\quad\quad\quad\quad \mathcal{T}(n')(\delta') := \mathcal{T}(n')(\delta') \sqcup m$
$(27):\ $ **until** $\mathcal{W} = \emptyset$

(a) a normal worklist algorithm Normal_k (b) our algorithm $\mathsf{Normal}_k/\mathsf{RSS}$

Fig. 3. A normal context-sensitive worklist algorithm Normal_k (left-hand side) and its RSS modification $\mathsf{Normal}_k/\mathsf{RSS}$ (right-hand side). These two algorithms are the same except for shaded regions. For brevity, we omit the usual definition of $\hat{\mathcal{F}}$, which updates the worklist in addition to computing the flow equation's body.

system. However, because the algorithm prunes only spurious returns that definitely do not happen in the real executions of the program, our algorithm does not miss any real executions.

$\mathsf{Normal}_k/\mathsf{RSS}$ is always at least as precise as Normal_k. Because our technique prunes some (worklist-level) computations that occur along invalid return paths, it improves the precision. The actual precision of $\mathsf{Normal}_k/\mathsf{RSS}$ varies depending on the worklist order, but is no worse than that of Normal_k.

Example 3. Consider the program in Fig 1 again, and suppose the current worklist is $\{1, 5\}$. When analyzing the program with Normal_0, the fixpoint-solving follows both spurious return paths, regardless of the worklist order,

$$1 \to 2 \to 3 \to 6 \tag{1}$$
$$5 \to 2 \to 3 \to 4 \tag{2}$$

because of multiple returns from node 3. When analyzing with $\mathsf{Normal}_0/\mathsf{RSS}$, there are two possibilities, depending on the worklist order:

1. When $\mathsf{Normal}_0/\mathsf{RSS}$ selects node 1 first: Then the fixpoint iteration sequence may be $1; 2; 3; 4; 5; 2; 3; 6$. This sequence involves the spurious path (1)

(because the second visit to node 2 uses the information from node 1 as well as from node 5), but not (2). $\mathsf{Normal}_0/\mathsf{RSS}$ is more precise than Normal_0.

2. When $\mathsf{Normal}_0/\mathsf{RSS}$ selects node 5 first: Then the fixpoint iteration sequence may be $5; 2; 3; 6; 1; 2; 3; 4; 5; 2; 3; 6$. This computation involves both spurious paths (1) and (2). With this iteration order, Normal_0 and $\mathsf{Normal}_0/\mathsf{RSS}$ have the same precision.

4 Experiments

We implemented our algorithm inside a realistic C analyzer [5,6]. Experiments with open-source programs show that $\mathsf{Normal}_k/\mathsf{RSS}$ for any k is very likely faster than Normal_k, and that even $\mathsf{Normal}_{k+1}/\mathsf{RSS}$ can be faster than Normal_k.

4.1 Setting Up

Normal_k is our underlying worklist algorithm, on top of which our industrialized static analyzer [5,6] for C is installed. The analyzer is an interval-domain-based abstract interpreter. The analyzer performs by default flow-sensitive and call-string-based context-sensitive global analysis on the supergraph of the input programs: it computes $\mathcal{T} = \mathit{Node} \rightarrow \mathit{State}$ where $\mathit{State} = \Delta \rightarrow \mathit{Mem}$. Mem denotes abstract memory $\mathit{Mem} = \mathit{Addr} \rightarrow \mathit{Val}$ where Addr denotes abstract locations that are either program variables or allocation sites, and Val denotes abstract values including $\hat{\mathbb{Z}}$ (interval domain), 2^{Addr} (addresses), and $2^{\mathit{AllocSite} \times \hat{\mathbb{Z}} \times \hat{\mathbb{Z}}}$ (array block, consisting of base address, offset, and size [6]).

We measured the net effects of avoiding spurious interprocedural cycles. Since our algorithmic technique changes the existing worklist order, performance differences between Normal_k and $\mathsf{Normal}_k/\mathsf{RSS}$ could be attributed not only to avoiding spurious cycles but also to the changed worklist order. In order to measure the net effects of avoiding spurious cycles, we applied the same worklist order to both Normal_k and $\mathsf{Normal}_k/\mathsf{RSS}$. The order (between nodes) that we used is a reverse topological order between procedures on the call graph: a node n of a procedure f precedes a node m of a procedure g if f precedes g in the reverse topological order in the call graph. If f and g are the same procedure, the order between the nodes are defined by the weak topological order [3] on the control flow graph of the procedure. Note that this ordering itself contains the "prioritize callees over call-sites" feature and we don't explicitly need the delaying call technique (lines 12-13 in Fig 3.(b)) in $\mathsf{Normal}_k/\mathsf{RSS}$. Hence the worklist order for Normal_k and $\mathsf{Normal}_k/\mathsf{RSS}$ are the same.[4]

We have analyzed 11 open-source software packages. Table 2 shows our benchmark programs as well as their raw analysis results. All experiments were done on a Linux 2.6 system running on a Pentium4 3.2 GHz box with 4 GB of main memory.

[4] In fact, the order described here is the one our analyzer uses by default, which consistently shows better performance than naive worklist management scheme (BFS/DFS) or simple "wait-at-join" techniques (e.g., [6]).

Table 2. Benchmark programs and their raw analysis results. Lines of code (**LOC**) are given before preprocessing. The number of nodes in the supergraph(**#nodes**) is given after preprocessing. **k** denotes the size of call-strings used for the analysis. Entries with ∞ means missing data because of our analysis running out of memory.

Program	LOC	#nodes	k-call-strings	#iterations		time	
				Normal	Normal/RSS	Normal	Normal/RSS
spell-1.0	2,213	782	0	33,864	5,800	60.98	8.49
			1	31,933	10,109	55.02	13.35
			2	57,083	15,226	102.28	19.04
barcode-0.96	4,460	2,634	0	22,040	19,556	93.22	84.44
			1	33,808	30,311	144.37	134.57
			2	40,176	36,058	183.49	169.08
httptunnel-3.3	6,174	2,757	0	442,159	48,292	2020.10	191.53
			1	267,291	116,666	1525.26	502.59
			2	609,623	251,575	5983.27	1234.75
gzip-1.2.4a	7,327	6,271	0	653,063	88,359	4601.23	621.52
			1	991,135	165,892	10281.94	1217.58
			2	1,174,632	150,391	18263.58	1116.25
jwhois-3.0.1	9,344	5,147	0	417,529	134,389	4284.21	1273.49
			1	272,377	138,077	2445.56	1222.07
			2	594,090	180,080	8448.36	1631.07
parser	10,900	9,298	0	3,452,248	230,309	61316.91	3270.40
			1	∞	∞	∞	∞
bc-1.06	13,093	4,924	0	1,964,396	412,549	23515.27	3644.13
			1	3,038,986	1,477,120	44859.16	12557.88
			2	∞	∞	∞	∞
less-290	18,449	7,754	0	3,149,284	1,420,432	46274.67	20196.69
			1	∞	∞	∞	∞
twolf	19,700	14,610	0	3,028,814	139,082	33293.96	1395.32
			1	∞	∞	∞	∞
tar-1.13	20,258	10,800	0	4,748,749	700,474	75013.88	9973.40
			1	∞	∞	∞	∞
make-3.76.1	27,304	11,061	0	4,613,382	2,511,582	88221.06	44853.49
			1	∞	∞	∞	∞

4.2 Results

We use two performance measures: (1) *#iterations* is the total number of iterations during the worklist algorithm. The number directly indicates the amount of computation; (2) *time* is the CPU time spent during the analysis.

Fig 4(a) compares the analysis time between $\mathsf{Normal}_k/\mathsf{RSS}$ and Normal_k for $k = 0, 1, 2$. In this comparison, $\mathsf{Normal}_k/\mathsf{RSS}$ reduces the analysis time of Normal_k by 7%-96%.

- When $k = 0$ (context-insensitive) : $\mathsf{Normal}_0/\mathsf{RSS}$ has reduced the analysis time by, on average, about 74% against Normal_0. For most programs, the analysis time has been reduced by more than 50%. There is one exception: `barcode`. The analysis time has been reduced by 9%. This is because `barcode` has unusual call structures: it does not call a procedure many times, but calls many different procedures one by one. So, the program contains few butterfly cycles.

- When $k = 1$: $\mathsf{Normal}_1/\mathsf{RSS}$ has reduced the analysis time by, on average, about 60% against Normal_1. Compared to the context-insensitive case, for all programs, cost reduction ratios have been slightly decreased. This is mainly because, in our analysis, Normal_0 costs more than Normal_1 for most programs (`spell`, `httptunnel`, `jwhois`). For `httptunnel`, in Table 2, the analysis time (2020.10 s) for $k = 1$ is less than the time (1525.26 s) for $k = 0$. This means that performance problems by butterfly cycles is much more severe when $k = 0$ than that of $k = 1$, because by increasing context-sensitivity some spurious paths can be removed.
- When $k = 2$: $\mathsf{Normal}_2/\mathsf{RSS}$ has reduced the analysis time by, on average, 69% against Normal_2. Compared to the case of $k = 1$, the cost reduction ratio has been slightly increased for most programs. In the analysis of Normal_2, since the equation system is much larger than that of Normal_1, our conjecture is that the size of butterfly cycles is likely to get larger. Since larger butterfly cycles causes more serious problems (Section 2), our RSS algorithm is likely to greater reduce useless computation.

Fig 4(b) compares the performance of $\mathsf{Normal}_{k+1}/\mathsf{RSS}$ against Normal_k for $k = 0, 1$. The result shows that, for all programs except `barcode`, $\mathsf{Normal}_{k+1}/\mathsf{RSS}$ is likely faster than Normal_k. Since $\mathsf{Normal}_{k+1}/\mathsf{RSS}$ can be even faster than Normal_k, if memory cost permits, we can consider using $\mathsf{Normal}_{k+1}/\mathsf{RSS}$ instead of Normal_k.

Table 3 compares the precision between Normal_0 and $\mathsf{Normal}_0/\mathsf{RSS}$. In order to measure the increased precision, we first joined all the memories associated with each program point (*Node*). Then we counted the number of constant intervals (*#const*, e.g., $[1, 1]$), finite intervals (*#finite*, e.g., $[1, 5]$), intervals with one infinity (*#open*, e.g., $[-1, +\infty)$ or $(-\infty, 1]$), and intervals with two infinity (*#top*, $(-\infty, +\infty)$) from interval values ($\hat{\mathbb{Z}}$) and array blocks ($2^{AllocSite \times \hat{\mathbb{Z}} \times \hat{\mathbb{Z}}}$) contained in the joined memory. The constant interval and top interval indicate the most precise and imprecise values, respectively. The results show that $\mathsf{Normal}_0/\mathsf{RSS}$ is more precise (`spell`, `barcode`, `httptunnel`, `gzip`) than Normal_0 or the precision is the same (`jwhois`).

Table 3. Comparison of precision between Normal_0 and $\mathsf{Normal}_0/\mathsf{RSS}$

Program	Analysis	*#const*	*#finite*	*#open*	*#top*
spell-1.0	Normal_0	345	88	33	143
	$\mathsf{Normal}_0/\mathsf{RSS}$	345	89	35	140
barcode-0.96	Normal_0	2136	588	240	527
	$\mathsf{Normal}_0/\mathsf{RSS}$	2136	589	240	526
httptunnel-3.3	Normal_0	1337	342	120	481
	$\mathsf{Normal}_0/\mathsf{RSS}$	1345	342	120	473
gzip-1.2.4a	Normal_0	1995	714	255	1214
	$\mathsf{Normal}_0/\mathsf{RSS}$	1995	716	255	1212
jwhois-3.0.1	Normal_0	2740	415	961	1036
	$\mathsf{Normal}_0/\mathsf{RSS}$	2740	415	961	1036

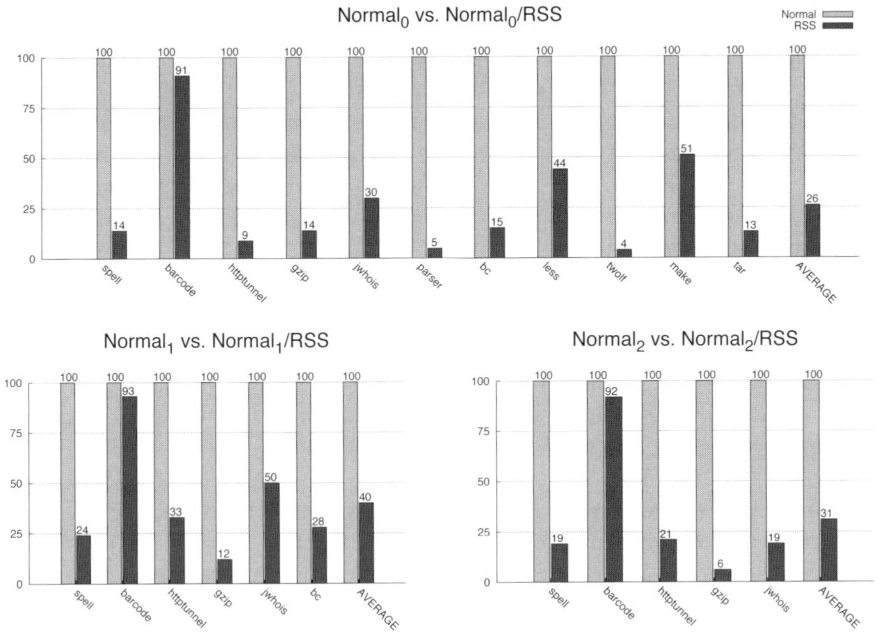

(a) Comparison of *#iterations* between Normal_k and $\mathsf{Normal}_k/\mathsf{RSS}$, for $k = 0, 1, 2$.

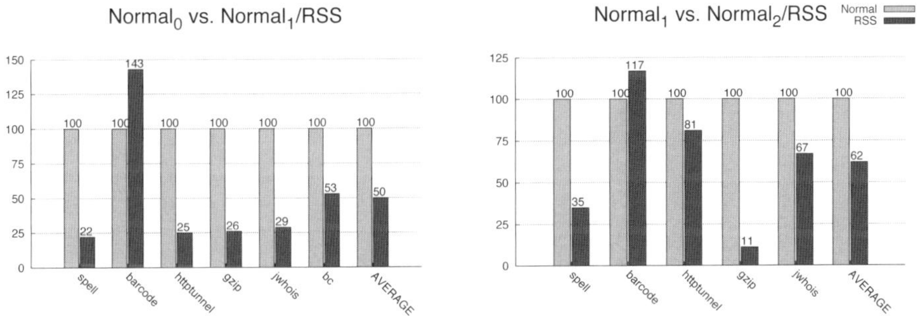

(b) Comparison of *#iterations* between Normal_k and $\mathsf{Normal}_{k+1}/\mathsf{RSS}$, for $k = 0, 1$.

Fig. 4. Net effects of avoiding spurious cycles

5 Conclusion

We have presented a simple algorithmic technique to alleviate substantial inefficiency in global static analysis caused by large spurious interprocedural cycles. Such cycles are identified as a major reason for the folklore problem in static analysis that less precise analyses sometimes are slower. Although this inefficiency might not come to the fore when analyzing small programs, globally analyzing medium or large programs makes it outstanding. The proposed algorithmic technique reduces the analysis time by 7%-96% for open-source benchmarks.

Though tuning the precision of static analysis can in principle be controlled solely by redesigning the underlying abstract semantics, our algorithmic technique is a simple and orthogonal leverage to effectively shift the analysis cost/precision balance for the better. The technique's correctness is obvious enough to avoid the burden of a safety proof that would be needed if we newly designed the abstract semantics.

Acknowledgements. I am grateful to Wontae Choi, Yungbum Jung, Will Klieber, Soonho Kong, and Daejun Park for their helpful comments and suggestions. I would like to especially thank Deokhwan Kim and Kwangkeun Yi for their very kindhearted help in writing this paper. I am also thankful to anonymous referees for helpful comments.

This work was supported by the Engineering Research Center of Excellence Program of Korea Ministry of Education, Science and Technology(MEST) / Korea Science and Engineering Foundation(KOSEF) (R11-2008-007-01002-0) and the Brain Korea 21 Project, School of Electrical Engineering and Computer Science, Seoul National University in 2009.

References

1. Balakrishnan, G., Reps, T.: Analyzing memory accesses in x86 binary executables. In: Duesterwald, E. (ed.) CC 2004. LNCS, vol. 2985, pp. 5–23. Springer, Heidelberg (2004)
2. Blanchet, B., Cousot, P., Cousot, R., Feret, J., Mauborgne, L., Miné, A., Monniaux, D., Rival, X.: A static analyzer for large safety-critical software. In: Proceedings of the ACM SIGPLAN-SIGACT Conference on Programming Language Design and Implementation, pp. 196–207 (2003)
3. Bourdoncle, F.: Efficient chaotic iteration strategies with widenings. In: Proceedings of the International Conference on Formal Methods in Programming and their Applications, pp. 128–141 (1993)
4. Chambers, C., Dean, J., Grove, D.: Frameworks for intra- and interprocedural dataflow analysis. Technical report, Department of Computer Science and Engineering, University of Washington (1996)
5. Jhee, Y., Jin, M., Jung, Y., Kim, D., Kong, S., Lee, H., Oh, H., Park, D., Yi, K.: Abstract interpretation + impure catalysts: Our Sparrow experience. Presentation at the Workshop of the 30 Years of Abstract Interpretation, San Francisco (January 2008), `http://www.ropas.snu.ac.kr/~kwang/paper/30yai-08.pdf`
6. Jung, Y., Kim, J., Shin, J., Yi, K.: Taming false alarms from a domain-unaware C analyzer by a bayesian statistical post analysis. In: Hankin, C., Siveroni, I. (eds.) SAS 2005. LNCS, vol. 3672, pp. 203–217. Springer, Heidelberg (2005)
7. Karkare, B., Khedker, U.P.: An improved bound for call strings based interprocedural analysis of bit vector frameworks. ACM Trans. on Programming Languages and Systems 29(6), 38 (2007)

8. Khedker, U.P., Karkare, B.: Efficiency, precision, simplicity, and generality in interprocedural data flow analysis: Resurrecting the classical call strings method. In: Hendren, L. (ed.) CC 2008. LNCS, vol. 4959, pp. 213–228. Springer, Heidelberg (2008)
9. Martin, F.: PAG - an efficient program analyzer generator. International Journal on Software Tools for Technology Transfer 2(1), 46–67 (1998)
10. Martin, F.: Experimental comparison of call string and functional approaches to interprocedural analysis. In: Jähnichen, S. (ed.) CC 1999. LNCS, vol. 1575, pp. 63–75. Springer, Heidelberg (1999)
11. Reps, T., Horwitz, S., Sagiv, M.: Precise interprocedural dataflow analysis via graph reachability. In: Proceedings of The ACM SIGPLAN-SIGACT Symposium on Principles of Programming Languages, pp. 49–61 (1995)
12. Rival, X., Mauborgne, L.: The trace partitioning abstract domain. ACM Trans. on Programming Languages and System 29(5), 26–51 (2007)
13. Sagiv, M., Reps, T., Horwitz, S.: Precise interprocedural dataflow analysis with applications to constant propagation. Theoretical Computer Sicence 167(1-2), 131–170 (1996)
14. Sharir, M., Pnueli, A.: Two approaches to interprocedural data flow analysis. In: Program Flow Analysis: Theory and Applications, ch. 7. Prentice-Hall, Englewood Cliffs (1981)
15. Sridharan, M., Bodík, R.: Refinement-based context-sensitive points-to analysis for java. In: Proceedings of the ACM SIGPLAN-SIGACT Conference on Programming Language Design and Implementation, pp. 387–400 (2006)
16. Whaley, J., Lam, M.S.: Cloning-based context-sensitive pointer alias analysis using binary decision diagrams. In: Proceedings of the ACM SIGPLAN-SIGACT Conference on Programming Language Design and Implementation, pp. 131–144 (2004)

Abstract Transformers for Thread Correlation Analysis

Michal Segalov[1], Tal Lev-Ami[1], Roman Manevich[2], Ramalingam Ganesan[3], and Mooly Sagiv[1]

[1] Tel Aviv University
{tla,segalovm,msagiv}@post.tau.ac.il
[2] University of California Los Angeles
rumster@cs.ucla.edu
[3] Microsoft Research India
grama@microsoft.com

Abstract. We present a new technique for speeding up static analysis of (shared memory) concurrent programs. We focus on analyses that compute *thread correlations*: such analyses infer invariants that capture correlations between the local states of different threads (as well as the global state). Such invariants are required for verifying many natural properties of concurrent programs.

Tracking correlations between different thread states, however, is very expensive. A significant factor that makes such analysis expensive is the cost of applying abstract transformers. In this paper, we introduce a technique that exploits the notion of *footprints* and *memoization* to compute individual abstract transformers more efficiently.

We have implemented this technique in our concurrent shape analysis framework. We have used this implementation to prove properties of fine-grained concurrent programs with a shared, mutable, heap in the presence of an unbounded number of objects and threads. The properties we verified include memory safety, data structure invariants, partial correctness, and linearizability. Our empirical evaluation shows that our new technique reduces the analysis time significantly (e.g., by a factor of 35 in one case).

1 Introduction

This paper is concerned with analysis and verification of (shared memory) concurrent programs. We present a new technique that makes such analyses more efficient. The technique presented in this paper speeds up the verification significantly (e.g., reducing the verification time from 56,347 seconds to 1,596 seconds — a 35 fold speed-up — for one program).

One key abstraction technique for dealing with the state space explosion problem in analyzing concurrent programs is thread-modularity (see, e.g., [7]), which works by abstracting away correlations between the local states of different threads. Unfortunately, thread-modular analysis fails when the proof of a desired property relies on invariants connecting the local states of different threads, which is the case in several natural examples.

Z. Hu (Ed.): APLAS 2009, LNCS 5904, pp. 30–46, 2009.

Thread-Correlation Analysis. Hence, we focus on analysis using abstractions that track correlations between pairs of (abstract) thread states (e.g., see [11,5,2]). The abstract domain elements, in our analysis, essentially represent invariants of the form $\forall t, e \,.\, \bigvee_{i=1}^{n} \varphi_i[t, e]$ where t and e are universally quantified thread variables and $\varphi_i[t, e]$ are formulas taken from a finite, but usually large, set of candidates (describing some relation between the states of threads t and e). In our experience, we found such abstractions to be sufficiently precise for verifying the programs and properties of interest, but the corresponding analyses were quite time-consuming.

Abstract Transformers. The idea of using abstractions that correlate states of different threads is not new. In this paper we address the question of how to define precise, yet efficient, transformers for such domains, a question that has not been systematically studied before. This is, however, an important question because, as we found, the cost of applying abstract transformers is one of the main reasons why thread-correlation analyses are expensive. The abstract transformer corrresponding to a statement must determine how the execution of the statement by some thread affects the invariant computed by the analysis so far. The transformer must consider all possible (abstract) states of the executing thread, and identify the effect of the statement execution on all possible (abstract) states of any pair of threads. This introduces a non-linear factor that makes the transformer computation expensive. One of our key contributions is a set of techniques for computing the abstract transformer more efficiently.

Implementation and Evaluation. We have implemented the techniques described in this paper in our framework for concurrent shape analysis. We have used this implementation to verify properties, such as memory safety, preservation of data structure invariants, and linearizability [13], of fine-grained concurrent programs, especially those with dynamically-allocated concurrent data structures. Such data-structures are important building blocks of concurrent systems and are becoming part of standard libraries (e.g., JDK 1.6). Automatic verification of these algorithms is challenging because they often contain fine-grained concurrency with benign data races, low-level synchronization operations such as `CAS`, and destructive pointer-updates which require accurate alias analysis. Furthermore, the data-structure can grow in an unbounded fashion and the number of threads concurrently updating it can also grow in an unbounded fashion.

Our empirical evaluation shows that our optimizations lead to significant reduction in the analysis time.

Main Contributions. Our contribution is not specific to shape analysis and can be used for other analyses of concurrent programs as well. For this reason, we describe our techniques in a simple setting, independent of shape analysis. Specifically, we present our ideas using a simple abstract domain for concurrent programs. This domain formalizes our notion of thread correlation by abstracting concrete states, which capture correlations between the states of all threads, into abstract states that capture only correlations between the states of every pair of threads. (Our implementation, however, realizes these ideas in a shape analysis and our empirical results concern this concurrent shape analysis.)

The main contributions of this paper are:

Sound Transformer. We define a sound abstract post operator (transformer) for the new abstract domain from the concrete sequential semantics. The transformer reasons rather precisely about interference between threads.

Transformer Optimizations. We present two refinements to the computation of the above transformers that lead to significant speedups.

Implementation. We have implemented an analysis based on the above ideas and used it to automatically verify properties of several concurrent data structure implementations.

Evaluation. We present an empirical evaluation of our techniques and show the advantages of the optimizations to the abstract transformer computation. For example, for a lock-free implementation of a concurrent set using linked lists [18], our optimizations reduce the analysis time from 56,347 CPU seconds to 1,596 — a 35 fold speed-up. We have also analyzed erroneous mutations of concurrent algorithms and our tool quickly found errors in all of the incorrect variations.

Outline of the rest of this paper. Sec. 2 presents an overview of our analysis in a semi-formal way. Sec. 3 formalizes our analysis using the theory of abstract interpretation [6]. Sec. 4 defines optimizations to the transformers. Sec. 5 evaluates the effectiveness of our optimizations on realistic benchmarks. Sec. 6 concludes with discussion of related works. Proofs and elaborations are found in [21].

2 Overview

In this section, we explain our approach informally, using an adaptation of a very simple example originally constructed to show the limitations of concurrent separation logic [19]. We use this example to motivate the need for tracking thread correlations and show the difficulties in computing postconditions efficiently. Fig. 1 shows a concurrent program with producer threads and consumer threads communicating via a single-object buffer, `b`, and a global flag `empty`. For simplicity, instead of locks or semaphores, we use the `await` construct, which atomically executes the then-clause when the await-condition holds.

2.1 The Need for Thread Correlations

In this example, the system consists of an unbounded number of producer and consumer threads. Each producer allocates a new object, transfers it to a single consumer via the buffer, and the consumer uses the object and then deallocates the object. Our goal is to verify that `use(c)` and `dispose(c)` operate on objects that have not been deallocated. (This also verifies that an object is not deallocated more than once.)

One way to verify properties of concurrent systems is by establishing a global invariant on the reachable configurations and show that the invariant entails the

```
Boolean empty = true;
Object b = null;
```

```
produce() {
[1]   Object p = new();
[2]   await (empty) then {
        b = p; empty = false;
      }
[3] }
```

```
consume() {
      Object c;
      // Boolean x;
[4]   await (!empty) then {
        c = b; empty = true;
      }
[5]   use(c);
      // x = f(c);
[6]   dispose(c);
      // use(x);
[7] }
```

Fig. 1. A concurrent program implementing a simple protocol between a producer thread and a consumer thread transferring objects in a single-element buffer. The commented out lines are only used and explained in Sec. 4.

required properties (e.g., see [1]). In our program, we need to show that the following property holds:

$$\forall t \,.\, pc[t] \in \{5, 6\} \Rightarrow a(c[t]) \;, \qquad (1)$$

where t ranges over threads, $pc[\mathrm{t}]$ $c[t]$ denote the program counter and value of the variable c of thread t, and $a(c[t])$ is true iff $c[t]$ points to an object that has not yet been disposed. For simplicity, we assume that the set of local variables is the same for all threads (and is the union of local variables of all threads).

This verification requires the computation of an inductive invariant that implies (1). In particular, the invariant should guarantee that the dispose command executed by one consumer thread does not dispose an object used by another consumer thread and that an object that a producer places in the buffer is not a disposed object. A natural inductive invariant that implies (1) is:

$$\forall t, e \,.\, \begin{pmatrix} pc[t] \in \{5, 6\} \Rightarrow a(c[t]) & \wedge \;\; (i) \\ \neg empty \Rightarrow a(b) & \wedge \;\; (ii) \\ pc[t] = 2 \Rightarrow a(p[t]) & \wedge \;\; (iii) \\ t \neq e \wedge pc[t] = 2 \Rightarrow p[t] \neq c[e] & \wedge \;\; (iv) \\ t \neq e \wedge pc[t] \in \{5, 6\} \Rightarrow c[t] \neq c[e] & (v) \end{pmatrix} \qquad (2)$$

This invariant ensures that dispose operations executed by threads cannot affect locations pointed-to by producer threads that are waiting to transfer their value to the buffer and also cannot affect the values of other consumer threads that have not yet disposed their values. Here e is a thread that represents the environment in which t is executed. Specifically: (i) describes the desired verification property; (ii) is the buffer invariant, which is required in order to prove that (i) holds when a consumer copies the value from the buffer into its local pointer c; (iii) establishes the producer properties needed to establish the buffer invariant. The most interesting parts of this invariant are the *correlation invariants* (iv) and (v), describing the potential correlations between local states of two arbitrary threads and the content of the (global) heap. These ensure that the invariant is inductive, e.g., (v) ensures that (i) is *stable*: deallocations by different threads cannot affect it, if it already holds. Notice that the correlation invariants cannot be inferred by pure thread-modular approaches. Our work goes beyond pure thread-modular analysis [8] by explicitly tracking these correlations.

2.2 Automatically Inferring Correlation Invariants

In this paper, we define an abstract interpretation algorithm that automatically infers inductive correlation invariants. The main idea is to infer normalized invariants of the form:

$$\forall t, e \,.\, \bigvee_{i=1}^{n} \varphi_i[t,e] \tag{3}$$

where t and e are universally quantified thread variables and $\varphi_i[t,e]$ are formulas taken from a finite, but usually large, set of candidates. We will refer to each $\varphi_i[t,e]$ as a *ci-disjunct* (Correlation-Invariant Disjunct). As in predicate abstraction and other powerset abstractions, the set of ci-disjuncts is computed by successively adding more ci-disjuncts, starting from the singleton set containing a ci-disjunct describing t and e in their initial states. For efficiency, $\varphi_i[t,e]$ are usually asymmetric in the sense that they record rather precise information on the current thread t and a rather coarse view of other threads, represented by e.

For this program, we can use conjunctions of atomic formulas describing: (i) that t and e are different, (ii) the program counter of t; (iii) (in)equalities between local pointers of t and e, and between local pointers of t and global pointers; (iv) allocations of local pointers of t and global pointers; and (v) the value of the Boolean `empty`.

Thus, the invariant (2) can be written as:

$$\forall t, e \,.\, \begin{pmatrix} t \neq e \wedge \\ pc[t] = 5 \wedge \\ c[t] \neq c[e] \wedge c[t] \neq b \wedge c[e] \neq b \wedge \\ a(c[t]) \wedge a(c[e]) \wedge a(b) \wedge \\ \neg empty \end{pmatrix} \bigvee \begin{pmatrix} t \neq e \wedge \\ pc[t] = 6 \wedge \\ c[t] \neq c[e] \wedge c[t] \neq b \wedge c[e] \neq b \wedge \\ a(c[t]) \wedge a(c[e]) \wedge a(b) \wedge \\ \neg empty \end{pmatrix} \bigvee \cdots \tag{4}$$

where the ci-disjuncts describe cases of a consumer thread t that copied the value from the buffer, (which has since been refilled), and has either used the value locally or not. The other disjuncts are not shown.

2.3 Computing Postconditions Efficiently

The iterative procedure successively adds ci-disjuncts describing the reachable states after applying an atomic action to the formula representing the current set of reachable states, until a fixed point is reached. We compute the abstract transformer for an atomic action by identifying its effect on every ci-disjunct $\varphi_i[t,e]$. This is non-trivial since a transition by one thread can affect the global state (and the view of the environment of another thread) and, hence, a ci-disjunct involving other threads.

To compute the effect of a transition on a ci-disjunct $\varphi_i[t, e]$, we need to account for the following three possibilities: (i) The executing thread is t; (ii) The executing thread is e; or (iii) The executing thread is some other thread ex. The most challenging case is (iii). In this case, the ci-disjunct does not contain information about the local state of the executing thread ex. Applying an abstract transformer without any information about ex's local state can lead to imprecise results. Instead, we exploit the information available in the current set of ci-disjuncts. Specifically, the executing thread ex must itself satisfy some ci-disjunct $\varphi_j[ex, t']$. The situation with case (ii) is similar since only limited information is available about the environment thread in the ci-disjunct and it is handled similarly.

Thus, our transformer works as follows: we consider every pair of ci-disjuncts φ_i and φ_j and apply a "mini-transformer" to this pair. The mini-transformer first checks to see if the two ci-disjuncts are consistent with each other. (E.g., if they imply conflicting values for the global variable `empty`, they cannot correspond to ci-disjuncts from the same concrete state.) If so, it uses the information available about the executing thread from φ_i to determine how the global state will change as a result of the transition, and identifies how that alters ci-disjunct φ_j.

In our experiments, the above abstraction was precise enough to verify the programs analyzed, yet quite slow. One of the key factors for the inefficiency is the quadratic explosion in the transformer, as the transformer has to consider all pairs of ci-disjuncts and the number of ci-disjuncts can become very large.

Our key contributions include effective techniques for making the transformer more efficient by reducing this quadratic factor in common cases, usually without affecting precision. These techniques are analogous to techniques used in interprocedural analysis.

In the rest of this section, let us consider the application of the mini-transformer described above to ci-disjuncts φ_j (corresponding to an executing thread ex) and φ_i (corresponding to two other threads t and e).

The first optimization technique, called *summarizing effects*, is based on the following observation. Typically, φ_i can be expressed in the form $\varphi_i^p \wedge \varphi_i^r$, where φ_i^r (the *frame*) cannot be affected by the execution of ex. We refer to φ_i^p as the *footprint* of φ_i. E.g., purely local properties of t or e will usually be in the frame. If the transition by ex transforms φ_i^p into $\varphi_i^{p'}$, then the transformation of the complete ci-disjunct is given by $\varphi_i^{p'} \wedge \varphi_i^r$. Next, we note that distinct disjuncts φ_i and φ_k may have the same footprint. In this case, it suffices to compute the transformation of the footprint only once.

E.g., consider the first two ci-disjuncts of (4). These ci-disjuncts have the same footprint since they differ only in the program counter value of t which cannot be altered by the execution of ex. Typically, the number of distinct footprints created by a set of ci-disjuncts is much smaller than the number of ci-disjuncts, which leads to significant efficiency gains. This optimization is similar to the interprocedural analysis technique where information at the calling context not modified by the call can be transmitted across the procedure call. In section 4, we show the conditions under which this technique can be used to make the transformer more efficient without affecting precision.

The *summary abstraction* optimization applies to ci-disjunct φ_j and exploits the locality of the transformer. We abstract away information not used by the transition from φ_j (corresponding to the executing thread), constructing its footprint φ_j^f and use it for the mini-transformer. As distinct ci-disjuncts can have the same footprint, this decreases the number of ci-disjuncts passed to the mini-transformer.

One point to note here is that information not used or modified by an atomic action may still be used by the mini-transformer to check for consistency between the two ci-disjuncts. If such information is omitted from the footprint, we still get a sound transformer, though there may be a loss in precision. However, we found that this heuristic can be used to significantly reduce the computation time while maintaining a precise-enough abstraction. In general, an analysis designer can choose the information to be omitted from the footprint appropriately to achieve the desired tradeoff.

3 An Abstract Interpretation for Correlation Invariants

In this section, we formalize our analysis, which tracks correlations between pairs of threads, in the framework of abstract interpretation [6].

3.1 The Concrete Semantics (C, TR)

A concurrent program is a parallel composition of concurrently executing threads, where each thread is associated with an identifier from an unbounded set *Tid*. The threads communicate through a global store *Glob*, which is shared by all threads. In addition, each thread has its own local store, *Loc*, which includes the thread's program counter. A concrete state of the program consists of a global store and an assignment of a local store to each thread identifier. We denote the set of all concrete states by $\Sigma = (\mathit{Tid} \to \mathit{Loc}) \times \mathit{Glob}$ and the concrete domain by $C = 2^{\Sigma}$. Given a state σ, let σ^G represent the global store of σ and let $\sigma^L[t]$ represent the local store of thread t in σ.

The relation $tr \subseteq (\mathit{Loc} \times \mathit{Glob}) \times (\mathit{Loc} \times \mathit{Glob})$ describes a step that a thread can take, given its local store and a global store. We write $x \rightsquigarrow y$ as shorthand for $(x, y) \in tr$. Let $\sigma^L[t \mapsto l]$ denote a state that is identical to σ^L, except that the local store of thread t is l. The concrete transition relation is defined as

$$TR = \{((\rho, g), (\rho[t \mapsto l'], g') \mid t \in \mathit{Tid} \,.\, (\rho[t], g) \rightsquigarrow (l', g'), \} \ . \qquad (5)$$

3.2 The Abstract Semantics (CI, TR_{CI})

We now present an abstraction to deal with an unbounded number of threads. As we saw in Sec. 2, tracking information about a single thread in the style of thread-modular analysis [7] can be imprecise. This motivates the following abstract domain. We define an abstraction that records correlations between the local stores of two different threads and a global store. Let $CID \equiv Loc \times Glob \times Loc$ denote the set of such correlations. We will refer to an element of CID as a ci-disjunct. We define the abstract domain CI to be the powerset 2^{CID}.

The abstraction of a single concrete state is given by

$$\beta_{CI}(\sigma) = \{(\sigma^L[t], \sigma^G, \sigma^L[e]) \mid t, e \in Tid, t \neq e\} \ . \tag{6}$$

Note that a ci-disjunct $(\sigma^L[t], \sigma^G, \sigma^L[e])$ represents the state from the perspective of two threads: t, which we call the primary thread, and e, which we call the secondary thread. We say that $(\sigma^L[t], \sigma^G, \sigma^L[e])$ is a ci-disjunct generated by threads t and e.

The abstraction of a set of states $\alpha_{CI}: C \to CI$ and the concretization $\gamma_{CI}: CI \to C$ are:

$$\alpha_{CI}(X) \equiv \bigcup_{\sigma \in X} \beta_{CI}(\sigma) \ , \qquad \gamma_{CI}(R) \equiv \{\sigma \mid \beta_{CI}(\sigma) \subseteq R\} \ .$$

Composing With Other Abstractions. Note that when Loc and $Glob$ are finite sets, CI gives us a finite abstraction. In Section 3.3, we show how to compose the above abstraction with a subsequent abstraction to create other finite, tractable, abstract domains. For the sake of exposition, we first show how to define a sound transformer for the simple domain CI before we consider such an extension.

An Abstract Transformer. We define the abstract transformer $TR_{CI} : CI \to CI$ as follows:

$$TR_{CI}(R) \equiv \bigcup_{d \in R} tr_{CI}^{direct}(d) \cup TR_{CI}^{ind}(R) \ . \tag{7}$$

The function $tr_{CI}^{direct} : CID \to 2^{CID}$ captures the effect of a transition by a thread t on a ci-disjunct whose primary thread is t. Abusing terminology, if threads t_p and t_s satisfy $\phi(t_p, t_s)$, where $\phi \in CID$, then after a transition by thread t_p, the threads will satisfy $tr_{CI}^{direct}(\phi)(t_p, t_s)$.

$$tr_{CI}^{direct}(\ell_p, g, \ell_s) \equiv \{(\ell_p', g', \ell_s) \mid (\ell_p, g) \rightsquigarrow (\ell_p', g')\}. \tag{8}$$

The function TR_{CI}^{ind} captures what we call the *indirect effects*: i.e., the effect of a transition by some thread t on ci-disjuncts whose primary thread is not t. As a first attempt, let us consider the following candidate definition for TR_{CI}^{ind}:

$$TR_{CI}^{ind}(R) = \bigcup_{(\ell_1, g, \_) \in R, (\ell_2, g, \ell_3) \in R} \{(\ell_2, g', \ell_3) \mid (\ell_1, g) \rightsquigarrow (\ell_1', g')\} \ .$$

Here, the transition $(\ell_1, g) \rightsquigarrow (\ell_1', g')$ by one thread changes the global state to g'. As a result, a ci-disjunct (ℓ_2, g, ℓ_3) may be transformed to (ℓ_2, g', ℓ_3). While the above definition is a sound definition, it is not very precise. In fact, this definition defeats the purpose of tracking thread correlations because it does not check to see if the ci-disjunct (ℓ_2, g, ℓ_3) is "consistent" with the executing ci-disjunct. We say that two ci-disjuncts x and y are consistent if there exists $\sigma \in \Sigma$ such that $\{x, y\} \subseteq \beta_{CI}(\sigma)$.

We first define some notation. Let *CIMap* denote $Loc \times Glob \rightarrow 2^{Loc}$. Define function $map : CI \rightarrow CIMap$ by $map(R) \equiv \lambda(\ell, g).\{\ell_e \mid (\ell, g, \ell_e) \in R\}$. Function *map* is bijective and *CI* and *CIMap* are isomorphic domains. Given $R \in CI$, let $R(\ell, g) \equiv map(R)(\ell, g)$ and $par(R) \equiv \{(\ell, g, R(\ell, g)) \mid \exists \ell_e.(\ell, g, \ell_e) \in R\}$. We refer to an element of $par(R)$ as a *cluster*. A cluster (e.g., $(\ell_1, g, \{\ell_2, \ell_3\})$) represents a set of ci-disjuncts with the same first and second component (e.g., $\{(\ell_1, g, \ell_2), (\ell_1, g, \ell_3)\}$). $par(R)$ partitions a set of ci-disjuncts R into clusters.

We define TR_{CI}^{ind} as follows:

$$TR_{CI}^{ind}(R) = \bigcup_{c_e, c_t \in par(R)} tr_{CI}^{indirect}(c_e, c_t) \ . \tag{9}$$

$$\begin{aligned} & tr_{CI}^{indirect}((\ell_1, g_1, e_1), (\ell_2, g_2, e_2)) \equiv \\ & \quad \textbf{if} \quad (g_1 = g_2 \wedge \ell_1 \in e_2 \wedge \ell_2 \in e_1) \\ & \quad \textbf{then} \ \{(\ell_2, g_1', \ell_3) \mid (\ell_1, g_1) \rightsquigarrow (\ell_1', g_1'), \ell_3 \in (e_1 \cap e_2) \cup \{\ell_1'\}\} \\ & \quad \textbf{else} \ \{\} \ . \end{aligned} \tag{10}$$

The first parameter of $tr_{CI}^{indirect}$ is a cluster representing the executing thread, and the second is a cluster representing thread(s) on which we compute the interference. We call this the *tracked thread.* The if-condition is a consistency check between two clusters. If the condition is false, then the clusters are inconsistent: i.e., a ci-disjunct from the first cluster and a ci-disjunct from the second cluster can not arise from the same concrete state. Hence, the transformer produces no new ci-disjunct.

Theorem 1 (Soundness). *The abstract transformer* TR_{CI} *is sound, i.e., for all* $R \in CI$, $TR(\gamma_{CI}(R)) \subseteq \gamma_{CI}(TR_{CI}(R))$.

Note that the transformer is not guaranteed to be the most-precise transformer [6]. In terms of efficiency, we can see that the expensive part of the transformer is the application of $tr_{CI}^{indirect}$, which operates over pairs of elements in $par(R)$, requiring a quadratic number of queries to tr.

3.3 Composing with Other Abstractions

In this section, we show how we can compose the abstraction *CI* defined in the previous section with other abstractions of *Loc* and/or *Glob* to create other, more tractable, abstract domains. This can be used to create finite state abstractions even if *Loc* and/or *Glob* are infinite-state.

Abstract Domain. Let $(2^{Loc}, \alpha_P, \gamma_P, Loc_P)$ be a Galois Connection we want to use to abstract the primary thread's local state. Let $(2^{Glob}, \alpha_G, \gamma_G, Glob_G)$ be a Galois Connection we want to use to abstract the global state. Let $(2^{Loc}, \alpha_S, \gamma_S, Loc_S)$ be a Galois Connection for abstracting the secondary thread's local state.

Let $ACID = Loc_P \times Glob_G \times Loc_S$. Let $ACI = 2^{ACID}$, with the Hoare powerdomain ordering. (Since *ACID* is already ordered, it is possible for several elements of ACI to represent the same concrete set of states, which we allow as a convenience.) We use ACI as an abstraction of CI, with the abstraction function $\alpha_{ACI} : CI \to ACI$ defined by:

$$\alpha_{ACI}(S) = \{(\alpha_P(\{\ell_e\}), \alpha_G(\{g\}), \alpha_S(\{\ell_t\})) \mid (\ell_e, g, \ell_t) \in S\}.$$

We use the first local store (Loc_P) as the primary source of information about locals.The second local store (Loc_S) is used primarily to express correlation invariants (and to check for consistency between different ci-disjuncts). (This can be seen in the definition of the abstract transformers presented earlier.) Thus, in practice, the domain Loc_P is richer and captures more information than the domain Loc_S.

Abstracting basic transitions. Recall that $\rightsquigarrow \subseteq (Loc \times Glob) \times (Loc \times Glob)$ represents a single step transition by a thread. Let $\rightsquigarrow_a \subseteq (Loc_P \times Glob_G) \times (Loc_P \times Glob_G)$ be a sound abstraction of this relation: i.e., abusing notation, $\rightsquigarrow_a$ should satisfy $\gamma \circ \rightsquigarrow_a \supseteq \rightsquigarrow \circ \gamma$. More precisely, we want

$$\{(x, y) \mid (\ell_e, g_a) \rightsquigarrow_a (\ell'_e, g'_a), x \in \gamma_P(\ell'_e), y \in \gamma_G(g'_a)\} \supseteq \\ \{(\ell', g') \mid \ell \in \gamma_P(\ell_e), g \in \gamma_G(g_a), (\ell, g) \rightsquigarrow (\ell', g')\} \ .$$

Abstract Transformer. We now present a sound abstract transformer TR_{ACI} for the domain ACI, which is very similar to the transformer for domain CI defined in the previous section. In particular, equations 7 and 9 defining the transformer remain the same as before. The function tr^{direct} is the same as before, except that $\rightsquigarrow$ is replaced by $\rightsquigarrow_a$ as follows:

$$tr^{direct}_{ACI}(\ell_p, g, \ell_s) \equiv \{(\ell'_p, g', \ell_s) \mid (\ell_p, g) \rightsquigarrow_a (\ell'_p, g')\}. \tag{11}$$

The definition of function $tr^{indirect}$, however, is a bit more complex.

We define the abstract transformer in terms of a sound consistency-check operation for comparing elements across different abstract domains as follows, where the indices i and j are either P or S. Let $\approx_{i,j} \subseteq Loc_i \times Loc_j$ be such that

$$\gamma_i(x) \cap \gamma_j(y) \neq \{\} \Rightarrow x \approx_{i,j} y.$$

We define a corresponding relation $\overline{\in}_{i,j} \subseteq Loc_i \times 2^{Loc_j}$ by

$$x \mathrel{\overline{\in}_{i,j}} S \text{ iff } \exists y \in S . x \approx_{i,j} y.$$

We will omit the indices i, j if no confusion is likely. Informally, $x \approx y$ indicate that x and y may represent the same concrete (local) state.

$$\begin{aligned} & tr^{indirect}_{ACI}((\ell_1, g_1, e_1), (\ell_2, g_2, e_2)) \equiv \\ & \quad \text{let } g = g_1 \sqcap g_2 \text{ in} \\ & \quad \{(\ell_2, g', \ell_s) \mid \ell_1 \mathrel{\overline{\in}} e_2, \ell_2 \mathrel{\overline{\in}} e_1, (\ell_1, g) \rightsquigarrow_a (\ell'_1, g'), (\ell_s \in e_2 \wedge \ell_s \mathrel{\overline{\in}} e_1) \vee (\ell_s = \ell'_1)\} \end{aligned} \tag{12}$$

Note that the above definition closely corresponds to equation 10, except that $\in$ is replaced by a corresponding sound approximation $\overline{\in}$.

Theorem 2. *The abstract transformer TR_{ACI} is sound.*

4 Efficiently Computing Indirect Effects

As mentioned earlier, the expensive part of computing transformers is the computation of indirect effects. We now present a couple of techniques for making this computation more efficient. (The techniques we present are inspired by well-known optimization techniques used in inter-procedural analysis.)

4.1 Abstracting the Executing Cluster

The computation of indirect effects, $tr^{indirect}(c_e, c_t)$, determines how a single transition by a thread e (described by a cluster c_e) transforms another cluster c_t (describing the state of another thread t). However, not all of the information in the clusters c_e and c_t is *directly* used in the computation of indirect effects. This lets us abstract away some of the information, say, from c_e to construct c'_e and compute $tr^{indirect}(c'_e, c_t)$ to determine the indirect effects. We refer to c'_e as the *footprint* of c_e. This helps speed up the computation because different clusters $c_1, \cdots, c_k$ can have the same footprint c_f: in such a case, it is sufficient to compute the indirect effect due to the single footprint c_f, instead of the k different clusters. We call this technique *summary abstraction*. The notion of a footprint can be applied to ci-disjuncts (as in the example below) or, equivalently, to clusters (as in our formalism).

Example 1. We first illustrate the value of this technique using an example from the single buffer algorithm in Fig. 1 with the commented lines added. In Fig. 2 every box represents a ci-disjunct. We consider states with 3 threads $C1$, $C2$ and $C3$. The boxes under the column labelled Ci, Cj represents ci-disjuncts with primary thread Ci and secondary thread Cj. However, not all ci-disjuncts are shown. The abstraction includes the program counter of the primary thread (shown in the lower left corner) but not of the secondary thread. c_i represents the value of c in thread Ci: it points to nothing if it is null (the initial value), and a hollow circle if it points to an allocated object, and a filled circle if it points to an object that has been deallocated. c_i and c_j point to different circles to indicate that they are not aliased. The value of x of thread $C1$ is shown as x_1 (true) or $!x_1$ (false).

We now consider the transition due to the execution of the statement `dispose(c)` by C1. The tracked thread is C2. Fig. 2(a) depicts some of the

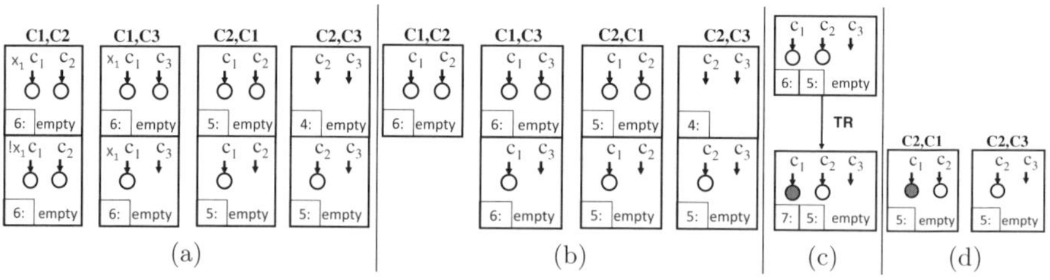

Fig. 2. Abstract states for summary abstraction

input ci-disjuncts. The ci-disjuncts in the leftmost column differ only in the value of x_1. Fig. 2(b) represents the ci-disjuncts from Fig. 2(a) after the application of summary abstraction, which abstracts away x_1 (since the executed statement does not use x). As a result, the two ci-disjuncts of the first column are now represented by a single footprint. Fig. 2(c) depicts the application of the transformer to the state obtained by combining two ci-disjuncts (the executing ci-disjunct $C1, C2$ and the tracked ci-disjunct $C2, C3$). Note that the left program counter is that of C1, and the right one is that of C2. Finally, Fig. 2(d) depicts the resulting ci-disjuncts where C2 is the primary thread. □

We now present a modified version of the transformer TR_{CI}^{ind} that incorporates this optimization. Let *Cluster* denote the set of all clusters. Our modified definition is parameterized by a function $fp_E : Cluster \rightarrow Cluster$ that abstracts away some information from the executing cluster c_e to construct its "footprint" c'_e. However, the only property required of fp_E for soundness is that $fp_E(x) \sqsupseteq x$ (for all x), where the ordering $\sqsupseteq$ is the ordering on the domain ACI (treating a cluster as a set of ci-disjuncts). Given a set S of clusters, let $\overline{fp_E}(S)$ denote $\{fp_E(c) \mid c \in S\}$. Given such a function, we define:

$$TR_E^{ind}(R) = \cup_{e \in \overline{fp_E}(par(R))} \cup_{t \in par(R)} tr_{ACI}^{indirect}(e, t).$$

Theorem 3. *If for all x, $fp_E(x) \sqsupseteq x$, then TR_E^{ind} is a sound approximation of TR_{CI}^{ind}: $TR_E^{ind}(R) \sqsupseteq TR_{CI}^{ind}(R)$.*

Note that analysis designers can define fp_E so that the above technique is an optimization (with no loss in precision, i.e., $tr_E^{indirect}(e,t) = tr^{indirect}(e,t)$), or they can define a more aggressive absraction function that leads to greater speedups with a potential loss in precision. Thus, the parameter fp_E acts as a precision-efficiency tradeoff switch.

In our implementation, we used a definition of fp_E such that $fp_E(c_e)$ is the part of c_e that is read or written by the executed statement (transition).

4.2 Exploiting Frames for the Tracked Cluster

The technique described above for the executing cluster can be used for the tracked cluster as well, but with some extensions. The modified technique involves decomposing the tracked cluster c_t into two parts: the part c_t^{fp} that is directly used to determine the indirect effect, and the part c_t^{fr} that is neither used nor modifed by the indirect effect. We refer to c_t^{fp} as the *footprint* and to c_t^{fr} as the *frame*. Unlike in the earlier case, we require the frame now because the goal of the indirect effect is to determine the updated value of the tracked cluster. We call this technique *summarizing effects*.

Example 2. We demonstrate the summarizing effects technique on the algorithm in Fig. 1. A set of ci-disjuncts are depicted in Fig. 3(a). The notation used is the same as that in Fig. 2. Consider the execution of `dispose(c)` by C1. C2 is the tracked thread. Note that the ci-disjuncts in the third column of Fig. 3(a) differ

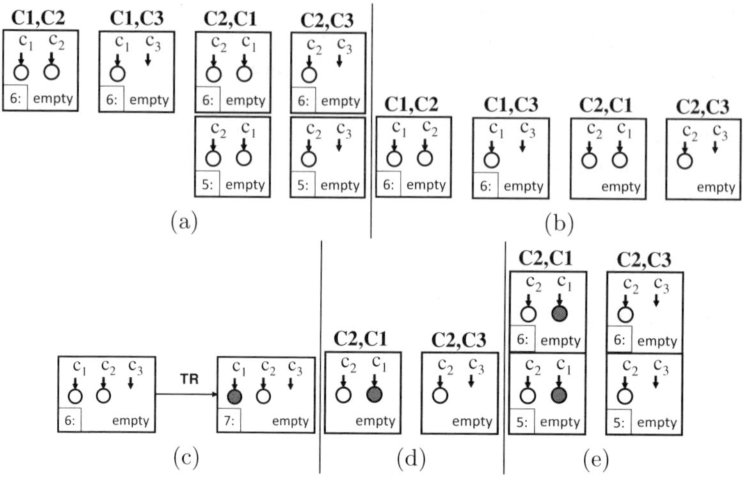

Fig. 3. Abstract states for summarizing effects

only by C2's program counter. This is also true for the ci-disjuncts in the fourth column.We define the frame of a ci-disjunct to consist of its program counter and the footprint to consist of everything else. Fig. 3(b) shows ci-disjuncts after we replaced the tracked ci-disjunctsby their footprints. Fig. 3(c) shows the application of the transformer on the information gathered from all the ci-disjuncts considered. Fig. 3(d) depicts the states after they are projected back to the *CID* domain and before the frame is restored. Finally, we use the frame from Fig. 3(a) on Fig. 3(d) and get the abstract state in Fig. 3(e). □

We now present a modified form of our earlier transformer, parameterized by a couple of functions. Given functions $frame_T : Cluster \to Cluster$ and $fp_T : Cluster \to Cluster$ we define:

$$\begin{aligned} TR^{ind}_T(R) = &\text{ let } C = par(R) \text{ in} \\ &\text{ let } TC = \{(fp_T(c), frame_T(c)) \mid c \in C\} \text{ in} \\ &\textstyle\bigcup_{e \in C} \bigcup_{(p,r) \in TC} (r \sqcap tr^{indirect}_{ACI}(e,p)). \end{aligned}$$

Note that the above technique is similar in spirit to the inter-procedural analysis technique of abstracting away information about the caller that is not visible to the callee when the callee is analyzed and restoring this information at the return site (see e.g., [14]). Furthermore, to achieve an efficiency gain with this definition, we need to *save and reuse* the value of $tr^{indirect}_{ACI}(e,p)$ when different clusters have the same footprint p. This is analogous to the technique of *memoization* in interprocedural analysis. In our context, we can capture this by rewriting the last line of the above definition as follows:

$$\bigcup_{p \in dom(TC)} (\cup_{e \in C} tr^{indirect}_{ACI}(e,p)) \otimes \{r \mid (p,r) \in TC\}$$

where $dom(TC) = \{p \mid (p,r) \in TC\}$ and $S_1 \otimes S_2 = \{x \sqcap y \mid x \in S_1, y \in S_2\}$..

Theorem 4. *Let* $frame_T$ *and* fp_T *satisfy (for all* x, y*) (a)* $fp_T(x) \sqsupseteq x$*, (b)* $frame_T(x) \sqsupseteq x$*, and (c)* $frame_T(x) \sqsupseteq tr^{indirect}(y, x)$*. Then,* TR_T^{ind} *is a sound approximation of* TR_{CI}^{ind}*:* $TR_T^{ind}(R) \sqsupseteq TR_{CI}^{ind}(R)$*.*

In our implementation, the local store of the tracked thread is abstracted into the frame and omitted from the footprint. (For heap-manipulating programs, any regions of the heap that are private to the tracked thread can be handled similarly.)

5 Evaluation

We have implemented our ideas in a framework for concurrent shape analysis. Our implementation may be seen as an instantiation of the framework in Sec. 3.3, obtained by composing the thread correlation abstraction (in Sec. 3.2) with TVLA [16], an abstraction for shape analysis, and its extension HeDec [17]. We use a flow-sensitive and context-sensitive shape analysis. Context sensitivity is maintained by using call-strings.

We have used our implementation to verify properties such as memory safety, data structure invariants, and linearizability for several highly concurrent state-of-the-art practical algorithms.

Our evaluation indeed confirms the need for extra precision in tracking thread correlations, without which the analysis fails to verify the specified properties. Our evaluation also confirms the value of the optimizations described in this paper. Tab. 1 summarizes the verified data structures and the speedups gained from the use of summarizing effects and summarizing abstraction techniques. Our benchmarks are all concurrent sets implemented by sorted linked lists. More details can be found in an accompanying technical report [21].

We analyzed variants of these programs with intentionally added bugs (e.g., missing synchronization, changing the synchronization order). Our analysis found all these bugs and reported a problem (as expected, since our analysis is sound).

Note that the speedup is particularly high for the first two programs (namely [18] and its optimized variant). These are also the examples where the analysis took most time. We believe this confirms the non-linear speedups achieved by

Table 1. Experiments performed on a machine with a 2.4Ghz Intel Q6600 32 bit processor and 4Gb memory running Linux with JDK 1.6

	Time (seconds)				Speedup		
Algorithm	Standard	Summar.	Abs.	Both	Summar.	Abs.	Both
Concurrent Set [18]	56,347	19,233	2,402	1,596	2.93	23.46	35.30
Optimized Concurrent Set	46,499	18,981	2,061	1,478	2.45	22.57	31.45
Lazy List Set [10]	963	679	460	390	1.42	2.09	2.47
CAS-based set [23]	13,182	8,710	4,223	2,975	1.51	3.12	4.43
DCAS-based set [23]	861	477	446	287	1.80	1.93	3.00
Hand over Hand Set [12]	686	577	444	398	1.19	1.54	1.73

the techniques: we optimize a quadratic algorithm, thus we expect to gain more as the examples become bigger. These algorithms were expensive to analyze since they were interprocedural, and used a large number of pointer variables and Boolean fields. Summarizing effects significantly reduced the blow-up due to context sensitivity and summarizing abstraction was able to reduce blow-ups due to local Boolean fields.

6 Related Work

In this paper we have presented techniques for speeding up analysis (abstract interpretation) of concurrent programs. One of the recent works in this area is [7], which presents the idea of thread-modular verification for model checking systems with finitely-many threads. However, in many natural examples tracking correlations between different thread states is necessary, and our work focuses on abstractions that track such correlations. The work on Environment Abstraction [5] presents a *process-centric abstraction* framework that permits capturing thread-correlations. Our abstract domain is similar in spirit. The novelty of our work, however, is in the definition of the transformers and its optimizations, and its application to concurrent shape analysis.

Resource invariants [19] enable the use of thread-modular analysis to verify concurrent programs without tracking thread correlations. One of the challenges in automating such verification is inferring resource invariants. [8] and [3] present techniques for inferring resource invariants. These techniques apply to programs with coarse-grained concurrency. Our implementation, however, handles *fine-grained* concurrency, including non-blocking or lock-free algorithms. [4], and more recently [22], present semi-automated algorithms for verifying programs with fine-grained concurrency, using a combination of separation-logic, shape abstractions, and rely-guarantee reasoning. While powerful, this approach requires programmers to provide annotations describing the abstract effects of the atomic statements of a thread.

The abstract states in our analysis represent quantified invariants. Quantified invariants have been previously used in Indexed Predicate Abstraction [15] and in Environment Abstraction [5]. A similar quantified invariants approach has also been used in the analysis of heap properties [20] and properties of collections [9] in sequential programs.

The work described in this paper is a continuation of [2]. The new contributions of this paper are: we introduce a new, simple, abstract domain for capturing correlations between pairs of threads and systematically study the question of defining a precise, yet efficient, transformer for this domain, and present new techniques for computing transformers efficiently for this domain; we also present an empirical evaluation of our approach that shows that our techniques lead to a dramatic reduction in verification time (compared to our earlier work) while still being able to prove the same properties.

References

1. Ashcroft, E.: Proving assertions about parallel programs. J. Comput. Syst. Sci. 10(1), 110–135 (1975)
2. Berdine, J., Lev-Ami, T., Manevich, R., Ramalingam, G., Sagiv, M.: Thread quantification for concurrent shape analysis. In: Gupta, A., Malik, S. (eds.) CAV 2008. LNCS, vol. 5123, pp. 399–413. Springer, Heidelberg (2008)
3. Calcagno, C., Distefano, D., Vafeiadis, V.V.: Bi-abductive resource invariant synthesis. In: Hu, Z. (ed.) APLAS 2009. LNCS, vol. 5904, pp. 259–274. Springer, Heidelberg (2009)
4. Calcagno, C., Parkinson, M.J., Vafeiadis, V.: Modular safety checking for fine-grained concurrency. In: Riis Nielson, H., Filé, G. (eds.) SAS 2007. LNCS, vol. 4634, pp. 233–248. Springer, Heidelberg (2007)
5. Clarke, E.M., Talupur, M., Veith, H.: Proving Ptolemy right: The environment abstraction framework for model checking concurrent systems. In: Ramakrishnan, C.R., Rehof, J. (eds.) TACAS 2008. LNCS, vol. 4963, pp. 33–47. Springer, Heidelberg (2008)
6. Cousot, P., Cousot, R.: Systematic design of program analysis frameworks. In: POPL, pp. 269–282. ACM Press, New York (1979)
7. Flanagan, C., Qadeer, S.: Thread-modular model checking. In: Ball, T., Rajamani, S.K. (eds.) SPIN 2003. LNCS, vol. 2648, pp. 213–224. Springer, Heidelberg (2003)
8. Gotsman, A., Berdine, J., Cook, B., Sagiv, M.: Thread-modular shape analysis. In: PLDI, pp. 266–277 (2007)
9. Gulwani, S., McCloskey, B., Tiwari, A.: Lifting abstract interpreters to quantified logical domains. In: POPL, pp. 235–246 (2008)
10. Heller, S., Herlihy, M., Luchangco, V., Moir, M., Scherer, W., Shavit, N.: A lazy concurrent list-based set algorithm. In: Anderson, J.H., Prencipe, G., Wattenhofer, R. (eds.) OPODIS 2005. LNCS, vol. 3974, pp. 3–16. Springer, Heidelberg (2006)
11. Henzinger, T.A., Jhala, R., Majumdar, R.: Race checking by context inference. In: PLDI, pp. 1–13 (2004)
12. Herlihy, M., Shavit, N.: The Art of Multiprocessor Programming. M. Kaufmann, San Francisco (2008)
13. Herlihy, M., Wing, J.M.: Linearizability: a correctness condition for concurrent objects. TOPLAS 12(3) (1990)
14. Knoop, J., Steffen, B.: The interprocedural coincidence theorem. In: Pfahler, P., Kastens, U. (eds.) CC 1992. LNCS, vol. 641, pp. 125–140. Springer, Heidelberg (1992)
15. Lahiri, S.K., Bryant, R.E.: Predicate abstraction with indexed predicates. TOCL 9(1), 1–29 (2007)
16. Lev-Ami, T., Sagiv, M.: TVLA: A system for implementing static analyses. In: Palsberg, J. (ed.) SAS 2000. LNCS, vol. 1824, pp. 280–302. Springer, Heidelberg (2000)
17. Manevich, R., Lev-Ami, T., Sagiv, M., Ramalingam, G., Berdine, J.: Heap decomposition for concurrent shape analysis. In: Alpuente, M., Vidal, G. (eds.) SAS 2008. LNCS, vol. 5079, pp. 363–377. Springer, Heidelberg (2008)
18. Michael, M.M.: High performance dynamic lock-free hash tables and list-based sets. In: SPAA, pp. 73–82 (2002)
19. O'Hearn, P.W.: Resources, concurrency, and local reasoning. Theor. Comput. Sci. 375(1-3), 271–307 (2007)

20. Podelski, A., Wies, T.: Boolean heaps. In: Hankin, C., Siveroni, I. (eds.) SAS 2005. LNCS, vol. 3672, pp. 268–283. Springer, Heidelberg (2005)
21. Segalov, M., Lev-Ami, T., Manevich, R., Ramalingam, G., Sagiv, M.: Efficiently inferring thread correlations. TR-09-59203 (January 2009)
22. Vafeiadis, V.: Shape-value abstraction for verifying linearizability. In: Jones, N.D., Müller-Olm, M. (eds.) VMCAI 2009. LNCS, vol. 5403, pp. 335–348. Springer, Heidelberg (2009)
23. Vechev, M., Yahav, E.: Deriving linearizable fine-grained concurrent objects. In: PLDI, pp. 125–135 (2008)

Scalable Context-Sensitive Points-to Analysis Using Multi-dimensional Bloom Filters

Rupesh Nasre[1], Kaushik Rajan[2], R. Govindarajan[1], and Uday P. Khedker[3]

[1] Indian Institute of Science, Bangalore, India
[2] Microsoft Research, Bangalore, India
[3] Indian Institute of Technology, Bombay, India
nasre@csa.iisc.ernet.in, kaushik@msr.microsoft.com,
govind@serc.iisc.ernet.in, uday@cse.iitb.ac.in

Abstract. Context-sensitive points-to analysis is critical for several program optimizations. However, as the number of contexts grows exponentially, storage requirements for the analysis increase tremendously for large programs, making the analysis non-scalable. We propose a scalable flow-insensitive context-sensitive inclusion-based points-to analysis that uses a specially designed multi-dimensional bloom filter to store the points-to information. Two key observations motivate our proposal: (*i*) points-to information (between pointer-object and between pointer-pointer) is sparse, and (*ii*) moving from an *exact* to an *approximate* representation of points-to information only leads to reduced precision without affecting correctness of the *(may-points-to)* analysis. By using an approximate representation a multi-dimensional bloom filter can significantly reduce the memory requirements with a probabilistic bound on loss in precision. Experimental evaluation on SPEC 2000 benchmarks and two large open source programs reveals that with an average storage requirement of 4MB, our approach achieves almost the same precision (98.6%) as the exact implementation. By increasing the average memory to 27MB, it achieves precision upto 99.7% for these benchmarks. Using Mod/Ref analysis as the client, we find that the client analysis is not affected that often even when there is some loss of precision in the points-to representation. We find that the *NoModRef* percentage is within 2% of the exact analysis while requiring 4MB (maximum 15MB) memory and less than 4 minutes on average for the points-to analysis. Another major advantage of our technique is that it allows to trade off precision for memory usage of the analysis.

1 Introduction

Pointer analysis enables many compiler optimization opportunities and remains as one of the most important compiler analyses. For client analyses, both precision and speed of the underlying pointer analysis play a vital role. Several context-insensitive algorithms have been shown to scale well for large programs [1][2][3][4]. However, these algorithms are significantly less precise for real world programs compared to their context-sensitive counterparts[5][6][7][8]. Unfortunately,

Z. Hu (Ed.): APLAS 2009, LNCS 5904, pp. 47–62, 2009.

context-sensitive pointer analysis improves precision at the cost of high — often unacceptable — storage requirement and analysis time. These large overheads are an artifact of the large number of contexts that a program might have. For example, the SPEC2000 benchmark *eon* has 19K pointers if we do not consider context information but the number increases to 417K pointers if we consider all context-wise pointers. Scaling a context sensitive points-to analysis is therefore a challenging task. Recent research (see Related Work in Section 5) has focused on the scalability aspect of context-sensitive points-to analysis and achieves moderate success in that direction[9][4]. However, the memory requirements are still considerably large. For instance, in [9], most of the larger benchmarks require over 100 MB for points-to analysis. Hence, scalability still remains an issue. Also, none of the current analyses provide a handle to the user to control the memory usage of a points-to analysis. Such a feature will be useful when analyzing a program in a memory constrained environment.

The objective of a context-sensitive points-to analysis is to construct, for each pointer and context, a set containing all the memory locations (pointees) that the pointer can point to in that context. This paper proposes a new way of representing points-to information using a special kind of bloom filter[10] that we call a multi-dimensional bloom filter.

A bloom filter is a compact, and approximate, representation (typically in the form of bit vectors) of a set of elements which trades off some precision for significant savings in memory. It is a lossy representation that can incur false positives, i.e., an element not in the set may be answered to be in the set. However, it does not have false negatives, i.e., no element *in the set* would be answered as *not in the set*. To maintain this property, the operations on a bloom filter are restricted so that items can only be added to the set but can never be deleted[1]. Our motivation for using bloom filters for context-sensitive flow-insensitive points to analysis stems from the following three key observations.

- ***Conservative static analysis:*** As with any other compiler analysis, static points-to analysis tends to be conservative as correctness is an absolute requirement. Thus, in case of static may-points-to analysis, a pointer not pointing to a variable at run time can be considered otherwise, but not vice-versa. As a bloom filter does not have false negatives, a representation that uses bloom filters is safe. A bloom filter can only (falsely) answer that a pointer points to a few extra pointees. This only makes the analysis less precise and does not pose any threat to correctness. Further, as a bloom filter is designed to efficiently trade off precision for space it is an attractive representation to enable scalability of points-to analysis.
- ***Sparse points-to information:*** The number of pointees that each context-wise pointer (pointer under a given context) actually points to is many orders of magnitude less than both the number of context-wise pointers and the total number of potential pointees. Hence, though the points-to set can potentially be very large, in practice, it is typically small and sparse. A bloom filter is

[1] Some modified bloom filter structures[11] have been proposed that can support deletion but they do so at the expense of introducing false negatives.

ideally suited to represent data of this kind. When the set is sparse, a bloom filter can significantly reduce the memory requirement with a probabilistically low bound on loss in precision.
- ***Monotonic data flow analysis:*** As long as the underlying analysis uses a monotonic iterative data flow analysis, the size of the points-to set can only increase monotonically. This makes a bloom filter a suitable choice as monotonicity guarantees that there is no need to support deletions.

The above observations make a bloom filter a promising candidate for representing points-to information. However, using the bloom filter as originally proposed in [10] is not efficient for a context sensitive analysis. We therefore extend the basic bloom filter to a multi-dimensional bloom filter (*multibloom*) to enable efficient storage and manipulation of context aware points-to information. The added dimensions correspond to *pointers*, *calling contexts*, and *hash functions*. The bloom filter is extended along the first two dimensions (pointers and calling contexts) to support all the common pointer manipulation operations ($p = q$, $p = \&q$, $p = *q$ and $*p = q$) and the query operation $DoAlias(p, q)$ efficiently. The third dimension (hash functions) is essential to control loss in precision. We theoretically show and empirically observe that larger the number of hash functions, lower is the loss in precision. In effect, multibloom significantly reduces the memory requirement with a very low probabilistically bound loss in precision. The compact representation of points-to information allows the context sensitive analysis to scale well with the program size.

The major contributions of this paper are:

- We propose a multi-dimensional bloom filter (*multibloom*) that can compactly represent the points-to information with almost no loss in precision.
- Using extended bloom filter operations, we develop a context-sensitive flow-insensitive points-to analysis for C programs in the LLVM compilation infrastructure.
- We show that by using multibloom, a user can control the total memory requirement of a compiler analysis, unlike in most other analyses.
- We demonstrate the effectiveness of multibloom through experimental evaluation on 16 SPEC 2000 benchmarks and 2 real world applications. With less than 4MB memory on average (maximum 15MB), multibloom achieves more than 98% precision, taking less than 4 minutes per benchmark on average.
- We also evaluate precision of a client Mod/Ref analysis. We find that using *multibloom*, the *NoModRef* percentage is within 1.3% of the exact analysis while requiring 4MB memory and 4 minutes on average for the points-to analysis.

2 Background

General purpose languages like C pose many challenges to the compiler community. Use of pointers hinders many compiler optimizations. Pointers with multiple indirections, pointers to functions, etc. only add to these challenges. For analyzing such

```
void main() {
  S1: p1 = f(&x);
      p3 = p1;
  S2: p2 = f(&y);
}
```

```
int *f(int *a) {
    int *u, *v;
  S3: u = g(&x);
  S4: v = g(&y);
    return a;
}
```

```
int *g(int *b) {
    return b;
}
```

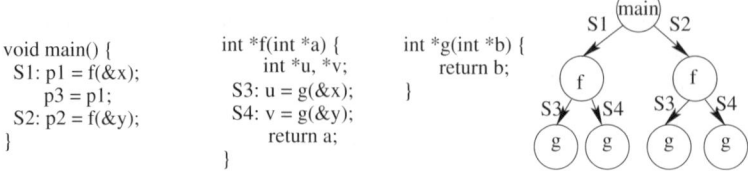

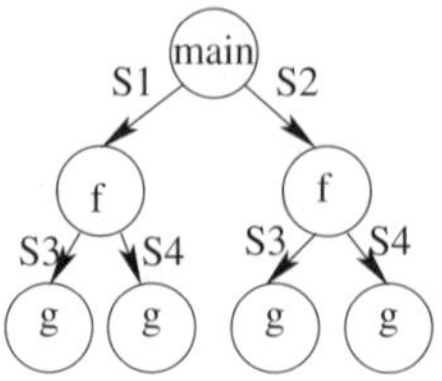

Fig. 1. Example program and its invocation graph

complicated programs, however, it is sufficient to assume that all pointer statements in the program are represented using one of the four basic forms: address-of assignment ($p = \&q$), copy assignment ($p = q$), load assignment ($p = *q$) and store assignment ($*p = q$)[12] (we describe how these statements are handled by our analysis in Section 3). Our analysis handles all aspects of C (including recursion), except variable number of arguments.

2.1 Context-Sensitive Points-to Analysis

A context-sensitive points-to analysis distinguishes between various calling contexts of a program and thus, is able to more accurately determine the points-to information compared to the context-insensitive version [5]. This precision, however, comes at a price: storing the number of contexts, which is huge in a large C program. Consider the example program and its invocation graph shown in Figure 1. The invocation graph shows that for different contexts, function f has 2 instances and function g has 4 instances. The number of distinct paths from $main$ to the leaf nodes in the graph is equal to the number of different contexts the program has. In general, the number of contexts in a program can be exponential in terms of the number of functions. For instance, the number of methods in the open source program *pmd* is 1971, but it has 10^{23} context-sensitive paths[9]. Therefore, for a context-sensitive points-to analysis, the number of points-to tuples can be exponential (in the number of functions in the program). The exponential blow up in the number of contexts, typically results in an exponential blow up in the storage requirement for exact representation of context-wise points-to tuples.

Reducing the storage requirements of a context-sensitive points-to analysis has attracted much research in pointer analysis. Several novel approaches have been proposed for scalable pointer analyses (see Section 5 for related work). Despite these advances, absolute values of memory and time required are substantially high. For instance, in [9], all the benchmarks having more than 10K methods (*columba*, *gantt*, *jxplorer*, *jedit*, *gruntspud*) require over 100MB of memory. For the benchmarks we evaluate, we find that the number of pointers increases by 1 or 2 orders of magnitude if we track them in a context-wise manner. So it is possible that the memory and time requirements of a context-sensitive analysis will be a few orders of magnitude higher than a context insensitive analysis.

Our goal, in this paper, is to reduce this storage and execution time requirement of a context-sensitive points-to analysis. This is achieved by using a variant of bloom filter, which sacrifices a small amount of precision. As we shall see in the next subsection, once the user fixes the size of a bloom filter, he/she can estimate a probabilistic bound on the loss in precision as a function of the average number of pointees of a pointer (in a given context).

2.2 Bloom Filter

A bloom filter is a probabilistic data structure used to store a set of elements and test the membership of a given element[10]. In its simplest form, a bloom filter is an array of N bits. An element e belonging to the set is represented by setting the kth bit to 1, where $h(e) = k$ and h is the hash function mapping element e to k^{th} bit. For instance, if the hash function is $h_1(e) = (3*e+5)\%N$, and if $N = 10$, then for elements $e = 13$ and 100, the bits 4 and 5 are set. Membership of an element e is tested by using the same hash function. Note that element 3 also hashes to the same location as 13. This introduces false positives, as the membership query would return *true* for element 3 even if it is not inserted. Note, however, that there is no possibility of false negatives, since we never reset any bit.

The false positive rate can be reduced drastically by using multiple hash functions. Thus, if we use two hash functions for the above example, with $h_2(e) = (\lfloor e/2 \rfloor + 9)\%N$, then the elements $e = 13,\ 100$ get hashed to bits $5,\ 9$. Note that a membership query to 3 would return *false* as location 0 (corresponding to $h_2(3)$) is 0, even though location 4 (corresponding to $h_1(3)$) is set. Thus, using multiple hash functions the false positives can be reduced.

The false positive rate P for a bloom filter of size N bits after n elements are added to the filter with d hash functions is given by Equation 1 (from [10]).

$$P = \frac{(1/2)^d}{(1 - \frac{nd}{N})} \tag{1}$$

This is under the assumption that the individual hash functions are *random* and different hash functions are *independent*. Unlike traditional data structures used in points-to analysis[5][8], time to insert elements in a bloom filter and to check for their membership is independent of the number of elements in the filter.

3 Points-to Analysis Using Bloom Filters

A points-to tuple $\langle p, c, x\rangle$ represents a pointer p pointing to variable x in calling context c. A context is defined by a sequence of functions and their call-sites. A naive implementation stores context-sensitive points-to tuples in a bloom filter by hashing the tuple $\langle p, c, x\rangle$ and setting that bit in the bloom filter. This simple operation takes care of statements only of the form $p = \&x$. Other pointer statements, like $p = q$, $p = *q$, and $*p = q$ require additional care. For example, for handling $p = q$ type of statements, the points-to set of q has to be copied to p. While bloom filter is very effective for existential queries, it is inefficient for universal queries like "*what is the points-to set of pointer p under context c?*".

One way to solve this problem is to keep track of the set of all pointees (objects). This way, the query $FindPointsTo(p, c)$ to find the points-to set for a pointer p under context c is answered by checking the bits that are set for each of the pointees. Although this is possible in theory, it requires storing all possible pointees, making it storage inefficient. Further, going through all of them every time to process a $p = q$ operation makes this strategy time inefficient. Further complications arise if we want to support a context-sensitive $DoAlias$ query. Therefore, we propose an alternative design that has more dimensions than a conventional bloom filter in order to support the pointer operations.

3.1 Multi-dimensional Bloom Filter

Our proposed multi-dimensional bloom filter (multibloom) is a generalization of the basic bloom filter introduced in Section 2.2. It has 4 dimensions, one each for pointers, contexts, hash functions and a bit vector along the fourth dimension. It is represented as $mb[P][C][D][B]$. The configuration of a multibloom is specified by a 7-tuple $\langle P, C, D, B, M_p, M_c, H\rangle$ where P is the number of entries for pointers, C is the number of entries for contexts, D is the number of hash functions, B is the bit-vector size for each hash function, M_p is the function mapping pointers, M_c is the function mapping contexts and H is the family of hash functions. The first 4 entries (P, C, D, B) denote the number of unique values that can be taken along each dimension. For example $C = 16$ would mean that the multibloom has space for storing the pointee set for 16 contexts in which a pointer is accessed. We will have to map every context of a given pointer to one among 16 entries. The total size of the structure is $Size = P \times C \times D \times B$. Functions M_p and M_c map the pointer p and context c to integers $Pidx$ and $Cidx$ in the range $[0, P-1]$ and $[0, C-1]$ respectively. A family of hash functions $H{=}(h_1, h_2, \cdots, h_D)$ map the pointee x to D integers $Hidx_1, Hidx_2, \cdots, Hidx_D$ respectively. These play the same role as the hash functions in Section 2.2.

Given a points-to tuple $\langle p, c, x\rangle$, it is entered into the multibloom as follows. $Pidx$, $Cidx$ and $(Hidx_1, Hidx_2, \cdots, Hidx_D)$ are obtained using M_p, M_c and H respectively. The tuple is added to multibloom by setting the following D bits:

$$mb\,[Pidx]\,[Cidx]\,[i]\,[Hidx_i] = 1,\ \forall i \in [1, D]$$

Extending Bloom Filter Operations for $p = q$ Statement. While processing $p = q$ type of statement under context c, all we need to do is to find the $B \times D$ source bits from the multibloom that correspond to pointer q under the context c and bitwise-OR it with the $B \times D$ destination bits corresponding to pointer p under context c. This logically copies the pointees of q on to p without having to universally quantify all the pointees that q points to. The pseudo-code is given in Algorithm 1.

Example. Consider the program fragment given in the first column of Figure 2. Consider a multibloom with configuration

$$\langle P, C, D, B, M_p, M_c, H\rangle = \langle 3, 1, 2, 8, I, C_0, (h_1, h_2)\rangle$$

Algorithm 1. Handling statement $p = q$ under context c in multibloom, with D hash functions and a B bit vector

$Pidx_{src} = M_p[q]$, $Cidx_{src} = M_c[c]$
$Pidx_{dst} = M_p[p]$, $Cidx_{dst} = M_c[c]$
for $i = 1$ to D **do**
  for $j = 1$ to B **do**
    $mb[Pidx_{dst}][Cidx_{dst}][i][j] = mb[Pidx_{dst}][Cidx_{dst}][i][j]$
      $\vee\ mb[Pidx_{src}][Cidx_{src}][i][j]$
  end for
end for

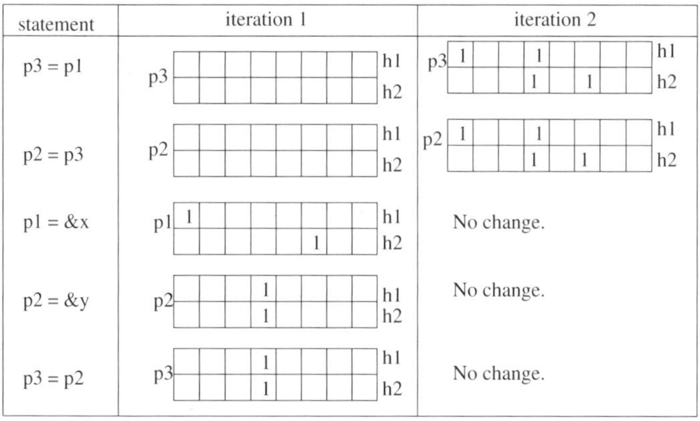

Fig. 2. Example program to illustrate points-to analysis using bloom filters. First column shows the program statements. Later columns show the state of bloom filters for different pointers after successive iterations over constraints until a fix-point is reached.

The map M_p is an identity function I that returns a different value for $p1$, $p2$ and $p3$. The two hash functions h_1 and h_2 are defined as $h_1(x) = 0,\ h_2(x) = 5,\ h_1(y) = 3$ *and* $h_2(y) = 3$. C_0 maps every context to entry 0, since $C = 1$. As there is only one entry for context and each statement modifies one pointer, we illustrate the multibloom as 3 bloom filters. For clarity, we depict the multibloom as multiple 2-dimensional arrays in Figure 2. Initially, all the bits in the buckets of each pointer are set to 0. The state of bloom filters after every iteration (the analysis is flow-insensitive) for the example code is shown in Figure 2.

Extending Bloom Filter Operations for $*p = q$ and $p = *q$. There are two ways to handle statements of the form $*p = q$ and $p = *q$. One way is to extend the above strategy by adding more dimensions to the multibloom. This is extensible to multiple levels of indirection. This strategy would add more dimensions to our 4-dimensional bloom filter, one for each pointer dereference. Clearly, this adds to storage and analysis time requirements. The second way is to conservatively assume that a pointer to a pointer points to the universal set of pointees and process the statement conservatively. The number of pointers to pointers is much less in programs compared to single-level pointers. Therefore, depending on the application, one may be willing to lose some precision by this conservative estimate. To obtain a good balance of storage requirement, analysis time and precision, we employ a combination of the above two techniques. We extend multibloom for two-level pointers (**p) and use the conservative strategy (universal set of pointees) for higher-level pointers (***p, ****p and so on). The conservative strategy results in little precision loss considering that less than 1% of all dynamic pointer statements contain more than two levels of pointer indirections (obtained empirically).

Extending multibloom for two-level pointers makes it look like $mb[P][S][C][D][B]$ where S is the number of entries for pointers that are pointees of a two-level pointer. For single-level pointers, S is 1. For two-level pointers S is configurable. For higher-level pointers S is 1 and an additional bit is set to indicate that the pointer points to the universal set of pointees.

To handle load statement $p = *q$ where p is a single-level pointer and q is a two-level pointer, all the cubes $mb[Q][i]$ (i.e., $C \times D \times B$ bits) corresponding to pointer q, $\forall i = 1..S$ are bitwise-ORed to get a resultant cube. Note that $S = 1$ for the result, i.e., the result is for a single-level pointer. This cube is then bitwise-ORed with that of p, i.e., with $mb[P][1]$. This makes p point to the pointees pointed to by all pointers pointed to by q.

To handle store statement $*q = p$ where p is a single-level pointer and q is a two-level pointer, the cube $mb[P][1]$ of p is bitwise-ORed with each cube $mb[Q][i]$ of q, $\forall i = 1..S$. It makes each pointer pointed to by q point to the pointees pointed to by p.

Handling context-sensitive load/store statements requires a modification to address-of assignment $p = \&q$. If p is a two-level pointer, then to process the address-of statement in context c, $D \times B$ bits of q are bitwise-ORed with $D \times B$ bits of p in the appropriate hash entry for q (see example below).

For mapping a pointer onto the range $1..S$, we need a mapping function M_s. The multibloom configuration is thus extended to include S and M_s.

Example. Consider the program fragment given in the first column of Figure 3. Consider a multibloom with configuration

$$\langle P, S, C, D, B, M_p, M_s, M_c, H\rangle = \langle 5, 2, 1, 1, 8, I, h_s, -, (h)\rangle$$

The map M_p is an identity function I that returns a different value for $p1$ through $p5$ The hash function h is defined as $h(x) = 1 \ and \ h(y) = 4$. The mapping function h_s is defined as $h_s(p1) = 1 \ and \ h_s(p2) = 2$. Initially, all bits in the buckets for each pointer are set to 0. The state of bloom filters after each statement is processed is shown in the second column of Figure 3. Third column describes the multibloom operation. Note that the above strategy of using an additional dimension for two-level pointers can be extended to include more dimensions to accommodate higher-level pointers.

Storage Requirement of Multibloom. A quick analysis explains why multibloom is space efficient. Consider the SPEC 2000 benchmark *parser* which has about 10K pointers and an average of 3 pointees per context-wise pointer, on an

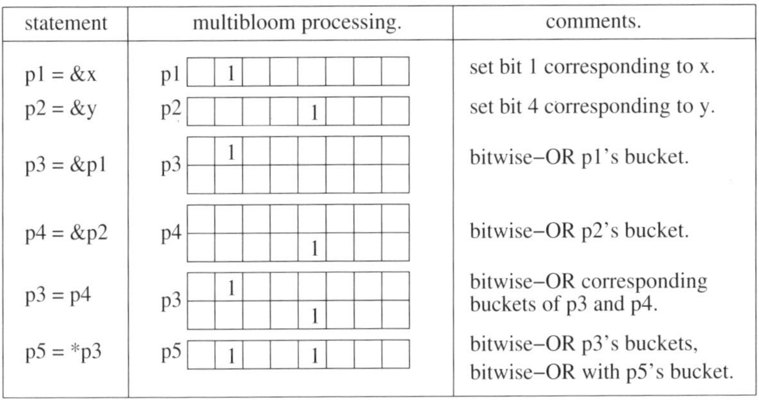
statement
multibloom processing.
comments.
p1 = &x
p1
1
set bit 1 corresponding to x.
p2 = &y
p2
1
set bit 4 corresponding to y.
p3 = &p1
p3
1
bitwise–OR p1's bucket.
p4 = &p2
p4
1
bitwise–OR p2's bucket.
p3 = p4
p3
1
1
bitwise–OR corresponding buckets of p3 and p4.
p5 = *p3
p5
1
1
bitwise–OR p3's buckets, bitwise–OR with p5's bucket.

Fig. 3. Example program to illustrate handling load/store statements. First column shows the program statements. Second column shows the bloom filter state after each statement is processed. Third column describes the multibloom operation.

average about 16 contexts per pointer, and around 20% two- or higher-level runtime pointer-statements. Consider a multibloom with $P = 10\text{K}$, $S = 5$, $C = 8$, $D = 8$ and $B = 50$. The total memory requirement for the multibloom is $10\text{K} \times (0.2 \times 5 + 0.8 \times 1) \times 8 \times 8 \times 50$ bits $= 4.32\text{MB}$. This is much less than what a typical analysis would require, which is at least a few tens of megabytes for a program having 10K pointers.

To measure the false positive rate we will now try to map the values back from a 4-dimensional multibloom to a 2-dimensional bloom filter so that we can apply Equation 1. As there are 16 contexts on an average per pointer and $C = 8$, on average 2 contexts would map to a given context bin. Therefore the number of entries per bloom filter would be twice the average number of pointees per context-wise pointer. Now assuming the representation across pointers is more or less uniform, we can use the equation with $N = B \times D = 400$, $d = D = 8$, $n = 3 \times 2 = 6$ (average number of contexts per bin multiplied by average number of pointees per context-wise pointer). This gives a false positive rate of 0.5% per Equation 1. In practice we find that the loss in precision is not perceivable at all. The *NoAlias* percentage, a metric used in [13] (explained in Section 4), in this case for the approximate representation is exactly the same as that for an exact representation which takes significantly higher amounts of memory.

3.2 Querying the Multibloom

The ultimate goal of alias analysis is to answer whether two pointers p and q alias with each other either in a specific calling context or in a context-insensitive manner. We describe below how multibloom can be used to answer these queries.

Context-Sensitive Query. A context-sensitive query is of type $DoAlias(q_1, q_2, c)$. To answer this query we need to first extract the $B \times D$ bit sets

Algorithm 2. Handling context-sensitive $DoAlias(q_1, q_2, c)$

```
Pidx_q1 = M_p [q1], Cidx_q1 = M_c [c]
Pidx_q2 = M_p [q2], Cidx_q2 = M_c [c]
for i = 1 to D do
  hasPointee = false
  for j = 1 to B do
    if mb [Pidx_q1] [Cidx_q1] [i] [j] == mb [Pidx_q2] [Cidx_q2] [i] [j] == 1 then
      hasPointee = true
      break
    end if
  end for
  if hasPointee == false then
    return NoAlias
  end if
end for
return MayAlias
```

Algorithm 3. Handling context-insensitive $DoAlias(q_1, q_2)$

```
for c = 1 to C do
  if DoAlias(q1, q2, c) == MayAlias then
    return MayAlias
  end if
end for
return NoAlias
```

that belong to q_1 and q_2 under the context c. For each hash function the algorithm needs to determine if the corresponding bit vectors have at least one common bit with the value 1. If no such bit exists for any one hash function, then q_1 and q_2 do not alias. The pseudo-code is given in Algorithm 2. Note that this procedure is for single level pointers. In case q_1 and q_2 are higher-level pointers, the outermost for-loop of the procedure needs to be run for each value of s where $s \in [1..S]$.

Context-Insensitive Query. A context-insensitive query will be of type $DoAlias(q_1, q_2)$. The query is answered by iterating over all possible values of the context c and calling the context-sensitive version of DoAlias: $DoAlias(q_1, q_2, c)$. Only if under no context do q_1 and q_2 alias, it concludes that there is no alias. The pseudo-code is shown in Algorithm 3.

4 Experimental Evaluation

4.1 Implementation Details and Experimental Setup

All our implementation is done in the LLVM compiler infrastructure[13] and the analysis is run as a post linking phase. We implement two points-to analyses, one which has an exact representation (without false positives) of the points-to set and the other uses our proposed multiblooom representation. For an exact representation we store pointees per context for a pointer using STL vectors[14]. Both versions are implemented by extending Andersen's algorithm [15] for context-sensitivity. They are flow-insensitive and field-insensitive implementations that use an invocation graph based approach. Each aggregate (like arrays and structures) is represented using a single memory location. Neither version implements optimizations like offline variable substitution[16].

Table 1. Benchmark characteristics

Bench -mark	KLOC	Total Inst	Pointer Inst	No. of Fns
gcc	222.185	328425	119384	1829
perlbmk	81.442	143848	52924	1067
vortex	67.216	75458	16114	963
eon	17.679	126866	43617	1723
httpd	125.877	220552	104962	2339
sendmail	113.264	171413	57424	1005
parser	11.394	35814	11872	356
gap	71.367	118715	39484	877
vpr	17.731	25851	6575	228
crafty	20.657	28743	3467	136
mesa	59.255	96919	26076	1040
ammp	13.486	26199	6516	211
twolf	20.461	49507	15820	215
gzip	8.618	8434	991	90
bzip2	4.650	4832	759	90
mcf	2.414	2969	1080	42
equake	1.515	3029	985	40
art	1.272	1977	386	43

Table 2. Sensitivity to parameter S

Bench -mark	Memory (KB)		Precision	
	$S=1$	$S=5$	$S=1$	$S=5$
gcc	220973	302117.00	84.2	85.3
perlbmk	99346.9	143662.00	89.3	90.6
vortex	44756.4	62471.00	91	91.5
eon	108936	131552.00	96.3	96.8
httpd	221633	233586.00	92.8	93.2
sendmail	122310	127776.00	90.2	90.4
parser	23511.4	43093.10	97	98
gap	74914.8	84551.70	96.7	97.4
vpr	15066.4	23676.60	93.6	94.2
crafty	10223.9	10891.20	96.9	97.6
mesa	50389.7	55066.90	99.2	99.4
ammp	12735.8	15282.90	99.1	99.2
twolf	29037.2	33663.10	99.1	99.3
gzip	2807	3005.9	90.6	90.9
bzip2	2128.51	2333.82	87.7	88
mcf	2122.09	3758.17	94.5	94.5
equake	2245.6	3971.50	97.6	97.7
art	1090.72	1693.82	88.6	88.6

We evaluate performance over 16 C/C++ SPEC 2000 benchmarks and two large open source programs: *httpd* and *sendmail*. Their characteristics are given in Table 1. *KLOC* is the number of Kilo lines of code, *Total Inst* is the total number of static LLVM instructions, *Pointer Inst* is the number of static pointer-type LLVM instructions and *No. of Fns* is the number of functions in the benchmark. The LLVM intermediate representations of SPEC 2000 benchmarks and open source programs were run using *opt* tool of LLVM on an Intel Xeon machine with 2GHz clock, 4MB L2 cache and 3GB RAM. To quantify the loss in precision with a multibloom implementation, we use the *NoAlias* percentage metric used in LLVM. It is calculated by making a set of alias queries for all pairs of pointer variables within each function in a program and counting the number of queries that return *NoAlias*. Larger the *NoAlias* percentage, more precise is the analysis (upper bounded by the precision of the exact analysis).

We evaluate the performance of a multibloom for many different configurations and compare it with the exact implementation. In all evaluated configurations we

Table 3. Precision (*NoAlias* %) vs Memory (in KB). *OOM* means *Out Of Memory*.

Bench -mark	Precision (*NoAlias* %)					Memory (KB)				
		multibloom					multibloom			
	exact	4-4-10 tiny	8-8-10 small	8-12-50 medium	8-16-100 large	exact	4-4-10 tiny	8-8-10 small	8-12-50 medium	8-16-100 large
gcc	OOM	71.8	79.6	83.4	85.3	OOM	3956	15445	113577	302117
perlbmk	OOM	75.3	85.0	89.3	90.6	OOM	1881	7345	54008	143662
vortex	OOM	85.7	90.1	91.2	91.5	OOM	818	3194	23486	62471
eon	96.8	81.5	88.9	94.3	96.8	385284	3059	11942	87814	233586
httpd	93.2	90.1	92.1	92.9	93.2	225513	1673	6533	48036	127776
sendmail	90.4	85.6	88.2	90.3	90.4	197383	1723	6726	49455	131552
parser	98.0	65.8	97.3	97.9	98.0	121588	565	2204	16201	43094
gap	97.5	88.2	93.5	96.7	97.4	97863	1107	4323	31786	84552
vpr	94.2	85.9	93.9	94.1	94.2	50210	310	1211	8901	23677
crafty	97.6	97.1	97.6	97.6	97.6	15986	143	557	4095	10892
mesa	99.4	89.6	96.6	99.1	99.4	8261	721	2816	20702	55067
ammp	99.2	98.4	99.0	99.2	99.2	5844	201	782	5746	15283
twolf	99.3	96.7	99.1	99.3	99.3	1594	441	1721	12656	33664
gzip	90.9	88.8	90.5	90.8	90.9	1447	42	164	1205	3205
bzip2	88.0	84.8	88.0	88.0	88.0	519	31	120	878	2334
mcf	94.5	91.3	94.3	94.5	94.5	220	50	193	1413	3759
equake	97.7	96.9	97.7	97.7	97.7	161	52	204	1494	3972
art	88.6	86.6	88.4	88.6	88.6	42	23	87	637	1694

allow the first dimension (P) to be equal to the number of unique pointers. We empirically found that the number of entries S for pointers pointed to by two-level pointers gives a good trade off between memory and precision for $S = 5$. The hash family H, the context mapper M_c and the pointer-location mapper M_s are derived from the in-built pseudo random number generator. Many different combinations were tried for the other three dimensions: $C = (4, 8, 16)$, $B = (10, 20, 50, 100)$ and $D = (4, 8, 12, 16)$. From now on, when we report the results, we refer to the multibloom configuration by the tuple $(C - D - B)$. Below we report the results for select configurations that showed interesting behavior.

4.2 Tradeoff between Precision, Memory and Analysis Time

In Tables 3-4 we report the precision, time and memory requirements for various benchmarks. We compare 4 different multibloom configurations namely *tiny t* (4-4-10), *small s* (8-8-10), *medium m* (8-12-50) and *large l* (8-16-100) with *exact* which does not have any false positives.

Three out of the 18 benchmarks run out of memory when we run an exact analysis, highlighting the need for a scalable context-sensitive points-to analysis. All the multibloom configurations ran to completion successfully for these three benchmarks. The *tiny* configuration indicates significant reduction in both memory and analysis time. The memory requirement is three orders less, while the access time is reduced to about one-fourth for all benchmarks which take at least 20 seconds.

Table 4. Precision (*NoAlias* %) vs Time (in sec). *OOM* means *Out Of Memory*. *t* is *tiny*, *s* is *small*, *m* is *medium* and *l* is *large* configuration.

Bench -mark	Precision (*NoAlias* %)					Time (s)				
		multibloom					multibloom			
	exact	t	s	m	l	exact	t	s	m	l
gcc	OOM	71.8	79.6	83.4	85.3	OOM.	791.705	3250.627	10237.702	27291.303
perlbmk	OOM	75.3	85.0	89.3	90.6	OOM.	76.277	235.207	2632.044	5429.385
vortex	OOM	85.7	90.1	91.2	91.5	OOM.	95.934	296.995	1998.501	4950.321
eon	96.8	81.5	88.9	94.3	96.8	231.166	39.138	118.947	1241.602	2639.796
httpd	93.2	90.1	92.1	92.9	93.2	17.445	7.180	15.277	52.793	127.503
sendmail	90.4	85.6	88.2	90.3	90.4	5.956	3.772	6.272	25.346	65.889
parser	98.0	65.8	97.3	97.9	98.0	55.359	9.469	31.166	145.777	353.382
gap	97.5	88.2	93.5	96.7	97.4	144.181	5.444	17.469	152.102	419.392
vpr	94.2	85.9	93.9	94.1	94.2	29.702	5.104	18.085	88.826	211.065
crafty	97.6	97.1	97.6	97.6	97.6	20.469	2.636	9.069	46.899	109.115
mesa	99.4	89.6	96.6	99.1	99.4	1.472	1.384	2.632	10.041	23.721
ammp	99.2	98.4	99.0	99.2	99.2	1.120	1.008	2.592	15.185	38.018
twolf	99.3	96.7	99.1	99.3	99.3	0.596	0.656	1.152	5.132	12.433
gzip	90.9	88.8	90.5	90.8	90.9	0.348	0.192	0.372	1.808	4.372
bzip2	88.0	84.8	88.0	88.0	88.0	0.148	0.144	0.284	1.348	3.288
mcf	94.5	91.3	94.3	94.5	94.5	0.112	0.332	0.820	5.036	12.677
equake	97.7	96.9	97.7	97.7	97.7	0.224	0.104	0.236	1.104	2.652
art	88.6	86.6	88.4	88.6	88.6	0.168	0.164	0.408	2.404	6.132

The precision (in terms of *NoAlias* percentage) is within 7% for *tiny* of an exact analysis on average. At the other end, *medium* and *large* configurations achieve full precision for all the benchmarks with significant savings in memory requirement for those requiring at least 15MB memory. However, this comes at a price in terms of analysis time. Thus *medium* and *large* are good configuration to use if precision is an absolute requirement. Even for the larger benchmarks they will lead to termination as they still provide a compact storage.

The *small* configuration proves to be an excellent trade off point. It achieves a good precision (within 1.5%) on average and achieves more than 10-fold memory reduction for benchmarks requiring more than 10MB memory for an exact analysis. It takes around the same amount of time on benchmarks that terminate with exact analysis. It should be noted that for smaller benchmarks (*mesa*, *ammp*, *twolf*, *gzip*, *bzip2*, *mcf*, *equake* and *art*) the configuration *small* requires more time than *exact* configuration. However, for larger benchmarks we see significant improvements in analysis time using bloom filter. One unique advantage of using multibloom is the user-control over various parameters to trade off precision for memory or vice versa. To reduce memory requirement for *medium* and *large*, we experimented with smaller values of S. The results for $S = 1$ versus $S = 5$ are given in Table 2 (memory in KB and precision as *NoAlias* percentage). We observe that with at most 1% reduction in average precision, we can obtain around 18% reduction in average memory requirement. In summary, a multibloom representation

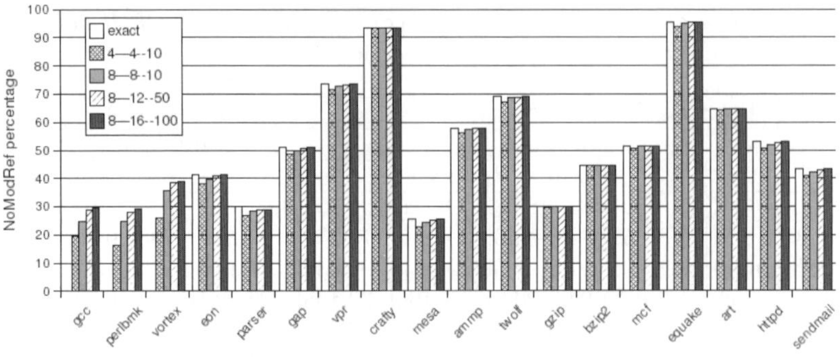

Fig. 4. Mod/Ref client analysis

guarantees a compact storage representation for context-sensitive points-to analysis and allows the user to pick the configuration depending on whether analysis time or accuracy is more desirable.

4.3 Mod/Ref Analysis as a Client to Points-to Analysis

Next we analyze how the loss in precision in the points-to analysis due to false positives affect the client analyses. We use the Mod/Ref analysis as the client of our multibloom based points-to analysis. For a query $GetModRef(callsite, pointer)$, the Mod/Ref analysis checks whether *callsite* reads or modifies the memory pointed to by *pointer*. It has four outcomes: (i) *NoModRef*: *call-site* does not read from or write to memory pointed to by *pointer*, (ii) *Ref*: *call-site* reads from the memory pointed to by *pointer*, (iii) *Mod*: *call-site* writes to (and does not read from) the memory pointed to by *pointer*, and (iv) *ModRef*: *call-site* reads from and writes to the memory pointed to by *pointer*. $ModRef$ is most conservative and should be returned when it is not possible to establish otherwise for a safe analysis. The more precise an approximate points-to analysis the more often will it answer *NoModRef* (upper bounded by an *exact analysis*). Figure 4 shows percentage of queries answered *NoModRef* by the analysis. From the figure, it can be seen that the *NoModRef* percentage with multibloom is 96.9% of the exact analysis even with a *tiny* configuration. For *small* configuration, it improves further to 98.7%. This shows that a client analysis is hardly affected due to loss in precision by using an approximate representation, while still enjoying the benefits of reduced memory and time requirements.

An important aspect of using multibloom is the provision of selecting a configuration on need basis. For more precise analysis, one can trade off memory and speed requirements by choosing larger values for C, D and B. For scalable analyses, one can reduce these values trading off some precision.

5 Related Work

Many scalable pointer analysis algorithms are context- and flow-insensitive [1]. As scalability became an important factor with increasing code size, interesting mechanisms were introduced to approximate the precision of a full blown context-sensitive and flow-sensitive analysis. [17] proposed *one level flow* to improve precision of context-insensitive, flow-insensitive analyses, still maintaining the scalability. Later, several inclusion-based scalable analyses were proposed [2][3][4], based on some novel data structures for points-to analysis like BDD. Similar to ours, several context-sensitive but flow-insensitive analyses have been recently proposed. Since inclusion-based analyses are costly, several unification-based algorithms were introduced, trading off precision for speed [1], [18]. Several context-sensitive algorithms proposed earlier [5][6][7][8] are flow-sensitive. Flow-sensitivity adds to precision but typically makes the analysis non-scalable. The idea of *bootstrapping* [19] enables context- and flow-sensitive algorithms to scale.

Various enhancements have also been made to the original Andersen's inclusion-based algorithm: online cycle elimination[20] to break dependence cycles on the fly, offline variable substitution[16] to reduce the number of pointers tracked during the analysis, location equivalence[21] and semi-sparse flow-sensitivity[22]. These enhancements are orthogonal to the usage of bloom filters. One can implement a points-to analysis with, for instance, online cycle elimination with points-to tuples stored in bloom filters and enjoy combined benefits.

Several novel data structures have been used in the last decade to scale points-to analysis, like ROBDD[2][23][9], ZBDD[24]. These data structures store exact representation of the points-to information and have no false positives. In contrast, bloom filters are useful for storing information in an approximate way. Also, our multibloom filter approach provides the user to control the memory requirement with a probabilistic lower bound on the loss in precision. Optimistic results for pointer analysis hint that bloom filters would be very useful for other compiler analyses as well.

6 Conclusions

In this paper we propose the use of multi-dimensional bloom filter for storing points-to information. The proposed representation, though, may introduce false positives, significantly reduces the memory requirement and provides a probabilistic lower bound on loss of precision. As our multibloom representation introduces only false positives, but no false negatives, it ensures safety for (may-)points-to analysis. We demonstrate the effectiveness of multibloom on 16 SPEC 2000 benchmarks and 2 real world applications. With average 4MB memory, multibloom achieves almost the same (98.6%) precision as the exact analysis taking about average 4 minutes per benchmark. Using Mod/Ref analysis as the client, we find that the client analysis is not affected that often even with some loss of precision in points-to representation. Our approach, for the first time, provides user a control on the memory requirement, yet giving a probabilistic lower bound on the loss in precision. As a future work, it would be interesting to see the effect of approximation introduced using bloom filters with the approximations introduced in control-flow analyses such as kCFA or in unification of contexts.

References

1. Steensgaard, B.: Points-to analysis in almost linear time. In: POPL (1996)
2. Berndl, M., Lhotak, O., Qian, F., Hendren, L., Umanee, N.: Points-to analysis using BDDs. In: PLDI (2003)
3. Heintze, N., Tardieu, O.: Ultra-fast aliasing analysis using CLA: A million lines of C code in a second. In: PLDI (2001)
4. Lhotak, O., Hendren, L.: Scaling Java points-to analysis using spark. In: Hedin, G. (ed.) CC 2003. LNCS, vol. 2622, pp. 153–169. Springer, Heidelberg (2003)
5. Emami, M., Ghiya, R., Hendren, L.J.: Context-sensitive interprocedural points-to analysis in the presence of function pointers. In: PLDI (1994)
6. Landi, W., Ryder, B.G., Zhang, S.: Interprocedural modification side effect analysis with pointer aliasing. In: PLDI (1993)
7. Whaley, J., Rinard, M.: Compositional pointer and escape analysis for java programs. In: OOPSLA (1999)
8. Wilson, R.P., Lam, M.S.: Efficient context-sensitive pointer analysis for C programs. In: PLDI (1995)
9. Whaley, J., Lam, M.S.: Cloning-based context-sensitive pointer alias analysis using binary decision diagrams. In: PLDI (2004)
10. Bloom, B.H.: Space/time trade-offs in hash coding with allowable errors. Communications of the ACM 13(7), 422–426 (1970)
11. Fan, L., Cao, P., Almeida, J., Broder, A.Z.: Summary cache: a scalable wide-area web cache sharing protocol. In: SIGCOMM (1998)
12. Rugina, R., Rinard, M.: Pointer analysis for multithreaded programs. In: PLDI (1999)
13. The LLVM compiler infrastructure, `http://llvm.org`
14. Standard Template Library, `http://en.wikipedia.org/wiki/Standard_Template_Library`
15. Andersen, L.O.: Program analysis and specialization for the C programming language. PhD Thesis (1994)
16. Rountev, A., Chandra, S.: Offline variable substitution for scaling points-to analysis. In: PLDI (2000)
17. Das, M.: Unification-based pointer analysis with directional assignments. In: PLDI (2000)
18. Fahndrich, M., Rehof, J., Das, M.: Scalable context-sensitive flow analysis using instantiation constraints. In: PLDI (2000)
19. Kahlon, V.: Bootstrapping: a technique for scalable flow and context-sensitive pointer alias analysis. In: PLDI (2008)
20. Faehndrich, M., Foster, J.S., Su, Z., Aiken, A.: Partial online cycle elimination in inclusion constraint graphs. In: PLDI (1998)
21. Hardekopf, B., Lin, C.: Exploiting pointer and location equivalence to optimize pointer analysis. In: Riis Nielson, H., Filé, G. (eds.) SAS 2007. LNCS, vol. 4634, pp. 265–280. Springer, Heidelberg (2007)
22. Hardekopf, B., Lin, C.: Semi-sparse flow-sensitive pointer analysis. In: POPL (2009)
23. Zhu, J., Calman, S.: Symbolic pointer analysis revisited. In: PLDI (2004)
24. Lhotak, O., Curial, S., Amaral, J.N.: Using ZBDDs in points-to analysis. In: Adve, V., Garzarán, M.J., Petersen, P. (eds.) LCPC 2007. LNCS, vol. 5234, pp. 338–352. Springer, Heidelberg (2008)

A Short Cut to Optimal Sequences

Akimasa Morihata

JSPS research fellow, University of Tokyo
morihata@ipl.t.u-tokyo.ac.jp

Abstract. We propose a method for easily developing efficient programs for finding optimal sequences, such as the maximum weighted sequence of a set of feasible ones. We formalize a way to derive efficient algorithms from naive enumerate-and-choose-style ones by *shortcut fusion*, which is a program transformation for eliminating intermediate data structures passed between functions. In addition, we propose a set of transformations for exploiting our shortcut fusion law. As an implementation of our method, we introduce a library for finding optimal sequences. The library consists of proposed transformations, together with functions useful for describing desirable sequences, so that naive enumerate-and-choose-style programs will be automatically improved.

1 Introduction

Suppose that we are preparing an emergency knapsack, in which we would like to put as many useful items as possible. How can we find the best way to do this? In fact, this is the 0-1 knapsack problem [1], a problem for finding the most valuable collection of items among those whose total weight is less than a limit. The following recurrence equation specifies this problem, where w yields the weight of each item and $\geq_{value}$ compares collections by the total values of the items.

$$\begin{aligned} knap([\,], u) &= [\,] \\ knap(a : x, u) &= \textbf{if } w(a) \leq u \wedge (a : knap(x, u - w(a))) \geq_{value} knap(x, u) \\ &\ \textbf{then } a : knap(x, u - w(a)) \textbf{ else } knap(x, u) \end{aligned}$$

Given items x and a limit u, $knap(x, u)$ returns the best collection of items, and memoization of $knap$ brings a well-known dynamic programming algorithm.

We often attempt at efficiently finding the best solution as the case above. However, it is difficult to develop efficient algorithms, because their correctness highly depends on details of problems. For example, if we consider a variant of the 0-1 knapsack problem in which we regard flashlights as more valuable when there are also spare batteries in the knapsack, the recurrence equation above is no longer correct. When we want to exclude collections containing too many items, we cannot naively reuse the recurrence equation, either.

In this paper, we propose a method for easily developing efficient programs for finding optimal sequences. We consider naive programs in an enumerate-and-choose manner, such as the following.

$$knapsack(x, u) = max_{\geq_{value}}(lessWeighted_u(subsequences(x)))$$

Z. Hu (Ed.): APLAS 2009, LNCS 5904, pp. 63–78, 2009.

This program describes the optimal sequence by three parts: *subsequences*, which enumerates all subsequences (subsets) of the items; $lessWeighted_u$, which filters out sequences that are heavier than the limit; and $maximum_{\geq_{value}}$, which chooses the most valuable sequence. From such a naive and inefficient program, our method derives an efficient one that enumerates only a small number of sequences. As a result, we are able to develop efficient programs in the same way, even for variants of the problem such as the ones mentioned above.

In Sect. 3, we formalize a method for deriving efficient algorithms by *shortcut fusion* [2,3]. Given a pair of functions, a producer and a consumer of an intermediate result, shortcut fusion collapses the producer-consumer pair into a function by eliminating the intermediate result. We propose a shortcut fusion law that derives efficient algorithms by fusing a maximization operation with an enumeration of feasible solutions. In addition, we introduce program transformations for exploiting our shortcut fusion law. From natural descriptions of optimal sequences, the transformations derive programs for which our shortcut fusion law is applicable.

In Sect. 4, we introduce a Haskell library for enumerating optimal sequences. The library consists of proposed transformations, together with functions useful for describing desirable sequences, so that naive enumerate-and-choose-style programs will be automatically improved. Therefore, users are able to develop efficient programs with little algorithmic insight. The transformation is implemented using *RULES pragma* [4], which is an extension of the Glasgow Haskell Compiler[1]. The library is available from the author's website[2].

We discuss related works and give a conclusion in Sect. 5. Because of space limitations, we omit some of the materials, including proofs and examples, which are available in the technical report [5].

2 Preliminary

2.1 Basic Notions

We basically borrow notations from Haskell [6]. We use lambda notation, and for example, the identity function *id* is defined as $id \stackrel{\text{def}}{=} (\lambda x.\, x)$. A function f taking a value of type A and resulting in a value of type B is written by $f :: A \to B$, for example, $id :: \forall a.\, a \to a$. We omit parentheses for function applications, which precede operator applications; thus, $a + f\ x$ is equivalent to $a + f(x)$. Operators might be sectioned, i.e., we write $(+)\ 1\ 4$ or $(+4)\ 1$ instead of $1 + 4$. $(\circ)$ is the function composition operator and its definition is $(f \circ g)\ x \stackrel{\text{def}}{=} f\ (g\ x)$. We only consider terminating functions and no undefined value is taken into account.

We consider sequences (lists) constructed from two constructors: the empty sequence $[]$ and the left-extension operator $(:)$. We also consider uniform sets constructed from the empty set $\emptyset$, the singleton operator $\{\cdot\}$, and the union operator $(\cup)$. We assume that equality checking is available on set elements. We use the standard functions shown in Fig. 1.

[1] The Glasgow Haskell Compiler: available from `http://www.haskell.org/ghc/`

[2] `http://www.ipl.t.u-tokyo.ac.jp/~morihata/DPSH.tar.gz`

$$\begin{array}{llll} \mathit{fst}\ (a,b) \overset{\text{def}}{=} a & & \mathit{snd}\ (a,b) \overset{\text{def}}{=} b & \\ \mathit{map}_{Set}\ f\ x \overset{\text{def}}{=} \{f\ a \mid a \in x\} & & \mathit{filter}_{Set}\ p\ x \overset{\text{def}}{=} \{a \mid a \in x \wedge p\ a\} & \\ \mathit{map}_{List}\ f\ [] & \overset{\text{def}}{=} [] & \mathit{foldr}\ f\ e\ [] & \overset{\text{def}}{=} e \\ \mathit{map}_{List}\ f\ (a:x) & \overset{\text{def}}{=} f\ a : \mathit{map}_{List}\ f\ x & \mathit{foldr}\ f\ e\ (a:x) & \overset{\text{def}}{=} f\ a\ (\mathit{foldr}\ f\ e\ x) \end{array}$$

Fig. 1. Definitions of Standard Functions

A binary relation $\preceq$ is called *preorder* if it satisfies reflexivity $\forall a.\, a \preceq a$ and transitivity $\forall a\,b\,c.\, (a \preceq b \wedge b \preceq c) \Rightarrow a \preceq c$. A preorder $\preceq$ is said to be *total* if $\forall a\,b.\, a \preceq b \vee b \preceq a$ holds. A preorder $\sim$ is called *equivalence relation* if it satisfies symmetry $a \sim b \Rightarrow b \sim a$. Given a preorder $\preceq$, we associate a *dictionary order* (also called *lexicographic order*) $\preceq^*$ in the way that $[] \preceq^* y$ holds for any y and $(a : x) \preceq^* (b : y) \overset{\text{def}}{\Leftrightarrow} a \preceq b \wedge x \preceq^* y$. Given a preorder $\preceq$ and a function f, $\preceq_f$ denotes another preorder defined by $a \preceq_f b \overset{\text{def}}{\Leftrightarrow} f(a) \preceq f(b)$. An *intersection* of two preorders $\preceq$ and $\ll$ is defined by $a\ (\preceq \cap \ll)\ b \overset{\text{def}}{\Leftrightarrow} a \preceq b \wedge a \ll b$. A *lexicographic composition* of two preorders $\preceq$ and $\ll$, denoted by $\preceq ; \ll$, is defined by $a(\preceq ; \ll)b \overset{\text{def}}{\Leftrightarrow} a \ll b \wedge (\neg(b \ll a) \vee a \preceq b)$. Intuitively, $\preceq ; \ll$ compares operands by $\ll$ first, and by $\preceq$ afterwards if they are equivalent on $\ll$.

2.2 Shortcut Fusion

In functional programming, we frequently use intermediate structures for gluing functions. Use of intermediate structures improves modularity and clarity of programs but reduces efficiency because their production and consumption is costly. *Shortcut fusion* [2,3] (also called *shortcut deforestation*) is a program transformation for eliminating intermediate structures.

Theorem 1 (shortcut fusion [2]). *Let build $g \overset{\text{def}}{=} g\ (:)\ []$; then the following equation holds, if the function g has the type $g :: \forall \beta.\, (a \to \beta \to \beta) \to \beta \to \beta$.*

$$\mathit{foldr}\ f\ e\ (\mathit{build}\ g) = g\ f\ e \qquad \square$$

The key to shortcut fusion is the composition of a well-structured producer and a well-structured consumer. Well-structured producers are specified by *foldr*, which replaces sequence constructors by its parameters. Well-structured consumers, so-called *build forms*, are *build* with functions of a certain polymorphic type. *build* captures all the constructors on intermediate sequences, as guaranteed from the type requirement, and thus, we can eliminate the intermediate sequence by supplying the function g with the parameters of *foldr*. The strength of shortcut fusion is its suitability for mechanization. Fusion is accomplished by just canceling *foldr* and *build* out once programs are specified by well-structured producers and consumers. It is worth noting that shortcut fusion was generalized to the *acid rain theorem* [7], which eliminates not only intermediate sequences but also intermediate trees.

As an example, consider the program to compute the square-sum, namely $\mathit{sum}\ (\mathit{map}_{List}\ \mathit{sq}\ x)$ where $\mathit{sq}\ a \overset{\text{def}}{=} a^2$, and let us eliminate the intermediate sequence produced by map_{List} using shortcut fusion. An apparent way to derive a build form is to extract all constructors appearing in the result of the producer. Extracting (:) and [] in the right-hand-side expressions of the definition of map_{List}, we obtain the following.

$$\begin{aligned} map'_{List}\ f\ []\ c\ n &\stackrel{\text{def}}{=} n \\ map'_{List}\ f\ (a : x)\ c\ n &\stackrel{\text{def}}{=} c\ (f\ a)\ (map'_{List}\ f\ x\ c\ n) \end{aligned}$$

Then, $map_{List}\ sq\ x = build\ (map'_{List}\ sq\ x)$ holds and $map'_{List}\ sq\ x$ has the type $\forall\beta.\,(Int \to \beta \to \beta) \to \beta \to \beta$. Moreover, *sum* is equivalent to $foldr\ (+)\ 0$. Therefore, from Theorem 1,

$$sum\ (map_{List}\ sq\ x) = map'_{List}\ sq\ x\ (+)\ 0$$

holds, and we obtain the following equations after inlining (+) and 0.

$$\begin{aligned} sum\ (map_{List}\ sq\ []) &= 0 \\ sum\ (map_{List}\ sq\ (a : x)) &= sq\ a + sum\ (map_{List}\ sq\ x) \end{aligned}$$

We can see that no intermediate sequences are left.

3 Deriving Efficient Algorithms by Shortcut Fusion

Our aim is to solve problems to find the optimal sequence. We use maximals to specify optimality. Given a preorder $\preceq$, $\mathsf{maximals}_{\preceq}$ extracts all the *maximals*, namely elements that are not strictly smaller than others.

$$\mathsf{maximals}_{\preceq}\ X \stackrel{\text{def}}{=} \{a \mid a \in X \wedge \forall b \in X.\, a \preceq b \Rightarrow b \preceq a\}$$

Monotonicity is an important property for efficiently enumerating maximals.

Definition 1 (complete monotonicity). *Sequence extension is said to be* completely monotonic *on a preorder $\preceq$ if both $x \preceq y \Rightarrow (a : x) \preceq (a : y)$ and $x \precnsim y \Rightarrow (a : x) \precnsim (a : y)$ hold, where $v \precnsim w \stackrel{\text{def}}{\Leftrightarrow} v \preceq w \wedge \neg(w \preceq v)$.* □

Intuitively, complete monotonicity means that sequence extension preserves the order. Then, maximals of longer sequences can be obtained by extending the maximals of shorter ones.

3.1 A Short Cut to Optimal Sequences

Let us consider finding the optimal subsequence of a given sequence. It is natural to describe the optimal subsequence as $\mathsf{maximal}_{\preceq} \circ subsequences$, where $\preceq$ specifies the criterion of optimality and *subsequences* enumerates all subsequences.

$$\begin{aligned} subsequences\ [] &\stackrel{\text{def}}{=} \{[]\} \\ subsequences\ (a : x) &\stackrel{\text{def}}{=} \mathbf{let}\ r = subsequences\ x\ \mathbf{in}\ r \cup map_{Set}\ (a{:})\ r \end{aligned}$$

We would like to derive an efficient program from this description. Notice that *subsequences* generates intermediate results, namely candidates of optimal sequences, that will be consumed by $\mathsf{maximal}_{\preceq}$. Our objective is to eliminate this enumerated candidates by shortcut fusion.

First, let us prepare a build form of *subsequences*. Since the intermediate results consist of $(\cup)$, $\{\cdot\}$, $\emptyset$, $(:)$, and $[]$, we attempt to extract them. However, it is impossible because map_{Set} performs iterations over a set made by *subsequences*, and the extraction obstructs these iterations. *Freezing* technique [8,9] is effective for this case. We freeze the functions that obstruct the extraction of constructors, namely $map_{Set}\ (a{:})$ in this case, and regard them as constructors. Then, we successfully obtain the following build form.

$$\begin{array}{l} subsequences\ x = subsequences'\ x\ (\cup)\ \{\cdot\}\ \emptyset\ (\lambda a.\ map_{Set}\ (a{:}))\ (:)\ []\\ \quad \textbf{where}\\ \qquad subsequences'\ []\ j\ s\ e\ m\ c\ n \qquad = s\ n\\ \qquad subsequences'\ (a:x)\ j\ s\ e\ m\ c\ n = \textbf{let}\ r = subsequences'\ x\ j\ s\ e\ m\ c\ n\\ \qquad \qquad \qquad \qquad \qquad \qquad \qquad \quad \textbf{in}\ j\ r\ (m\ a\ r) \end{array}$$

In fact, freezing $(\lambda a.\ map_{Set}\ (a{:}))$ is commonly effective for finding optimal sequences; therefore, we name it *extend* and freeze it for all cases.

$$extend\ a\ x \stackrel{\text{def}}{=} map_{Set}\ (a{:})\ x$$

The reason freezing *extend* is appropriate can be explained from the isomorphism between set-generating functions and nondeterministic computations. From the viewpoint of nondeterministic computation, *extend* is simply the sequence extension operation, and it is rather natural to recognize *extend* as a constructor.

Now, let gen be the function that supplies constructors, together with *extend*, to a function of a certain polymorphic type.

$$\begin{array}{l} \mathsf{gen} :: \forall a. \left(\forall \beta\ \gamma. \begin{array}{l} (\gamma \to \gamma \to \gamma) \to (\beta \to \gamma) \to \gamma \to \\ (a \to \gamma \to \gamma) \to (a \to \beta \to \beta) \to \beta \to \gamma \end{array} \right) \to \{[a]\}\\ \mathsf{gen}\ g \stackrel{\text{def}}{=} g\ (\cup)\ \{\cdot\}\ \emptyset\ extend\ (:)\ [] \end{array}$$

Then, we can derive an efficient algorithm in a shortcut manner.

Theorem 2 (a short cut to optimal sequence). *For a function g of the appropriate type,*

$$\begin{array}{l} \mathsf{maximals}_{\preceq}\ (\mathsf{gen}\ g)\\ \quad = g\ (\lambda x\, y.\ \mathsf{maximals}_{\preceq}\ (x \cup y))\ \{\cdot\}\ \emptyset\ (\lambda a.\ \mathsf{maximals}_{\preceq} \circ extend\ a)\ (:)\ [] \end{array}$$

holds, provided that sequence extension is completely monotonic on $\preceq$. □

Theorem 2 states that if a problem is specified by a composition of a function of a build form and a maximization operation satisfying complete monotonicity, we can derive an efficient program in a shortcut manner. The derived program is efficient in the sense that it uses maximization operations (namely $\mathsf{maximals}$) instead of joining operations (namely $\cup$), and thus, it enumerates only the maximals, instead of all the candidates, during the computation. It is worth remarking that several methods [10,11,12] have been proposed for deriving build forms and they are also useful for our case.

3.2 Deriving Shortcutable Programs

We have introduced our shortcut fusion law, namely Theorem 2. It is worth stressing that the law requires complete monotonicity. However, it is generally difficult to confirm complete monotonicity; moreover, a problem description seldom forms a composition of a producer and a maximization operation.

Recall the 0-1 knapsack problem. The following is an enumerate-and-choose-style description of the problem, where u is the limit of weight, and val and w respectively specify the value and the weight of each item.

$$\begin{aligned} &\mathit{knapsack}\ x\ u\ \mathit{val}\ w\ = \mathsf{maximals}_{\preceq}\ (\mathit{filter}_{\mathit{Set}}\ \mathit{less}_u\ (\mathit{subsequences}\ x)) \\ &\quad \textbf{where}\ a \preceq b \overset{\mathrm{def}}{\Leftrightarrow} \mathit{sum}\ (\mathit{map}_{\mathit{List}}\ \mathit{val}\ a) \leq \mathit{sum}\ (\mathit{map}_{\mathit{List}}\ \mathit{val}\ b) \\ &\qquad\quad \mathit{less}_u\ x \overset{\mathrm{def}}{=} \mathit{weight}\ x \leq u \\ &\qquad\quad \mathit{weight}\ x \overset{\mathrm{def}}{=} \mathit{sum}\ (\mathit{map}_{\mathit{List}}\ w\ x) \end{aligned}$$

We previously derived a build form of *subsequence* and sequence extension is completely monotonic on $\preceq$. However, we cannot apply Theorem 2 to *knapsack* because $\mathit{filter}_{\mathit{Set}}$ blocks the connection of $\mathsf{maximals}_{\preceq}$ to *subsequences*. It is possible to fuse $\mathsf{maximals}_{\preceq}$ and $\mathit{filter}_{\mathit{Set}}$, as $\mathsf{maximals}_{\preceq} \circ \mathit{filter}_{\mathit{Set}}\ \mathit{less}_u = \mathsf{maximals}_{\ll}$ where $a \ll b \overset{\mathrm{def}}{\Leftrightarrow} (\neg \mathit{less}_u\ a \wedge \mathit{less}_u\ b) \vee (\mathit{less}_u\ a = \mathit{less}_u\ b \wedge a \preceq b)$; however, such a naive transformation would ruin monotonicity, and in fact, sequence extension is not completely monotonic on $\ll$.

To resolve this difficulty and exploit Theorem 2, we propose a set of laws. Each law identifies or prepares an order on which sequence extension is completely monotonic and pushes a maximization on the order toward producers. Then, we finally obtain a program to which Theorem 2 is applicable.

First, we show two trivial cases where complete monotonicity holds.

Lemma 1. *Sequence extension is completely monotonic on the order* $\leq_{sum}$. □

Lemma 2. *Sequence extension is completely monotonic on* $\preceq^*$ *for any total preorder* $\preceq$. □

The next lemma is useful when the objective value of a sequence is computed from the value of each of its component.

Lemma 3. *For any function* f*, sequence extension is completely monotonic on a preorder* $\preceq_{\mathit{map}_{\mathit{List}}\ f}$ *if so is on* $\preceq$. □

The value of each component may depend on its context. To capture such cases, we use a function *mapAccumR*, which behaves like a combination of $\mathit{map}_{\mathit{List}}$ and *foldr*.

$$\begin{aligned} &\mathit{mapAccumR}\ f\ e\ []\ \overset{\mathrm{def}}{=} (e, []) \\ &\mathit{mapAccumR}\ f\ e\ (a:x) \overset{\mathrm{def}}{=} \textbf{let}\ (s, y) = \mathit{mapAccumR}\ f\ e\ x \\ &\qquad\qquad\qquad\qquad\qquad\quad (s', b) = f\ s\ a \\ &\qquad\qquad\qquad\qquad\quad\ \ \textbf{in}\ (s', b : y) \end{aligned}$$

We can extract a maximization that satisfies complete monotonicity and push it toward producers when component values can be specified by *mapAccumR*.

Lemma 4. *Given a preorder* $\ll \stackrel{\text{def}}{=} \preceq_{snd \circ mapAccumR\, f\, e}$,

$$\mathsf{maximals}_{\ll} = \mathsf{maximals}_{\ll} \circ \mathsf{maximals}_{\ll \cap =_{foldr\ f'\ e}}$$

holds, where $f'\ a\ s \stackrel{\text{def}}{=} fst\ (f\ s\ a)$*; moreover, sequence extension is completely monotonic on* $\ll \cap =_{foldr\ f'\ e}$ *if so is on* $\preceq$. □

Note that the order $\ll \cap =_{foldr\ f'\ e}$ compares sequences by $\ll$ only if they yield the same value by $foldr\ f'\ e$. In other words, sequences are classified by their $foldr\ f'\ e$ values and compared inside each class. The underlying idea is to specify a safe classification in which complete monotonicity holds in each class. It is worth remarking that the classification by $foldr\ f'\ e$ determines the efficiency of programs that will be derived. The coarser classification yields enumeration of less number of sequences.

Next, let us consider filtering operations.

Lemma 5. *Given a predicate* $p = q \circ foldr\ f\ e$,

$$\mathsf{maximals}_{\preceq} \circ \mathit{filter}_{Set}\ p = \mathsf{maximals}_{\preceq} \circ \mathit{filter}_{Set}\ p \circ \mathsf{maximals}_{\preceq \cap =_{foldr\ f\ e}}$$

holds, and sequence extension is completely monotonic on $\preceq \cap =_{foldr\ f\ e}$ *if so is on* $\preceq$. □

Lemma 5 works similar to Lemma 4. It enables us to push a maximization operation satisfying monotonicity toward producers.

We can derive more efficient programs for certain kinds of filtering operations, such as *suffix-closed* [13] cases.

Definition 2 (suffix-closed). *A predicate* p *is said to be* suffix-closed *if* $p\,(a : x)$ *implies* $p\ x$. □

A typical example of suffix-closed predicates is a predicate that checks whether a sequence is shorter than a limit. Such requirements frequently occur in practice, and the following lemma provides an effective way to deal with them.

Lemma 6. *For a suffix-closed predicate* $p = q \circ foldr\ f\ e$,

$$\begin{aligned}&\mathit{filter}_{Set}\ p = \mathit{filter}_{Set}\ p \circ \mathsf{maximals}_{\lessdot}\\ &\quad \textbf{where}\ x \lessdot y \stackrel{\text{def}}{=} (p\ x \wedge p\ y \wedge x =_{foldr\ f\ e} y) \vee (\neg(p\ x) \wedge p\ y) \vee\\ &\qquad\qquad\qquad (\neg(p\ x) \wedge \neg(p\ y) \wedge (y = [\,] \vee (y = b : w \wedge x = a : u \wedge u \lessdot w)))\end{aligned}$$

holds, and sequence extension is completely monotonic on $\lessdot$. □

If p is suffix-closed, all suffixes of a p-satisfying sequence satisfy p; therefore, it is unnecessary to consider extensions of sequences violating p for enumerating p-satisfying ones. $\mathsf{maximals}_{\lessdot}$ discard p-violators if there is a sequence satisfying p, and moreover, sequence extension is completely monotonic on $\lessdot$.

Finally, consider the case where given two criteria of better sequences, we want to find the best in one criterion among those that are the best in the other.

Lemma 7. *The following equation holds.*

$$\mathsf{maximals}_{\ll} \circ \mathsf{maximals}_{\preceq} = \mathsf{maximals}_{\ll} \circ \mathsf{maximals}_{\ll;\preceq}$$

Moreover, sequence extension is completely monotonic on the order $\ll;\preceq$ *if so is on both* $\ll$ *and* $\preceq$. □

Lemma 7 passes maximization on $\ll$ toward producers by introducing a lexicographic composition.

3.3 Solving 0-1 Knapsack Problem

Let us solve the 0-1 knapsack problem. Recall that $\mathit{filter}_{Set}\ \mathit{less}_u$ separates $\mathsf{maximals}_{\preceq}$ from the producer *subsequences*. Lemma 5 is effective for this case. Since $\mathit{less}_u = (\lambda w.\, w \le u) \circ \mathit{weight}$ and *weight* can be specified by *foldr*, we can push $\mathsf{maximals}_{\preceq \cap =_{weight}}$ to *subsequences*; moreover, sequence extension is completely monotonic on $\preceq \cap =_{weight}$. Then, we can apply Theorem 2. The derivation is summarized as follows.

$$
\begin{array}{l}
\mathit{knapsack}\ x\ u\ \mathit{val}\ w \\
\quad = \quad \{ \text{ definition } \} \\
\qquad \mathsf{maximals}_{\preceq}\ (\mathit{filter}_{Set}\ \mathit{less}_u\ (\mathit{subsequences}\ x)) \\
\quad = \quad \{ \ \mathit{weight} = \mathit{foldr}\ (\lambda a\, r.\, w\ a + r)\ 0, \text{ and Lemma 5 } \} \\
\qquad \mathsf{maximals}_{\preceq}\ (\mathit{filter}_{Set}\ \mathit{less}_u\ (\mathsf{maximals}_{\preceq \cap =_{weight}}\ (\mathit{subsequences}\ x))) \\
\quad = \quad \{ \ \mathit{subsequences}\ x = \mathsf{gen}\ (\mathit{subsequences}'\ x), \text{ and let } \preceq' \stackrel{\text{def}}{=} \preceq \cap =_{weight} \} \\
\qquad \mathsf{maximals}_{\preceq}\ (\mathit{filter}_{Set}\ \mathit{less}_u\ (\mathsf{maximals}_{\preceq'}\ (\mathsf{gen}\ (\mathit{subsequences}'\ x)))) \\
\quad = \quad \{ \text{ Theorem 2 (Lemmas 1, 3, and 5 prove complete monotonicity of } \preceq') \} \\
\qquad \mathsf{maximals}_{\preceq}\ (\mathit{filter}_{Set}\ \mathit{less}_u\ (\mathit{aux}\ x)) \\
\qquad\quad \textbf{where } \mathit{aux}\ []\ \stackrel{\text{def}}{=}\ \{[]\} \\
\qquad\qquad\quad\ \ \mathit{aux}\ (a : x) \stackrel{\text{def}}{=} \textbf{let } r = \mathit{aux}\ x \\
\qquad\qquad\qquad\qquad\qquad\quad \textbf{in } \mathsf{maximals}_{\preceq'}\ (r \cup \mathsf{maximals}_{\preceq'}\ (\mathit{extend}\ a\ r))
\end{array}
$$

The derived program is efficient in the sense that a collection of items is to be retained only if it is the most valuable one among those of the same weight.

When the weight of each item is positive, less_u is suffix-closed and hence Lemma 6 brings a more efficient program as follows.

$$
\begin{array}{l}
\mathit{knapsack}\ x\ u\ \mathit{val}\ w \\
\quad = \quad \mathsf{maximals}_{\preceq}\ (\mathit{filter}_{Set}\ \mathit{less}_u\ (\mathit{subsequences}\ x)) \\
\quad = \quad \{ \text{ Lemma 6, where let } \lessdot \text{ be the order defined in the lemma } \} \\
\qquad \mathsf{maximals}_{\preceq}\ (\mathsf{maximals}_{\lessdot}\ (\mathit{subsequences}\ x)) \\
\quad = \quad \{ \text{ Lemma 7 } \} \\
\qquad \mathsf{maximals}_{\preceq}\ (\mathsf{maximals}_{\preceq;\lessdot}\ (\mathit{subsequences}\ x)) \\
\quad = \quad \{ \ \mathit{subsequences}\ x = \mathsf{gen}\ (\mathit{subsequences}'\ x), \text{ and Theorem 2 } \} \\
\qquad \mathsf{maximals}_{\preceq}\ (\mathit{aux}\ x) \\
\qquad\quad \textbf{where } \mathit{aux}\ []\ \stackrel{\text{def}}{=}\ \{[]\} \\
\qquad\qquad\quad\ \ \mathit{aux}\ (a : x) \stackrel{\text{def}}{=} \textbf{let } r = \mathit{aux}\ x \\
\qquad\qquad\qquad\qquad\qquad\quad \textbf{in } \mathsf{maximals}_{\preceq;\lessdot}\ (r \cup \mathsf{maximals}_{\preceq;\lessdot}\ (\mathit{extend}\ a\ r))
\end{array}
$$

Lemmas 1, 3, 6, and 7 proves complete monotonicity of $\preceq\,;<$. $\mathsf{maximals}_{\preceq;<}$ extracts the maximum-valued ones among those of the same weight after discarding ones heavier than u. Therefore, with appropriate memoization, the derived program runs in $O(u \cdot n)$ time for a sequence of length n.

3.4 Memoization Issues

Memoization is one of the most important issue for efficient implementation of derived programs.

We can achieve memoization of maximal-enumeration steps, for example, *aux* in the derived program above, by preparing producers in a memoized manner. If the producer does not perform plural times of recursive calls for the same argument, maximal-enumeration steps will be done in a memoized manner because derived programs follow the recursion schema of the producer. It is sometimes non-trivial to prepare producers in a memoized manner. Since sequence-enumerations commonly follow certain patterns, it is effective to prepare finely-memoized producers for these patterns beforehand.

It is also required to memoize auxiliary functions, for example, *weight* and $sum \circ map_{List}\ val$ invoked from $\preceq$. Memoization of such functions can be usually achieved by retaining computed results for each candidate. For example, we can achieve memoization for *weight* by remembering *weight*-values for each candidate. We will introduce a variant of Theorem 2 that performs such memoization later in Sect. 4.2.

Another way to achieve memoization is to use existing methods, such as [14,15,16,17,18]. A main effect of our method is to derive recurrence equations from generate-and-choose-style descriptions, and in fact, the derived program above corresponds to the recurrence equation shown in the introduction. Therefore, our method can cooperate with existing methods that derive efficient programs from recurrence equations.

4 A Library for Finding Optimal Sequences

Based on our developed method, we implemented a Haskell library for finding optimal sequences. The library consists of functions that are useful for describing desirable sequences; moreover, the library consists of rewrite rules that automatically derive efficient programs.

4.1 Functions for Enumerating Desirable Sequences

Figure 2 shows definitions of some representative functions of our library.

First, the library contains the function gen, which is the key to our shortcut fusion law. We also implemented build forms of several sequence-enumeration patterns, for example, segs, subsequences, interleave, etc.

For filtering out infeasible sequences, we prepare two functions, constraint and always. constraint $p\ f\ e$ leaves sequences that satisfy $p \circ foldr\ f\ e$. always $p\ f\ e$ requires each sequence to satisfy $p \circ foldr\ f\ e$ for all its suffixes.

$$\mathsf{gen}\ g \stackrel{\text{def}}{=} g\ (\cup)\ \{\cdot\}\ \emptyset\ \mathit{extend}\ (:)\ []$$

$$\begin{aligned} \mathsf{inits}\ [] &\stackrel{\text{def}}{=} \{[]\} \\ \mathsf{inits}\ (a:x) &\stackrel{\text{def}}{=} \{[]\} \cup \mathit{extend}\ a\ (\mathsf{inits}\ x) \end{aligned}$$

$$\begin{aligned} \mathsf{tails}\ [] &\stackrel{\text{def}}{=} \{[]\} \\ \mathsf{tails}\ (a:x) &\stackrel{\text{def}}{=} \{a:x\} \cup \mathsf{tails}\ x \end{aligned}$$

$$\begin{aligned} \mathsf{segs}\ [] &\stackrel{\text{def}}{=} \{[]\} \\ \mathsf{segs}\ (a:x) &\stackrel{\text{def}}{=} \mathsf{inits}\ (a:x) \cup \mathsf{segs}\ x \end{aligned}$$

$$\begin{aligned} \mathsf{subsequences}\ [] &\stackrel{\text{def}}{=} \{[]\} \\ \mathsf{subsequences}\ (a:x) &\stackrel{\text{def}}{=} \mathbf{let}\ r = \mathsf{subsequences}\ x\ \mathbf{in}\ r \cup \mathit{extend}\ a\ r \end{aligned}$$

$$\begin{aligned} \mathsf{markingBy}\ \mathit{fs}\ [] &\stackrel{\text{def}}{=} \{[]\} \\ \mathsf{markingBy}\ \mathit{fs}\ (a:x) &\stackrel{\text{def}}{=} \mathbf{let}\ r = \mathsf{markingBy}\ \mathit{fs}\ x\ \mathbf{in}\ \textstyle\bigcup_{f \in \mathit{fs}} \mathit{extend}\ (f\ a)\ r \end{aligned}$$

$$\begin{aligned} \mathsf{interleave}\ []\ y &\stackrel{\text{def}}{=} \{y\} \\ \mathsf{interleave}\ x\ [] &\stackrel{\text{def}}{=} \{x\} \\ \mathsf{interleave}\ (a{:}x)\ (b{:}y) &\stackrel{\text{def}}{=} \mathit{extend}\ a\ (\mathsf{interleave}\ x\ (b{:}y)) \cup \mathit{extend}\ b\ (\mathsf{interleave}\ (a{:}x)\ y) \end{aligned}$$

$$\mathsf{constraint}\ p\ f\ e \stackrel{\text{def}}{=} \mathit{filter}_{\mathit{Set}}\ (p \circ \mathit{foldr}\ f\ e)$$

$$\mathsf{always}\ p\ f\ e \stackrel{\text{def}}{=} \mathit{filter}_{\mathit{Set}}\ (\lambda x.\ \textstyle\bigwedge_{y \in \mathsf{tails}\ x} p\ (\mathit{foldr}\ f\ e\ y))$$

$$\mathsf{maxBySum} \stackrel{\text{def}}{=} \mathsf{maximals}_{\leq_{\mathit{sum}}}$$

$$\mathsf{maxByMapSum}\ f \stackrel{\text{def}}{=} \mathsf{maximals}_{\leq_{\mathit{sum} \circ \mathit{map}_{\mathit{List}}\ f}}$$

$$\mathsf{maxByAccumSum}\ f\ e \stackrel{\text{def}}{=} \mathsf{maximals}_{\leq_{\mathit{sum} \circ \mathit{snd} \circ \mathit{mapAccumR}\ f\ e}}$$

$$\mathsf{maxByLexico} \stackrel{\text{def}}{=} \mathsf{maximals}_{\leq^*}$$

Fig. 2. Definitions of Some Library Functions

We prepare some maximal-extracting functions. maxBySum extracts the sequences of the maximum total sum; maxByMapSum and maxByAccumSum take auxiliary functions to specify the objective value of each sequence component; maxByLexico extracts the maximum on the dictionary order. Since no different sequences are equivalent or incomparable on the dictionary order, maxByLexico is useful, particularly when one of the optimal sequences is sufficient.

4.2 Rewrite Rules

The library functions are designed so that efficient programs will be derived from our laws, namely Theorem 2 with Lemmas 1–7. The derivation is mechanized using *RULES pragma* [4], which enables us to specify rewrite rules that will be repeatedly applied to programs at compile time.

We introduce another function maxIR that provides an intermediate representation of the derivation.

$$\mathsf{maxIR}\ f\ e\ (\preceq)\ k \stackrel{\text{def}}{=} k \circ \mathsf{maximals}_{\preceq_{\mathit{foldr}\ f\ e}}$$

The function $\mathsf{maxIR}\ f\ e\ (\preceq)\ k$ computes maximals on $\preceq_{foldr\ f\ e}$; in addition, it takes a finalizing computation k that will be applied after the maximization. We impose two properties on $\mathsf{maxIR}\ f\ e\ (\preceq)\ k$ for guaranteeing the correctness of our rewrite rules. Sequence extension must be completely monotonic on $\preceq_{foldr\ f\ e}$, and $\mathsf{maximals}_{\ll} \circ k \circ \mathsf{maximals}_{\preceq_{foldr\ f\ e}} = \mathsf{maximals}_{\ll} \circ k \circ \mathsf{maximals}_{\ll ; \preceq_{foldr\ f\ e}}$ must hold for any $\ll$. It is worth noting that our rewrite rules maintain the properties as confirmed in the technical report [5].

The strategy is to assemble a maxIR from the composition of library functions. First, $\mathsf{maxBySum}$ can be rewritten into maxIR by the following rewrite rule.

$$\mathsf{maxBySum} \rightsquigarrow \mathsf{maxIR}\ (+)\ 0\ (\leq)\ id$$

The translation is straightforward, and sequences are compared by its summation $\leq_{foldr\ (+)\ 0}$. Since no finalizing computation is necessary, the fourth parameter is the identity function id. The derived maxIR certainly satisfies the properties, as confirmed from Lemmas 1 and 7. The rewrite rule for $\mathsf{maxByMapSum}$ is similar.

$$\mathsf{maxByMapSum}\ f \rightsquigarrow \mathsf{maxIR}\ (\lambda a\, r.\ f\ a + r)\ 0\ (\leq)\ id$$

We translate $\mathsf{maxByAccumSum}$ to maxIR as follows, where $\mathsf{maxByAccumSum}'$ is an alias of $\mathsf{maxByAccumSum}$ for avoiding infinite rewriting.

$$\begin{aligned}\mathsf{maxByAccumSum}\ f\ e \rightsquigarrow \mathsf{maxIR}\ &(\lambda a\,(s,r).\,\mathbf{let}\ (t,b) = f\ s\ a\ \mathbf{in}\ (t, b+r))\ (e,0)\\ &(\leq_{snd} \cap =_{fst})\ (\mathsf{maxByAccumSum}'\ f\ e)\end{aligned}$$

This rule is an implementation of Lemma 4. Let $f'\ a\ s \stackrel{\text{def}}{=} fst\ (f\ s\ a)$ and $\ll \stackrel{\text{def}}{=} \leq_{sum \circ snd \circ mapAccumR\ f\ e}$. The maxIR computes pairs that consist of values of $foldr\ f'\ e$ and $sum \circ snd \circ mapAccumR\ f\ e$; thus, the right-hand-side expression of the rule exactly corresponds to $\mathsf{maxByAccumSum}'\ f\ e \circ \mathsf{maximals}_{\ll \cap =_{foldr\ f'\ e}}$. As required, $\ll \cap =_{foldr\ f'\ e}$ satisfies complete monotonicity from Lemma 4.

The rule for $\mathsf{maxByLexico}$ is the following, where Lemma 2 assures complete monotonicity.

$$\mathsf{maxByLexico} \rightsquigarrow \mathsf{maxIR}\ (:)\ []\ (\leq^*)\ id$$

Since always can be regarded as a filtering operation using a suffix-closed predicate, it can be rewritten to maxIR based on Lemma 6 as follows.

$$\begin{aligned}&\mathsf{always}\ p\ f\ e \rightsquigarrow\\ &\quad \mathsf{maxIR}\ (\lambda a\,(v,r).\,(f\ a\ v, p\ (f\ a\ v) \wedge r))\ (e, p\ e)\ (=_{fst} ; \leq_{snd})\ (\mathsf{always}'\ p\ f\ e)\end{aligned}$$

Note that *True* is larger than *False* and always' is an alias of always.

We have introduced rules to translate library functions into maxIR, except for $\mathsf{constraint}$ and $\mathsf{producers}$. Next, let us consider their compositions.

It is easy to provide a rule for the composition of two $\mathsf{constraints}$.

$$\begin{aligned}&\mathsf{constraint}\ p_1\ f_1\ e_1 \circ \mathsf{constraint}\ p_2\ f_2\ e_2 \rightsquigarrow\\ &\quad \mathsf{constraint}\ (\lambda(r_1,r_2).\,p_1\ r_1 \wedge p_2\ r_2)\ (\lambda a\,(r_1,r_2).\,(f_1\ a\ r_1, f_2\ a\ r_2))\ (e_1,e_2)\end{aligned}$$

The following is an implementation of Lemma 5 and deals with the composition of maxIR and constraint.

$$\begin{array}{l}\mathsf{maxIR}\ f\ e\ (\preceq)\ k \circ \mathsf{constraint}\ p\ g\ z \rightsquigarrow \\ \quad \mathsf{maxIR}\ (\lambda a\,(r,s).\,(f\ a\ r, g\ a\ s))\ (e,z)\ (\preceq_{fst} \cap =_{snd}) \\ \qquad (k \circ \mathsf{maximals}_{\preceq_{foldr\ f\ e}} \circ \mathsf{constraint}\ p\ g\ z)\end{array}$$

The left-hand side corresponds to $k \circ \mathsf{maximals}_{\preceq_{foldr\ f\ e}} \circ filter_{Set}\ (p \circ foldr\ g\ z)$, and the right-hand side pushes maximization on $\preceq_{foldr\ f\ e} \cap =_{foldr\ g\ z}$ to producers. This rule maintains the properties of maxIR, as confirmed by Lemmas 5 and 7.

The composition of two maxIRs can be fused as follows.

$$\begin{array}{l}\mathsf{maxIR}\ f_1\ e_1\ (\preceq)\ k_1 \circ \mathsf{maxIR}\ f_2\ e_2\ (\ll)\ k_2 \rightsquigarrow \\ \quad \mathsf{maxIR}\ (\lambda a\,(r_1,r_2).\,(f_1\ a\ r_1, f_2\ a\ r_2))\ (e_1,e_2)\ (\preceq_{fst}\ ;\ \ll_{snd}) \\ \qquad (k_1 \circ \mathsf{maximals}_{\preceq_{foldr\ f\ e}} \circ k_2)\end{array}$$

The correctness of this rule can be confirmed by Lemma 7 and the properties of maxIR. Again, this rewrite rule maintains the properties of maxIR.

So far, we have introduced rules to put functions together and assemble a maxIR. Then, our shortcut fusion law will derive an efficient program.

$$\begin{array}{l}\mathsf{maxIR}\ f\ e\ (\preceq)\ k\ (\mathsf{gen}\ g) \rightsquigarrow k\ (map_{Set}\ fst\ (g\ m\ \{\cdot\}\ \emptyset\ \eta\ f'\ ([\,],e))) \\ \quad \mathsf{where}\ f'\ a\ (x,r) = (a:x, f\ a\ r) \\ \qquad\quad m\ x\ y = \mathsf{maximals}_{\preceq_{snd}}\ (x \cup y) \\ \qquad\quad \eta\ a = \mathsf{maximals}_{\preceq_{snd}} \circ map_{Set}\ (f'\ a)\end{array}$$

This is a variant of Theorem 2 and performs memoization of auxiliary functions, which has been encoded into the parameters f and e by preceding rewrite rules. It is worth stressing that complete monotonicity is assured from the properties of maxIR, and in fact, we have designed the rewrite rules so that they maintain complete monotonicity.

4.3 Experiments

To confirm the effectiveness of our library, we did some experiments. We report the results concerning the 0-1 knapsack problem.

It is easy to describe the 0-1 knapsack problem using our library.

$$\begin{array}{l}knapsack\ x\ u\ val\ w = \\ \quad \mathsf{maxByMapSum}\ val\ (\mathsf{always}\ (\leq u)\ (\lambda i\, r.\ w\ i + r)\ 0\ (subsequences\ x))\end{array}$$

This is straightforward coding of the problem description in Sect. 3.2. We assume the weight of each item to be positive.

It is also easy to specify its variants. As examples, let us solve the two variants of the 0-1 knapsack problem discussed in the introduction.

First, assume that a flashlight is twice as valuable when the knapsack contains a battery. This problem can be described using maxByAccumSum as follows,

Table 1. Computational Times of Programs for the 0-1 Knapsack Problem and the Variants (unit: second)

number of items	100	500	1000	2000	3000	5000	10000
handwritten	0.04	0.22	0.45	0.88	1.32	2.19	4.37
knapsack	0.03	0.15	0.28	0.54	0.80	1.32	2.61
knapsack′	0.09	0.46	0.88	1.68	2.48	4.20	8.46
knapsack″	0.09	0.50	1.00	1.99	2.98	4.93	10.11

where *battery* and *flashlight* respectively check for batteries and flashlights.

$$\begin{aligned}&\mathit{knapsack}'\ x\ u\ \mathit{val}\ w =\\&\quad \mathsf{maxByAccumSum}\ f\ \mathit{False}\ (\mathsf{always}\ (\leq u)\ (\lambda i\, r.\, w\ i + r)\ 0\ (\mathit{subsequences}\ x))\\&\qquad \textbf{where}\ f\ b\ i \stackrel{\text{def}}{=} (b \vee \mathit{battery}\ i, \textbf{if}\ b \wedge \mathit{flashlight}\ i\ \textbf{then}\ 2 \times \mathit{val}\ i\ \textbf{else}\ \mathit{val}\ i)\end{aligned}$$

The function f computes the value of each item by remembering the presence of a battery. It is assumed that batteries appear earlier than flashlights for simplicity.

It is sufficient to add one more always when the knapsack cannot contain more than, for example, ten items.

$$\begin{aligned}&\mathit{knapsack}''\ x\ u\ \mathit{val}\ w =\\&\quad \mathsf{maxByMapSum}\ \mathit{val}\ (\mathsf{always}\ (\leq u)\ (\lambda i\, r.\, w\ i + r)\ 0\\&\qquad\qquad\qquad (\mathsf{always}\ (\leq 10)\ (\lambda i\, s.\, 1 + s)\ 0\ (\mathit{subsequences}\ x)))\end{aligned}$$

We measured the computational times of these three programs. In addition, we prepared a handwritten textbook-program for the 0-1 knapsack problem for comparison. The environment of the experiments consists of Intel Quad-Core Xeon 3.0-GHz CPUs, 8-GB memory, Mac OS X, and the Glasgow Haskell Compiler 6.10.4. Note that all the programs use one core only. The computational times are averages of 100 executions, and exclude times for I/O. The value and weight of each item are integers generated uniformly and respectively range from -1000 to 10000 and from 10 to 50, u was 1000, and *battery* and *flashlight* are defined in an ad-hoc manner.

Table 1 lists the results. Although we have developed *knapsack* without considering its efficiency, it runs in time proportional to the list lengths; moreover, it is even faster than the handwritten code by virtue of the careful implementation of the library. It is worth noting that *knapsack* hardly runs in the absence of our rewrite rules; it generates too many subsequences, e.g., 2^{100} subsequences for a list of 100 elements. The variants, *knapsack′* and *knapsack″*, are slower than *knapsack*, yet they run in time proportional to the list lengths.

5 Discussion

We have proposed a method and implementation for easily finding optimal sequences. We formalized a shortcut-fusion-based method to derive efficient programs and introduced several laws for exploiting our shortcut fusion law. Based on our developed method, we introduced a Haskell library for enumerating optimal sequences. We implemented our transformations using RULES pragma to automatically improve programs on our library. Our experiments showed that programs on our library are easy to write and reasonably fast by virtue of embedded rewrite rules. It is worth remarking that our library naturally cooperates with other Haskell programs. We can write a part of a large system using our library, or use Haskell functions as parameters of our library functions.

The point of our method is to specify a classification such that complete monotonicity holds in each class; then, our shortcut fusion law derives a recurrence equation between the optimal solutions of subproblems. This contrasts with most of the current studies on systematically developing dynamic programming algorithms [14,15,16,17,18,19,20], where users are required to specify recurrence equations or some similar structures. As discussed in the introduction, developing an appropriate recurrence equation is not easy and takes algorithmic practice. For example, Gergerich et al. [19] proposed a domain-specific language for processing sequences, together with an efficient dynamic-programming-based evaluation procedure. In their framework, we can specify optimal sequences using tree grammars, which provide an abstraction of recurrence equations. Nevertheless, because the set of feasible solutions should be specified by a tree grammar, we should develop another tree grammar if we want to impose additional requirements. Our method provides a more modular way for developing dynamic programming algorithms.

We formalized derivation of efficient algorithms by shortcut fusion. Fusion-based program developments have been studied, and among others, Bird and de Moor did an intensive study on this topic [21,22,23,24], and yet their study has not been mechanized. Studies on maximum marking problems [25,26,27,28] reported that a class of problems is mechanically solvable once problems are described in specific forms. We aim at developing mechanizable and generic method by combining these studies with shortcut fusion. Our results correspond to a generalization of studies on maximum marking problems for problems to find optimal sequences. They discussed problems concerning more generic structures rather than sequences. Our results can be extended to problems to find optimal (possibly non-sequence) structures using the acid rain theorem [7].

A system for optimal path querying [29] was previously proposed. This work shares a central idea with the previous one, that is, deriving monotonicity condition from problem descriptions. A main difference is that this work is general-purpose, while the previous one proposes a domain-specific system. However, this work cannot deal with path problems when there are infinitely many paths.

Optimal segment problems have been intensively studied. Zantema [13] did an extensive study on longest segment problems and Mu [30] discussed maximum-sum and maximum-average segment problems. Our method cannot be used to derive the algorithms they introduced. Their algorithms use problem-specific knowledge, such as properties of segment problems, while our method works with little concern about such knowledge. Recently, Puchinger and Stuckey [31] proposed a method that automatically derives efficient branch-and-bound procedures from dynamic programming algorithms. Their method may be effective for introducing problem-specific knowledge to programs derived using our method.

Acknowledgement. The author is grateful to anonymous referees for their careful reviews, which were helpful to improve not only the presentation but also the implementation of the library. Thanks are also due to Shin-Cheng Mu for his valuable comments on an early draft. This research is supported by the Grant-in-Aid for JSPS research fellows 20 · 2411.

References

1. Cormen, T.H., Stein, C., Rivest, R.L., Leiserson, C.E.: Introduction to algorithms, 2nd edn. MIT Press, Cambridge (2001)
2. Gill, A., Launchbury, J., Peyton Jones, S.: A short cut to deforestation. In: FPCA 1993 Conference on Functional Programming Languages and Computer Architecture, pp. 223–232. ACM, New York (1993)
3. Gill, A.: Cheap deforestation for non-strict functional languages. PhD thesis, Department of Computing Science, Glasgow University (1996)
4. Peyton Jones, S., Tolmach, A., Hoare, T.: Playing by the rules: rewriting as a practical optimisation technique in GHC. In: Proceedings of 2001 ACM SIGPLAN Haskell Workshop. Technical Report UU-CS-2001-23, Institute of Information and Computing Sciences, Utrecht University, pp. 203–233 (2001)
5. Morihata, A.: Solving maximum weighted-sum problems for free. Technical Report METR 2009-20, Department of Mathematical Informatics, University of Tokyo (2009)
6. Peyton Jones, S. (ed.): Haskell 98 language and libraries: the revised report. Cambridge University Press, Cambridge (2003)
7. Takano, A., Meijer, E.: Shortcut deforestation in calculational form. In: Conference Record of FPCA 1995 SIGPLAN-SIGARCH-WG2.8 Conference on Functional Programming Languages and Computer Architecture, pp. 306–313. ACM, New York (1995)
8. Kühnemann, A., Glück, R., Kakehi, K.: Relating accumulative and non-accumulative functional programs. In: Middeldorp, A. (ed.) RTA 2001. LNCS, vol. 2051, pp. 154–168. Springer, Heidelberg (2001)
9. Voigtländer, J.: Concatenate, reverse and map vanish for free. In: Proceedings of the Seventh ACM SIGPLAN International Conference on Functional Programming (ICFP 2002), pp. 14–25. ACM, New York (2002)
10. Launchbury, J., Sheard, T.: Warm fusion: Deriving build-catas from recursive definitions. In: Conference Record of FPCA 1995 SIGPLAN-SIGARCH-WG2.8 Conference on Functional Programming Languages and Computer Architecture, pp. 314–323. ACM, New York (1995)
11. Chitil, O.: Type inference builds a short cut to deforestation. In: Proceedings of the 4th ACM SIGPLAN International Conference on Functional Programming, ICFP 1999, pp. 249–260. ACM, New York (1999)
12. Yokoyama, T., Hu, Z., Takeichi, M.: Calculation rules for warming-up in fusion transformation. In: The 2005 Symposium on Trends in Functional Programming, TFP 2005, pp. 399–412 (2005)
13. Zantema, H.: Longest Segment Problems. Sci. Comput. Program. 18(1), 39–66 (1992)

14. Cohen, H.N.: Eliminating redundant recursive calls. ACM Trans. Program. Lang. Syst. 5(3), 265–299 (1983)
15. Acar, U.A., Blelloch, G.E., Harper, R.: Selective memoization. In: Conference Record of POPL 2003: The 30th SIGPLAN-SIGACT Symposium on Principles of Programming Languages, pp. 14–25. ACM, New York (2003)
16. Liu, Y.A., Stoller, S.D.: Dynamic programming via static incrementalization. Higher-Order and Symbolic Computation 16(1-2), 37–62 (2003)
17. Liu, Y.A., Stoller, S.D., Li, N., Rothamel, T.: Optimizing aggregate array computations in loops. ACM Trans. Program. Lang. Syst. 27(1), 91–125 (2005)
18. Chin, W.-N., Khoo, S.-C., Jones, N.: Redundant call elimination via tupling. Fundam. Inform. 69(1-2), 1–37 (2006)
19. Giegerich, R., Meyer, C., Steffen, P.: A discipline of dynamic programming over sequence data. Sci. Comput. Program. 51(3), 215–263 (2004)
20. Kabanov, J., Vene, V.: Recursion schemes for dynamic programming. In: Uustalu, T. (ed.) MPC 2006. LNCS, vol. 4014, pp. 235–252. Springer, Heidelberg (2006)
21. de Moor, O.: Categories, Relations and Dynamic Programming. PhD thesis, Oxford University Computing Laboratory (1992)
22. de Moor, O.: A Generic Program for Sequential Decision Processes. In: Swierstra, S.D. (ed.) PLILP 1995. LNCS, vol. 982, pp. 1–23. Springer, Heidelberg (1995)
23. Bird, R.S., de Moor, O.: Algebra of Programming. Prentice-Hall, Englewood Cliffs (1996)
24. Bird, R.S.: Maximum marking problems. J. Funct. Program. 11(4), 411–424 (2001)
25. Arnborg, S., Lagergren, J., Seese, D.: Easy problems for tree-decomposable graphs. J. Algorithms 12(2), 308–340 (1991)
26. Borie, R.B., Parker, R.G., Tovey, C.A.: Automatic generation of linear-time algorithms from predicate calculus descriptions of problems on recursively constructed graph families. Algorithmica 7(5-6), 555–581 (1992)
27. Sasano, I., Hu, Z., Takeichi, M., Ogawa, M.: Make it practical: a generic linear-time algorithm for solving maximum-weightsum problems. In: Proceedings of the 5th ACM SIGPLAN International Conference on Functional Programming, ICFP 2000, pp. 137–149. ACM, New York (2000)
28. Sasano, I., Ogawa, M., Hu, Z.: Maximum marking problems with accumulative weight functions. In: Van Hung, D., Wirsing, M. (eds.) ICTAC 2005. LNCS, vol. 3722, pp. 562–578. Springer, Heidelberg (2005)
29. Morihata, A., Matsuzaki, K., Takeichi, M.: Write it recursively: a generic framework for optimal path queries. In: Proceedings of the 2008 ACM SIGPLAN International Conference on Functional Programming, ICFP 2008, pp. 169–178. ACM, New York (2008)
30. Mu, S.C.: Maximum segment sum is back: deriving algorithms for two segment problems with bounded lengths. In: Proceedings of the 2008 ACM SIGPLAN Symposium on Partial Evaluation and Semantics-based Program Manipulation, PEPM 2008, pp. 31–39. ACM, New York (2008)
31. Puchinger, J., Stuckey, P.J.: Automating branch-and-bound for dynamic programs. In: Proceedings of the 2008 ACM SIGPLAN Symposium on Partial Evaluation and Semantics-based Program Manipulation, PEPM 2008, pp. 81–89. ACM, New York (2008)

A Skeletal Parallel Framework with Fusion Optimizer for GPGPU Programming

Shigeyuki Sato and Hideya Iwasaki

Department of Computer Science
The University of Electro-Communications
sato@ipl.cs.uec.ac.jp, iwasaki@cs.uec.ac.jp

Abstract. Although today's graphics processing units (GPUs) have high performance and general-purpose computing on GPUs (GPGPU) is actively studied, developing GPGPU applications remains difficult for two reasons. First, both parallelization and optimization of GPGPU applications is necessary to achieve high performance. Second, the suitability of the target application for GPGPU must be determined, because whether an application performs well with GPGPU heavily depends on its inherent properties, which are not obvious from the source code. To overcome these difficulties, we developed a skeletal parallel programming framework for rapid GPGPU application developments. It enables programmers to easily write GPGPU applications and rapidly test them because it generates programs for both GPUs and CPUs from the same source code. It also provides an optimization mechanism based on fusion transformation. Its effectiveness was confirmed experimentally.

1 Introduction

It is more difficult to develop efficient parallel programs, because they are more complex than sequential ones due to interactions between processes. One approach to making parallel programming easier is *skeletal parallel programming* [1], in which parallel programs are built using *skeletons*, i.e., frequently used parallel computation patterns. Skeletons provide high-level abstraction and enable programmers to write parallel programs in a sequential manner.

Skeletal parallel programming has been studied from both theoretical and practical aspects. In the theoretical area, optimization based on *fusion* [2,3,4] has been studied [5,6,7]. In the practical area, skeleton libraries for distributed memory systems such as PC clusters have been developed [8,9,10,11]. However, not many practical applications rely on skeletal parallelism, which is a serious problem for skeletal parallel programming. To expand the area of its application, we applied skeletal parallelism to the programming for graphics processing units (GPUs).

The arithmetic performance and memory bandwidth of today's GPUs is ten times higher than that of today's CPUs, and the performance of GPUs is improving more rapidly than that of CPUs. This is why general-purpose computing on

Z. Hu (Ed.): APLAS 2009, LNCS 5904, pp. 79–94, 2009.

GPUs (GPGPU) [12,13] is being actively studied in the field of high-performance computing and why many GPGPU applications have been developed.

Development of a GPGPU application is difficult and troublesome for two reasons. First, only parallel programs that are well optimized for GPU architectures can fully utilize the performance of GPUs. The performance of a GPGPU program that does not sufficiently exploit a GPU's capabilities is often worse than that of a simple sequential one running on a CPU. Second, programmers need to determine whether the target application is suitable for GPGPU. For example, an application may not be able to achieve the good performance due to data transfer from main memory to video memory and GPU start-up time.

As an approach to these difficulties of GPGPU programming, we propose applying high-level abstraction of skeletons to hide the use of GPUs. We have developed a skeletal parallel programming framework with a fusion optimizer that enables programmers to easily write GPGPU applications and test them rapidly. The proposed framework is designed so as to be embedded in the C language, i.e., programmers can use the framework without any language extensions to C. In addition, programmers can write efficient parallel programs for both GPUs and CPUs as the same source code. Thus, the suitability for GPGPU can be tested rapidly. Our main contributions can be summarized as follows.

- We show that skeletal parallel programming can be applied to a practical framework for rapid GPGPU application development. We also illustrate its effectiveness through specific examples. The proposed framework is a practical application of skeletal parallel programming.
- We present that the proposed framework enables programmers to rapidly check the suitability of target applications for GPGPU. From the same source code, the framework generates three kinds of programs, namely a GPGPU program, a portable C++ parallel program with OpenMP, and a portable sequential C program.
- We present an implementation of the optimizer based on fusion transformation of skeletons and show its effectiveness for GPGPU applications. In the best case, an optimized GPGPU program ran 2.44 times faster than the non-optimized version.

2 Preliminaries

2.1 BMF and Skeletal Parallelism

In this paper, we regard data parallel primitives in the Bird-Meertens Formalism (BMF) [14] as skeletons for BMF-based skeletal parallel programming [15,16]. Throughout this paper, we use the notation of Haskell for describing the specifications of skeletons and other primitive operations.

Three important skeletons in BMF are map, reduce and zipwith.

$$\mathsf{map}\ f\ [x_1, x_2, \ldots, x_n] = [f\ x_1, f\ x_2, \ldots, f\ x_n]$$
$$\mathsf{reduce}\ (\oplus)\ [x_1, x_2, \ldots, x_n] = x_1 \oplus x_2 \oplus \cdots \oplus x_n$$
$$\mathsf{zipwith}\ f\ [x_1, x_2, \ldots, x_n]\ [y_1, y_2, \ldots, y_n] = [f\ x_1\ y_1, f\ x_2\ y_2, \ldots, f\ x_n\ y_n],$$

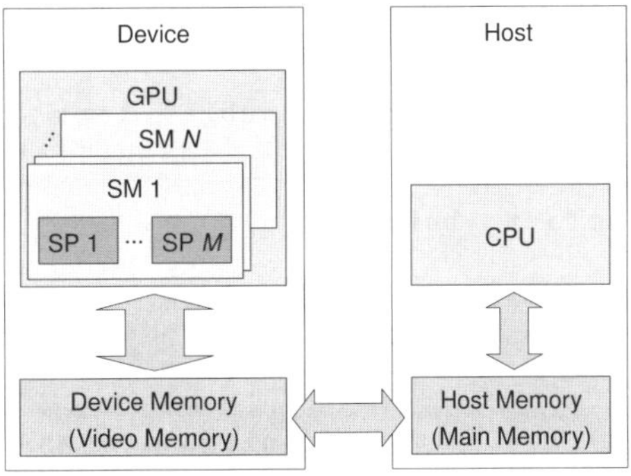

Fig. 1. CUDA hardware model

where $\oplus$ is an associative operator. We suppose that map, reduce, and zipwith are not given either empty or infinite lists.

We can transform a program into an efficient one by merging successive skeletons into a single one, e.g., map f (map g as) = map $(f \circ g)$ as. Such program transformation is called *fusion*, which is well-known in functional programming.

2.2 CUDA

CUDA is a general-purpose parallel computing architecture for GPUs. We briefly describe CUDA's features. Refer to the programming guide [17] for more details.

CUDA's hardware model is a distributed memory system that consists of host and device memory. These two kinds of memory are physically separated, as illustrated in Fig. 1. Host memory corresponds to main memory, while device memory corresponds to video memory. A GPU has several streaming processors (SMs), each of which consists of several scalar processor (SP) cores. Each SM supports multithreading.

Programmers use "C for CUDA"[1], an extended C language, to write GPGPU programs. Strictly speaking, CUDA is a subset of C++ with language extensions for using the device. These extensions include three additional function type qualifiers: `__global__`, `__device__`, and `__host__`. The `__global__` qualifier declares a function that is called from the host and executed in the device, the `__device__` qualifier declares one that is called from the device and executed in the device, and the `__host__` qualifier declares one that is called from the host and executed in the host. A function without one of these qualifiers is regarded to be qualified by `__host__`. A function qualified by both `__device__` and `__host__` is compiled for both the device and the host. `__global__` and `__device__` functions have several restrictions; e.g., they do not support the recursive call, the return type of each `__global__` function must be `void`, and a function pointer to a `__device__` function cannot be taken.

[1] In the rest of this paper, "C for CUDA" is simply called CUDA.

```
1  #include <skeleton.h>
2
3  double sqr(int x) { return (double) x*x; }
4  double add(double x, double y) { return x+y; }
5
6  double sqr_sum(int *buf, int n)
7  {
8    int *as[PTR_UNIT];      // declare wrapped array pointer
9    double *tmp[PTR_UNIT]; // declare wrapped array pointer
10   double res;
11
12   skel_new(as);           // initialize as
13   skel_new(tmp);          // initialize tmp
14   skel_wrap(as, buf, n); // wrap array pointed to by buf
15
16   map(sqr, as, tmp);       // square each element of as
17   reduce(add, tmp, &res); // sum up all elements of tmp
18
19   skel_del(as);  // dispose of wrapped array
20   skel_del(tmp); // dispose of wrapped array
21
22   return res;
23 }
```

Fig. 2. Program that computes square sum of integer list using framework

Because CUDA had made GPGPU easier than before, CUDA became most popular in GPGPU programming. Nevertheless, GPGPU programming with CUDA remains difficult. For instance, when a matrix multiplication program that is simply and sequentially coded for a CPU is ported to CUDA for a GPU without much modification, the ported program is 200–2000 times slower than the original one as shown in an experiment[2]. This suggests that GPGPU programming with CUDA needs very hardware-conscious programming.

3 Overview of Proposed Framework

We briefly describe how to write a program using the proposed framework. Figure 2 shows an example program that computes a square sum of a list that is represented by an array using the framework.

First, the header file is included (line 1) to enable use of the framework APIs. Wrapped array pointers, which will be described in Sect. 4.1, are declared (lines 8–9) and initialized by `skel_new` (lines 12–13). Then, an array is wrapped by `skel_wrap` (line 14), whose third parameter is the number of wrapped elements in the array. Then, the skeletons operate on the lists (lines 16–17), where the last parameter given to each skeleton is the destination for storing the result.

[2] Refer to Sect. 7 for details on the experimental environment.

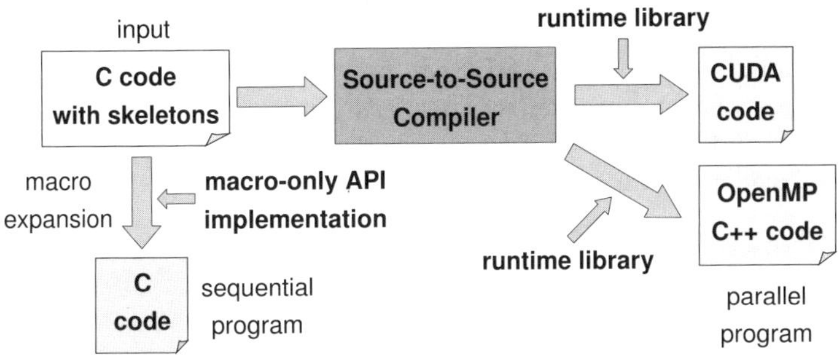

Fig. 3. Outline of proposed framework

Finally, `skel_del` disposes of the wrapped array that is no longer necessary (lines 19–20). With this framework, programmers can easily write GPGPU programs without any consideration of either hardware or parallelization.

The framework transforms a given program in which APIs of the framework are used. As shown in Fig. 3, it has three main components:

- a source-to-source compiler with a fusion optimizer for parallel programs,
- runtime libraries, and
- a macro-only API implementation for sequential programs.

The source-to-source compiler, which is the core of the framework, generates C code with skeletons into CUDA code for GPUs or C++ code with OpenMP for CPUs. Compiler driver scripts run a CUDA compiler or a C++ compiler with appropriate compile-time constants, and the generated code is compiled into executable code. The runtime libraries are used by the generated code. The macro-only API implementation is used for debugging and porting.

4 Design

4.1 Principles

C for Base Language. The framework was designed on the basis of the C language. Each API of the framework can be seen as a macro from the viewpoint of C programming, even though each API call and other parts of a program are transformed by our compiler for GPGPU. The framework also provides the macro-only implementation of each API to help users debug programs as on-CPU sequential C programs. Skeletons require no language extension to C. This is one of the great merits of our framework and skeletal parallel programming.

There are three reasons for selecting C as the base language. The first is CUDA's affinity for C: it is easy to translate C into CUDA because CUDA is an extended C language. The second and third reasons are the popularity and performance of C. In fact, many skeleton libraries [8,9,10,11,18] have been implemented in C/C++ for these two reasons.

Transparency. The framework is designed to have transparency, i.e., to hide the use of the GPU and distributed memory. This enables the framework to generate three kinds of programs: GPGPU programs, on-CPU parallel programs, and on-CPU sequential programs. Thus, transparency leads to portability. The transparency and portability of the framework owe much to the high-level abstraction of skeletons, an important advantage of skeletal parallel programming.

Pointer Contracts. The proposed framework imposes three *contracts*, i.e., promises that should be kept.

- A list passed to skeletons should be a wrapped array.
- Wrapped arrays should be accessed via only APIs of the framework.
- Every wrapped array pointer should have no alias.

If a skeleton received pointers into which the result of a computation was stored, memory copying between device and host would occur every time that skeleton was called. This would seriously degrade performance. This problem is caused by pointers that can freely access memory. To solve this problem, we introduce *wrapped arrays* to which access is restricted and *wrapped array pointers* that point to the head of a wrapped array, in contrast to the *raw pointers* and *raw arrays* natively supported in C.

Neither dereferencing nor pointer arithmetic against wrapped array pointers are permitted. They are only permitted to be passed to APIs. In addition, when part of a raw array is wrapped, the programmer must ensure that the area is not referred to by other pointers.

Because aliases make fusion optimization difficult, the framework forbids operations that may produce aliases of wrapped array pointers, e.g., assignment, indirect reference, passing to functions, and returning from functions.

4.2 APIs

The framework provides simple and natural APIs for C programmers. Table 1 shows the APIs with brief descriptions. Each skeleton is a procedure (a function with no return value) whose last parameter is the destination into which the result will be stored. The `mapls` and `maprs` APIs are introduced because C does not support partial application. The `generate` API is introduced because of its efficient construction of lists and synergy with fusion.

The APIs do not depend on list element types and have as polymorphic behaviors as macros.

Functions passed to skeletons are defined in C without special function type qualifiers even though skeletons are executed on GPUs. This enables programmers to transparently reuse functions.

No operations that change the length of a list are provided. Thus, the length of the resulting list of a skeleton call is automatically determined once the list length is set by `skel_wrap` or `generate`. Programmers need not be concerned about the list length because the framework appropriately propagates the length in the implementation of skeletons.

Table 1. API list (function identifier, wrapped array pointer, raw pointer, wrapped array, and raw array are abbreviated as FI, WAP, RP, WA, and RA, respectively)

API	Brief description
`map(FI f, WAP as, WAP bs)`	map
`reduce(FI op, WAP as, RP a)`	reduce
`zipwith(FI f, WAP as, WAP bs, WAP cs)`	zipwith
`mapls(FI f, RP∪WAP a, WAP bs, WAP cs)`	map $(\lambda x.f\ a\ x)\ bs$
`maprs(FI f, RP∪WAP a, WAP bs, WAP cs)`	map $(\lambda x.f\ x\ a)\ bs$
`generate(FI f, int n, WAP as)`	map $f\ [0, \ldots, n-1]$
`skel_new(WAP as)`	initializing WAP
`skel_del(WAP as)`	disposing of WA
`skel_wrap(WAP dst, RP src, int n)`	wrapping RA
`skel_unwrap(WAP as)`	unwrapping WA
`skel_dup_contents(RP dst, WAP src)`	copying WA to RA
`skel_get_element(RP dst, WAP src, int i)`	getter for WA
`skel_set_element(WAP dst, int i, RP src)`	setter for WA

The APIs do not include memory allocation operations. Instead, runtime libraries automatically allocate memory when a skeleton first accesses a wrapped array pointer. Hence, `skel_del` does nothing unless memory has been allocated.

For implementation reasons, the APIs have the following restrictions.

- A list element type must not include the pointer type.
- Each API call must be an expression statement.
- A function argument passed to a skeleton must be the function identifier.
- Functions passed to skeletons have the same restrictions as `__device__` functions in CUDA.
- Binary operators passed to `reduce` must be associative and commutative.

The first restriction comes from the fact that the framework does not support serialization. The second restriction is needed for the macro-only API implementation. For instance, a skeleton call in an expression causes a syntax error if the skeleton is implemented as a macro of a **for** loop. The third restriction helps both CUDA and C++ compilers to inline functions passed to skeletons. A function passed to a skeleton can be inlined only if it can be statically determined. The fourth restriction is needed because functions passed to skeletons are executed on GPUs. The last restriction is necessary to achieve efficient implementations of skeletons on GPUs. If commutative and associative operators are given, the reduction algorithm can be optimized for GPUs by using the Harris algorithm [19]. This restriction is not particularly severe because frequently used operators have commutativity.

5 Fusion Transformation

Two functions, which are not explicitly used by programmers, are used for intermediate representation of skeletons. They are introduced to implement the fusion transformation in a uniform way.

$$\mathsf{zipwith}_k\ f\ [x_1^1,\ldots,x_n^1]\cdots[x_1^k,\ldots,x_n^k] = [f\ x_1^1\ \cdots\ x_1^k,\ldots,f\ x_n^1\ \cdots\ x_n^k]$$
$$\mathsf{reduce}_k\ (\oplus)\ f\ [x_1^1,\ldots,x_n^1]\cdots[x_1^k,\ldots,x_n^k] = (f\ x_1^1\ \cdots\ x_1^k) \oplus \cdots \oplus (f\ x_n^1\ \cdots\ x_n^k)$$

$\mathsf{zipwith}_k$ returns a list zipping corresponding elements of given lists with a function f. reduce_k returns a value of folding with $\oplus$ the result of zipping corresponding elements of given lists with f. The following three equations hold.

$$\mathsf{map} = \mathsf{zipwith}_1 \qquad \mathsf{zipwith} = \mathsf{zipwith}_2 \qquad \mathsf{reduce}\ (\oplus) = \mathsf{reduce}_1\ (\oplus)\ id,$$

where id is the identity function.

The fusion rules for map, reduce, and zipwith are as follows.

$$\mathsf{map}\ f\ (\mathsf{zipwith}_k\ g\ as^1\ \cdots\ as^k) \longrightarrow \mathsf{zipwith}_k\ (f \circ g)\ as^1\ \cdots\ as^k$$
$$\mathsf{reduce}\ (\oplus)\ (\mathsf{zipwith}_k\ f\ as^1\ \cdots\ as^k) \longrightarrow \mathsf{reduce}_k\ (\oplus)\ f\ as^1\ \cdots\ as^k$$
$$\mathsf{zipwith}\ f\ (\mathsf{zipwith}_i\ g\ as^1\ \cdots\ as^i)\ (\mathsf{zipwith}_j\ h\ bs^1\ \cdots\ bs^j)$$
$$\longrightarrow \mathsf{zipwith}_{i+j}\ \phi\ as^1\ \cdots\ as^i\ bs^1\ \cdots\ bs^j$$
$$\mathbf{where}\ \phi\ x^1\ \cdots\ x^i\ y^1\ \cdots\ y^j = f\ (g\ x^1\ \cdots\ x^i)\ (h\ y^1\ \cdots\ y^j)$$

Using these rules and the definitions of skeletons, we can express skeleton fusion results in terms of only $\mathsf{zipwith}_k$ and reduce_k. Therefore, implementations of $\mathsf{zipwith}_k$ and reduce_k should suffice for the framework.

From the perspective of efficiency, we implemented $\mathsf{zipwith}_k$ and reduce_k in imperative algorithms using loops for arrays.

$$\mathsf{step}_k\ i\ f\ [x_1^1,\ldots,x_n^1]\cdots[x_1^k,\ldots,x_n^k] = f\ x_i^1\ \cdots\ x_i^k$$

$\mathsf{step}_k\ i\ as_1\ \cdots\ as_k\ (i = 1,\ldots,n)$ is used at each iteration step that computes the i-th element of the result of $\mathsf{zipwith}_k\ as_1\ \cdots\ as_k$. Therefore, parallelization of $\mathsf{zipwith}_k$ can be implemented with loop splitting, and parallelization of reduce_k can be implemented with loop splitting and tree reduction.

The second parameter function of step_k, f, is composed of the functions passed to skeletons. Hence, the function can be constructed in a bottom-up manner from a tree structure of skeleton calls (a *skeleton tree*). Construction of $[0,\ldots,n-1]$ in `generate` can be avoided by using the value of the first parameter of step_k. Thus, if skeleton trees have been constructed, fusion is straightforward.

6 Implementation

6.1 Compiler

The source-to-source compiler was implemented using the COINS[3] compiler infrastructure. The `cfront` component of COINS translates C source code into high-level intermediate representation (HIR), which is a kind of abstract syntax tree, and the `hir2c` component translates HIR into C source code. Program transformation for skeletons was mainly implemented at the HIR level.

There are four steps in the compilation process.

[3] `http://coins-project.is.titech.ac.jp/international/`

1. The C source code with skeletons is translated into HIR by `cfront`.
2. The fusion optimizer constructs skeleton trees from the HIR and then performs HIR-to-HIR transformation.
3. The transformed HIR is translated into C code by `hir2c`. Then, `__device__`, `__host__`, and `inline` are appended to the prototype declarations of all functions passed to skeletons for CUDA code generation. For C++ code, `inline` are appended.
4. Code is generated from each skeleton tree and merged into the code generated in Step 3. Then, runtime libraries are included.

In the generated CUDA code, implementation of specific skeletons consists of two function templates, i.e., an entry function template and a `__global__` function template. First, the entry function template is called from a point of a skeleton call. In the entry function template, array length check, memory allocation, memory copy, and some preparations for CUDA are performed. In addition, depending on the array length, the execution of the skeleton body is switched to either GPUs or CPUs. Second, if the body is determined to be executed on GPUs, the `__global__` function template for the skeleton body, which includes parallel loops with some optimization techniques on CUDA, is called. The generated C++ code with OpenMP is similar, except that it does not use a `__global__` function template. These function templates are strongly typed. If compilation by our compiler and compilation of the generated code succeed, the use of skeletons is type-safe. Such generative approach reduces overhead and overcomes restrictions of `__device__` functions.

6.2 Fusion Optimizer

The fusion optimizer

1. finds *safely fusible* skeleton calls, whose fusion preserves the semantics of the program,
2. constructs a skeleton tree from each sequence of those calls, and
3. rewrites the HIR by using the result of the fusion.

Steps 1 and 2 are done by *fusion analyzer*, which is part of the fusion optimizer.

The algorithm of the fusion optimizer is based on a *greedy fusion strategy*, which fuses as many skeleton calls as possible regardless of recomputation. In fact, recomputation is not bad or sometimes good even though it seems to waste resources. In particular, recomputation is good for GPUs because arithmetic operations are much faster than memory accesses on GPUs. For instance, a recomputation of generate often performs better than a store/load of the results because it avoids construction of lists and memory accesses. Moreover, reducing skeleton calls is good for GPUs because GPUs take more time to start up. Therefore, we decided to recompute skeletons rather than to store/load the results in the fusion optimization process.

In addition to the above properties of GPUs, the greedy fusion strategy is used because light-weight functions rather than heavy-weight ones are often passed to

```
1 {
2     map(f, as, bs);
3     map(g, bs, ds);
4     zipwith(op, cs, ds, es);
5     map(h, bs, bs);
6     reduce(oq, es, &r);
7     skel_del(es);
8 }
```

(a) Before fusion

```
1 {
2
3     ds = zipwith_1 (g ∘ f) as
4
5     bs = zipwith_1 (h ∘ f) as
6     r = reduce_2 oq op cs ds
7     skel_del(es);
8 }
```

(b) After fusion (psuedo)

Fig. 4. Example of fusion optimization

skeletons and a skeleton call given a heavy-weight function is rarely fused with many other skeleton calls.

A target of the fusion analyzer is a basic block, which is a series of statements that does not include jumps or labels but can include function calls. The fusion optimizer performs a local optimization. Hence, the analysis is performed within each basic block.

In a basic block, the fusion analyzer (1) finds a skeleton call, s, (2) constructs U_s, where U_s is a set of all successive skeleton calls that use the result of s, and (3) checks whether the result of s is not used except for members of U_s. Then, (4) if the validation in (3) succeeds, a set of skeleton calls that are *safely fusible* with s is U_s; otherwise $\emptyset$. Finally, (5) s is fused[4] with every member of U_s. The fusion process proceeds to the next skeleton call of s.

Figure 4 shows an example of fusion optimization. When `map` (line 2) is s, $U_s = \{$`map` (line 3), `map` (line 5)$\}$. Because the result of `map` (line 2) is overwritten in line 5, i.e., that is not used any more, `map` (line 2) is fused with both `map` (line 3) and `map` (line 5). In this case, mapping `f` to `as` is computed twice on the basis of the greedy fusion strategy. Similarly, when `map` (line 3) is s, $U_s = \{$`zipwith` (line 4)$\}$. However, `map` (line 3) cannot be fused with `zipwith` (line 4) because the result of `map` (line 3), i.e., `ds`, is not deleted.

6.3 API Implementation

The wrapped array pointer was implemented by using a fixed-length array of pointers, each of which is of a pointer type to the list element type. The pointer array consists of a pointer to host memory, a pointer to device memory, and the length of the list in the case of CUDA code. The wrapped array pointer type behaves like a `struct` type that has parametric polymorphism. Although this solution seems to be ad hoc, both language extension to C and the use of void pointers were avoided.

A device pointer is extracted from each wrapped array pointer passed to skeletons within the implementation of each skeleton. Then, the array in the

[4] More precisely, the fusion analyzer only constructs skeleton trees.

device is directly accessed in the execution of the skeleton body. Therefore, the overhead of wrapped array pointers is small.

The polymorphism of the APIs was implemented with the void pointer type for the compiler. First, the prototype declarations of the APIs were defined using the void pointer type in the header file. Then, the API calls are rewritten to calls of function templates that implement the APIs by the compiler. After that, the void pointer type of the APIs is not used. These function templates have strongly typed polymorphism.

7 Experimental Results

It is difficult to determine the properties of a GPGPU application simply by analyzing the algorithms or reading the source code. Thus, it is of great use to generate programs for GPUs and CPUs from the same source code to compare their performance. To demonstrate the effectiveness of the proposed framework from this viewpoint, we tested four applications[5].

N-Body (NB): This is an N-body simulation using the Euler method in two-dimensional space. Two lists (positions and velocities of bodies) are updated every step. An element in each list is a pair of `double` numbers. Its time complexity is $O(tn^2)$, where n is the number of bodies and t is the number of steps.

Numerical Integration (NI): This computes $\int_a^b x \log x \cos x \, \mathrm{d}x$ in $2n$ divisions (x is `double`) by using Simpson's rule. Its time complexity is $O(n)$.

Matrix Multiplication (MM): This computes AB, where A is an $m \times n$ matrix and B is an $n \times m$ matrix whose elements are `double`. A and B are represented as row and column vectors respectively. AB is computed with inner products of row and column vectors. Its time complexity is $O(m^2n)$.

Correlation Coefficient (CC): This computes the Pearson product-moment correlation coefficient from two sequences of samples whose lengths are n. Each sequence is represented as a list of `double`. Its time complexity is $O(n)$.

The experiments were performed on a PC with an Intel Core 2 Duo E8500 CPU (3.16 GHz, L2 cache 6 MB) and a NVIDIA GeForce GTX 280 GPU (via PCI-Express 2.0). The main memory was DDR2-800 4 GB. The video memory of the GPU was 1 GB. The operating system was Ubuntu 7.10 (32-bit). We used CUDA SDK 2.0 (driver version 177.67) and GNU C++ 4.2.1 (including OpenMP) for compiling on-CPU programs. Each binary was created in `-O3` optimization level.

For each application, we used four programs.

skel-GPU-gen: An on-GPU skeleton program whose input data is generated on the GPU with generate.

skel-GPU-trans: An on-GPU skeleton program whose input data is generated sequentially on the CPU and transferred to device memory.

skel-CPU-par: An on-CPU skeleton program with OpenMP. It can be generated from the same source code used for skel-GPU-gen by our framework.

[5] Refer to Table 2 for the number of skeleton calls used in each application.

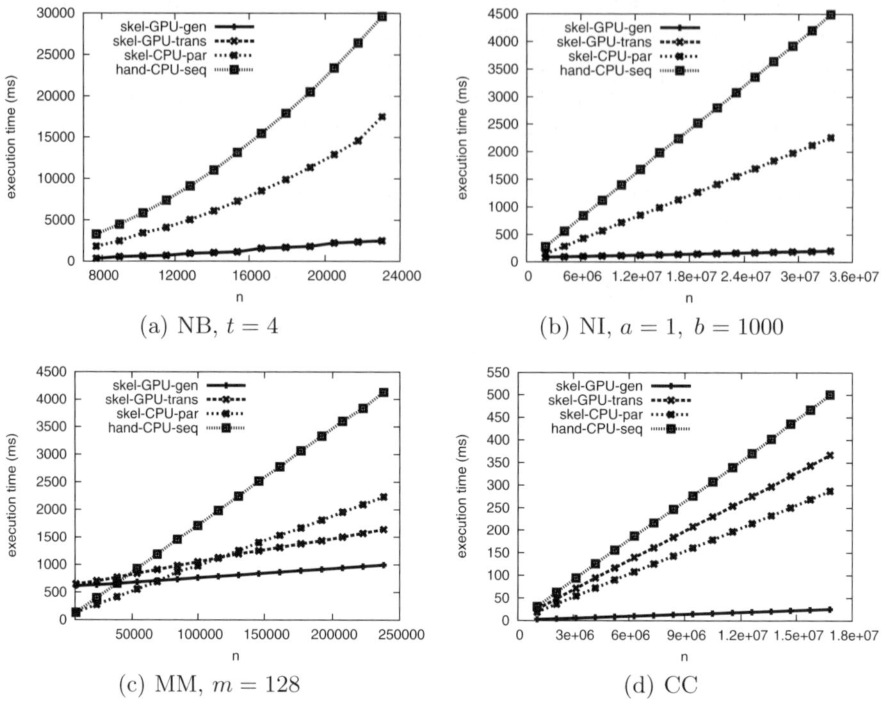

Fig. 5. Execution time of four applications against input data size for skel-GPU-gen, skel-GPU-trans, skel-CPU-par, and hand-CPU-seq

hand-CPU-seq: A simple hand-coded sequential program in C++ that performs the same computation as skel-CPU-par after fusion optimization in a sequential manner on the CPU without using our framework.

Fusion optimization was applied to all skeleton programs. Because the macro-only API implementation does not support fusion optimization, we did not use the sequential on-CPU program of each skeleton program generated by the proposed framework. Instead, we used hand-CPU-seq in the experiments.

As shown in Fig. 5, NB and NI had the same tendency: skel-GPU-gen and skel-GPU-trans showed almost the same results and were always better than skel-CPU-par and hand-CPU-seq. From these results, we can see that NB and NI are suitable for GPGPU. For MM, skel-GPU-gen and skel-GPU-trans were better than skel-CPU-par and hand-CPU-seq when the amount of input data was large. This means that the suitability of MM for GPGPU depends on the amount of input data. For CC, skel-GPU-trans was always worse than skel-CPU-par: CC is not suitable for GPGPU due to the transfer of input data.

For all applications, skel-GPU-gen had the best performance except for MM on small input data. This shows that the framework is able to exploit the potential of the GPU. Depending on the application and amount of input data,

Table 2. Effects of fusion optimization on skel-GPU-gen. Number of skeleton calls was statically counted in source code, not counted at runtime

Application	NB	NI	MM	CC
Number of skeleton calls (before/after)	5/4	10/2	4/3	12/7
Maximum speed up (times)	1.00	1.48	1.71	2.44

Table 3. Overhead of skel-GPU-gen compared to hand-GPU-gen on large input data

Application	NB	NI	MM	CC
skel-GPU-gen (%)	27.3 s (100.00)	3.84 s (100.25)	994 ms (108.86)	25.3 ms (116.93)
hand-GPU-gen (%)	27.3 s (100.00)	3.83 s (100.00)	913 ms (100.00)	21.7 ms (100.00)

skel-GPU-trans may be slower than skel-CPU-par. This is due to the inherent properties of the application. It is quite difficult to determine the inherent properties of an application without running the programs. An important and distinguishing point of the proposed framework is that programmers can easily identify such properties by generating programs for both GPUs and CPUs from the same source code and comparing their performance.

Table 2 shows the effects of fusion optimization on skel-GPU-gen under the same condition as the benchmarks in Fig. 5. For each application, the maximum speed up was achieved at largest input data and the minimum was caused at nearly least input data. Overall, the fusion optimization had good effects on the performance in GPGPU.

Table 3 shows the overhead of skel-GPU-gen compared to hand-GPU-gen: a hand-coded parallel program in CUDA whose input data was generated on the GPU. The hand-GPU-gen programs of NB, NI, and CC were optimized so as to reuse functions passed to skeletons. The hand-GPU-gen program of MM was mainly implemented using the DGEMM subroutine of the CUBLAS library, which is an implementation of basic linear algebra subprograms on CUDA. The overhead was examined when the amount of input data was larger than or equal to the maximum in the benchmarks in Fig. 5. For NB and NI, which are suitable for GPGPU, there was very little overhead. For MM, although CUBLAS is a well optimized library, there was a little overhead. For CC, because hand-GPU-gen avoided recomputation efficiently and elaborately, there was the largest overhead of the four applications.

8 Related Work and Discussion

8.1 Skeletal Parallel Programming

Many skeletal parallel programming environments provide skeletons as libraries. Muesli [8], eSkel [9], Quaff [10], and SkeTo [11] are libraries implemented in C/C++ with MPI for distributed memory systems such as PC clusters. BlockLib

[18] is a library implemented in C equipped with C preprocessor macros for the Cell Broadband Engine processor. Our framework differs from these approaches in that the target is GPGPU.

Some implementations have optimization mechanisms for skeleton calls. The FAN skeleton framework [20] supports automatic rule-based program transformation; however, the transformation is ad hoc and requires many rules. Grelck and Scholz [21] presented three optimizers that merge with-loops, which are used for array skeletons, in a SaC [22] compiler. Their optimizer was focused on multi-dimensional different-bounds arrays. SkeTo supports an optimizer [23] that partially implements Hu et al.'s fusion [5,6] for BMF-based list skeletons. The SkeTo optimizer does not support zipwith fusion at all, which ours supports.

8.2 GPGPU Programming

Stream programming [24] has been proposed for efficiently exploiting stream processors. Brook for GPUs [25] supports stream programming for GPUs.

MapReduce [26,27] is a programming model that efficiently exploits large-scale PC clusters in the back-end of search engines. MapReduce systems for GPUs have been developed; Mars [28] is optimized for CUDA, and Merge [29] dispatches tasks to both GPUs and CPUs.

Stream programming is similar to BMF-based skeletal programming from the viewpoint that both compose operations of a specific data structure. However, in stream programming, the data structure is restricted to streams, while BMF can be extended to various data structures. MapReduce resembles BMF-based skeletal programming because both use higher-order functions. However, MapReduce does not treat the composition of higher-order functions. Therefore, BMF-based skeletal parallel programming, like our framework, has higher abstraction and wider generality than stream programming and MapReduce.

Lee et al. [30] proposed an embedded language and its online compiler for using GPUs in Haskell. Although they employed the idea of skeletons, their main challenge is to use GPUs with monads in Haskell. Their approach differs from ours in two respects: it had significant overhead and it did not support fusion optimization. Lee et al. [31] developed OpenMP optimized for CUDA, which is directive-based approach compared to our skeletal approach.

9 Conclusion

We have developed a skeletal parallel programming framework for GPGPU programming that has a fusion optimizer. The framework enables rapid GPGPU application development.

There are two directions for future work. One is to add other skeletons to enrich applications. More applications can be described using our framework if scan and shift are introduced. Thus, we will demonstrate expressiveness of skeletons. The other is to improve the fusion analyzer. In the current implementation, the fusion optimization is a local optimization. The fusion optimizer can perform a more powerful global optimization if the fusion analyzer gathers data flow among basic blocks. In addition, we want to enhance the fusion analyzer to check some part of contracts and restrictions of APIs at compile time.

Acknowledgments. We wish to thank Masato Takeichi, Kenetsu Hanabusa, Zhenjiang Hu, Kiminori Matsuzaki, and other POP members in Tokyo for their fruitful discussions. This work was partially supported by Grant-in-Aid for Scientific Research (20500029) from the Japan Society of the Promotion of Science.

References

1. Cole, M.I.: Algorithmic Skeletons: Structured Management of Parallel Computation. MIT Press, Cambridge (1989)
2. Wadler, P.: Deforestation: Transforming programs to eliminate trees. In: Ganzinger, H. (ed.) ESOP 1988. LNCS, vol. 300, pp. 344–358. Springer, Heidelberg (1988)
3. Chin, W.: Safe Fusion of Functional Expressions. In: 7th ACM Conference on Lisp and Functional Programming, pp. 11–20. ACM Press, New York (1992)
4. Gill, A., Launchbury, J., Peyton Jones, S.L.: A Short Cut to Deforestation. In: Conference on Functional Programming Languages and Computer Architecture, pp. 223–232 (1993)
5. Hu, Z., Iwasaki, H., Takeichi, M.: An Accumulative Parallel Skeleton for All. In: Le Métayer, D. (ed.) ESOP 2002. LNCS, vol. 2305, pp. 83–97. Springer, Heidelberg (2002)
6. Iwasaki, H., Hu, Z.: A New Parallel Skeleton for General Accumulative Computations. International Journal of Parallel Programming 32, 398–414 (2004)
7. Emoto, K., Matsuzaki, K., Hu, Z., Takeichi, M.: Domain-Specific Optimization Strategy for Skeleton Programs. In: Kermarrec, A.-M., Bougé, L., Priol, T. (eds.) Euro-Par 2007. LNCS, vol. 4641, pp. 705–714. Springer, Heidelberg (2007)
8. Kuchen, H.: A Skeleton Library. In: Monien, B., Feldmann, R.L. (eds.) Euro-Par 2002. LNCS, vol. 2400, pp. 85–124. Springer, Heidelberg (2002)
9. Benoit, A., Cole, M., Gilmore, S., Hillston, J.: Flexible Skeletal Programming with eSkel. In: Cunha, J.C., Medeiros, P.D. (eds.) Euro-Par 2005. LNCS, vol. 3648, pp. 761–770. Springer, Heidelberg (2005)
10. Falcou, J., Sérot, J., Chateau, T., Lapreste, J.T.: QUAFF: efficient C++ design for parallel skeletons. Parallel Comput. 32(7-8), 604–615 (2006)
11. Matsuzaki, K., Emoto, K., Iwasaki, H., Hu, Z.: A Library of Constructive Skeletons for Sequential Style of Parallel Programming. In: 1st International Conference on Scalable Information Systems, vol. 13 (2006)
12. Luebke, D., Harris, M., Krüger, J., Purcell, T., Govindaraju, N., Buck, I., Woolley, C., Lefohn, A.: GPGPU: General-Purpose Computation on Graphics Hardware. In: ACM SIGGRAPH 2004 Course Notes (2004)
13. Owens, J.D., Luebke, D., Govindaraju, N., Harris, M., Krüger, J., Lefohn, A.E., Purcell, T.J.: A Survey of General-Purpose Computation on Graphics Hardware. Comput. Graph. Forum 26(1), 80–113 (2007)
14. Bird, R.: Lecture Notes on Theory of Lists. STOP Summer School on Constructive Algorithmics (1987)
15. Skillicorn, D.B.: The Bird-Meertens Formalism as a Parallel Model. In: Software for Parallel Computation. NATO ASI Series F, vol. 106, pp. 120–133 (1993)
16. Gorlatch, S.: Systematic Efficient Parallelization of Scan and Other List Homomorphisms. In: Fraigniaud, P., Mignotte, A., Robert, Y., Bougé, L. (eds.) Euro-Par 1996. LNCS, vol. 1124, pp. 401–408. Springer, Heidelberg (1996)

17. NVIDIA Corporation: NVIDIA CUDA™ Programming Guide Version 2.2 (2009)
18. Ålind, M., Eriksson, M.V., Kessler, C.W.: BlockLib: A Skeleton Library for Cell Broadband Engine. In: 1st International Workshop on Multicore Software Engineering, pp. 7–14 (2008)
19. Harris, M.: Optimizing Parallel Reduction in CUDA. Technical report, NVIDIA Corporation (2007), http://developer.download.nvidia.com/compute/cuda/1_1/Website/projects/reduction/doc/reduction.pdf
20. Aldinucci, M., Gorlatch, S., Lengauer, C., Pelagatti, S.: Towards Parallel Programming by Transformation: The FAN Skeleton Framework. Parallel Algorithms Appl. 16, 87–121 (2001)
21. Grelck, C., Scholz, S.: Merging compositions of array skeletons in SAC. Parallel Comput. 32(7-8), 507–522 (2006)
22. Scholz, S.B.: Single Assignment C: efficient support for high-level array operations in a functional setting. J. Funct. Program. 13(6), 1005–1059 (2003)
23. Matsuzaki, K., Kakehi, K., Iwasaki, H., Hu, Z., Akashi, Y.: A Fusion-Embedded Skeleton Library. In: Danelutto, M., Vanneschi, M., Laforenza, D. (eds.) Euro-Par 2004. LNCS, vol. 3149, pp. 644–653. Springer, Heidelberg (2004)
24. Kapasi, U., Dally, W.J., Rixner, S., Owens, J.D., Khailany, B.: The Imagine Stream Processor. In: 20th IEEE International Conference on Computer Design, pp. 282–288 (2002)
25. Buck, I., Foley, T., Horn, D., Sugerman, J., Fatahalian, K., Houston, M., Hanrahan, P.: Brook for GPUs: Stream Computing on Graphics Hardware. ACM Trans. Graph. 23, 777–786 (2004)
26. Dean, J., Ghemawat, S.: MapReduce: Simplified Data Processing on Large Clusters. In: 6th Symposium on Operating System Design and Implementation, pp. 137–150 (2004)
27. Dean, J., Ghemawat, S.: MapReduce: Simplified Data Processing on Large Clusters. Commun. ACM 51, 107–113 (2008)
28. He, B., Fang, W., Luo, Q., Govindaraju, N.K., Wang, T.: Mars: A MapReduce Framework on Graphics Processors. In: 17th International Conference on Parallel Architectures and Compilation Techniques, pp. 260–269 (2008)
29. Linderman, M.D., Collins, J.D., Wang, H., Meng, T.H.: Merge: A Programming Model for Heterogeneous Multi-Core Systems. In: 13th International Conference on Architectural Support for Programming Languages and Operating Systems, pp. 287–296 (2008)
30. Lee, S., Chakravarty, M.M.T., Grover, V., Keller, G.: GPU Kernels as Data-Parallel Array Computations in Haskell. In: Workshop on Exploiting Parallelism using GPUs and other Hardware-Assisted Methods (2009)
31. Lee, S., Min, S.J., Eigenmann, R.: OpenMP to GPGPU: A Compiler Framework for Automatic Translation and Optimization. In: 14th ACM SIGPLAN Symposium on Principles and Practice of Parallel Programming, pp. 101–110 (2009)

Witnessing Purity, Constancy and Mutability

Ben Lippmeier

Department of Computer Science
Australian National University
Ben.Lippmeier@anu.edu.au

Abstract. Restricting destructive update to values of a distinguished reference type prevents functions from being polymorphic in the mutability of their arguments. This restriction makes it easier to reason about program behaviour during transformation, but the lack of polymorphism reduces the expressiveness of the language. We present a System-F style core language that uses dependently kinded proof witnesses to encode information about the mutability of values and the purity of computations. We support mixed strict and lazy evaluation, and use our type system to ensure that only computations without visible side effects are suspended.

1 Introduction

Suppose we are writing a library that provides a useful data structure such as linked lists. A Haskell-style definition for the list type would be:

$$\textbf{data}\ \mathit{List}\ \ a = \mathit{Nil}\ \mid\ \mathit{Cons}\ \ a\ (\mathit{List}\ \ a)$$

The core language of compilers such as GHC is based around System-F [15]. Here is the translation of the standard *map* function to this representation, complete with type abstractions and applications:

$$\begin{aligned}
&\mathit{map} :: \forall a\ b.\ (a \to b) \to \mathit{List}\ \ a \to \mathit{List}\ \ b\\
&\mathit{map} = \Lambda a.\ \Lambda b.\ \lambda(f : a \to b).\ \lambda(\mathit{list} : \mathit{List}\ \ a).\\
&\qquad \textbf{case}\ \mathit{list}\ \textbf{of}\\
&\qquad\qquad \mathit{Nil} \qquad\qquad \to \mathit{Nil}\ \ b\\
&\qquad\qquad \mathit{Cons}\ \ x\ \ xs \to \mathit{Cons}\ \ b\ (f\ \ x)\ (\mathit{map}\ \ a\ b\ f\ \ xs)
\end{aligned}$$

Say we went on to define some other useful list functions, and then decided that we need one to destructively insert a new element into the middle of a list. In Haskell, side effects are carefully controlled and we would need to introduce a monad such as ST or IO [8] to encapsulate the effects due to the update. Destructive update is also limited to distinguished types such as *STRef* and *IORef*. We cannot use our previous list type, so will instead change it to use an *IORef*.

$$\textbf{data}\ \mathit{List}\ \ a = \mathit{Nil}\ \mid\ \mathit{Cons}\ \ a\ (\mathit{IORef}\ \ (\mathit{List}\ \ a))$$

Z. Hu (Ed.): APLAS 2009, LNCS 5904, pp. 95–110, 2009.

Unfortunately, as we have changed the structure of our original data type, we can no longer use the previous definition of *map*, or any other functions we defined earlier. We must go back and refactor each of these function definitions to use the new type. We must insert calls to *readIORef* and use monadic sequencing combinators instead of vanilla let and where-expressions. However, doing so introduces explicit data dependencies into the core program. This in turn reduces the compiler's ability to perform optimisations such as deforestation and the full laziness transform [6], which require functions to be written in the "pure", non-monadic style. It appears that we need *two* versions of our list structure and its associated functions, an immutable version that can be optimised, and a mutable one that can be updated.

Variations of this problem are also present in ML and O'Caml. In ML, mutability is restricted to *ref* and *array* types [11]. In O'Caml, record types can have mutable fields, but variant types cannot [9]. Similarly to Haskell, in these languages we are forced to insert explicit reference types into the definitions of mutable data structures, which makes them incompatible with the standard immutable ones. This paper shows how to avoid this problem:

- We present a System-F style core language that uses region and effect typing to guide program optimisation. Optimisations that depend on purity can be performed on the the pure fragments of the program.
- We use region variables and dependently kinded witnesses to encode mutability polymorphism. This allows arbitrary data structures to be mutable without changing the structure of their value types.
- We use call-by-value evaluation as default, but support lazy evaluation via a primitive *suspend* operator. We use witnesses of purity to ensure that only pure function applications can be suspended.

Our goals are similar to those of Benton and Kennedy [3], but as in [15] we use a System-F based core language instead of a monadic one. Type inference and translation from source to core is discussed in [10].

2 Regions, Effects and Mutability Constraints

In Haskell and ML, references and arrays are distinguished values, and are the only ones capable of being destructively updated. This means that the structure of mutable data is necessarily different from the structure of constant data, which makes it difficult to write polymorphic functions that act on both. For example, if we use *IORef Int* as the type of a mutable integer and *Int* as the type of a constant integer, then we would need *readIORef* to access the first, but not the second. On the other hand, if we were to treat all data as mutable, then every function would exhibit a side effect. This would prevent us from using code-motion style optimisations that depend on purity.

Instead, we give integers the type $Int\ r$, where r is a region variable, and constrain r to be mutable or constant as needed. Our use of region variables is similar to that by Talpin and Jouvelot [16], where the variable r is a name for a set of locations in the store where a run-time object may lie. We do not use regions for controlling allocation as per [17], due to the difficulty of statically determining when objects referenced by suspended computations can be safely deallocated. We define region variables to have kind %, and use this symbol because pictorially it is two circles separated by a line, a mnemonic for "this, or that". The kind of value types is *, so the *Int* type constructor has kind $\mathit{Int} :: \% \to *$. The type of a literal integer such as '5' is:

$$5 \ :: \ \forall (r : \%).\, \mathit{Int}\ r$$

In our System-F style language, type application corresponds to instantiation, and '5' is the name of a function that allocates a new integer object into a given region. Note that unlike [16] we do not use allocation effects. This prevents us from optimising away some forms of duplicated computation, such as described in §7 of [4], but also simplifies our type system. For the rest of this paper we will elide explicit kind annotations on binders when they are clear from context.

2.1 Updating Integers

To update an integer we use the *updateInt* function which has type:

$$\mathit{updateInt} \ :: \forall r_1\ r_2.\, \mathit{Mutable}\ r_1 \Rightarrow \mathit{Int}\ r_1 \to \mathit{Int}\ r_2 \xrightarrow{\mathit{Read}\ r_2\ \vee\ \mathit{Write}\ r_1} ()$$

This function reads the value of its second integer argument, and uses this to overwrite the value of the first. As in [16] we annotate function types with their latent effects. We organise effects as a lattice and collect atomic effects with the $\vee$ operator. We use $\bot$ as the effect of a pure function, and unannotated function arrows are taken to have this effect. We also use a set-like subtraction operator where the effect $\sigma \setminus \sigma'$ contains the atomic effects that appear in σ but not σ'. We use ! as the kind of effects, so *Read* has kind $\mathit{Read} :: \% \to !$. The symbol ! is a mnemonic for "something's happening!".

Returning to the type of *updateInt*, $\mathit{Mutable}\ r_1$ is a *region constraint* that ensures that only mutable integers may be updated. When we call this function we must pass a *witness* to the fact that this constraint is satisfied, a point we will discuss further in §3.

When the number of atomic effects becomes large, using the above syntax for effects becomes cumbersome. Due to this we sometimes write effect terms after the body of the type instead:

$$\begin{aligned} \mathit{updateInt} \ &:: \ \forall r_1\ r_2.\, \mathit{Mutable}\ r_1 \Rightarrow \mathit{Int}\ r_1 \to \mathit{Int}\ r_2 \xrightarrow{e_1} () \\ &\rhd\ e_1 = \mathit{Read}\ r_2 \vee \mathit{Write}\ r_1 \end{aligned}$$

The symbol $\rhd$ is pronounced "with". Note that the effect variable e_1 is not quantified. It has been introduced for convenience only and is not a parameter of the type.

2.2 Updating Algebraic Data

Along with primitive types such as *Int*, the definition of an algebraic data type can also contain region variables. For example, we define our lists as follows:

$$\textbf{data}\ List\ r\ a = Nil\ \mid\ Cons\ a\ (List\ r\ a)$$

This definition is similar to the one from §1 except that we have also applied the *List* constructor to a region variable. This variable identifies the region that contains the list cells, and can be constrained to be constant or mutable as needed. The definition also introduces data constructors that have the following types:

$$\begin{aligned} &Nil && :: \forall r\ a.\ List\ r\ a \\ &Cons && :: \forall r\ a.\ a \to List\ r\ a \to List\ r\ a \end{aligned}$$

In the type of *Nil*, the fact that r is quantified indicates that this constructor allocates a new *Nil* object. Freshly allocated objects do not alias with existing objects, so they can be taken to be in any region. On the other hand, in the type of *Cons*, the type of the second argument and return value share the same region variable r, which means the new cons-cell is allocated into the same region as the existing cells. For example, evaluation of the following expression produces the store objects shown below.

$$\begin{aligned} &list :: List\ r_5\ (Int\ r_6) \\ &list = Cons\ r_5\ (Int\ r_6)\ (2\ r_6)\ (Cons\ r_5\ (Int\ r_6)\ (3\ r_6)\ (Nil\ r_5)) \end{aligned}$$

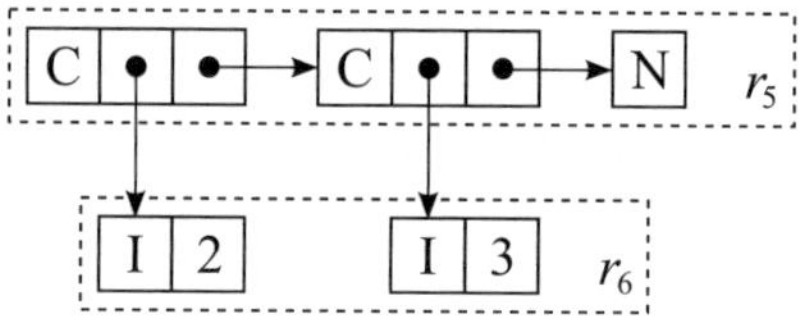

As the list cells and integer elements are in different regions, we can give them differing mutabilities. If the type of *list* was constrained as follows, then we would be free to update the integer elements, but not the spine.

$$list :: Const\ r_5 \Rightarrow Mutable\ r_6 \Rightarrow List\ r_5\ (Int\ r_6)$$

The definition of an algebraic type also introduces a set of update operators, one for each updatable component of the corresponding value. For our list type, as we could usefully update the head and tail pointers in a cons-cell, we get the following operators:

$$\begin{aligned} &update_{Cons,0} && :: \forall r\ a.\ Mutable\ r \Rightarrow List\ r\ a \to a \xrightarrow{Write\ r} () \\ &update_{Cons,1} && :: \forall r\ a.\ Mutable\ r \Rightarrow List\ r\ a \to List\ r\ a \xrightarrow{Write\ r} () \end{aligned}$$

These operators both take a list and a new value. If the list contains an outer cons-cell, then the appropriate pointer in that cell is updated to point to the new value. If the list is not a cons, then a run-time error is raised.

3 Witnesses and Witness Construction

The novel aspect of our core language is that it uses dependently kinded witnesses to manage information about purity, constancy and mutability. A witness is a special type that can occur in the term being evaluated, and its occurrence guarantees a particular property of the program. The System-Fc [15] language uses a similar mechanism to manage information about non-syntactic type equality. Dependent kinds were introduced by the Edinburgh Logical Framework (LF) [1] which uses them to encode logical rules.

Note that although our formal operational semantics manipulates witnesses during reduction, in practice they are only used to reason about the program during compilation, and are not needed at runtime. Our compiler erases witnesses before code generation, along with all other type information.

3.1 Region Handles

We write witnesses with an underline, and the first we discuss are the region allocation witnesses $\underline{\rho_n}$. These are also called *region handles* and are introduced into the program with the **letregion** r **in** t expression. Reduction of this expression allocates a fresh handle $\underline{\rho}$ and substitutes it for all occurrences of the variable r in t. To avoid problems with variable capture we require all bound variables r in the initial program to be distinct. Although region handles are not needed at runtime, we can imagine them to be operational descriptions of physical regions of the store, perhaps incorporating a base address and a range. For example, the following program adds two to its argument, while storing an intermediate value in a region named r_3.

$$\begin{aligned} addTwo &:: \forall r_1\ r_2.\ Int\ r_1 \xrightarrow{Read\, r_1} Int\ r_2 \\ addTwo &= \Lambda r_1\ r_2.\ \lambda(x : Int\ r_1). \\ &\qquad \mathbf{letregion}\ r_3\ \mathbf{in}\ succ\ r_3\ r_2\ (succ\ r_1\ r_3\ x) \end{aligned}$$

This program makes use of the primitive *succ* function that reads its integer argument and produces a new value into a given region:

$$succ :: \forall r_1\ r_2.\ Int\ r_1 \xrightarrow{Read\, r_1} Int\ r_2$$

Note the phase distinction between region variables r_n and region handles $\underline{\rho_n}$. Region handles are bound by region variables. As no regions exist in the store before execution, region handles may not occur in the initial program. Also, although the outer call to *succ* reads a value in r_3, this effect is not observable by calling functions, so is masked and not included in the type signature of *addTwo*. This is similar to the system of [17].

3.2 Witnesses of Constancy and Mutability

The constancy or mutability of values in a particular region is represented by the witnesses $\underline{\mathsf{const}\ \rho}$ and $\underline{\mathsf{mutable}\ \rho}$. Once again, these witnesses may not occur in the initial program. Instead, they are created with the *MkConst* and *MkMutable* witness type constructors which have the following kinds:

$$\begin{array}{ll} \mathit{MkConst} & :: \Pi(r : \%).\ \mathit{Const}\ r \\ \mathit{MkMutable} & :: \Pi(r : \%).\ \mathit{Mutable}\ r \end{array}$$

Both constructors take a region handle and produce the appropriate witness. To ensure that both $\underline{\text{const}\ \rho_n}$ and $\underline{\text{mutable}\ \rho_n}$ for the same $\underline{\rho_n}$ cannot be created by a given program, we require the mutability of a region to be set at the point it is introduced. We introduce new regions with **letregion**, so extend this construct with an optional witness binding that specifies the desired mutability. If a function accesses values in a given region, and does not possess either a witness of constancy or mutability for that region, then it cannot assume either. For example, the following function computes the length of a list by destructively incrementing a local accumulator, then copying out the final value.

$$\begin{array}{l} \mathit{length} :: \forall a\ r_1\ r_2.\ \mathit{List}\ r_1\ a \xrightarrow{\mathit{Read}\ r_1} \mathit{Int}\ r_2 \\ \mathit{length} = \Lambda a\ r_1\ r_2.\ \lambda(\mathit{list} : \mathit{List}\ r_1\ a). \\ \quad \mathbf{letregion}\ r_3\ \mathbf{with}\ \{w = \mathit{MkMutable}\ r_3\}\ \mathbf{in} \\ \quad \mathbf{let}\ (\mathit{acc} : \mathit{Int}\ r_3) = 0\ r_3 \\ \quad\quad (\mathit{length}' : ...) \\ \quad\quad\quad = \lambda(\mathit{xx} : \mathit{List}\ r_1\ a). \\ \quad\quad\quad\quad \mathbf{case}\ \mathit{xx}\ \mathbf{of} \\ \quad\quad\quad\quad\quad \mathit{Nil} \rightarrow \mathit{copyInt}\ r_3\ r_2\ \mathit{acc} \\ \quad\quad\quad\quad\quad \mathit{Cons}\ \_\ \mathit{xs} \rightarrow \mathbf{let}\ (\_ : ()) = \mathit{incInt}\ r_3\ w\ \mathit{acc} \\ \quad\quad\quad\quad\quad\quad \mathbf{in}\ \mathit{length}'\ \mathit{xs} \\ \quad \mathbf{in}\ \ \mathit{length}'\ \mathit{list} \end{array}$$

where

$$\begin{array}{ll} \mathit{copyInt} & :: \forall r_1\ r_2.\ \mathit{Int}\ r_1 \xrightarrow{\mathit{Read}\ r_1} \mathit{Int}\ r_2 \\ \mathit{incInt} & :: \forall r_1.\ \mathit{Mutable}\ r_1 \Rightarrow \mathit{Int}\ r_1 \xrightarrow{\mathit{Read}\ r_1 \vee \mathit{Write}\ r_1} () \end{array}$$

The set after the **with** keyword binds an optional witness type variable. If the region variable bound by the **letregion** is r, then the right of the witness binding must be either *MkConst* r or *MkMutable* r. The type constructors *MkConst* and *MkMutable* may not occur elsewhere in the program. The *length* function above makes use of *incInt* which requires its integer argument to be in a mutable region, and we satisfy this constraint by passing it our witness to the fact.

3.3 Laziness and Witnesses of Purity

Although we use call-by-value evaluation as the default, we can suspend the evaluation of an arbitrary function application with the *suspend* operator:

$$\mathit{suspend} :: \forall a\ b\ e.\ \mathit{Pure}\ e \Rightarrow (a \xrightarrow{e} b) \rightarrow a \rightarrow b$$

suspend takes a parameter function of type $a \xrightarrow{e} b$, its argument of type a, and defers the application by building a thunk at runtime. When the value of the thunk is demanded, the contained function will be applied to its argument, yielding a result of type b. As per [7], values are demanded when they are used as the function in an application, or are inspected by a case-expression or primitive operator such as *update*. The constraint *Pure e* indicates that we must also provide a witness that the application to be suspended is observably pure. Witnesses of purity are written $\underline{\text{pure } \sigma}$ where σ is some effect. They can be created with the *MkPurify* witness type constructor. For example, the following function computes the successor of its argument, but only when the result is demanded:

$$\begin{aligned} succL &:: \forall r_1\ r_2.\ Const\ r_1 \Rightarrow Int\ r_1 \xrightarrow{Read\ r_1} Int\ r_2 \\ succL &= \Lambda r_1\ r_2\ (w : Const\ r_1).\ \lambda(x : Int\ r_1). \\ &\quad\ suspend\ (Int\ r_1)\ (Int\ r_2)\ (Read\ r_1)\ (MkPurify\ r_1\ w) \\ &\qquad\quad (succ\ r_1\ r_2)\ x \end{aligned}$$

MkPurify takes a witness that a particular region is constant, and produces a witness proving that a read from that region is pure. It has the following kind:

$$MkPurify\ :: \Pi(r : \%).\ Const\ r \rightarrow\ Pure\ (Read\ r)$$

Reads of constant regions are pure because it does not matter when the read takes place, the same value will be returned each time. Note that in our system there are several ways of writing the effect of a pure function. As mentioned in §2.1 the effect term $\bot$ is manifestly pure. However, we can also treat any other effect as pure if we can produce a witness of the appropriate kind. For example, $Read\ r_5$ is pure if we can produce a witness of kind $Pure\ (Read\ r_5)$.

3.4 Witness Joining and Explicit Effect Masking

Purity constraints extend naturally to higher order functions. Here is the definition of a lazy map function, *mapL*, which constructs the first list element when called, but only constructs subsequent elements when they are demanded:

$$\begin{aligned} mapL &:: \forall a\ b\ r_1\ r_2\ e. \\ &\quad\ Const\ r_1 \Rightarrow Pure\ e \Rightarrow (a \xrightarrow{e} b) \rightarrow List\ r_1\ a \rightarrow List\ r_2\ b \end{aligned}$$

$$\begin{aligned} &mapL \\ &= \Lambda a\ b\ r_1\ r_2\ e\ (w_1 : Const\ r_1)\ (w_2 : Pure\ e). \\ &\quad \lambda(f : a \xrightarrow{e} b)\ (list : List\ r_1\ a). \\ &\quad \textbf{mask}\ (MkPureJoin\ (Read\ r_1)\ e\ (MkPurify\ r_1\ w_1)\ w_2)\ \textbf{in} \\ &\quad \textbf{case}\ list\ \textbf{of} \\ &\qquad Nil \qquad\quad \rightarrow Nil\ r_2 \\ &\qquad Cons\ x\ xs \rightarrow Cons\ r_2\ b\ (f\ x) \\ &\qquad\qquad\qquad\qquad (suspend\ (List\ r_1\ a)\ (List\ r_2\ b)\ \bot\ MkPure \\ &\qquad\qquad\qquad\qquad\qquad (mapL\ a\ b\ r_1\ r_2\ e\ w_1\ w_2\ f)\ xs) \end{aligned}$$

The inner case-expression in this function has the effect $Read\ r_1 \vee e$. The first part is due to inspecting the list constructors, and the second is due to the application of the argument function f to the list element x. However, as the recursive call to *mapL* is suspended, *mapL* itself must be pure. One way to satisfy this constraint would be to pass a witness showing that $Read\ r_1 \vee e$ is pure directly to *suspend*. This works, but leaves *mapL* with a type that contains this (provably pure) effect term. Instead, we have chosen to explicitly mask this effect in the body of *mapL*. This gives *mapL* a manifestly pure type, and allows us to pass a trivial witness to *suspend* to show that the recursive call is pure.

The masking is achieved with the **mask** δ **in** t expression, which contains a witness of purity δ and a body t. The type and value of this expression is the same as for t, but its effect is the effect of t minus the terms which δ proves are pure. In our *mapL* example we prove that $Read\ r_1 \vee e$ is pure by combining two other witnesses, w_1 which proves that the list cells are in a constant region, and w_2 which proves that the argument function itself is pure. They are combined with the *MkPureJoin* witness type constructor which has the following kind:

$$MkPureJoin :: \Pi(e_1 : !).\ \Pi(e_2 : !).\ Pure\ \ e_1 \rightarrow Pure\ \ e_2 \rightarrow\ \ Pure\,(e_1 \vee e_2)$$

The masking expression in our example also uses *MkPure*, which introduces a witness that the effect $\bot$ is pure. Note that our type for *mapL* now contains exactly the constraints that are *implicit* in a lazy language such as Haskell. In Haskell, all algebraic data is constant, and all functions are pure. In our language, we can suspend function applications as desired, but doing so requires the functions and data involved to satisfy the usual constraints of lazy evaluation.

4 Language

We are now in a position to formally define our core language and its typing rules. The structure of the language is given in Fig. 1. Most has been described previously, so we only discuss the aspects not covered so far. Firstly, we use $\diamondsuit$ as the result kind of witness kind constructors, so a constructor such as *Mutable* has kind $Mutable :: \% \rightarrow \diamondsuit$. This says that a witness of kind $Mutable\ \ r$ guarantees a property of a region, where $\diamondsuit$ refers to the guarantee.

We use use τ_i as binders for value types, σ_i as binders for effect types, and δ_i as binders for type expressions that construct witness types. Δ_i refers to constructed witnesses of the form $\underline{\rho}$, $\underline{\text{const}\ \rho}$, $\underline{\text{mutable}\ \rho}$ or $\underline{\text{pure}\ \sigma}$. φ_i can refer to any type expression.

The values in our term language are identified with v. Weak values, v°, consist of the values as well as suspended function applications $suspend\ \ \overline{\varphi}\ v_1^\circ\ v_2^\circ$. A suspension is only forced when its (strong) value is demanded by using it as the function in an application, the discriminant of a case expression, or as an argument to a primitive operator such as *update*. Store locations l_i are discussed in §4.2. The other aspects of our term language are standard. Recursion can be introduced via **fix** in the usual way, but we omit it to save space. To simplify the presentation we require the alternatives in a case-expression to be exhaustive.

4.1 Typing Rules

In Fig. 2 the judgement form $\Gamma \vdash_{\mathrm{K}} \kappa :: \kappa'$ reads: with type environment Γ, kind κ has kind κ'. We could have added a super-kind stratum containing $\diamondsuit$, but inspired by [12] we cap the hierarchy in this way to reduce the volume of typing rules.

Symbol Classes

$a, r, e, w \;\rightarrow$ (type variable) $\quad T \rightarrow$ (type constructor)

$x \;\rightarrow$ (value variable) $\quad K \rightarrow$ (data constructor)

Kinds

$$\begin{array}{lll} \kappa ::= & \kappa\ \varphi \mid \Pi(a : \kappa_1).\ \kappa_2 & \text{(kinds)} \\ \mid & * \mid \% \mid\ ! \mid \Diamond & \text{(base kinds)} \\ \mid & \mathit{Const} \mid \mathit{Mutable} \mid \mathit{Pure} & \text{(kind constrs)} \end{array}$$

Types

$\varphi, \tau, \sigma, \delta, \Delta$

$$\begin{array}{lll} ::= & a \mid \forall(a : \kappa).\ \tau \mid \varphi_1\ \varphi_2 \mid (\rightarrow) \mid () \mid T & \text{(types)} \\ \mid & \sigma_1 \vee \sigma_2 \mid \bot \mid \mathit{Read} \mid \mathit{Write} & \text{(effects)} \\ \mid & \mathit{MkConst} \mid \mathit{MkMutable} \mid \mathit{MkPure} \mid \mathit{MkPurify} \mid \mathit{MkPureJoin} & \text{(witness constrs)} \\ \mid & \underline{\rho} \mid \underline{\text{const}\ \rho} \mid \underline{\text{mutable}\ \rho} \mid \underline{\text{pure}\ \sigma} & \text{(witnesses)} \end{array}$$

Terms

$$\begin{array}{lll} t & ::= & v \mid t\ \varphi \mid t_1\ t_2 \mid \textbf{letregion}\ r\ \textbf{with}\ \{\overline{w = \delta}\}\ \textbf{in}\ t \mid K\ \overline{\varphi}\ \overline{t} \\ & \mid & \textbf{case}\ t\ \textbf{of}\ \overline{K\ \overline{x : \tau} \rightarrow t'} \mid \mathit{update}_{K,i}\ \overline{\varphi}\ t_1\ t_2 \mid \mathit{suspend}\ \overline{\varphi}\ t_1\ t_2 \\ & \mid & \textbf{mask}\ \delta\ \textbf{in}\ t \end{array}$$

$$\begin{array}{lll} v^\circ, u^\circ & ::= & v \mid \mathit{suspend}\ \overline{\varphi}\ v_1^\circ\ v_2^\circ \qquad \text{(weak values)} \\ v, u & ::= & x \mid l \mid () \mid \Lambda(a : \kappa).\ t \mid \lambda(x : \tau).\ t \qquad \text{(values)} \end{array}$$

Derived Forms

$\kappa_1 \rightarrow \kappa_2 \overset{\text{def}}{=} \Pi(\_ : \kappa_1).\ \kappa_2 \qquad \textbf{let}\ (x : \tau) = t_1\ \textbf{in}\ t_2 \overset{\text{def}}{=} (\lambda(x : \tau).\ t_2)\ t_1$

$\kappa \Rightarrow \tau \overset{\text{def}}{=} \forall(\_ : \kappa).\ \tau \qquad \textbf{letregion}\ r\ \textbf{in}\ t \overset{\text{def}}{=} \textbf{letregion}\ r\ \textbf{with}\ \emptyset\ \textbf{in}\ t$

Store Typing

$\Sigma ::= l : \tau \mid \underline{\rho} \mid \underline{\text{const}\ \rho} \mid \underline{\text{mutable}\ \rho}$

Type Environment

$\Gamma ::= a : \kappa \mid x : \tau$

Fig. 1. Core Language

$$\boxed{\Gamma \vdash_{\mathrm{K}} \kappa :: \kappa'}$$

$$\frac{\kappa \in \{*,\ \%,\ !,\ \Diamond\}}{\Gamma \vdash_{\mathrm{K}} \kappa :: \kappa}\ \text{(KsRefl)} \qquad \frac{\Gamma \vdash_{\mathrm{K}} \kappa_1 :: \kappa_{11} \rightarrow \kappa_{12} \quad \Gamma \vdash_{\mathrm{K}} \varphi :: \kappa_{11}}{\Gamma \vdash_{\mathrm{K}} \kappa_1\ \varphi :: \kappa_{12}}\ \text{(KsApp)}$$

$$\Gamma \vdash_{\mathrm{K}} \mathit{Const} :: \% \rightarrow \Diamond \qquad \Gamma \vdash_{\mathrm{K}} \mathit{Mutable} :: \% \rightarrow \Diamond \qquad \Gamma \vdash_{\mathrm{K}} \mathit{Pure} :: !\ \rightarrow \Diamond$$

Fig. 2. Kinds of Kinds

$$\boxed{\Gamma \mid \Sigma \vdash_{\mathrm{T}} \varphi :: \kappa}$$

$$\Gamma,\ a : \kappa \mid \Sigma \vdash_{\mathrm{T}} a :: \kappa \ (\text{KiVar})$$

$$\Gamma \mid \Sigma,\ \underline{\rho} \vdash_{\mathrm{T}} \underline{\rho} :: \% \ (\text{KiHandle}) \qquad \Gamma \mid \Sigma \vdash_{\mathrm{T}} \bot :: ! \ (\text{KiBot})$$

$$\frac{a \notin fv(\Gamma) \quad \Gamma \vdash_{\mathrm{K}} \kappa_1 :: \kappa_1' \quad \Gamma,\ a : \kappa_1 \mid \Sigma \vdash_{\mathrm{T}} \tau :: \kappa_2}{\Gamma \mid \Sigma \vdash_{\mathrm{T}} \forall(a : \kappa_1).\ \tau :: \kappa_2} \ (\text{KiAll}) \qquad \frac{\Gamma \mid \Sigma \vdash_{\mathrm{T}} \sigma_1 :: ! \quad \Gamma \mid \Sigma \vdash_{\mathrm{T}} \sigma_2 :: !}{\Gamma \mid \Sigma \vdash_{\mathrm{T}} \sigma_1 \vee \sigma_2 :: !} \ (\text{KiJoin})$$

$$\frac{\Gamma \mid \Sigma \vdash_{\mathrm{T}} \varphi_1 :: \Pi(a : \kappa_1).\ \kappa_2 \quad \Gamma \mid \Sigma \vdash_{\mathrm{T}} \varphi_2 :: \kappa_1}{\Gamma \mid \Sigma \vdash_{\mathrm{T}} \varphi_1\ \varphi_2 :: \kappa_2[\varphi_2/a]} \ (\text{KiApp})$$

$$\Gamma \mid \Sigma,\ \underline{\mathrm{const}\ \rho} \vdash_{\mathrm{T}} \underline{\mathrm{const}\ \rho} :: \mathit{Const}\ \underline{\rho} \qquad (\text{KiConst})$$

$$\Gamma \mid \Sigma,\ \underline{\mathrm{mutable}\ \rho} \vdash_{\mathrm{T}} \underline{\mathrm{mutable}\ \rho} :: \mathit{Mutable}\ \underline{\rho} \qquad (\text{KiMutable})$$

$$\Gamma \mid \Sigma \vdash_{\mathrm{T}} \underline{\mathrm{pure}\ \bot} :: \mathit{Pure}\ \bot \qquad (\text{KiPure})$$

$$\Gamma \mid \Sigma,\ \underline{\mathrm{const}\ \rho} \vdash_{\mathrm{T}} \underline{\mathrm{pure}\ (\mathit{Read}\ \rho)} :: \mathit{Pure}\ (\mathit{Read}\ \underline{\rho}) \qquad (\text{KiPurify})$$

$$\frac{\Gamma \mid \Sigma \vdash_{\mathrm{T}} \underline{\mathrm{pure}\ \sigma_1} :: \mathit{Pure}\ \sigma_1 \quad \Gamma \mid \Sigma \vdash_{\mathrm{T}} \underline{\mathrm{pure}\ \sigma_2} :: \mathit{Pure}\ \sigma_2}{\Gamma \mid \Sigma \vdash_{\mathrm{T}} \underline{\mathrm{pure}\ (\sigma_1 \vee \sigma_2)} :: \mathit{Pure}\ (\sigma_1 \vee \sigma_2)} \qquad (\text{KiPureJoin})$$

$$\begin{array}{llll}
\Gamma \mid \Sigma \vdash_{\mathrm{T}} (\to) & :: * \to * \to\ ! \to * & \Gamma \mid \Sigma \vdash_{\mathrm{T}} () & :: * \\
\Gamma \mid \Sigma \vdash_{\mathrm{T}} \mathit{Bool} & :: \% \to * & \Gamma \mid \Sigma \vdash_{\mathrm{T}} \mathit{Read} & :: \% \to\ ! \\
\Gamma \mid \Sigma \vdash_{\mathrm{T}} \mathit{MkConst} & :: \Pi(r : \%).\ \mathit{Const}\ r & \Gamma \mid \Sigma \vdash_{\mathrm{T}} \mathit{Write} & :: \% \to\ ! \\
\Gamma \mid \Sigma \vdash_{\mathrm{T}} \mathit{MkMutable} & :: \Pi(r : \%).\ \mathit{Mutable}\ r & \Gamma \mid \Sigma \vdash_{\mathrm{T}} \mathit{MkPure} & :: \mathit{Pure}\ \bot
\end{array}$$

$$\Gamma \mid \Sigma \vdash_{\mathrm{T}} \mathit{MkPurify} :: \Pi(r : \%).\ \mathit{Const}\ r \to \mathit{Pure}\ (\mathit{Read}\ r)$$

$$\Gamma \mid \Sigma \vdash_{\mathrm{T}} \mathit{MkPureJoin} :: \Pi(e_1 : !).\ \Pi(e_2 : !).\ \mathit{Pure}\ e_1 \to \mathit{Pure}\ e_2 \to \mathit{Pure}\ (e_1 \vee e_2)$$

Fig. 3. Kinds of Types

In Fig. 3 the judgement form $\Gamma \mid \Sigma \vdash_{\mathrm{T}} \varphi :: \kappa$ reads: with type environment Γ and store typing Σ, type φ has kind κ. We discuss store typings in §4.3.

In Fig. 4 the judgement form $\Gamma \mid \Sigma \vdash t :: \tau ; \sigma$ reads: with type environment Γ and store typing Σ, term t has type τ and effect σ. In TyLetRegion the premise "$\overline{\delta_i}$ well formed" refers to the requirement discussed in §3.2 that the witness introduced by a **letregion** must concern the bound variable r. In TyUpdate and TyAlt, the meta-function ctorTypes(T) returns a set containing the types of the data constructors associated with type constructor T.

4.2 Dynamic Semantics

During evaluation, all updatable data is held in the store (also known as the heap), which is defined in Fig. 5. The store contains bindings that map abstract

$$\boxed{\Gamma \mid \Sigma \vdash t :: \tau \,;\, \sigma}$$

$$\Gamma,\, x : \tau \mid \Sigma \vdash x :: \tau \,;\, \bot \;\text{(TyVar)} \qquad \Gamma \mid \Sigma,\, l : \tau \vdash l :: \tau \,;\, \bot \;\text{(TyLoc)}$$

$$\Gamma,\, K : \tau \mid \Sigma \vdash K :: \tau \,;\, \bot \;\text{(TyCtor)} \qquad \Gamma \mid \Sigma \vdash () :: () \,;\, \bot \;\text{(TyUnit)}$$

$$\frac{\Gamma,\, a : \kappa \mid \Sigma \vdash t_2 :: \tau_2 \,;\, \sigma_2}{\Gamma \mid \Sigma \vdash \Lambda(a : \kappa).\, t_2 :: \forall(a : \kappa).\, \tau_2 \,;\, \sigma_2} \;\text{(TyAbsT)}$$

$$\frac{\Gamma \mid \Sigma \vdash t_1 :: \forall(a : \kappa_{11}).\, \varphi_{12} \,;\, \sigma_1 \qquad \Gamma \mid \Sigma \vdash_{\mathrm{T}} \varphi_2 :: \kappa_{11}}{\Gamma \mid \Sigma \vdash t_1\ \varphi_2 :: \varphi_{12}[\varphi_2/a] \,;\, \sigma_1[\varphi_2/a]} \;\text{(TyAppT)}$$

$$\frac{\Gamma,\, x : \tau_1 \mid \Sigma \vdash t :: \tau_2 \,;\, \sigma}{\Gamma \mid \Sigma \vdash \lambda(x : \tau_1).\, t :: \tau_1 \xrightarrow{\sigma} \tau_2 \,;\, \bot} \;\text{(TyAbs)}$$

$$\frac{\Gamma \mid \Sigma \vdash t_2 :: \tau_{11} \,;\, \sigma_2 \qquad \Gamma \mid \Sigma \vdash t_1 :: \tau_{11} \xrightarrow{\sigma} \tau_{12} \,;\, \sigma_1}{\Gamma \mid \Sigma \vdash t_1\ t_2 :: \tau_{12} \,;\, \sigma_1 \vee \sigma_2 \vee \sigma} \;\text{(TyApp)}$$

$$\frac{\begin{array}{c}\overline{\delta_i}\ \text{well formed} \quad r \notin fv(\tau) \quad \Gamma \vdash_{\mathrm{K}} \kappa_i :: \Diamond \\ \Gamma,\, r : \%,\, \overline{w_i : \kappa_i} \mid \Sigma \vdash t :: \tau \,;\, \sigma \qquad \Gamma \mid \Sigma \vdash_{\mathrm{T}} \delta_i :: \kappa_i\end{array}}{\Gamma \mid \Sigma \vdash \textbf{letregion}\ r\ \textbf{with}\ \{\overline{w_i = \delta_i}\}\ \textbf{in}\ t :: \tau \,;\, \sigma \setminus (\mathit{Read}\ r \vee \mathit{Write}\ r)}$$
(TyLetRegion)

$$\frac{\Gamma \mid \Sigma \vdash t :: T\ \varphi\ \overline{\varphi'} \,;\, \sigma \qquad \overline{\Gamma \mid \Sigma \vdash p_i \to t_i :: T\ \varphi\ \overline{\varphi'} \to \tau \,;\, \sigma_i'}^{\,n}}{\Gamma \mid \Sigma \vdash \textbf{case}\ t\ \textbf{of}\ \overline{p \to t} :: \tau \,;\, \sigma \vee \mathit{Read}\ \varphi \vee \sigma_0' \vee \sigma_1' ... \vee \sigma_n'} \;\text{(TyCase)}$$

$$\frac{\begin{array}{ll}\Gamma \mid \Sigma \vdash_{\mathrm{T}} \delta :: \mathit{Mutable}\ \varphi & \Gamma \mid \Sigma \vdash t' :: \tau_i[\varphi/r][\overline{\varphi'/a}] \,;\, \sigma' \\ \Gamma \mid \Sigma \vdash t :: T\ \varphi\ \overline{\varphi'} \,;\, \sigma & K :: \forall(r : \%)(\overline{a : \kappa}).\overline{\tau} \to T\ r\ \overline{a} \in \mathrm{ctorTypes}(T)\end{array}}{\Gamma \mid \Sigma \vdash \mathit{update}_{K,i}\ \varphi\ \overline{\varphi'}\ \delta\ t\ t' :: () \,;\, \sigma \vee \sigma' \vee \mathit{Write}\ \varphi}$$
(TyUpdate)

$$\frac{\Gamma \mid \Sigma \vdash_{\mathrm{T}} \delta :: \mathit{Pure}\ \sigma \quad \Gamma \mid \Sigma \vdash t_1 :: \tau_{11} \xrightarrow{\sigma} \tau_{12} \,;\, \sigma_1 \quad \Gamma \mid \Sigma \vdash t_2 :: \tau_{11} \,;\, \sigma_2}{\Gamma \mid \Sigma \vdash \mathit{suspend}\ \tau_{11}\ \tau_{12}\ \sigma\ \delta\ t_1\ t_2 :: \tau_{12} \,;\, \sigma_1 \vee \sigma_2}$$
(TySuspend)

$$\frac{\Gamma \mid \Sigma \vdash t :: \tau \,;\, \sigma \quad \Gamma \mid \Sigma \vdash_{\mathrm{T}} \delta :: \mathit{Pure}\ \sigma'}{\Gamma \mid \Sigma \vdash \textbf{mask}\ \delta\ \textbf{in}\ t :: \tau \,;\, \sigma \setminus \sigma'} \;\text{(TyMaskPure)}$$

$$\boxed{\Gamma \mid \Sigma \vdash p \to t :: \tau \to \tau' \,;\, \sigma}$$

$$\frac{\begin{array}{r}\theta = [\varphi/r\ \overline{\varphi'/a}] \\ K :: \forall(r : \%)(\overline{a : \kappa}).\overline{\tau} \to T\ r\ \overline{a} \in \mathrm{ctorTypes}(T) \quad \Gamma,\, \overline{x : \theta(\tau)} \mid \Sigma \vdash t :: \tau' \,;\, \sigma\end{array}}{\Gamma \mid \Sigma \vdash K\ \overline{x} \to t :: T\ \varphi\ \overline{\varphi'} \to \tau' \,;\, \sigma}$$
(TyAlt)

Fig. 4. Types of Terms

$$
\begin{array}{lll}
l & \rightarrow & \text{(store location)} \\
\rho & \rightarrow & \text{(region handle)} \\
o & ::= & \rho \mid \text{const } \rho \mid \text{mutable } \rho \qquad \text{(property)} \\
\pi & ::= & l \mid () \mid \Lambda(a : \kappa).t \mid \lambda(x : \tau).t \mid \textit{suspend } \overline{\varphi}\ \pi\ \pi' \qquad \text{(store value)} \\
\mu & ::= & C_K\ \overline{\pi} \qquad \text{(store object)} \\
H : & & \{\ l \overset{\rho}{\mapsto} \mu\ \} + \{\ o\ \} \qquad \text{(store)}
\end{array}
$$

Fig. 5. Stores and Store Objects

store locations to store objects. Each store object consists of a constructor tag C_K and a list of store values $\overline{\pi}$, where each value can be a location, unit value, abstraction or suspension. Each binding is annotated with a region handle ρ that specifies the region that the binding belongs to. Note that store *objects* can be usefully updated, but store *values* can not.

The store also contains *properties* that specify how bindings in the various regions may be used. The properties are ρ, (const ρ) and (mutable ρ). The last two indicate whether a binding in that region may be treated as constant, or updated. When used as a property, a region handle ρ indicates that the corresponding region has been created and is ready to have bindings allocated into it. Note that the region handles of store bindings and properties are not underlined because those occurrences are not used as types.

In Fig. 6 the judgement form $H; \delta \rightsquigarrow \delta'$ reads: with store H, witness δ produces witness δ'. Operationally, properties can be imagined as protection flags on regions of the store — much like the read, write and execute bits in a hardware page table. The witness constructors *MkConst* and *MkMutable* test for these properties, producing a type-level artefact showing that the property was set. If we try to evaluate either constructor when the desired property is *not* set, then the evaluation becomes stuck.

In Fig. 7 the judgement form $H; t \longrightarrow H'; t'$ reads: in heap H term t reduces to a new heap H' and term t'. In EvLetRegion the propOf meta-function maps a witness to its associated store property. Also, note that the premise of EvLetRegion is always true, and produces the required witnesses and properties from the given witness constructions $\overline{\delta_i}$.

4.3 Soundness

In the typing rules we use a store typing Σ that models the state of the heap as the program evaluates. The store typing contains the type of each store location, along with witnesses to the current set of store properties. We say the store typing *models* the store, and write $\Sigma \models H$, when all members of the store typing correspond to members of the store. Conversely, we say the store is *well typed*, and write $\Sigma \vdash H$ when it contains all the bindings and properties predicted by the store typing. Both the store and store typing grow as the program evaluates, and neither bindings, properties or witnesses are removed once added.

Store bindings can be modified by the *update* operator, but the typing rules for update ensure that bindings retain the types predicted by the store typing.

$$\frac{H \;;\; \delta \rightsquigarrow \delta'}{H \;;\; E_w[\delta] \rightsquigarrow E_w[\delta']} \qquad \begin{array}{lcl} E_w & ::= & [\,] \mid \mathit{MkPurify}\ \rho\ E_w \\ & \mid & \mathit{MkPureJoin}\ \sigma_1\ \sigma_2\ E_w\ E_w \end{array}$$

$$H[\ \mathrm{const}\ \rho\ ]\ ;\ \mathit{MkConst}\ \underline{\rho} \rightsquigarrow \underline{\mathrm{const}\ \rho} \qquad \text{(EwConst)}$$

$$H[\ \mathrm{mutable}\ \rho\ ]\ ;\ \mathit{MkMutable}\ \underline{\rho} \rightsquigarrow \underline{\mathrm{mutable}\ \rho} \qquad \text{(EwMutable)}$$

$$H \;;\; \mathit{MkPure} \rightsquigarrow \underline{\mathrm{pure}\ \bot} \qquad \text{(EwPure)}$$

$$H \;;\; \mathit{MkPurify}\ \ \underline{\rho}\ \underline{\mathrm{const}\ \rho} \rightsquigarrow \underline{\mathrm{pure}\ (\mathit{Read}\ \ \rho)} \qquad \text{(EwPurify)}$$

$$H \;;\; \mathit{MkPureJoin}\ \ \sigma_1\ \sigma_2\ \underline{\mathrm{pure}\ \sigma_1}\ \underline{\mathrm{pure}\ \sigma_2} \rightsquigarrow \underline{\mathrm{pure}\ (\sigma_1 \vee \sigma_2)} \qquad \text{(EwPureJoin)}$$

Fig. 6. Witness Construction

$$\frac{e \longrightarrow e'}{E_v[e] \longrightarrow E_v[e']} \qquad \begin{array}{lcll} E_v & ::= & [\,] \mid E_v\ \varphi \mid E_v\ t_2 \mid v\ E_v \mid \mathbf{case}\ E_v\ \mathbf{of}\ \overline{alt} & \\ & \mid & K\ \overline{\varphi}\ E_v\ t_1\ ... & \mid K\ \overline{\varphi}\ v_0\ E_v\ ... \mid ... \\ & \mid & \mathit{update}_{K,i}\ \ \overline{\varphi}\ E_v\ t_2 & \mid \mathit{update}_{K,i}\ \ \overline{\varphi}\ l\ E_v \\ & \mid & \mathit{suspend}\ \ \overline{\varphi}\ E_v\ t_2 & \mid \mathit{suspend}\ \ \overline{\varphi}\ v\ E_v \end{array}$$

$$H \;;\; (\Lambda(a :: \kappa).\ t)\ \varphi \ \longrightarrow\ H \;;\; t[\varphi/a] \qquad \text{(EvTAppAbs)}$$

$$H \;;\; (\lambda(x :: \tau).\ t)\ v^\circ \ \longrightarrow\ H \;;\; t[v^\circ/x] \qquad \text{(EvAppAbs)}$$

$$\frac{H,\ \overline{\mathrm{propOf}(\Delta_i)}\ ;\ \overline{\delta_i[\underline{\rho}/r] \rightsquigarrow \Delta_i} \qquad \rho\ \mathrm{fresh}}{H \;;\; \mathbf{letregion}\ r\ \mathbf{with}\ \{\overline{w_i = \delta_i}\}\ \mathbf{in}\ t \ \longrightarrow\ H,\ \rho,\ \overline{\mathrm{propOf}(\Delta_i)}\ ;\ t[\overline{\Delta_i/w_i}][\underline{\rho}/r]} \qquad \text{(EvLetRegion)}$$

$$H[\rho]\ ;\ K\ \underline{\rho}\ \overline{\varphi}\ \overline{v^\circ} \ \longrightarrow\ H,\ l \overset{\rho}{\mapsto} C_K\ \overline{v^\circ}\ ;\ l \qquad l\ \mathrm{fresh} \qquad \text{(EvAlloc)}$$

$$H[l \overset{\rho}{\mapsto} C_K\ \overline{v^\circ}]\ ;\ \mathbf{case}\ l\ \mathbf{of}\ ...K\ \overline{x} \to t... \ \longrightarrow\ H \;;\; t[\overline{v^\circ}/\overline{x}] \qquad \text{(EvCase)}$$

$$\frac{H \;;\; \delta \rightsquigarrow \delta'}{H \;;\; \mathit{update}\ \ \overline{\varphi}\ \delta\ t\ t' \longrightarrow H \;;\; \mathit{update}\ \ \overline{\varphi}\ \delta'\ t\ t'} \qquad \text{(EvUpdateW)}$$

$$\begin{array}{l} H[\ \mathrm{mutable}\ \rho\ ],\ l \overset{\rho}{\mapsto} C_K\ \overline{v^\circ}^{\,n}\ ;\ \mathit{update}_{K,i}\ \ \overline{\varphi}\ \underline{\mathrm{mutable}\ \rho}\ \ l\ u^\circ \\ \qquad\qquad \longrightarrow\ H,\ l \overset{\rho}{\mapsto} C_K\ v_0..u_i^\circ..v_n\ ;\ () \end{array} \qquad \text{(EvUpdate)}$$

$$\begin{array}{l} H[\ \mathrm{mutable}\ \rho\ ],\ l \overset{\rho}{\mapsto} C_K\ \overline{v^\circ}\ ;\ \mathit{update}_{K',i}\ \ \overline{\varphi}\ \underline{\mathrm{mutable}\ \rho}\ \ l\ u^\circ \\ \qquad\qquad \longrightarrow\ H\ ;\ \mathrm{fail} \qquad\qquad K \neq K' \end{array} \qquad \text{(EvFail)}$$

$$\frac{H \;;\; \delta \rightsquigarrow \delta'}{H \;;\; \mathit{suspend}\ \ \overline{\varphi}\ \delta\ t\ t' \longrightarrow H \;;\; \mathit{suspend}\ \ \overline{\varphi}\ \delta'\ t\ t'} \qquad \text{(EvSuspendW)}$$

$$H \;;\; \mathit{suspend}\ \ \tau\ \tau'\ \sigma\ \underline{\mathrm{pure}\ \sigma}\ (\lambda(x : \tau).\ t)\ v^\circ \ \longrightarrow\ H \;;\; t[v^\circ/x] \qquad \text{(EvSuspend)}$$

$$H \;;\; \mathbf{mask}\ \delta\ \mathbf{in}\ t \ \longrightarrow\ H \;;\; t \qquad \text{(EvMask)}$$

Fig. 7. Term Evaluation

The rule TyLoc of Fig. 4 and KiHandle, KiConst, KiMutable and KiPurify of Fig. 3 ensure that if a location or witness occurs in the term, then it also occurs in the store typing. Provided the store typing models the store, this also means that the corresponding binding or property is present in the store. From the evaluation rules in Fig. 7, the only term that adds properties to the store is **letregion**, and when it does, it also introduces the corresponding witnesses into the expression. The well-formedness restriction on **letregion** guarantees that a witnesses of mutability and constancy for the same region cannot be created. This ensures that if we have, say, the witness $\underline{\mathrm{const}\ \rho}$ in the term, then there is *not* a (mutable ρ) property in the store. This means that bindings in those regions can never be updated, and it is safe to suspend function applications that read them.

Our progress and preservation theorems are stated below. We do not prove these here, but [10] contains a proof for a similar system. The system in this paper supports full algebraic data types, whereas the one in [10] is limited to booleans. Also, here we include a $r \notin fv(\tau)$ premise in the TyLetRegion rule, which makes the presentation easier. See [10] for a discussion of this point.

Progress. If $\emptyset \mid \Sigma \vdash t :: \tau\ ; \sigma$ and $\Sigma \models H$ and $\Sigma \vdash H$ and nofab(t) then either $t \in$ Value or for some H', t' we have ($H; t \longrightarrow H'; t'$ and nofab(t') or $H; t \longrightarrow H'$; fail).

Preservation. If $\Gamma \mid \Sigma \vdash t :: \tau\ ; \sigma$ and $H; t \longrightarrow H'; t'$ then for some Σ', σ' we have $\Gamma \mid \Sigma' \vdash t' :: \tau\ ; \sigma'$ and $\Sigma' \supseteq \Sigma$ and $\Sigma' \models H'$ and $\Sigma' \vdash H'$ and $\Gamma \mid \Sigma \vdash \sigma' \sqsubseteq \sigma$.

In the Progress Theorem, "nofab" is short for "no fabricated region witnesses", and refers to the syntactic constraint that *MkConst* and *MkMutable* may only appear in the witness binding of a **letregion** and not elsewhere in the program. We could perhaps recast these two constructors as separate syntactic forms of **letregion**, and remove the need for nofab, but we have chosen not to do this because we prefer the simpler syntax.

In the Preservation Theorem, note that the latent effect of the term reduces as the program progresses. The $\sqsubseteq$ relationship on effects is defined in the obvious way, apart from the following extra rule:

$$\frac{\Gamma \mid \Sigma \vdash_{\mathrm{T}} \delta :: \mathit{Pure}\ \sigma}{\Gamma \mid \Sigma \vdash \sigma \sqsubseteq \bot} \quad \text{(SubPurify)}$$

This says that if we can construct a witness that a particular effect is pure, then we can treat it as such. This allows us to erase read effects on constant regions during the proof of Preservation. It is needed to show that forcing a suspension does not have a visible effect, and that we can disregard explicitly masked effect terms when entering into the body of a mask-expression.

5 Related Work

The inspiration for our work has been to build on the monadic intermediate languages of [18], [3] and [13]. Note that for our purposes, the difference between using effect and monadic typing is largely syntactic. We prefer effect typing because it mirrors our operational intuition more closely, but [19] gives a translation between the two. Our system extends the previous languages with region, effect and mutability polymorphism, which improves the scope of optimisations that can be performed. In [4] and [2], Benton *et al* present similar monadic languages that include region and effect polymorphism, but do not consider mutability polymorphism or lazy evaluation.

The Capability Calculus [5] provides region based memory management, whereby a capability is associated with each region, and an expression can only access a region when it holds its capability. When the region is deallocated, its associated capability is revoked, ensuring soundness. The capabilities of [5] have similarities to the witnesses of our system, but theirs are not reified in the term being evaluated, and we do not allow ours to be revoked.

The BitC [14] language permits any location, whether on the stack, heap or within data structures to be mutated. Its operational semantics includes an explicit stack as well as a heap, and function arguments are implicitly copied onto the stack during application. BitC includes mutability annotations, but does not use region or effect typing.

6 Conclusion and Future Work

We have presented a System-F style intermediate language that supports mutability polymorphism as well as lazy evaluation, and uses dependently kinded witnesses to track the purity of effects and the mutability and constancy of regions. One of the current limitations of our system is that the results of all case alternatives must have the same type. This prevents us from choosing between, say, a mutable and a constant integer. In future work we plan to provide a new region constraint *Blocked* that represents the fact that an object could be in either a mutable or constant region. We would permit such objects to be read, but not updated, and computations that read them could not be suspended. Doing so would likely require introducing a notion of subtyping into the system, so the types of all alternatives could be coerced to a single upper bound.

The system presented in this paper has been implemented in the prototype Disciplined Disciple Compiler (DDC) which can be obtained from the `haskell.org` website.

References

1. Avron, A., Honsell, F., Mason, I.A.: An overview of the Edinburgh Logical Framework. In: Current Trends in Hardware Verification and Automated Theorem Proving, pp. 323–340. Springer, Heidelberg (1989)
2. Benton, N., Buchlovsky, P.: Semantics of an effect analysis for exceptions. In: Proc. of TLDI 2007, pp. 15–26. ACM, New York (2007)
3. Benton, N., Kennedy, A.: Monads, effects and transformations. Electronic Notes in Theoretical Computer Science, pp. 1–18. Elsevier, Amsterdam (1999)

4. Benton, N., Kennedy, A., Beringer, L., Hofmann, M.: Relational semantics for effect-based program transformations with dynamic allocation. In: Proc. of PPDP, pp. 87–96. ACM, New York (2007)
5. Crary, K., Walker, D., Morrisett, G.: Typed memory management in a calculus of capabilities. In: Proc. of POPL, pp. 262–275. ACM, New York (1999)
6. de Medeiros Santos, A.L.: Compilation by Transformation in Non-Strict Functional Languages. PhD thesis, University of Glasgow (1995)
7. Launchbury, J.: A natural semantics for lazy evaluation. In: Proc. of POPL, pp. 144–154. ACM, New York (1993)
8. Launchbury, J., Jones, S.P.: Lazy functional state threads. In: Proc. of PLDI, pp. 24–35. ACM, New York (1994)
9. Leroy, X., Doligez, D., Garrigue, J., Rémy, D., Vouillon, J.: The Objective Caml system, release 3.11, documentation and user's manual. Technical report, INRIA (2008)
10. Lippmeier, B.: Type Inference and Optimisation for an Impure World. PhD thesis, Australian National University (June 2009) (submitted)
11. MacQueen, D.B.: Standard ML of New Jersey. In: Małuszyński, J., Wirsing, M. (eds.) PLILP 1991. LNCS, vol. 528, pp. 1–13. Springer, Heidelberg (1991)
12. Peyton Jones, S., Meijer, E.: Henk: a typed intermediate language. In: Proc. of the Workshop on Types in Compilation (1997)
13. Peyton Jones, S., Shields, M., Launchbury, J., Tolmach, A.: Bridging the gulf: a common intermediate language for ML and Haskell. In: Proc. of POPL, pp. 49–61. ACM, New York (1998)
14. Shapiro, J., Sridhar, S., Doerrie, S.: BitC language specification. Technical report, The EROS Group and Johns Hopkins University (2008)
15. Sulzmann, M., Chakravarty, M.M.T., Jones, S.P., Donnelly, K.: System-F with type equality coercions. In: Proc. of TLDI. ACM, New York (2007)
16. Talpin, J.-P., Jouvelot, P.: The type and effect discipline. In: Proc. of Logic in Computer Science, pp. 162–173. IEEE, Los Alamitos (1992)
17. Tofte, M., Birkedal, L., Elsman, M., Hallenberg, N., Olesen, T.H., Sestoft, P.: Programming with regions in the MLKit (revised for version 4.3.0). Technical report, IT University of Copenhagen, Denmark (January 2006)
18. Tolmach, A.: Optimizing ML using a hierarchy of monadic types. In: Leroy, X., Ohori, A. (eds.) TIC 1998. LNCS, vol. 1473, pp. 97–115. Springer, Heidelberg (1998)
19. Wadler, P., Thiemann, P.: The marriage of effects and monads. ACM Trans. Computation and Logic 4(1), 1–32 (2003)

On the Decidability of Subtyping with Bounded Existential Types*

Stefan Wehr and Peter Thiemann

Institut für Informatik, Universität Freiburg
{wehr,thiemann}@informatik.uni-freiburg.de

Abstract. Bounded existential types are a powerful language feature for modeling partial data abstraction and information hiding. However, existentials do not mingle well with subtyping as found in current object-oriented languages: the subtyping relation is already undecidable for very restrictive settings.

This paper considers two subtyping relations defined by extracting the features specific to existentials from current language proposals (JavaGI, WildFJ, and Scala) and shows that both subtyping relations are undecidable. One of the two subtyping relations remains undecidable even if bounded existential types are removed.

With the goal of regaining decidable type checking for the JavaGI language, the paper also discusses various restrictions including the elimination of bounded existentials from the language as well as possible amendments to regain some of their features.

1 Introduction

Cardelli and Wegner [5] introduced bounded existential types to obtain a fine-grained modeling instrument for structured and partial data abstraction and information hiding, thus generalizing the concept of an abstract data type modeled with a plain existential type [12]. Language designers and type theorists rely on bounded existentials in diverse areas such as object-oriented languages [1], module systems [19], and functional languages [10].

In the realm of object-oriented languages, bounded existential types have found uses for modeling object-oriented languages in general [2], as well as for modeling specific features such as Java wildcards [3,20,21]. Only a few languages (e.g., Scala [13]) make bounded existential types in full generality available to the programmer. Also, the initial design of JavaGI [23] includes bounded existential types and provides interface types (i.e., the ability to form types from interface names) as a special case supported by syntactic sugar. Building directly on bounded existential types has several advantages compared to interface types: they properly generalize interface types, they encompass Java wildcards, and they have meaningful uses with interfaces abstracting over families of types. Thus, despite the complexity that they introduce in a type system, bounded existential types initially appear like a worthwhile feature.

* A preliminary version of this work was presented at FTfJP 2008 [24].

Z. Hu (Ed.): APLAS 2009, LNCS 5904, pp. 111–127, 2009.

Unfortunately, it turns out that subtyping —and hence type checking— for JavaGI is undecidable in the presence of general bounded existential types. Furthermore, subtyping for bounded existential types as used to encode Java wildcards is also undecidable. This article proves both of these undecidability results. Moreover, it also shows that replacing JavaGI's existentials with plain interface types does not regain decidability of subtyping.

1.1 Contributions and Overview

After refreshing some background on the JavaGI language in Sec. 2, Sec. 3 defines the calculus $\mathcal{EX}_{impl}$ that models the essential aspects of subtyping and bounded existential types in JavaGI. Subtyping in $\mathcal{EX}_{impl}$ is shown to be undecidable by reduction from Post's Correspondence Problem [18]. Further, the section defines the calculus $\mathcal{IT}_{impl}$ by replacing existential types in $\mathcal{EX}_{impl}$ with plain interface types. Subtyping in $\mathcal{IT}_{impl}$ is also undecidable but various restrictions exist that ensure decidability.

Sec. 4 considers the calculus $\mathcal{EX}_{uplo}$ supporting existentials with lower and upper bounds. Subtyping in $\mathcal{EX}_{uplo}$ is also undecidable, as shown by reduction from subtyping in $F^D_\leq$, a restricted form of the polymorphic λ-calculus extended with subtyping [14]. The results in this section are relevant to Scala [13], formal systems for modeling Java wildcards [20, 4, 3], and JavaGI's full type system.

Sec. 5 explores alternative design options for JavaGI that avoid bounded existential types but keep the remaining features. Finally, Sec. 6 reviews related work and Sec. 7 concludes. Detailed proofs may be found in an accompanying technical report [26].

2 Background

JavaGI [23, 25] is a conservative extension of Java 1.5. It generalizes Java's interface concept to incorporate the essential features of Haskell type classes [8, 22]. The generalization allows for retroactive and type-conditional interface implementations, binary methods, static methods in interfaces, default implementations for interface methods, and multi-headed interfaces (interfaces over families of types). Furthermore, JavaGI's initial design generalizes Java-like interface types to bounded existential types. This section only discusses the features relevant to this paper, namely retroactive interface implementations and existential types.

2.1 Retroactive Interface Implementations

Retroactive interface implementations allow programmers to implement an interface for some class without changing the source code of the class. For example, Java rejects the use of a `for`-loop to iterate over the characters of a string because the class `String` does not implement the interface `Iterable`:[1]

[1] Java's enhanced `for`-loop allows to iterate over arrays and all types implementing the `Iterable<X>` interface, which contains a single method `Iterator<X> iterator()`.

```
implementation Iterable<Character> [String] {
  public Iterator<Character> iterator() {
    return new Iterator<Character>() {
      private int index = 0;
      public boolean hasNext() { return index < length(); }
      public Character next() { return charAt(index++); }
    };
  }
}
```

Fig. 1. Retroactive implementation of the `Iterable` interface

```
for (Character c : "21 is only half the truth") { ... } // illegal in Java
```

As a class definition in Java must specify all interfaces that the class implements and the definition of `java.lang.String` is fixed, there is no hope of getting this code to work. A JavaGI programmer can overcome this restriction by adding implementations for interfaces to an existing class at any time, retroactively, without modifying the source code of the class.

For example, the *implementation definition* shown in Fig. 1 specifies that the *implementing type* `String`, enclosed in square brackets `[]`, implements the interface `Iterable<Character>`.[2] The definition of the `iterator` method can use the methods `length` and `charAt` because they are part of `String`'s public interface.

2.2 Bounded Existential Types

Java uses the name of an interface as an *interface type* to denote the set of all types implementing the interface. Instead of interface types, the initial design of JavaGI features *bounded existential types* [5] and provides syntactic sugar for recovering interface types. For example, the interface type `List<String>` abbreviates the existential type ∃ `X` **`where`** `X` **`implements`** `List<String> . X`. The *implementation constraint* "`X` **`implements`** `List<String>`" restricts instantiations of the type variable `X` to types that implement the interface `List<String>`. Thus, the existential type denotes the set of all types implementing `List<String>`, exactly like the synonymous interface type. (The occurrence of "`List<String>`" in the implementation constraint does not abbreviate an existential type.)

Existentials are more general than interface types. For instance, the existential ∃ `X` **`where`** `X` **`implements`** `List<String>, X` **`implements`** `Set<String> . X` denotes the set of all types that implement both `List<String>` and `Set<String>`. Java supports such intersections of interface types only for specifying bounds of type variables. Existentials also encompass Java wildcards [21, 20, 4, 3]. For instance, the existential type ∃ `X` **`where`** `X` **`extends`** `Number . List<X>` corresponds to the wildcard type `List<?` **`extends`** `Number>`.[3]

[2] The implementation ignores the `remove` method of the `Iterator` interface.
[3] Because `List` is an interface, ∃ `X` **`where`** `X` **`extends`** `Number . List<X>` stands for ∃ `X,L` **`where`** `X` **`extends`** `Number, L` **`implements`** `List<X> . L`.

The initial design of JavaGI allows implementation definitions for existentials. For example, given an interface `I`, a programmer may write an implementation definition to specify that all types implementing `List<X>` also implement `I`.

```
implementation<X> I [List<X>] { /* implement methods of I */ }
```

Such a definition is feasible only if all methods of `I` can be implemented using only methods of the `List` interface. The example also demonstrates that JavaGI supports *generic implementation definitions*, which are parameterized by type variables.

3 Subtyping Existential Types with Implementation Constraints

This section introduces $\mathcal{EX}_{impl}$, a subtyping calculus with existentials ($\mathcal{EX}$) and implementation constraints (*impl*). The calculus is a subset of Core-JavaGI [23]. It does not model all aspects of JavaGI's initial design, but contains only those features that make subtyping undecidable. In particular, the syntax of existentials is restricted such that all existentials are encodings of interface types. Consequently, undecidability of subtyping also holds for $\mathcal{IT}_{impl}$, a variant of $\mathcal{EX}_{impl}$ where interface types ($\mathcal{IT}$) replace existentials.

3.1 Definition of $\mathcal{EX}_{impl}$

Fig. 2 defines the syntax along with the entailment and subtyping relations of $\mathcal{EX}_{impl}$. An implementation constraint P has the form $X\ \texttt{implements}\ I\texttt{<}\overline{T}\texttt{>}$ and constrains the type variable X to types that implement the interface $I\texttt{<}\overline{T}\texttt{>}$. An interface without type parameters is written I instead of $I\texttt{<}\bullet\texttt{>}$.[4]

A type T is either a type variable X or a bounded existential type of the form $\exists X\ \texttt{where}\ X\ \texttt{implements}\ I\texttt{<}\overline{T}\texttt{>}\,.\,X$. For simplicity, there are no class types, existentials have a single quantified type variable X, they have exactly one constraint $X\ \texttt{implements}\ I\texttt{<}\overline{T}\texttt{>}$, and the body of an existential must be the quantified type variable. Existentials are considered equal up to renaming of bound type variables.

A definition *def* in $\mathcal{EX}_{impl}$ is either an interface or an implementation definition. Interface and implementation definitions do not have method signatures or bodies, because methods do not matter for the entailment and subtyping relations of $\mathcal{EX}_{impl}$. Moreover, $\mathcal{EX}_{impl}$ does not support interface inheritance. An implementation definition $\texttt{implementation<}\overline{X}\texttt{>}\ I\texttt{<}\overline{T}\texttt{>}\ \texttt{[}J\texttt{<}\overline{U}\texttt{>]}$ implicitly assumes that $\overline{X} = \mathsf{ftv}(J\texttt{<}\overline{U}\texttt{>})$.[5]

The entailment relation $\Theta; \Delta \Vdash T\ \texttt{implements}\ I\texttt{<}\overline{T}\texttt{>}$ expresses that type T implements interface $I\texttt{<}\overline{T}\texttt{>}$. It relies on a program environment Θ, which is a finite set of definitions *def*, and a type environment Δ, which is a finite set of

---

[4] The notation $\overline{\xi}$ abbreviates a sequence $\xi_1, \ldots, \xi_n$ of syntactic entities with $\bullet$ standing for the empty sequence. Sometimes, the sequence $\overline{\xi}$ stands for the set $\{\overline{\xi}\}$.

[5] The notation $\mathsf{ftv}(\xi)$ denotes the set of type variables free in ξ.

Syntax

$$
\begin{array}{rcl}
P, Q, R & ::= & X \ \texttt{implements}\ I\texttt{<}\overline{T}\texttt{>} \\
T, U, V, W & ::= & X \mid \exists X\ \texttt{where}\ P \,.\, X \\
\mathit{def} & ::= & \texttt{interface}\ I\texttt{<}\overline{X}\texttt{>} \mid \texttt{implementation}\texttt{<}\overline{X}\texttt{>}\ I\texttt{<}\overline{T}\texttt{>}\ [I\texttt{<}\overline{T}\texttt{>}]
\end{array}
$$

$$X, Y, Z \in \mathit{TyvarName} \qquad I, J \in \mathit{IfaceName}$$

$\Theta; \Delta \Vdash T\ \texttt{implements}\ I\texttt{<}\overline{T}\texttt{>}$

$$\text{E}_1\text{-IMPL}\quad \frac{\texttt{implementation}\texttt{<}\overline{X}\texttt{>}\ I\texttt{<}\overline{T}\texttt{>}\ [U] \in \Theta}{\Theta; \Delta \Vdash [\overline{V/X}]\,(U\ \texttt{implements}\ I\texttt{<}\overline{T}\texttt{>})} \qquad \text{E}_1\text{-LOCAL}\quad \frac{P \in \Delta}{\Theta; \Delta \Vdash P}$$

$\Theta; \Delta \vdash T \leq T$

$$\text{S}_1\text{-REFL}\quad \Theta; \Delta \vdash T \leq T \qquad \text{S}_1\text{-TRANS}\quad \frac{\Theta; \Delta \vdash T \leq U \qquad \Theta; \Delta \vdash U \leq V}{\Theta; \Delta \vdash T \leq V}$$

$$\text{S}_1\text{-OPEN}\quad \frac{\Theta; \Delta, P \vdash X \leq T \qquad X \notin \mathsf{ftv}(\Theta, \Delta, T)}{\Theta; \Delta \vdash (\exists X\ \texttt{where}\ P \,.\, X) \leq T} \qquad \text{S}_1\text{-ABSTRACT}\quad \frac{\Theta; \Delta \Vdash [T/X]P}{\Theta; \Delta \vdash T \leq (\exists X\ \texttt{where}\ P \,.\, X)}$$

Fig. 2. Syntax, entailment, and subtyping for $\mathcal{EX}_{impl}$

constraints P, where Δ, P abbreviates $\Delta \cup \{P\}$. A type implements an interface either because it corresponds to an instance of a suitable implementation definition (rule E₁-IMPL) or because the type environment contains the constraint (rule E₁-LOCAL).[6]

The subtyping relation $\Theta; \Delta \vdash T \leq U$ states that T is a subtype of U. It is reflexive and transitive as usual. Rule S₁-OPEN opens an existential on the left-hand side of the subtyping relation by moving its constraint into the type environment. The premise $X \notin \mathsf{ftv}(\Theta, \Delta, T)$ ensures that the existentially quantified type variable is sufficiently fresh and does not escape from its scope. Rule S₁-ABSTRACT deals with existentials on the right-hand side of the subtyping relation. It states that T is a subtype of some existential if the constraint of the existential holds after substituting T for the existentially quantified type variable.

As part of a type soundness proof for Core-JavaGI, we verified that the subtyping relation of $\mathcal{EX}_{impl}$ supports the usual principle of subsumption: we can always promote the type of an expression to some supertype without causing runtime errors.

3.2 Undecidability of Subtyping in $\mathcal{EX}_{impl}$

The undecidability of subtyping in $\mathcal{EX}_{impl}$ follows by reduction from Post's Correspondence Problem (PCP). It is well known that PCP is undecidable [7, 18].

[6] The notation $[\overline{T/X}]$ stands for the capture-avoiding substitution replacing each X_i with T_i.

Definition 1 (PCP). *Let $\{(u_1, v_1) \dots, (u_n, v_n)\}$ be a set of pairs of non-empty words over some finite alphabet Σ with at least two elements. A solution of PCP is a sequence of indices $i_1 \dots i_r$ such that $u_{i_1} \dots u_{i_r} = v_{i_1} \dots v_{i_r}$. The decision problem asks whether such a solution exists.*

Theorem 2. *Subtyping in $\mathcal{EX}_{impl}$ is undecidable.*

Proof. Let $\mathcal{P} = \{(u_1, v_1), \dots, (u_n, v_n)\}$ be a particular instance of PCP over the alphabet Σ. We can encode $\mathcal{P}$ as an equivalent subtyping problem in $\mathcal{EX}_{impl}$ as follows. First, words over Σ must be represented as types in $\mathcal{EX}_{impl}$.

```
interface E       // empty word ε
interface L<X>    // letter, for every L ∈ Σ
```

Words $u \in \Sigma^*$ are formed with these interfaces through nested existentials. For example, the word AB is represented by

$$\exists X \,\texttt{where}\, X \,\texttt{implements}\,\texttt{A<}\exists Y \,\texttt{where}\, Y \,\texttt{implements}\,\texttt{B<} \\ \exists Z \,\texttt{where}\, Z \,\texttt{implements}\,\texttt{E}\,.\, Z\texttt{>}\,.\,Y\texttt{>}\,.\,X$$

The abbreviation $I\texttt{<}\overline{T}\texttt{>}$ stands for the type $\exists X \,\texttt{where}\, X \,\texttt{implements}\, I\texttt{<}\overline{T}\texttt{>}\,.\,X$. Using this notation, the word AB is represented by A<B<E>>.

Formally, we define the representation of a word u as $[\![u]\!] := u \# \texttt{E}$, where $u \# T$ is the concatenation of a word u with a type T:

$$\varepsilon \# T := T \qquad\qquad Lu \# T := L\texttt{<}u \# T\texttt{>}$$

Two interfaces are required to model the search for a solution of PCP:

```
interface S<X,Y>    // search state
interface G         // search goal
```

The type $\texttt{S<}[\![u]\!], [\![v]\!]\texttt{>}$ represents a particular search state where we have already accumulated indices $i_1, \dots, i_k$ such that $u = u_{i_1} \dots u_{i_k}$ and $v = v_{i_1} \dots v_{i_k}$. To model valid transitions between search states, we define implementations of S for all $i \in \{1, \dots, n\}$ as follows:

$$\texttt{implementation<X,Y> S<}u_i\#\texttt{X, }v_i\#\texttt{Y> [S<X,Y>]} \tag{1}$$

The type G represents the goal of a search, as expressed by the following implementation:

$$\texttt{implementation<X> G [S<X,X>]} \tag{2}$$

To get the search running we ask whether there exists some $i \in \{1, \dots, n\}$ such that $\Theta_{\mathcal{P}}; \emptyset \vdash \texttt{S<}[\![u_i]\!], [\![v_i]\!]\texttt{>} \leq \texttt{G}$ is derivable. The program $\Theta_{\mathcal{P}}$ consists of the interfaces and implementations just defined. In the extended version [26], we prove a lemma showing that $\mathcal{P}$ has a solution if, and only if, there exists some $i \in \{1, \dots, n\}$ such that $\Theta_{\mathcal{P}}; \emptyset \vdash \texttt{S<}[\![u_i]\!], [\![v_i]\!]\texttt{>} \leq \texttt{G}$ is derivable. □

Syntax

$$\varphi ::= \forall \overline{X}.\, I\texttt{<}\overline{T}\texttt{>} \leq I\texttt{<}\overline{T}\texttt{>}$$
$$T, U, V, W ::= X \mid I\texttt{<}\overline{T}\texttt{>}$$
$$X, Y, Z \in \mathit{TyvarName} \qquad I, J \in \mathit{IfaceName}$$

$\Phi \vdash T \leq T$

S2-REFL
$$\Phi \vdash T \leq T$$

S2-TRANS
$$\frac{\Phi \vdash T \leq U \qquad \Phi \vdash U \leq V}{\Phi \vdash T \leq V}$$

S2-IMPL
$$\frac{(\forall \overline{X}.\, T \leq U) \in \Phi}{\Phi \vdash [\overline{V/X}]T \leq [\overline{V/X}]U}$$

Fig. 3. Syntax and subtyping for $\mathcal{IT}_{impl}$

Example. Suppose the PCP instance $\mathcal{P} = \{(u_1, v_1), (u_2, v_2)\}$ with $u_1 = \texttt{A}$, $u_2 = \texttt{ABA}$, $v_1 = \texttt{AA}$, and $v_2 = \texttt{B}$ is given. The instance has the solution $1, 2, 1$ because $u_1 u_2 u_1 = v_1 v_2 v_1 = \texttt{AABAA}$. The program $\Theta_{\mathcal{P}}$ for the $\mathcal{EX}_{impl}$ encoding of this problem looks like this:

```
interface E              interface A<X>     interface B<X>
interface S<X,Y>         interface G
implementation<X,Y> S<A<X>,        A<A<Y>>>   [S<X,Y>]          // (1)
implementation<X,Y> S<A<B<A<X>>>, B<Y>>       [S<X,Y>]          // (2)
implementation<X>   G                         [S<X,X>]          // (3)
```

We then need to ask whether there exists some $i \in \{1, 2\}$ such that $\Theta_{\mathcal{P}}; \emptyset \vdash \texttt{S<}[\![u_i]\!], [\![v_i]\!]\texttt{>} \leq \texttt{G}$ is derivable. Verifying that such a derivation exists for $i = 1$ is left as an exercise to the reader.

3.3 Undecidability without Existential Types

The proof of undecidability of subtyping in $\mathcal{EX}_{impl}$ reveals that subtyping remains undecidable even if plain interface types replace existentials. To make this claim concrete, Fig. 3 defines the calculus $\mathcal{IT}_{impl}$, which essentially is a version of $\mathcal{EX}_{impl}$ with plain interface types instead of existentials. The simplify the syntax, $\mathcal{IT}_{impl}$ drops interface definitions altogether and uses subtyping schemes instead of implementation definitions: a *subtyping scheme* $\varphi = \forall \overline{X}.\, J\texttt{<}\overline{T}\texttt{>} \leq I\texttt{<}\overline{U}\texttt{>}$ corresponds to an implementation definition $\texttt{implementation<}\overline{X}\texttt{>}\ I\texttt{<}\overline{U}\texttt{>}\ \texttt{[}J\texttt{<}\overline{T}\texttt{>]}$. Such a subtyping scheme implicitly assumes that $\overline{X} = \mathsf{ftv}(J\texttt{<}\overline{T}\texttt{>})$. $\mathcal{IT}_{impl}$ also replaces constraint entailment and the rules S1-OPEN and S1-ABSTRACT with a single rule S2-IMPL. The symbol Φ ranges over finite sets of subtyping schemes φ.

Theorem 3. *Subtyping in $\mathcal{IT}_{impl}$ is undecidable.*

Proof. Similar to the proof of Theorem 2.

The rest of this section investigates decidable fragments of $\mathcal{IT}_{impl}$. It starts with the observation that the undecidability proofs of subtyping in $\mathcal{EX}_{impl}$ and $\mathcal{IT}_{impl}$ rely on two main ingredients:

Cyclic interface subtyping. Implementation definitions in $\mathcal{EX}_{impl}$ (or subtyping schemes in $\mathcal{IT}_{impl}$) allow the introduction of cycles in the subtyping graph of interfaces. Consider one of the implementations defined by Equation (1) on page 116: it states that $\texttt{S<}u_i \,\#\, \texttt{X}, v_i \,\#\, \texttt{Y>}$ is a supertype of $\texttt{S<X, Y>}$. In the reduction from PCP, such cycles are used to encode the individual steps in the search for a solution.

Multiple instantiation subtyping. Implementation definitions in $\mathcal{EX}_{impl}$ (or subtyping schemes in $\mathcal{IT}_{impl}$) allow to introduce two different instantiations of the same interface as supertypes of some other interface. Consider again the implementations defined by Equation (1): for $u_i \neq u_j$ or $v_i \neq v_j$ the implementations state that $\texttt{S<}u_i \,\#\, \texttt{X}, v_i \,\#\, \texttt{Y>} \neq \texttt{S<}u_j \,\#\, \texttt{X}, v_j \,\#\, \texttt{Y>}$ are both supertypes of $\texttt{S<X, Y>}$. In the reduction from PCP, multiple instantiation subtyping encodes the choice between different pairs (u_i, v_i) and (u_j, v_j).

An obvious way to obtain decidable subtyping for $\mathcal{IT}_{impl}$ is to restrict the set of subtyping schemes Φ such that, for all types T, only a finite set of T-supertypes is derivable from Φ.

Definition 4. *The* set of T-supertypes derivable from Φ, *written* $\mathcal{S}_{T,\Phi}$, *is defined as the smallest set closed under the following rules:*

$$T \in \mathcal{S}_{T,\Phi} \qquad\qquad \frac{(\forall \overline{X}.\, V \leq U) \in \Phi \qquad [\overline{W/X}]V \in \mathcal{S}_{T,\Phi}}{[\overline{W/X}]U \in \mathcal{S}_{T,\Phi}}$$

Restriction 1. The set $\mathcal{S}_{T,\Phi}$ must be finite for all types T.

Theorem 5. *Under Restriction 1, subtyping in $\mathcal{IT}_{impl}$ is decidable.*

Proof. See the extended version [26]. □

Here is a restriction that eliminates cyclic interface subtyping.

Definition 6. *A finite set of subtyping schemes Φ is contractive if, and only if, there exists no sequence $\varphi_1, \ldots, \varphi_n \in \Phi$ such that $\varphi_i = \forall \overline{X_i}.\, I_i\texttt{<}\overline{T_i}\texttt{>} \leq J_i\texttt{<}\overline{U_i}\texttt{>}$ for all $i = 1, \ldots, n$ and $J_i = I_{i+1}$ for all $i = 1, \ldots, n-1$ and $J_n = I_1$.*

Restriction 2. The set Φ must be contractive.

Lemma 7. *Restriction 2 implies Restriction 1.*

Proof. See the extended version [26]. □

Remark. Restriction 1 does not imply Restriction 2. Consider the set $\Phi = \{\forall \bullet .\, I \leq I\}$, which obviously meets Restriction 1 but is not contractive.

The next restriction is strictly stronger than Restriction 2.

Restriction 3. For all $\varphi_1, \varphi_2 \in \Phi$ is must hold that $\varphi_1 = \forall \overline{X}.\, I_1\texttt{<}\overline{T}\texttt{>} \leq J_1\texttt{<}\overline{U}\texttt{>}$ and $\varphi_2 = \forall \overline{Y}.\, I_2\texttt{<}\overline{V}\texttt{>} \leq J_2\texttt{<}\overline{W}\texttt{>}$ imply $J_1 \neq I_2$.

The last restriction considered eliminates multiple instantiation subtyping.

Restriction 4. If $\Phi \vdash I{<}\overline{T}{>} \leq J{<}\overline{U}{>}$ and $\Phi \vdash I{<}\overline{T}{>} \leq J{<}\overline{V}{>}$ then it must hold that $\overline{U} = \overline{V}$.

Lemma 8. *Restriction 4 implies Restriction 1.*

Proof. See the extended version [26]. □

Remark. Neither Restriction 1 nor Restriction 2 implies Restriction 4 as demonstrated by $\Phi = \{\forall \bullet . I \leq J{<}A{>}, \forall \bullet . I \leq J{<}B{>}\}$. Moreover, Restriction 4 does not imply Restriction 2 as demonstrated by $\Phi' = \{\forall \bullet . I \leq J, \forall \bullet . J \leq I\}$.

4 Subtyping Existential Types with Upper and Lower Bounds

This section considers the calculus $\mathcal{EX}_{uplo}$, which is similar in spirit to $\mathcal{EX}_{impl}$, but supports upper and lower bounds (*uplo*) for type variables but no implementation constraints. Other researchers [20,4,3] use formal systems very similar to $\mathcal{EX}_{uplo}$ for modeling Java wildcards [21]. It is not the intention of $\mathcal{EX}_{uplo}$ to provide another formalization of wildcards, but rather to expose the essential ingredients that make subtyping undecidable in a calculus as simple as possible. Scala [13] as well as the initial design of the full JavaGI language employ existential types with upper and lower bounds as a replacement for Java wildcards.

4.1 Definition of $\mathcal{EX}_{uplo}$

Fig. 4 defines the syntax and the entailment and subtyping relations of $\mathcal{EX}_{uplo}$. A class type N is either `Object` or an instantiated generic class $C{<}\overline{X}{>}$, where the type arguments must be type variables. A type T is a type variable, a class type, or an existential. Unlike in $\mathcal{EX}_{impl}$, existentials in $\mathcal{EX}_{uplo}$ may quantify over several type variables, they support multiple constraints, and the body of an existential must be a class type. A constraint P places either an upper bound ($X\,\texttt{extends}\,T$) or a lower bound ($X\,\texttt{super}\,T$) on a type variable X. Type environments Δ are finite set of constraints P with Δ, P standing for $\Delta \cup \{P\}$.

Class definitions and inheritance are omitted from $\mathcal{EX}_{uplo}$. The only assumption is that every class name C comes with a fixed arity that is respected when applying C to type arguments. There are some further (implicit) restrictions:

(1) If $T = \exists \overline{X}\,\texttt{where}\,\overline{P} . N$, then $\overline{X} \neq \bullet$ and $\overline{X} \subseteq \mathsf{ftv}(N)$. That is, an existential must abstract over at least one type variable and all its bounded type variables must appear in the body type N.
(2) If $T = \exists \overline{X}\,\texttt{where}\,\overline{P} . N$ and $P \in \overline{P}$, then $P = Y\,\texttt{extends}\,T$ or $P = Y\,\texttt{super}\,T$ with $Y \in \overline{X}$. That is, only bound variables may be constrained.
(3) A type variable must not have both upper and lower bounds.[7]

[7] Modeling Java wildcards requires upper and lower bounds for the same type variable in certain situations.

Syntax

$$
\begin{aligned}
N, M &::= C\texttt{<}\overline{X}\texttt{>} \mid \texttt{Object} \\
T, U, V, W &::= X \mid N \mid \exists \overline{X}\,\texttt{where}\,\overline{P}\,.\,N \\
P, Q, R &::= X\,\texttt{extends}\,T \mid X\,\texttt{super}\,T
\end{aligned}
$$

$$X, Y, Z \in \mathit{TyvarName} \qquad C, D \in \mathit{ClassName}$$

$\Delta \Vdash T\,\texttt{extends}\,T \qquad \Delta \Vdash T\,\texttt{super}\,T$

$$\text{E3-EXTENDS}\ \frac{\Delta \vdash T \leq U}{\Delta \Vdash T\,\texttt{extends}\,U} \qquad \text{E3-SUPER}\ \frac{\Delta \vdash U \leq T}{\Delta \Vdash T\,\texttt{super}\,U}$$

$\Delta \vdash T \leq T$

$$\text{S3-REFL}\ \Delta \vdash T \leq T \qquad \text{S3-TRANS}\ \frac{\Delta \vdash T \leq U \quad \Delta \vdash U \leq V}{\Delta \vdash T \leq V} \qquad \text{S3-OBJECT}\ \Delta \vdash T \leq \texttt{Object} \qquad \text{S3-EXTENDS}\ \frac{X\,\texttt{extends}\,T \in \Delta}{\Delta \vdash X \leq T}$$

$$\text{S3-SUPER}\ \frac{X\,\texttt{super}\,T \in \Delta}{\Delta \vdash T \leq X} \qquad \text{S3-OPEN}\ \frac{\Delta, \overline{P} \vdash N \leq T \quad \overline{X} \cap \mathsf{ftv}(\Delta, T) = \emptyset}{\Delta \vdash \exists \overline{X}\,\texttt{where}\,\overline{P}\,.\,N \leq T} \qquad \text{S3-ABSTRACT}\ \frac{T = [\overline{U/X}]N \quad (\forall i)\ \Delta \Vdash [\overline{U/X}]P_i}{\Delta \vdash T \leq \exists \overline{X}\,\texttt{where}\,\overline{P}\,.\,N}$$

Fig. 4. Syntax, entailment, and subtyping for $\mathcal{EX}_{uplo}$

These three restrictions simplify the formulation of a variant of $\mathcal{EX}_{uplo}$'s subtyping relation without an explicit rule for transitivity (see the extended version [26]).

Constraint entailment ($\Delta \Vdash T\,\texttt{extends}\,U$ and $\Delta \Vdash U\,\texttt{super}\,T$) uses subtyping ($\Delta \vdash T \leq U$) to check that the constraint given holds. The subtyping rules for $\mathcal{EX}_{uplo}$ are similar to those for $\mathcal{EX}_{impl}$, except that `Object` is now a supertype of every type and that rules S3-EXTENDS and S3-SUPER use assumptions from Δ. Moreover, rule S3-ABSTRACT possibly needs to "guess" some of the types $\overline{U}$ because, unlike in $\mathcal{EX}_{impl}$, existentials in $\mathcal{EX}_{uplo}$ may quantify over more than one type variable.

4.2 Undecidability of Subtyping in $\mathcal{EX}_{uplo}$

To get a feeling how subtyping derivations in $\mathcal{EX}_{uplo}$ may lead to infinite regress, consider the goal $\{X\,\texttt{extends}\,\neg U\} \vdash X \leq \neg C\texttt{<}X\texttt{>}$, where U is defined as $\exists X\,\texttt{where}\,X\,\texttt{extends}\,\neg C\texttt{<}X\texttt{>}\,.\,C\texttt{<}X\texttt{>}$ and the notation $\neg T$ is an abbreviation for $\exists X\,\texttt{where}\,X\,\texttt{super}\,T\,.\,D\texttt{<}X\texttt{>}$ such that X is fresh. Searching for a derivation of this goal quickly leads to a subgoal of the form $\{X\,\texttt{extends}\,\neg U, Z\,\texttt{super}\,U\} \vdash X \leq \neg C\texttt{<}X\texttt{>}$, where Z is a fresh type variable introduced by rule S3-OPEN. The details are left as an exercise to the reader.

The undecidability proof of subtyping in $\mathcal{EX}_{uplo}$ is by reduction from $F^D_{\leq}$ [14], a restricted version of $F_{\leq}$ [5]. Pierce defines $F^D_{\leq}$ for his undecidability proof of $F_{\leq}$ subtyping [14]. Fig. 5 recapitulates $F^D_{\leq}$'s syntax and subtyping relation. Let n be

Syntax

$$\tau^+ ::= \mathsf{Top} \mid \forall \alpha_0 {\le} \tau_0^- \dots \alpha_n {\le} \tau_n^- \,.\, \neg\, \tau^-$$
$$\tau^- ::= \alpha \mid \forall \alpha_0 \dots \alpha_n \,.\, \neg\, \tau^+$$
$$\Gamma^- ::= \emptyset \mid \Gamma^-, \alpha {\le} \tau^-$$

$\Gamma^- \vdash \sigma^- \le \tau^+$

D-TOP
$$\Gamma \vdash \tau \le \mathsf{Top}$$

D-VAR
$$\frac{\tau \ne \mathsf{Top} \qquad \Gamma \vdash \Gamma(\alpha) \le \tau}{\Gamma \vdash \alpha \le \tau}$$

D-ALL-NEG
$$\frac{\Gamma, \alpha_0 {\le} \phi_0 \dots \alpha_n {\le} \phi_n \vdash \tau \le \sigma}{\Gamma \vdash \forall \alpha_0 \dots \alpha_n \,.\, \neg\, \sigma \le \forall \alpha_0 {\le} \phi_0 \dots \alpha_n {\le} \phi_n \,.\, \neg\, \tau}$$

Fig. 5. Syntax and subtyping for $F_{\le}^{D}$

a fixed natural number. A type τ is either an n-positive type, τ^+, or an n-negative type, τ^-, where n stands for the number of type variables (minus one) bound at the top-level of the type. An n-negative type environment Γ^- associates type variables α with upper bounds τ^-. The polarity (+ or −) characterizes at which positions of a subtyping judgment a type or type environment may appear. For readability, the polarity is often omitted and n is left implicit.

An *n-ary subtyping judgment* in $F_{\le}^{D}$ has the form $\Gamma^- \vdash \sigma^- \le \tau^+$, where Γ^- is an n-negative type environment, σ^- is an n-negative type, and τ^+ is an n-positive type. Only n-negative types appear to the left and only n-positive types appear to the right of the $\le$ symbol. The subtyping rule D-ALL-NEG compares two quantified types $\sigma = \forall \alpha_0 \dots \alpha_n \,.\, \neg\, \sigma'$ and $\tau = \forall \alpha_0 {\le} \tau_0 \dots \alpha_n {\le} \alpha_n \,.\, \neg\, \tau'$ by swapping the left- and right-hand sides of the subtyping judgment and checking $\tau' \le \sigma'$ under the extended environment $\Gamma, \alpha_0 {\le} \tau_0 \dots \alpha_n {\le} \tau_n$. The rule is correct with respect to $F_{\le}$ because we may interpret every $F_{\le}^{D}$ type as an $F_{\le}$ type:

$$\forall \alpha_0 \dots \alpha_n \,.\, \neg\, \sigma' \equiv \forall \alpha_0 {\le} \mathsf{Top} \dots \forall \alpha_n {\le} \mathsf{Top}. \forall \beta {\le} \sigma' \,.\, \beta \ (\beta \text{ fresh})$$
$$\forall \alpha_0 {\le} \tau_0 \dots \alpha_n {\le} \alpha_n \,.\, \neg\, \tau' \equiv \forall \alpha_0 {\le} \tau_0 \dots \forall \alpha_n {\le} \tau_n . \forall \beta {\le} \tau' \,.\, \beta \qquad (\beta \text{ fresh})$$

Using these abbreviations, every $F_{\le}^{D}$ subtyping judgment can be read as an $F_{\le}$ subtyping judgment. The subtyping relations in $F_{\le}^{D}$ and $F_{\le}$ coincide for judgments in their common domain [14].

It is sufficient to consider only *closed judgments.* A type τ is closed under Γ if $\mathsf{ftv}(\tau) \subseteq \mathsf{dom}(\Gamma)$ (where $\mathsf{dom}(\alpha_1 {\le} \tau_1, \dots, \alpha_n {\le} \tau_n) = \{\alpha_1, \dots, \alpha_n\}$) and, if $\tau = \forall \alpha_0 {\le} \tau_0 \dots \alpha_n {\le} \tau_n \,.\, \neg\, \sigma$, then no α_i appears free in any τ_j. A type environment Γ is closed if $\Gamma = \emptyset$ or $\Gamma = \Gamma', \alpha {\le} \tau$ with Γ' closed and τ closed under Γ'. A judgment $\Gamma \vdash \tau \le \sigma$ is closed if Γ is closed and τ, σ are closed under Γ.

These notions are sufficient to state the central theorem of this section and sketch its proof.

Theorem 9. *Subtyping in $\mathcal{EX}_{uplo}$ is undecidable.*

Proof. The proof is by reduction from $F_{\le}^{D}$. Fig. 6 defines a translation from $F_{\le}^{D}$ types, type environments, and subtyping judgments to their corresponding $\mathcal{EX}_{uplo}$ forms. The translation of an n-ary subtyping judgment assumes the

$$
\begin{aligned}
[\![\mathsf{Top}]\!]^+ &= \texttt{Object} \\
[\![\forall \alpha_0 {\le} \tau_0^- \ldots \alpha_n {\le} \tau_n^- \,.\, \neg\, \tau^-]\!]^+ &= \neg\, \exists Y, \overline{X^{\alpha_i}} \;\texttt{where}\; X^{\alpha_0}\; \texttt{extends}\; [\![\tau_0]\!]^- \ldots \\
&\qquad X^{\alpha_n}\; \texttt{extends}\; [\![\tau_n]\!]^-, Y\; \texttt{extends}\; [\![\tau]\!]^- \\
&\qquad .\, C^{n+2}\texttt{<}Y, \overline{X^{\alpha_i}}\texttt{>} \\
[\![\alpha]\!]^- &= X^\alpha \\
[\![\forall \alpha_0 \ldots \alpha_n \,.\, \neg\, \tau^+]\!]^- &= \neg\, \exists Y, \overline{X^{\alpha_i}} \;\texttt{where}\; Y\; \texttt{extends}\; [\![\tau]\!]^+ \,.\, C^{n+2}\texttt{<}Y, \overline{X^{\alpha_i}}\texttt{>} \\
[\![\emptyset]\!]^- &= \emptyset \\
[\![\Gamma, \alpha {\le} \tau^-]\!]^- &= [\![\Gamma]\!]^-, X^\alpha\; \texttt{extends}\; [\![\tau]\!]^- \\
[\![\Gamma^- \vdash \tau^- \le \sigma^+]\!] &= [\![\Gamma]\!]^- \vdash [\![\tau]\!]^- \le [\![\sigma]\!]^+
\end{aligned}
$$

Fig. 6. Reduction from $F_{\le}^{D}$ to $\mathcal{EX}_{uplo}$

existence of two $\mathcal{EX}_{uplo}$ classes: C^{n+2} accepts $n+2$ type arguments, and D^1 takes one type argument. The superscripts in $[\![\cdot]\!]^+$ and $[\![\cdot]\!]^-$ indicate whether the translation acts on positive or negative entities.

As before, a negated type, written $\neg\, T$, is an abbreviation for an existential with a single `super` constraint: $\neg\, T \equiv \exists X \;\texttt{where}\; X \;\texttt{super}\; T \,.\, D^1\texttt{<}X\texttt{>}$, where X is fresh. The `super` constraint simulates the behavior of the $F_{\le}^{D}$ subtyping rule D-ALL-NEG, which swaps the left- and right-hand sides of subtyping judgments.

An n-positive type $\forall \alpha_0 {\le} \tau_0^- \ldots \alpha_n {\le} \tau_n^- \,.\, \neg\, \tau^-$ is translated into a negated existential. The existentially quantified type variables $X^{\alpha_0}, \ldots, X^{\alpha_n}$ correspond to the universally quantified type variables $\alpha_0, \ldots, \alpha_n$. The bound $[\![\tau]\!]^-$ of the fresh type variable Y represents the body $\neg\, \tau^-$ of the original type. We cannot use $[\![\tau]\!]^-$ directly as the body because existentials in $\mathcal{EX}_{uplo}$ have only class types as their bodies. The translation for n-negative types is similar to the one for n-positive types. It is easy to see that the $\mathcal{EX}_{uplo}$ types in the image of the translation meet the restrictions defined in Sec. 4.1. Type environments and subtyping judgments are translated in the obvious way.

We now need to verify that $\Gamma \vdash \tau \le \sigma$ is derivable in $F_{\le}^{D}$ if and only if $[\![\Gamma \vdash \tau \le \sigma]\!]$ is derivable in $\mathcal{EX}_{uplo}$. The "$\Rightarrow$" direction is an easy induction on the derivation of $\Gamma \vdash \tau \le \sigma$. The "$\Leftarrow$" direction requires more work because the transitivity rule S3-TRANS (Fig. 4) involves an intermediate type which is not necessarily in the image of the translation. Hence, a direct proof by induction on the derivation of $[\![\Gamma \vdash \tau \le \sigma]\!]$ fails. To solve this problem, we give an equivalent definition of the $\mathcal{EX}_{uplo}$ subtyping relation that does not include an explicit transitivity rule. See the extended version [26] for details and the full proof. □

5 Lessons Learned

What are the consequences of this investigation for the design of JavaGI? While bounded existential types are powerful and unify several diverse concepts, they complicate the metatheory of JavaGI's initial design considerably. Also, subtyping with existential types is undecidable in the general case, as demonstrated in the two preceding sections.

There are three alternatives for dealing with this problem: (1) Accept that the subtyping relation is undecidable. (2) Restrict existentials such that subtyping becomes decidable. (3) Remove existentials from JavaGI altogether.

The first alternative (opted for by the Scala compiler) is pragmatic and readily implementable by imposing a resource limit on the subtype checker to avoid divergence. Consequently, the subtyping algorithm would become incomplete with respect to its specification.

The second alternative turns out not to be viable. It is feasible to come up with a set of restrictions that keep the subtyping relation defined in Sec. 3 decidable. (Sec. 3.3 investigated such restrictions for plain interface types.) For the subtyping relation defined in Sec. 4, however, we were not able to identify sensible restrictions without giving up either lower or upper bounds (which are essential for encoding Java wildcards). Moreover, restricting existential types so that subtyping becomes decidable would make an already complex type system even more complicated. In addition, such restrictions tend to be difficult to communicate to users of the language.

The third alternative comes with the realization that existentials may not be worth the trouble. JavaGI's main contribution is its very general and powerful interface concept (which this paper does not explore, but see [23, 25]). While existential types are related to this concept, they are not at the heart of it. In fact, we conducted several real-world case studies using our implementation of JavaGI without a need for full-blown existential types arising [25].

Under these circumstances, it appears that the price of having bounded existential types at the core of JavaGI is too high. Hence, the current, revised version of JavaGI elides bounded existential types because of their poor power/cost ratio but retains all other features of the previous design. Thus, it gives up some of the power in favor of simplicity.

Several already existing features make up for the lack of existentials. More specifically, the revised design copes with most uses of existentials from Sec. 1: parametric polymorphism in combination with multiple subtyping constraints (as already present in Java) allows to emulate the composition of interface types in most situations; direct support for wildcards avoids their encoding through existential types;[8] JavaGI's `implements` constraints in combination with parametric polymorphism allow the specification of meaningful types for interfaces over families of types.

[8] It is an open question whether subtyping for Java wildcards is decidable (see Sec. 6 for details). Of course, the inclusion of wildcards in JavaGI is a concession to ensure backwards compatibility with Java 1.5. An embedding of JavaGI's generalized interface concept in other languages such as C# could easily drop support for wildcards. Thus, the decidability question for wildcards is not intrinsic to decidability of subtyping in JavaGI.

Even the revised design has to accept compromises to avoid undecidability. Sec. 3.3 reveals that subtyping remains undecidable even if plain interface types replace existentials. The real culprit for undecidability is the ability to provide implementation definitions with interface types acting as implementing types.

Disallowing such implementation definitions completely is a rather severe restriction because it prevents useful implementation definitions such as the one given for `List<X>` in Sec. 2.2. Instead, the revised design allows interfaces as implementing types but it imposes the equivalent of Restriction 3 from Sec. 3.3: if an interface is used as an implementing type then no retroactive implementation can be provided for this interface.[9]

Sometimes, even this restriction is too strict. For example, the use of `List<X>` as an implementing type in Sec. 2.2 prevents retroactive implementations of the `List` interface. *Abstract implementation definitions* are a potential cure. They look similar to non-abstract implementation definitions but do not contribute to constraint entailment and subtyping, so the restriction just explained does not apply. The details of abstract implementation definitions are explained elsewhere [25].

6 Related Work

Kennedy and Pierce [9] investigate undecidability of subtyping under multiple instantiation inheritance and declaration-site variance. They prove that the general case is undecidable and present three decidable fragments. The proof in Sec. 3 is similar to theirs, although undecidability has different causes: Kennedy and Pierce's system is undecidable because of contravariant generic types, expansive class tables, and multiple instantiation inheritance, whereas undecidability of our system is due to implementation definitions for existentials (or interface types), which cause cyclic interface and multiple instantiation subtyping.

Pierce [14] proves undecidability of subtyping in $F_{\leq}$ by a chain of reductions from the halting problem for two-counter Turing machines. An intermediate link in this chain is the subtyping relation of $F_{\leq}^{D}$, which is also undecidable. Our proof in Sec. 4 works by reduction from $F_{\leq}^{D}$ and is inspired by a reduction given by Ghelli and Pierce [6], who study bounded existential types in the context of $F_{\leq}$ and show undecidability of subtyping. Crucial to the undecidability proof of $F_{\leq}^{D}$ is rule D-ALL-NEG: it extends the typing context and essentially swaps the sides of a subtyping judgment. In $\mathcal{EX}_{uplo}$, rule S3-OPEN and rule S3-ABSTRACT together with lower bounds on type variables play a similar role.

Torgersen and coworkers [20] present WildFJ as a model for Java wildcards using existential types. The authors do not prove WildFJ sound. Cameron and coworkers [4] define a similar calculus ∃J and prove soundness. However, ∃J is not a full model for Java wildcards because it does not support lower bounds for type variables. The same authors present with TameFJ [3] a sound calculus supporting

[9] Restriction 2 is more flexible then Restriction 3 but the latter simplifies the detection of ambiguities arising through conflicting implementation definitions and it allows for an efficient implementation of dynamic method lookup.

all essential features of Java wildcards. WildFJ's and TameFJ's subtyping rules are similar to the ones of $\mathcal{EX}_{uplo}$ defined in Sec. 4, so the conjecture is that subtyping in WildFJ and TameFJ is also undecidable. The rule XS-ENV of TameFJ is roughly equivalent to the rules S3-OPEN and S3-ABSTRACT of $\mathcal{EX}_{uplo}$.

Decidability of subtyping for Java wildcards is still an open question [11]. One step in the right direction might be the work of Plümicke, who solves the problem of finding a substitution s such that $sT \leq sU$ for Java types T, U with wildcards [17, 16]. Our undecidability result for $\mathcal{EX}_{uplo}$ does not imply undecidability for Java subtyping with wildcards. The proof of this claim would require a translation from subtyping derivations in $\mathcal{EX}_{uplo}$ to subtyping derivations in Java with wildcards, which is not addressed in this paper. In general, existentials in $\mathcal{EX}_{uplo}$ are strictly more powerful than Java wildcards. For example, the existential $\exists X.C\texttt{<}X, X\texttt{>}$ cannot be encoded as the wildcard type $C\texttt{<?,?>}$ because the two occurrences of ? denote two distinct types.

The programming language Scala [13] supports existential types in its latest release to provide better interoperability with Java libraries using wildcards and to address the avoidance problem [15, Chapter 8]. The subtyping rules for existentials (Sec. 3.2.10 and Sec. 3.5.2 of the specification [13]) are very similar to the ones for $\mathcal{EX}_{uplo}$. This raises the question whether Scala's subtyping relation with existentials is decidable.

A recent article [25] reports on practical experience with the revised design of JavaGI. It discusses several case studies and describes the implementation of a compiler and a runtime system for JavaGI, which employs the restrictions discussed in Sec. 5.

7 Conclusion

The paper investigated decidability of subtyping with bounded existential types in the context of JavaGI, Java wildcards, and Scala. It defined two calculi $\mathcal{EX}_{impl}$ and $\mathcal{EX}_{uplo}$ featuring bounded existential types in two variations and proved undecidability of subtyping for both calculi. Subtyping is also undecidable for $\mathcal{II}_{impl}$, a simplified version of $\mathcal{EX}_{impl}$ without existentials. The paper also suggested a revised version of JavaGI that avoids fully general existentials without giving up much expressivity. The revised version of JavaGI is available at `http://www.informatik.uni-freiburg.de/~wehr/javagi/`.

Acknowledgments

We thank the anonymous FTfJP 2008 and APLAS 2009 reviewers for feedback on earlier versions of this article.

References

1. Abadi, M., Cardelli, L.: A Theory of Objects. Springer, Heidelberg (1996)
2. Bruce, K.B., Cardelli, L., Pierce, B.C.: Comparing object encodings. Information and Computation 155(1-2), 108–133 (1999)

3. Cameron, N., Drossopoulou, S., Ernst, E.: A model for Java with wildcards. In: Vitek, J. (ed.) ECOOP 2008. LNCS, vol. 5142, pp. 2–26. Springer, Heidelberg (2008)
4. Cameron, N., Ernst, E., Drossopoulou, S.: Towards an existential types model for Java wildcards. In: FTfJP, informal proceedings (2007), http://www.doc.ic.ac.uk/~ncameron/papers/cameron_ftfjp07_full.pdf
5. Cardelli, L., Wegner, P.: On understanding types, data abstraction, and polymorphism. ACM Comput. Surv. 17, 471–522 (1985)
6. Ghelli, G., Pierce, B.: Bounded existentials and minimal typing. Theoretical Computer Science 193(1-2), 75–96 (1998)
7. Hopcroft, J.E., Motwani, R., Ullman, J.D.: Introduction to Automata Theory, Languages, and Computation, 3rd edn. Addison Wesley, Reading (2006)
8. Kaes, S.: Parametric overloading in polymorphic programming languages. In: Ganzinger, H. (ed.) ESOP 1988. LNCS, vol. 300, pp. 131–144. Springer, Heidelberg (1988)
9. Kennedy, A.J., Pierce, B.C.: On decidability of nominal subtyping with variance. In: FOOL/WOOD, informal proceedings (January 2007), http://foolwood07.cs.uchicago.edu/program/kennedy-abstract.html
10. Läufer, K.: Type classes with existential types. J. Funct. Program. 6(3), 485–517 (1996)
11. Mazurak, K., Zdancewic, S.: Type inference for Java 5: Wildcards, F-bounds, and undecidability (2006), http://www.cis.upenn.edu/~stevez/note.html
12. Mitchell, J.C., Plotkin, G.D.: Abstract types have existential types. ACM TOPLAS 10(3), 470–502 (1988)
13. Odersky, M.: The Scala language specification version 2.7. Draft (April 2008), http://www.scala-lang.org/docu/files/ScalaReference.pdf
14. Pierce, B.C.: Bounded quantification is undecidable. Information and Computation 112(1), 131–165 (1994)
15. Pierce, B.C. (ed.): Advanced Topics in Types and Programming Languages. MIT Press, Cambridge (2005)
16. Plümicke, M.: Typeless programming in Java 5.0 with wildcards. In: 5th PPPJ. ACM, New York (2007)
17. Plümicke, M.: Java type unification with wildcards. In: Seipel, D., Hanus, M., Wolf, A. (eds.) INAP/WLP 2007. LNCS (LNAI), vol. 5437, pp. 223–240. Springer, Heidelberg (2009)
18. Post, E.L.: A variant of a recursivley unsolvable problem. Bulletin of the American Mathematical Society 53, 264–268 (1946)
19. Russo, C.V.: Types for Modules. PhD thesis, Edinburgh University, Edinburgh, Scotland, LFCS Thesis ECS–LFCS–98–389 (1998)
20. Torgersen, M., Ernst, E., Hansen, C.P.: Wild FJ. In: FOOL, informal proceedings (2005), http://homepages.inf.ed.ac.uk/wadler/fool/program/14.html
21. Torgersen, M., Ernst, E., Hansen, C.P., von der Ahé, P., Bracha, G., Gafter, N.: Adding wildcards to the Java programming language. Journal of Object Technology 3(11), 97–116 (2004)
22. Wadler, P., Blott, S.: How to make ad-hoc polymorphism less ad-hoc. In: Proc. 16th ACM Symp. POPL, Austin, Texas, USA. ACM Press, New York (1989)
23. Wehr, S., Lämmel, R., Thiemann, P.: JavaGI: Generalized interfaces for Java. In: Ernst, E. (ed.) ECOOP 2007. LNCS, vol. 4609, pp. 347–372. Springer, Heidelberg (2007)

24. Wehr, S., Thiemann, P.: Subtyping existential types. In: 10th FTfJP, informal proceedings (2008), `http://www.informatik.uni-freiburg.de/~wehr/publications/subex.pdf`
25. Wehr, S., Thiemann, P.: JavaGI in the battlefield: Practical experience with generalized interfaces. In: Proc. 8th GPCE, Denver, Colorado, USA. ACM, New York (2009)
26. Wehr, S., Thiemann, P.: On the decidability of subtyping with bounded existential types (extended edition). Technical report, Universität Freiburg (September 2009), `ftp://ftp.informatik.uni-freiburg.de/documents/reports/report250/report00250.ps.gz`

Fractional Ownerships for Safe Memory Deallocation

Kohei Suenaga and Naoki Kobayashi

Tohoku University*

Abstract. We propose a type system for a programming language with memory allocation/deallocation primitives, which prevents memory-related errors such as double-frees and memory leaks. The main idea is to augment pointer types with fractional ownerships, which express both capabilities and obligations to access or deallocate memory cells. By assigning an ownership to each pointer type constructor (rather than to a variable), our type system can properly reason about list/tree-manipulating programs. Furthermore, thanks to the use of fractions as ownerships, the type system admits a polynomial-time type inference algorithm, which serves as an algorithm for automatic verification of lack of memory-related errors. A prototype verifier has been implemented and tested for C programs.

1 Introduction

In programming languages with manual memory management (like C and C++), a misuse of memory allocation/deallocation primitives often causes serious, hard-to-find bugs. We propose a new type-based method for static verification of lack of such memory-related errors. More precisely, we construct a type system that guarantees that well-typed programs do not suffer from memory leaks (forgetting to deallocate memory cells), double frees (deallocating memory cells more than once), and illegal read/write accesses to deallocated memory. We then construct a polynomial-time type inference algorithm, so that programs can be verified without any type annotations.

The key idea of our type system is to assign *fractional ownerships* to pointer types. An ownership ranges over the set of rational numbers in $[0, 1]$, and expresses both a capability (or permission) to access a pointer, and an obligation to deallocate the memory referred to by the pointer. As in Boyland's fractional permissions [1], a non-zero ownership expresses a permission to dereference the pointer, and an ownership of 1 expresses a permission to update the memory cell referenced by the pointer. In addition, a non-zero ownership expresses an obligation to eventually deallocate (the cell referenced by) the pointer, and an ownership of 1 also expresses a permission to deallocate the pointer. (Therefore, if one has a non-zero ownership less than 1, one has to eventually combine it with other ownerships to obtain an ownership of 1, to fulfill the obligation to deallocate the pointer).

---

* Suenaga's Current Affiliation: IBM Research.

Z. Hu (Ed.): APLAS 2009, LNCS 5904, pp. 128–143, 2009.

Ownerships are also used in Heine and Lam's static analysis for detecting memory leaks [2], although their ownerships range over integer values $\{0, 1\}$. The most important deviation from their system is that our type system assigns an ownership to each *pointer type constructor*, rather than to a variable. For example, $\mathbf{int}\ \mathbf{ref}_1\ \mathbf{ref}_1$ is the type of a pointer to a pointer to an integer, such that both the pointers can be read/written, and must be deallocated through the pointer. $\mathbf{int}\ \mathbf{ref}_0\ \mathbf{ref}_1$ is the type of a pointer to an pointer to an integer, such that only the first pointer can be read/written, and must be deallocated. The type $\mu\alpha.(\alpha\ \mathbf{ref}_1)$ (where $\mu\alpha.\tau$ is a recursive type) describes a pointer to a list structure shown in Figure 1, where the pointer holds the ownerships of all the pointers reachable from it. This allows us to properly reason about list- and tree-manipulating programs, unlike Heine and Lam's analysis.

For example, consider the following program, written in an ML-like language (but with memory deallocation primitive `free`).

`fun freeall(x) =`	`freeall`$: \mu\alpha.(\alpha\ \mathbf{ref}_1) \to \mu\alpha.(\alpha\ \mathbf{ref}_0)$
`  if null(x)`	$x : \mu\alpha.(\alpha\ \mathbf{ref}_1)$
`  then skip`	$x : \mu\alpha.(\alpha\ \mathbf{ref}_0)$
`  else let y = *x in`	$x : \mu\alpha.(\alpha\ \mathbf{ref}_1)$
`         (freeall(y);`	$x : (\mu\alpha.(\alpha\ \mathbf{ref}_0))\ \mathbf{ref}_1, y : \mu\alpha.(\alpha\ \mathbf{ref}_1)$
`          free(x)`	$x : (\mu\alpha.(\alpha\ \mathbf{ref}_0))\ \mathbf{ref}_1, y : \mu\alpha.(\alpha\ \mathbf{ref}_0)$
`         )`	$x : \mu\alpha.(\alpha\ \mathbf{ref}_0), y : \mu\alpha.(\alpha\ \mathbf{ref}_0)$

The function `freeall` takes as an argument a pointer `x` to a list structure, and deallocates all the pointers reachable from `x`. The righthand side shows the type of function `freeall`, as well as the types assigned to `x` and `y` before execution of each line. (Our type system is flow-sensitive, so that different types are assigned at different program points.) In the type of `freeall` on the first line, $\mu\alpha.(\alpha\ \mathbf{ref}_1)$ and $\mu\alpha.(\alpha\ \mathbf{ref}_0)$ are the types of x before and after the call of the function. The type $\mu\alpha.(\alpha\ \mathbf{ref}_0)$ means that `x` holds no ownerships when the function returns (which implies that all the pointers reachable from `x` will be deallocated inside the function).

The type assignment at the beginning of the function indicates that all the memory cells reachable from `x` should be deallocated through variable `x`. In the then-branch, `x` is a null pointer, so that all the ownerships are cleared to 0. In the else-branch, $\mathbf{let}\ y = *x\ \mathbf{in} \cdots$ transfers a part of the ownerships held by `x` to `y`; after that, `x` has type $(\mu\alpha.(\alpha\ \mathbf{ref}_0))\ \mathbf{ref}_1$, indicating that x holds only the ownership of the pointer stored in `x`. The other ownerships (of the pointers that are reachable from `x`) are now held by `y`. After the recursive call to `freeall`, all the ownerships held by `y` become empty. Finally, after `free(x)`, the ownership of `x` also becomes empty.

The type system with fractional ownerships prevents: (i) memory leaks by maintaining the invariant that the total ownership for each memory cell is 1 until the cell is deallocated and by ensuring the ownerships held by a variable are empty at the end of the scope of the variable, (ii) double frees by ensuring that the ownership for a cell is consumed when the cell is deallocated, and

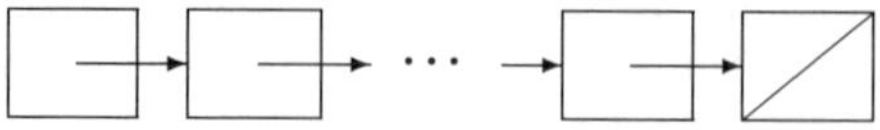

Fig. 1. List-like structure

(iii) illegal access to deallocated cells by requiring that a non-zero ownership is required for read/write operations.

Thanks to the use of fractional ownerships, the type inference problem can be reduced to a linear programming problem over rational numbers, which can be solved in polynomial time. If ownerships were integer-valued, the type inference problem would be reduced to an integer linear programming problem, which is NP-hard.[1] Furthermore, fractional ownerships make the type system more expressive: see Example 3 in Section 3.

Based on the type system sketched above, we have implemented a verifier for C programs, and tested it for programs manipulating lists, trees, doubly-linked lists, etc.

The rest of this paper is structured as follows. Section 2 introduces a simple imperative language that has only pointers as values. Section 3 presents our type system with fractional ownerships, proves its soundness, and discusses type inference issues. Section 4 discusses extensions to deal with data structures. Section 5 reports a prototype implementation of our type-based verification algorithm. Section 6 discusses related work, including Ueda's work [3] on fractional capabilities for GHC, to which our type system seems closely related, despite the differences of the target languages. Section 7 concludes the paper.

2 Language

This section introduces a simple imperative language with primitives for memory allocation/deallocation. For the sake of simplicity, the only values are (possibly null) pointers. See Section 4 for extensions of the language and the type system to deal with other language constructs.

The syntax of the language is given as follows.

Definition 1 (commands, programs)

$$\begin{array}{rl} s\ (commands) ::= & \mathbf{skip} \mid *x \leftarrow y \mid s_1; s_2 \mid \mathbf{free}(x) \mid \mathbf{let}\ x = \mathbf{malloc}()\ \mathbf{in}\ s \\ & \mid \mathbf{let}\ x = \mathbf{null}\ \mathbf{in}\ s \mid \mathbf{let}\ x = y\ \mathbf{in}\ s \mid \mathbf{let}\ x = *y\ \mathbf{in}\ s \\ & \mid \mathbf{ifnull}(x)\ \mathbf{then}\ s_1\ \mathbf{else}\ s_2 \mid f(x_1, \ldots, x_n) \\ & \mid \mathbf{assert}(x = y) \mid \mathbf{assert}(x = *y) \\ d\ (definitions) ::= & f(x_1, \ldots, x_n) = s \end{array}$$

A program is a pair (D, s), where D is a set of definitions.

[1] With the recent advance of SAT solvers, it may still be the case that the integer linear programming problem generated by the type inference can be solved efficiently in practice; that may be left as a subject for further investigation.

The command **skip** does nothing. $*x \leftarrow y$ updates the target of x (i.e., the contents of the memory cell pointed to by x) with the value of y. The command $s_1; s_2$ is a sequential execution of s_1 and s_2. The command $\mathbf{free}(x)$ deallocates (the cell referenced by) the pointer x. The command $\mathbf{let}\ x = e\ \mathbf{in}\ s$ evaluates e, binds x to the value of e, and executes s. The expression **malloc**() allocates a memory cell and returns a pointer to it. The expression **null** denotes a null pointer. $*y$ dereferences the pointer y. The command $\mathbf{ifnull}(x)\ \mathbf{then}\ s_1\ \mathbf{else}\ s_2$ executes s_1 if x is null, and executes s_2 otherwise. The command $f(x_1, \ldots, x_n)$ calls function f. We require that $x_1, \ldots, x_n$ are mutually distinct variables. (This does not lose generality, as we can replace $f(x, x)$ with $\mathbf{let}\ y = x\ \mathbf{in}\ f(x, y)$.) There is no return value of a function call; values can be returned only by reference passing. The commands $\mathbf{assert}(x = y)$ and $\mathbf{assert}(x = *y)$ do nothing if the equality holds, and aborts the program otherwise. These are introduced to simplify the type system and the proof of its soundness in Section 3. Usually, assert commands can be automatically inserted during the transformation from a surface language (like C) into our language; for example, $\mathbf{assert}(x = y)$ is automatically inserted at the end of a let-expression $\mathbf{let}\ x = y\ \mathbf{in} \cdots$. Separate pointer analyses may also be used to insert assertions; in general, insertion of more assertions makes our analysis more precise.

Remark 1. Notice that unlike in C (and like in functional languages), variables are immutable; they are initialized in let-expressions, and are never re-assigned afterwards. The declaration `int x = 1; ...` in C is expressed as:

$$\mathbf{let}\ \&x = \mathbf{malloc}()\ \mathbf{in}\ (*\&x \leftarrow 1; \cdots ; \mathbf{free}(\&x))$$

in our language. Here, $\&x$ is treated as a variable name.

Operational Semantics. We assume that there is a countable set $\mathcal{H}$ of *heap addresses*. A run-time state is represented by a triple $\langle H, R, s \rangle$, where H is a mapping from a finite subset of $\mathcal{H}$ to $\mathcal{H} \cup \{\mathbf{null}\}$, R is a mapping from a finite set of variables to $\mathcal{H} \cup \{\mathbf{null}\}$. Intuitively, H models the heap memory, and R models local variables stored in stacks or registers. The set of *evaluation contexts* is defined by $E ::= [\,] \mid E; s$. We write $E[s]$ for the command obtained by replacing $[\,]$ in E with s.

Figure 2 shows the transition rules for run-time states. In the figure, $f\{x \mapsto v\}$ denotes the function f' such that $dom(f) = dom(f') \cup \{x\}$, $f'(x) = v$, and $f'(y) = f(y)$ for every $y \in dom(f) \setminus \{x\}$. $[x'/x]s$ denotes the command obtained by replacing x in s with x'. $\tilde{x}$ abbreviates a sequence $x_1, \ldots, x_n$. In the rules for let-expressions, we require that $x' \notin dom(R)$. In the rule for **malloc**, the contents v of the allocated cell can be any value in $\mathcal{H} \cup \{\mathbf{null}\}$. There are three kinds of run-time errors: **NullEx** for accessing null pointers, **Error** for illegal read/write/free operations on deallocated pointers, and **AssertFail** for assertion failures. The type system in this paper will prevent only the errors expressed by **Error**. In the rules for assertions on the last line, the relation $H, R \models P$ is defined by: $H, R \models x = y$ iff $R(x) = R(y)$, and $H, R \models x = *y$ iff $R(x) = H(R(y))$.

$$\frac{}{\langle H, R, E[\mathbf{skip}; s]\rangle \longrightarrow_D \langle H, R, E[s]\rangle}$$

$$\frac{R(x) \in dom(H)}{\langle H, R, E[*x \leftarrow y]\rangle \longrightarrow_D \langle H\{R(x) \mapsto R(y)\}, R, E[\mathbf{skip}]\rangle}$$

$$\frac{R(x) \in dom(H) \cup \{\mathbf{null}\}}{\langle H, R, E[\mathbf{free}(x)]\rangle \longrightarrow_D \langle H \setminus \{R(x)\}, R, E[\mathbf{skip}]\rangle}$$

$$\frac{x' \notin dom(R)}{\langle H, R, E[\mathbf{let}\ x = \mathbf{null}\ \mathbf{in}\ s]\rangle \longrightarrow_D \langle H, R\{x' \mapsto \mathbf{null}\}, E[[x'/x]s]\rangle}$$

$$\frac{}{\langle H, R, E[\mathbf{let}\ x = y\ \mathbf{in}\ s]\rangle \longrightarrow_D \langle H, R\{x' \mapsto R(y)\}, E[[x'/x]s]\rangle}$$

$$\frac{}{\langle H, R, E[\mathbf{let}\ x = *y\ \mathbf{in}\ s]\rangle \longrightarrow_D \langle H, R\{x' \mapsto H(R(y))\}, E[[x'/x]s]\rangle}$$

$$\frac{h \notin dom(H)}{\langle H, R, E[\mathbf{let}\ x = \mathbf{malloc}()\ \mathbf{in}\ s]\rangle \longrightarrow_D \langle H\{h \mapsto v\}, R\{x' \mapsto h\}, E[[x'/x]s]\rangle}$$

$$\frac{}{\langle H, R\{x \mapsto \mathbf{null}\}, E[\mathbf{ifnull}(x)\ \mathbf{then}\ s_1\ \mathbf{else}\ s_2]\rangle \longrightarrow_D \langle H, R\{x \mapsto \mathbf{null}\}, E[s_1]\rangle}$$

$$\frac{R(x) \neq \mathbf{null}}{\langle H, R, E[\mathbf{ifnull}(x)\ \mathbf{then}\ s_1\ \mathbf{else}\ s_2]\rangle \longrightarrow_D \langle H, R, E[s_2]\rangle}$$

$$\frac{R(x) = \mathbf{null}}{\langle H, R, E[*x \leftarrow y]\rangle \longrightarrow_D \mathbf{NullEx}} \qquad \frac{R(y) = \mathbf{null}}{\langle H, R, E[\mathbf{let}\ x = *y\ \mathbf{in}\ s]\rangle \longrightarrow_D \mathbf{NullEx}}$$

$$\frac{R(x) \notin dom(H) \cup \{\mathbf{null}\}}{\langle H, R, E[*x \leftarrow y]\rangle \longrightarrow_D \mathbf{Error}} \qquad \frac{R(y) \notin dom(H) \cup \{\mathbf{null}\}}{\langle H, R, E[\mathbf{let}\ x = *y\ \mathbf{in}\ s]\rangle \longrightarrow_D \mathbf{Error}}$$

$$\frac{R(x) \notin dom(H) \cup \{\mathbf{null}\}}{\langle H, R, E[\mathbf{free}(x)]\rangle \longrightarrow_D \mathbf{Error}} \qquad \frac{f(\tilde{y}) = s \in D}{\langle H, R, E[f(\tilde{x})]\rangle \longrightarrow_D \langle H, R, E[[\tilde{x}/\tilde{y}]s]\rangle}$$

$$\frac{H, R \models P}{\langle H, R, E[\mathbf{assert}(P)]\rangle \longrightarrow_D \langle H, R, E[\mathbf{skip}]\rangle} \qquad \frac{H, R \not\models P}{\langle H, R, E[\mathbf{assert}(P)]\rangle \longrightarrow_D \mathbf{AssertFail}}$$

Fig. 2. Transition Rules

Note that the function call $f(x_1, \ldots, x_n)$ is just replaced by the function's body. Thus, preprocessing is required to handle functions in C: A function call `x = f(y)` in C is simulated by $f(y, \&x)$ in our language (where $\&x$ is a variable name), and a C function definition `f(y) {s; return v;}` is simulated by:

$$f(y, r) = \mathbf{let}\ \&y = \mathbf{malloc}()\ \mathbf{in}\ (*\&y \leftarrow y; s; *r \leftarrow v; \mathbf{free}(\&y)).$$

Here, the malloc and free commands above correspond to the allocation and deallocation of a stack frame.

3 Type System

This section introduces a type system that prevents memory leaks, double frees, and illegal read/write operations.

3.1 Types

The syntax of types is given by:

$$\begin{array}{l}\tau \text{ (value types) } ::= \alpha \mid \tau\ \mathbf{ref}_f \mid \mu\alpha.\tau \\ \sigma \text{ (function types) } ::= (\tau_1, \ldots, \tau_n) \to (\tau_1', \ldots, \tau_n')\end{array}$$

We often write $\top$ for $\mu\alpha.\alpha$, which describes pointers carrying no ownerships. The metavariable f ranges over rational numbers in $[0, 1]$. It is called an *ownership*, and represents both a capability and an obligation to read/write/free a pointer.

α is a type variable, which gets bound by the recursive type constructor $\mu\alpha$. The type $\tau\ \mathbf{ref}_f$ describes a pointer whose ownership is f, and also expresses the constraint that the value obtained by dereferencing the pointer should be used according to τ. For example, if x has type $\top\ \mathbf{ref}_1\ \mathbf{ref}_1$, not only the pointer x but also the pointer stored in the target of the pointer x must be eventually deallocated through x.

Type $(\tau_1, \ldots, \tau_n) \to (\tau_1', \ldots, \tau_n')$ describes a function that takes n arguments. The types $\tau_1, \ldots, \tau_n, \tau_1', \ldots, \tau_n'$ describe how ownerships on arguments are changed by the function: the type of the i-th argument is τ_i at the beginning of the function, and it is τ_i' at the end of the function.

The semantics of (value) types is defined as a mapping from the set $\{0\}^*$ (the set of finite sequences of the symbol 0) to the set of rational numbers. Intuitively, the type $[\![\tau]\!](\epsilon)$ of a pointer represents the ownership for the memory cell directly pointed to by the pointer, and $[\![\tau]\!](0^k)$ represents the ownership for the memory cell reached by k hops of pointer traversals. (If the language is extended with structures with n elements as discussed in Section 4, $[\![\tau]\!]$ should be extended to a mapping from $\{0, \ldots, , n-1\}^*$ to the set of rational numbers.)

Definition 2 *The mapping* $[\![\cdot]\!]$ *from the set of closed types to* $\{0\}^* \to [0, 1]$ *is the least function that satisfies the following conditions.*

$$[\![\tau\ \mathbf{ref}_f]\!](\epsilon) = f \qquad [\![\tau\ \mathbf{ref}_f]\!](0w) = [\![\tau]\!](w) \qquad [\![\mu\alpha.\tau]\!] = [\![[\mu\alpha.\tau/\alpha]\tau]\!]$$

(Here, the order between functions from S to T is defined by: $f \leq_{S\to T} g$ if and only if $\forall x \in S. f(x) \leq_T g(x)$.) We write $\tau \approx \tau'$, if $[\![\tau]\!] = [\![\tau']\!]$.

Note that $\top (= \mu\alpha.\alpha) \approx \mu\alpha.(\alpha\ \mathbf{ref}_0)$, and $\mu\alpha.\tau \approx [\mu\alpha.\tau/\alpha]\tau$.

We write $\mathbf{empty}(\tau)$ if all the ownerships in τ are 0. We say that a type τ is *well-formed* if $[\![\tau]\!](w) \geq c \times [\![\tau]\!](w0)$ for every $w \in \{0\}^*$. Here, we let c be the constant 1/2, but the type system given below remains sound as long as c is a positive (rational) number. In the rest of this paper, we consider only types that satisfy the well-formedness condition. See Remark 2 for the reason why the well-formedness is required.

3.2 Typing

A type judgment is of the form $\Theta; \Gamma \vdash s \Rightarrow \Gamma'$, where Θ is a finite mapping from (function) variables to function types, Γ and Γ' are finite mappings from variables to value types. Γ describes the ownerships held by each variable before the execution of s, while Γ' describes the ownerships after the execution of s. For example, we have $\Theta; x : \top\ \mathbf{ref}_1 \vdash \mathbf{free}(x) \Rightarrow x : \top\ \mathbf{ref}_0$. Note that a variable's type describes how the variable should be used, and not necessarily the status of the value stored in the variable. For example, $x : \top\ \mathbf{ref}_0$ does not mean that the memory cell pointed to by x has been deallocated; it only means that deallocating the cell through x (i.e., executing $\mathbf{free}(x)$) is disallowed. There may be another variable y of type $\tau\ \mathbf{ref}_1$ that holds the same pointer as x.

Typing rules are shown in Figure 3. $\tau \approx \tau_1 + \tau_2$ and $\tau_1 + \tau_2 \approx \tau_1' + \tau_2'$ mean $[\![\tau]\!] = [\![\tau_1]\!] + [\![\tau_2]\!]$ and $[\![\tau_1]\!] + [\![\tau_2]\!] = [\![\tau_1']\!] + [\![\tau_2']\!]$ respectively. In the rule for assignment $*x \leftarrow y$, we require that the ownership of x is 1 (see Remark 2). The ownerships of τ' must be empty, since the value stored in $*x$ is thrown away by the assignment. The ownerships of y (described by τ) is divided into τ_1, which will be transferred to x, and τ_2, which remains in y.

In the rule for **free**, the ownership of x is changed from 1 to 0. τ must be empty, since x can no longer be dereferenced. In the rule for **malloc**, the ownership of x is 1 at the beginning of s, indicating that x must be deallocated. At the end of s, we require that the ownership of x is 0, since x goes out of the scope. Note that this requirement does not prevent the allocated memory cell from escaping the scope of the let-expression: For example, $\mathbf{let}\ x = \mathbf{malloc}()\ \mathbf{in}\ *y \leftarrow x$ allows the new cell to escape through variable y. The ownership of x is empty at the end of the let-expression, since the ownership has been transferred to y.

In the rule for dereferencing ($\mathbf{let}\ x = *y\ \mathbf{in}\ \cdots$), the ownership of y must be non-zero. The ownerships stored in the target of the pointer y, described by τ, are divided into τ_1 and τ_2. At the end of the let-expression, the ownerships held by x must be empty (which is ensured by $\mathbf{empty}(\tau_1')$), since x goes out of scope.

In the rule for **null**, there is no constraint on the type of x, since x is a null pointer. In the rule for conditionals, any type may be assigned to x in the then-branch. Thanks to this, $\mathbf{ifnull}(x)\ \mathbf{then\ skip\ else\ free}(x)$ is typed as follows.

$$\frac{\Theta; x : \top\ \mathbf{ref}_0 \vdash \mathbf{skip} \Rightarrow x : \top\ \mathbf{ref}_0 \qquad \Theta; x : \top\ \mathbf{ref}_1 \vdash \mathbf{free}(x) \Rightarrow x : \top\ \mathbf{ref}_0}{\Theta; x : \top\ \mathbf{ref}_1 \vdash \mathbf{ifnull}(x)\ \mathbf{then\ skip\ else\ free}(x) \Rightarrow x : \top\ \mathbf{ref}_0}$$

The rules for assertions allow us to shuffle the ownerships held by the same pointers.

Remark 2. The well-formedness condition approximates the condition: $\forall w \in \{\mathtt{0}\}^*.([\![\tau]\!](w) = 0 \Rightarrow [\![\tau]\!](w\mathtt{0}) = 0)$. Types that violate the condition (like $(\top\ \mathbf{ref}_1)\ \mathbf{ref}_0$) make the type system unsound. For example, consider the following command s (here, some let-expressions are inlined):

$$\mathbf{let}\ y = x\ \mathbf{in}\ (*y \leftarrow \mathbf{null}; \mathbf{assert}(x = y); \mathbf{free}(*x); \mathbf{free}(x)).$$

If we ignore the well-formedness condition, we can derive $\Theta; x : (\top\ \mathbf{ref}_1)\ \mathbf{ref}_1 \vdash s \Rightarrow x : (\top\ \mathbf{ref}_0)\ \mathbf{ref}_0$ from $\Theta; x : (\top\ \mathbf{ref}_1)\ \mathbf{ref}_0, y : (\top\ \mathbf{ref}_0)\ \mathbf{ref}_1 \vdash s' \Rightarrow x : (\top\ \mathbf{ref}_0)\ \mathbf{ref}_0, y : (\top\ \mathbf{ref}_0)\ \mathbf{ref}_0$ where s' is the body of s. However, the judgment is semantically wrong: the memory cell referenced by $*x$ is not deallocated by s

$$\frac{}{\Theta; \Gamma \vdash \mathbf{skip} \Rightarrow \Gamma} \qquad \frac{\Theta; \Gamma \vdash s_1 \Rightarrow \Gamma'' \qquad \Gamma'' \vdash s_2 \Rightarrow \Gamma'}{\Theta; \Gamma \vdash s_1; s_2 \Rightarrow \Gamma'}$$

$$\frac{\tau \approx \tau_1 + \tau_2 \qquad \mathbf{empty}(\tau')}{\Theta; \Gamma, x : \tau' \ \mathbf{ref}_1, y : \tau \vdash *x \leftarrow y \Rightarrow \Gamma, x : \tau_1 \ \mathbf{ref}_1, y : \tau_2}$$

$$\frac{\mathbf{empty}(\tau)}{\Theta; \Gamma, x : \tau \ \mathbf{ref}_1 \vdash \mathbf{free}(x) \Rightarrow \Gamma, x : \tau \ \mathbf{ref}_0} \qquad \frac{\begin{array}{c}\Theta; \Gamma, x : \tau \ \mathbf{ref}_1 \vdash s \Rightarrow \Gamma', x : \tau' \ \mathbf{ref}_0 \\ \mathbf{empty}(\tau) \qquad \mathbf{empty}(\tau')\end{array}}{\Theta; \Gamma \vdash \mathbf{let}\ x = \mathbf{malloc}()\ \mathbf{in}\ s \Rightarrow \Gamma'}$$

$$\frac{\begin{array}{c}\Theta; \Gamma, x : \tau_1, y : \tau_2 \vdash s \Rightarrow \Gamma', x : \tau_1' \\ \tau \approx \tau_1 + \tau_2 \qquad \mathbf{empty}(\tau_1')\end{array}}{\Theta; \Gamma, y : \tau \vdash \mathbf{let}\ x = y\ \mathbf{in}\ s \Rightarrow \Gamma'} \qquad \frac{\begin{array}{c}\Theta; \Gamma, x : \tau_1, y : \tau_2 \ \mathbf{ref}_f \vdash s \Rightarrow \Gamma', x : \tau_1' \\ f > 0 \qquad \tau \approx \tau_1 + \tau_2 \qquad \mathbf{empty}(\tau_1')\end{array}}{\Theta; \Gamma, y : \tau \ \mathbf{ref}_f \vdash \mathbf{let}\ x = *y\ \mathbf{in}\ s \Rightarrow \Gamma'}$$

$$\frac{\Theta; \Gamma, x : \tau \vdash s \Rightarrow \Gamma', x : \tau'}{\Theta; \Gamma \vdash \mathbf{let}\ x = \mathbf{null}\ \mathbf{in}\ s \Rightarrow \Gamma'} \qquad \frac{\Theta; \Gamma, x : \tau' \vdash s_1 \Rightarrow \Gamma' \qquad \Theta; \Gamma, x : \tau \vdash s_2 \Rightarrow \Gamma'}{\Theta; \Gamma, x : \tau \vdash \mathbf{ifnull}(x)\ \mathbf{then}\ s_1\ \mathbf{else}\ s_2 \Rightarrow \Gamma'}$$

$$\frac{\tau_1 + \tau_2 \approx \tau_1' + \tau_2'}{\Theta; \Gamma, x : \tau_1, y : \tau_2 \vdash \mathbf{assert}(x = y) \Rightarrow \Gamma, x : \tau_1', y : \tau_2'}$$

$$\frac{\tau_1 + \tau_2 \approx \tau_1' + \tau_2'}{\Theta; \Gamma, x : \tau_1, y : \tau_2 \ \mathbf{ref}_f \vdash \mathbf{assert}(x = *y) \Rightarrow \Gamma, x : \tau_1', y : \tau_2' \ \mathbf{ref}_f}$$

$$\frac{\Theta(f) = (\tilde{\tau}) \rightarrow (\tilde{\tau}')}{\Theta; \Gamma, \tilde{x} : \tilde{\tau} \vdash f(\tilde{x}) \Rightarrow \Gamma, \tilde{x} : \tilde{\tau}'} \qquad \frac{\Gamma \approx \Gamma_1 \qquad \Gamma' \approx \Gamma_1' \qquad \Theta; \Gamma_1 \vdash s \Rightarrow \Gamma_1'}{\Theta; \Gamma \vdash s \Rightarrow \Gamma'}$$

$$\frac{\begin{array}{c}\Theta; \tilde{x} : \tilde{\tau} \vdash s : \tilde{x} : \tilde{\tau}' \qquad \Theta(f) = \tilde{\tau} \rightarrow \tilde{\tau}' \\ (\text{for each } f(\tilde{x}) = s \in D) \\ \mathit{dom}(\Theta) = \mathit{dom}(D)\end{array}}{\vdash D : \Theta} \qquad \frac{\vdash D : \Theta \qquad \Theta; \emptyset \vdash s \Rightarrow \emptyset}{\vdash (D, s)}$$

Fig. 3. Typing Rules

Fig. 4. Snapshots of the heap during the execution of the program in Remark 2. The lefthand side and the righthand side show the states before and after executing $*y \leftarrow$ **null** respectively. The rightmost cell will be leaked.

(see Figure 4). The well-formedness condition ensures that if a variable (say, x) has an ownership of a pointer (say, p) reachable from x, then the variable must hold a fraction of ownerships for all the pointers between x and p, so that the pointers cannot be updated through aliases.

Example 1. Recall the example in Section 1.
The part **let** $y = *x$ **in** $(\texttt{freeall}(y); \textbf{free}(x))$ is typed as follows.

$$\dfrac{\dfrac{\Theta; x:\tau, y:\mu\alpha.(\alpha\ \textbf{ref}_1) \vdash \texttt{freeall}(y) \Rightarrow x:\tau, y:\top \quad \Theta; x:\tau, y:\top \vdash \textbf{free}(x) \Rightarrow \Theta_0}{\Theta; x:(\mu\alpha.(\alpha\ \textbf{ref}_0))\ \textbf{ref}_1, y:\mu\alpha.(\alpha\ \textbf{ref}_1) \vdash (\texttt{freeall}(y); \textbf{free}(x)) \Rightarrow \Theta_0}}{\Theta; x:\mu\alpha.(\alpha\ \textbf{ref}_1) \vdash \textbf{let}\ y = *x\ \textbf{in}\ (\texttt{freeall}(y); \textbf{free}(x)) \Rightarrow x:\top}$$

Here, $\tau = (\mu\alpha.(\alpha\ \textbf{ref}_0))\ \textbf{ref}_1$, $\Theta = \texttt{freeall} : (\mu\alpha.(\alpha\ \textbf{ref}_1)) \to (\top)$, and $\Theta_0 = x:\top, y:\top$.

Example 2. The following function destructively appends two lists p and q, and stores the result in $*r$.

$$\begin{aligned}\mathsf{app}(p,q,r) = {} & \textbf{ifnull}(p)\ \textbf{then}\ *r \leftarrow q \\ & \textbf{else}\ (*r \leftarrow p; (\textbf{let}\ x = *p\ \textbf{in}\ \mathsf{app}(x,q,p)); \textbf{assert}(p = *r))\end{aligned}$$

app has type $(\tau_1, \tau_1, \top\ \textbf{ref}_1) \to (\top, \top, \tau_1)$, where $\tau_1 = \mu\alpha.(\alpha\ \textbf{ref}_1)$. The else-part is typed as follows.

$$\dfrac{\Theta; \Gamma_1 \vdash *r \leftarrow p \Rightarrow \Gamma_1 \qquad \dfrac{\Theta; \Gamma_1 \vdash s \Rightarrow \Gamma_2 \quad \Theta; \Gamma_2 \vdash \textbf{assert}(p = *r) \Rightarrow p:\top, q:\top, r:\tau_1}{\Theta; \Gamma_1 \vdash s; \textbf{assert}(p = *r) \Rightarrow p:\top, q:\top, r:\tau_1}}{\Theta; \Gamma_1 \vdash *r \leftarrow p; s; \textbf{assert}(p = *r) \Rightarrow p:\top, q:\top, r:\tau_1}$$

Here, $s = \textbf{let}\ x = *p\ \textbf{in}\ \mathsf{app}(x,q,p)$, and $\Theta, \Gamma_1, \Gamma_2$ are given by:

$$\begin{aligned}&\Theta = \mathsf{app} : (\tau_1, \tau_1, \top\ \textbf{ref}_1) \to (\top, \top, \tau_1)\\ &\Gamma_1 = p:\tau_1, q:\tau_1, r:\top\ \textbf{ref}_1 \qquad \Gamma_2 = p:\tau_1, q:\top, r:\top\ \textbf{ref}_1\end{aligned}$$

Example 3. Consider the following functions f and g:

$$\begin{aligned}f(x) &= \textbf{let}\ y = x\ \textbf{in}\ g(x,y); \textbf{assert}(x = y)\\ g(x,y) &= \textbf{let}\ z = *x\ \textbf{in}\ \textbf{let}\ w = *y\ \textbf{in}\ \textbf{skip}\end{aligned}$$

Then, f and g can be given types $\top\ \textbf{ref}_1 \to \top\ \textbf{ref}_1$ and $(\top\ \textbf{ref}_{0.5}, \top\ \textbf{ref}_{0.5}) \to (\top\ \textbf{ref}_{0.5}, \top\ \textbf{ref}_{0.5})$. Without fractional types, f is not typable because the ownership of x cannot be split into the first and second arguments of g. Although the situation above is not likely to occur so often in actual sequential programs, we expect that fractional ownerships will play a more fundamental role in a multi-threaded setting, where ownerships for shared variables need to be split for multi-threads.

3.3 Type Soundness

The soundness of our type system is stated as follows.

Theorem 1. *If* $\vdash (D, s)$*, then the following conditions hold.*

1. $\langle \emptyset, \emptyset, s\rangle \not\longrightarrow_D^* \textbf{Error}$.
2. *If* $\langle \emptyset, \emptyset, s\rangle \longrightarrow_D^* \langle H, R, \textbf{skip}\rangle$*, then* $H = \emptyset$.

The first condition means that there is no illegal read/write/free access to deallocated memory. The second condition means that well-typed programs do not leak memory. See the longer version [4] for the proof.

3.4 Type Inference

By Theorem 1, verification of lack of memory-related errors is reduced to type inference. For the purpose of automated type inference, we restrict the syntax of types to those of the form $(\mu\alpha.\alpha\ \mathbf{ref}_{f_1})\ \mathbf{ref}_{f_2}$. This restriction makes the type system slightly less expressive, by precluding types like $\mu\alpha.(\alpha\ \mathbf{ref}_{0.5}\ \mathbf{ref}_{0.7})$. The restriction, however, does not seem so restrictive for realistic programs: in fact, all the correct programs we have checked so far (including those given in this paper) are typable in the restricted type system.

Given a program written in our language, type inference proceeds as follows.

1. For each n-ary function f, prepare a type template

$$((\mu\alpha.\alpha\ \mathbf{ref}_{\eta_{f,1,1}})\ \mathbf{ref}_{\eta_{f,1,2}}, \ldots, (\mu\alpha.\alpha\ \mathbf{ref}_{\eta_{f,n,1}})\ \mathbf{ref}_{\eta_{f,n,2}})$$
$$\rightarrow ((\mu\alpha.\alpha\ \mathbf{ref}_{\eta'_{f,1,1}})\ \mathbf{ref}_{\eta'_{f,1,2}}, \ldots, (\mu\alpha.\alpha\ \mathbf{ref}_{\eta'_{f,n,1}})\ \mathbf{ref}_{\eta'_{f,n,2}}),$$

   where $\eta_{f,i,j}$ and $\eta'_{f,i,j}$ are variables to denote unknown ownerships. Also, for each program point p and for each variable x live at p, prepare a type template $(\mu\alpha.\alpha\ \mathbf{ref}_{\eta_{p,x,1}})\ \mathbf{ref}_{\eta_{p,x,2}}$.
2. Generate linear inequalities on ownership variables based on the typing rules and the well-formedness condition.
3. Solve the linear inequalities. If the inequalities have a solution, the program is well-typed.

The number of ownership variables and linear inequalities is quadratic in the size of the input program. Since linear inequalities (over rational numbers) can be solved in time polynomial in the size of the inequalities, the whole algorithm runs in time polynomial in the size of the input program.

4 Extensions and Limitations

We have so far considered a very simple language which has only pointers as values. This section discusses extensions of the type system for other language features (mainly of the C language).

It is straightforward to extend the type system to handle primitive types such as integers and floating points. For structures with n elements (for the sake of simplicity, assume that each element has the same size as a pointer), we can introduce a type of the form $(\tau_0 \times \cdots \times \tau_{n-1})\ \mathbf{ref}_{w_0,\ldots,w_{n-1},f}$ as the type of a pointer to a structure. Here, τ_i is the type of the i-th element of the structure, f denotes the obligation to deallocate the structure, and w_i is a capability to read/write the i-th element; thus, an ownership has been split into a free obligation and read/write capabilities. Then the rules for pointer dereference and pointer arithmetics are given by:

$$\frac{\begin{array}{c}\Theta; \Gamma, x : \tau_{0,x}, y : (\tau_{0,y} \times \tau_1 \times \cdots \times \tau_{n-1})\ \mathbf{ref}_{w_0,\ldots,w_{n-1},f} \vdash s \Rightarrow \Gamma', x : \tau' \\ w_0 > 0 \qquad \tau_0 \approx \tau_{0,x} + \tau_{0,y} \qquad \mathbf{empty}(\tau')\end{array}}{\Theta; \Gamma, y : (\tau_0 \times \tau_1 \times \cdots \times \tau_{n-1})\ \mathbf{ref}_{w_0,\ldots,w_{n-1},f} \vdash \mathbf{let}\ x = *y\ \mathbf{in}\ s \Rightarrow \Gamma'}$$

```
fun delnext(p) =
```

$$p : \tau_P \times \tau_N \ \mathbf{ref}_{1,1,1}$$

```
  let nextp = p+1 in
```

$$p : \tau_P \times \top \ \mathbf{ref}_{1,0,1}, \mathtt{nextp} : \tau_N \times \top \ \mathbf{ref}_{1,0,0}$$

```
  let next = *nextp in
```

$$p : \tau_P \times \top \ \mathbf{ref}_{1,0,1}, \mathtt{nextp} : \top \times \top \ \mathbf{ref}_{1,0,0}, \mathtt{next} : \tau_N$$

```
  let nnp = next+1 in
```

$$p : \tau_P \times \top \ \mathbf{ref}_{1,0,1}, \mathtt{nextp} : \top \times \top \ \mathbf{ref}_{1,0,0}, \mathtt{next} : \top \times \top \ \mathbf{ref}_{1,0,1}, \mathtt{nnp} : \tau_N \times \top \ \mathbf{ref}_{1,0,0}$$

```
  let nn = *nnp in
```

$$p : \tau_P \times \top \ \mathbf{ref}_{1,0,1}, \mathtt{nextp} : \top \times \top \ \mathbf{ref}_{1,0,0}, \mathtt{next} : \top \times \top \ \mathbf{ref}_{1,0,1}, \mathtt{nnp} : \top \times \top \ \mathbf{ref}_{1,0,0}, \mathtt{nn} : \tau_N$$

```
  *nn <- p;
```

$$p : \tau_P \times \top \ \mathbf{ref}_{1,0,1}, \mathtt{nextp} : \top \times \top \ \mathbf{ref}_{1,0,0}, \mathtt{next} : \top \times \top \ \mathbf{ref}_{1,0,1}, \mathtt{nnp} : \top \times \top \ \mathbf{ref}_{1,0,0}, \mathtt{nn} : \tau_N$$

```
  *nextp <- nn
```

$$p : \tau_P \times \top \ \mathbf{ref}_{1,0,1}, \mathtt{nextp} : \tau_N \times \top \ \mathbf{ref}_{1,0,0}, \mathtt{next} : \top \times \top \ \mathbf{ref}_{1,0,1}, \mathtt{nnp} : \top \times \top \ \mathbf{ref}_{1,0,0}, \mathtt{nn} : \top$$

```
  assert(nnp=next+1);
```

$$p : \tau_P \times \top \ \mathbf{ref}_{1,0,1}, \mathtt{nextp} : \tau_N \times \top \ \mathbf{ref}_{1,0,0}, \mathtt{next} : \top \times \top \ \mathbf{ref}_{1,1,1}, \mathtt{nnp} : \top \times \top \ \mathbf{ref}_{0,0,0}, \mathtt{nn} : \top$$

```
  free(next)
```

$$p : \tau_P \times \top \ \mathbf{ref}_{1,0,1}, \mathtt{nextp} : \tau_N \times \top \ \mathbf{ref}_{1,0,0}, \mathtt{next} : \top \times \top \ \mathbf{ref}_{0,0,0}, \mathtt{nnp} : \top \times \top \ \mathbf{ref}_{0,0,0}, \mathtt{nn} : \top$$

```
  assert(nextp=p+1);
```

$$p : \tau_P \times \tau_N \ \mathbf{ref}_{1,1,1}, \mathtt{nextp} : \top \times \top \ \mathbf{ref}_{0,0,0}, \mathtt{next} : \top \times \top \ \mathbf{ref}_{0,0,0}, \mathtt{nnp} : \top \times \top \ \mathbf{ref}_{0,0,0}, \mathtt{nn} : \top$$

Fig. 5. A function manipulating a doubly-linked list and its typing

$$\frac{\begin{array}{c}\Theta; \Gamma, x : (\tau_{i,x} \times \cdots \times \tau_{n-1,x}, \top, \ldots, \top) \ \mathbf{ref}_{w_{i,x},\ldots,w_{n-1,x},0,\ldots,0,0}, \\ y : (\tau_{0,y} \times \cdots \times \tau_{n-1,y}) \ \mathbf{ref}_{w_{0,y},\ldots,w_{n-1,y},f} \vdash s \Rightarrow \Gamma', x : \tau_x \\ \forall j \in \{0, \ldots, i-1\}.(\tau_{j,y} \approx \tau_j \wedge w_j = w_{j,y}) \\ \forall j \in \{i, \ldots, n-1\}.(\tau_j \approx \tau_{j,y} + \tau_{j,x} \wedge w_j = w_{j,x} + w_{j,y}) \qquad \mathbf{empty}(\tau_x)\end{array}}{\Theta; \Gamma, y : (\tau_0 \times \cdots \times \tau_{n-1}) \ \mathbf{ref}_{w_0,\ldots,w_{n-1},f} \vdash \mathbf{let}\ x = y + i\ \mathbf{in}\ s \Rightarrow \Gamma'}$$

For example, consider the function `delnext` in Figure 5. It takes a doubly-linked list as shown in Figure 6, and deletes the next element of p. The function is given the type $(\tau_P \times \tau_N) \ \mathbf{ref}_{1,1,1} \rightarrow (\tau_P \times \tau_N) \ \mathbf{ref}_{1,1,1}$, where $\tau_P = \mu\alpha.((\alpha \times \top) \ \mathbf{ref}_{1,1,1})$ and $\tau_N = \mu\alpha.((\top \times \alpha) \ \mathbf{ref}_{1,1,1})$. The type $(\tau_P \times \tau_N) \ \mathbf{ref}_{1,1,1}$ means that the first element of `p` holds the capabilities and obligations on the cells reachable through the backward pointers, and the second element holds those on the cells reachable through the forward pointers.

An array of primitive values can be treated as one big reference cell, assuming that array boundary errors are prevented by other methods (such as dynamic checks or static analyses). At this moment, however, we do not know how to deal with arrays of pointers.

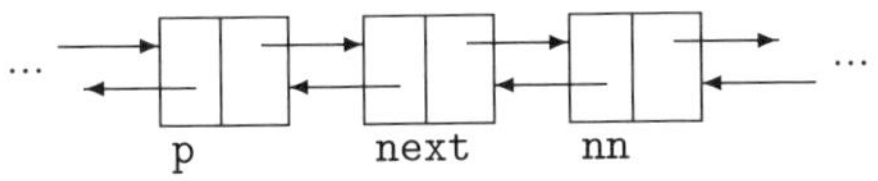

Fig. 6. A doubly-linked list given as an input of `delnext`. The cell `next` is removed and deallocated.

A dereference of a function pointer in C can be replaced with a non-deterministic choice of the functions it may point to, by using a standard flow analysis. It is not clear, however, how to deal with higher-order functions in functional languages, especially those stored in reference cells.

Cast operations can be handled in a conservative manner. For example, a pointer to a structure of type $(\tau_0 \times \cdots \times \tau_{n-1})$ $\mathbf{ref}_{w_0,\ldots,w_{n-1},f}$ can be casted to a pointer of type $(\tau_0 \times \cdots \times \tau_{m-1})$ $\mathbf{ref}_{w_0,\ldots,w_{m-1},f'}$ (if $m \leq n$). An integer can be casted to a pointer with 0 ownership (but it is useless).

Besides arrays of pointers and higher-order functions, one of the major limitations of our type system is that it cannot deal with cyclic structures well. The only type that can be assigned to cyclic lists of arbitrary length is $\top$: Notice that if we assign $\mu\alpha.(\alpha\ \mathbf{ref}_f)$ to the cycle, then an ownership f can be extracted for *each path* (e.g., ϵ, 00, 0000, ... for the cell on the lefthand side). We have to maintain the invariant that $f + f + f + \cdots \leq 1$, so that f must be 0. Thus, although a cyclic list can be constructed, it is useless as there is no ownership. Note, however, that this limitation does not apply to the case of doubly-linked lists, since cycles in doubly-linked lists are formed by two kinds of pointers; forward and backward pointers (recall the example in Figure 5). In order to handle cyclic lists, we need to extend pointer types to $\tau\ \mathbf{ref}_f^P$, which means that the pointer is an element of the set P or has an ownership f. The pointer type $\tau\ \mathbf{ref}_f$ is then just a special case of $\tau\ \mathbf{ref}_f^{\{\mathtt{NULL}\}}$.

5 Preliminary Experiments

We have implemented a prototype verifier for C programs, and tested it for several programs. The implementation, written in Objective Caml, is available at `http://www.kb.ecei.tohoku.ac.jp/~suenaga/mallocfree/`. As a linear programming solver, we used GLPK 4.15 wrapped by ocaml-glpk 0.1.5. The implementation is based on the type system described in Section 3, with the extension for structures discussed in Section 4.

The limitations of the current implementation are: (i) Unsound treatment of arrays of pointers (recall the discussion in Section 4): An array of pointers is handled as an array of size 1; (ii) Poor error reporting: when a program is ill-typed, the current system does produce some diagnostic information to indicate a possible location of a bug, but it is probably incomprehensible for end-users; (iii) Lack of support of several C statements: for example, a function call of the form `f(&x->f)` has to be manually rewritten to a sequence of statements

benchmark	LOC	Time (total)	Time (LP)	NASSERT	SIZE_LP	NVAR
ll-app	62	0.09	0.002	2	196	403
ll-reverse	67	0.10	0.002	2	217	430
ll-search	70	0.09	0.002	1	192	398
ll-merge	69	0.10	0.003	3	227	460
dl-insert	80	0.14	0.011	9	806	954
dl-delete	87	0.15	0.014	8	919	1134
bt-insert	64	0.09	0.003	0	188	479
authfd.c	6463	0.44	0.07	16	739	5408
cdrom.c	13429	26.49	19.85	14	35197	47185

Fig. 7. Benchmark result. The meaning of each column is as follows. LOC: the number of lines of code. Time (total): total execution time (sec). Time (LP): execution time for solving linear inequalities (sec). NASSERT: the number of manually-inserted assertions. SIZE_LP: the number of linear inequality constraints (after preprocessing of trivial constraints). NVAR: the number of variables contained in generated linear inequalities.

`p = &x->f; f(p); assert(&x->f, p);` and (iv) Need for manual insertion of assertions (**assert**$(x = y)$ and **assert**$(x = *y)$ in Section 2).

Figure 7 shows the result of the experiments. We used a machine with an Intel(R) Xeon(R) 3.00Hz CPU, 4MB cache and 8GB memory. The programs used for the experiments are described as follows:

– **ll-app**, **ll-reverse** and **ll-search** create lists, perform specific operations on the lists (append for **ll-app**, reverse for **ll-reverse**, and list search for **ll-search**), and deallocate the lists.

– **dl-insert** and **dl-remove** create doubly-linked lists, insert or delete a cell, and deallocate the doubly-linked lists.

– **bt-insert** constructs a binary tree, performs an insertion, and then deallocates the tree.

– **authfd.c** is a preprocessed file taken from `openssh-5.2p1`. (A large part of the preprocessed file consists of type declarations; the rest of the code consists of about 600 lines.)

– **cdrom.c** is a *fragment*[2] of Linux device driver `/drivers/cdrom/cdrom.c`.

All the programs have been verified correctly. It is worth noting that the programs manipulating doubly-linked lists could be verified. The benchmark results show that our analysis is reasonably fast, even for **cdrom.c**, which consists of 13K LOC.

Note that only 14 assertions were required for **cdrom.c**. (Thus, although the microbenchmarks used in this experiment are quite small, they are actually tricky programs.) All of those assertions were of the form `assert(p=NULL)`, except the following assertion, which asserts that `prev` points to the previous element of `cdi` in a singly-linked list.

[2] For the rest of the driver code, we have not yet checked whether it is typable by appropriate insertion of assertion commands.

```
while (cid && cdi != unreg){
  assert(cdi, prev->next); prev = cdi; cdi = prev->next;}
```

This suggests that most of the assertions manually inserted in the experiments above can be automatically inferred by a rather straightforward intra procedural analysis like the one mentioned in Section 2 (except those for doubly-linked lists, which require knowledge of the data structure invariant).

6 Related Work

There are a lot of studies and tools to detect or prevent memory-related errors. They are classified into static and dynamic analyses. Here we focus on static analysis techniques.

We have already discussed Heine and Lam's work [2] in Section 1. They use polymorphism on ownerships to make the analysis context-sensitive, which would be applicable to our type system. Dor, Rodeh, and Sagiv [5] use shape analysis techniques to verify lack of memory-related errors in list-manipulating programs. Unlike ours, their analysis can also detect null-pointer dereferences. Advantages of our type system over their analysis are the simplicity and efficiency. It is not clear whether their analysis can be easily extended to handle procedure calls and data structures (e.g., trees and doubly-linked lists) other than singly-linked lists in an efficient manner. Orlovich and Rugina [6] proposed a backward dataflow analysis to detect memory leaks. Their analysis does not detect double-frees and illegal accesses to deallocated memory. Xie and Aiken [7] use a SAT solver to detect memory leaks. Their analysis is unsound for loops and recursion. Boyapati et al. [8] uses ownership types for safe memory management for real-time Java, but their target is region-based memory management, and assume explicit type annotations. Swamy et al. [9] also developed a language with safe manual memory management. Unlike C, their language requires programmers to provide various annotations (such as whether a pointer is aliased or not).

Yang et al. [10,11] applied separation logic to automated verification of pointer safety in systems code. The efficiency of their verification method [10] seems comparable to ours. However, they do not deal with doubly linked lists ([10], Section 2).[3] Like our technique, their tool cannot handle arrays of pointers.

Other potential advantages of our type-based approach are: (i) By allowing programmers to declare ownership types, they may serve as good specifications of functions or modules, and also enhance modular verification, (ii) Our approach can probably be extended to deal with multi-threaded programs, along the line of previous work using fractional capabilities [1,12,13], and (iii) There is a clear proof of soundness of the analysis, based on a standard technique for proving type soundness (see the longer version [4]). A main limitation of our approach is that our type system cannot properly handle cycles (recall the discussion in Section 4) and value-dependent (or, path-sensitive) behaviors. In practice, therefore, a combination of our technique with other techniques would be useful.

[3] Berdine et al. [11] can handle doubly linked lists, but the verification tool is much slower according to their experimental results.

Technically, our type system is based on the notion of ownerships and fractional permissions/capabilities. Although there are many pieces of previous work that use ownerships and fractional capabilities, our work is original in the way they are integrated into a type system (in particular, pointer types that can represent an ownership of each memory cell reachable from a pointer, and typing rules that allow automated inference of such pointer types). The idea of fractional capabilities can be traced back to Ueda's work [3] on GHC (a concurrent logic programming language). He extended input/output modes to capabilities ranging over $[-1, 1]$, and used them to guarantee that there is no leakage of memory cells for storing constructors. Our type system actually seems closer to his system than to other later fractional capability systems [1,12,13]. In particular, his system assigns a capability (or, an ownership in our terminology) to each node reachable from a variable (just as our type system assigns an ownership to each pointer reachable from a variable), and the unification constraint $X = Y$ between variables plays a role similar to our assert commands. Nevertheless, the details are different: our ownerships range over $[0, 1]$ while theirs range over $[-1, 1]$, and both the well-formedness conditions on types, and the constraints imposed by the type systems are different. This seems to come from the differences in the language primitives: sequential vs concurrent compositions, and pointers vs unification variables. Note that, for example, updating a pointer does not consume any capability, while writing to a unification variable consumes a write capability.

Boyland [1] used fractional permissions (for read/write operations) to prevent race conditions in multi-threaded programs. Terauchi [12,13] later found another advantage of using fractions: inference of fractional permissions (or capabilities) can be reduced to a linear programming problem (rather than integer linear programming), which can be solved in polynomial time. The type system of this paper mainly exploits the latter advantage. In their work [1,12,13], a fractional capability is assigned to an abstract location (often called a region), while our type system assigns a fractional ownership to each access path from a variable. More specifically, in their work [1,12,13], a pointer type is represented as $\tau\ \mathbf{ref}_{\rho_i}$ with a separate map $\{\rho_1 \mapsto f_1, \ldots, \rho_n \mapsto f_n\}$ from abstract locations to fractions, whereas our pointer type $\tau\ \mathbf{ref}_f$ may be regarded as a kind of existential type $\exists \rho :: \{\rho \mapsto f\}.\tau\ \mathbf{ref}_\rho$. The former approach is not suitable for the purpose of our analysis: for example, without existential types, all the elements in a list are abstracted to the same location, so that a separate ownership cannot be assigned to each element of the list. Our pointer types (e.g. of the form $\mu\alpha.\alpha\ \mathbf{ref}_{0.5}\ \mathbf{ref}_1$) seem to have some similarity with the notion of fractional permissions with nesting [14], as both can express ownerships for nested data structures. Boyland [14] gives the semantics of fractional permissions with nesting, but does not discuss their application to program analysis.

7 Conclusion

We have proposed a new type system that guarantees lack of memory-related errors. The type system is based on the notion of fractional ownerships, and is equipped with a polynomial-time type inference algorithm. The type system is quite simple (especially compared with previous techniques for analyzing similar properties), yet it can be used to verify tricky pointer-manipulating programs. It is left for future work to carry out more experiments to evaluate the effectiveness of the type system, and to construct a practical memory-leak verification tool for C programs.

Acknowledgment. We would like to especially thank Toshihiro Wakatake and Kensuke Mano. Some of the ideas in this paper came from discussions with them. We would also like to thank anonymous referees for valuable comments, especially for pointing out a close connection to Ueda's work, and members of our research group for comments and discussions.

References

1. Boyland, J.: Checking interference with fractional permissions. In: Cousot, R. (ed.) SAS 2003. LNCS, vol. 2694, pp. 55–72. Springer, Heidelberg (2003)
2. Heine, D.L., Lam, M.S.: A practical flow-sensitive and context-sensitive C and C++ memory leak detector. In: Proc. of PLDI, pp. 168–181 (2003)
3. Ueda, K.: Resource-passing concurrent programming. In: Kobayashi, N., Pierce, B.C. (eds.) TACS 2001. LNCS, vol. 2215, pp. 95–126. Springer, Heidelberg (2001)
4. Suenaga, K., Kobayashi, N.: Fractional ownerships for safe memory deallocation. A longer version (2009), `http://www.kb.ecei.tohoku.ac.jp/~koba/papers/malloc.pdf`
5. Dor, N., Rodeh, M., Sagiv, S.: Checking cleanness in linked lists. In: Palsberg, J. (ed.) SAS 2000. LNCS, vol. 1824, pp. 115–135. Springer, Heidelberg (2000)
6. Orlovich, M., Rugina, R.: Memory leak analysis by contradiction. In: Yi, K. (ed.) SAS 2006. LNCS, vol. 4134, pp. 405–424. Springer, Heidelberg (2006)
7. Xie, Y., Aiken, A.: Context- and path-sensitive memory leak detection. In: ACM SIGSOFT International Symposium on Foundations of Software Engineering, pp. 115–125 (2005)
8. Boyapati, C., Salcianu, A., Beebee, W.S., Rinard, M.C.: Ownership types for safe region-based memory management in real-time Java. In: Proc. of PLDI, pp. 324–337 (2003)
9. Swamy, N., Hicks, M.W., Morrisett, G., Grossman, D., Jim, T.: Safe manual memory management in Cyclone. Sci. Comput. Program. 62(2), 122–144 (2006)
10. Yang, H., Lee, O., Berdine, J., Calcagno, C., Cook, B., Distefano, D., O'Hearn, P.W.: Scalable shape analysis for systems code. In: Gupta, A., Malik, S. (eds.) CAV 2008. LNCS, vol. 5123, pp. 385–398. Springer, Heidelberg (2008)
11. Berdine, J., Calcagno, C., Cook, B., Distefano, D., O'Hearn, P.W., Wies, T., Yang, H.: Shape analysis for composite data structures. In: Damm, W., Hermanns, H. (eds.) CAV 2007. LNCS, vol. 4590, pp. 178–192. Springer, Heidelberg (2007)
12. Terauchi, T.: Checking race freedom via linear programming. In: Proc. of PLDI, pp. 1–10 (2008)
13. Terauchi, T., Aiken, A.: A capability calculus for concurrency and determinism. ACM Trans. Prog. Lang. Syst. 30(5) (2008)
14. Boyland, J.: Semantics of fractional permissions with nesting. UWM EECS Technical Report CS-07-01 (2007)

Ownership Downgrading for Ownership Types

Yi Lu, John Potter, and Jingling Xue

Programming Languages and Compilers Group
School of Computer Science and Engineering
University of New South Wales, Sydney
{ylu,potter,jingling}@cse.unsw.edu.au

Abstract. Ownership types support information hiding by providing object-based encapsulation. However the static restrictions they impose on object accessibility can limit the expressiveness of ownership types. In order to deal with real applications, it is sometimes necessary to admit mechanisms for dynamically exposing otherwise encapsulated information. The need for policies and mechanisms to control such information flow, known as downgrading or declassification, has been well covered in the security literature.

This paper proposes a flexible ownership type system for object-level access control. It still maintains privacy of owned data, but allows information to be dynamically exposed where appropriate through an explicit declassification operation. The key innovation is an owners-as-downgraders policy, implemented via a simple language construct, which allows an object to be made more widely accessible by downgrading its ownership to its owner's owner.

1 Introduction

Traditional class-level private declarations in Java-like programming languages are inadequate for hiding object instances or restricting access to them. For instance, the underlying object in a private field can be accidentally exposed by assignments, calls or method returns. *Ownership types* [26,11,10] are a widely accepted technique for providing object-based encapsulation by partitioning all objects into a structure called the *ownership tree*. In such type systems, the *owners-as-dominators* property guarantees that an object is only accessible within the encapsulation provided by its owner. This prevents unwanted representation exposure and protects against deliberate attacks.

This form of strong encapsulation is too inflexible in practice; for example, it impedes the use of common coding idioms and design patterns such as iterators and observers. A number of proposals have been made for improving the expressiveness of ownership types (as reviewed in Section 5). They explore ways to increase object accessibility by exposing otherwise encapsulated objects. While these approaches vary in their detail, they all require object exposure to be statically determined, being fixed at the time of object creation. Hence object accessibility is fixed for the lifetime of the object.

Z. Hu (Ed.): APLAS 2009, LNCS 5904, pp. 144–160, 2009.

However, to deal with real applications, it is sometimes necessary to admit mechanisms for dynamically exposing otherwise encapsulated information. A long-standing problem in information security is how to specify and enforce expressive security policies that hide information while also permitting information release (called downgrading or declassification) where appropriate [7].

In this paper, we present a new ownership type system for object-level access control. While it still protects object instances like other ownership type systems do, it can allow programmers to intentionally expose encapsulated objects at runtime through an explicit declassification operation. Compared to other ownership type systems where an object's accessibility is statically and solely determined by its creator, our type system allows object accessibility to be changed dynamically by its *dynamic owner*. Compared to other downgrading policies in information security (where downgrading is controlled based on code authority [25] or conditions [7] or actions [19]), our type system enforces a downgrading policy based on object ownership, called *owners-as-downgraders*. The owners-as-downgraders property highlights what is a natural role for an owner—access to an object must be sufficiently authorized by its owners. With the ability to encapsulate objects as well as to expose them, we provide a more flexible and expressive ownership type system for object access control, which allows programmers to express design intent more precisely.

The paper is organized as follows: Section 2 gives a brief introduction to ownership types. Section 3 provides an informal overview of our proposed model. An example is presented with a detailed description to illustrate the use of our type system. Section 4 presents a core object-oriented language to allow us to formalize the static semantics, dynamic semantics and some important properties. Section 5 discusses related work, and Section 6 briefly concludes the paper.

2 Object Encapsulation with Static Ownership

We first give a brief overview of the classic approach to *static ownership* and before introducing our concept of *dynamic ownership* in Section 3.

Earlier object encapsulation systems, such as *Islands* [16] and *Balloons* [3], use full encapsulation techniques to forbid both incoming and outgoing references to an object's internal representation. Ownership types [11,10,8] provide a more flexible mechanism than previous systems; instead of full encapsulation, they allow outgoing references while still restricting incoming ones. The work on ownership types emanated from some general principles for *Flexible Alias Protection* [26] and the use of dominator trees in structuring object graphs [28].

In ownership type systems, each object has one fixed owning object, called the owner or *static owner*, bound statically at object creation. Often, the term *context* is used in the ownership types literature [11,9] to refer to ownership parameters in types. In the following example, the first context parameter `o` of class `Author` is the owner of an author object. Other context parameters such as `p` are optional; they are used to type references outside the current encapsulation.

Types are formed by binding actual context parameters to the formal parameters of a class. In the following example, the owner of book can be declared to be the current object/context **this**.

```
class Author<o,p> {
  Book<this> book;
  Date<p> deadline;
}
// client code
Author<owner,world> author = new Author<owner,world>();
... = author.book; // error
```

Ownership partitions all objects in the heap into an *ownership tree*, rooted at the special context **world**. Ownership types support information hiding by providing statically enforceable object encapsulation based on the ownership tree. The key technical mechanism used here is the hiding of object identity; ownership type systems ensure that the identity of an object can only be propagated (via class parameters) to its owned objects. In order to declare a type for a reference, one must be able to identify the owner that encapsulates the object, so that objects outside an encapsulation boundary can never identify the owner of encapsulated objects. The **world** context is globally nameable, so that objects owned by **world** are accessible from anywhere in the program.

For example, in the `Author` class, the author may want to hide his book from unauthorized access. In Java, this can be done by declaring the `book` field to be private. However such a class-level private declaration does not prevent the underlying object instance from being referenced from outside, because a reference to the object may easily be leaked by assignments to fields of other objects, bindings to calls, or method returns. In ownership types, the owner of `book` can be declared to be the current context **this**, which is different from object to object. It is impossible to name **this** to give the correct type of an author's `book` from outside. Thus, any attempted access (reference) to the book from client code via the expression `author.book` is a type error.

Ownership types can be considered as an access control system where owners are security levels for object instances. The **world** context is the lowest security level, so that accesses to objects owned by **world** are not restricted. However, unlike pre-defined security levels in conventional security systems, owners are also normal objects (except **world**) which may be owned by other objects. The following *owners-as-dominators* property guarantees that any access from outside to an object's internal representation must be made via the object's owner.

Property 1 (Static Encapsulation)
If object A accesses object B then $A \preceq owner(B)$.

This property states that an object can only be accessed from within its static owner. The function *owner(B)* denotes the static owner of *B*. The symbol $\preceq$, often called *inside* (or *dominated by*), denotes the reflexive and transitive closure of the ownership relation. This property implies that both accessibility for an object (the set of objects that can reference it) and its reference capability (the set of objects it can reference) is determined by the object's position in the ownership tree. This, in turn is defined by the object's static owner, which remains fixed for its lifetime. This fixed ownership has limited utility in applications that require a more flexible access control policy, such as when information needs to be released at runtime.

3 Object Exposure with Dynamic Ownership

In this section, we give an informal introduction to our type system. We first introduce our concept of dynamic ownership in Section 3.1, and then explain how to safely expose objects using dynamic ownership in Section 3.2. Finally, we illustrate our type system with an example, showing that it is more flexible and expressive than static ownership types.

3.1 Dynamic Encapsulation

In order to support a more flexible and dynamic access policy, we introduce a concept of dynamic ownership which separates an object's *dynamic owner* from its static owner. This separation enables the object's dynamic owner to be changed (downgraded) at runtime while its static owner remains fixed after creation. Like previous ownership types, the static owner of an object defines its fixed position in the ownership tree, hence determines the capability of the object. Unlike previous ownership types, object accessibility is determined by its dynamic owner rather than static owner. Thus the accessibility of an object may be changed at runtime by downgrading its dynamic ownership. Here is a simple illustration.

```
class Author<o> {
  [this]Book<o> book = new Book<o>();
}
```

Each type in our system is a (classic) ownership type prefixed with a dynamic owner. The dynamic owner of the variable `book` is the current context `[this]`. The dynamic owner of a new object is not explicitly specified, because the initial dynamic owner is always the same as its static owner; in this example the implicit dynamic owner for the new book is `o`, the static owner of the new book (and of the current author).

The assignment on variable `book` being OK implies `[o]Book<o>` is a subtype of `[this]Book<o>`. This subtyping is safe because it never exposes objects; the set of objects that can access **this** is a subset of the objects that can access `o`. In this example, the new object becomes less accessible when it is assigned to the variable `book` (our type system requires **this** to be inside `o`). This is typical of access control mechanisms in security applications where it is safe to increase the security level by restricting the number of subjects that may access an object. We used a similar mechanism in previous work [20] on the variance of object access modifiers. In this paper, we focus on how to expose objects using dynamic ownership. We now state the encapsulation property for our new system with dynamic ownership.

Property 2 (Dynamic Encapsulation)
If object A accesses object B then $A \preceq$ downer(B).

The function *downer(B)* denotes the dynamic owner of *B*. This property is more general than static encapsulation, because the dynamic ownership of an object can be changed at runtime by controlled downgrading, which will be discussed in the next section.

3.2 Dynamic Exposure

An object may be exposed by downgrading its dynamic ownership, i.e. promoting its dynamic owner up the ownership tree so the object becomes more accessible. Like most information security systems [7], in our system downgrading only occurs via an explicit expose operation in order to avoid accidental leaking of sensitive information. Below is a simple example of the expose operation.

```
class Author<o> {
  [this]Book<this> bookInWriting;
  [o]Book<*> release() {
    ...
    return expose bookInWriting;
  }
}
```

The reference in the field bookInWriting is encapsulated within the current object as suggested by its dynamic owner ([**this**]). Classic ownership type systems would never allow such a reference to be leaked outside. However, in our type system, we allow programmers to release this reference via the explicit expose operation (for example, the author may wish to release the book after he has finished writing it). In the above code, **expose** bookInWriting downgrades the dynamic ownership of the book reference by promoting its dynamic owner from **this** to o (we know o owns **this**). This enables the reference to be accessed by the owner of the current object or other objects within it.

The * symbol (similar to Java's ? wildcard for generics) can be thought of as an abstract owner; they have become common in ownership-based type systems [21,20,6]. Abstract owners are useful when the actual owners are unknown to the current context. Only context arguments (including the static owner) of a type may be abstract; dynamic owners can never be abstract as they determine if the object is accessible in the current context. In the example, the return type of the method release is [o]Book<*>, which implies that the receiver of the method call only needs to know o in order to access the released book (without having to know its static owner).

The following property states the effect of object exposure. An expose operation allows the exposed object to be accessed from within the downgrader's owner.

Property 3 (Object Exposure)
If object A has exposed object B, then owner(A) $\preceq$ downer(B).

Not surprisingly, our type system requires that the dynamic owner of the exposed object to be known to the downgrader (which is always the current object). This means that the object to be exposed is dynamically owned by the downgrader or the downgrader's owners. The static owner of an exposed object is not restricted by the type system; typically it can be abstracted by $*$. Note that, since the capability of an object is determined by its static ownership, its capability won't be affected by any downgrading. Moreover, an `expose` operation may promote an object's dynamic ownership by at most one level up the ownership tree. For an object to be exposed through more than one level, it must go through a sequence of expose operations, authorized by a sequence of downgraders up an ownership branch. That *B is a downgrader of A* means either B has exposed A via an explicit expose operation, or B has the authority to expose A (i.e. it is the current dynamic owner of A). The *owners-as-downgraders* property states our authorization policy on object exposure.

Property 4 (Owners-as-Downgraders)
For two objects A and B, if owner(A) $\preceq$ B $\preceq$ downer(A), then B must be a downgrader of A.

Since *owner(A)* and *downer(A)* are identical when A is created, we know A has been exposed if *downer(A)* is outside *owner(A)*. That is, the object has become more accessible than was allowed by its creator. If A is exposed, then all A's transitive owners up to *downer(A)* (exclusively) must have authorized the exposure via explicit expose operations.

Our type system strictly subsumes classic ownership types; the owners-as-dominators property is the same owners-as-downgraders without downgrading. In other words, ownership programs are special cases of our programs where no expose operation is used; in that case, the dynamic owner of every object is fixed, remaining identical to its static owner.

3.3 A Publisher Example

In this section, we sketch a scenario for book publishing which involves multiple steps of exposure of an object. The sample code, given in Figure 1, is kept simple, to highlight the idea of ownership downgrading. Figure 2 illustrates the steps of exposure and the change of object accessibility in the system after each exposure.

In this example, there are two top-level objects, a publisher and a reader. The reader reads books published by the publisher. Inside the publisher, there are an author and an editor, whose jobs are, respectively, writing and reviewing books for the publisher. A book object is owned by the author. Their ownership relation is fixed as suggested by their static owners. But the accessibility of the book changes at runtime due to the use of object exposure.

In the code, we use some defaults for declaring types. Context arguments of a type may be omitted if they are all abstract; for instance, `[p]Book` is a

```
class Publisher<o> {
 Author<this> author;
 Editor<this> editor;
 [this]Book book;
 [o]Book release() {
   book = author.release();
   editor.edit(book);
   ...
   if (finishedEditing(book))
     return expose book;
 }
}
```

```
class Author<p> {
 Book<this> book;
 [p]Book release() {
   ...
   if (finishedWriting(book))
     return expose book;
 }
}
// a reader client
Publisher<world> publisher;
[world]Book book; book =
publisher.release();
read(book);
```

Fig. 1. A Publisher Example

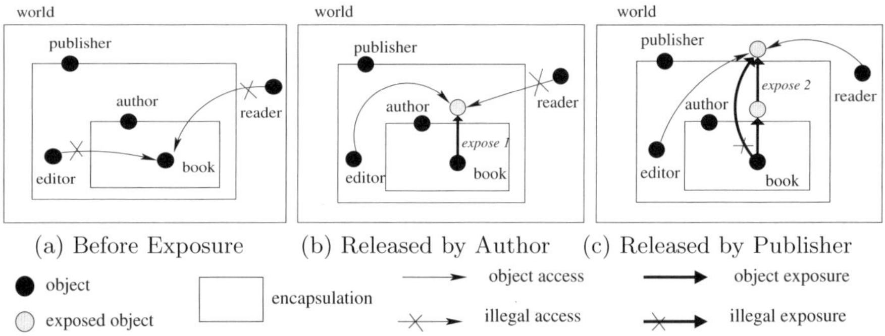

Fig. 2. Step by Step Exposure

shorthand for `[p]Book<*>`. Also, the dynamic owner of a type may be omitted if it is the same as the static owner (which must not be abstract); for instance, `Author<this>` is a shorthand for `[this]Author<this>`.

In the class `Author` the book is owned by the author, initially it cannot be accessed from outside the author. In Figure 2(a), the book object is encapsulated inside the author's context, so that accesses on it from the editor or the reader are prevented by the type system (as shown by crossed arrow lines in the figure). However, the author may release the book to the publisher (its owner) after he finishes writing it. An expose operation is used in the `release()` method to expose the book to the publisher. The book becomes dynamically owned by the publisher as suggested by the dynamic owner of the return type `[p]Book`.

After the first exposure, the book object is accessible within the publisher: it can be accessed by the editor but not the reader, as shown in Figure 2(b). The editor can now do some editing on the book. The second exposure is defined in the `Publisher` class. The publisher will release the book after the editor finishes editing it. Another expose operation is used by the publisher to expose the book;

the book becomes dynamically owned by the **world**. After the second exposure, the book object is accessible by any object in the program so that the reader can start reading the book now, as shown in Figure 2(c).

In our type system, it is necessary to expose the book twice in order to release the book to the reader. Our owners-as-downgraders policy ensures that such exposure must be authorized (via the explicit expose operations) by both the author and the publisher. The crossed thick line in Figure 2(c) indicates that it is not possible to directly expose the book to the reader in a single step.

The ability to encapsulate objects and expose them allows our programs to express useful aspects of designer intent. The publisher example shows that we can use object exposure to enforce a logical sequence of actions in a certain order. This is like an assured pipeline in information flow security. When the author is writing the book, he does not want any interference from outside, so the book object is kept private by the author until writing is finished. After the book is released to the publisher, the editor may edit the book in collaboration with the author. The book remains private to the publisher until editing is finished. The reader may not read the book, until the publisher publishes it. In practice, as the book is exposed, the type of the reference should be restricted to a more limited interface, e.g. to prevent readers editing the book.

4 The Formal System

In this section, we present a core object-oriented language which allows us to formalize the type system, semantics and the main results of the type system. We show that our owners-as-downgraders property can be checked syntactically by a type system. The abstract syntax and typing rules follow the conventions used in our previous papers [20,22], which extend *Featherweight Java* [17] with field assignment and ownership information.

Table 1 gives the abstract syntax of the source language, with the extensions used by the type system having grey background as they are not available to programmers. The extensions include the syntax for type environments and existential contexts. Type environments Γ record the assumed ownership ordering between context parameters, and the types of variables. Existential contexts are used by the type system to name contexts which are hidden from the current environment. The expression e may be a concrete context only if e is this, otherwise e is an existential context (hence not a well-formed context by the rules in Table 4). The special existential context ? represents a concrete unknown context: an anonymous Skolemisation; it is only used in type instantiation in class member lookup (see [L-DEF] in Table 7) to prevent unsound binding. Types with existential context ? have restricted *bindability* (see [T-SUB] in Table 3), because ? is not a well-formed context in the current environment (see [A-ID]). Conventional existential types use some form of pack/unpack or close/open pairing to distinguish between typing contexts where the existential type is visible or not. Our use of the context abstraction $*$ in the language syntax and the existential context ? in the type system is somewhat akin to the use of pack/unpack mechanisms for existential types, but simpler. In particular, we avoid introducing new

Table 1. Abstract Syntax for Source Language and Type System

T	$::= [\mathsf{D}]\mathsf{O}$	variable types
O	$::= \mathsf{C}\langle\overline{\mathsf{K}}\rangle$	object types
K, D	$::= \mathsf{X} \mid \mathsf{this} \mid \mathsf{world} \mid * \mid ? \mid e$	contexts
P	$::= \overline{\mathsf{L}}\; e$	programs
L	$::= \mathsf{class}\ \mathsf{C}\langle\overline{\mathsf{X}}\rangle \lhd \mathsf{O}\ \{\overline{\mathsf{T}\ \mathsf{f}};\ \overline{\mathsf{M}}\}$	classes
M	$::= \mathsf{T}\ \mathsf{m}(\overline{\mathsf{T}\ \mathsf{x}})\ \{e\}$	methods
e	$::= \mathsf{x} \mid \mathsf{new}\ \mathsf{O} \mid e.\mathsf{f} \mid e.\mathsf{f} = e \mid e.\mathsf{m}(\overline{e}) \mid \mathsf{expose}\ e$	expressions
Γ	$::= \bullet \mid \Gamma, \mathsf{X} \preceq \mathsf{X} \mid \Gamma, \mathsf{x} : \mathsf{T}$	environments

Table 2. Judgements in Type System

Judgement	Meaning
$\Gamma \vdash \mathsf{O}$	O is a well-formed object type
$\vdash \mathsf{O} < \mathsf{O}'$	O is a subtype of O'
$\Gamma \vdash \mathsf{T}$	T is a well-formed variable type
$\Gamma \vdash \mathsf{T} <: \mathsf{T}'$	an expression of type T is bindable to a variable of type T'
$\Gamma \vdash \mathsf{K} \ll \mathsf{K}'$	K can be abstracted by K'
$\Gamma \vdash \mathsf{K}$	K is a well-formed context
$\Gamma \vdash \mathsf{K} \preceq \mathsf{K}'$	K is inside K'
$\vdash \mathsf{P}$	P is a well-formed program
$\vdash \mathsf{L}$	L is a well-formed class
$\Gamma \vdash \mathsf{M}$	M is a well-formed method
$\Gamma \vdash_{\mathsf{K}} e : \mathsf{T}$	expression e is of type T
$\mathsf{H}; e \Downarrow_{\mathsf{K}} \mathsf{H}'; e'$	e is reduced to e' in context K, and heap H is updated to be H'

names for contexts into environments by keeping them anonymous. The details of existential contexts can be found in [20]; we do not discuss them in full detail in this paper.

4.1 Static Semantics

The judgements used in the type system are give in Table 2, together with their meanings. Table 3 provides rules for type well-formedness, subtyping rules for object (value) types and variable types, as well as the rules for context abstraction. Directly borrowed from [20], we use a separate judgement for bindability to handle types with existential contexts, which only occur after field or method lookup by the type system (see Table 7). The well-formedness [TYPE] rule is somewhat unconventional; it allows the introduction of context abstraction $*$ into types, via the bindability requirement. Well-formed object types, [OBJECT], only use concrete contexts; by requiring the owner context of an object type to be inside any other context parameters, we ensure that any type accessed from within has an owner that contains the current object, as required for the encapsulation property. [A-ID] ensures that the existential contexts abstract nothing, because

Table 3. Types, Subtype, Binding and Abstraction Rules

Rule	Definition
[OBJECT]	$\dfrac{\lvert\overline{\mathsf{K}}\rvert = arity(\mathsf{C}) \quad \Gamma \vdash \overline{\mathsf{K}} \quad \overline{\mathsf{K}} = \mathsf{K}, ... \quad \Gamma \vdash \mathsf{K} \preceq \overline{\mathsf{K}}}{\Gamma \vdash \mathsf{C}\langle\overline{\mathsf{K}}\rangle}$
[O-SUB]	$\dfrac{\mathsf{class}\ \mathsf{C}\langle\overline{\mathsf{X}}\rangle \lhd \mathsf{O}\ ...}{\vdash \mathsf{C}\langle\overline{\mathsf{K}}\rangle < \mathsf{O}[\overline{\mathsf{K}/\mathsf{X}}]}$
[O-RFL]	$\dfrac{}{\vdash \mathsf{O} < \mathsf{O}}$
[O-TRA]	$\dfrac{\vdash \mathsf{O} < \mathsf{O}'' \quad \vdash \mathsf{O}'' < \mathsf{O}'}{\vdash \mathsf{O} < \mathsf{O}'}$
[TYPE]	$\dfrac{\Gamma \vdash \mathsf{D} \quad \Gamma \vdash \mathsf{O}' \quad \Gamma \vdash [\mathsf{D}]\mathsf{O}' <: [\mathsf{D}]\mathsf{O}}{\Gamma \vdash [\mathsf{D}]\mathsf{O}}$
[T-SUB]	$\dfrac{\Gamma \vdash \overline{\mathsf{K} \ll \mathsf{K}'} \quad \Gamma \vdash \mathsf{D}' \preceq \mathsf{D}}{\Gamma \vdash [\mathsf{D}]\mathsf{C}\langle\overline{\mathsf{K}}\rangle <: [\mathsf{D}']\mathsf{C}\langle\overline{\mathsf{K}'}\rangle}$
[T-TRA]	$\dfrac{\vdash \mathsf{O} < \mathsf{O}'' \quad \Gamma \vdash [\mathsf{D}]\mathsf{O}'' <: [\mathsf{D}']\mathsf{O}'}{\Gamma \vdash [\mathsf{D}]\mathsf{O} <: [\mathsf{D}']\mathsf{O}'}$
[ABSTRACT]	$\dfrac{}{\Gamma \vdash \mathsf{K} \ll *}$
[A-ID]	$\dfrac{\Gamma \vdash \mathsf{K}}{\Gamma \vdash \mathsf{K} \ll \mathsf{K}}$

Table 4. Context and Inside Rules

Rule	Definition
[CONTEXT]	$\dfrac{\mathsf{K} \in \Gamma}{\Gamma \vdash \mathsf{K}}$
[WORLD]	$\dfrac{}{\Gamma \vdash \mathsf{world}}$
[C-OWN]	$\dfrac{}{\Gamma \vdash \mathsf{K} \preceq owner_\Gamma(\mathsf{K})}$
[C-ENV]	$\dfrac{\mathsf{K} \preceq \mathsf{K}' \in \Gamma}{\Gamma \vdash \mathsf{K} \preceq \mathsf{K}'}$
[C-WLD]	$\dfrac{}{\Gamma \vdash \mathsf{K} \preceq \mathsf{world}}$
[C-TRA]	$\dfrac{\Gamma \vdash \mathsf{K} \preceq \mathsf{K}'' \quad \Gamma \vdash \mathsf{K}'' \preceq \mathsf{K}'}{\Gamma \vdash \mathsf{K} \preceq \mathsf{K}'}$
[C-RFL]	$\dfrac{\Gamma \vdash \mathsf{K}}{\Gamma \vdash \mathsf{K} \preceq \mathsf{K}}$

they are not valid contexts by [CONTEXT] in Table 4. Combined with [T-SUB] this ensures that bindability is not reflexive, because existential types can only occur on the right-hand side of the binding relation. The use of bindability in typing field assignment and method argument binding (see [E-ASS], [E-CAL] in Table 6) prevents existential contexts from being associated with the target of a binding. Substitutions used in this type system are postfixed in order to be distinct from the prefixed dynamic owners. For instance, $\mathsf{O}[\overline{\mathsf{K}/\mathsf{X}}]$ substitutes $\overline{\mathsf{K}}$ for $\overline{\mathsf{X}}$ in O.

Table 4 defines well-formed contexts and context ordering for concrete contexts. Direct ownership is captured in [C-OWN] by looking up the static owner from the type of the context via [L-OWN]. The only direct ownership relation available in static semantics is for the this context; it is owned by the first context parameter of its type (see [CLASS]). this is the only context that is given a static type; at runtime, this is bound to the location of the target object.

The rules for well-formed program definitions and declarations are in Table 5. In the [CLASS] rule, each class defines its own environment formed from its formal contexts and the type of this and super objects. The owner parameter (the first context parameter X) has to be inside all other context parameters, just like the classic ownership types [11,9]. The only direct ownership relation

Table 5. Program, Class and Method Rules

[PROGRAM] $$\frac{\vdash \overline{L} \qquad \bullet \vdash e : T}{\vdash \overline{L}\ e}$$

[CLASS] $$\frac{\begin{array}{c}\overline{X} = X, \ldots \qquad \Gamma = X \preceq \overline{X}, \mathsf{this} : [X]C\langle\overline{X}\rangle, \mathsf{super} : [X]O \qquad \Gamma \vdash [X]O, \overline{T} \\ \Gamma \vdash \overline{M} \qquad owner_\Gamma(\mathsf{this}) = owner_\Gamma(\mathsf{super}) \qquad \overline{f} \cap dom(flds_\Gamma(\mathsf{super})) = \bullet\end{array}}{\mathsf{class}\ C\langle\overline{X}\rangle \lhd O\ \{\overline{T\ f};\ \overline{M}\}}$$

[METHOD] $$\frac{\begin{array}{c}\Gamma, \overline{x : T} \vdash_{\mathsf{this}} e : T'' \qquad \Gamma \vdash T, \overline{T} \qquad \Gamma \vdash T'' <: T \\ mth(\Gamma(\mathsf{super}), \mathsf{this}, m) = T'\ \overline{T'} \quad \Longrightarrow \quad \Gamma \vdash T <: T' \qquad \Gamma \vdash \overline{T' <: T}\end{array}}{\Gamma \vdash T\ m(\overline{T\ x})}$$

known to the class, that is $\mathsf{this} \preceq X$, is not included in the class environment; instead, we capture it in the [C-OWN] rule to make it generally derivable. A bullet symbol is used to denote something null or empty. For instance, in $\bullet \vdash e : T$ in [PROGRAM], the environment of the expression does not exist. For simplicity, we often simply omit the bullets.

Table 6 defines expression types. Each expression judgement is attached with a context ($\vdash_K$), which is the current context where the expression is evaluated (the target object of the current call). In the static semantics, it is bound to the this context in class methods (see [METHOD]); in the dynamic semantics, it is bound to the location of the current object. It is omitted in [PROGRAM], because the main method does not have a target object; because world context is never used as a target object. The most interesting typing rule is [E-XPO], where an object may be exposed. Since a dynamic owner is only authorized to expose an object it directly owns, this rule insists an object can only be exposed, by promoting its dynamic owner one level up in the ownership tree, if its dynamic owner is the current context. Otherwise, there is no exposure.

Table 7 defines auxiliary definitions to be used by the type system. We put substitutions and lookups in the auxiliary definitions to keep the type rules simple. When accessing the fields or methods via an expression e, we determine their types, given the type of e. These in turn use [L-DEF] to find a correct substitution for parameters of T's class, where $*$ is replaced by ?. This is similar to the usual unpack/open for conventional existential types. The major difference is that we do not introduce fresh context variables into the current environment. Instead, we keep the existential context anonymous by using a special symbol ?. This technique eliminates the need for the pack/close operation, since anonymous contexts do not have to be bound to an environment, they naturally become global (see [20] for more details).

4.2 Dynamic Semantics and Properties

The extended syntax and features used by the dynamic semantics are given in Table 8. Ownership information, including both static and dynamic owners, is only needed in static type checking so that they may be erased after type checking. The expose operations may be erased too, because they only affect

Table 6. Expression Rules

[E-VAR] $$\frac{}{\Gamma \vdash_K x : \Gamma(x)}$$

[E-NEW] $$\frac{\Gamma \vdash O \qquad O = C\langle D, ...\rangle}{\Gamma \vdash_K \mathsf{new}\ O : [D]O}$$

[E-SEL] $$\frac{flds^K_\Gamma(e)(f) = T \qquad \Gamma \vdash T}{\Gamma \vdash_K e.f : T}$$

[E-ASS] $$\frac{\Gamma \vdash_K e.f : T \qquad \Gamma \vdash_K e' : T' \qquad \Gamma \vdash T' <: T}{\Gamma \vdash_K e.f = e' : T}$$

[E-CAL] $$\frac{mth^K_\Gamma(e, m) = T\ \overline{T}\ ... \qquad \Gamma \vdash_K \overline{e : T'} \qquad \Gamma \vdash \overline{T' <: T} \qquad \Gamma \vdash T}{\Gamma \vdash_K e.m(\overline{e}) : T}$$

[E-XPO] $$\frac{\Gamma \vdash_K e : [D]O \qquad D = K \implies D' = owner_\Gamma(D) \qquad D \neq K \implies D' = D}{\Gamma \vdash_K \mathsf{expose}\ e : [D']O}$$

Table 7. Auxiliary Definitions for Lookup

[L-OWN] $$\frac{\Gamma \vdash_K e : [D]C\langle K', ..\rangle}{owner^K_\Gamma(e) = K'}$$

[L-FLD'] $$\frac{def(O, K) = ... \lhd O'\ \{\overline{T\ f};\ ...\}}{flds(O, K) = \overline{f\ T}, flds(O', K)}$$

[L-DYN] $$\frac{\Gamma \vdash_K e : [D]O}{downer^K_\Gamma(e) = D}$$

[L-MTH] $$\frac{\Gamma \vdash_K e : [D]O}{mth^K_\Gamma(e, m) = mth(O, e, m)}$$

[L-DEF] $$\frac{L = \mathsf{class}\ C\langle\overline{X}\rangle ... \qquad \overline{K'} = \overline{K}[?/*] \qquad L' = L[\overline{K'/X}, K/\mathsf{this}]}{def(C\langle\overline{K}\rangle, K) = L'}$$

[L-MTH'] $$\frac{def(O, K) = ...\ T\ m(\overline{T\ x})\ \{e\}\ ...}{mth(O, K, m) = T\ \overline{T}\ \overline{x}\ \ e}$$

[L-FLD] $$\frac{\Gamma \vdash_K e : [D]O}{flds^K_\Gamma(e) = flds(O, e)}$$

[L-MTH''] $$\frac{def(O, K) = ... \lhd O'\ \{...\ ; \overline{M}\} \qquad m \notin \overline{M}}{mth(O, K, m) = mth(O', K, m)}$$

dynamic owners; expose e becomes just e after erasure. However, in order to formalize the key properties of the type system, we need to establish a connection between the static and dynamic semantics by including ownership and exposures in the dynamic semantics.

Locations are annotated with the type of the object they refer to, as well as a list of dynamic owners which records the history of exposures of this object. The dynamic owners of a location may be extended over time through exposures. The list is used to prove Theorem 4. The last element in the dynamic owners list of a location is the current dynamic owner of the object, i.e., the downgrader who currently has the authority to expose the object. The advantage of not storing the type information in the heap is that we can look up type information directly from the location itself without referring to the heap (see [E-LOC]). All locations are annotated with their owners and type; but we may omit them wherever that information is not used.

Expressions are extended with locations, which indirectly extends contexts with locations. A heap is a mapping from locations to objects; an object maps its fields to locations. A few auxiliary definitions are included in Table 9 to help formalize the properties. We have used some shorthand for simplicity. $\Gamma \vdash e <: T$

Table 8. Extended Syntax with Dynamic Features

$l, l_O^{\overline{D}}$	locations	$o ::= \overline{f \mapsto l}$	objects
$e ::= ... \mid l$	expressions	$H ::= \overline{l \mapsto o}$	heaps

Table 9. Auxiliary Definitions for Dynamic Semantics

$$\text{[E-LOC]}\quad \frac{}{\Gamma \vdash_K l_O^{\overline{D},D} : [D]O}$$

$$\text{[L-XPO]}\quad \frac{}{\mathsf{downgraders}(l_O^{\overline{D}}) = \overline{D}}$$

$$\text{[HEAP]}\quad \frac{\begin{array}{c}\forall l \in \mathsf{dom}(H)\ \cdot \\ H(l) = \overline{f \mapsto l} \qquad \mathsf{flds}(l) = \overline{f\ T} \\ \vdash \overline{l : T'} \qquad \vdash \overline{T' <: T}\end{array}}{\vdash H}$$

means $\Gamma \vdash_K e : T'$ and $\Gamma \vdash T' <: T$. We may omit $\bullet$ in judgements and lookup functions; for example, $\vdash_K e : T$ means $\bullet \vdash_K e : T$. We may also omit the current context K where it is not used.

The dynamic semantics are defined in a big step fashion in Table 10. The context K in $\Downarrow_K$ refers to the target object of the current call; the main method does not have a target object. At the time of method invocation in [R-CAL], the target object of the body of the invoked method is l. The variable this is not substituted in $e'[\overline{l/x}]$. Instead, this is replaced by l in the substitution provided by the lookup function $\mathsf{mth}(l, m)$. In [R-XPO], if the current object K is the same as the last dynamic owner of l (i.e, K is the current authorizing downgrader for l), then the exposure is authorized and the dynamic owner of l is promoted to $\mathsf{owner}(D)$. The exposure is completed by an appending of $\mathsf{owner}(D)$ to the end of the dynamic owner list that is attached to the location of the object. Otherwise, the exposure has insufficient authorization; the object l and its dynamic owner list remains unchanged.

The operational semantics for field operations are obvious. In [R-NEW], to create an object, we adopt the default field initialization scheme from MOJO [6]. We first create a new object at a fresh address in the heap; then we initialize the fields with default object creation. Object creation is a recursive process in an atomic step. MOJO's default field initialization simplifies the formalism because it avoid nulls; otherwise we would need to allow for null errors. In this paper, we focus on the correctness of object exposure, rather than concerning ourselves with a more complex, but realistic model for object initialization.

Finally, we formalize some of the key properties of the type system, including a standard type preservation result in Theorem 1. Theorems 2-4 directly correspond to the properties introduced informally in Section 3.

Theorem 1 (Preservation). *Given* $\vdash H$ *and* $\vdash_K e : T$, *If* $H; e \Downarrow_K H'; l$ *then* $\vdash H'$ *and* $\vdash l <: T$.

Theorem 2 (Encapsulation)
Given $\vdash H$ *and* $\vdash_K e : T$, *if* $H; e \Downarrow_K H'; l$ *then* $\vdash K \preceq \mathsf{downer}(l)$.

Table 10. A Big Step Semantics

$$[\text{R-SEL}] \quad \frac{H; e \Downarrow_K H'; l}{H; e.f \Downarrow_K H'; H'(l)(f)}$$

$$[\text{R-NEW}] \quad \frac{\begin{array}{c} l \notin dom(H) \qquad H_1 = H, l_O^D \mapsto \bullet \qquad \overline{f\ T} = flds(l) \\ \forall i \in 1..|\overline{f}| \quad \cdot \quad H_i; \mathsf{new}\ T_i \Downarrow_K H_{i+1}; l_i \\ O = C\langle D, ...\rangle \qquad H' = H_{|\overline{f}|+1}[l_O^D \mapsto \overline{f \mapsto l}] \end{array}}{H; \mathsf{new}\ O \Downarrow_K H'; l}$$

$$[\text{R-ASS}] \quad \frac{H; e \Downarrow_K H'; l \qquad H'; e' \Downarrow_l H''; l'}{H; e.f = e' \Downarrow_K H''[l \mapsto H''(l)[f \mapsto l']]; l'}$$

$$[\text{R-CAL}] \quad \frac{\begin{array}{c} H; e \Downarrow_K H_1; l \qquad mth(l, m) = ...\overline{x}\ e' \\ \forall i \in 1..|\overline{x}| \quad \cdot \quad H_i; e_i \Downarrow_K H_{i+1}; l_i \\ H_{|\overline{x}|+1}; e'[\overline{l/x}] \Downarrow_l H'; l' \end{array}}{H; e.m(\overline{e}) \Downarrow_K H'; l'}$$

$$[\text{R-XPO}] \quad \frac{\begin{array}{c} H; e \Downarrow_K H'; l \qquad \vdash_K l : [D]O \qquad D \neq K \implies H'' = H' \\ D = K \implies H'' = H'[l_O^{downgraders(l), owner(D)}/l] \end{array}}{H; \mathsf{expose}\ e \Downarrow_K H''; l}$$

Theorem 3 (Exposure)
Given $\vdash H$ *and* $\vdash_K \mathsf{expose}\ e : T$, *if* $H; \mathsf{expose}\ e \Downarrow_K H'; l$, *then* $\vdash owner(K) \preceq downer(l)$.

Theorem 4 (Owners-as-downgraders)
Given $\vdash H$ *and* $l, l' \in H$, *if* $\vdash owner(l) \preceq l' \preceq downer(l)$ *then* $l' \in downgraders(l)$.

5 Discussion and Related Work

In this paper, we have focused on techniques for exposing objects safely at runtime in a statically typed language. Any object may become accessible to any other object, given sufficient downgrading. Our type system ensures that owners must explicitly authorize downgrading; this highlights the role of the owner – only the owner can authorize the objects it owns to be accessed from outside. Like security types with downgrading [30,25,7,19], our type system does not track downgrading information. In other words, we cannot tell, from the types, whether an object has-been-exposed or may-be-exposed. However, in many applications where stronger static assumptions are needed (for instance, program verification and reasoning about object invariants), we may still want to retain fixed object ownership so that certain objects can never be exposed. A simple extension to our system would allow us to model (ownership-traditional) never-to-be-exposed objects in addition to may-be-exposed objects, but that is not a concern of this paper. Never-to-be-exposed objects are just a special case of may-be-exposed objects where downgrading is not allowed.

Our formalization is built upon classic tree-based ownership types [11,10,9] for simplicity. Modern extensions to ownership types have been studying richer structures than per-context ownership trees. For instance, *Ownership Domains* [1] allow programmers to further partition contexts into domains for finer-grained access control, and MOJO [6] replaces ownership tree with multiple ownership for more precise reasoning about effects. We believe that the object exposure technique introduced in this paper could be applied in those systems too.

Syntactic overhead for our types is that of ownership types plus an extra dynamic owner for each type. As we have seen in our earlier example, with carefully selected defaults type annotations can be reduced. Moreover, the ideas of *Generic Ownership* [27] can also be employed here to reduce the burden of type annotations in the presence of class type parameters. As for other ownership type systems, ours allows separate compilation. It is statically checkable and does not require any runtime support.

There have been a variety of ownership type systems seeking to improve the expressiveness of the classic ownership types by relaxing the owners-as-dominators property. JOE [9] allows internal contexts to be exposed through read-only local variables. Ownership Domains [1] uses final fields to expose internal contexts. Lexical scoping has been used to give inner class instances special access privileges to their outer objects [8,5]. Both SOT [10] and [20] offer separation of accessibility and capability of an object. Such separation allows the creator of an object to decide its accessibility independently from its position in the ownership tree, and also implies object access need not be authorized by its owner. All these techniques increase nameability of internal contexts, but object accessibility remains statically determined, being fixed at creation for the object's lifetime. None of these approaches can dynamically expose an encapsulated object at runtime as in this paper.

We have focused on object instance access control with object ownership. Beside access control, the idea of object ownership has been proved to be useful in other applications. *OOFX* [14], JOE [9] and *MOJO* [6] combine effects and some forms of ownership. These systems focus on reasoning about read and write effects in order to syntactically control interference in the program. *Boogie* [18], *Universes* [13], *Effective Ownership* [21] and *Oval* [22] use the ownership structure to confine object dependency in order to support localized reasoning about object invariants. These systems typically do not hide information as they do not restrict read access or reference; object invariants can only be violated by mutations. They enforce an owners-as-modifiers property.

Ownership transfer has been supported in a number of systems which permits the owner of an object to be changed when necessary. However, they either cannot be enforced statically, or have to enforce some form of uniqueness of reference. *Islands* [16] uses strict unique references with destructive reads to permit transfer. *External uniqueness* [12] is a flexible form of uniqueness for ownership types which permits internal sharing without compromising uniqueness of external reference; it supports ownership transfer by combining external uniqueness with destructive reads and borrowing. *AliasJava* [2] supports ownership transfer using destructive field reads and lent variables. Beside these type systems, *UUT* [24] combines a type system and static analysis to enforce temporary uniqueness for ownership transfer. Program logics, such as Boogie [4,18,23], can allow dynamic ownership, but require program verification to check ownership properties.

Our owners-as-downgraders property essentially enforces a downgrading policy based on object ownership. Unlike most security types for secure information flow [7,19], our type system does not consider covert channels [30], hence we do not enforce a conventional *noninterference* property (we could have done so, but it is not a concern of this paper). Our downgrading policy may be considered as a special case of intransitive noninterference [15,29], where special downgrading paths exist in a security lattice. With our owners-as-downgraders property, such downgrading paths are upward branches in the ownership tree.

6 Conclusion

In this paper, we have proposed an expressive ownership type system, which encapsulates object privacy while also permitting information release where appropriate. In this new system, objects may expose their owned information via an explicit operation. We have shown an example where object encapsulation and exposure capture useful aspects of designer intent. With the ability to change object accessibility at runtime, we have provided a more dynamic and expressive model for object access control in ownership types.

References

1. Aldrich, J., Chambers, C.: Ownership domains: Separating aliasing policy from mechanism. In: Odersky, M. (ed.) ECOOP 2004. LNCS, vol. 3086, pp. 1–25. Springer, Heidelberg (2004)
2. Aldrich, J., Kostadinov, V., Chambers, C.: Alias annotations for program understanding. In: Proceedings of the 17th annual ACM SIGPLAN Conference on Object-Oriented Programming, Systems, Languages, and Applications, pp. 311–330 (2002)
3. Almeida, P.S.: Balloon types: Controlling sharing of state in data types. In: Aksit, M., Matsuoka, S. (eds.) ECOOP 1997. LNCS, vol. 1241, pp. 32–59. Springer, Heidelberg (1997)
4. Barnett, M., DeLine, R., Fähndrich, M., Leino, K.R.M., Schulte, W.: Verification of object-oriented programs with invariants. In: Eisenbach, S., Leavens, G.T., Müller, P., Poetzsch-Heffter, A., Poll, E. (eds.) Formal Techniques for Java-like Programs (FTfJP) (July 2003); Published as Technical Report 408 from ETH Zurich
5. Boyapati, C., Liskov, B., Shrira, L.: Ownership types for object encapsulation. In: Proceedings of the 30th ACM SIGPLAN-SIGACT Symposium on Principles of Programming Languages, pp. 213–223. ACM Press, New York (2003)
6. Cameron, N., Drossopoulou, S., Noble, J., Smith, M.: Multiple Ownership. In: OOPSLA (October 2007)
7. Chong, S., Myers, A.C.: Security policies for downgrading. In: ACM Conference on Computer and Communications Security, pp. 198–209 (2004)

8. Clarke, D.: Object Ownership and Containment. PhD thesis, School of Computer Science and Engineering, The University of New South Wales, Sydney, Australia (2001)
9. Clarke, D., Drossopoulou, S.: Ownership, encapsulation and disjointness of type and effect. In: OOPSLA (2002)
10. Clarke, D., Noble, J., Potter, J.: Simple ownership types for object containment. In: Knudsen, J.L. (ed.) ECOOP 2001. LNCS, vol. 2072, p. 53. Springer, Heidelberg (2001)
11. Clarke, D., Potter, J., Noble, J.: Ownership types for flexible alias protection. In: OOPSLA (1998)
12. Clarke, D., Wrigstad, T.: External uniqueness is unique enough. In: Cardelli, L. (ed.) ECOOP 2003. LNCS, vol. 2743. Springer, Heidelberg (2003)
13. Dietl, W., Müller, P.: Universes: Lightweight ownership for JML. Journal of Object Technology, JOT (2005)
14. Greenhouse, A., Boyland, J.: An object-oriented effects system. In: Guerraoui, R. (ed.) ECOOP 1999. LNCS, vol. 1628, pp. 205–229. Springer, Heidelberg (1999)
15. Haigh, J.T., Young, W.D.: Extending the noninterference version of mls for sat. IEEE Trans. on Software Engineering SE-13(2), 141–150 (1987)
16. Hogg, J.: Islands: aliasing protection in object-oriented languages. In: Proceedings of Conference on Object-Oriented Programming Systems, Languages, and Applications, pp. 271–285. ACM Press, New York (1991)
17. Igarashi, A., Pierce, B., Wadler, P.: Featherweight Java: A minimal core calculus for Java and GJ. In: OOPSLA, pp. 132–146 (1999)
18. Leino, K.R.M., Müller, P.: Object invariants in dynamic contexts. In: Odersky, M. (ed.) ECOOP 2004. LNCS, vol. 3086, pp. 491–515. Springer, Heidelberg (2004)
19. Li, P., Zdancewic, S.: Downgrading policies and relaxed noninterference. In: POPL, pp. 158–170 (2005)
20. Lu, Y., Potter, J.: On ownership and accessibility. In: Thomas, D. (ed.) ECOOP 2006. LNCS, vol. 4067, pp. 99–123. Springer, Heidelberg (2006)
21. Lu, Y., Potter, J.: Protecting representation with effect encapsulation. In: POPL. ACM Press, New York (2006)
22. Lu, Y., Potter, J., Xue, J.: Validity invariants and effects. In: Ernst, E. (ed.) ECOOP 2007. LNCS, vol. 4609, pp. 202–226. Springer, Heidelberg (2007)
23. Microsoft Research. Towards a Verifying Compiler: The Spec# Approach (2006)
24. Müller, P., Rudich, A.: Ownership transfer in universe types. In: OOPSLA, pp. 461–478 (2007)
25. Myers, A.C.: JFlow: Practical mostly-static information flow control. In: Symposium on Principles of Programming Languages, pp. 228–241 (1999)
26. Noble, J., Vitek, J., Potter, J.: Flexible alias protection. In: Jul, E. (ed.) ECOOP 1998. LNCS, vol. 1445, p. 158. Springer, Heidelberg (1998)
27. Potanin, A., Noble, J., Clarke, D., Biddle, R.: Generic ownership for generic Java. In: OOPSLA (2006)
28. Potter, J., Noble, J., Clarke, D.: The ins and outs of objects. In: ASWEC. IEEE Press, Los Alamitos (1998)
29. Roscoe, A.W., Goldsmith, M.H.: What is intransitive noninterference? In: CSFW, pp. 228–238 (1999)
30. Sabelfeld, A., Myers, A.C.: Language-based information-flow security. IEEE Journal on Selected Areas in Communications 21(1) (2003)

A Fresh Look at Separation Algebras and Share Accounting*

Robert Dockins[1], Aquinas Hobor[2], and Andrew W. Appel[1]

[1] Princeton University
[2] National University of Singapore

Abstract. *Separation Algebras* serve as models of Separation Logics; *Share Accounting* allows reasoning about concurrent-read/exclusive-write resources in Separation Logic. In designing a Concurrent Separation Logic and in mechanizing proofs of its soundness, we found previous axiomatizations of separation algebras and previous systems of share accounting to be useful but imperfect. We adjust the axioms of separation algebras; we demonstrate an operator calculus for constructing new separation algebras; we present a more powerful system of share accounting with a new, simple model; and we provide a reusable Coq development.

1 Introduction

Separation logic is an elegant solution to the pointer aliasing problem of Hoare logic. We have been using separation logic to examine the metatheory of C minor enhanced with primitives for shared-memory concurrency [6,5]. Along the way, we developed a generic library of constructions and proof techniques for separation logic. Here we explain two related parts of our toolkit: separation algebras and share models. **Contribution 0:** Our proofs are machine checked in Coq.[1]

Calcagno, O'Hearn and Yang [4] present a semantics of separation logic based on structures they call "separation algebras." Although Calcagno's definition is adequate for their purposes, we found it too limiting in some ways and too permissive in others. **Contribution 1:** We make several alterations to the definition of separation algebras to produce a class of objects that have more pleasing mathematical properties and that are better suited to the task of generating useful separation logics.

Different separation logics often require different separation algebra models, but verifying that a complex object is a separation algebra can be both tedious and surprisingly difficult. **Contribution 2:** We demonstrate an operator calculus for rapidly constructing a wide variety of new separation algebras.

We also revisit share accounting, which is used to reason about read-sharing concurrent protocols. Share accounting allows a process to "own" some share of

* Supported in part by National Science Foundation grant CNS-0627650 and a Lee Kuan Yew Postdoctoral Fellowship.

[1] The Coq development corresponding to this paper is part of the Mechanized Semantic Library, available at `http://msl.cs.princeton.edu/`

Z. Hu (Ed.): APLAS 2009, LNCS 5904, pp. 161–177, 2009.

a memory location: the full share gives read/write/deallocate permissions, while a partial share gives only the read permission. **Contribution 3:** We present a new share model that is superior to those by Bornat et al. [1] and Parkinson [8].

2 Separation Algebras

Calcagno, O'Hearn, and Yang [4] introduced the notion of a *separation algebra*, which they defined as "a cancellative, partial commutive monoid." That is, a separation algebra (SA) is a tuple $\langle A, \oplus, u \rangle$ where A is a set, $\oplus$ is a partial binary operation on A and u is an element of A satisfying the following axioms:

$$x \oplus y = y \oplus x \tag{1}$$

$$x \oplus (y \oplus z) = (x \oplus y) \oplus z \tag{2}$$

$$u \oplus x = x \tag{3}$$

$$x_1 \oplus y = x_2 \oplus y \;\rightarrow\; x_1 = x_2 \tag{4}$$

The primary interest of a separation algebra is that it can be used to build a separation logic [11]. However, for most of this paper, we are going to consider separation algebras as first-class objects and investigate their properties.

We wish to construct our models in Coq. Dealing with partial functions in Coq can be tricky, since the function space of Coq's metatheory contains only computable total functions.[2] We would like to be able to construct models whose combining operation is not computable. Therefore, we adopt a convention from philosophical logic, where it is common to give the semantics of substructural connectives in terms of 3-place relations rather than binary functions [10].

We recast the separation algebra ideas of Calcagno et al. in this relational setting by considering the *join relation* $J(x, y, z)$, usually written suggestively as $x \oplus y = z$. The partiality of the $\oplus$ operation follows from the fact that for a given x and y we are not guaranteed that there is some z such that $x \oplus y = z$. Reinterpreted in this setting, we say that $\langle A, J \rangle$, (where A is a carrier set and J is a three-place relation on A) is a separation algebra provided that:

$$x \oplus y = z_1 \;\rightarrow\; x \oplus y = z_2 \;\rightarrow\; z_1 = z_2 \tag{5}$$

$$x_1 \oplus y = z \;\rightarrow\; x_2 \oplus y = z \;\rightarrow\; x_1 = x_2 \tag{6}$$

$$x \oplus y = z \;\rightarrow\; y \oplus x = z \tag{7}$$

$$x \oplus y = a \;\rightarrow\; a \oplus z = b \;\rightarrow\; \exists c.\; y \oplus z = c \wedge x \oplus c = b \tag{8}$$

$$\exists u.\; \forall x.\; u \oplus x = x \tag{9}$$

That is, $\oplus$ is a functional relation (5), it is cancellative (6), commutative (7), associative (8), and has a unit u (9).

We are justified in calling this object "the" unit because the cancellation axiom guarantees that it must be unique. In addition, the unit is exactly the unique element u satisfying $u \oplus u = u$, again by the cancellation axiom.

[2] Uncomputable functions can be built if one assumes the axiom of description.

3 The Algebra of Separation Algebras

A new separation algebra can be built by applying operators to preexisting SAs.

Definition 1 (SA product operator). *Let $\langle A, J_A\rangle$ and $\langle B, J_B\rangle$ be SAs. Then the product SA is $\langle A \times B, J\rangle$, where J is defined componentwise:*

$$J((x_a, x_b), (y_a, y_b), (z_a, z_b)) \equiv J_A(x_a, y_a, z_a) \wedge J_B(x_b, y_b, z_b) \tag{10}$$

Definition 2 (SA function operator). *Let A be a set and let $\langle B, J_B\rangle$ be a SA. Then the function SA is $\langle A \to B, J\rangle$, where J is defined pointwise:*

$$J(f, g, h) \equiv \forall a \in A.\ J_B(f(a), g(a), h(a)) \tag{11}$$

The SA product and the SA function operators are isomorphic to special cases of the general indexed product (*i.e.*, dependent function space) operator.

Definition 3 (SA indexed product operator). *Let I be a set, called the index set, and let P be a mapping from I to separation algebras. Then the indexed product SA is $\langle \Pi x : I.\ P(x), J\rangle$ where J is defined pointwise:*

$$J(f, g, h) \equiv \forall i \in I.\ J_{P(i)}(f(i), g(i), h(i)) \tag{12}$$

What about the disjoint union operator? Can it be constructed? Unfortunately, it cannot. Suppose we have two SAs $\langle A, J_A\rangle$, $\langle B, J_B\rangle$. We would like to define $\langle A + B, J\rangle$ such that J is the smallest relation satisfying:

$$J_A(x, y, z) \to J(inl\ x, inl\ y, inl\ z) \quad \text{for all } x, y, z \in A \tag{13}$$

$$J_B(x, y, z) \to J(inr\ x, inr\ y, inr\ z) \quad \text{for all } x, y, z \in B \tag{14}$$

Here $A + B$ is the disjoint union of A and B with *inl* and *inr* as the left and right injections. This structure cannot be a separation algebra under the original axioms: if u_A and u_B are the units of A and B, then both $inl\ u_A$ and $inr\ u_B$ satisfy $u \oplus u = u$. We noted the unit u is the unique element satisfying this equation, so $inl\ u_A = u = inr\ u_B$. However, this is a contradiction as the injection functions for disjoint union always produce unequal elements. The generalization of disjoint union to the indexed sum fails for the same reason.

One option for dealing with this problem is to use the "almost" disjoint sum, which is the disjoint sum of the nonunit elements together with a single unit. This solution is adequate, but not entirely satisfactory; it combines two distinct operations (the disjoint sum and the combining of units) which are better understood separately. In other words, the construction is not *compositional.*

There is good news, however: we can slightly relax the SA axioms to allow the desired construction. Recall the SA axiom for the existence of a unit:

$$\exists u.\ \forall x.\ u \oplus x = x \tag{9}$$

If we simply swap the order of the quantifiers in this axiom, we get a weaker statement which says that every element of the SA has an associated unit:

$$\forall x.\ \exists u_x.\ u_x \oplus x = x \tag{15}$$

To distinguish these species of separation algebras, we call SAs defined by axioms 5, 6, 7, 8, and 9 *Single-unit Separation Algebras* (SSA), we call SAs defined by axioms 5, 6, 7, 8, and 15 *Multi-unit Separation Algebras* (MSA). Note that axiom 9 implies axiom 15, and thus the SSAs are a strict subset of the MSAs.

Although the relaxation to multiple units is common in the tradition of relevant logic [10], it is significant here because it enables a number of additional operators, including naïve indexed sums and the *discrete* separation algebra.

Definition 4 (MSA indexed sum operator). *Let I be a set, called the index set. Let S be a mapping from I to separation algebras. Then the indexed sum MSA is $\langle \Sigma i : I.\ S(i), J \rangle$ such that J is the least relation satisfying:*

$$J_{S(i)}(x, y, z) \rightarrow J(inj_i(x), inj_i(y), inj_i(z)) \quad \text{for all } i \in I; x, y, z \in S(i) \quad (16)$$

Here inj_i is the injection function associated with i. As with products, if $|I| = 2$, the indexed sum is isomorphic to the disjoint union operator.

Definition 5 (discrete MSA). *Let A be a set. Then the discrete MSA is $\langle A, J \rangle$ where J is defined as the smallest relation satisfying:*

$$J(x, x, x) \quad \text{for all } x \in A \quad (17)$$

The discrete MSA has a join relation that holds only when all three arguments are equal: *every* element of the discrete MSA is a unit. The discrete MSA is useful for constructing MSAs over tuples where only some of the components have interesting joins; the other components can be turned into discrete MSAs. Note the *compositionality* of this construction using the discrete and product operators together. With SSAs, one would instead have to "manually" construct an appropriate tupling operator because the discrete SA is not available.

Sometimes we wish to coerce an MSA into an SSA; the *lifting operator* removes all the units from an MSA and replaces them with a new unique unit.[3]

Definition 6 (MSA lifting operator). *Let $\langle A, J_A \rangle$ be a multi-unit separation algebra. Define A^+ to be the subset of A containing all the nonunit elements, $A^+ = \{x \in A | \neg(x \oplus x = x)\}$. Let $\bot$ be a distinguished element such that $\bot \notin A$. Then the lifting SA is $\langle A^+ \cup \{\bot\}, J \rangle$ where J is the least relation satisfying:*

$$J(\bot, x, x) \quad \text{for all } x \in A^+ \cup \{\bot\} \quad (18)$$

$$J(x, \bot, x) \quad \text{for all } x \in A^+ \cup \{\bot\} \quad (19)$$

$$J_A(x, y, z) \rightarrow J(x, y, z) \quad \text{for all } x, y, z \in A^+ \quad (20)$$

Note that the "almost" disjoint union described above can be constructed using the lifting operator applied to the naïve disjoint sum operator on MSAs. Again compositionality is increased by working with MSAs.

The above operators can construct many kinds of separation algebras. The associated Coq development includes a number of additional operators (*e.g.*, lists, subsets, bijections, etc.) that we have also found useful.

---

[3] Considered as a functor from **MSA** to **SSA**, the lifting operator is left adjoint to the inclusion functor from **SSA** to **MSA**.

Table 1. A model of HBI given a SA

Assume we have a MSA $\langle A, J\rangle$. The following is a model of HBI (a Hilbert-style axiomatization of the logic of bunched implications). `Prop` is the type of Coq propositions, and the right-hand sides are stated in Coq's metalogic.

$$\begin{aligned}
\mathit{formula} &\equiv A \to \texttt{Prop} \\
a \models p &\equiv p(a) \\
p \vdash q &\equiv \forall a.\ a \models p \to a \models q
\end{aligned}$$

$$\begin{aligned}
\top &\equiv \lambda a.\ \texttt{True} \\
\bot &\equiv \lambda a.\ \texttt{False} \\
p \wedge q &\equiv \lambda a.\ a \models p \wedge a \models q \\
p \vee q &\equiv \lambda a.\ a \models p \vee a \models q \\
p \to q &\equiv \lambda a.\ a \models p \to a \models q \\
\mathbf{emp} &\equiv \lambda a.\ a \oplus a = a \\
p * q &\equiv \lambda a.\ \exists a_1.\exists a_2.\ a_1 \oplus a_2 = a \wedge a_1 \models p \wedge a_2 \models q \\
p \mathrel{-\!\!*} q &\equiv \lambda a.\ \forall a_1.\forall a'.\ a_1 \oplus a = a' \to a_1 \models p \to a' \models q
\end{aligned}$$

4 Inducing a Separation Logic

The purpose of a separation algebra is to generate a separation logic, that is, a Hoare-style program logic where the assertion language is the logic of bunched implications (BI). Calcagno et al. demonstrated that their interpretation leads to a Boolean BI algebra, a model of BI. Here we demonstrate that we are still generating models for the desired class of logics despite relaxing the unit axiom.

We too will interpret formulae of separation logic as predicates on the elements of a separation algebra (equivalently, members of the powerset). In Coq we simply define the formulae as `A -> Prop`, where `A` is the type of elements in the MSA, and `Prop` is the type of propositions in Coq's metatheory.

We have chosen to directly link our models to the proof theory of BI by showing[4] a soundness proof with respect to the system HBI, a Hilbert-style axiomatic system for the (propositional) logic of bunched implications [9, Table 2]. The definitions which give rise to HBI are summarized in table 1; they are quite standard, except for the definition of the empty proposition **emp**.

Ordinarily, one defines **emp** as the predicate which accepts only the unit of the SSA. However, by relaxing the unit axiom we allow multiple units, each of which must be characterized. Recall that an MSA is a set of equivalence classes distinguished by unique units, each of which satisfies the equation $u \oplus u = u$. In fact, only units satisfy that equation, so we define **emp** as the predicate that accepts any element x provided that $x \oplus x = x$. This subsumes the ordinary definition in the event that the unit is unique. More importantly, however, from this definition we can prove that **emp** is the unit for separating conjunction.

[4] The accompanying Coq development contains the full set of definitions and proofs.

Thus we see that relaxing the unit axiom does not take us outside the class of models of the logic of bunched implications.

5 Useful Restrictions of SAs

Positivity. Calcagno et al.'s definition of separation algebras [4] permits very strange logics that do not correspond well to the common view that the formulae in separation logic describe resources.

Consider the structure $\langle \{0,1,2\}, +_3 \rangle$, of the integers with addition modulo 3. This structure satisfies the separation algebra axioms given in the previous section and the integer 0 is the unique unit. The problem is that the following holds: $1 +_3 2 = 0$. The resource 1 combines with the resource 2 to give the "empty" resource 0. Stated another way, we can *split* the empty resource 0 to get two *nonempty* resources 1 and 2. By analogy to physics, 1 and 2 act as a resource/antiresource pair that annihilate each other when combined.

This is not at all how one expects resources to behave. If one has, for example, an empty pile of bricks and splits it into two piles, one expects to have two empty piles. One does *not* expect to get one pile of bricks and another pile of antibricks.

The existence of antiresources is particularly troublesome because it interacts badly with the frame rule, a ubiquitous feature of separation logic. A program with no resources can write to memory! Proof: it splits the empty permission, obtaining a write and an anti-write permission. Using the frame rule, it "frames out" the antipermission, giving it the permission to perform a write.

Calcagno et al. resolve this problem by requiring that all actions be "local." The locality condition captures the requirement that actions must be compatible with the frame rule; as a side-effect, the locality condition ensures that any "negative" resources that may exist cannot be used for any interesting purpose. The ultimate consequence is that proving the required locality properties is more difficult (if not impossible) in SAs with negative resources.

We prefer to directly rule out this troublesome class of separation algebras by disallowing negative resources. We require that SAs be *positive* by adding the following positivity axiom:

$$a \oplus b = c \;\rightarrow\; c \oplus c = c \;\rightarrow\; a \oplus a = a \tag{21}$$

That is, whenever two elements join to create a unit element, these joined elements must themselves be units (and hence the same element). This axiom rules out separation algebras such as the addition-modulo-3 example above. Furthermore, this axiom is preserved by the all the SA operators we examined above, which means we have not lost the ground we gained by relaxing the unit axiom.

One of most compelling reasons for including (21) in the axiom base is that all the nontoy SAs known to the authors (that is, those which can be used to reason about some computational system), including all five examples listed by Calcagno et al. [4], satisfy this axiom.[5]

[5] Brotherson and Calcagno [3] investigate *Classical* BI, whose models have *negative*, or *dual*, elements. However, the combination of an element with its dual gives the distinguished element ∞, which is not necessarily the unit, so (21) may still hold.

The positivity axiom also allows us to make a connection to order theory. We define an ordering relation on the elements of a separation algebra:

$$a \preceq b \quad \equiv \quad \exists x.\ a \oplus x = b \tag{22}$$

This relation is reflexive and transitive, which makes it a preorder. The preorder $\preceq$ is antisymmetric, and thus a partial order, if and only if axiom (21) holds.

Disjointness. The *disjointness* property is that no nonempty share joins with itself. If a separation logic over program heaps lacks disjointness then unusual things can happen when defining predicates about inductive data in a program heap. For example, without disjointness, the "obvious" definition of a formula to describe binary trees in fact describes directed acyclic graphs [1].

Disjointness is easy to axiomatize:

$$a \oplus a = b \ \rightarrow \ a = b \tag{23}$$

The disjointness axiom requires that any SA element that joins with itself be a unit. Equivalently, it says that any nonunit element cannot join with itself (is disjoint). This axiom captures the same idea as Parkinson's "disjoint" axiom [8]:

$$\ell \mapsto_s v * \ell \mapsto_s v \ \leftrightarrow \ \text{false} \tag{24}$$

The primary difference is that our axiom is on separation *algebras*, whereas Parkinson's axiom is on separation *logic*.

As with the positivity axiom, the disjointness axiom is preserved by the SA operators presented in the previous section. It also implies positivity. The converse does not hold: disjointness is strictly stronger than positivity.

To see why disjointness (23) implies positivity (21), consider the following proof sketch. Assume $a \oplus b = c$ and $c \oplus c = c$ for some a, b, and c; we wish to show $a \oplus a = a$. Then the following hold (modulo some abuse of notation):

$$\begin{array}{lll}
c \oplus c & = c & \text{assumed} \\
(a \oplus b) \oplus (a \oplus b) & = a \oplus b & \text{subst. } a \oplus b = c \\
(a \oplus a) \oplus (b \oplus b) & = a \oplus b & \text{comm. and assoc.} \\
(a \oplus a) \oplus b & = a \oplus b & \text{disjointness} \\
a \oplus a & = a & \text{cancellation}
\end{array}$$

The converse fails: consider the structure $\langle \mathbb{N}, + \rangle$ of natural numbers with addition. This fulfills the SA axioms, including positivity. However, every natural number $i > 0$ falsifies the disjointness axiom.

Two alternative ways of formulating the disjointness property are inspired by order theory and provide additional insight. First, if $a \oplus b = c$, then any lower bound of a and b is a unit:

$$a \oplus b = c \ \rightarrow \ d \preceq a \ \rightarrow \ d \preceq b \ \rightarrow \ d \oplus d = d \tag{25}$$

Second, $a \oplus b$ is minimal in the following sense:

$$a \oplus b = c \;\rightarrow\; a \preceq d \;\rightarrow\; b \preceq d \;\rightarrow\; d \preceq c \;\rightarrow\; c = d \tag{26}$$

This implies that if a and b join and have a least upper bound, then it is $a \oplus b$.

Cross-split. The alternative formulations of disjointness bring up an interesting point about separation algebras: even for two elements in the same equivalence class, there is no guarantee that either least upper bounds or greatest lower bounds exist. The lack of greatest lower bounds (*i.e.*, intersections), in particular, proved to be troublesome in Hobor et al.'s proof of soundness of a concurrent separation logic for Concurrent C minor [6,5], when they needed to track permissions being transferred between threads. At the time they were using a modified version of Parkinson's share model (discussed below) in which intersections did not always exist. This failure resulted in an unpleasant workaround and spurred development of the alternate model discussed in section 7.

The particular property required was as follows: suppose a single resource can be split in two different ways; then one should be able to divide the original resource into *four* pieces that respect the original splittings.

$$\begin{array}{l} a \oplus b = z \;\wedge\; c \oplus d = z \rightarrow \\ \exists\; ac,\; ad,\; bc,\; bd. \\ \quad ac \oplus ad = a \;\wedge\; bc \oplus bd = b \;\wedge \\ \quad ac \oplus bc = c \quad\wedge\; ad \oplus bd = d \end{array} \tag{27}$$

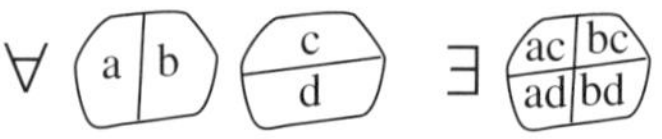

That is, if an element can be split in two different ways, then there should be four subelements that partition the original element and respect the splittings. We call this property the cross-split axiom and, as with positivity and disjointness, this property is preserved by the separation algebra operators.[6]

Splittability. Another frequently desirable property of SAs is *infinite splittability*, which is a useful property for reasoning about the kinds of resource sharing that occur in divide-and-conquer style computations. Splittability means that we can take any element of the SA and split it into two pieces that recombine into the original. To avoid degenerate splittings, both the split pieces must be nonempty if the original was nonempty. Thus, a SA is infinitely splittable if there exists a function `split` that calculates such a splitting.

$$\texttt{split}\ x = (x_1, x_2) \;\rightarrow\; x_1 \oplus x_2 = x \tag{28}$$

$$\texttt{split}\ x = (x_1, x_2) \;\rightarrow\; x_1 \oplus x_1 = x_1 \rightarrow x \oplus x = x \tag{29}$$

$$\texttt{split}\ x = (x_1, x_2) \;\rightarrow\; x_2 \oplus x_2 = x_2 \rightarrow x \oplus x = x \tag{30}$$

There are reasonable separation logics that have models where disjointness, cross-split, and/or infinite splittability are false. We present these axioms because we (and others such as Parkinson) found them useful in separation logic

[6] To pull an intersection property through the lifting operator, one needs to apply lifts only where there is a computable test for units, or use the axiom of description.

proofs and metaproofs, and because any separation algebra built with our operator calculus can inherit them for free if desired. In contrast, every nontoy separation algebra used for reasoning about computational systems and known to the authors satisfies the positivity axiom (21). In our own work we find that adding the disjointness axiom (which implies positivity) to the SA axiom base to be quite convenient and suggest that "disjoint" MSAs, defined by axioms 5, 6, 7, 8, 15 and 23, are very natural structures for reasoning in this domain.

6 Shares

An important application of separation algebras is to model Hoare logics of programming languages with mutable memory. We generate an appropriate separation logic by choosing the correct semantic model, that is, the correct separation algebra. A natural choice is to simply take the program heaps as the elements of the separation algebra together with some appropriate join relation.

In most of the early work in this direction, heaps were modeled as partial functions from addresses to values. In those models, two heaps join iff their domains are disjoint, the result being the union of the two heaps. However, this simple model is too restrictive, especially when one considers concurrency. It rules out useful and interesting protocols where two or more threads agree to share *read* permission to an area of memory.

There are a number of different ways to do the necessary permission accounting. Bornat et al. [1] present two different methods; one based on fractional permissions, and another based on token counting. Parkinson, in chapter 5 of his thesis [8], presents a more sophisticated system capable of handling both methods. However, this model has some drawbacks, which we shall address below.

Fractional permissions are used to handle the accounting situations that arise from concurrent divide-and-conquer algorithms. In such algorithms, a worker thread has read-only permission to the dataset and it needs to divide this permission among various child threads. When a child thread finishes, it returns its permission to its parent. Child threads, in turn, may need to split their permissions among their own children and so on. In order to handle any possible pattern of divide-and-conquer, splitting must be possible to an unbounded depth.

The token-counting method is intended to handle the accounting problem that arises from reader-writer locks. When a reader acquires a lock, it receives a "share token," which it will later return when it unlocks. The lock tracks the number of active readers with an integer counter that is incremented when a reader locks and decremented when a reader unlocks. When the reader count is positive there are outstanding read tokens; when it is zero there are no outstanding readers and a writer may acquire the lock.

Here we will show how each of the above accounting systems arises from the choice of a "share model," and we present our own share model which can handle both accounting methods and avoids a pitfall found in Parkinson's model.

Suppose we have a separation algebra $\langle S, J_S \rangle$ of *shares*. If L and V are sets of addresses and values, respectively, we can define a SA over heaps as follows:

$$H \equiv L \rightarrow (S \times V_=)_\perp \tag{31}$$

This equation is quite concise but conceals some subtle points. The operators in this equation are the operators on SAs defined in § 3. We let $V_=$ be the "discrete" MSA over values (i.e., values V with the trivial join relation) and $S \times V_=$ is the MSA over pairs of shares and values.Next we construct the "lifted" SSA $(S \times V_=)_\perp$, which removes the unit values and adds a new, distinguished unit $\perp$. This requires values to be paired only with nonunit shares. Finally, $L \rightarrow (S \times V_=)_\perp$ builds the function space SSA. Thus, heaps are partial functions from locations to pairs of nonunit shares and values.[7]

Now we can define the points-to operator of separation logic as:

$$\ell \mapsto_s v \equiv \lambda h.\ h(\ell) = (s, v) \wedge (\forall \ell'. \ell \neq \ell' \rightarrow h(\ell') = \perp) \tag{32}$$

Here, $\ell \in L$ is an address, $v \in V$ is a value, and $s \in S^+$ is a nonunit share. In English, $\ell \mapsto_s v$ means "the memory location at address ℓ contains v, I have share s at this location, and I have no permission at any other locations." Now the exact behavior of the points-to operator depends only on the share model S.

An important property of this definition is that the separation algebra on shares lifts in a straightforward way through the separation logic:

$$s_1 \oplus s_2 = s \leftrightarrow (\ell \mapsto_s v \leftrightarrow \ell \mapsto_{s_1} v * \ell \mapsto_{s_2} v) \tag{33}$$

Thus we can use properties of our share model in the separation logic.

We can produce a separation logic very similar to the ones studied by Reynolds [11] and by Ishtiaq and O'Hearn [7] by choosing S to be the SA over Booleans with the smallest join relation such that "false" is the unique unit.

Definition 7 (Boolean shares). *The Boolean share model is* $\langle \{\circ, \bullet\}, J \rangle$ *where* J *is the least relation satisfying* $J(\circ, x, x)$ *and* $J(x, \circ, x)$ *for all* $x \in \{\circ, \bullet\}$.

Here $\circ$ and $\bullet$ stand for "false" and "true", respectively. This share model is unsophisticated: one either has unrestricted permission or no permission at all. Note that the lifting operator removes $\circ$, leaving $\bullet$ as the only legal annotation. This justifies omitting the annotation, resulting in the more familiar $\ell \mapsto v$.

Boyland proposed a model which takes shares as fractions in the interval $[0, 1]$ as shares [2]. Although Boyland works in the reals, the rationals suffice.

Definition 8 (Fractional shares). *The fractional share model is* $\langle [0, 1] \cap \mathbb{Q}, + \rangle$ *where* $+$ *is the restriction of addition to a partial operation on* $[0, 1]$.

The main advantage of the fractional share model is that it is infinitely splittable. The splitting function is simple: to split a share s, let $s_1 = s_2 = s/2$. The fractional share model satisfies the positivity axiom but not the disjointness axiom, which leads to the problems noticed by Bornat et al. [1, §13.1].

Bornat et al. also examined the *token factory* model, where a central authority starts with total ownership and then lends out permission tokens. The authority

[7] Our heaps are quite similar those defined by Bornat et al. [1, §10.1]. Their "partial commutative semigroup" of shares arises here from the nonunit elements of a SA.

counts the outstanding tokens; when the count is zero, all have returned. A slight modification of Bornat's construction yields a suitable model:

Definition 9 (Counting shares). *The counting share model is $\langle \mathbb{Z} \cup \{\bot\}, J\rangle$ where J is defined as the least relation satisfying:*

$$J(\bot, x, x) \quad \text{for all } x \in \mathbb{Z} \cup \{\bot\} \tag{34}$$

$$J(x, \bot, x) \quad \text{for all } x \in \mathbb{Z} \cup \{\bot\} \tag{35}$$

$$(x < 0 \vee y < 0) \wedge ((x + y \geq 0) \vee (x < 0 \wedge y < 0)) \rightarrow J(x, y, x + y) \quad \text{for all } x, y \in \mathbb{Z} \tag{36}$$

This definition sets up the nonnegative integers as token factories and negative integers as tokens. To absorb a token back into a factory, the integers are simply added. The token factory has collected all its tokens when its share is zero. Like the fractional model, the counting model satisfies positivity but not disjointness.

This share model validates the following logical axioms:

$$\ell \mapsto_n v \quad \leftrightarrow \quad (\ell \mapsto_{n+m} v * \ell \mapsto_{-m} v) \quad \text{for } n \geq 0 \text{ and } m > 0 \tag{37}$$

$$\ell \mapsto_{-(n+m)} v \quad \leftrightarrow \quad (\ell \mapsto_{-n} v * \ell \mapsto_{-m} v) \quad \text{for } n, m > 0 \tag{38}$$

$$(\ell \mapsto_0 v * \ell \mapsto_n v) \quad \leftrightarrow \quad \text{false} \tag{39}$$

Equation (37) says that a token factory with n tokens outstanding can be split into a token (of size m) and a new factory, which has $n + m$ tokens outstanding. Furthermore the operation is reversable: a token and its factory can be recombined to get a factory with fewer outstanding tokens. Equation (38) says that the tokens themselves may be split and merged. Finally, equation (39) says that it is impossible to have both a full token factory (with no outstanding tokens) and any other share of the same location (whether a factory or a token).

If one only utilizes tokens of size one, then equations (37)–(39) describe the sorts of share manipulations required for a standard reader-writer lock. Other token sizes allow more subtle locking protocols where, for example, one thread may acquire the read tokens of several others and release them all at once.

In his thesis, Parkinson defines a more sophisticated share model that can support both the splitting and the token counting use cases.

Definition 10 (Parkinson's named shares). *Parkinson's named share model is given by $\langle \mathcal{P}(\mathbb{N}), \uplus\rangle$, where $\mathcal{P}(\mathbb{N})$ is the set of subsets of the natural numbers and $\uplus$ is disjoint union.*[8]

This model satisfies the disjointness axiom, and thus positivity. It also satisfies the cross-split axiom: the required subshares are calculated by set intersection.

In order to support the token-counting use case, Parkinson considers the finite and cofinite subsets of $\mathbb{N}$. These sets can be related to the counting model given above by considering the cardinality of the set (or set complement, for cofinite sets). We will see the details of this embedding later.

[8] That is, the union of disjoint sets rather than discriminated union.

Unfortunately, this share model is not infinitely splittable, since there is no way to split a singleton set into two nonempty subsets. Therefore we cannot define a total function which calculates the splitting of a share in this model, and this makes it difficult to support the parallel divide-and-conquer use case.

We can fix this problem by restricting the model to include only the *infinite* subsets of $\mathbb{N}$ (and the empty set). We can split an infinite set s by enumerating its elements and generating s_1 from those in even positions and s_2 from the those in odd positions. Then s_1 and s_2 are infinite, disjoint, and partition s.

Unfortunately, restricting to infinite subsets means that we cannot use finite and cofinite sets to model token counting. This problem can be solved, at the cost of some complication, with an embedding into the infinite sets [8].

The problem with *that* solution is that the infinite subsets of $\mathbb{N}$ are also not closed under set intersection, which means the share model no longer satisfies the cross split axiom. To see why this axiom fails, consider splitting $\mathbb{N}$ into the primes/nonprimes and the even/odd numbers. All four sets are infinite, but the set $\{2\}$ of even primes is finite and thus not in the share model.

Hobor suggested further restricting the model by reasoning about equivalence classes of subsets of $\mathbb{N}$, where two subsets are equivalent when their symmetric difference is finite; but developing this model in Coq was difficult [5].

We will present a new model with all the right properties: disjointness axiom, cross-split axiom, infinitely splittable, supports token counting, and is straightforward to represent in a theorem prover. As a bonus, we also achieve a decidable test for share equality.

7 Binary Tree Share Model

Before giving the explicit construction of our share model, we shall take a short detour to show how we can induce a separation algebra from a lattice.

Definition 11 (Lattice SA). *Let $\langle A, \sqsubseteq, \sqcap, \sqcup, 0, 1\rangle$ be a bounded distributive lattice. Then, $\langle A, J\rangle$ is a separation algebra where J is defined as:*

$$J(x, y, z) \quad \equiv \quad x \sqcup y = z \ \wedge \ x \sqcap y = 0 \tag{40}$$

Disjointness follows from the right conjunct of the join relation; cross split follows from the existence of greatest lower bounds. It also has a unique unit, 0.

It is interesting to note that all of the share models we have examined thus far that satisfy the disjointness axiom are instances of this general construction.[9] The Boolean share model is just the lattice SA derived from the canonical 2-element Boolean algebra, and Parkinson's model (without the restriction to infinite subsets) is the separation algebra derived from the powerset Boolean algebra. Restricting Parkinson's model to infinite sets as described above buys the ability to do infinite splitting at the price of destroying part of the structure of the lattice. Below we show that paying this price is unnecessary.

---

[9] This is not *necessarily* so. There exist disjoint SAs which are not distributive lattices.

If the structure is additionally a Boolean algebra, then we can make the following pleasant connection:

$$x \preceq y \;\leftrightarrow\; x \sqsubseteq y \tag{41}$$

That is, the lattice order coincides with the SA order. The forward direction holds for any bounded distributive lattice. The backward direction relies on the complement operator to construct the witness $(\neg x \sqcap y)$ for the existential quantifier in the definition of $\preceq$. Any bounded distributive lattice satisfying (41) is a Boolean algebra; the witness of $\preceq$ gives the complement for x when $y = 1$.

Trees. Now we can restate our goal; we wish to construct a bounded distributive lattice which supports splitting and token counting. This means we must support a splitting function and we must be able to embed the finite and cofinite subsets of the naturals. We can build a model of shares supporting all these operations by starting with a very simple data structure: the humble binary tree. We consider binary trees with Boolean-valued leaves and unlabeled internal nodes.

$$\tau ::= \circ \mid \bullet \mid \widehat{\tau\;\tau} \tag{42}$$

We use an empty circle $\circ$ to represent a "false" leaf and the filled circle $\bullet$ to represent a "true" leaf. Thus $\bullet$ is a tree with a single leaf, $\widehat{\circ\,\bullet}$ is a tree with one internal node and two leaves, etc.

We define the ordering on trees as the least relation $\sqsubseteq$ satisfying:

$$\circ \sqsubseteq \circ \tag{43}$$

$$\circ \sqsubseteq \bullet \tag{44}$$

$$\bullet \sqsubseteq \bullet \tag{45}$$

$$\circ \cong \widehat{\circ\;\circ} \tag{46}$$

$$\bullet \cong \widehat{\bullet\;\bullet} \tag{47}$$

$$x_1 \sqsubseteq x_2 \quad\rightarrow\quad y_1 \sqsubseteq y_2 \quad\rightarrow\quad \widehat{x_1\;y_1} \sqsubseteq \widehat{x_2\;y_2} \tag{48}$$

Here, $x \cong y$ is defined as $x \sqsubseteq y \wedge y \sqsubseteq x$. The intuitive meaning is that $x \sqsubseteq y$ holds iff x has a $\circ$ in at least every position y does once we expand leaf nodes using the congruence rules until the trees are the same shape. The congruence rules allow us to "fold up" any subtree which has the same label on all its leaves.

This relation is reflexive and transitive; however it is not antisymmetric because of the structural congruence rules. We can get around this by working only with the "canonical" trees. A tree is canonical if it is the tree with the fewest nodes in the equivalence class generated by $\cong$. Canonical trees always exist and are unique, and the ordering relation is antisymmetric on the domain of canonical trees. Therefore we can build a partial order using the canonical Boolean-labeled binary trees with the above ordering relation.

The details of canonicalization are straightforward but tedious, so we will work informally up to congruence. In the formal Coq development, however, we give a full account of canonicalization and show all the required properties. The short story is that we normalize trees after every operation by finding and reducing all the subtrees which can be reduced by one of the congruence rules.

Our next task is to implement the lattice operations. The trees ∘ and • are the least and greatest element of the partial order, respectively. The least upper bound of two trees is calculated as the pointwise disjunction of Booleans (expanding the trees as necessary to make them the same shape). For example,  $\sqcup$ 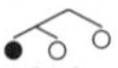 $\cong$  $\sqcup$  $\cong$  $\cong$ . Likewise, the greatest lower bound is found by pointwise conjunction, so that  $\sqcap$  $\cong$  $\sqcap$ 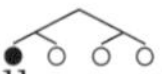 $\cong$  $\cong$ 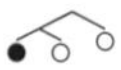. Finally, this structure is a Boolean algebra as well as a distributive lattice, and the complement operation is pointwise Boolean complement: $\neg$  $\cong$ . The Boolean algebra axioms can be verified by simple inductive arguments over the structure of the trees.

We can also define a decidable test for equality by simply checking structural equality of trees. Trees form a lattice, and thus a decision procedure for equality also yields a test for the lattice order. In contrast, Parkinson's model over arbitrary subsets of $\mathbb{N}$ lacks both decidable equality and decidable ordering.

In addition to the lattice operations, we require an operation to split trees. Given some tree s, we wish to find two trees s_1 and s_2 such that $s_1 \sqcup s_2 \cong s$ and $s_1 \sqcap s_2 \cong \circ$ and both $s_1 \not\cong \circ$ and $s_2 \not\cong \circ$ provided that $s \not\cong \circ$. We can calculate s_1 and s_2 by recursively replacing each • leaf in s with  and  respectively.

We can usefully generalize this procedure by defining the "relativization" operator $x \bowtie y$, which replaces every • leaf in x with the tree y. This operator is associative with identity •. It distributes over $\sqcup$ and $\sqcap$ on the left, and is injective for non-∘ arguments.

$$x \bowtie \bullet = x = \bullet \bowtie x \tag{49}$$

$$x \bowtie \circ = \circ = \circ \bowtie x \tag{50}$$

$$x \bowtie (y \bowtie z) = (x \bowtie y) \bowtie z \tag{51}$$

$$x \bowtie (y \sqcup z) = (x \bowtie y) \sqcup (x \bowtie z) \tag{52}$$

$$x \bowtie (y \sqcap z) = (x \bowtie y) \sqcap (x \bowtie z) \tag{53}$$

$$x \bowtie y_1 = x \bowtie y_2 \rightarrow x = \circ \vee y_1 = y_2 \tag{54}$$

$$x_1 \bowtie y = x_2 \bowtie y \rightarrow x_1 = x_2 \vee y = \circ \tag{55}$$

Given this operator, we can more succinctly define the split of x as returning the pair containing $x \bowtie$  and $x \bowtie$ . The required splitting properties follow easily from this definition and the above properties of $\bowtie$.

If this were the only use of the relativization, however, it would hardly be worthwhile to define it. Instead, the main purpose of this operator is to allow us to glue together arbitrary methods for partitioning permissions. In particular, we can split or perform token counting on any nonempty permission we obtain, no matter how it was originally generated. In addition, we only have to concentrate on how to perform accounting of the full permission • because we can let the $\bowtie$ operator handle relativizing to some other permission of interest.

Following Parkinson, we will consider finite and cofinite sets of the natural numbers to support token counting. This structure has several nice properties. First, it is closed under set intersection, set union and set complement and it contains $\mathbb{N}$ and $\emptyset$; in other words, it forms a sub-Boolean algebra of the powerset Boolean algebra over $\mathbb{N}$. Furthermore the cardinalities of these sets can be mapped to the integers in following way:

$$[\![p]\!]_{\mathbb{Z}} = \begin{cases} -|p| & \text{when } p \text{ is finite and nonempty} \\ |\mathbb{N} \backslash p| & \text{when } p \text{ is cofinite} \end{cases} \tag{56}$$

The cardinalities of disjoint (co)finite sets combine in exactly the way defined by the counting share model (equation 36).

We can embed the (co)finite subsets of $\mathbb{N}$ into our binary tree model by encoding the sets as right-biased trees[10] (trees where the left subtree of each internal node is always a leaf). Such trees form a list of Booleans together with one extra Boolean, the rightmost leaf in the tree. Then the ith Boolean in the list encodes whether the natural number i is in the set. The final terminating Boolean stands for all the remaining naturals. If it is $\circ$, the set is finite and does not contain the remaining naturals, and if it is $\bullet$ the set is infinite and contains all the remaining naturals. This interpretation is consistent with the congruence rules that allow you to unfold the rightmost terminating Boolean into a arbitrarily long list of the same Boolean value.

For example, the finite set $\{0, 2\}$ is encoded in tree form as . The coset $\mathbb{N}\backslash\{0, 2\}$ is encoded as 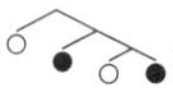. And, of course,  $\oplus$  $= \bullet$.

This encoding is in fact a Boolean algebra homomorphism; GLBs, LUBs, complements and the top and bottom elements are preserved. This homomorphism allows us to transport the token counting results on (co)finite sets to binary trees. We write $[\![p]\!]_{\mathcal{T}} = s$ when s is the tree encoding the (co)finite set p.

Now we can define a more sophisticated points-to operator which allows us to incorporate token counting along with permission splitting.

$$\ell \mapsto_{s,n} v \equiv \lambda h.\ \exists p.\ h(\ell) = (s \bowtie [\![p]\!]_{\mathcal{T}}, v) \wedge [\![p]\!]_{\mathbb{Z}} = n \wedge \forall \ell'. \ell \neq \ell' \rightarrow h(\ell') = \bot \tag{57}$$

Then $\ell \mapsto_{s,n} v$ means that ℓ contains value v and we have a portion of the permission s indexed by n. If n is zero, we have all of s. If n is positive, we have a token factory over s with n tokens missing, and if n is negative, we have a token of s (of size $-n$).

This points-to operator satisfies the following logical axioms:

$$(\ell \mapsto_{s,0} v * \ell \mapsto_{s,n} v) \quad \leftrightarrow \quad \text{false} \tag{58}$$

$$s_1 \oplus s_2 = s \quad \rightarrow \quad ((\ell \mapsto_{s_1,0} v * \ell \mapsto_{s_2,0} v) \quad \leftrightarrow \quad \ell \mapsto_{s,0} v) \tag{59}$$

$$n_1 \oplus n_2 = n \quad \rightarrow \quad ((\ell \mapsto_{s,n_1} v * \ell \mapsto_{s,n_2} v) \quad \leftrightarrow \quad \ell \mapsto_{s,n} v) \tag{60}$$

$$\ell \mapsto_{s,n} v \quad \rightarrow \quad \exists! s'.\ \ell \mapsto_{s,n} v \quad \leftrightarrow \quad \ell \mapsto_{s',0} v \tag{61}$$

[10] We could just as well have used left-biased trees.

Equation (58) generalizes both the disjointness axiom from Parkinson (24) and the disjointness axiom for token factories (39). Likewise, equation (59) generalizes the share axiom (33). Essentially, if we fix $n = 0$ we get back the simpler definition of the points-to operator from above as a special case. In equation (60), $n_1 \oplus n_2 = n$ refers to the token counting join relation on integers defined in equation 36, and this axiom generalizes the token factory axioms (37) and (38). Both of those axioms follow as a special case when we fix $s = \top$. Finally, equation (61) allows one to project a tokenized share into a nontokenized share (one where $n = 0$). This might be useful if one needs to perform share splitting on a share which was derived from a token factory, for example.

This collection of axioms allow fluid reasoning about both the token-counting and splitting use cases, which enables a unified way to do flexible and precise permission accounting.

8 Conclusion

We have presented a new formulation of multi-unit separation algebras which we find easier to use than the original definition by Calcagno et al. [4]. The original definition is both too restrictive (it rules out desirable constructions, including the naïve disjoint sum and the discrete SA) and too permissive (it allows badly-behaved "exotic" SAs). We examined a variety of operators over separation algebras that allow us to easily construct complicated separation algebras from simpler ones, and have shown an example of their utility.

We have also constructed a new solution to the share accounting problem. Our share model based on Boolean-labeled binary trees fully supports both the splitting and token counting use cases for read sharing, and yet still validates the cross split axiom; it also enjoys a decidable equality test. No previously published system for share accounting has all these properties. Parkinson's model [8] comes closest, but suffers from the inability to find splittings for some shares and lacks decidable equality.

We have implemented the constructions discussed in this paper and proved their relevant properties using the proof assistant Coq.[3]

References

1. Bornat, R., Calcagno, C., O'Hearn, P., Parkinson, M.: Permission accounting in separation logic. In: POPL 2005: Proc. of the 32nd ACM SIGPLAN-SIGACT Symp. on Principles of Programming Languages, pp. 259–270 (2005)
2. Boyland, J.: Checking interference with fractional permissions. In: Cousot, R. (ed.) SAS 2003. LNCS, vol. 2694, pp. 55–72. Springer, Heidelberg (2003)
3. Brotherston, J., Calcagno, C.: Classical BI: a logic for reasoning about dualising resources. In: POPL 2009: Proc. of the 36th ACM SIGPLAN-SIGACT Symp. on Principles of Programming Languages, pp. 328–339 (2009)
4. Calcagno, C., O'Hearn, P.W., Yang, H.: Local action and abstract separation logic. In: LICS 2007: Proceedings of the 22nd IEEE Symp. on Logic in Computer Science, pp. 366–378 (2007)

5. Hobor, A.: Oracle Semantics. PhD thesis, Princeton University (2008)
6. Hobor, A., Appel, A.W., Zappa Nardelli, F.: Oracle semantics for concurrent separation logic. In: Drossopoulou, S. (ed.) ESOP 2008. LNCS, vol. 4960, pp. 353–367. Springer, Heidelberg (2008)
7. Ishtiaq, S.S., O'Hearn, P.W.: BI as an assertion language for mutable data structures. In: POPL 2001: Proc. of the 28th ACM SIGPLAN-SIGACT Symposium on Principles of Programming Languages, pp. 14–26 (2001)
8. Parkinson, M.: Local Reasoning for Java. PhD thesis, Univ. of Cambridge (2005)
9. Pym, D.J., O'Hearn, P.W., Yang, H.: Possible worlds and resources: the semantics of BI. Theor. Comput. Sci. 315(1), 257–305 (2004)
10. Restall, G.: An Introduction to Substructural Logics. Routledge, London (2000)
11. Reynolds, J.C.: Separation logic: A logic for shared mutable data structures. In: LICS 2002: Proc. of the 17th Annual IEEE Symp. on Logic in Computer Science, pp. 55–74 (2002)

Weak Updates and Separation Logic

Gang Tan[1], Zhong Shao[2], Xinyu Feng[3], and Hongxu Cai[4]

[1] Lehigh University
[2] Yale University
[3] Toyota Technological Institute at Chicago
[4] Google Inc.

Abstract. Separation Logic (SL) provides a simple but powerful technique for reasoning about imperative programs that use shared data structures. Unfortunately, SL supports only "strong updates", in which mutation to a heap location is safe only if a unique reference is owned. This limits the applicability of SL when reasoning about the interaction between many high-level languages (e.g., ML, Java, C#) and low-level ones since these high-level languages do not support strong updates. Instead, they adopt the discipline of "weak updates", in which there is a global "heap type" to enforce the invariant of type-preserving heap updates. We present SL^W, a logic that extends SL with reference types and elegantly reasons about the interaction between strong and weak updates. We also describe a semantic framework for reference types; this framework is used to prove the soundness of SL^W.

1 Introduction

Reasoning about mutable, aliased heap data structures is essential for proving properties or checking safety of imperative programs. Two distinct approaches perform such kind of reasoning: Separation Logic, and a type-based approach employed by many high-level programming languages.

Extending Hoare Logic, the seminal work of Separation Logic (SL [10, 13]) is a powerful framework for proving properties of low-level imperative programs. Through its separating conjunction operator and frame rule, SL supports local reasoning about heap updates, storage allocation, and explicit storage deallocation.

SL supports "strong updates": as long as a unique reference to a heap cell is owned, the heap-update rule of SL allows the cell to be updated with any value:

$$\overline{\{(e \mapsto -) * \mathtt{p}\}[e] := e'\{(e \mapsto e') * \mathtt{p}\}} \quad (1)$$

In the above heap-update rule, there is no restriction on the new value e'. Hereafter, we refer to heaps with strong updates as *strong heaps*. Heap cells in strong heaps can hold values of different types at different times of program execution.

Most high-level programming languages (e.g., Java, C#, and ML), however, support only "weak updates". In this paradigm, programs can perform only type-preserving heap updates. There is a global "heap type" that tells the type of every allocated heap location. The contents at a location have to obey the prescribed type of the location in

Z. Hu (Ed.): APLAS 2009, LNCS 5904, pp. 178–193, 2009.

the heap type, at any time. Managing heaps with weak updates is a simple and type-safe mechanism for programmers to access memory. As an example, suppose an ML variable has type "τ ref" (i.e., it is a reference to a value of type τ). Then any update through this reference with a new value of type τ is type safe and does not affect other types, even in the presence of aliases and complicated points-to relations. Hereafter, we refer to heaps with weak updates as *weak heaps*.

This paper is concerned with the interaction between strong and weak updates. Strong-update techniques are more precise and powerful, allowing destructive memory updates and explicit deallocation. But aliases and uniqueness have to be explicitly tracked. Weak-update techniques allow type-safe management of memory without tracking aliases, but types of memory cells can never change. A framework that mixes strong and weak updates enables a trade-off between precision and scalability.

Such a framework is also useful for reasoning about *multilingual programs*. Most real-world programs are developed in multiple programming languages. Almost all high-level languages provide foreign function interfaces for interfacing with low-level C code (for example, the OCaml/C FFI, and the Java Native Interface). Real-world programs consist of a mixture of code in both high-level and low-level languages. A runtime state for such a program conceptually contains a union of a weak heap and a strong heap. The weak heap is managed by a high-level language (e.g., Java), accepts type-preserving heap updates, and is garbage-collected. The strong heap is managed by a low-level language, accepts strong updates, and its heap cells are manually recollected. To check the safety and correctness of multilingual programs, it is of practical value to have one framework that accommodates both strong and weak updates.

Since Separation Logic (SL) supports strong heaps, one natural thought to mix strong and weak updates is to extend SL with types so that assertions can also describe weak heaps. That is, in addition to regular SL assertions, we add $\{e \mapsto \tau\}$, which specifies a heap with a single cell and the cell holds a value of type τ. This scheme, however, would encounter two challenges.

First, allowing general reference types in $\{e \mapsto \tau\}$ would make SL unsound. An example demonstrating this point is as follows:

$$\{\{x \mapsto 4\} * \{y \mapsto \text{even ref}\}\}\ [x] := 3\ \{\{x \mapsto 3\} * \{y \mapsto \text{even ref}\}\} \tag{2}$$

The example is an instantiation of the heap-update rule in (1) and uses the additional assertion $\{e \mapsto \tau\}$. The precondition states that y points to a heap cell whose contents are of type "even ref" (i.e., a reference to an even integer). Therefore, the precondition is met on a heap where y points to x. However, the postcondition will not hold on the new heap after the update because x will point to an odd number. Therefore, the above rule is sound only if y does not point to x.

The second challenge of adding types to SL is how to prove its soundness with mixed SL assertions and types. Type systems are usually proved sound following a syntactic approach [19], where types are treated as syntax. Following the tradition of Hoare Logic, SL's soundness is proved through a denotational model, and SL assertions are interpreted semantically. There is a need to resolve the conflict between syntactic and semantic soundness proofs.

In this paper, we propose a hybrid logic, SL^W, which mixes SL and a type system. Although the logic is described in a minimal language and type system, it makes a solid

$$\begin{array}{rrcl} (\mathit{Command}) & c & ::= & \cdots \mid x := [e] \mid [x] := e \mid x := \mathsf{alloc}(e) \mid \mathsf{free}(e) \\ (\mathit{Expression}) & e & ::= & x \mid v \mid op(e_1, \ldots, e_n) \\ (\mathit{Value}) & v & ::= & n \mid \ell \end{array}$$

Fig. 1. Language syntax

step toward a framework that reasons about the interaction between high-level and low-level languages. The most significant technical aspects of the logic are as follows:

- SL^W extends SL with a simple type system. It employs SL for reasoning about strong updates, and employs the type system for weak updates. Most interestingly, SL^W mixes SL assertions and types, and accommodates cross-boundary pointers (from weak to strong heaps and vice versa). This is achieved by statically maintaining the distinction between pointers to weak heaps and pointers to strong heaps. SL^W is presented in Section 2.
- To resolve the conflict between syntactic types and semantic assertions, we propose a semantic model of types. Our model of reference types follows a fixed-point approach and allows us to define a denotational model of SL^W and prove its soundness. The model of SL^W is presented in Section 3.

2 SL^W: Separation Logic with Weak Updates

We next describe SL^W, an extension of SL that incorporates reasoning over weak heaps. In Section 2.1, we describe a minimal language that enables us to develop SL^W. Rules of SL^W are presented in Section 2.2 and examples of using the logic in Section 2.3.

We first describe some common notations. For a map f, we write $f[x \rightsquigarrow y]$ for a new map that agrees with f except it maps x to y. For two finite maps f_1 and f_2, $f_1 \uplus f_2$ is the union of f_1 and f_2 when their domains are disjoint, and undefined otherwise. We write $f \setminus X$ for a new map after removing elements in X from the domain of f. We write $\vec{x}$ for a sequence of xs and ε for an empty sequence.

2.1 Language Syntax and Semantics

Figure 1 presents the syntax of the programming language in which we will develop SL^W. The language is the imperative language used by Hoare [6], augmented with a set of commands for manipulating heap data structures. It is similar to the one used in Reynolds' presentation of SL [13]. Informally, the command "$x := [e]$" loads the contents at location e into variable x; "$[x] := e$" updates the location at x with the value e; "$x := \mathsf{alloc}(e)$" allocates a new location, initializes it with e, and assigns the new location to x; "$\mathsf{free}(e)$" deallocates the location e.

In the syntax, we use n for integers, x for variables, ℓ for heap locations, and op for arithmetic operators. We assume there is an infinite number of variables and locations.

Figure 2 presents a formal operational semantics of the language. A state consists of a map $\mathtt{r}$ from variables to values, a heap h, and a sequence of commands. Commands bring one state to another state and their semantics is formally defined by a step relation $\longmapsto$. We write $\longmapsto^*$ for the reflexive and transitive closure of $\longmapsto$.

$$\begin{array}{lll}
(State) & s & ::= (\mathtt{r}, h, \vec{c}) \\
(Locals) & \mathtt{r} & ::= Var \rightarrow Value \\
(Heap) & h & ::= \{\ell_1 \mapsto v_1, \ldots, \ell_n \mapsto v_n\}
\end{array}$$

$(\mathtt{r}, h, c \cdot \vec{c_1}) \longmapsto (\mathtt{r}_2, h_2, \vec{c_2})$		
if $c =$	then $(\mathtt{r}_2, h_2, \vec{c_2}) =$	
...	...	
$x := [e]$	$(\mathtt{r}[x \rightsquigarrow h(\ell)], h, \vec{c_1})$	when $\mathtt{r}(e) = \ell$ and $\ell \in \mathrm{dom}(h)$
$[x] := e$	$(\mathtt{r}, h[\ell \rightsquigarrow \mathtt{r}(e)], \vec{c_1})$	when $\mathtt{r}(x) = \ell$ and $\ell \in \mathrm{dom}(h)$
$x :=$ alloc(e)	$(\mathtt{r}[x \rightsquigarrow \ell], h \uplus \{\ell \mapsto \mathtt{r}(e)\}, \vec{c_1})$	when $\ell \notin \mathrm{dom}(h)$
free(e)	$(\mathtt{r}, h \setminus \{\ell\}, \vec{c_1})$	when $\mathtt{r}(e) = \ell$ and $\ell \in \mathrm{dom}(h)$

$$\text{where } \mathtt{r}(e) = \begin{cases} \mathtt{r}(x) & \text{when } e = x \\ v & \text{when } e = v \\ op(\mathtt{r}(e_1), \ldots, \mathtt{r}(e_n)) & \text{when } e = op(e_1, \ldots, e_n) \end{cases}$$

Fig. 2. Operational semantics

A state may have no next state, i.e., "getting stuck". For example, a state whose next instruction to execute is $[x] := e$ gets stuck when x does not represent a location or the location is not in the domain of the state's heap. A state is a terminal state when the sequence of commands is empty.

Definition 1. *(Stuck and terminal states)*

$$\begin{array}{ll}
\mathrm{stuck}(s) & \triangleq \neg(\exists s'.\, s \longmapsto s') \\
\mathrm{terminal}(r, h, \vec{c}) & \triangleq \vec{c} = \varepsilon
\end{array}$$

Below we define the usual notions of safety and termination:

Definition 2. *(Safety and termination)*

$$\mathrm{safe}(s) \triangleq \forall s'.\, \left((s \longmapsto^* s') \wedge \neg\mathrm{terminal}(s')\right) \Rightarrow \exists s''.\, s' \longmapsto s''$$

$$\mathrm{terminate}(s) \triangleq \forall s'.\, s \longmapsto^* s' \Rightarrow \exists s''.\, s' \longmapsto^* s'' \wedge \mathrm{terminal}(s'')$$

2.2 The Logic SL^{W}

Figure 3 presents assertions and types used in SL^{W}. Assertions in SL^{W} include all formulas in predicate calculus (not shown in the figure), and all SL formulas. The only additional assertion form in SL^{W} is $\{e : \tau\}$, which denotes that e has type τ.

SL^{W} is equipped with a simple type system that classifies integers and locations. Although the type system does not include many types in high-level languages, by including reference types it is already sufficient to show interesting interactions between strong and weak heaps. Reference types are the most common types when high-level languages interoperate with low-level languages because in this setting most data are passed by references.

$$
\begin{array}{rrcl}
(\textit{Assertion}) & \mathsf{p} & ::= & \cdots \mid \mathsf{emp} \mid \{e_1 \mapsto e_2\} \mid \mathsf{p}_1 * \mathsf{p}_2 \mid \mathsf{p}_1 -\!\!* \mathsf{p}_2 \mid \boxed{\{e : \tau\}} \\
(\textit{Type}) & \tau & ::= & \mathsf{int} \mid \mathsf{ref} \mid \mathsf{wref}\ \tau \\
(\textit{HeapType}) & \Psi & ::= & \{\ell_1 : \tau_1, \ldots, \ell_n : \tau_n\} \\
(\textit{LocalVarType}) & \Gamma & ::= & \{x_1 : \tau_1, \ldots, x_n : \tau_n\}
\end{array}
$$

Fig. 3. Assertions and types

$\boxed{\Psi, \Gamma \vdash e : \tau}$

$$
\frac{x \in \mathrm{dom}(\Gamma)}{\Psi, \Gamma \vdash x : \Gamma(x)} \qquad \frac{}{\Psi, \Gamma \vdash n : \mathsf{int}} \qquad \frac{}{\Psi, \Gamma \vdash \ell : \mathsf{ref}}
$$

$$
\frac{\Psi(\ell) = \tau}{\Psi, \Gamma \vdash \ell : \mathsf{wref}\ \tau} \qquad \frac{\forall i \in [1..n].\ \Psi, \Gamma \vdash e_i : \mathsf{int}}{\Psi, \Gamma \vdash op(e_1, \ldots, e_n) : \mathsf{int}}
$$

Fig. 4. Typing rules for expressions

Type int is for all integers and ref for all locations. Type "wref τ" is for locations in a weak heap, but not in a strong heap. A heap type Ψ tells the type of every location in a weak heap; mathematically, it is a finite map from locations to types. Given heap type Ψ, location ℓ has type "wref τ" if $\Psi(\ell)$ equals τ. A local variable type, Γ, tells the type of local variables.

Figure 4 presents typing rules for expressions, which are unsurprising. Notice that the typing rule for "wref τ" requires that the location ℓ is in the domain of the heap type Ψ and $\Psi(\ell)$ has to be the same as τ. This rule and the later weak-update rule enforce type-preserving updates on weak heaps.

The following schematic diagram helps to understand the relationship between weak heaps, strong heaps, local variables, assertions and various kinds of types in SL^{W}:

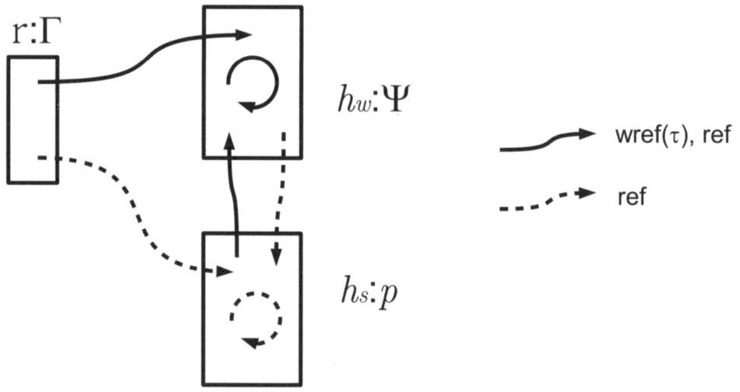

As shown in the diagram, SL^{W} conceptually divides a heap into a weak heap h_w and a strong heap h_s. The weak heap is specified by a heap type Ψ, and the strong heap by SL formula p. Pointers to weak-heap cells (in solid lines) have type "wref τ" or ref. Pointers to strong heap cells (in dotted lines) can have only type ref.

Figure 5 presents rules for checking commands. These rules use the judgment $\Psi \vdash \{\Gamma, \mathsf{p}\}\ \vec{c}\ \{\Gamma', \mathsf{p}'\}$. In this judgment, Ψ, Γ and p are preconditions and specify

$\boxed{\Psi \vdash \{\Gamma,\, \mathsf{p}\}\, \vec{c}\, \{\Gamma',\, \mathsf{p}'\}}$ ***(Well-formed statements)***

$$\frac{\Psi,\Gamma \vdash e : \mathsf{ref} \quad \Psi,\Gamma \vdash y : \tau}{\Psi \vdash \{\Gamma,\, \{e \mapsto y\}\}\; x := [e]\; \{\Gamma[x \rightsquigarrow \tau],\, x = y \wedge \{e \mapsto x\}\}}\;(\text{S-LOAD})$$
where $x \notin \mathsf{FV}(e)$

$$\frac{\Psi,\Gamma \vdash x : \mathsf{ref}}{\Psi \vdash \{\Gamma,\, \{x \mapsto -\}\}\; [x] := e\; \{\Gamma,\, \{x \mapsto e\}\}}\;(\text{S-UPDATE})$$

$$\frac{}{\Psi \vdash \{\Gamma,\, \mathsf{emp}\}\; x := \mathsf{alloc}(e)\; \{\Gamma[x \rightsquigarrow \mathsf{ref}],\, \{x \mapsto e\}\}}\;(\text{S-ALLOC})$$
where $x \notin \mathsf{FV}(e)$

$$\frac{\Psi,\Gamma \vdash e : \mathsf{ref}}{\Psi \vdash \{\Gamma,\, \{e \mapsto -\}\}\; \mathsf{free}(e)\; \{\Gamma,\, \mathsf{emp}\}}\;(\text{S-FREE})$$

$$\frac{\Psi \vdash \{\Gamma,\, \mathsf{p}\}\, \vec{c}\, \{\Gamma',\, \mathsf{p}'\}}{\Psi \vdash \{\Gamma,\, \mathsf{p} * \mathsf{p}_1\}\, \vec{c}\, \{\Gamma',\, \mathsf{p}' * \mathsf{p}_1\}}\;(\text{FRAME})$$
where no variable occurring free in p_1 is modified by $\vec{c}$

↑ THE WORLD OF STRONG HEAPS

↓ THE WORLD OF WEAK HEAPS

$$\frac{\Psi,\Gamma \vdash e : \mathsf{wref}\ \tau}{\Psi \vdash \{\Gamma,\, \mathsf{emp}\}\; x := [e]\; \{\Gamma[x \rightsquigarrow \tau],\, \mathsf{emp}\}}\;(\text{W-LOAD})$$

$$\frac{\Psi,\Gamma \vdash x : \mathsf{wref}\ \tau \quad \Psi,\Gamma \vdash e : \tau}{\Psi \vdash \{\Gamma,\, \mathsf{emp}\}\; [x] := e\; \{\Gamma,\, \mathsf{emp}\}}\;(\text{W-UPDATE})$$

$$\frac{\Psi,\Gamma \vdash e : \tau}{\Psi \vdash \{\Gamma,\, \mathsf{emp}\}\; x := \mathsf{alloc}(e)\; \{\Gamma[x \rightsquigarrow \mathsf{wref}\ \tau],\, \mathsf{emp}\}}\;(\text{W-ALLOC})$$

Fig. 5. Rules for commands (Rules for assignments, conditional statements, loops, and sequencing are the same as the ones in Hoare Logic and are omitted)

conditions on the weak heap, local variables, and the strong heap respectively. Postconditions are Γ' and p'; they specify conditions on local variables and the strong heap of the state after executing $\vec{c}$. Readers may wonder why there is no postcondition specification of the weak heap. As common in mutable-reference type systems, the implicit semantics of the judgment is that there exists an extended heap type $\Psi' \supseteq \Psi$ and the weak heap of the poststate should satisfy Ψ'. In terms of type checking, the particular Ψ' does not matter. The formal semantics of the judgment will be presented in Section 3.

Rules in Figure 5 are divided into two groups. One group is for the world of strong heaps, and another for the world of weak heaps. The rules for strong heaps are almost the same as the corresponding ones in standard SL, except that they also update Γ when necessary.

Operational semantics: $(\mathtt{r}, h, \mathsf{s2w}(x) \cdot \vec{c}) \longmapsto (\mathtt{r}, h, \vec{c})$

Rule: $$\frac{\Psi, \Gamma \vdash x : \mathsf{ref} \quad \Psi, \Gamma \vdash e : \tau}{\Psi \vdash \{\Gamma,\ \{x \mapsto e\}\}\ \mathsf{s2w}(x)\ \{\Gamma[x \rightsquigarrow \mathsf{wref}\ \tau],\ \mathsf{emp}\}}\ \text{S2W}$$

Fig. 6. Rule for converting a location from the strong heap to the weak heap

$$\frac{\vdash \{\Gamma'_1, \mathrm{p}'_1\} \Rightarrow \{\Gamma_1, \mathrm{p}_1\} \quad \Psi \vdash \{\Gamma_1, \mathrm{p}_1\}\ \vec{c}\ \{\Gamma_2, \mathrm{p}_2\} \quad \vdash \{\Gamma_2, \mathrm{p}_2\} \Rightarrow \{\Gamma'_2, \mathrm{p}'_2\}}{\Psi \vdash \{\Gamma'_1, \mathrm{p}'_1\}\ \vec{c}\ \{\Gamma'_2, \mathrm{p}'_2\}}\ \text{WEAKENING}$$

$\boxed{\vdash \{\Gamma, \mathrm{p}\} \Rightarrow \{\Gamma', \mathrm{p}'\}}$

$$\frac{}{\vdash \{\Gamma, \mathrm{p}\} \Rightarrow \{\Gamma, \mathrm{p} \wedge \{x : \Gamma(x)\}\}}\ \text{W1} \qquad \frac{\vdash \mathrm{p} \Rightarrow \mathrm{p}'}{\vdash \{\Gamma, \mathrm{p}\} \Rightarrow \{\Gamma, \mathrm{p}'\}}\ \text{W2}$$

Fig. 7. Weakening rules

The rules for weak heaps are the ones that one would usually find in a type system for mutable-reference types. The weak-update rule W-UPDATE requires that the pointer be of type "wref τ", and that the new value be of type τ. This rule enforces type-preserving updates. Once these conditions hold, Γ remains unchanged after the update. Notice in this rule there is no need to understand separation and aliases as the S-UPDATE rule does. The W-ALLOC rule does not need to extend the heap type Ψ because Ψ is only a precondition. When proving the soundness of the rule, we need to find a new Ψ' that extends Ψ and is also satisfied by the new weak heap after the allocation. Finally, there is no rule for free(e) in the world of weak heaps. Weak heaps should be garbage-collected.[1]

Figures 6 and 7 present some rules that show the interaction between weak and strong heaps. Figure 6 adds a new instruction "s2w(x)" for converting a location from a strong heap to a weak heap. Operationally, this instruction is a no-op (so it is an annotation, rather than a "real" instruction). Its typing rule, however, involves transforming the ownership in the strong heap to a pointer of weak-reference types. Notice that there is no rule for converting a location from the weak heap to the strong heap; this is similar to deallocation in weak heaps and requires the help of garbage collectors.

Figure 7 presents weakening rules. Rule W1 converts type information in Γ to information in assertion p. This is useful since information in Γ might be overwritten due to assignments to variables. One of examples in later sections will show the use of this rule. Rule W2 uses the premise $\vdash \mathrm{p} \Rightarrow \mathrm{p}'$; any valid SL formula $\mathrm{p} \Rightarrow \mathrm{p}'$ is acceptable.

2.3 Examples

We now show a few examples that demonstrate the use of SL^{W}. In these examples, we assume an additional type even for even integers. For clarity, we will also annotate

[1] We do not formally consider the interaction between garbage collectors and weak heaps. When considering a garbage collector, SL^{W} has to build in an extra level of indirection for cross-boundary references from strong heaps to weak heaps as objects in weak heaps may get moved (this is how the JNI implements Java references in native code). We leave this as future work.

the allocation instruction to indicate whether the allocation happens in the strong heap or in the weak heap. We write $x := \mathsf{alloc}_{\mathrm{S}}(e)$ for a strong-heap allocation. We write $x := \mathsf{alloc}_{\mathrm{W},\tau}(e)$ for a weak-heap allocation, and the intended type for e is τ. These annotations help in guiding the type checking of SL^{W}.

The first example shows how the counterexample in the introduction (formula (2) on page 179) plays out in SL^{W}. The following program first initializes the heap to a form such that y points to a location of type "wref even" and x points to 4, and then performs a heap update through x. The whole program is checkable in SL^{W} with respect to any heap type (remember the heap type specifies the *initial* weak heap). Below we also include conditions of the form "Γ, p" between instructions.

$$
\begin{array}{lll}
 & \{\}, \ \mathsf{emp} & \\
z := \mathsf{alloc}_{\mathrm{W},\mathsf{even}}(2) & & \\
 & \{z : \mathsf{wref\ even}\}, \ \mathsf{emp} & \\
y := \mathsf{alloc}_{\mathrm{S}}(z) & & \\
 & \{y : \mathsf{ref}, z : \mathsf{wref\ even}\}, \ \{y \mapsto z\} & \text{by rule (w1)} \\
 & \{y : \mathsf{ref}, z : \mathsf{wref\ even}\}, \ \{y \mapsto z\} \wedge \{z : \mathsf{wref\ even}\} & \text{by rule (w2)} \\
 & \{y : \mathsf{ref}, z : \mathsf{wref\ even}\}, \ \exists v.\ \{y \mapsto v\} \wedge \{v : \mathsf{wref\ even}\} & \\
z := 0 & & \\
 & \{y : \mathsf{ref}, z : \mathsf{int}\}, \ \exists v.\ \{y \mapsto v\} \wedge \{v : \mathsf{wref\ even}\} & \\
x := \mathsf{alloc}_{\mathrm{S}}(4) & & \\
 & \{x : \mathsf{ref}, y : \mathsf{ref}, z : \mathsf{int}\}, \ \exists v.\ (\{y \mapsto v\} \wedge \{v : \mathsf{wref\ even}\}) * \{x \mapsto 4\} & \\
[x] := 3 & & \\
 & \{x : \mathsf{ref}, y : \mathsf{ref}, z : \mathsf{int}\}, \ \exists v.\ (\{y \mapsto v\} \wedge \{v : \mathsf{wref\ even}\}) * \{x \mapsto 3\} &
\end{array}
$$

Different from the counterexample, the condition before "[x] := 3" limits where y can point to. In particular, y cannot point to x because (1) by the type of v, variable y must point to a weak-heap location; (2) x represents a location in the strong heap. Therefore, the update through x does not invalidate the type of v. We could easily construct an example where y indeed points to x. But in that case the type of v would be ref, which would also not be affected by updates through x.

One of the motivations of SL^{W} is to reason about programs where code in high-level languages interacts with low-level code. Prior research [4, 14] has shown that it is error prone when high-level code interoperates with low-level code. All kinds of errors may occur. One common kind of errors occurs when low-level code makes type misuses of references that point to objects in the weak heap. For instance, in the JNI, types of all references to Java objects are conflated into one type in native code—`jobject`. Consequently, there is no static checking of whether native code uses these Java references in a type-safe way. Type misuses of these Java references can result in silent memory corruption or unexpected behavior.

The first example already demonstrates how SL^{W} enables passing pointers from high-level to low-level code. In the example, the first allocation is on the weak heap and can be thought of as an operation by high-level code. Then, the location is passed to the low level by being stored in the strong heap. Unlike foreign function interfaces where types of cross-boundary references are conflated into a single type in low-level code, SL^{W} can track the accurate types of those references and enable type safety.

The next example demonstrates how low-level code can initialize a data structure in the strong heap, and then transfer that structure to the weak heap so that the structure is usable by high-level code.

$$\begin{array}{l} \quad \{\}, \ \mathsf{emp} \\ x := \mathsf{alloc_s}(4) \\ \quad \{x : \mathsf{ref}\}, \ \{x \mapsto 4\} \\ y := \mathsf{alloc_s}(x) \\ \quad \{x : \mathsf{ref}, y : \mathsf{ref}\}, \ \{x \mapsto 4\} * \{y \mapsto x\} \\ \mathsf{s2w}(x) \\ \quad \{x : \mathsf{wref\ even}, y : \mathsf{ref}\}, \ \{y \mapsto x\} \\ \mathsf{s2w}(y) \\ \quad \{x : \mathsf{wref\ even}, y : \mathsf{wref\ (wref\ even)}\}, \ \mathsf{emp} \end{array}$$

3 Soundness of $\mathrm{SL^W}$

Soundness of $\mathrm{SL^W}$ is proved by a semantic approach. We first describe a semantic model for weak-reference types. Based on this model, semantics of various concepts in $\mathrm{SL^W}$ are defined. Every rule in $\mathrm{SL^W}$ is then proved as a lemma according to the semantics.

3.1 Modeling Weak-Reference Types

Intuitively, a type is a set of values. This suggests that a semantic type should be a predicate of the metatype "*Value* → *Prop*". However, this idea would not support weak-reference types. To see why, let us examine a naïve model where "wref τ" in a heap h would denote a set of locations ℓ such that $h(\ell)$ is of type τ. This simple model is unfortunately unsound, which is illustrated by the following example:

1. Create a reference of type "wref even", and let the reference be x.
2. Copy x to y. By the naïve model, a reference of type "wref even" also has type "wref int" (because an even number is also an integer). Let "wref int" be the type of y.
3. Update the reference through y with an odd integer, say 3. As y has the type "wref int", updating it with an odd integer is legal.
4. Dereference x. Alas, the dereference returns 3, although the type of x implies a result of an even number!

The problem with the naïve model is that, with aliases, it allows inconsistent views of memory. In the foregoing example, x and y have inconsistent views on the same memory cell. To address this problem, $\mathrm{SL^W}$ uses a heap type Ψ to type check a location. This follows the approach of Tofte [16] and Harper [5]. An example Ψ is as follows:

$$\Psi = \{\ell_0 : \mathsf{even},\ \ell_1 : \mathsf{int},\ \ell_2 : \mathsf{wref\ even},\ \ell_3 : \mathsf{wref\ int}\} \tag{3}$$

A heap type Ψ helps to define two related concepts, informally stated below (their formal semantic definitions will be presented in a moment):

(i) A location ℓ is of type "wref τ" if and only if $\Psi(\ell)$ equals τ.

(ii) A heap h is consistent with Ψ if for every ℓ, the value $h(\ell)$ has type $\Psi(\ell)$. For the example Ψ, it means that $h(\ell_0)$ should be an even number, $h(\ell_1)$ should be an integer, $h(\ell_2)$ should be of type "wref even", ...

The heap type Ψ prevents aliases from having inconsistent views of the heap. Aliases have to agree on their types because the types have to agree with the type in Ψ. In particular, the example showing the unsoundness of the naïve model would not work in the above model because, in step 3 of the example, y cannot be cast from type "wref even" to "wref int": type "wref even" implies that $\Psi(y) = \mathsf{even}$, which is a different type from int.

A subtlety of the above model is the denotation of "wref τ" depends on the heap type Ψ, but is *independent* of the heap h. A weak-reference type is connected to the heap h only indirectly, through the consistency relation between h and Ψ.

Example 3. Let $h = \{\ell_0 \mapsto 4,\ \ell_1 \mapsto 3,\ \ell_2 \mapsto \ell_0,\ \ell_3 \mapsto \ell_1\}$. It is consistent with the example Ψ in (3). To see this, 4 at location ℓ_0 is an even number and 3 at location ℓ_1 is an integer. At location ℓ_2, ℓ_0 is of type "wref even" because, by (i), this is equivalent to $\Psi(\ell_0) = \mathsf{even}$—a true statement. Similarly, the value ℓ_1 at location ℓ_3 is of type "wref int". □

Formalizing a set of semantic predicates following (i) and (ii) directly, however, would encounter difficulties because of a circularity in the model: by (ii), Ψ is a map from locations to types; by (i), the model of types takes Ψ as an argument—Ψ is necessary to decide if a location belongs to "wref τ". If defined naïvely, the model would result in inconsistent cardinality, as described by Ahmed [1].

We next propose a fixed-point approach. We rewrite the heap type Ψ as a recursive equation. After adding Ψ as an argument to types, the example in (3) becomes:

$$\Psi = \{\ell_0 : \mathsf{even}(\Psi),\ \ell_1 : \mathsf{int}(\Psi),\ \ell_2 : (\mathsf{wref\ even})(\Psi),\ \ell_3 : (\mathsf{wref\ int})(\Psi)\} \tag{4}$$

Notice that Ψ appears on both the left and the right side of the equation. Once Ψ is written as a recursive equation, it follows that any fixed point of the following functional is a solution to the equation (4):

$$\lambda\Psi.\{\ell_0 : \mathsf{even}(\Psi),\ \ell_1 : \mathsf{int}(\Psi),\ \ell_2 : (\mathsf{wref\ even})(\Psi),\ \ell_3 : (\mathsf{wref\ int})(\Psi)\} \tag{5}$$

To get a fixed point of (5), we follow the indexed model of recursive types by Appel and McAllester [2]. We first introduce some domains:

$$\begin{array}{rcl} (\mathit{SemHeapType})\ \mathtt{F} & \in & \mathit{Loc} \rightharpoonup \mathit{SemIType} \\ (\mathit{SemIType})\ \mathtt{t} & \in & \mathit{SemHeapEnv} \to \mathit{Nat} \to \mathit{Value} \to \mathit{Prop} \\ (\mathit{SemHeapEnv})\ \phi & \in & \mathit{Loc} \rightharpoonup \mathit{Nat} \to \mathit{Value} \to \mathit{Prop} \end{array}$$

We use $\mathtt{F}$ for a semantic heap type (it is the metatype of the denotation of heap types, as we will see). It maps locations to indexed types. An important point is that from $\mathtt{F}$ we can define $\lambda\phi,\ell.\ \mathtt{F}(\ell)\ \phi$, which has the metatype $\mathit{SemHeapEnv} \to \mathit{SemHeapEnv}$.

Therefore, a semantic heap type is effectively a functional similar to the one in (5), and a fixed point of F is of the metatype *SemHeapEnv*.

A semantic type t is a predicate over the following arguments: ϕ is a semantic heap environment; k is a natural-number index; v is a value. The heap environment $\phi \in SemHeapEnv$ is used in our model of WRef(t) to constrain reference types. The index k comes from the indexed model and is a technical device that enables us to define the fixed point of a semantic heap type F.

Following the indexed model, we introduce a notion of contractiveness.

Definition 4. *(Contractiveness)*

$$\begin{aligned} \mathsf{contractive}(F) &\triangleq \forall \ell \in \mathrm{dom}(F).\ \mathsf{contractive}(F(\ell)) \\ \mathsf{contractive}(t) &\triangleq \forall \phi, k, j \leq k, v.\ (t\ \phi\ j\ v) \leftrightarrow (t\ (\mathsf{approx}(k,\phi))\ j\ v) \\ \mathsf{approx}(k,\phi) &\triangleq \lambda \ell, j, v.\ j < k \wedge \phi\ l\ j\ v. \end{aligned}$$

We define $(\wp \mathrm{F}) = \lambda\phi,\ell.\ \mathrm{F}(\ell)\ \phi$. That is, it turns F into a functional of type $SemHeapEnv \rightarrow SemHeapEnv$.

Theorem 5. *If* contractive(F)*, then the following* μF *is the least fixed point*[2] *of the functional* $(\wp F)$*:*

$$\mu F \triangleq \lambda \ell, k, v.\ (\wp F)^{k+1}(\bot)\ \ell\ k\ v,$$

where $\bot = \lambda \ell, k, v.$ false*, and* $(\wp F)^{k+1}$ *applies the functional* $k+1$ *times.*

The theorem is proved by following the indexed model of recursive types [2]. We present the proof in our technical report [15].

The following lemma is an immediate corollary of Theorem 5.

Lemma 6. *For any contractive F, any* ℓ, k, v*, we have* $\big(F(\ell)\ (\mu F)\ k\ v\big) \leftrightarrow \big((\mu F)(\ell)\ k\ v\big)$

Most of the semantic types ignore the ϕ argument. For example,

$$\mathrm{Even} \triangleq \lambda \phi, k, v.\ \exists u.\ v = 2 \times u.$$

We use capitalized Even to emphasize that it is a predicate, instead of the syntactic type even. The model of weak-reference types uses the argument ϕ.

Definition 7. $\mathrm{WRef}(t) \triangleq \lambda \phi, k, \ell.\ \forall j < k, v.\ \phi\ \ell\ j\ v \leftrightarrow t\ \phi\ j\ v$

In words, a location ℓ is of type WRef(t) under heap environment ϕ, if $\phi(\ell)$ equals t approximately, with index less than k.

Example 8. Let $\mathrm{F}_0 = \{\ell_0 : \mathrm{Even},\ \ell_1 : \mathrm{WRef(Even)}\}$. Then "WRef(Even) $(\mu \mathrm{F}_0)\ k\ \ell_0$" holds for any k. To see this, for any $j < k$ and v, we have

$$(\mu \mathrm{F}_0)\ \ell_0\ j\ v \leftrightarrow \mathrm{F}_0(\ell_0)(\mu \mathrm{F}_0) j\ v \leftrightarrow \mathrm{Even}\ (\mu \mathrm{F}_0)\ j\ v$$

The first step is by lemma 6, and the second is by the definition of F_0 at location ℓ_0. We can similarly show "WRef(WRef(Even)) $(\mu \mathrm{F}_0)\ k\ \ell_1$" holds. □

Note that the definition of WRef(t) is more general than the "wref τ" type in $\mathrm{SL^W}$, as τ is syntactically defined, while t can be any (contractive) semantic predicate.

---

[2] Since F is contractive in the sense that "$\mathrm{F}(\ell)\ \phi\ k\ w$" performs only calls to ϕ on arguments smaller than k, it is easy to show by induction that any two fixed points of F are identical; therefore, the least fixed point of F is also its greatest fixed point.

Heap allocation. We need an additional idea to cope with heap allocation in the weak heap. Our indexed types take the fixed point of a semantic heap type F as an argument. But F changes after heap allocation. For example, from

$$\mathtt{F} = \{\ell_0 : \text{Even},\ \ell_1 : \text{WRef(Even)}\} \text{ to } \mathtt{F}' = \{\ell_0 : \text{Even},\ \ell_1 : \text{WRef(Even)}, \ell_2 : \text{Even}\},$$

after ℓ_2 is allocated and initialized with an even number.

After a new heap location is allocated, any value that has type t before allocation should still have the same type after allocation. This is the monotonicity condition maintained by type systems. To model it semantically, our idea is to quantify explicitly outside of the model of types over all future semantic heap types and assert that the type in question is true over the fixed point of any future semantic heap type.

First is a semantic notion of type-preserving heap extension from F to F′:

Definition 9. $F' \geq F \ \triangleq$
$\quad \mathsf{contractive}(F') \wedge \mathsf{contractive}(F) \wedge \forall \ell \in \mathrm{dom}(F), \phi, k, v.\ F'(\ell)\ \phi\ k\ v \leftrightarrow F(\ell)\ \phi\ k\ v$

Lemma 10. *The relation $F' \geq F$ is reflexive, anti-symmetric, and transitive (thus a partial order).*

Next, we define the consistency relation between h and F, and also a relation that states a value v is of type t under F. Both relations quantify over all future semantic heap types, and require that the type in question be true over the fixed point of any future semantic heap type.

Definition 11. $\models h : F \ \triangleq\ \mathrm{dom}(h) \subseteq \mathrm{dom}(F) \wedge \forall \ell \in \mathrm{dom}(h). F \models h(\ell) : F(\ell)$
$\qquad F \models v : t \ \triangleq\ \forall F' \geq F. \forall k.\ t\ (\mu F')\ k\ v$

With our model, the following theorem for memory operations can be proved (please see our technical report [15] for proofs).

Theorem 12.

(i) (Read) *If* $\models h : F$, *and* $\ell \in \mathrm{dom}(h)$, *and* $F \models \ell : \mathrm{WRef}(t)$, *then* $F \models h(\ell) : t$.
(ii) (Write) *If* $\models h : F$, *and* $\ell \in \mathrm{dom}(h)$, *and* $F \models \ell : \mathrm{WRef}(t)$, *and* $F \models v : t$, *then* $\models h[\ell \rightsquigarrow v] : F$.
(iii) (Allocation) *If* $\models h : F$, *and* $F \models v : t$, *and* $\mathsf{contractive}(t)$, *and* $\ell \notin \mathrm{dom}(F)$, *then* $\models h \uplus \{\ell \mapsto v\} : F \uplus \{\ell \mapsto t\}$.

3.2 Semantic Model of $\mathrm{SL^W}$

To show the soundness of $\mathrm{SL^W}$, we define semantics for judgments in $\mathrm{SL^W}$ and then prove each rule as a lemma according to the semantics. Figure 8 presents definitions that are used in the semantics.

The semantics of types is unsurprising. In particular, the semantics of $[\![\mathsf{wref}\ \tau]\!]$ is defined in terms of the predicate $\mathrm{WRef}(t)$ in Definition 7. All these types are contractive. The semantics of Ψ and Γ is just the point-wise extension of the semantics of types.

$\boxed{[\![\tau]\!] \in \mathit{SemIType}}$

$[\![\mathsf{int}]\!] \triangleq \lambda\phi,k,v.\ \exists n.v = n.$ $[\![\mathsf{ref}]\!] \triangleq \lambda\phi,k,v.\ \exists\ell.v = \ell.$ $[\![\mathsf{wref}\ \tau]\!] \triangleq \mathrm{WRef}([\![\tau]\!])$

$\boxed{[\![\Psi]\!] \in \mathit{Loc} \rightharpoonup \mathit{SemIType}}$ $[\![\{\ell_1 : \tau_1, \ldots, \ell_n : \tau_n\}]\!] \triangleq \{\ell_1 : [\![\tau_1]\!], \ldots, \ell_n : [\![\tau_n]\!]\}$

$\boxed{[\![\Gamma]\!] \in \mathit{Var} \rightharpoonup \mathit{SemIType}}$ $[\![\{x_1 : \tau_1, \ldots, x_n : \tau_n\}]\!] \triangleq \{x_1 : [\![\tau_1]\!], \ldots, x_n : [\![\tau_n]\!]\}$

$\boxed{\mathtt{F}, \mathtt{r}, h \models \mathtt{p}}$

$$
\begin{aligned}
&\mathtt{F},\mathtt{r},h \models \{e:\tau\} \triangleq \mathtt{F} \models \mathtt{r}(e) : [\![\tau]\!] \\
&\mathtt{F},\mathtt{r},h \models \mathsf{emp} \triangleq \mathrm{dom}(h) = \emptyset \\
&\mathtt{F},\mathtt{r},h \models \{e_1 \mapsto e_2\} \triangleq \mathrm{dom}(h) = \mathtt{r}(e_1) \wedge h(\mathtt{r}(e_1)) = \mathtt{r}(e_2) \\
&\mathtt{F},\mathtt{r},h \models \mathtt{p}_1 * \mathtt{p}_2 \triangleq \exists h_1,h_2.\ (h = h_1 \uplus h_2) \wedge (\mathtt{F},\mathtt{r},h_1 \models \mathtt{p}_1) \wedge (\mathtt{F},\mathtt{r},h_2 \models \mathtt{p}_2) \\
&\mathtt{F},\mathtt{r},h \models \mathtt{p}_1 \mathrel{-\!\!*} \mathtt{p}_2 \triangleq \forall h_1.\ ((\mathrm{dom}(h_1) \cap \mathrm{dom}(h) = \emptyset) \wedge (\mathtt{F},\mathtt{r},h_1 \models \mathtt{p}_1)) \Rightarrow (\mathtt{F},\mathtt{r},h_1 \uplus h \models \mathtt{p}_2)
\end{aligned}
$$

$$
\begin{aligned}
&\mathtt{F} \models \mathtt{r} : \Gamma \quad \triangleq \forall x \in \mathrm{dom}(\Gamma).\ \mathtt{F} \models \mathtt{r}(x) : [\![\Gamma(x)]\!] \\
&\mathtt{r},h \models \mathtt{F} * \mathtt{p} \triangleq \exists h_1,h_2.\ (h = h_1 \uplus h_2) \wedge (\mathrm{dom}(h_1) = \mathrm{dom}(\mathtt{F})) \wedge (\models h_1 : \mathtt{F}) \wedge (\mathtt{F},\mathtt{r},h_2 \models \mathtt{p})
\end{aligned}
$$

Fig. 8. Semantic definitions

The predicate "$\mathtt{F},\mathtt{r},h \models \mathtt{p}$" interprets the truth of assertion p. When p is a standard SL formula, the interpretation is the same as the one in SL. When p is $\{e:\tau\}$, the interpretation depends on F. Notice that the interpretation of $\{e:\tau\}$ is independent of the heap; it is a pure assertion (that is, it does not depend on the strong heap).

The definition of $\mathtt{F} \models \mathtt{r} : \Gamma$ is the point-wise extension of $\mathtt{F} \models v : t$ to local variable types. The definition of "$\mathtt{r},h \models \mathtt{F} * \mathtt{p}$" splits the heap into two parts. One for the weak heap, which should satisfy F, and the other for the strong heap, which is specified by p.

With the above definitions, we are ready to define the semantics of the judgments in $\mathrm{SL^W}$. The following definitions interpret "$\Psi,\Gamma \vdash e:\tau$", "$\vdash \mathtt{p} \Rightarrow \mathtt{p}'$", and "$\vdash \{\Gamma,\ \mathtt{p}\} \Rightarrow \{\Gamma',\ \mathtt{p}'\}$".

Definition 13.

$$\Psi,\Gamma \models e:\tau \triangleq \forall F \geq [\![\Psi]\!].\ \forall r.\ F \models r:\Gamma \Rightarrow F \models r(e) : [\![\tau]\!].$$

$$\models p \Rightarrow p' \triangleq \forall F,r,h.\ (F,r,h \models p) \Rightarrow (F,r,h \models p')$$

$$
\begin{aligned}
&\models \{\Gamma,\ p\} \Rightarrow \{\Gamma',\ p'\} \triangleq \\
&\quad \forall F,r,h.\ (F \models r:\Gamma \wedge r,h \models F * p) \Rightarrow (F \models r:\Gamma' \wedge r,h \models F * p')
\end{aligned}
$$

Now we are ready to interpret $\Psi \vdash \{\Gamma,\ \mathtt{p}\}\ \vec{c}\ \{\Gamma',\ \mathtt{p}'\}$. Following Hoare Logic, we define both partial and total correctness:

Definition 14. *(Partial and total correctness)*

$$\begin{array}{l}\Psi \models_{\mathrm{p}} \{\Gamma,\, p\}\,\vec{c}\,\{\Gamma',\, p'\} \triangleq \\ \quad \forall F \geq [\![\Psi]\!], r, h.\ \big((F \models r : \Gamma) \wedge (r, h \models F * p)\big) \Rightarrow \\ \quad\quad \mathrm{safe}(r, h, \vec{c}) \wedge \\ \quad\quad \big(\forall r', h'.\ (r, h, \vec{c}) \longmapsto^{*} (r', h', \varepsilon) \Rightarrow \exists F' \geq F.\ (F' \models r' : \Gamma') \wedge (r', h' \models F' * p')\big)\end{array}$$

$$\begin{array}{l}\Psi \models_{\mathrm{t}} \{\Gamma,\, p\}\,\vec{c}\,\{\Gamma',\, p'\} \triangleq \\ \quad (\Psi \models_{\mathrm{p}} \{\Gamma,\, p\}\,\vec{c}\,\{\Gamma',\, p'\}) \wedge \\ \quad \big(\forall F \geq [\![\Psi]\!], r, h.\ \big((F \models r : \Gamma) \wedge (r, h \models F * p)\big) \Rightarrow \mathrm{terminate}(r, h, \vec{c})\big)\end{array}$$

In the partial-correctness interpretation, it assumes a state that satisfies the condition $\{\Gamma, \mathrm{p}\}$ and requires that the state be safe (see Definition 2 on page 181 for safety). In addition, it requires that, for any terminal state after the execution of $\vec{c}$, we must be able to find a new semantic heap type F' so that $\mathrm{F}' \geq \mathrm{F}$ and the new state satisfies $\{\Gamma', \mathrm{p}'\}$. Note that F' may be larger than F due to allocations in $\vec{c}$. The total-correctness interpretation requires termination in addition to the requirements of partial correctness.

Theorem 15. *All rules in Figures 5, 6 and 7 are sound for both partial and total correctness.*

The proof uses Theorem 12. It is largely straightforward and omitted. We refer interested readers to our technical report [15] for the proof.

4 Related Work

We discuss related work in three categories: (1) work related to language interoperation; (2) work related to integrating SL with type systems; and (3) work related to semantic models of types.

Most work in language interoperation focuses on the design and implementation of foreign function interfaces. Examples are plenty. Given a multilingual program, one natural question is how to reason about the program as a whole. This kind of reasoning requires models, program analyzers, and program logics that can work across language boundaries. Previous work has addressed the question of how to model the interoperation between dynamically typed languages and statically typed languages [9], and the interoperation between two safe languages when they have different systems of computational effects [18]. By integrating SL and type systems, SL^{W} can elegantly reason about properties of heaps that are shared by high-level and low-level code.

Previous systems of integrating SL with type systems [11, 8] assume that programs are well-typed according to a syntactic type system, and SL is then used as an add-on to reason about more properties of programs. Honda *et al*'s program logic [7, 20] for higher-order languages supports reference types but also requires a separate type system (in addition to the Hoare assertions); Reus *et al* [12] presented an extension of separation logic for supporting higher-order store (i.e., references to higher-order functions), but their logic does not support weak heaps which we believe embodies the key feature of reference types (i.e., the ability to perform safe updates without knowing the exact aliasing relation). Compared to previous systems, SL^W targets the interoperation between high-level and low-level code. It allows cross-boundary references and mixes SL formulas and types.

The soundness of SL^W is justified by defining a semantic model, notably for types. Ahmed [1] and Appel *et al* [3] presented a powerful index-based semantic model for a rich type system with ML-style references. They rely on constructing a "dependently typed" global heap type to break the circularity discussed in Section 3. Our current work, in contrast, simply takes a fixed point of the recursively defined heap type predicate and avoids building any dependently typed data structures. Our work also differs from theirs in that we are reasoning about reference types in a program logic. Appel *et al.* [3] can also support impredicative polymorphism which is not addressed in our current work.

5 Discussion and Future Work

This work aims toward a framework for reasoning about language interoperation, but a lot remains to be done. A realistic high-level language contains many more language features and types. We do not foresee much difficulty in incorporating language features and types at the logic level as their modeling is largely independent from the interaction between weak and strong heaps. One technical concern is how to extend our semantic model to cover a complicated type system, including function types and OO classes.

SL^W does not formally consider the effect of a garbage collector. A garbage collector would break the crucial monotonicity condition of the weak heap that our semantic model relies on. We believe a possible way to overcome this problem is to use a region-based type system [17]. A garbage collector would also imply that there cannot be direct references from strong heaps to weak heaps; an extra level of indirection has to be added.

6 Conclusion

In his survey paper of Separation Logic [13], Reynolds asked *"whether the dividing line between types and assertions can be erased"*. This paper adds evidence that the type-based approach has its unique place when ensuring safety in weak heaps and when reasoning about the interaction between weak and strong heaps. The combination of types and SL provides a powerful framework for checking safety and verifying properties of multilingual programs.

Acknowledgments

We thank anonymous referees for suggestions and comments on an earlier version of this paper. Gang Tan is supported in part by NSF grant CCF-0915157. Zhong Shao is supported in part by a gift from Microsoft and NSF grants CCF-0524545 and CCF-0811665. Xinyu Feng is supported in part by NSF grant CCF-0524545 and National Natural Science Foundation of China (grant No. 90818019).

References

[1] Ahmed, A.J.: Semantics of Types for Mutable State. PhD thesis, Princeton University (2004)
[2] Appel, A.W., McAllester, D.: An indexed model of recursive types for foundational proof-carrying code. ACM Trans. on Prog. Lang. and Sys. 23(5), 657–683 (2001)
[3] Appel, A.W., Mellies, P.-A., Richards, C.D., Vouillon, J.: A very modal model of a modern, major, general type system. In: POPL 2007, pp. 109–122. ACM Press, New York (2007)
[4] Furr, M., Foster, J.S.: Checking type safety of foreign function calls. ACM Trans. Program. Lang. Syst. 30(4), 1–63 (2008)
[5] Harper, R.: A simplified account of polymorphic references. Information Processing Letters 57(1), 15–16 (1996)
[6] Hoare, C.A.R.: An axiomatic basis for computer programming. Commun. ACM 12(10), 578–580 (1969)
[7] Honda, K., Yoshida, N., Berger, M.: An observationally complete program logic for imperative higher-order frame rules. In: LICS 2005, June 2005, pp. 270–279 (2005)
[8] Krishnaswami, N., Birkedal, L., Aldrich, J., Reynolds, J.: Idealized ML and its separation logic (July 2007)
[9] Matthews, J., Findler, R.B.: Operational semantics for multi-language programs. In: Proc. 34th ACM Symp. on Principles of Prog. Lang., pp. 3–10 (2007)
[10] O'Hearn, P.W., Reynolds, J.C., Yang, H.: Local reasoning about programs that alter data structures. In: Fribourg, L. (ed.) CSL 2001. LNCS, vol. 2142, pp. 1–19. Springer, Heidelberg (2001)
[11] Parkinson, M.: Local reasoning for Java. PhD thesis, University of Cambridge Computer Laboratory, Oxford. Tech Report UCAM-CL-TR-654 (November 2005)
[12] Reus, B., Schwinghammer, J.: Separation logic for higher-order store. In: Ésik, Z. (ed.) CSL 2006. LNCS, vol. 4207, pp. 575–590. Springer, Heidelberg (2006)
[13] Reynolds, J.C.: Separation logic: A logic for shared mutable data structures. In: Proc. LICS 2002, July 2002, pp. 55–74 (2002)
[14] Tan, G., Croft, J.: An empirical security study of the native code in the JDK. In: 17th Usenix Security Symposium, pp. 365–377 (2008)
[15] Tan, G., Shao, Z., Feng, X., Cai, H.: Weak updates and separation logic (June 2009), http://www.cse.lehigh.edu/~gtan/paper/WUSL-tr.pdf
[16] Tofte, M.: Type inference for polymorphic references. Inf. and Comp. 89(1), 1–34 (1990)
[17] Tofte, M., Talpin, J.-P.: Region-based memory management. Information and Computation 132(2), 109–176 (1997)
[18] Trifonov, V., Shao, Z.: Safe and principled language interoperation. In: Swierstra, S.D. (ed.) ESOP 1999. LNCS, vol. 1576, pp. 128–146. Springer, Heidelberg (1999)
[19] Wright, A.K., Felleisen, M.: A syntactic approach to type soundness. Information and Computation 115(1), 38–94 (1994)
[20] Yoshida, N., Honda, K., Berge, M.: Logical reasoning for higher-order functions with local state. In: Seidl, H. (ed.) FOSSACS 2007. LNCS, vol. 4423, pp. 361–377. Springer, Heidelberg (2007)

Proving Copyless Message Passing

Jules Villard[1], Étienne Lozes[1], and Cristiano Calcagno[2]

[1] LSV, ENS Cachan, CNRS
[2] Imperial College, London

Abstract. Handling concurrency using a shared memory and locks is tedious and error-prone. One solution is to use message passing instead. We study here a particular, contract-based flavor that makes the ownership transfer of messages explicit. In this case, ownership of the heap region representing the content of a message is lost upon sending, which can lead to efficient implementations. In this paper, we define a proof system for a concurrent imperative programming language implementing this idea and inspired by the Singularity OS. The proof system, for which we prove soundness, is an extension of separation logic, which has already been used successfully to study various ownership-oriented paradigms.

Introduction

Asynchronous message passing often suffers from two drawbacks: contents of messages have to be copied, and deadlocks can be tricky to avoid. However, if messages to-be live in the same address space, the first issue can be resolved by sending a mere pointer to the memory region where the message is stored instead of issuing a copy. This implementation is sound provided that the emitting thread loses ownership over the message, *i.e.* does not access it for reading or writing after emission.

The goal of this paper is to give a semantics and a proof theory for this way of programming. Our idealized programming language allows memory manipulation and asynchronous communications ruled by contracts, a basic form of session types, following the ideas of `Sing#`. Our proof system is based on separation logic [12], which has already been used to specify and prove various ownership-based paradigms [10,4]. Contracts play an essential role in this proof system: message invariants are associated to every contract's message, in the same spirit as resource invariants in concurrent separation logic [10]. Moreover, we show that they can ensure the absence of memory leaks when channels are closed.

To better illustrate copyless message passing, consider the following code snippet, where x, y can be thought of as buffers, and e, e' as the two endpoints of a channel:

```
(e,e') = open();
send(e,x);
y = receive(e');
close(e,e');
```

In a copying implementation, a whole copy of the buffer x would be allocated, and its address stored in y, whereas in copyless message passing, the whole code would be equivalent to `x = y`.

Z. Hu (Ed.): APLAS 2009, LNCS 5904, pp. 194–209, 2009.

Our first contribution is the proof of soundness for our proof system: provable programs do not fault on memory accesses, are race free, and are contract obedient. However, and unlike for concurrent separation logic, it cannot entail the absence of memory leaks, due to the possibility of non-local leaks when channels are closed.

Finding a semantics that both establishes the soundness of our proof system and corresponds to the intended behaviour was challenging, because the standard semantics for separation logic is a local semantics, for which for instance the equivalence between the code above and `x = y` would not hold. Our second contribution is to propose a new approach for defining such a semantics. Indeed, we define a *local* semantics based on abstract separation logic [5], for which our proof system is sound, and then restrict it to a *global* semantics, also sound by restriction. However, neither the local nor the global semantics reflect the intended semantics faithfully.

Our third contribution is to state and prove a more general result that entails the validity of the pointer-passing implementation and the absence of memory leaks. This result, which we christen the transfers erasure property, relates the global semantics to the intended semantics in a non-trivial way, and allows to state that programs p for which the Hoare triple $\{\mathsf{emp}\}\ p\ \{\mathsf{emp}\}$ is valid are leak free under some conditions on the contracts.

We first introduce the language and its main features by a small motivating example. We then present the programming language and our proof system in Sec. 2, and demonstrate how to prove the example. Sec. 3 gives an overview of the main ingredients of our semantics. We develop the semantics in more details in Sec. 4, leading to a soundness result for our logic. Sec. 5 is devoted to the transfers erasure property.

Related work. The Singularity operating system [6] is a prominent application of contract-based copyless message passing ideas. It can safely run processes sharing a unique address space without memory protection. Executables are written in the `Sing#` programming language, which supports (copyless) message passing primitives. Ownership violations are detected at compile-time using static analysis techniques, and communications are ruled by contracts. Our work can be seen as an abstract model of `Sing#`, though some differences between the two are worth noting: we chose to be able to detect memory leaks, while `Sing#` is equipped with a garbage collector, and we support complete mobility of channels, similar to π-calculus, whereas `Sing#` provides internal mobility only. Finally, as our language is not full-fledged, we did not provide mechanisms for error handling, for example when one endpoint is abruptly closed.

Concurrent Separation Logic [10] and the logic of Gotsman & al. for locks in the heap [7] inspired our work. While the former cannot handle an unbounded number of resources, it would surely have been possible to encode message passing commands in the toy programming language of the latter. However, contracts seem of such a different nature that it appeared simpler to take message passing instructions as primitive. More importantly, the local semantics used in these works is an over-approximation of the intended semantics, as the exchange of shared resources involves a possible non-deterministic change of the resource content provided it still respects some invariant. The transfers erasure property cannot be established in these approaches.

Contracts may be viewed as session types [13]. However, the approach is different in this work, as our main concern with contracts is how they can help us to prove that channels do not leak memory, and not how they can prove the absence of communication errors (although this certainly is an interesting topic for future work). Session types were also used on top of Java in SessionJ [9], but this does not address the problem of copyless message passing.

Pym and Tofts [11], and O'Hearn and Hoare [8] have defined two other logics for resource aware message passing programs. However, their respective models differ significantly from ours as they are based on process algebras, and are not centered around memory management.

1 Programming Language

1.1 Contracts

Contracts describe the behavior of channels. A channel is asynchronous, bi-directional, and has two endpoints, distinguished for ease of reference: the serving endpoint and the client endpoint. Contracts are state machines describing what sends (`!`) and receives (`?`) are allowed in a given state. They are written from the server's point of view, the client's one being dual. Each message sent over the channel is described by a message identifier. Moreover, each message identifier is annotated with an invariant (between brackets) for proofs' purpose. These invariants are separation logic formulas, and replace `Sing#` messages' types. Their syntax and purpose will be explained in the next sections.

The contract `C` below describes the protocol implemented by our example. It has three states, three transitions, and three messages may trigger these transitions.

```
contract C {
  message ack       [emp]
  message cell      [val ↦ X]
  message close_me  [src ↦^ep (C{end}, −) ∧ src = val]

  initial state transfer { !cell --> wait_ack;
                           !close_me --> end; }
  state wait_ack { ?ack --> transfer; }
  final state end {} }
```

`ack` is a message used for synchronization purpose only, whereas `cell` and `close_me` respectively carry (the addresses of) a list's head and an endpoint. On a channel following `C`, the serving endpoint would be able to perform as many sequences of sending a memory cell and then waiting for an acknowledgment as it wishes, and will eventually send a `close_me` message to go to the final state `end`. This protocol can be used to send a linked list over the channel until it is empty, and finally request a closing of the channel, as we will see next.

1.2 Sending a List Cell By Cell

The imperative programming language we use features standard variable and memory manipulation. We moreover use `send(m, e, x)` to send message m with value x over endpoint e and `x = receive(m, f)` to retrieve this value through f, provided it is the other end of the channel (*i.e.* f is the *peer* of e). Intuitively, `send` and `receive` are asynchronous communications, and act as enqueuing and dequeuing over one of the two queues that are shared by two coupled endpoints (one queue for each direction). Endpoints are allocated on the heap upon channel creation (`(e,f)=open(C)`) and closed together (`close(e,f)`). This differs from most implementations, where endpoints can be closed independently, but this case an implicit message is sent to notify the closing of one of the endpoint to the other; in our setting, such a message has to be sent explicitly.

Let us now give a program implementing contract `C`. The serving endpoint e is held by the `putter` program, which communicates with `getter`. The program is given a list starting at the address x that it sends cell by cell over e. `getter` disposes the cells one by one, and when the list becomes empty, `putter` sends its endpoint over itself so that `getter` may close the channel. Comments (lines starting with `//` and annotations between brackets) are elements of the proof and will be explained later.

```
putter(e,x) [e,x ⊩ e ↦^ep (C{transfer}, X) * list(x)] {
  local t;
  while (x != 0) {
    // e,x,t ⊩ x ↦ Y * list(Y) * e ↦^ep (C{transfer}, X)
    t = *x;
    send(cell, e, x);
    // e,x,t ⊩ list(t) * e ↦^ep (C{wait_ack}, X)
    x = t;
    receive(ack, e); }
  // e,x,t ⊩ e ↦^ep (C{transfer}, X)
  send(close_me, e, e); } [e,x ⊩ emp]

getter(f) [f ⊩ f ↦^ep (C̄{transfer}, Y)] {
  local x, e = 0;
  // 0 = x,e,f
  while (e == 0) {
    // O ⊩ f ↦^ep (C̄{transfer}, Y) * e = 0
    switch receive {
    x = receive(cell, f): {
      // O ⊩ f ↦^ep (C̄{wait_ack}, Y) * e = 0 * x ↦ -
      free(x)
      // O ⊩ f ↦^ep (C̄{wait_ack}, Y) * e = 0
      send(ack, f); }
    e = receive(close_me, f): {} }}
  // O ⊩ e ↦^ep (C{end}, f) * f ↦^ep (C̄{end}, e)
  close(e, f); } [f ⊩ emp]

main() [x ⊩ list(x)] {
  local e,f;
  (e,f) = open(C);
  // x,e,f ⊩ list(x) * e ↦^ep (C{transfer}, f) * f ↦^ep (C̄{transfer}, e)
  putter(e,x); || getter(f); } [x ⊩ emp]
```

2 A Separation Logic for Copyless Message Passing

2.1 Syntax of Programs

We assume infinite sets $\mathit{Var} = \{e, f, x, y, \dots\}$, $\mathit{Loc} = \{l, \dots\}$, $\mathit{Endpoint} = \{\varepsilon, \dots\}$, $\mathit{MsgId} = \{m, \dots\}$, $\mathit{State} = \{a, b, \dots\}$ and $\mathit{Val} = \{v, \dots\}$ of respectively variables, memory locations, endpoints, message identifiers, contracts' states and values. All sets but values are pairwise disjoint, and $Loc \uplus Endpoint \uplus \{0\} \subseteq Val$. The grammar of expressions, boolean expressions, atomic commands and programs is as follows:

$$E ::= x \in Var \mid v \in Val \qquad\qquad B ::= E = E \mid B \text{ and } B \mid \text{not } B$$

$$\begin{aligned} c ::= {} & \text{assume(B)} \mid \texttt{x = E} \mid \texttt{x = new()} \mid \texttt{*E = E} \mid \texttt{x = *E} \mid \text{free (E)} \\ & \mid \texttt{(e,f) = open(C)} \mid \text{close (E,E)} \mid \text{send(m, E, E)} \mid \texttt{x = receive (m, E)} \end{aligned}$$

$$p ::= c \mid p;\ p \mid p \parallel p \mid p + p \mid p^* \mid \text{local } \texttt{x} \text{ in } p$$

`assume(B)` blocks unless B holds, and does nothing otherwise. Compound commands are standard and are in order sequential and parallel composition, non-deterministic choice, Kleene iteration and local variable creation. `switch receive` is defined as a non-deterministic choice of the `{x=receive(m,E); p}` for every `x = receive(m,E):` p of its body. We leave the similar definitions of `while` loops and `if` statements to the attention of the reader. In our example of Sec. 1.2, subroutines `putter` and `getter` should actually be inlined to fit our model, as it does not feature procedure calls. We write $v(E)$ the set of variables that appear in expression E.

Contracts. A contract is an edge-labeled oriented graph. Vertices are called *states*, and every contract C distinguishes an initial state $\text{init}(C)$ and a set of final states $\text{final}(C)$. Labels are either send label $!m$ or receive label $?m$, where m is a message identifier. We write $\bar{C}$ for the dual of contract C, *i.e.* C where ! and ? are swapped.

A contract specification is given by a map $m \mapsto I_m$ from message identifiers to precise separation logic formulas (to be defined soon). I_m is called the invariant of the message. Only special variables `val` and `src` can appear free in I_m.

2.2 Syntax of the Logic

We assume an extra infinite set $LVar = \{X, Y, \ldots\}$ of logical variables distinct from the program's variables. We extend the grammar of expressions to allow them to contain logical variables. The assertion language is then as follows:

$$\begin{aligned} A ::= {} & \mathsf{emp}_s \mid \mathsf{own}(x) \mid E = E && \text{stack predicates} \\ & \mid \mathsf{emp}_h \mid \mathsf{emp}_{ep} \mid E \mapsto E \mid E \overset{ep}{\mapsto} (C\{a\}, E) && \text{heaps predicates} \\ & \mid \neg A \mid A \wedge A \mid \exists X.\, A \mid A * A \mid A \mathrel{-\!\!*} A && \text{connectives} \end{aligned}$$

All predicates and connectives are standard, except emp_{ep} and $E \overset{ep}{\mapsto} (C\{a\}, E)$. Before defining the semantics of the logic, let us define some useful shorthands.

We will write emp for $\mathsf{emp}_h \wedge \mathsf{emp}_{ep}$ and, for instance, $E \mapsto -$ for $\exists X.\, E \mapsto X$. In this work, we use variables as resources [2] without permissions for simplicity, thus forbidding concurrent reads. When $O = x_1, \ldots, x_n$, we will write, as usual, $O \Vdash A$ as a shorthand for $(\mathsf{own}(x_1) * \ldots * \mathsf{own}(x_n)) \wedge A$. Moreover, to avoid cumbersome notations in formulas, we will sometimes allow reads to the same variable in the stack in two disjoint states, *i.e.* have formulas of the form $x \Vdash A(x) * B(x)$. They should be understood as $x \Vdash \exists X.\, x = X \wedge (A(X) * B(X))$.

2.3 Basic Memory Model

Formulas are interpreted over a subset Σ^{wf} of the set Σ of basic memory pre-states (s, h, k) defined by:

$$\Sigma \triangleq \mathit{Stack} \times \mathit{CHeap} \times \mathit{EHeap} \qquad \mathit{Stack} \triangleq \mathit{Var} \rightharpoonup \mathit{Val} \qquad \mathit{CHeap} \triangleq \mathit{Loc} \rightharpoonup \mathit{Val}$$

$$\mathit{EHeap} \triangleq \mathit{Endpoint} \rightharpoonup \mathit{Contract} \times \mathit{State} \times \mathit{Endpoint}$$

It is equipped with a composition law $\circ$ of a separation algebra (see Sec. 3.1) defined as the disjoint union $\uplus$ of each of the components of the pre-states: $(s, h, k) \circ (s', h', k') \triangleq (s \uplus s', h \uplus h', k \uplus k')$. *Stack* and *CHeap* (cell heap) are standard, and *EHeap* (endpoint heap) works in the same way as *CHeap* but is used to represent endpoints.

We define *memory states* Σ^{wf} as the elements of Σ that satisfy the axioms

$$\begin{array}{rl} \textbf{Dual} & k(\varepsilon) = (C, a, \varepsilon') \;\&\; k(\varepsilon') = (C', b, \varepsilon'') \Rightarrow \varepsilon'' = \varepsilon \;\&\; C' = \bar{C} \\ \textbf{Irreflexive} & k(\varepsilon) = (-, -, \varepsilon') \Rightarrow \varepsilon \neq \varepsilon' \\ \textbf{Injective} & k(\varepsilon_1) = (-, -, \varepsilon_1') \;\&\; k(\varepsilon_2) = (-, -, \varepsilon_2') \;\&\; \varepsilon_1 \neq \varepsilon_2 \Rightarrow \varepsilon_1' \neq \varepsilon_2' \end{array}$$

We restrict $\circ$ to a new operation $\bullet$ on memory states defined only when $\sigma \circ \sigma' \in \Sigma^{\mathsf{wf}}$. We will write $\sigma \sharp \sigma'$ when this is the case. Let us now give the satisfaction relation $\vDash$ between states in Σ^{wf} and formulas. We write $[\![x]\!]s$ to denote $s(x)$ if $x \in \mathit{dom}(s)$, and $[\![v]\!]s$ denotes v.

$$\begin{array}{lll} (s,h,k) \vDash E_1 = E_2 & \text{iff} & v(E_1, E_2) \subseteq \mathit{dom}(s) \;\&\; [\![E_1]\!]s = [\![E_2]\!]s \\ (s,h,k) \vDash \mathsf{emp}_{\spadesuit} & \text{iff} & \mathit{dom}(\spadesuit) = \emptyset \quad (\spadesuit \in \{s, h, k\}) \\ (s,h,k) \vDash \mathsf{own}(x) & \text{iff} & \mathit{dom}(s) = \{x\} \\ (s,h,k) \vDash E_1 \mapsto E_2 & \text{iff} & v(E_1, E_2) \subseteq \mathit{dom}(s) \;\&\; \mathit{dom}(h) = \{[\![E_1]\!]s\} \\ & & \;\&\; \mathit{dom}(k) = \emptyset \;\&\; h([\![E_1]\!]s) = [\![E_2]\!]s \\ (s,h,k) \vDash E_1 \overset{ep}{\mapsto}(C\{a\}, E_2) & \text{iff} & v(E_1, E_2) \subseteq \mathit{dom}(s) \;\&\; \mathit{dom}(k) = \{[\![E_1]\!]s\} \\ & & \;\&\; \mathit{dom}(h) = \emptyset \;\&\; k([\![E_1]\!]s) = (C, a, [\![E_2]\!]s) \\ \sigma \vDash \neg A & \text{iff} & \sigma \nvDash A \\ \sigma \vDash A_1 \wedge A_2 & \text{iff} & \sigma \vDash A_1 \;\&\; \sigma \vDash A_2 \\ \sigma \vDash \exists X.\, A & \text{iff} & \exists v \in \mathit{Val}.\, \sigma \vDash A[X \leftarrow v] \\ \sigma \vDash A_1 * A_2 & \text{iff} & \exists \sigma_1, \sigma_2.\, \sigma = \sigma_1 \bullet \sigma_2 \;\&\; \sigma_1 \vDash A_1 \;\&\; \sigma_2 \vDash A_2 \\ \sigma \vDash A \mathrel{-\!\!*} B & \text{iff} & \forall \sigma' \sharp \sigma.\, \sigma' \vDash A \text{ implies } \sigma \bullet \sigma' \vDash B \end{array}$$

2.4 Proof System

Our proof system is based on the framework of abstract separation logic. We extend the rules of separation logic (frame rule, composition rules and the standard small axioms for all pointer instructions) with four new small axioms for channel instructions. We abbreviate $I_m[\mathtt{src} \leftarrow E_1, \mathtt{val} \leftarrow E_2]$ as $I_m(E_1, E_2)$. Figure 1 presents all the rules. Among these four new small axioms, the one for send deserves a special attention, as we can derive two different small axioms from it: $\{O \Vdash E \overset{ep}{\mapsto}(C\{a\}, \varepsilon) * I_m(E, F)\}$ send(m,E,F) $\{O \Vdash E \overset{ep}{\mapsto}(C\{a\}, \varepsilon)\}$ that accounts for the most standard sending (taking $A = E \overset{ep}{\mapsto}(C\{b\}, \varepsilon)$), and sending the endpoint over itself is accounted by $\{O \Vdash E \overset{ep}{\mapsto}(C\{a\}, \varepsilon) * (E \overset{ep}{\mapsto}(C\{b\}, \varepsilon) \mathrel{-\!\!*} I_m(E, F))\}$ send(m,E,F) $\{O \Vdash \mathsf{emp}\}$ (taking $A = \mathsf{emp}$). We will write $\vdash \{A\}\; \mathsf{p}\; \{B\}$ when this triple is derivable.

$$\frac{\boldsymbol{x} = v(B)}{\{\boldsymbol{x} \Vdash \boldsymbol{x} = \boldsymbol{v}\}\ \text{assume(B)}\ \{\boldsymbol{x} \Vdash \boldsymbol{x} = \boldsymbol{v} \wedge B\}} \qquad \{x, O \Vdash E = v \wedge \mathsf{emp}\}\ \texttt{x = E}\ \{x, O \Vdash x = v \wedge \mathsf{emp}\}$$

$$\{x \Vdash \mathsf{emp}\}\ \texttt{x = new()}\ \{x \Vdash x \mapsto -\} \qquad \{O \Vdash E \mapsto - \wedge F = v\}\ \texttt{*E = F}\ \{O \Vdash E \mapsto v\}$$

$$\{x, O \Vdash E = v \wedge v \mapsto v'\}\ \texttt{x = *E}\ \{x, O \Vdash x = v' \wedge v \mapsto v'\} \qquad \{O \Vdash E \mapsto -\}\ \texttt{free(E)}\ \{O \Vdash \mathsf{emp}\}$$

$$\frac{i = \mathrm{init}(C)}{\{e, f \Vdash \mathsf{emp}\}\ \texttt{(e,f) = open(C)}\ \{e, f \Vdash e \overset{ep}{\mapsto}(C\{i\}, f) * f \overset{ep}{\mapsto}(\bar{C}\{i\}, e)\}}$$

$$\frac{a \in \mathrm{final}(C)}{\{O \Vdash E \overset{ep}{\mapsto}(C\{a\}, E') * E' \overset{ep}{\mapsto}(\bar{C}\{a\}, E)\}\ \texttt{close(E,E')}\ \{O \Vdash \mathsf{emp}\}}$$

$$\frac{a \xrightarrow{!m} b \in C}{\{O \Vdash E \overset{ep}{\mapsto}(C\{a\}, \varepsilon) * (E \overset{ep}{\mapsto}(C\{b\}, \varepsilon) \mathrel{-\!\!*} (I_m(E, F) * A))\}\ \texttt{send(m,E,F)}\ \{O \Vdash A\}}$$

$$\frac{a \xrightarrow{?m} b \in C}{\{O, x \Vdash E \overset{ep}{\mapsto}(C\{a\}, \varepsilon)\}\ \texttt{x = receive(m,E)}\ \{O, x \Vdash E \overset{ep}{\mapsto}(C\{b\}, \varepsilon) * I_m(\varepsilon, x)\}} \qquad \frac{\{A\}\ p\ \{B\}}{\{A * F\}\ p\ \{B * F\}}$$

$$\frac{A' \Rightarrow A \quad \{A\}\ p\ \{B\} \quad B \Rightarrow B'}{\{A'\}\ p\ \{B'\}} \qquad \frac{\{A_i\}\ p\ \{B_i\} \quad \text{all i in } I}{\{\bigsqcap_{i \in I} A_i\}\ p\ \{\bigsqcap_{i \in I} B_i\}} \qquad \frac{\{A_i\}\ p\ \{B_i\} \quad \text{all i in } I}{\{\bigsqcup_{i \in I} A_i\}\ p\ \{\bigsqcup_{i \in I} B_i\}}$$

$$\frac{\{A\}\ p\ \{B\} \quad \{A'\}\ p'\ \{B'\}}{\{A * A'\}\ p \parallel p'\ \{B * B'\}} \qquad \frac{\{A\}\ p\ \{A'\} \quad \{A'\}\ p'\ \{B\}}{\{A\}\ p; p'\ \{B\}} \qquad \frac{\{A\}\ p\ \{B\} \quad \{A\}\ p'\ \{B\}}{\{A\}\ p + p'\ \{B\}}$$

$$\frac{\{I\}\ p\ \{I\}}{\{I\}\ p^*\ \{I\}} \qquad \frac{\{\mathsf{own}(z) * A\}\ p[x \leftarrow z]\ \{\mathsf{own}(z) * B\}}{\{A\}\ \text{local}\, x \text{ in } p\ \{B\}}\ z \text{ fresh}$$

Fig. 1. Proof System Rules

2.5 Back to the Example

We now highlight some steps of the proof that the program p presented at Sec. 1.2 satisfies the Hoare triple $\{x \Vdash \mathrm{list}(x)\}\ p\ \{x \Vdash \mathsf{emp}\}$. Bracketed formulas are used to denote the pre and post-condition of a program. We start with the precondition $x \Vdash \mathrm{list}(x)$, where $\mathrm{list}(x)$ is the inductive list predicate verifying emp if $x = 0$ and $\exists X. x \mapsto X * \mathrm{list}(X)$ otherwise. Before entering the parallel composition, we obtain $x, e, f \Vdash \mathrm{list}(x) * e \overset{ep}{\mapsto}(C\{\mathtt{transfer}\}, f) * f \overset{ep}{\mapsto}(\bar{C}\{\mathtt{transfer}\}, e)$. To apply the rule for parallel composition, we have to split the state into two. `putter` will get resources $e, x \Vdash e \overset{ep}{\mapsto}(C\{\mathtt{transfer}\}, -) * \mathrm{list}(x)$ and `getter` $f \Vdash f \overset{ep}{\mapsto}(\bar{C}\{\mathtt{transfer}\}, -)$. The next important step is after the loop, at line 9; we are left with just the endpoint e, which we send in a `close_me` message. According to $I_{\mathtt{close\_me}}$ and the rule of `send` with $A = \mathsf{emp}$, the post-condition of `putter` is thus $e, x \Vdash \mathsf{emp}$.

The proof of the `getter` program follows the same lines. Crucially, after receiving the `close_me` message, we can deduce that we have received the *peer* of f thanks to **Dual** and the use of the `src` variable in $I_{\mathtt{close\_me}}$. This allows the CLOSE rule to fire up. At the end of the parallel composition, we thus obtain empty heaps $x \Vdash \mathsf{emp}$ which concludes the proof.

3 Soundness

We now turn to proving that the proof system is sound and giving an accurate semantics for programs. As the soundness of concurrent separation logic itself has proven hard to establish in the past [3], we base our work on abstract separation logic, which allows us to deduce the soundness of our proof system from the sole soundness of its axioms. But this only resolves half of our concerns, for concurrent separation logic is not fit to describe synchrony issues, for example that sends must happen before receives, nor does it entail a pointer passing semantics, without transfers (the transfers erasure property). In this section, we explain how to remedy this by extending the basic memory model.

As even an informal presentation of our semantics relies heavily on abstract separation logic [5], we begin this section by a short introduction to this framework.

3.1 Abstract Separation Logic in a Nutshell

A *separation algebra* is a cancellative, partial, commutative monoid $(\Sigma, \bullet, u)$ where cancellative means that the partial function $\sigma \bullet (\cdot) : \Sigma \rightharpoonup \Sigma$ is injective; one may write either $\sigma_1 \sharp \sigma_2$ or $\sigma_1 \perp \sigma_2$ when $\sigma_1 \bullet \sigma_2$ is defined, $\sigma \preceq \sigma'$ if there is σ_1 such that $\sigma' = \sigma \bullet \sigma_1$, and denote the unique such σ_1 by $\sigma' - \sigma$ when it exists. $(\mathcal{P}(\Sigma)^\top, \sqsubseteq)$ denotes the powerset of Σ ordered by inclusion, extended with a greatest element $\top$. The operator $*$ defined by $A * B = \{\sigma_0 \bullet \sigma_1 \mid \sigma_0 \sharp \sigma_1 \,\&\, \sigma_0 \in A \,\&\, \sigma_1 \in B\}$ if $A, B \neq \top$, $\top$ otherwise, defines a commutative ordered monoid $(\mathcal{P}(\Sigma)^\top, *, \emptyset, \sqsubseteq)$. A property A is *precise* if for all σ, there is at most one $\sigma' \preceq \sigma$ in A.

We will later define the semantics of all atomic commands as local functions. A *local function* $f : \Sigma \to \mathcal{P}(\Sigma)^\top$ is a total function such that for all $\sigma, \sigma' \in \Sigma$, if $\sigma \sharp \sigma'$ then $f(\sigma \bullet \sigma') \sqsubseteq \{\sigma\} * f(\sigma')$. $f \sqsubseteq g$ denotes the pointwise order on local functions. Composition $f; g$ of local functions is performed using the obvious lifting of g to $\mathcal{P}(\Sigma)^\top$: $(f; g)(\sigma) \triangleq \bigsqcup\{g(\sigma') \mid \sigma' \in f(\sigma)\}$ or $\top$ if $f(\sigma) = \top$. A *specification* ϕ is a set of pairs (A, B) in $\mathcal{P}(\Sigma)$. We write $f \vDash \phi$ and say that f satisfies ϕ when $f(A) \sqsubseteq B$ for every $(A, B) \in \phi$. The best local action of ϕ is defined by $bla[\phi](\sigma) = \bigsqcap_{\sigma' \preceq \sigma, \sigma' \in A, (A,B) \in \phi} \{\sigma - \sigma'\} * B$. It is local, satisfies its specification, and is the greatest such local function for the pointwise order on local functions [5].

Lemma 1. *Basic memory states* $(\Sigma^{\mathsf{wf}}, \bullet, u)$ *and pre-states* $(\Sigma, \circ, u)$*, where* $u = (\emptyset, \emptyset, \emptyset)$*, are separation algebras.*

A simple way to obtain a soundness result for our proof system would thus be to define the semantics of all atomic commands as the best local actions of their specifications. Using the trace semantics we will present soon, all proof rules would be sound. As we will explain now, this would lead to a very coarse semantics without synchronization that over-approximates the communications. In particular, as mentionned in the introduction, sending a message with value x and immediately retrieving it in y would not be equivalent to simply assigning x to y.

3.2 Trace Semantics and Global Semantics

Syntactic traces. Let us define the traces $T(p)$ of a program p as a set of sequences of *actions* $\alpha \in \{c, \mathrm{norace}(c_1, c_2), \mathrm{n}_x, \mathrm{d}_x\}$ for all commands c, c_1, c_2, following the original approach of abstract separation logic extended with the treatment of local variables: n_x allocates $x \in \mathit{Var}$ on the stack and d_x disposes it.

$$T(\alpha) = \{\alpha\} \qquad T(p_1 + p_2) = T(p_1) \cup T(p_2) \qquad T(p^*) = (T(p))^*$$

$$T(p_1; p_2) = \{tr_1; tr_2 \mid tr_i \in T(p_i)\} \qquad T(p_1 \parallel p_2) = \{tr_1 \; zip \; tr_2 \mid tr_i \in T(p_i)\}$$

$$T(\text{local x in } p) = \{\mathrm{n}_z; T(p[x \leftarrow z]); \mathrm{d}_z \mid z \text{ fresh in } p\}$$

Parallel composition is treated as a syntactic interleaving of commands. We force all racy programs to fault by placing $\mathrm{norace}(c_1, c_2)$ each time c_1 and c_2 may be executed simultaneously. This command will check that c_1 and c_2 can execute on disjoint portions of the state. *zip* is thus defined by $\varepsilon \; zip \; tr = tr \; zip \; \varepsilon = tr$ in the base case, and by $(c_1; tr_1) \, zip \, (c_2; tr_2) = \mathrm{norace}(c_1, c_2); ((c_1; (tr_1 \, zip \, (c_2; tr_2))) \cup (c_2; (c_1; tr_1) \, zip \, tr_2))$.

Semantics. The denotational semantics of traces is the composition of the interpretation of atomic actions: $[\![\alpha]\!] = (\![\alpha]\!)$ and $[\![tr_1; tr_2]\!] = [\![tr_1]\!]; [\![tr_2]\!]$. This assumes that a semantics $(\![c]\!)$ is defined for all primitive commands, which we will give later. The semantics of $\mathrm{norace}(c_1, c_2)$ is the local function $norace((\![c_1]\!), (\![c_2]\!))$, defined by

$$norace(f, g)(\hat{\sigma}) \triangleq \begin{cases} \{\hat{\sigma}\} & \text{if } \exists \hat{\sigma}_f, \hat{\sigma}_g. \, \hat{\sigma}_f \bullet \hat{\sigma}_g = \hat{\sigma} \;\&\; f(\hat{\sigma}_f) \neq \top \;\&\; g(\hat{\sigma}_g) \neq \top \\ \top & \text{otherwise} \end{cases}$$

Finally, the semantics of stack bookkeeping actions n_x and d_x are defined as the best local actions $(\![\mathrm{n}_x]\!) \triangleq n_x \triangleq bla[\mathsf{emp}_s, \mathsf{own}(x)]$ and $(\![\mathrm{d}_x]\!) \triangleq d_x \triangleq bla[\mathsf{own}(x), \mathsf{emp}_s]$.

Following this approach is essential for deriving easily the soundness of the parallel rule: $[\![p \parallel p']\!](\sigma \bullet \sigma') \sqsubseteq [\![p]\!](\sigma) * [\![p']\!](\sigma')$. The downside is that parallel threads have to work on disjoint memory states, hence receiving a message cannot be blocking and must be non-deterministic. This poses two challenges: how to synchronize concurrent actions and how to model inter-threads communication.

Successive semantics. Our approach here relies on three successive refinements of the semantics defined by the small axioms of our proof system.

The first one enriches the memory model and the communication primitives so that, at any point in the execution, the history of all past communications, including the contents of all messages, can be observed in the resulting states. This is covered in Sec. 4. However, this semantics is still local so we cannot link the histories of two corresponding endpoints yet, as one of them may reside outside of the current heap. Moreover, `send` and `receive` still act respectively as a disposal and a non-deterministic creation of the message's contents.

The next step is thus to consider programs as wholes. In this case, we can observe the whole state at every point of the execution. In particular, both endpoints of every opened channel will always be present. We may now restrict the states produced by the commands to *legal* ones, *i.e.* states where receives have happened after the corresponding send, and where contents of sent and received messages match (intuitions about how this will be performed are introduced in the next two subsections). This will automatically restrict traces in the same way: a receive preceding the corresponding send will produce an empty set of legal states. This is also how `assume(B)` works: it blocks executions where B does not hold.

The third and final semantics is the same as the global one, except that the communications are not loggued, thus achieving a pure pointer-passing semantics.

We will explain now what information histories will have to contain in the h.p. model. The formal definition of legal states can be found in Sec. 5.

3.3 Synchronization

Concurrent separation logic uses critical sections to synchronize and communicate between processes. In this case, the synchronization may be performed at the syntactic trace level, by considering only *well-formed* traces, in which two critical sections over the same resource are never interleaved [5]. This syntactic synchronization is possible because resources are not part of the expression language, and determining whether two critical sections refer to the same resource can be done just by looking at the resource identifier. This is not the case for channel communication, as retrieving which endpoint is used for sending or receiving involves evaluating an expression, which cannot be done at the trace level.

Instead, we rule out ill-synchronized traces at the semantics level by making them block when executed. To achieve this, we must add information to the endpoints in the model, namely how many messages have been sent and how many have been received on this endpoint (see Sec. 3.5), and modify `send` and `receive` to increment these counters. Legal states will thus be such that any endpoint ε must have received less than what its peer has sent. This ensures that traces where a `receive` happens when there is no pending message inside the channel will block.

3.4 Communication

In concurrent separation logic, communication is achieved by passing pieces of states around using conditional critical regions: acquiring a shared resource is modeled by an allocation (roughly, $(\!|\mathrm{acquire}\ r|\!)(\sigma) = \{\sigma\} * I_r$), and releasing it is modeled by deallocation of the part of memory corresponding to the invariant. Acquiring a resource is thus non-deterministic, as the resource r may be acquired in any state satisfying the resource invariant I_r, and not the state in which it was left after the last release. The local semantics of `receive` suffer from the same caveat.

The semantics to which we aspire should be more precise and ensure that the contents of what is received match what was sent. For this purpose, we have chosen to "log" a copy of the message contents that is sent or non-deterministically received in the thread-local heap. To describe "logging", we enrich the model with *timestamps*: each cell and endpoint is tagged with a timestamp $\tau \in \mathcal{T}$ and a direction $\dagger \in \{?, !\}$. We will note $[\tau^\dagger]\hat{\sigma}$ for the memory state formed of a single log using timestamp τ. Sending $\hat{\sigma}$ will deallocate it and allocate the log $[\tau^!]\hat{\sigma}$, whereas the corresponding `receive` will allocate $\hat{\sigma}' \bullet [\tau^?]\hat{\sigma}'$ for the same timestamp τ and some guessed $\hat{\sigma}'$. Then, the memory state $[\tau^!]\hat{\sigma} \bullet [\tau^?]\hat{\sigma}'$ will be declared legal if and only if $\hat{\sigma} = \hat{\sigma}'$, which will ensure the coherence of communications in the global semantics.

Moreover, we have to provide a mechanism for choosing which timestamp should be used for logging for each message, and the endpoint's owner that will issue a message should locally choose its timestamp. We thus attach to every channel a pair of *histories*

$(\ell_!, \ell_?)$ where $\ell_!, \ell_?$ contain a list of the successive (distinct) timestamps at which the messages respectively sent and received (from the serving endpoint point of view) will have to be logged. Both endpoints will be equipped with these histories upon creation (the client endpoint will be equipped with the dual pair $(\ell_?, \ell_!)$) in order to log the same message with the same timestamp when it is sent and received.

Finally, histories can also be used to check that the value and message identifier of a message is the same on both endpoints involved. This could have been part of the logging mechanism, but it has turned out to be simpler to consider it apart.

3.5 Refined Model

Adding up what has been informally described above, we obtain the following *history preserving memory model* $\hat{\Sigma}$ defined from histories $\mathit{Hist} \triangleq (\mathit{MsgId} \times \mathit{Val} \times \mathcal{T})^\omega$:

$$\begin{aligned} \hat{\Sigma} &\triangleq \mathit{Stack} \times \mathit{C\hat{H}eap} \times \mathit{E\hat{H}eap} \\ \mathit{C\hat{H}eap} &\triangleq \mathit{Loc} \times \mathcal{T}^{\{?,!\}} \rightharpoonup \mathit{Val} \\ \mathit{E\hat{H}eap} &\triangleq \mathit{Endpoint} \times \mathcal{T}^{\{?,!\}} \rightharpoonup \mathit{Contract} \times \mathit{State} \times \mathit{Endpoint} \times \mathbb{N}^2 \times \mathit{Hist}^2 \end{aligned}$$

Timestamps τ form an infinite set $\mathcal{T}$, disjoint from previously defined sets, from which we define *polarized* timestamps $\mathcal{T}^{\{?,!\}} \triangleq (\mathcal{T} \times \{?,!\}) + \{\mathbf{now}\}$. We extend Val to contain $\mathcal{T}$. For simplicity, we may write $\mathbf{now}^!$ and $\mathbf{now}^?$ for $\mathbf{now}$.

$(\hat{\Sigma}, \circ, u)$ defines a separation algebra where $\circ$ denotes disjoint union of (tuples of) partial functions. To distinguish heaps of the basic and h.p. model, we adopt a hat notation, and let $\hat{h}, \hat{k}, \ldots$ range over $\mathit{C\hat{H}eap}$, $\mathit{E\hat{H}eap}$.

We define the projection $\mathrm{now} : \hat{\Sigma} \to \Sigma$ which associates to a state $\hat{\sigma} = (s, \hat{h}, \hat{k}) \in \hat{\Sigma}$ the state $\sigma = (s, h, k)$ where $h = \hat{h}(\cdot, \mathbf{now})$ and k is $\hat{k}(\cdot, \mathbf{now})$ where histories and counters have been erased. We can now define what it means for a program executing on h.p. states to satisfy a Hoare triple.

Definition 1 (Semantic Hoare Triple).
- *If* $A, B \in \mathcal{P}(\Sigma)$ *and* $f : \hat{\Sigma} \to \mathcal{P}(\hat{\Sigma})^\top$, *we write* $\langle\langle A \rangle\rangle\ f\ \langle\langle B \rangle\rangle$ *iff* $\forall \hat{\sigma}.\ \mathrm{now}(\hat{\sigma}) \in A$ *implies* $\mathrm{now}(f(\hat{\sigma})) \sqsubseteq B$.
- *We write* $\vDash \{A\}\ p\ \{B\}$ *iff* $\forall tr \in T(p).\ \langle\langle A \rangle\rangle\ [\![tr]\!]\ \langle\langle B \rangle\rangle$.

4 Semantics of Programs

4.1 Refined Assertions

We now show how to interpret the logic in the refined model, so as to give a semantics of commands from logical specifications and state the soundness theorem later on.

We let $ts(\ell)$ denote the set of timestamps that appear in ℓ. If ℓ is a history list and i is an integer, $\ell[i]$ represents the ith item of ℓ. We write $\mathit{logs}(\hat{\sigma})$ to denote the set of polarized timestamps that appear in $\hat{\sigma}$, *i.e.* $\mathrm{snd}(\mathit{dom}(\hat{h})) \cup \mathrm{snd}(\mathit{dom}(\hat{k}))$.

If $\hat{\sigma} = (s, \hat{h}, \hat{k})$, we write $\hat{\sigma}\lfloor_{\tau^\dagger}$ (resp. $\hat{\sigma}\lfloor_T$) to denote the pre-state at timestamp $\tau^\dagger$ defined by restricting $\hat{h}$ and $\hat{k}$ to the timestamp $\tau^\dagger$ (resp. the set of polarized timestamps T). This gives a semantics for formulas over $\hat{\Sigma}$: for any $\hat{\sigma} \in \hat{\Sigma}$, and for any A, $\hat{\sigma} \vDash A$ if and only if (1) $\mathit{logs}(\hat{\sigma}) \subseteq \{\mathbf{now}\}$ and (2) $\hat{\sigma}\lfloor_{\mathbf{now}} \vDash A$.

We now extend the logic to be able to talk about logged cells. Note that, within a memory state, the same location may be allocated with a different content for different timestamps, which we call conflicting cells. For $\hat{\sigma} = (s, \hat{h}, \hat{k})$ and a polarized timestamp $\tau^\dagger$, we write $\langle\tau^\dagger\rangle\hat{\sigma}$ for the set of states that result from $\hat{\sigma}$ by tagging all cells with timestamp $\tau^\dagger$, for any possible resolution of conflicting cells. Formally, $\hat{\sigma}' = (s, \hat{h}', \hat{k}') \in \langle\tau^\dagger\rangle\hat{\sigma}$ if $logs(\hat{\sigma}') = \{\tau^\dagger\}$ and for all $l \in Loc$ (resp. for all $\varepsilon \in Endpoint$) there is a timestamp $\tau'^\ddagger$ such that $\hat{h}'(l, \tau^\dagger) = \hat{h}(l, \tau'^\ddagger)$ (resp. $\hat{k}'(\varepsilon, \tau^\dagger) = \hat{k}(\varepsilon, \tau'^\ddagger)$). When there are no conflicting cells, that is when $\langle\tau^\dagger\rangle\hat{\sigma} = \{\hat{\sigma}_0\}$, we write $[\tau^\dagger]\hat{\sigma}$ to denote $\hat{\sigma}_0$. Finally, we write $\langle\tau^\dagger\rangle A$ to denote $\bigsqcup\{\langle\tau^\dagger\rangle\hat{\sigma} \mid \hat{\sigma} \vDash A\}$, and $\langle\tau_1^\dagger * \tau_2^\ddagger\rangle A$ to denote the set of states $\{[\tau_1^\dagger]\hat{\sigma} \bullet [\tau_2^\ddagger]\hat{\sigma} \mid \hat{\sigma} \vDash A\}$.

Finally, we restrict h.p. memory states to well-formed ones in the same way as for memory states, and limit the composition of states so that the logged content of a message is never split into two, nor extended by the frame rule, thus preventing two distinct messages from being logged at the same timestamp.

Definition 2 (H.P. memory states). *The separation subalgebra $(\hat{\Sigma}^{\mathsf{wf}}, \bullet, \hat{u})$ of well-formed h.p. memory states is the subalgebra of $(\hat{\Sigma}, \circ, \hat{u})$ obtained by restricting $\hat{\Sigma}$ to states $\hat{\sigma}$ such that* $\mathrm{now}(\hat{\sigma}) \in \Sigma^{\mathsf{wf}}$*, and strengthening the compatibility relation $\perp$ by:* ***AtomicLogs****: $\hat{\sigma} \bullet \hat{\sigma}'$ is defined if $\hat{\sigma} \circ \hat{\sigma}' \in \hat{\Sigma}^{\mathsf{wf}}$ and for all $\dagger \in \{?, !\}$ and $\tau \neq$* **now**, $[\mathbf{now}](\hat{\sigma}\lfloor_{\tau^\dagger}) \vDash \mathsf{emp}$ *or* $[\mathbf{now}](\hat{\sigma}'\lfloor_{\tau^\dagger}) \vDash \mathsf{emp}$.

Lemma 2. *$(\hat{\Sigma}^{\mathsf{wf}}, \bullet, \hat{u})$ is a separation algebra.*

Finally, we extend the satisfaction relation of Sec. 2.3 to h.p. states by overloading every predicate but $\overset{ep}{\mapsto}$ and every constructor in the obvious way. We overload $\overset{ep}{\mapsto}$ with two new meanings:

$$(s, \hat{h}, \hat{k}) \vDash E \overset{ep}{\mapsto} (C\{a\}, E', n_?, n_!, \ell_?, \ell_!) \text{ iff}$$
$$\begin{cases} \quad v(E, E') \subseteq dom(s) \;\&\; dom(\hat{k}) = \{(\llbracket E \rrbracket s, \mathbf{now})\} \;\&\; dom(\hat{h}) = \emptyset \\ \;\&\; \hat{k}(\llbracket E \rrbracket s, \mathbf{now}) = (C, a, \llbracket E' \rrbracket s, n_?, n_!, \ell_?, \ell_!) \end{cases}$$
$$(s, \hat{h}, \hat{k}) \vDash E \overset{ep}{\mapsto} (C\{a\}, E') \text{ iff } \exists n_?, n_!, \ell_?, \ell_!.\, (s, \hat{h}, \hat{k}) \vDash E \overset{ep}{\mapsto} (C\{a\}, E', n_?, n_!, \ell_?, \ell_!)$$

4.2 Refined Small Axioms

We define the semantics $(\!|c|\!) : \hat{\Sigma}^{\mathsf{wf}} \to \mathcal{P}(\hat{\Sigma}^{\mathsf{wf}})^\top$ of an atomic command c as the best local action of a specification $\hat{\phi}$ over $\hat{\Sigma}^{\mathsf{wf}}$. For most of the commands, $\hat{\phi}$ is simply the specification ϕ given by the small axiom associated to it in the proof system, interpreted over $\hat{\Sigma}^{\mathsf{wf}}$ (according to the already mentioned interpretation of $\hat{\sigma} \vDash A$: $logs(\hat{\sigma}) = \{\mathbf{now}\}$ and $\mathrm{now}(\hat{\sigma}) \vDash A$). The only commands for which $\hat{\phi} \neq \phi$ are `open`, `send` and `receive`, which need to deal with histories.

The semantics of `open` is the simplest one. As mentioned in Sec. 3.4, the histories attached to the endpoints are guessed when they are created, and dual histories should match; moreover, the queues' counters are initialized to zero. The refined small axiom for `open` is hence the following:

$$\frac{i = \mathsf{init}(C)}{\{e, f \Vdash \mathsf{emp}\}\ \texttt{(e,f) = open(C)}\ \{e, f \Vdash e \overset{ep}{\mapsto} (C\{i\}, f, 0, 0, \ell, \ell') * f \overset{ep}{\mapsto} (\bar{C}\{i\}, e, 0, 0, \ell', \ell)\}}$$

$$\{O \Vdash E \overset{ep}{\mapsto}(C\{a\}, \varepsilon, n_?, n_!, \ell_?, \ell_!) \wedge E' = v\}$$
$$\texttt{enq(E,E')}$$
$$\{O \Vdash E \overset{ep}{\mapsto}(C\{a\}, \varepsilon, n_?, n_! + 1, \ell_?, \ell_!) \wedge E' = v \wedge \ell_![n_!] = (-, v, -)\}$$

$$\{O, x \Vdash E \overset{ep}{\mapsto}(C\{a\}, \varepsilon, n_?, n_!, \ell_?, \ell_!)\}$$
$$\texttt{x = deq(E)}$$
$$\{O, x \Vdash E \overset{ep}{\mapsto}(C\{a\}, \varepsilon, n_? + 1, n_!, \ell_?, \ell_!) \wedge \ell_?[n_?] = (-, x, -)\}$$

$$\frac{a \xrightarrow{\dagger m} b \in C}{\{O \Vdash E \overset{ep}{\mapsto}(C\{a\}, \varepsilon, n_?, n_!, \ell_?, \ell_!)\} \ \texttt{contract}^\dagger\texttt{(m,E)} \ \{O \Vdash E \overset{ep}{\mapsto}(C\{b\}, \varepsilon, n_?, n_!, \ell_?, \ell_!) \wedge \ell_\dagger[n_\dagger] = (m, -, -)\}}$$

$$\{O, x \Vdash E \overset{ep}{\mapsto}(C\{a\}, \varepsilon, n_?, n_!, \ell_?, \ell_!)\}$$
$$\texttt{x = cur\_ts}^\dagger\texttt{(E)}$$
$$\{O, x \Vdash E \overset{ep}{\mapsto}(C\{a\}, \varepsilon, n_?, n_!, \ell_?, \ell_!) \wedge \ell_\dagger[n_\dagger - 1] = (-, -, x)\}$$

$$\{O, e \Vdash E \overset{ep}{\mapsto}(C\{a\}, \varepsilon, n_?, n_!, \ell_?, \ell_!)\} \ \texttt{e = peer(E)} \ \{O, e \Vdash E \overset{ep}{\mapsto}(C\{a\}, \varepsilon, n_?, n_!, \ell_?, \ell_!) \wedge e = \varepsilon\}$$

$$\{O \Vdash E = \varepsilon \wedge E' = v \wedge \mathsf{emp}\} \ \texttt{new(m,E,E')} \ \{O \Vdash E = \varepsilon \wedge E' = v \wedge I_m(\varepsilon, v)\}$$

$$\{O \Vdash I_m(E, E')\} \ \texttt{free(m,E,E')} \ \{O \Vdash \mathsf{emp}\} \qquad \frac{\hat{\sigma} \vDash O \Vdash I_m(E, E') \wedge t = \tau}{\{\hat{\sigma}\} \ \texttt{log}^\dagger\texttt{(m,E,E',t)} \ \{\langle \mathbf{now} * \tau^\dagger \rangle \hat{\sigma}\}}$$

Fig. 2. Small axioms of the sub-atomic operations

The semantics of `send` and `receive` are more complex: they are the composition of several sub-atomic operations that perform basic tasks.

$$\texttt{send(m, E, E')} \triangleq \texttt{atomic}\{\ \texttt{contract}^!\texttt{(m,E); enq(E,E'); local t in \{}$$
$$\texttt{t = cur\_ts}^!\texttt{(E); log}^!\texttt{(m,E,E',t); free(m,E,E');\}}\}$$
$$\texttt{x = receive(m,E)} \triangleq \texttt{atomic}\{\texttt{contract}^?\texttt{(m,E); x = deq(E);}$$
$$\texttt{local t,e in \{ t = cur\_ts}^?\texttt{(E); e = peer(E);}$$
$$\texttt{new(m,e,x); log}^?\texttt{(m,e,x,t);\}}\}$$

Intuitively, $\texttt{contract}^\dagger$ checks whether the contract authorizes the communication, `enq` and `deq` are the pure pointer passing counterparts of `send` and `receive`, $\texttt{cur\_ts}^\dagger$ selects in the history which timestamp to use for logging the current communication, `peer(E)` retrieves the peer of E, $\texttt{log}^\dagger$ logs a copy of the part of the heap that is transferred, and `new` and `free` allocate and deallocate this transferred heap. Fig 2 presents the small axioms defining these sub-atomic operations.

4.3 Soundness

In order to establish the soundness for the whole proof system, all we have to do is to establish the soundness of all atomic commands with respect to their coarse small axioms. We say that a local function f over $\hat{\Sigma}^{\mathsf{wf}}$ satisfies a specification ϕ over Σ^{wf} and write $f \vDash \phi$ if for all $(A, B) \in \phi$, $\langle\langle A \rangle\rangle\ f\ \langle\langle B \rangle\rangle$. Let $\mathrm{now}^{-1}(A)$ denote the set of all $\hat{\sigma} \in \hat{\Sigma}^{\mathsf{wf}}$ such that $\hat{\sigma} = \hat{\sigma}\downharpoonright_{\mathbf{now}}$ and $\mathrm{now}(\hat{\sigma}) \in A$.

Definition 3 (Implementation). *A specification $\hat{\phi}$ over $\hat{\Sigma}^{\mathsf{wf}}$ implements a specification ϕ over Σ^{wf} if* $\forall (A, B) \in \phi. \exists (\hat{A}, \hat{B}) \in \hat{\phi}. \mathrm{now}^{-1}(A) \sqsubseteq \hat{A}\ \&\ \mathrm{now}(\hat{B}) \sqsubseteq B$.

Lemma 3. *If $\hat{\phi}$ implements ϕ, then for all local function f, $f \vDash \hat{\phi}$ implies $f \vDash \phi$.*

We can show that the refined small axiom of `open` implements the corresponding coarse axiom, and that sub-atomic commands implement some specifications which, composed together, allow us to derive the coarse small axioms of `send` and `receive`. Abstract separation logic allows us to conclude that our proof system is sound.

Lemma 4 (Soundness for atomic commands). *If $\{A\}\ c\ \{B\}$ is an axiom of our proof system then for all $\hat{\sigma}$ such that* $\mathrm{now}(\hat{\sigma}) \vDash A$, $\mathrm{now}((\!|c|\!)(\hat{\sigma})) \sqsubseteq B$.

Theorem 1 (Soundness). $\vdash \{A\}\ p\ \{B\}$ *implies* $\vDash \{A\}\ p\ \{B\}$.

We can easily derive from this theorem that in every provable program, there is no memory violation or race, and contracts are respected. Memory leaks are not yet guaranteed to be avoided: this is the purpose of the transfers erasure property.

5 Transfers Erasure Property

In this section, we relate the transferring, local semantics we introduced for establishing the soundness of our proof system to the intended non-transferring, global semantics. Defining the non-transferring semantics is rather simple thanks to our decomposition of `send` and `receive` in sub-atomic operations. `check_inv` is added so that $\mathtt{send}_g^{nt}$ still faults whenever the invariant of the message is not satisfied.

Definition 4 (Non-transferring semantics). *The non-transferring semantics $(\!|.|\!)^{nt}$ is the semantics that differs from $(\!|.|\!)$ by erasing transfers in* `send` *and* `receive`*:*

$$\mathtt{send(m,E,E')}^{nt} \triangleq \mathtt{atomic}\ \{\ \mathtt{contract^!(m,E);enq(E,E');check\_inv(m,E,E');}\ \}$$

$$\mathtt{x=receive(m,E)}^{nt} \triangleq \mathtt{atomic}\ \{\mathtt{contract^?(m,E);\ x\ =\ deq(E);}\ \}$$

$$c^{nt} \triangleq c \quad \textit{otherwise}$$

where `check_inv(m,E,E')` *is the best local action defined by the Hoare triples $\{\hat{\sigma}\}$ check_inv(m,E,E') $\{\hat{\sigma}\}$ for all $\hat{\sigma}$ satisfying $I_m(E,E')$.*

In order to relate $(\!|.|\!)$ and $(\!|.|\!)^{nt}$, we first need to restrict them to well-interleaved local traces, otherwise many undesired executions would have to be considered: a receive may precede a send, or the message that is sent may not necessarily be the same as the one that is received. This can be observed directly on the resulting memory states thanks to histories, so restricting the semantics to legal states is enough to rule out executions that do not comply with the intended global semantics.

Let $UL(\hat{\sigma})$ denote the set of unmatched logs of $\hat{\sigma}$, that is $UL(\hat{\sigma}) = \{\tau^\dagger \in logs(\hat{\sigma}) \mid \tau^{\bar{\dagger}} \notin logs(\hat{\sigma})\}$, and let $transfer(\hat{\sigma})$ denote $\hat{\sigma}\lfloor_{UL(\hat{\sigma})}$. A state $\hat{\sigma}$ is *partitioned* if and only if $\langle \mathbf{now} \rangle transfer(\hat{\sigma}) = \{\hat{\sigma}_0\}$ and $\hat{\sigma}\lfloor_{\mathbf{now}} \perp \hat{\sigma}_0$. When this is the case, the closure of $\hat{\sigma}$ is defined as $closure(\hat{\sigma}) \triangleq \hat{\sigma}\lfloor_{\mathbf{now}} \bullet [\mathbf{now}]transfer(\hat{\sigma})$. A legal state should always be partitioned (intuitively, a cell cannot be both in transfer and owned by a thread), the logged contents of dual messages should match, and the read history of any endpoint should have been played at most up to the same point as the write history of its peer. Moreover, all timestamps should be different, except dual timestamps.

Definition 5 (Legal state). *A state* $\hat{\sigma} = (s, \hat{h}, \hat{k})$ *is* legal *when it satisfies*

Partitions $\hat{\sigma} \in \hat{\Sigma}^{\mathsf{wf}}$ *is partitioned*

DualMatch $\forall \tau.\ [\mathbf{now}](\hat{\sigma}\lfloor_{\tau?}) \vDash \neg\mathsf{emp} \Rightarrow \hat{\sigma}\lfloor_{\tau!} = \hat{\sigma}\lfloor_{\tau?}$

Asynch $closure(\hat{\sigma}) \vDash \begin{pmatrix} \varepsilon \overset{ep}{\mapsto}(-, \varepsilon', n_?, -, -, -) * \\ \varepsilon' \overset{ep}{\mapsto}(-, \varepsilon, -, n_!, -, -) * \mathsf{true} \end{pmatrix} \Rightarrow n_! \geq n_?$

DisjointLogs $\forall \varepsilon, \varepsilon', \varepsilon''.\ \begin{cases} k(\varepsilon) = (-, -, -, -, \ell_?, \ell_!)\ \&\ k(\varepsilon') = (-, \varepsilon'', -, -, \ell'_?, \ell'_!) \\ \&\ \varepsilon \neq \varepsilon'\ \&\ \varepsilon \neq \varepsilon'' \end{cases}$

$\Rightarrow$ *all timestamps appearing in* $ts(\ell_?)$, $ts(\ell_!)$, $ts(\ell'_?)$, $ts(\ell'_!)$ *are distinct*

The global semantics is then defined as $(\!|c|\!)_g(\hat{\sigma}) \triangleq \{\hat{\sigma}' \in (\!|c|\!)(\hat{\sigma}) \mid \hat{\sigma}' \text{ legal}\}$ if $(\!|c|\!)(\hat{\sigma}) \neq \top$, $\top$ otherwise. The global non-transferring semantics $(\!|.|\!)_g^{nt}$ is defined the same way. Our aim is to show that the global semantics is the same as the non-transferring one, up to a closure that brings back cells that are being transferred. It might be a surprise that this result does not hold without some particular restrictions on the contracts that ensure that no messages are lost when a channel is closed. We do not give the most general condition on contracts that achieves this non-leaking property, but rather provide a sufficient condition that is easy to check syntactically on the contract. These restrictions are very similar to those used in Singularity. A contract is *deterministic* if any two distinct edges with the same source have different labels. It is *positional* if every two edges with the same source are labeled with either two sends or two receives. A state is *synchronizing* if every graph cycle that goes through it contains at least one send and one receive.

Definition 6. *A contract is* non-leaking *if it is deterministic, positional, and every final state is a synchronizing state.*

For instance, the contract of the example is non-leaking, but would be leaking if all states were merged in a single state.

Theorem 2. *For any provable program* p *with non-leaking contracts, for all* $tr \in T(p)$, $[\![tr]\!]_g^{nt}(u) = closure([\![tr]\!]_g(u))$.

Remark 1. In particular, if $\vdash \{\mathsf{emp}\}\ p\ \{\mathsf{emp}\}$ and p terminates, then p does not fault on memory accesses nor leaks memory for any of the considered semantics.

We establish this result by induction on tr with a stronger inductive property. Due to lack of space, we do not detail the rather involved proof. One hard part of the proof, as mentioned earlier, is to establish that no memory is leaked when a channel is closed. Since non-leaking contracts are deterministic and positional, it can be proved that channels are in fact half-duplex. Moreover, as contracts are respected, in any reachable memory state, and for any coupled endpoints $\varepsilon, \varepsilon'$ of this state, the list of unread messages by ε, if not empty, is the same as the one labeling a read path from the contract's state of ε to the one of ε'. We then prove the absence of memory leak by the following argument: as a channel is closed if and only if the two endpoints are in the same final state, their histories may differ only from a read or a write cycle in the contract, and since final states are synchronizing, this cycle must be the empty cycle.

Conclusion and Future Work

We presented a proof system for copyless message passing ruled by contracts, illustrating how contracts may facilitate the work of the `Sing#` compiler in the static analysis that verifies the absence of ownership violations. We established the soundness of the proof system with respect to an over-approximating local semantics where message exchanges are unsynchronized, and restricted it to a global semantics for which we established the transfers erasure property.

We illustrated our proof system on a small and rather simple example. We focused on the foundations of our proof system in this work, but we wish to tackle more case-studies in the future. We moreover plan to automate the proof inference using an existing tools like `Smallfoot` [1]. Another challenging application of our proof system could be to prove a distributed garbage collector synchronized by message passing, for which the transfers erasure property would potentially be an important issue.

References

1. `http://www.dcs.qmul.ac.uk/research/logic/theory/projects/smallfoot/`
2. Bornat, R., Calcagno, C., Yang, H.: Variables as Resource in Separation Logic. Electronic Notes in Theoretical Computer Science 155, 247–276 (2006)
3. Brookes, S.: A semantics for concurrent separation logic. TCS 375(1-3), 227–270 (2007)
4. Calcagno, C., Parkinson, M., Vafeiadis, V.: Modular Safety Checking for Fine-Grained Concurrency. In: Riis Nielson, H., Filé, G. (eds.) SAS 2007. LNCS, vol. 4634, pp. 233–248. Springer, Heidelberg (2007)
5. Calcagno, C., O'Hearn, P., Yang, H.: Local action and abstract separation logic. In: 22nd LICS, pp. 366–378 (2007)
6. Fähndrich, M., Aiken, M., Hawblitzel, C., Hodson, O., Hunt, G.C., Larus, J.R., Levi, S.: Language support for fast and reliable message-based communication in Singularity OS. In: EuroSys (2006)
7. Gotsman, A., Berdine, J., Cook, B., Rinetzky, N., Sagiv, M.: Local reasoning for storable locks and threads. In: Shao, Z. (ed.) APLAS 2007. LNCS, vol. 4807, pp. 19–37. Springer, Heidelberg (2007)
8. Hoare, T., O'Hearn, P.: Separation logic semantics for communicating processes. Electron. Notes Theor. Comput. Sci. 212, 3–25 (2008)
9. Hu, R., Yoshida, N., Honda, K.: Session-based distributed programming in java. In: Vitek, J. (ed.) ECOOP 2008. LNCS, vol. 5142, pp. 516–541. Springer, Heidelberg (2008)
10. O'Hearn, P.W.: Resources, concurrency, and local reasoning. TCS 375(1-3), 271–307 (2007)
11. Pym, D., Tofts, C.: A Calculus and logic of resources and processes. Formal Aspects of Computing 18(4), 495–517 (2006)
12. Reynolds, J.C.: Separation logic: A logic for shared mutable data structures. In: LICS 2002 (2002)
13. Takeuchi, K., Honda, K., Kubo, M.: An Interaction-Based Language and Its Typing System. LNCS, pp. 398–398. Springer, Heidelberg (1994)

On Stratified Regions

Roberto M. Amadio

Université Paris Diderot, Paris 7

Abstract. Type and effect systems are a tool to analyse statically the behaviour of programs with effects. We present a proof based on the so called reducibility candidates that a suitable stratification of the type and effect system entails the termination of the typable programs. The proof technique covers a simply typed, multi-threaded, call-by-value lambda-calculus, equipped with a variety of scheduling (preemptive, cooperative) and interaction mechanisms (references, channels, signals).

Keywords: Types and effects, Termination, Reducibility candidates.

1 Introduction

In the framework of functional programs, the relationship between type systems and termination has been extensively studied through the Curry-Howard correspondence. It would be interesting to extend these techniques to programs with *effects*. By effect we mean the possibility of executing operations that modify the state of a system such as reading/writing a reference or sending/receiving a message.

Usual type systems as available, *e.g.*, in various dialects of the ML programming language, are too poor to account for the behaviour of programs with effects. A better approximation is possible if one abstracts the state of a system in a certain number of *regions* and if the types account for the way programs act on such regions. So-called *type and effect* systems [9] are an interesting formalisation of this idea and have been successfully used to analyse statically the problem of heap-memory deallocation [11]. On the other hand, the proof-theoretic foundations of such systems are largely unexplored. Only recently, it has been shown [4] that a *stratification* of the regions entails termination in a certain higher-order language with cooperative threads and references. Our purpose here is to revisit this result trying to clarify and extend both its scope and its proof technique (a more technical comparison is delayed to section 4). We refer to [4] for a tentative list of papers referring to a notion of stratification for programs with side effects. Perhaps the closest works in spirit are those that have adapted the reducibility candidates techniques to the π-calculus [12,10]. Those works exhibit type systems for the π-calculus that guarantee the termination of the usual continuation passing style translations of typed *functional* languages into the π-calculus. However, as pointed out by one of the authors of *op.cit* in [6], they are not very successful in handling state sensitive programs. The approach here is a bit different: one starts with a higher-order typed functional language

Z. Hu (Ed.): APLAS 2009, LNCS 5904, pp. 210–225, 2009.

which is known to be terminating and then one determines to what extent side-effects can be added while preserving termination. Yet in another direction, we notice that a notion of region stratification has been used in [3] to guarantee the polynomial time reactivity of a first-order timed/synchronous language.

We outline the contents of the paper. In section 2, we introduce a λ-calculus with *regions*. Regions are an abstraction of dynamically generated values such as references, channels, and signals, and the reduction rules of the calculus are given in such a way that the reduction rules for references, channels, and signals can be simulated by those given for regions. In section 3, we describe a simple *type and effect* system along the lines of [9]. In this discipline, types carry information on the regions on which the evaluated expressions may read or write. The discipline allows to write in a region r values that have an effect on the region r itself. In turn, this allows to simulate recursive definitions and thus to produce non terminating behaviours. In section 4, following [4], we describe a stratification of the regions. The idea is that regions are ordered and that a value written in a region may only produce effects in smaller regions. We then propose a new reducibility candidates interpretation (see, *e.g.*, [7] for a good survey) entailing the termination of typable programs. In section 5, we enrich the language with the possibility to generate new threads and to react to the termination of the computation. The language we consider is then *timed/synchronous* in the sense that a computation is regarded as a possibly infinite sequence of instants. An instant ends when the calculus cannot progress anymore (cf. timed/synchronous languages such as Timed CCS [8] and ESTEREL [5]). We extend the stratified typing rules to this language and show by means of a translation into the core language that typable programs terminate. We also show that a fixed-point combinator can be *defined* and *typed* so that recursive calls are allowed as long as they arise at a later instant. This differs from [4] where a fixed-point combinator is *added* to the language potentially compromising the termination property.

We refer to the report [1] for the full proofs.

2 A λ-Calculus with Regions

We consider a λ-calculus with *regions*. Regions are *abstractions* of dynamically generated 'pointers' which, depending on the context, are called references, channels, or signals. Given a program with operators to generate dynamically values (such as ref in the ML language or ν in the π-calculus), one may simply introduce a distinct region for every occurrence of such operators. This amounts to collapse all the 'pointers' generated by the operator at run time into one constant. The resulting language simulates the original one as long as the values written into regions do not erase those already there. In particular, termination for the language with regions entails termination for the original language.

We notice that ordinary type system for programs with dynamic values perform a similar abstraction: all the values that are generated by an operator are assigned the same type. For instance, typing $\nu x\ P$ in the π-calculus will reduce to typing the process P in a context where the name x is associated with a suitable type A. In the corresponding language with regions, one will replace the name x with a region r and type $[r/x]P$ ($[r/x]$ is the substitution) in a region context where r is associated with A.

To summarise, termination for the language with regions entails termination for the original calculi and moreover ordinary type system implicitly abstract dynamically generated values into regions. Therefore, we argue that one can carry on the main type theoretic arguments at the level of regions rather than at the more detailed level of dynamically generated values.[1]

2.1 Syntax

We consider the following syntactic categories:

$x, y, \ldots$	(variables)
$r, s, \ldots$	(regions)
$e, e', \ldots$	(finite sets of regions)
$A ::= \mathbf{1} \mid \mathsf{Reg}_r A \mid (A \xrightarrow{e} A)$	(types)
$\Gamma ::= x_1 : A_1, \ldots, x_n : A_n$	(context)
$R ::= r_1 : A_1, \ldots, r_n : A_n$	(region context)
$M ::= x \mid r \mid * \mid \lambda x.M \mid MM \mid \mathsf{get}(M) \mid \mathsf{set}(M, M)$	(terms)
$V ::= r \mid * \mid \lambda x.M$	(values)
$v, v', \ldots$	(sets of value)
$S ::= (r \Leftarrow v) \mid S, S$	(stores)
$X ::= M \mid S$	(stores or terms)
$P ::= X \mid X, P$	(programs)

We briefly comment the notation: $\mathbf{1}$ is the terminal (unit) type with value $*$; $\mathsf{Reg}_r A$ is the type of a region r containing values of type A; $A \xrightarrow{e} B$ is the type of functions that when given a value of type A may produce a value of type B and an effect on the regions in e; get is the operator to read *some* value in a region and set is the operator to *insert* a value in a region.

We write $[N/x]M$ for the substitution of N for x in M. If $R = r_1 : A_1, \ldots, r_n : A_n$ then $dom(R) = \{r_1, \ldots, r_n\}$. If $r \in dom(R)$ then we write $R(r)$ for the type A such that $r : A$ occurs in R. We also define the term $\mathsf{reg}_r M$ as an abbreviation for $(\lambda x.r)(\mathsf{set}(r, M))$. Thus the difference between $\mathsf{set}(r, M)$ and $\mathsf{reg}_r M$ is that in the first case we return $*$ while in the second we return r. When writing a program $P = X_1, \ldots, X_n$ we regard the symbol ',' as associative and commutative, or equivalently we regard a program as a multi-set of terms and stores. We write $(r \Leftarrow V)$ for $(r \Leftarrow \{V\})$. We shall identify the store $(r \Leftarrow v_1), (r \Leftarrow v_2)$ with the store $(r \Leftarrow v_1 \cup v_2)$. We denote with $dom(S)$ the set of regions r such that $(r \Leftarrow v)$ occurs in S and define $S(r)$ as the set $\{V \mid (r \Leftarrow V) \text{ occurs in } S\}$.

[1] Incidentally, it seems much easier to produce denotational models of languages with regions than for the original languages with dynamic values so that one can hope to find models that do provide insight into the type systems.

2.2 Reduction

A call-by value *evaluation context* E is defined as:

$$E ::= [\,] \mid EM \mid VE \mid \mathsf{get}(E) \mid \mathsf{set}(E, M) \mid \mathsf{set}(V, E)$$

An *elementary* evaluation context is defined as:

$$El ::= [\,]M \mid V[\,] \mid \mathsf{get}([\,]) \mid \mathsf{set}([\,], M) \mid \mathsf{set}(V, [\,])$$

An evaluation context can be regarded as the finite composition (possibly empty) of elementary evaluation contexts. The *reduction* on programs is defined as follows:

$$\frac{}{E[(\lambda x.M)V] \to E[[V/x]M]} \qquad \frac{}{E[\mathsf{get}(r)], (r \Leftarrow V) \to E[V], (r \Leftarrow V)}$$

$$\frac{}{E[\mathsf{set}(r, V)] \to E[*], (r \Leftarrow V)} \qquad \frac{P \to P'}{P, P'' \to P', P''}$$

Note that the semantics of set amounts to *add* rather than to *update* a binding between a region and a value. Hence a region can be bound at the same time to several values (possibly infinitely many) and the semantics of get amounts to select non-deterministically one of them.

As already mentioned, the notion of region is intended to simulate some familiar programming concepts such as references, channels, or signals. Specifically: (i) when writing a reference, we replace the previously written value (if any), (ii) when reading a (unordered, unbounded) channel we consume (remove from the store) the value read, and finally (iii) the values written in a signal persist within an instant and disappear at the end of it.[2] One can easily formalise the reduction rules for references, channels, and signals, and check that (within an instant) each reduction step is simulated by at least one reduction step in the calculus with regions. Thus, typing disciplines that guarantee termination for the calculus with regions will guarantee the same property when adapted to references, channels, or signals.

3 Types and Effects: Unstratified Case

We introduce a simple *type and effect* system along the lines of [9]. The following rules define when a region context R is *compatible* with a type A (judgement $R \downarrow A$):

$$\frac{}{R \downarrow \mathbf{1}} \qquad \frac{R \downarrow A \quad R \downarrow B \quad e \subseteq dom(R)}{R \downarrow (A \xrightarrow{e} B)} \qquad \frac{r : A \in R}{R \downarrow \mathsf{Reg}_r A}$$

[2] Signals arise in timed/synchronous models where the computation is regulated by a notion of instant or phase (see section 5).

The compatibility relation is just introduced to define when a region context is well formed (judgement $R \vdash$) and when a type and effect is well-formed with respect to a region context (judgements $R \vdash A$ and $R \vdash (A, e)$).

$$\frac{\forall r \in dom(R) \;\; R \downarrow R(r)}{R \vdash} \qquad \frac{R \vdash \quad R \downarrow A}{R \vdash A} \qquad \frac{R \vdash A \quad e \subseteq dom(R)}{R \vdash (A, e)}$$

A more informal way to express the condition is to say that a judgement $r_1 : A_1, \ldots, r_n : A_n \vdash B$ is well formed provided that: (1) all the region names occurring in the types $A_1, \ldots, A_n, B$ belong to the set $\{r_1, \ldots, r_n\}$ and (2) all types of the shape $\mathsf{Reg}_{r_i} C$ with $i \in \{1, \ldots, n\}$ and occurring in the types $A_1, \ldots, A_n, B$ are such that $C = A_i$. For instance, the reader may verify that $r : 1 \xrightarrow{\{r\}} 1 \vdash \mathsf{Reg}_r 1 \xrightarrow{\{r\}} 1$ can be derived while $r_1 : \mathsf{Reg}_{r_2}(1 \xrightarrow{\{r_2\}} 1), r_2 : 1 \xrightarrow{\{r_1\}} 1 \vdash$ cannot. Also it can be easily checked that the following properties hold:

$$\begin{array}{ll}
R \vdash \mathbf{1} & \text{iff } R \vdash \\
R \vdash \mathsf{Reg}_r A & \text{iff } R \vdash \text{ and } R(r) = A \\
R \vdash A \xrightarrow{e} B & \text{iff } R \vdash, R \vdash A, R \vdash B, \text{ and } e \subseteq dom(R) \\
R \vdash & \text{iff } \forall r \in dom(R) \;\; R \vdash R(r)
\end{array}$$

The subset relation on effects induces a *subtyping* relation on types and on pairs of types and effects which is defined as follows (judgements $R \vdash A \leq A'$, $R \vdash (A, e) \leq (A', e')$):

$$\frac{R \vdash A}{R \vdash A \leq A} \qquad \frac{\begin{array}{c} R \vdash A' \leq A \quad R \vdash B \leq B' \\ e \subseteq e' \subseteq dom(R) \end{array}}{R \vdash (A \xrightarrow{e} B) \leq (A' \xrightarrow{e'} B')} \qquad \frac{\begin{array}{c} R \vdash A \leq A' \\ e \subseteq e' \subseteq dom(R) \end{array}}{R \vdash (A, e) \leq (A', e')}$$

We notice that the transitivity rule:

$$\frac{R \vdash A \leq B \qquad R \vdash B \leq C}{R \vdash A \leq C}$$

can be derived via a simple induction on the height of the proofs. The subtyping rule trades flexibility against precision of the type system. For instance, suppose $A_1 = \mathbf{1} \xrightarrow{e_1} \mathbf{1}$ and $A_2 = \mathbf{1} \xrightarrow{e_2} \mathbf{1}$ and we want to define the type B of the functionals that take a value V_1 of type A_1 and a value V_2 of type A_2 and compute either $V_1 *$ or $V_2 *$. We can define $B = A_1 \xrightarrow{\emptyset} (A_2 \xrightarrow{e_1 \cup e_2} \mathbf{1})$. The reader can check that both $\lambda x.\lambda y.x*$ and $\lambda x.\lambda y.y*$ have type B *provided* the subtyping rule is used. Incidentally, we note that [4] seems to 'forget' the subtyping rule. While there are no particular problems to provide a reducibility candidates interpretation for this rule, we notice that without it the following diverging ML expression $\mathsf{let}\ l = \mathsf{ref}(\lambda x.x)\ \mathsf{in}\ l := \lambda x.!lx; !l()$, which is given in *op.cit.* to motivate the stratification of regions does *not* type already in the ordinary unstratified type and effect system because $(\lambda x.x)$ has type $\mathbf{1} \xrightarrow{\emptyset} \mathbf{1}$ but not $\mathbf{1} \xrightarrow{\{r\}} \mathbf{1}$ where r is the region associated with the reference l.

We now turn to the typing rules for the terms. We shall write $R \vdash x_1 : A_1, \ldots, x_n : A_n$ if $R \vdash$ and $R \vdash A_i$ for $i = 1, \ldots, n$. Note that in the following rules we always refer to the *same* region context R.

$$\frac{R \vdash \Gamma \quad x : A \in \Gamma}{R; \Gamma \vdash x : (A, \emptyset)} \qquad \frac{R \vdash \Gamma \quad r : A \in R}{R; \Gamma \vdash r : (\mathsf{Reg}_r A, \emptyset)} \qquad \frac{R \vdash \Gamma}{R; \Gamma \vdash * : (\mathbf{1}, \emptyset)}$$

$$\frac{R; \Gamma, x : A \vdash M : (B, e)}{R; \Gamma \vdash \lambda x.M : (A \xrightarrow{e} B, \emptyset)} \qquad \frac{R; \Gamma \vdash M : (A \xrightarrow{e_2} B, e_1) \quad R; \Gamma \vdash N : (A, e_3)}{R; \Gamma \vdash MN : (B, e_1 \cup e_2 \cup e_3)}$$

$$\frac{R; \Gamma \vdash M : (\mathsf{Reg}_r A, e)}{R; \Gamma \vdash \mathsf{get}(M) : (A, e \cup \{r\})} \qquad \frac{R; \Gamma \vdash M : (\mathsf{Reg}_r A, e_1) \quad R; \Gamma \vdash N : (A, e_2)}{R; \Gamma \vdash \mathsf{set}(M, N) : (\mathbf{1}, e_1 \cup e_2 \cup \{r\})}$$

$$\frac{R; \Gamma \vdash M : (A, e) \quad R \vdash (A, e) \leq (A', e')}{R; \Gamma \vdash M : (A', e')}$$

Finally, we extend the typing rules to stores and general multi-threaded programs. To this end, it is convenient to introduce a constant behaviour type $\mathbf{B}$ which is the type we give to multi-sets of threads and/or stores which are not supposed to return a value but just to interact via side-effects. We will use $\alpha, \alpha', \ldots$ to denote either an ordinary type A or this new behaviour type $\mathbf{B}$.

$$\frac{r : A \in R \quad \forall V \in v \;\; R; \Gamma \vdash V : (A, \emptyset)}{R; \Gamma \vdash (r \Leftarrow v) : (\mathbf{B}, \emptyset)} \qquad \frac{R; \Gamma \vdash X_i : (\alpha_i, e_i) \quad i = 1, \ldots, n \geq 1}{R; \Gamma \vdash X_1, \ldots, X_n : (\mathbf{B}, e_1 \cup \cdots \cup e_n)}$$

Remark 1. The derived typing rule for $\mathsf{reg}_r M$ is as follows:

$$\frac{r : A \in R \quad R; \Gamma \vdash M : (A, e)}{R; \Gamma \vdash \mathsf{reg}_r M : (\mathsf{Reg}_r A, e \cup \{r\})}$$

One can derive a more traditional 'effect-free' type system by *erasing all the effects* from the types and the typing judgements. Note that in the resulting system the subtyping rules are useless. We shall write $\vdash^{ef}$ for provability in this system. This 'weaker' type system suffices to state a decomposition property of the terms which is proven by induction on the structure of the term.

Proposition 1 (decomposition). *If $R; \vdash^{ef} M : A$ is a well-typed closed term then exactly one of the following situations arises where E is an evaluation context:*

1. *M is a value.*
2. *$M = E[\Delta]$ and Δ has the shape $(\lambda x.N)V$, $\mathsf{set}(r, V)$, or $\mathsf{get}(r)$.*

3.1 Basic Properties of Typing and Evaluation

We observe some basic properties: (i) one can weaken both the type and region contexts, (ii) typing is preserved when we replace a variable with an effect-free term of the same type, and (iii) typing is preserved by reduction. If S is a store and e is a set of regions then $S_{|e}$ is the store S restricted to the regions in e.

Proposition 2 (basic properties, unstratified). *The following properties hold:*

weakening. *If* $R;\Gamma \vdash M : (A, e)$ *and* $R, R' \vdash \Gamma, \Gamma'$ *then* $R, R'; \Gamma, \Gamma' \vdash M : (A, e)$.

substitution. *If* $R;\Gamma, x : A \vdash M : (B, e)$ *and* $R;\Gamma \vdash N : (A, \emptyset)$ *then* $R;\Gamma \vdash [N/x]M : (B, e)$.

subject reduction. *Let* $\mathbf{M}$ *denote a sequence* $M_1, \ldots, M_n$. *If* $R, R'; \vdash \mathbf{M}, S : (\mathbf{B}, e)$, $R \vdash e$, *and* $\mathbf{M}, S \to \mathbf{M}', S'$ *then* $R, R'; \vdash \mathbf{M}', S' : (\mathbf{B}, e)$, $S_{|dom(R')} = S'_{|dom(R')}$, *and* $\mathbf{M}, S_{|dom(R)} \to \mathbf{M}', S'_{|dom(R)}$. *Moreover, if* $\mathbf{M} = M$ *and* $R, R' \vdash M : (A, e)$ *then* $\mathbf{M}' = M'$ *and* $R, R' \vdash M' : (A, e)$.

The weakening and substitution properties are shown directly by induction on the proof height. Concerning subject reduction, it is useful to notice that if a term M, of type and effect (A, e), is ready to read/write the region r then $r \in e$. This follows from an analysis of the evaluation context. Then we prove the assertion by case analysis on the reduction rule applied, relying on the substitution property.

Remark 2. The subject reduction property is formulated so as to make clear that the type and effect system indeed delimits the interactions a term may have with the store. Note that a term may refer to regions which are not explicitly mentioned in its type and effect. For instance, consider $M = (\lambda f.*)(\lambda x.\mathsf{get}(r)x)$ and let $R = r : \mathbf{1} \xrightarrow{\emptyset} \mathbf{1}$. Then $R; \emptyset \vdash M : (\mathbf{1}, \emptyset)$, $\emptyset \vdash (\mathbf{1}, \emptyset)$ but $\emptyset; \emptyset \not\vdash M : (\mathbf{1}, \emptyset)$. The subject reduction property guarantees that such a term will only read/write regions included in the region context needed to type its type and effect.

3.2 Recursion

In our (unstratified) calculus, we can write in a region r a functional value $\lambda x.M$ where M reads from the region r itself. For instance, $\mathsf{reg}_r(\lambda x.(\mathsf{get}(r))x)$.

This kind of circularity leads to diverging computations such as:

$$\begin{array}{ll} \mathsf{get}(\mathsf{reg}_r \lambda x.\mathsf{get}(r)x)* & \to \mathsf{get}(r)*, (r \Leftarrow \lambda x.\mathsf{get}(r)x) \to \\ (\lambda x.\mathsf{get}(r)x)*, (r \Leftarrow \lambda x.\mathsf{get}(r)x) & \to \mathsf{get}(r)*, (r \Leftarrow \lambda x.\mathsf{get}(r)x) \to \cdots \end{array}$$

It is well known that this phenomenon can be exploited to simulate recursive definitions. Specifically, we define:

$$\mathsf{fix}_r f.M = \lambda x.(\mathsf{get}(\mathsf{reg}_r(\lambda x.[\lambda x.\mathsf{get}(r)x/f]M\ x)))\ x \tag{1}$$

By a direct application of the typing rules and proposition 2(substitution), one can derive a rule to type $\mathsf{fix}_r f.M$.

Proposition 3 (type fixed-point). *The following typing rule for the fixed point combinator is derived:*

$$\frac{\begin{array}{c} r : A \xrightarrow{e} B \in R \quad r \in e \\ R;\Gamma, f : A \xrightarrow{e} B \vdash M : (A \xrightarrow{e} B, \emptyset) \end{array}}{R;\Gamma \vdash \mathsf{fix}_r f.M : (A \xrightarrow{e} B, \emptyset)} \tag{2}$$

For a concrete example, assume basic operators on the integer type and let M be the factorial function: $M = \lambda x.\mathsf{if}\ x = 0\ \mathsf{then}\ 1\ \mathsf{else}\ x * f(x-1)$. Then compute $(\mathsf{fix}_r f.M)1$. In this case we have $e = \{r\}$ and $r : int \xrightarrow{r} int \in R$.

4 Types and Effects: Stratified Case

As we have seen, an unstratified simply typed calculus with effects may produce diverging computations. To avoid this, a natural idea proposed by G. Boudol in [4] is to *stratify* regions.

Intuitively, we fix a well-founded order on regions and we make sure that values stored in a region r can only produce effects on smaller regions. For instance, suppose V is a value with type $(\mathbf{1} \xrightarrow{\{r\}} \mathbf{1})$. Intuitively, this means that when applied to an argument $U : \mathbf{1}$, V may produce an effect on region $\{r\}$. Then the value V can only be stored in regions larger than r. We shall see that this stratification allows for an inductive definition of the values that can be stored in a given region.

The only change in the type system concerns the judgements $R \vdash$, $R \vdash A$, and $R \vdash (A, e)$ whose rules are redefined as follows:

$$\frac{}{\emptyset \vdash} \qquad \frac{R \vdash A \quad r \notin dom(R)}{R, r : A \vdash} \qquad \frac{R \vdash}{R \vdash \mathbf{1}}$$

$$\frac{R \vdash \quad r : A \in R}{R \vdash \mathsf{Reg}_r A} \qquad \frac{R \vdash A \quad R \vdash B \quad e \subseteq dom(R)}{R \vdash A \xrightarrow{e} B} \qquad \frac{R \vdash A \quad e \subseteq dom(R)}{R \vdash (A, e)}\ .$$

Proviso. Henceforth we shall use $\vdash$ to refer to provability in the stratified system and $\vdash^u$ for provability in the *unstratified* one. The former implies the latter since $R \vdash$ implies $R \vdash^u$ and $R \vdash A$ implies $R \vdash^u A$, while the other rules are unchanged.

4.1 Basic Properties Revisited

The main properties we have proven for the unstratified system can be specialised to the stratified one.

Proposition 4 (basic properties, stratified). *The following properties hold in the stratified system.*

weakening. *If* $R; \Gamma \vdash M : (A, e)$ *and* $R, R' \vdash \Gamma, \Gamma'$ *then* $R, R'; \Gamma, \Gamma' \vdash M : (A, e)$.

substitution. *If* $R; \Gamma, x : A \vdash M : (B, e)$ *and* $R; \Gamma \vdash N : (A, \emptyset)$ *then* $R; \Gamma \vdash [N/x]M : (B, e)$.

subject reduction. *If* $R, R'; \vdash \mathbf{M}, S : (\mathbf{B}, e)$, $R \vdash e$, *and* $\mathbf{M}, S \to \mathbf{M}', S'$ *then* $R, R'; \vdash \mathbf{M}', S' : (\mathbf{B}, e)$, $S_{|dom(R')} = S'_{|dom(R')}$, *and* $\mathbf{M}, S_{|dom(R)} \to \mathbf{M}', S'_{|dom(R)}$. *Moreover, if* $\mathbf{M} = M$ *and* $R, R'; \vdash M : (A, e)$ *then* $\mathbf{M}' = M'$ *and* $R, R'; \vdash M' : (A, e)$.

4.2 Interpretation

We describe a *reducibility candidates* interpretation that entails that typed programs terminate. We denote with SN the collection of strongly normalising single-threaded programs, *i.e.*, the programs of the shape M, S such that all reduction sequences terminate. We write $(M, S) \Downarrow (N, S')$ if $M, S \xrightarrow{*} N, S'$ and $N, S' \not\rightarrow$. We write $R' \geq R$, and say that R' extends R, if $R' \vdash$ and $R' = R, R''$ for some R''.

The starting idea is that the interpretation of $R \vdash$ is a set of stores and the interpretation of $R \vdash (A, e)$ is a set of terms. One difficulty is that the stores and the terms may depend on a region context R' which extends R. We get around this problem, by making the context R' explicit in the interpretation. Then the interpretation can be given directly by induction on the provability of the judgements $R \vdash$ and $R \vdash (A, e)$. This is a notable simplification with respect to the approach taken in [4] where a rather *ad hoc* well-founded order on judgements is introduced to define the interpretation.

A second characteristic of our approach is that the properties a thread must satisfy are specified with respect to a 'saturated' store which intuitively already contains all the values the thread may write into it. This approach simplifies the interpretation and provides a simple argument to extend the termination argument from single-threaded to multi-threaded programs. Indeed, if we a have a set of threads which are guaranteed to terminate with respect to a saturated store then their parallel composition will terminate too. To see this, one can reason by contradiction: if the parallel composition diverges then one thread must run infinitely often and, since the threads cannot modify the saturated store (what they write is already there), this contradicts the hypothesis that all the threads taken alone with the saturated store terminate.

Finally, minor technical differences with respect to [4] is that we interpret the subtyping rule (cf. discussion in section 3) and that our notion of reducibility candidate follows Girard rather than Stenlund-Tait (see [7] for a detailed comparison and references).

Region-context. Let $R = r_1 : A_1, \ldots, r_n : A_n$ and $R_{r_i} = r_1 : A_1, \ldots, r_{i-1} : A_{i-1}$, for $i = 1, \ldots, n$. We interpret a region-context R as a set of pairs $R' \vdash S$ where R' is a region-context which extends R and S is a 'saturated' store whose domain coincides with R:

$$\underline{R} = \{\ R' \vdash S \mid R' \geq R, \quad dom(S) = dom(R), \text{ and for } i = 1, \ldots, n \\ S(r_i) = \{V \mid R' \vdash V \in \underline{R_{r_i} \vdash (A_i, \emptyset)}\}\ \}$$

If $R' \geq R$ then $\underline{R}(R')$ is defined as the store S such that $R' \vdash S \in \underline{R}$. Note that, for $r \in dom(R)$ and $R = R_1, r : A, R_2$, $V \in \underline{R}(R')(r)$ means $R' \vdash V \in \underline{R_1 \vdash (A, \emptyset)}$.

Type and effect. We interpret a type and effect $R \vdash (A, e)$ as the set of pairs $R' \vdash M$ such that R' extends R, and M is a closed term typable with respect to R' and satisfying suitable properties (1-3 below):

$$\underline{R \vdash (A,e)} = \{R' \vdash M \mid \begin{array}{ll} (1) & R' \geq R, \quad R';\emptyset \vdash M : (A,e), \\ (2) & \text{for all } R'' \geq R'\ M, \underline{R}(R'') \in SN, \text{ and} \\ (3) & \text{for all } M', S', R'' \geq R' \quad (M, \underline{R}(R'')) \Downarrow (M', S') \\ & \quad \text{implies } S' = \underline{R}(R'') \text{ and } \mathcal{C}(A, R, R'', M')\ \} \end{array}$$

$$\begin{array}{l} \text{where: } \mathcal{C}(A,R,R'',M') \equiv \\ \quad (A = \mathbf{1} \quad \supset \quad M' = *) \wedge \\ \quad (A = \mathsf{Reg}_r B \quad \supset \quad M' = r) \wedge \\ \quad (A = A_1 \xrightarrow{e'} A_2 \quad \supset \quad M' = \lambda x.N \quad \wedge \\ \qquad\qquad \text{for all } R_1 \geq R'', R_1 \vdash V \in \underline{R \vdash (A_1, \emptyset)} \\ \qquad\qquad\quad \text{implies } R_1 \vdash M'V \in \underline{R \vdash (A_2, e')}\ ) \ . \end{array}$$

Suppose $R = r_1 : A_1, \ldots, r_n : A_n$. We note that the interpretation of R depends on the interpretation of $r_1 : A_1, \ldots, r_{i-1} : A_{i-1} \vdash A_i$ for $i = 1, \ldots, n$ and the interpretation of $R \vdash (A, e)$ depends on the interpretation of R and, when $A = A_1 \xrightarrow{e'} A_2$, on the interpretation of $R \vdash (A_1, \emptyset)$ and $R \vdash (A_2, e')$. It is easily verified that the definition of the interpretation is well founded by considering as measure the height of the proof of the interpreted judgement. We also note that such a well-founded definition would not be possible in the unstratified system. For instance, the interpretation of $r : A \vdash (A, \emptyset)$ where $A = \mathbf{1} \xrightarrow{r} \mathbf{1}$ should refer to a store containing values of type A. Finally, we stress that the interpretations of R and $R \vdash (A, e)$ actually contain terms typable in an extension R' of R but that their properties are stated with respect to a store whose domain is $dom(R)$. This is possible because the type and effect system does indeed delimit the effects a term may have when it is executed (cf. remark 2).

4.3 Basic Properties of the Interpretation

We say that a term M is *neutral* if it is not a λ-abstraction. The following proposition lists some basic properties of the interpretation. Similar properties arise in the reducibility candidates interpretations used for 'pure' functional languages, but the main point here is that we have to state them relatively to suitable stores. In particular, the extension/restriction property, which is perhaps less familiar, is crucial to prove the following soundness theorem 1.

Proposition 5 (properties interpretation). *The following properties hold.*

Weakening. *If* $R'' \geq R' \geq R$, $R \vdash (A, e)$, *and* $R' \vdash M \in \underline{R \vdash (A,e)}$ *then* $R'' \vdash M \in \underline{R \vdash (A,e)}$.

Extension/Restriction. *Suppose* $R'' \geq R' \geq R$ *and* $R \vdash (A, e)$. *Then* $R'' \vdash M \in \underline{R \vdash (A,e)}$ *if and only if* $R'' \vdash M \in \underline{R' \vdash (A,e)}$.

Subtyping. *If* $R \vdash (A,e) \leq (A',e')$ *then* $\underline{R \vdash (A,e)} \subseteq \underline{R \vdash (A',e')}$.

Strong normalisation. *If* $R' \vdash M \in \underline{R \vdash (A,e)}$ *and* $R'' \geq R'$ *then* $M, \underline{R}(R'') \in SN$.

Reduction closure. *If* $R' \vdash M \in \underline{R \vdash (A,e)}$, $R'' \geq R'$, *and* $M, \underline{R}(R'') \rightarrow M', S'$ *then* $R'' \vdash M' \in \underline{R \vdash (A,e)}$ *and* $S' = \underline{R}(R'')$.

Non-emptiness. *If* $R \vdash A$ *then there is a value* V *such that for all* $R' \geq R$ *and* $e \subseteq dom(R)$, $R' \vdash V \in \underline{R \vdash (A, e)}$.

Expansion closure. *Suppose* $R \vdash (A, e)$, $R' \geq R$, $R'; \emptyset \vdash M : (A, e)$, *and* M *is neutral. Then* $R' \vdash M \in \underline{R \vdash (A, e)}$ *provided that for all* $R'' \geq R', M', S'$ *such that* $M, \underline{R}(R'') \rightarrow M', S'$ *we have that* $R'' \vdash M' \in \underline{R \vdash (A, e)}$ *and* $S' = \underline{R}(R'')$.

PROOF HINT.

Weakening. We rely on proposition 4((syntactic) weakening) and the fact that, the properties the pairs $R' \vdash M$ must satisfy to belong to $\underline{R \vdash (A, e)}$, must hold for all the extensions $R'' \geq R'$.

Extension/Restriction. By definition, $\underline{R}(R'')$ coincides with $\underline{R'}(R'')$ on $dom(R)$. On the other hand, the proposition 4(subject reduction) guarantees that the reduction of a term of type and effect (A, e) will not depend and will not affect the part of the store whose domain is $dom(R') \backslash dom(R)$. We then prove the property by induction on the structure of the type A.

Subtyping. This is proven by induction on the the proof of $R \vdash A \leq A'$.

Strong normalisation. This follows immediately from the definition of the interpretation.

Reduction closure. We know that $M, \underline{R}(R'')$ must normalise to a value satisfying suitable properties and the same saturated store $\underline{R}(R'')$. Moreover, we know that the store can only grow during the reduction. We conclude applying the weakening property.

Non-emptiness/Expansion closure. These two properties are proven at once, by induction on the proof height of $R \vdash (A, e)$. We take as values: $*$ for the type $\mathbf{1}$, r for a type of the shape $\mathsf{Reg}_r B$, and the 'constant function' $\lambda x.V_2$ for a type of the shape $A_1 \xrightarrow{e_1} A_2$ where V_2 is the value inductively built for A_2. To prove $\lambda x.V_2 \in \underline{R \vdash (A_1 \xrightarrow{e_1} A_2, e)}$, we use the inductive hypothesis of expansion closure of $\underline{R \vdash (A_2, e_1)}$. □

4.4 Soundness of the Interpretation

By definition, if $R \vdash M \in \underline{R \vdash (A, e)}$ then $R; \vdash M : (A, e)$. We are going to show that the converse holds too. First we need to generalise the notion of reducibility to open terms.

Definition 1 (term interpretation). *We write* $R; x_1 : A_1, \ldots, x_n : A_n \models M : (B, e)$ *if whenever* $R' \geq R$ *and* $R' \vdash V_i \in \underline{R \vdash (A_i, \emptyset)}$ *for* $i = 1, \ldots, n$ *we have that* $R' \vdash [V_1/x_1, \ldots, V_n/x_n]M \in \underline{R \vdash (B, e)}$.

As usual, the main result can be stated as the soundness of the interpretation with respect to the typing rules. Since terms in the interpretation are strongly normalising relatively to a saturated store (cf. proposition 5), it follows that typable (closed) terms are strongly normalising.

Theorem 1 (soundness). *If* $R; \Gamma \vdash M : (B, e)$ *then* $R; \Gamma \models M : (B, e)$.

Proof hint. The proof goes by induction on the typing of the terms and exploits the properties of the interpretation stated in proposition 5. As usual, the case of the abstraction is proven by appealing to expansion closure and the case of application follows from the very interpretation of the functional types and reduction closure. The cases where we write or read from the store have to be handled with some care. We discuss a simplified situation. Suppose $R' \geq R = R_1, r : A, R_2$.

write. Suppose $R; \vdash \mathsf{set}(r, V) : (\mathbf{1}, \{r\})$ is derived from $R; \vdash V : (A, \emptyset)$. Then, by induction hypothesis, we know that $R' \vdash V \in \underline{R \vdash (A, \emptyset)}$. However, for maintaining the invariant that the saturated store is unchanged, we need to show that $R' \vdash V \in \underline{R_1 \vdash (A, \emptyset)}$, and this is indeed the case thanks to proposition 5(restriction).

read. Suppose we have $R'; \vdash \mathsf{get}(r) : (A, \{r\})$. Now notice that proposition 5(non-emptiness) guarantees that $\underline{R}(R')(r)$ is not empty. Thus $\mathsf{get}(r), \underline{R}(R')$ will reduce to $V, \underline{R}(R')$ for some value V such that $R' \vdash V \in \underline{R_1 \vdash (A, \emptyset)}$. However, what we need to show is that $R' \vdash V \in \underline{R \vdash (A, \emptyset)}$ and this is indeed the case thanks to proposition 5(extension). □

Corollary 1 (termination). (1) *The judgement $R; \vdash M : (A, e)$ is provable if and only if $R \vdash M \in \underline{R \vdash (A, e)}$.*
(2) *Every typable multi-threaded program $R; \vdash M_1, \ldots, M_n : (\mathbf{B}, e)$ terminates.*

Corollary 1(1), follows from theorem 1 taking the context Γ to be empty. Corollary 1(2) follows from the fact that each thread strongly normalizes with respect to a saturated store. Then its execution is not affected by the execution of other threads in parallel: all these parallel threads could do is to write in the saturated store values which are already there.

5 Extensions

In this section we sketch two extensions of our basic model. The first simple one (section 5.1) concerns the possibility of generating dynamically new threads while the second (section 5.2) is a bit more involved and it concerns the notion of timed/synchronous computation.

5.1 Thread Generation

In the presented system, the number of threads is constant. We describe a simple extension that allows to generate new threads during the execution. Namely, (1) we regard a multi-set of terms $M_1, \ldots, M_n$ as a term of behaviour type $\mathbf{B}$ and (2) we abstract terms of behaviour type $\mathbf{B}$ producing terms of type $(A \xrightarrow{e} \mathbf{B})$ for some type A, e (this formalisation is inspired by [2](chpt. 16)). It is straightforward to extend the rules for the formation of region contexts and types and for subtyping to take into account the behaviour type $\mathbf{B}$. Similarly, the typing rules for abstraction and application are extended to take into account the situation where the codomain of the functional space is $\mathbf{B}$. The full definition of this system is [1]. In this extended system, we can then type, *e.g.*, a term that after performing an input will start two threads in parallel: $(\lambda x.(M,N))\mathsf{get}(r)$ which would be written in, say, the π-calculus as $r(x).(M \mid N)$.

In order to show termination of this extended language, we have to define the interpretation of the judgement $R \vdash (\mathbf{B}, e)$. To this end, it is enough to extend the definition in section 4.2 by requiring that a term in $\overline{R \vdash (\mathbf{B}, e)}$ when run in the saturated store will indeed terminate without modifying the store and produce a multi-set of values. Formally, we add the condition '$A = \mathbf{B} \supset M' = V_1, \ldots, V_n, n \geq 1$' to the definition of the predicate $\mathcal{C}$. We can then lift our results to this system leaving the structure of the proofs unchanged.

5.2 Synchrony/Time

We consider a timed/synchronous extension of our language. Following an established tradition, we consider that the computation is divided into *instants* and that an instant ends when the computation cannot progress. Then we need at least an additional operator that allows to write programs that *react* to the end of the instant by changing their state in the following instant. We shall see that the termination of the typable programs can be obtained by mapping reductions in the extended language into reductions in the core language.

Syntax and Reduction. We extend the collection of terms as follows: $M ::= \cdots \mid M \triangleright M$, where the operator *else-next*, written $M \triangleright N$, tries to run M and, if it fails, runs N in the following instant (cf. [8]). We extend the evaluation contexts assuming: $E ::= \cdots \mid E \triangleright M$, and the *elementary* evaluation contexts assuming: $El ::= \cdots \mid [\,] \triangleright M$.

We define a simplification operator *red* that removes from a context all pending branches else-next:

$$
red(E) = \begin{cases} [\,] & \text{if } E = [\,] \\ red(E') & \text{if } E = E' \triangleright N \\ El[red(E')] & \text{otherwise, if } E = El[E'] \end{cases}
$$

We say that an evaluation context E is time insensitive if $red(E) = E$. We adapt the reduction rules defined in section 2 as follows:

$$
\begin{array}{ll}
E[(\lambda x.M)V] & \to red(E)[[V/x]M] \\
E[\mathsf{get}(r)], (r \Leftarrow V) & \to red(E)[V], (r \Leftarrow V) \\
E[\mathsf{set}(r, V)] & \to red(E)[*], (r \Leftarrow V)\ .
\end{array}
$$

Further, we have to describe how a program reacts to the end of the computation. This is specified by the relation $\xrightarrow{\mathsf{tick}}$ below:

$$\frac{}{V \xrightarrow{\text{tick}} V} \qquad \frac{}{S \xrightarrow{\text{tick}} S} \qquad \frac{M = E[\mathsf{get}(r)] \quad E \text{ time insensitive}}{M \xrightarrow{\text{tick}} M}$$

$$\frac{\begin{array}{c} M = E[E'[\Delta] \rhd N] \quad \Delta ::= V \mid \mathsf{get}(r) \\ E \text{ time insensitive} \end{array}}{M \xrightarrow{\text{tick}} E[N]} \qquad \frac{\begin{array}{c} P_i \xrightarrow{\text{tick}} P_i' \quad i = 1,2 \\ P_1, P_2 \not\rightarrow \end{array}}{P_1, P_2 \xrightarrow{\text{tick}} P_1', P_2'} .$$

For instance, we can write $(\lambda x.M)\mathsf{get}(r) \rhd N$ for a thread that tries to read a value from the region r in the first instant and if it fails it resumes the computation with N in the following instant. We can also write $* \rhd N$ for a thread that (unconditionally) stops its computation for the current instant and resumes it with N in the following instant.

Note that $P \xrightarrow{\text{tick}}$ only if $P \not\rightarrow$. The converse is in general false, but it holds for well-typed closed programs (details in [1]). Thus for well-typed closed programs the principle is that time passes (a $\xrightarrow{\text{tick}}$ transition is possible) exactly when the computation cannot progress (a $\rightarrow$ transition is impossible). Then termination is obviously a *very* desirable property of timed/synchronous programs.

Typing. The typing rules for the terms are extended as follows:

$$\frac{R; \Gamma \vdash M : (A, e) \quad R; \Gamma \vdash N : (A, e')}{R; \Gamma \vdash M \rhd N : (A, e)} .$$

Note that in typing $M \rhd N$ we only record the effect of the term M, that is we focus on the effects a term may produce in the first instant while neglecting those that may be produced at later instants.

Reduction. The decomposition proposition 1 can be lifted to the extended language. There is a third case to be considered besides the two arising in proposition 1 which corresponds to the situation where the redex is under the scope of an else-next. More precisely, in the third case a closed term M is decomposed as $E[E'[\Delta] \rhd N]$ where E is a time insensitive evaluation context and Δ has the shape V, $(\lambda x.N)V$, $\mathsf{set}(r, V)$, or $\mathsf{get}(r)$.

Focusing on the stratified case, one can adapt the weakening, substitution, and subject reduction properties whose proofs proceed as in proposition 4. The preservation of the type information by the passage of time (tick reduction) can be stated as follows.

> If $R; \vdash \mathbf{M}, S : (\mathbf{B}, e)$, and $\mathbf{M}, S \xrightarrow{\text{tick}} \mathbf{M}', S'$ then $S = S'$ and there is an effect e' such that $R; \vdash \mathbf{M}', S : (\mathbf{B}, e')$.

Notice that the effect of the reduced term might be incomparable with the effect of the term to be reduced. Still the following *context substitution* property allows to conclude that the resulting term is well-typed.

> If $R; \Gamma, x : A \vdash E[x] : (B, e)$ where x is not free in the evaluation context E and $R; \Gamma \vdash N : (A, e')$ then $R; \Gamma \vdash E[N] : (B, e \cup e')$.

Translation. We consider a translation that removes the else-next operator while preserving typing and reduction. Namely, we define a function $\langle \_ \rangle$ on terms such that $\langle M \triangleright N \rangle = \langle M \rangle$, $\langle x \rangle = x$, $\langle * \rangle = *$, $\langle r \rangle = r$, and which commutes with the other operators (abstraction, application, reading, and writing). Also the translation is extended to stores and programs in the obvious way: $\langle (r \Leftarrow V) \rangle = (r \Leftarrow \langle V \rangle)$, $\langle X_1, \ldots, X_n \rangle = \langle X_1 \rangle, \ldots, \langle X_n \rangle$.

Proposition 6 (simulation). (1) *If* $R;\Gamma \vdash M : (A, e)$ *then* $R;\Gamma \vdash \langle M \rangle : (A, e)$.
(2) *If* $R;\Gamma \vdash P : (\mathbf{B}, e)$ *then* $R;\Gamma \vdash \langle P \rangle : (\mathbf{B}, e)$.
(3) *If* $R; \vdash P : (\mathbf{B}, e)$ *and* $P \to P'$ *then* $\langle P \rangle \to \langle P' \rangle$.
(4) *A program* P *terminates if* $\langle P \rangle$ *terminates.*

The proof of this proposition is direct. In particular, to prove (3) we show that the translation commutes with the substitution and that the translation of an evaluation context is again an evaluation context.

Fixed-point, revisited. The typing rule (2) proposed for the fixed-point combinator cannot be applied in the stratified system as the condition $r : A \xrightarrow{e} B \in R$ and $r \in e$ cannot be satisfied. However, we can still type recursive calls that happen in a later instant.

Proposition 7 (type fixed-point, revisited). *The following typing rule for the fixed point combinator is derived in the stratified system*

$$\frac{R;\Gamma, f : A \xrightarrow{e \cup \{r\}} B \vdash M : (A \xrightarrow{e} B, \emptyset) \qquad r : A \xrightarrow{e} B \in R}{R;\Gamma \vdash \mathsf{fix}_r f.M : (A \xrightarrow{e \cup \{r\}} B, \emptyset)} \tag{3}$$

We prove this proposition by a direct application of the typing rules and the substitution property (details in [1]). To see a concrete example where the rule can be applied, consider a thread that at each instant writes an integer in a region r' (we assume a basic type *int* of integers):

$$M = \lambda x.(\lambda z. * \triangleright f(x+1))(\mathsf{set}(r', x))$$

Then, *e.g.*, $(\mathsf{fix}_r f.M)1$ is the infinite behaviour that at the *i-th* instant writes i in region r'. One can check the typability of $\mathsf{fix}_r f.M$ taking as (stratified) region context $R = r' : int, r : int \xrightarrow{\{r'\}} \mathbf{1}$.

6 Conclusion

We have introduced a λ-calculus with regions as an abstraction of a variety of concrete higher-order concurrent languages with specific scheduling and interaction mechanisms. We have described a stratified type and effect system and provided a new reducibility candidates interpretation for it which entails that typable programs terminate.

We have highlighted some relevant properties of the interpretation (proposition 5) which could be taken as the basis for an abstract definition of reducibility candidate. The latter is needed to interpret second-order (polymorphic) types (see, *e.g.*, [7]). We believe the proposed proof is both more general because it applies to a variety of interaction mechanisms and scheduling policies and simpler to understand because the interpretation is given by a direct induction on the proof system and because the invariant on the store is easier to manage (the store is not affected by the reduction). This is of course a subjective opinion and the reader who masters [4] may well find our revised treatment superfluous.

We have also lifted our approach to a timed/synchronous framework and derived a form of recursive definition which is useful to define behaviours spanning infinitely many instants.

Acknowledgements. The author was partially supported by ANR-06-SETI-010-02 and he is grateful to Gérard Boudol for several discussions on [4].

References

1. Amadio, R.: On stratified regions. Report ArXiv:0904.2076
2. Amadio, R., Curien, P.-L.: Domains and Lambda Calculi. Cambridge University Press, Cambridge
3. Amadio, R., Dabrowski, F.: Feasible reactivity in a synchronous π-calculus. In: Proc. ACM Principles and Practice of Declarative Programming, pp. 221–230 (2007)
4. Boudol, G.: Typing termination in a higher-order concurrent imperative language. In: Caires, L., Vasconcelos, V.T. (eds.) CONCUR 2007. LNCS, vol. 4703, pp. 272–286. Springer, Heidelberg (2007)
5. Berry, G., Gonthier, G.: The Esterel synchronous programming language. Science of computer programming 19(2), 87–152 (1992)
6. Deng, Y., Sangiorgi, D.: Ensuring termination by typability. Information and Computation 204(7), 1045–1082 (2006)
7. Gallier, J.: On Girard's Candidats de Reductibilité. In: Odifreddi (ed.) Logic and Computer Science, pp. 123–203. Academic Press, London (1990)
8. Hennessy, M., Regan, T.: A process algebra of timed systems. Information and Computation 117(2), 221–239 (1995)
9. Lucassen, J., Gifford, D.: Polymorphic effect systems. In: Proc. ACM-POPL (1988)
10. Sangiorgi, D.: Termination of processes. Math. Struct. in Comp. Sci. 16, 1–39 (2006)
11. Tofte, M., Talpin, J.-P.: Region-based memory management. Information and Computation 132(2), 109–176 (1997)
12. Yoshida, N., Berger, M., Honda, K.: Strong normalisation in the π-calculus. Information and Computation 191(2), 145–202 (2004)

Parallel Reduction in Resource Lambda-Calculus*

Michele Pagani[1] and Paolo Tranquilli[2]

[1] Dipartimento di Informatica – Università di Torino
pagani@di.unito.it
[2] Laboratoire PPS – Université Paris Diderot
ptranqui@pps.jussieu.fr

Abstract. We study the resource calculus – the non-lazy version of Boudol's λ-calculus with resources. In such a calculus arguments may be finitely available and mixed, giving rise to nondeterminism, modelled by a formal sum. We define parallel reduction in resource calculus and we apply, in such a nondeterministic setting, the technique by Tait and Martin-Löf to achieve confluence. Then, slightly generalizing a technique by Takahashi, we obtain a standardization result.

1 Introduction

In the '90s Boudol introduced resource calculus [1] – an extension of λ-calculus where arguments may come in limited availability and mixed together. Boudol's main motivation was studying a finer observational equivalence, arriving in particular to the one given by π-calculus via Milner's translation [2].

The main difference with ordinary λ-calculus is the renewal of the application of a function to an argument along two directions: on the one hand by introducing depletable arguments that must be used exactly once, on the other by letting the arguments come in multisets. Resource calculus is similar to Ehrhard and Regnier's differential λ-calculus [3]: the application of a function f to a linear argument corresponds, in the terminology of [3], to applying the derivative of f in 0 (which is a linear map) to that argument. Indeed, the second author shows in [4] that resource calculus corresponds to the intuitionistic minimal fragment of differential nets with promotion [5], exactly as λ-calculus corresponds to the intuitionistic minimal fragment of linear logic proof-nets [6]. This translation is therefore built on top of the *proofs-as-programs* correspondence, thus linking a language for nondeterministic programs with a new kind of nondeterministic proofs, the differential nets of differential linear logic.

Let us give a sample of resource calculus by means of an example. Let

$$\mathbf{I} := \lambda z.z \quad D := \lambda dz.z[d^!][d^!] \quad B := \lambda xy.\mathbf{I}[x^!, y^!] \quad M := \lambda b.b[(b[d^!][D[a]])^!][c^!],$$

where we follow the definition of the syntax as given in Figure 1(a). $\mathbf{I}$ is the standard λ-calculus identity. D is a standard λ-term too: it is $\lambda dz.zdd$. The slight

* Partially founded by the French ANR project blanc CHOCO, ANR-07-BLAN-0324.

Z. Hu (Ed.): APLAS 2009, LNCS 5904, pp. 226–242, 2009.

difference is only in the notation: we write the two arguments of z with a bang as superscript, emphasizing the fact that they are infinitely available arguments, and provide them as two distinct multiset singletons, delimited by brackets and called *bags*. This way of writing the application comes from Girard's linear logic [6]: indeed !-marked arguments (called *perpetual*) correspond exactly to exponential boxes (see [4]), the synchronized areas of proofs viable for non-linear operations (duplication and erasing). Along the same lines, the multiset bag constructor is semantically justified by several denotational models of linear logic, by their interpretation of the exponential modality.

Let us resume our example. The term B shows nondeterministic application: $\mathbf{I}$ is applied to a bag of two (infinitely available) terms, x and y. The term M is very like to the λ-term $\lambda b.b(bd(Da))c$, a nesting of two `if_then_else` with arguments d, Da and c (if b is fed with a boolean). All bags contain exactly one element, modelling deterministic λ-calculus application. However the bags $[D[a]]$ and, inside it, $[a]$ contain an element with no ! superscript, which sets the term apart from ordinary λ-calculus. This means that the argument $D[a]$ (resp. a) *must* be used exactly once by the function which is applied to $[D[a]]$ (resp. $[a]$). Let us evaluate $M[B^!]$ following the reduction of Definition 4.

$$\begin{aligned}
M[B^!] \rightarrow\ & B[(B[d^!][D[a]])^!][c^!] \rightarrow \big(\lambda y.\mathbf{I}[(B[d^!][D[a]])^!, y^!]\big)[c^!] && (1)\\
& \qquad\qquad\qquad\qquad \rightarrow \mathbf{I}[(B[d^!][D[a]])^!, c^!] \\
\rightarrow\ & B[d^!][D[a]] + c \rightarrow \big(\lambda y.\mathbf{I}[d^!, y^!]\big)[D[a]] + c \rightarrow \mathbf{I}[d^!, D[a]] + c && (2)\\
\rightarrow\ & D[a] + c \rightarrow \lambda z.z[a]1 + \lambda z.z1[a] + c. && (3)
\end{aligned}$$

The steps in line (1) of the example are akin to ordinary λ-calculus ones: we have a λ-abstraction fed with a bag containing exactly one infinitely available element. The step from line (1) to line (2) is a nondeterministic one, the argument of $\mathbf{I}$ being a bag with two elements, whence we have a sum of the two possible results. Sums intuitively correspond to a version of nondeterminism where the actual choice operation is left outside the calculus: the result of a term reduction will in general be a large formal sum of terms. The next steps in line (2) are again standard λ-calculus ones. The last term of line (2) has the nondeterministic redex $\mathbf{I}[d^!, D[a]]$. One could be tempted to contract the redex into $d + D[a]$, analogously to the previous nondeterministic step, but in this case the element $D[a]$ occurs linearly in the bag, hence only the choices using $D[a]$ exactly once are allowed. Specifically $\mathbf{I}[d^!, D[a]] \rightarrow D[a]$. Finally the last step has also a nondeterministic feature, this time due to a concurrency effect. Indeed in the redex $D[a]$, the function D encodes a pair where both the left and right components ask for the abstracted variable d. However the redex has only one linear occurrence of a available, for which the left and right components are in concurrency for fetching it. We thus have two possible outcomes, depending on which component takes linearly a while forcing the other to collapse to 1 i.e. the empty multiset.

In this paper we prove two basic properties of resource calculus — confluence (Theorem 4) and standardization (Theorem 6). Confluence does not contradict nondeterminism because the result of a nondeterministic reduction is a sum of

Λ:	M, N, L	$::= x \mid \lambda x.M \mid (MP)$	terms
Λ^{arg}:	$M^{(!)}, N^{(!)}$	$::= M \mid M^{!}$	arguments
Λ^{b}:	P, Q, R	$::= [M_1^{(!)}, \ldots, M_n^{(!)}]$	bags
$\Lambda^{(b)}$:	A, B	$::= M \mid P$	expressions

$\mu, \nu \in \mathbb{N}\langle\Lambda\rangle \quad \pi, \rho \in \mathbb{N}\langle\Lambda^{b}\rangle \quad \alpha, \beta, \gamma \in \mathbb{N}\langle\Lambda^{(b)}\rangle := \mathbb{N}\langle\Lambda\rangle \cup \mathbb{N}\langle\Lambda^{b}\rangle$ sums

(a) Grammar of terms, bags, expressions, sums.

$$\lambda x.(\textstyle\sum_i M_i) := \sum_i \lambda x.M_i \qquad [(\sum_i M_i)] \cdot P := \sum_i [M]_i \cdot P$$
$$(\textstyle\sum_i M_i)P := \sum_i M_i P \qquad [(\sum_i M_i)^{!}] \cdot P := [M_1^{!}, \ldots, M_k^{!}] \cdot P$$
$$M(\textstyle\sum_i P_i) := \sum_i MP_i.$$

(b) notation on $\mathbb{N}\langle\Lambda^{(b)}\rangle$.

Fig. 1. Syntax of resource calculus

terms. It remains meaningful, as it states that nondeterminism is really internal, and not caused by what an evaluator chooses to reduce. We achieve Theorem 4 by adapting the technique by Tait and Martin-Löf, using a suitable notion of parallel reduction (Definition 6). A similar result is in [3] where confluence of differential λ-calculus is proven. However our proof is somewhat simpler, using a notion of *development* (Definition 7) as defined by Takahashi [7] for λ-calculus. The result is at the same time proved for the *outer* reduction, which is meaningful for the standardization theorem.

A reduction step is *inner* if the redex to be contracted is under the scope of a bang, otherwise it is *outer* (Definition 5). Standardization states that every reduction chain can be split into a concatenation of outer steps followed by inner ones (Theorem 6). In λ-calculus such a result turned out to be fundamental for designing abstract machines computing (weak, head) normal forms, thus giving the theoretical justification of actual evaluators of functional languages. Although in our setting standardization does not give immediately a deterministic normalizing strategy (Example 1), it will help in implementing abstract machines for resource calculus, which can in turn also help in analyzing resource usage by ordinary λ-calculus programs [8]. Our proof of standardization adapts the one by Takahashi for λ-calculus, based on parallel reduction and inner parallel reduction [7]. Actually our notion of inner parallel reduction (Definition 8) is quite peculiar, possibly yielding a slight generalization of such technique.

We conclude the paper by discussing another, more atomic reduction of resource terms, called *baby-step* reduction in [4] (here Definition 10). Although confluence of baby-step reduction is an easy consequence of Theorem 4 (Theorem 7), we show how baby-step standardization fails in general, though it holds for normal and head normal forms (Theorem 8).

2 Syntax and Reduction

We will now introduce resource calculus. Though the "protagonists" are terms, for the ease of proofs it is best to present also other types of syntactic entities.

$$y\langle N/x\rangle := \begin{cases} N & \text{if } y = x, \\ 0 & \text{otherwise,} \end{cases} \qquad \begin{aligned} (\lambda y.M)\langle N/x\rangle &:= \lambda y.(M\langle N/x\rangle), \quad y \notin \mathrm{FV}(N) \cup \{x\}, \\ (MP)\langle N/x\rangle &:= M\langle N/x\rangle P + M(P\langle N/x\rangle), \end{aligned}$$

$$[M]\langle N/x\rangle := [M\langle N/x\rangle], \qquad 1\langle N/x\rangle := 0,$$

$$[M^!]\langle N/x\rangle := [M\langle N/x\rangle, M^!], \qquad (P\cdot R)\langle N/x\rangle := P\langle N/x\rangle\cdot R + P\cdot R\langle N/x\rangle.$$

(a) Linear substitution.

$$A\langle\!\langle N^{(!)}/x\rangle\!\rangle := \begin{cases} A\langle N/x\rangle & \text{if } N^{(!)} = N, \\ A\{x + N/x\} & \text{if } N^{(!)} = N^!, \end{cases}$$

$$A\langle\!\langle [N_1^{(!)}, \dots, N_k^{(!)}]/x\rangle\!\rangle := A\langle\!\langle N_1^{(!)}/x\rangle\!\rangle \cdots \langle\!\langle N_k^{(!)}/x\rangle\!\rangle, \quad x \notin \bigcup_{i=1}^{k} \mathrm{FV}(N_i^{(!)}).$$

(b) Argument and bag substitutions.

Fig. 2. Linear, argument and bag substitutions. Notice that the condition on bag substitution can always be achieved by renaming.

We thus introduce the calculus as a many-sorted one: the grammars for generating *terms* Λ and *bags* Λ^b (which are in fact multisets of *arguments* Λ^{arg}) is presented in Figure 1(a) together with their typical metavariables. $\Lambda^{(b)}$ (*expressions*) denotes either terms or bags. As we already mentioned, we also have formal sums, denoted by the $\mathbb{N}\langle\,.\,\rangle$ notation (as formal sums are the freely generated modules over natural numbers). However in $\mathbb{N}\langle\Lambda^{(b)}\rangle$, rather than taking freely generated sums, we allow only objects of the same sort to be summed.

Bags are multisets presented in multiplicative notation, so that $P\cdot Q$ is multiset union, and $1 = []$ is the empty bag. It must be noted though that we will never omit the dot $\cdot$, to avoid confusion with application.

The grammar for terms and bags does not include sums in any point, so that in a sense they may arise only on the "surface". However as an inductive notation (and *not* in the actual syntax) we extend all the constructors to sums as shown in Figure 1(b). In fact all constructors but the $(\cdot)^!$ are, as expected, linear. Notice the similarity between the equation $[(M + N)^!] = [M^!]\cdot[N^!]$ and $\mathrm{e}^{x+y} = \mathrm{e}^x\cdot\mathrm{e}^y$: this is not a coincidence, as Taylor expansion and semantics show well [9], and can be traced back to linear logic's *exponential isomorphism* $!A \otimes !B \cong !(A \& B)$.

There is no technical difficulty in defining α-equivalence and the set $\mathrm{FV}(\alpha)$ of free variables as in ordinary λ-calculus.

Definition 1 (Substitutions). *We define the following substitution operators.*

1. *$A\{N/x\}$ is the usual capture free substitution of N for x. It is extended to sums as in $\alpha\{\beta/x\}$ by linearity*[1] *in α and using the notations of Figure 1(b) for β. The form $A\{x + N/x\}$ is called* partial substitution.
2. *$A\langle N/x\rangle$ is the* linear substitution *defined inductively in Figure 2(a). It is extended to $\alpha\langle\beta/x\rangle$ by bilinearity in both α and β.*

[1] $F(A)$ (resp. $F(A, B)$) is extended by linearity (resp. bilinearity) by setting $F(\sum_i A_i) = \sum_i F(A_i)$ (resp. $F(\sum_i A_i, \sum_j B_j) = \sum_{i,j} F(A_i, B_j)$).

3. Argument substitution $A\langle\langle N^{(!)}/x\rangle\rangle$ *and its iteration* $A\langle\langle P/x\rangle\rangle$, *the* bag substitution, *are shown in Figure 2(b). Notice that* $A\langle\langle 1/x\rangle\rangle = A$. *Bag substitution is further generalized to* $\alpha\langle\langle\pi/x\rangle\rangle$ *by bilinearity in both* α *and* π.

As examples we show (supposing x not free in M, N):

$$\begin{aligned}
x[x^!]\,\{M+N/x\} &= (M+N)[(M+N)^!] = M[M^!,N^!]+N[M^!,N^!],\\
x[x^!]\langle M+N/x\rangle &= x[x^!]\langle M/x\rangle + x[x^!]\langle N/x\rangle\\
&= M[x^!]+x[M,x^!]+x[N,x^!]+N[x^!],\\
x[x^!]\langle\langle [M,N^!]/x\rangle\rangle &= M[x^!]\,\{x+N/x\}+x[M,x^!]\,\{x+N/x\}\\
&= M[N^!,x^!]+x[M,N^!,x^!]+N[M,N^!,x^!].
\end{aligned}$$

The definition of the linear substitution on a product of bags is clearly well defined regardless of the decomposition of the bag. On the other hand in order for the bag substitution to be well defined, we need to know that argument substitutions can be freely commuted. Commutation of linear substitutions is obtained from the so-called Schwartz lemma, a name due to linear substitution corresponding to partial derivation[2]. Both of the following lemmas are proved by structural induction (for details we refer to [3]).

Lemma 1 (Schwartz). *For* α *a sum of expressions,* μ, ν *sums of terms and* x, y *variables such that* $y \notin \mathrm{FV}(\mu)$*, we have*

$$\big(\alpha\langle\nu/y\rangle\big)\langle\mu/x\rangle = \big(\alpha\langle\mu/x\rangle\big)\langle\nu/y\rangle + \alpha\langle\nu\langle\mu/x\rangle/y\rangle.$$

In particular if $x \notin \mathrm{FV}(\nu)$ *then the second addend is* 0 *and the two substitutions commute.*

Lemma 2. *For* α, μ, ν, x, y *as in the above lemma, and moreover* $y \notin \mathrm{FV}(\nu)$*, we have*

$$\big(\alpha\,\{y+\nu/y\}\big)\langle\mu/x\rangle = \big(\alpha\langle\mu/x\rangle\big)\,\{y+\nu/y\} + \alpha\langle\nu\langle\mu/x\rangle/y\rangle\,\{y+\nu/y\}\,.$$

In particular if $x \notin \mathrm{FV}(\nu)$ *then the two commute.*

Furthermore we have, if $x \notin \mathrm{FV}(\mu) \cup \mathrm{FV}(\nu)$,

$$(\alpha\,\{x+\mu/x\})\,\{x+\nu/x\} = \alpha\,\{x+\mu+\nu/x\} = (\alpha\,\{x+\nu/x\})\,\{x+\mu/x\}\,.$$

Combined together, all the above implies that bag substitution is well defined, given its condition on the variable. We give another result we will need later.

Lemma 3. *If* $y \notin \mathrm{FV}(\mu) \cup \mathrm{FV}(\pi)$ *and* $x \neq y$*, then*

- $\alpha\langle\langle\pi/y\rangle\rangle\langle\mu/x\rangle = \alpha\langle\mu/x\rangle\langle\langle\pi/y\rangle\rangle + \alpha\langle\langle\pi\langle\mu/x\rangle/y\rangle\rangle$, *and*
- $\alpha\,\{0/y\}\,\langle\mu/x\rangle = \alpha\langle\mu/x\rangle\,\{0/y\}$.

[2] Indeed, notice the parallel between $\frac{\partial e^y}{\partial x} = \frac{\partial y}{\partial x}e^y$ and $[M^!]\langle N/x\rangle = [M\langle N/x\rangle]\cdot[M^!]$.

$$\frac{M \mathrel{\mathtt{R}} \mu}{\lambda x.M \mathrel{\mathtt{R}} \lambda x.\mu}\,\lambda \qquad \frac{M \mathrel{\mathtt{R}} \mu}{MP \mathrel{\mathtt{R}} \mu P}\,\mathtt{@l} \qquad \frac{P \mathrel{\mathtt{R}} \pi}{MP \mathrel{\mathtt{R}} M\pi}\,\mathtt{@r}$$

$$\frac{M \mathrel{\mathtt{R}} \mu}{[M]\cdot P \mathrel{\mathtt{R}} [\mu]\cdot P}\,\mathtt{bag}\ell \qquad \frac{M \mathrel{\mathtt{R}} \mu}{[M^!]\cdot P \mathrel{\mathtt{R}} [\mu^!]\cdot P}\,\mathtt{bag!} \qquad \frac{A \mathrel{\mathtt{R}} \alpha}{A+\beta \mathrel{\mathtt{R}} \alpha+\beta}\,\mathtt{sum}$$

Fig. 3. Rules defining the passing to the context of a relation R. For linear context, one just drops the bag! rule.

Proof. Sums pose no problems. Let us therefore reason, for the first point, by induction on $\pi = P$. For $P = 1$ it amounts to seeing $\alpha\langle\mu/x\rangle = \alpha\langle\mu/x\rangle + \alpha\langle\langle 0/y\rangle\rangle$. For $P = P'\cdot[L]$ we have by Schwartz lemma and inductive hypothesis:

$$\begin{aligned}\alpha\langle\langle P'/y\rangle\rangle\langle L/y\rangle\langle\mu/x\rangle &= \alpha\langle\langle P'/y\rangle\rangle\langle\mu/x\rangle\langle L/y\rangle + \alpha\langle\langle P'/y\rangle\rangle\langle L\langle\mu/x\rangle/y\rangle\\ &= \alpha\langle\mu/x\rangle\langle\langle P'\cdot[L]/y\rangle\rangle + \alpha\langle\langle (P'\langle\mu/x\rangle)\cdot[L]/y\rangle\rangle + \alpha\langle\langle P'\cdot([L]\langle\mu/x\rangle)/y\rangle\rangle\\ &= \alpha\langle\mu/x\rangle\langle\langle P/y\rangle\rangle + \alpha\langle\langle \big((P'\langle\mu/x\rangle)\cdot[L] + P'\cdot([L]\langle\mu/x\rangle)\big)/y\rangle\rangle\\ &= \alpha\langle\mu/x\rangle\langle\langle P/y\rangle\rangle + \alpha\langle\langle P\langle\mu/x\rangle/y\rangle\rangle.\end{aligned}$$

For $P = P'\cdot[L^!]$ we have by Lemma 2 and inductive hypothesis:

$$\begin{aligned}&\alpha\langle\langle P'/y\rangle\rangle\,\{y + L/y\}\,\langle\mu/x\rangle\\ &= \alpha\langle\langle P'/y\rangle\rangle\langle\mu/x\rangle\langle\langle L^!/y\rangle\rangle + \alpha\langle\langle P'/y\rangle\rangle\langle L\langle\mu/x\rangle/y\rangle\langle\langle L^!/y\rangle\rangle\\ &= \alpha\langle\mu/x\rangle\langle\langle P'\cdot[L^!]/y\rangle\rangle + \alpha\langle\langle P'\langle\mu/x\rangle\cdot[L^!]/y\rangle\rangle + \alpha\langle\langle P'\cdot[L\langle\mu/x\rangle, L^!]/y\rangle\rangle\\ &= \alpha\langle\mu/x\rangle\langle\langle P/y\rangle\rangle + \alpha\langle\langle (P'\cdot[L^!])\langle\mu/x\rangle/y\rangle\rangle = \alpha\langle\mu/x\rangle\langle\langle P/y\rangle\rangle + \alpha\langle\langle P\langle\mu/x\rangle/y\rangle\rangle.\end{aligned}$$

The second point is a straightforward induction on α. □

2.1 Relations

We will now introduce the relations defining reductions in resource calculus. Such relations will be in general defined by *rules* with premises and a conclusion. Such rules then *generate* the relation R, meaning that R is the least relation satisfying them, or equivalently is defined by *inferences*, i.e. trees made of such rules. A relation T *satisfies* the rules generating a relation R if such rules with T substituted for R are valid: then clearly R $\subseteq$ T. We will use this to avoid repeating identical steps in proofs by induction on the size of an inference of R. We denote composition of relations by juxtaposition, so that a RT b iff $\exists c$ s.t. a R c and c T b.

Definition 2 (Passing to the context). *A binary relation* R *on* $\mathbb{N}\langle\Lambda^{(b)}\rangle$ passes to the context *(resp. to the* linear context*) whenever it satisfies all the rules of Figure 3 (resp. all the rules but the* bag! *rule).*

Definition 3 (Compatibility). *We take a binary relation* R *on* $\mathbb{N}\langle\Lambda^{(b)}\rangle$ *to be* compatible *if it commutes with all constructors of* $\mathbb{N}\langle\Lambda^{(b)}\rangle$*, i.e. it satisfies all the*

$$\frac{}{x \; \mathtt{R} \; x}\;\texttt{var} \qquad \frac{M \; \mathtt{R} \; \mu \qquad P \; \mathtt{R} \; \pi}{MP \; \mathtt{R} \; \mu\pi}\;\overline{@} \qquad \frac{M \; \mathtt{R} \; \mu}{\lambda x.M \; \mathtt{R} \; \lambda x.\mu}\;\overline{\lambda}$$

$$\frac{}{1 \; \mathtt{R} \; 1}\;\texttt{bag1} \qquad \frac{M \; \mathtt{R} \; \mu \qquad P \; \mathtt{R} \; \pi}{[M]\cdot P \; \mathtt{R} \; [\mu]\cdot\pi}\;\overline{\mathsf{bag}\ell} \qquad \frac{M \; \mathtt{R} \; \mu \qquad P \; \mathtt{R} \; \pi}{[M^!]\cdot P \; \mathtt{R} \; [\mu^!]\cdot\pi}\;\overline{\mathsf{bag!}}$$

$$\frac{A_i \; \mathtt{R} \; \alpha_i, \qquad \text{for } 1 \leq i \leq k}{\sum_{i=1}^k A_i \; \mathtt{R} \; \sum_{i=1}^k \alpha_i}\;\overline{\texttt{sum}}$$

Fig. 4. Rules defining the compatibility for a relation $\mathtt{R}$. In $\overline{\texttt{sum}}$, $0 \leq k \neq 1$.

rules of Figure 4. We write of linear compatibility *when commutation is with all constructs but the* $(\cdot)^!$ *one: formally,* $\mathtt{R}$ *is linearly compatible if it satisfies all rules for compatibility but the* $\overline{\mathsf{bag!}}$ *one, which is replaced by*

$$\frac{P \; \mathtt{R} \; \pi}{[M^!]\cdot P \; \mathtt{R} \; [M^!]\cdot\pi}\;\overline{\mathsf{bag!}=}$$

Lemma 4. *A (linearly) compatible relation* $\mathtt{R}$ *is necessarily reflexive and passing to (linear) context.*

Proof. Reflexivity is evident as soon as one sees that equality is precisely the relation generated by the rules for both linear and regular compatibility. One then sees that all rules for passing to (linear) context are admissible under the rules for (linear) compatibility, by using reflexivity. □

We write that a relation is *sum-independent* if $\sum_i A_i \; \mathtt{R} \; \alpha$ implies that $\alpha = \sum_i \beta_i$ with $A_i \; \mathtt{R}^= \; \beta_i$ for all i, where $\mathtt{R}^=$ is the reflexive closure of $\mathtt{R}$. All the relations we study here are sum-independent, a notion capturing the fact that no interaction is possible between different addends of a sum. If the only rules introducing a sum on the left are among the two for passing to context ($\texttt{sum}$) or compatibility ($\overline{\texttt{sum}}$), the generated relation is clearly sum-independent.

Further, we speak of a *generalized rule* meaning a rule where all expressions in it are replaced by sums (using the notations of Figure 1(b) in the conclusion). A relation *strongly satisfies* a rule if it satisfies its generalized version.

Lemma 5. *The reflexive transitive closure* $\mathtt{R}^*$ *of a sum-independent relation* $\mathtt{R}$ *passing to (linear) context is sum-independent and (linearly) compatible.*

Proof. (sketch) Sum-independence is immediate. Then, by going through all passing to (linear) context rules, one sees that each one is strongly satisfied, which enables to easily check that also compatibility rules are. All single passages are carried out by inductions on the reduction length.

Lemma 6. *A (linearly) compatible sum-independent relation* $\mathtt{R}$ *strongly satisfies the rules for (linear) compatibility.*

Proof. (sketch) Straightforward check of all the rules.

Definition 4 (β-Reduction). *The β-reduction $\to$ is given by the rules for passing to the context (Figure 3) plus the following one:*

$$\frac{}{(\lambda x.M)P \to M\langle\langle P/x\rangle\rangle\,\{0/x\}}\ \mathtt{g}$$

For an example of reduction, see the one given in the introduction. In [4,10] this reduction is called the *giant-step* one (hence the name of the rule) to distinguish it from the baby-step one we will discuss in Section 5.

Definition 5 (Outer, Inner Reduction). *The* outer reduction *is the relation $\xrightarrow{\mathtt{o}}$ generated by the rule* g *of Definition 4 and the rules of passing the linear context (Figure 3 but the* bag! *rule). The* inner reduction *is the relation $\xrightarrow{\mathtt{i}}$ generated by the rules of passing the context and the following rule*

$$\frac{M \xrightarrow{\mathtt{o}} \mu}{[M^!]\cdot P \xrightarrow{\mathtt{i}} [\mu^!]\cdot P}\ \mathtt{in}$$

Informally, outer reduction is the one reducing linear redexes not inside a $(\cdot)^!$, inner is the rest. The rules we have provided for the inner reduction allow for more neat proofs. Notice the difference between $\xrightarrow{\mathtt{o}}$ and the λ-calculus head reduction: we have $\big(\lambda x.(\lambda y.y)[N^!]\big)[L^!] \xrightarrow{\mathtt{o}} (\lambda x.N)[L^!]$, which is false for head reduction. We will see in Example 1 how usual head redexes are not sufficient for reaching head normal forms, and linear arguments are to be taken into account as well. At this point we decided, mainly for the sake of elegance, to extend the notion to all *linear* redexes, even if under the scope of another linear redex.

Fact 1. We have that $\to = \xrightarrow{\mathtt{o}} \cup \xrightarrow{\mathtt{i}}$ as is expected: $\xrightarrow{\mathtt{o}} \cup \xrightarrow{\mathtt{i}}$ satisfies the rules of $\to$, and $\to$ those of both $\xrightarrow{\mathtt{o}}$ and $\xrightarrow{\mathtt{i}}$.

Fact 2. Using Lemma 6 one can also easily check that the relations $\xrightarrow{*}$, $\xrightarrow{\mathtt{i}*}$ and $\xrightarrow{\mathtt{o}*}$ are sum-independent and strongly satisfying all of the rules for (linear) compatibility.

3 Confluence

Definition 6 (Parallel reduction). *The* parallel reduction $\Rightarrow$ *(resp. the* parallel outer reduction $\overset{\mathtt{o}}{\Rightarrow}$*) is generated by the compatibility rules (resp. the linear compatibility rules) plus the following one:*

$$\frac{M \Rightarrow \mu \qquad P \Rightarrow \pi}{(\lambda x.M)P \Rightarrow \mu\langle\langle \pi/x\rangle\rangle\,\{0/x\}}\ \overline{\mathtt{g}}$$

Fact 3. $\Rightarrow$ and $\overset{\mathtt{o}}{\Rightarrow}$ are sum-independent and strongly satisfying all of their rules: by Lemma 6 only the new rule must be checked, which is immediate by multilinearity of the substitution operator.

We will thus be liberal when saying we apply one of the rules for parallel reduction, by allowing them with sums of expressions in the premises.

Lemma 7 (Closures coincide). *We have that* $\rightarrow \subseteq \Rightarrow \subseteq \xrightarrow{*}$. *In particular* $\xrightarrow{*} = \overset{*}{\Rightarrow}$ *The same holds for* $\xrightarrow{\circ}$ *and* $\overset{\circ}{\Rightarrow}$.

Proof. We show both inclusions by seeing that the right end satisfies the rules of the left one. For the first inclusion, by Lemma 4 just the $\mathtt{g}$ rule needs to be checked. This is straightforward by the $\overline{\mathtt{g}}$ rule and reflexivity of $\Rightarrow$ (Lemma 4). For the second inclusion, by Lemma 5 only the $\overline{\mathtt{g}}$ rule must be checked. Suppose therefore that $M \xrightarrow{*} \mu$ and $P \xrightarrow{*} \pi$. By compatibility of $\xrightarrow{*}$ (Lemma 5) we have $(\lambda x.M)P \xrightarrow{*} (\lambda x.\mu)\pi \xrightarrow{*} \mu\langle\langle\pi/x\rangle\rangle\,\{0/x\}$, where the last reduction (given by $\mathtt{g}$) is by compatibility with sum. The distinction between $\rightarrow$ and $\xrightarrow{\circ}$ is left to Lemma 5. ◻

Lemma 8 (Substitution for $\Rightarrow$). *For* $\alpha \Rightarrow \beta$ *and* $\pi \Rightarrow \sigma$ *we have* $\alpha\langle\langle\pi/x\rangle\rangle \Rightarrow \beta\langle\langle\sigma/x\rangle\rangle$ *and* $\alpha\,\{0/x\} \Rightarrow \beta\,\{0/x\}$. *The same holds for* $\overset{\circ}{\Rightarrow}$.

Proof. For the first result we reason by a primary induction on the size of π. We proceed by splitting over the last rule used to infer $\pi \Rightarrow \sigma$. The proof for $\overset{\circ}{\Rightarrow}$ proceeds almost identically, and we will highlight only its differences.
Case I ($\mathtt{bag1}$, $\pi = 1 = \sigma$). As $\alpha\langle\langle 1/x\rangle\rangle = \alpha \Rightarrow \beta = \beta\langle\langle 1/x\rangle\rangle$ we are done.
Case II ($\overline{\mathtt{bag!}}$, $\pi = [N^!]\cdot Q$). We have $\sigma = [\nu^!]\cdot\tau$ with $N \Rightarrow \nu$ ($\nu = N$ for $\overset{\circ}{\Rightarrow}$) and $Q \Rightarrow \tau$. Once we show that $\alpha\,\{x + N/x\} \Rightarrow \beta\,\{x + \nu/x\} = \beta\langle\langle[\nu^!]/x\rangle\rangle$ we would be done, as by inductive hypothesis on Q we would get

$$\alpha\langle\langle\pi/x\rangle\rangle = \alpha\,\{x + N/x\}\,\langle\langle Q/x\rangle\rangle \Rightarrow \beta\langle\langle[\nu^!]/x\rangle\rangle\langle\langle\tau/x\rangle\rangle = \beta\langle\langle\sigma/x\rangle\rangle.$$

We show it by induction on α. All but the base step for α a variable is trivial, as the substitution commutes with all the constructors, and $\Rightarrow$ is strongly compatible with them by Fact 3. For $\overset{\circ}{\Rightarrow}$, in the case $\alpha = [M^!]$, we have $\beta = \alpha$ and there is nothing to prove. If $\alpha = y = \beta$ we have

$$y\,\{x + N/x\} = y + \delta_{x,y}N \Rightarrow y + \delta_{x,y}\nu = y\langle\langle[\nu^!]/x\rangle\rangle.$$

Case III ($\overline{\mathtt{bag}\ell}$, $\pi = [N]\cdot Q$). As in the above case, we just need to show that $\alpha\langle N/x\rangle \Rightarrow \beta\langle\nu/x\rangle$ when $N \Rightarrow \nu$, as then the rest follows by inductive hypothesis on Q. Again we reason by a secondary induction on α, splitting on which rule was last used to infer $\alpha \Rightarrow \beta$. Apart the base cases $\mathtt{var}, \mathtt{bag1}$, the other cases uses secondary induction hypothesis and the strong compatibility of $\Rightarrow$ (resp. strong linear compatibility of $\overset{\circ}{\Rightarrow}$).
Subcase III.a ($\mathtt{var}$). We have $\alpha = y = \beta$, and $y\langle N/x\rangle = \delta_{x,y}N \Rightarrow \delta_{x,y}\nu = y\langle\langle[\nu]/x\rangle\rangle$.
Subcase III.b ($\overline{@}$). We have $\alpha = MR$ with $M \Rightarrow \mu$, $R \Rightarrow \rho$ and $\beta = \mu\rho$. Then

$$\alpha\langle N/x\rangle = M\langle N/x\rangle R + MR\langle N/x\rangle \Rightarrow \mu\langle\nu/x\rangle\rho + \mu\rho\langle\nu/x\rangle = (\mu\rho)\langle\nu/x\rangle.$$

$$
\begin{array}{rlr}
x^* := x, & & 1^* := 1, \\
(\lambda x.M)^* := \lambda x.M^*, & & [N]^* := [N^*], \\
(MP)^* := M^*P^* \quad \text{if } M \text{ is not an abstraction}, & & [N^!]^* := [(N^*)^!], \\
((\lambda x.M)P)^* := M^* \langle\!\langle P^*/x \rangle\!\rangle \{0/x\}, & & (P \cdot Q)^* := (P^* \cdot Q^*).
\end{array}
$$

Fig. 5. Inductive definition of developments

Subcase III.c ($\overline{\mathtt{g}}$). $\alpha = (\lambda y.M)R$, with $M \Rightarrow \mu$, $R \Rightarrow \rho$ and $\beta = \mu\langle\!\langle \rho/y \rangle\!\rangle \{0/y\}$, and by inductive hypothesis $M\langle N/x\rangle \Rightarrow \mu\langle \nu/x\rangle$ and $R\langle N/x\rangle \Rightarrow \rho\langle \nu/x\rangle$. Now, supposing $y \neq x$ and $y \notin \mathrm{FV}(N) \supseteq \mathrm{FV}(\nu)$,

$$
\begin{aligned}
\alpha\langle N/x\rangle &= (\lambda y.M\langle N/x\rangle)R + (\lambda y.M)(R\langle N/x\rangle) \\
&\Rightarrow \mu\langle \nu/x\rangle\langle\!\langle \rho/y \rangle\!\rangle \{0/y\} + \mu\langle\!\langle \rho\langle \nu/x\rangle/y \rangle\!\rangle \{0/y\} \\
&= \mu\langle\!\langle \rho/y \rangle\!\rangle\langle \nu/x\rangle \{0/y\} = \mu\langle\!\langle \rho/y \rangle\!\rangle \{0/y\} \langle \nu/x\rangle,
\end{aligned}
$$

where apart the inductive hypothesis we used Lemma 3.
Subcase III.d (otherwise). The other inductive steps are either trivial or easily carried over by using arguments like the above.
Case IV ($\overline{\mathtt{sum}}$, $\pi = P_1 + \cdots + P_k$). We have $\alpha\langle\!\langle \pi/x \rangle\!\rangle = \sum_i \alpha\langle\!\langle P_i/x \rangle\!\rangle$ and $\sigma = \sum_i \rho_i$ with $P_i \Rightarrow \rho_i$. We can apply inductive hypothesis k times and the $\overline{\mathtt{sum}}$ rule to get

$$
\alpha\langle\!\langle \pi/x \rangle\!\rangle = \textstyle\sum_i \alpha\langle\!\langle P_i/x \rangle\!\rangle \Rightarrow \sum_i \beta\langle\!\langle \rho_i/x \rangle\!\rangle = \beta\langle\!\langle \sigma/x \rangle\!\rangle.
$$

The result for $\alpha\{0/x\}$ is an easy induction on the derivation $\alpha \Rightarrow \beta$. □

Definition 7 (Developments α^* and $\alpha^{\circledast}$). *Given an expression A its* development $A^* \in \mathbb{N}\langle \Lambda^{(b)} \rangle$ *is defined inductively in Figure 5. The definition is extended to sums by linearity. The* linear development $\alpha^{\circledast}$ *is defined by the same inductive rules (just replace $*$ with $\circledast$), but for $[N^!]$ where $[N^!]^{\circledast} := [N^!]$.*

The name is due to the fact that it is a direct definition of the unique normal form one would get in proving the finite development theorem.

Lemma 9 (Main Lemma). *For any β such that $\alpha \Rightarrow \beta$ (resp. $\alpha \overset{\circ}{\Rightarrow} \beta$), we have $\beta \Rightarrow \alpha^*$ (resp. $\beta \overset{\circ}{\Rightarrow} \alpha^{\circledast}$).*

Proof. By induction on α, splitting on the last rule used for $\alpha \Rightarrow \beta$ (resp. $\alpha \overset{\circ}{\Rightarrow} \beta$). Again, we use only $\Rightarrow$, and we mark only where the proof differs for $\overset{\circ}{\Rightarrow}$.
Case I ($\mathtt{var}$, $\alpha = x$). As $\alpha^* = x = \beta$ and we are done.
Case II ($\overline{@}$, $\alpha = NP$). We have $\beta = \nu\pi$ with $N \Rightarrow \nu$ and $P \Rightarrow \pi$. By inductive hypothesis $\nu \Rightarrow N^*$ and $\pi \Rightarrow P^*$. We have two subcases.
Subcase II.a (N not an abstraction). We directly have $\nu\pi \Rightarrow N^*P^* = (NP)^*$ by a generalized $\overline{@}$ rule (Fact 3).

Subcase II.b ($N = \lambda x.L$). We have then that $\nu = \lambda x.\delta$ with $L \Rightarrow \delta \Rightarrow L^*$ by inductive hypothesis. Then by a generalized $\overline{\mathtt{g}}$ rule (Fact 3) we have $(\lambda x.\delta)\pi \Rightarrow L^*\langle\langle P^*/x\rangle\rangle\{0/x\} = \alpha^*$.
Case III ($\overline{\mathtt{g}}$, $\alpha = (\lambda x.L)P$). Again we have $L \Rightarrow \delta \Rightarrow L^*$ and $P \Rightarrow \pi \Rightarrow P^*$ by inductive hypothesis, where $\beta = \delta\langle\langle \pi/x\rangle\rangle\{0/x\}$. Then by Lemma 8 we have $\beta = \delta\langle\langle \pi/x\rangle\rangle\{0/x\} \Rightarrow L^*\langle\langle P^*/x\rangle\rangle\{0/x\} = \alpha^*$.
Case IV (Otherwise). The cases for $\overline{\mathtt{sum}}$ and $\mathtt{bag1}$ are trivial, while the ones for $\overline{\mathtt{bag}\ell}$ and $\overline{\mathtt{bag!}}$ (resp. $\overline{\mathtt{bag!=}}$ for $\overset{\mathtt{o}}{\Rightarrow}$) are analogous to the non-redex application (Subcase II.a). □

Theorem 4 (Confluence). *Both the β-reduction and the outer reductions are confluent.*

Proof. Lemma 9 gives strong confluence of $\Rightarrow$, which in turn gives strong confluence of $\overset{*}{\Rightarrow} = \overset{*}{\rightarrow}$ (Lemma 7), another way to say that $\rightarrow$ is confluent. The reasoning for $\overset{\mathtt{o}}{\rightarrow}$ is identical. □

We could similarly prove the same for $\overset{\mathtt{i}}{\rightarrow}$, though we restrain from doing so just because the proof would not have the same complete similarity as do the two for $\rightarrow$ and $\overset{\mathtt{o}}{\rightarrow}$.

4 Standardization

Definition 8 (Inner Parallel Reduction). *The* inner parallel reduction *is the relation* $\overset{\mathtt{i}}{\Rightarrow}$ *generated by the rule*

$$\frac{M \overset{\mathtt{o}*}{\longrightarrow} \nu \qquad \nu \overset{\mathtt{i}}{\Rightarrow} \mu \qquad P \overset{\mathtt{i}}{\Rightarrow} \pi}{[M^!]\cdot P \overset{\mathtt{i}}{\Rightarrow} [\mu^!]\cdot \pi}\ \overline{\mathtt{in}}$$

and those for compatibility (Figure 4) but the $\overline{\mathtt{bag!}}$ *rule.*

We excluded the $\overline{\mathtt{bag!}}$ as it is derivable from $\overline{\mathtt{in}}$, so that $\overset{\mathtt{i}}{\Rightarrow}$ is compatible anyway. Notice that $\overset{\mathtt{i}}{\Rightarrow} \not\subseteq \Rightarrow$, as the outer reduction in the premise of $\overline{\mathtt{in}}$ can go out of it. In fact it is an inductive definition of a "huge" relation: once the standardization theorem will be proved, but only then, it will turn out that $\overset{\mathtt{i}}{\Rightarrow} = \overset{\mathtt{i}*}{\longrightarrow}$.

Fact 5. Using Lemma 6, one sees that $\overset{\mathtt{i}}{\Rightarrow}$ is sum-independent and strongly satisfying all of its rules.

Lemma 10. *We have that* $\overset{\mathtt{i}}{\rightarrow} \subseteq \overset{\mathtt{i}}{\Rightarrow} \subseteq \overset{\mathtt{i}*}{\longrightarrow}$. *In particular* $\overset{\mathtt{i}*}{\longrightarrow} = \overset{\mathtt{i}*}{\Rightarrow}$.

Proof. By $\overline{\mathtt{in}}$ and the reflexivity of $\overset{\mathtt{i}}{\Rightarrow}$ (Lemma 4), $\overset{\mathtt{i}}{\Rightarrow}$ satisfies the $\mathtt{in}$ rule. Moreover $\overset{\mathtt{i}}{\Rightarrow}$ passes to the context (still Lemma 4), so $\overset{\mathtt{i}}{\Rightarrow}$ satisfies all rules generating $\overset{\mathtt{i}}{\rightarrow}$. We conclude $\overset{\mathtt{i}}{\rightarrow} \subseteq \overset{\mathtt{i}}{\Rightarrow}$.

Let us prove $\overset{\mathtt{i}}{\Rightarrow} \subseteq \overset{\mathtt{i}*}{\longrightarrow}$ by showing that $\overset{\mathtt{i}*}{\longrightarrow}$ enjoys the rules generating $\overset{\mathtt{i}}{\Rightarrow}$. Lemma 5 proves that $\overset{\mathtt{i}*}{\longrightarrow}$ is compatible. As for $\overline{\mathtt{in}}$, suppose $M \overset{\mathtt{o}*}{\longrightarrow} \nu$, $\nu \overset{\mathtt{i}*}{\longrightarrow} \mu$

and $P \xrightarrow{\texttt{i}*} \pi$, we must prove $[M^!]\cdot P \xrightarrow{\texttt{i}*} [\mu^!]\cdot\pi$. By an easy induction on the length of $M \xrightarrow{\texttt{o}*} \nu$ one has $[M^!] \xrightarrow{\texttt{i}*} [\nu^!]$, and by the compatibility of $\xrightarrow{\texttt{i}*}$ we have $[M^!]\cdot P \xrightarrow{\texttt{i}*} [\nu^!]\cdot P \xrightarrow{\texttt{i}*} [\mu^!]\cdot\pi$. □

Lemma 11 (Substitution for $\xrightarrow{\texttt{o}*}$). *For $\alpha \xrightarrow{\texttt{o}*} \beta$ and $\pi \xrightarrow{\texttt{o}*} \rho$ we have that $\alpha\langle\langle\pi/x\rangle\rangle \xrightarrow{\texttt{o}*} \beta\langle\langle\rho/x\rangle\rangle$ and $\alpha\,\{0/x\} \xrightarrow{\texttt{o}*} \beta\,\{0/x\}$.*

Proof. By Lemma 7, we have $\xrightarrow{\texttt{o}*} = \overset{\texttt{o}*}{\Rrightarrow}$, so we can reason with $\overset{\texttt{o}}{\Rrightarrow}$ only. Then a direct iteration of Lemma 8 (together with reflexivity of $\overset{\texttt{o}}{\Rrightarrow}$) yields $\alpha\langle\langle\pi/x\rangle\rangle \overset{\texttt{o}*}{\Rrightarrow} \beta\langle\langle\pi/x\rangle\rangle \overset{\texttt{o}*}{\Rrightarrow} \beta\langle\langle\sigma/x\rangle\rangle$, together with $\alpha\,\{0/x\} \overset{\texttt{o}*}{\Rrightarrow} \beta\,\{0/x\}$. □

Substitution on inner reductions is subtler: in general $\alpha \xrightarrow{\texttt{i}*} \beta$ and $\pi \xrightarrow{\texttt{i}*} \rho$ do not entail $\alpha\langle\pi/x\rangle \xrightarrow{\texttt{i}*} \beta\langle\rho/x\rangle$. For example take $M = y[(\mathbf{I}[x])^!]$ and $N = y[x^!]$, we have $M \xrightarrow{\texttt{i}*} N$ but $M\langle z/x\rangle \equiv y[\mathbf{I}[z],(\mathbf{I}[x])^!] \not\xrightarrow{\texttt{i}*} N\langle z/x\rangle \equiv y[z,x^!]$. However what suffices for standardization is the following lemma.

Lemma 12 (Substitution for $\overset{\texttt{i}}{\Rrightarrow}$). *Suppose $\alpha \overset{\texttt{i}}{\Rrightarrow} \beta$ and $\pi \overset{\texttt{i}}{\Rrightarrow} \rho$, then there is $\beta_o \in \mathbb{N}\langle\Lambda^{(b)}\rangle$ such that $\alpha\langle\langle\pi/x\rangle\rangle \xrightarrow{\texttt{o}*} \beta_o \overset{\texttt{i}}{\Rrightarrow} \beta\langle\langle\rho/x\rangle\rangle$. Moreover $\alpha\,\{0/x\} \overset{\texttt{i}}{\Rrightarrow} \beta\,\{0/x\}$.*

Proof. The proof of $\alpha\,\{0/x\} \overset{\texttt{i}}{\Rrightarrow} \beta\,\{0/x\}$ is a straightforward induction on the derivation of $\alpha \overset{\texttt{i}}{\Rrightarrow} \beta$, using Fact 5 and, for the $\overline{\texttt{in}}$ rule case, Lemma 11. As for $\alpha\langle\langle\pi/x\rangle\rangle \xrightarrow{\texttt{o}*} \beta_o \overset{\texttt{i}}{\Rrightarrow} \beta\langle\langle\rho/x\rangle\rangle$, we do induction on the derivation of $\pi \overset{\texttt{i}}{\Rrightarrow} \rho$. As usual, we will use Fact 5 implicitly. We split in cases, depending on the last rule inferring $\pi \overset{\texttt{i}}{\Rrightarrow} \rho$. The case `bag1` is trivial, and the case $\overline{\texttt{sum}}$ is an easy consequence of the linearity in π and the induction hypothesis.

Case I ($\overline{\texttt{in}}$). We have $\pi = [N^!]\cdot Q$, $\rho = [\nu^!]\cdot\tau$ and $N \xrightarrow{\texttt{o}*} \nu_o \overset{\texttt{i}}{\Rrightarrow} \nu$, $Q \overset{\texttt{i}}{\Rrightarrow} \tau$. Once we have proved that $\alpha\langle\langle N^!/x\rangle\rangle \xrightarrow{\texttt{o}*} \beta_o \overset{\texttt{i}}{\Rrightarrow} \beta\langle\langle[\nu^!]/x\rangle\rangle$, we would be done, as by Lemma 11 and inductive hypothesis on Q we would have

$$\alpha\langle\langle N^!/x\rangle\rangle\langle\langle Q/x\rangle\rangle \xrightarrow{\texttt{o}*} \beta_o\langle\langle Q/x\rangle\rangle \xrightarrow{\texttt{o}*} \beta_{oo} \overset{\texttt{i}}{\Rrightarrow} \beta\langle\langle[\nu^!]/x\rangle\rangle\langle\langle Q/x\rangle\rangle = \beta\langle\langle\rho/x\rangle\rangle.$$

The proof of $\alpha\langle\langle N^!/x\rangle\rangle \xrightarrow{\texttt{o}*} \beta_o \overset{\texttt{i}}{\Rrightarrow} \beta\langle\langle[\nu^!]/x\rangle\rangle$ is by induction on the derivation $\alpha \overset{\texttt{i}}{\Rrightarrow} \beta$.

Subcase I.a (`var`). If $\alpha = \beta = y$, then by compatibility $\alpha\,\{x+N/x\} = y + \delta_{x,y}N \xrightarrow{\texttt{o}*} y + \delta_{x,y}\nu_o \overset{\texttt{i}}{\Rrightarrow} y + \delta_{x,y}\nu = \beta\langle\langle[\nu^!]/x\rangle\rangle$.

Subcase I.b ($\overline{\texttt{in}}$). We have $\alpha = [M^!]\cdot R$, $\beta = [\mu^!]\cdot\rho'$ and $M \xrightarrow{\texttt{o}*} \mu_o \overset{\texttt{i}}{\Rrightarrow} \mu$, $R \overset{\texttt{i}}{\Rrightarrow} \rho'$. By Lemma 11 and inductive hypothesis on $\mu_o \overset{\texttt{i}}{\Rrightarrow} \mu$ and $R \overset{\texttt{i}}{\Rrightarrow} \rho'$, we have $M\langle\langle N^!/x\rangle\rangle \xrightarrow{\texttt{o}*} \mu_o\langle\langle N^!/x\rangle\rangle \xrightarrow{\texttt{o}*} \mu_{oo} \overset{\texttt{i}}{\Rrightarrow} \mu\langle\langle[\nu^!]/x\rangle\rangle$ and $R\langle\langle N^!/x\rangle\rangle \xrightarrow{\texttt{o}*} \rho_o \overset{\texttt{i}}{\Rrightarrow} \rho'\langle\langle[\nu^!]/x\rangle\rangle$. By compatibility of $\xrightarrow{\texttt{o}*}$ and a generalized $\overline{\texttt{in}}$ rule we have

$$[(M\langle\langle N^!/x\rangle\rangle)^!]\cdot R\langle\langle N^!/x\rangle\rangle \xrightarrow{\texttt{o}*} [(M\langle\langle N^!/x\rangle\rangle)^!]\cdot\rho_o \overset{\texttt{i}}{\Rrightarrow} [(\mu\langle\langle[\nu^!]/x\rangle\rangle)^!]\cdot\rho'\langle\langle[\nu^!]/x\rangle\rangle.$$

Subcase I.c ($\overline{@}$). We have $\alpha = MR$, $\beta = \mu\rho'$ and $M \stackrel{\mathtt{i}}{\Rightarrow} \mu$, $R \stackrel{\mathtt{i}}{\Rightarrow} \rho'$. By induction hypothesis we have $M\langle\!\langle N^!/x\rangle\!\rangle \stackrel{\mathtt{o*}}{\longrightarrow} \mu_o \stackrel{\mathtt{i}}{\Rightarrow} \mu\langle\!\langle[\nu^!]/x\rangle\!\rangle$ and $R\langle\!\langle N^!/x\rangle\!\rangle \stackrel{\mathtt{o*}}{\longrightarrow} \rho'_o \stackrel{\mathtt{i}}{\Rightarrow} \rho'\langle\!\langle[\nu^!]/x\rangle\!\rangle$. We conclude by strong compatibility $M\langle\!\langle N^!/x\rangle\!\rangle R\langle\!\langle N^!/x\rangle\!\rangle \stackrel{\mathtt{o*}}{\longrightarrow} \mu_o\rho'_o \stackrel{\mathtt{i}}{\Rightarrow} \mu\langle\!\langle[\nu^!]/x\rangle\!\rangle\rho'\langle\!\langle[\nu^!]/x\rangle\!\rangle$.

Subcase I.d (Otherwise). The case $\overline{\mathtt{bag}\ell}$ is similar to the previous $\overline{@}$ case; $\mathtt{bag1}$ is trivial and $\overline{\lambda}$, $\overline{\mathtt{sum}}$ are easy consequences of the induction hypothesis.

Case II ($\overline{\mathtt{bag}\ell}$). We have $\pi = [N]{\cdot}Q$, $\rho = \nu{\cdot}\tau$, with $N \stackrel{\mathtt{i}}{\Rightarrow} \nu$ and $Q \stackrel{\mathtt{i}}{\Rightarrow} \tau$. As in the previous case, once we prove that $\alpha\langle N/x\rangle \stackrel{\mathtt{o*}}{\longrightarrow} \beta_o \stackrel{\mathtt{i}}{\Rightarrow} \beta\langle\!\langle[\nu]/x\rangle\!\rangle$ we would have concluded, as by Lemma 11 and inductive hypothesis on $Q \stackrel{\mathtt{i}}{\Rightarrow} \tau$, we have $\alpha\langle N/x\rangle\langle\!\langle Q/x\rangle\!\rangle \stackrel{\mathtt{o*}}{\longrightarrow} \beta_o\langle\!\langle Q/x\rangle\!\rangle \stackrel{\mathtt{o*}}{\longrightarrow} \beta_{oo} \stackrel{\mathtt{i}}{\Rightarrow} \beta\langle\!\langle[\nu]/x\rangle\!\rangle\langle\!\langle\tau/x\rangle\!\rangle = \beta\langle\!\langle\rho/x\rangle\!\rangle$. We do induction on the derivation of $\alpha \stackrel{\mathtt{i}}{\Rightarrow} \beta$.

Subcase II.a ($\mathtt{var}$). If $\alpha = \beta = y$, then by compatibility $\alpha\langle N/x\rangle = \delta_{x,y}N \stackrel{\mathtt{i}}{\Rightarrow} \delta_{x,y}\nu = \beta\langle\nu/x\rangle$.

Subcase II.b ($\overline{\mathtt{in}}$). If $\alpha = [M^!]{\cdot}Q$, $\beta = [\mu^!]{\cdot}\tau$ and $M \stackrel{\mathtt{o*}}{\longrightarrow} \mu_o$, $\mu_o \stackrel{\mathtt{i}}{\Rightarrow} \mu$, $Q \stackrel{\mathtt{i}}{\Rightarrow} \tau$, then Lemma 11 gives $M\langle N/x\rangle \stackrel{\mathtt{o*}}{\longrightarrow} \mu_o\langle N/x\rangle$, and induction hypothesis yields $\mu_o\langle N/x\rangle \stackrel{\mathtt{o*}}{\longrightarrow} \mu_{oo} \stackrel{\mathtt{i}}{\Rightarrow} \mu\langle\nu/x\rangle$ and $Q\langle N/x\rangle \stackrel{\mathtt{o*}}{\longrightarrow} \tau_o \stackrel{\mathtt{i}}{\Rightarrow} \tau\langle\nu/x\rangle$. By strong compatibility and $\overline{\mathtt{in}}$, we have

$$\alpha\langle N/x\rangle = [M\langle N/x\rangle, M^!]{\cdot}Q + [M^!]{\cdot}Q\langle N/x\rangle \stackrel{\mathtt{o*}}{\longrightarrow} [\mu_{oo}, M^!]{\cdot}Q + [M^!]{\cdot}\tau_o$$
$$\stackrel{\mathtt{i}}{\Rightarrow} [\mu\langle\nu/x\rangle, \mu^!]{\cdot}\tau + [\mu^!]{\cdot}\tau\langle\nu/x\rangle = \beta\langle\nu/x\rangle.$$

Subcase II.c ($\overline{\mathtt{bag}\ell}$). If $\alpha = [M]\cdot Q$, $\beta = [\mu]\cdot\tau$ and $M \stackrel{\mathtt{i}}{\Rightarrow} \mu$, $Q \stackrel{\mathtt{i}}{\Rightarrow} \tau$, then induction hypothesis yields $M\langle N/x\rangle \stackrel{\mathtt{o*}}{\longrightarrow} \mu_o \stackrel{\mathtt{i}}{\Rightarrow} \mu\langle\nu/x\rangle$ and $Q\langle N/x\rangle \stackrel{\mathtt{o*}}{\longrightarrow} \tau_o \stackrel{\mathtt{i}}{\Rightarrow} \tau\langle\nu/x\rangle$. Strong compatibility of $\stackrel{\mathtt{o*}}{\longrightarrow}$ yields $[M\langle N/x\rangle]{\cdot}Q \stackrel{\mathtt{o*}}{\longrightarrow} [\mu_o]{\cdot}Q$ and $[M]{\cdot}[Q\langle N/x\rangle] \stackrel{\mathtt{o*}}{\longrightarrow} [M]{\cdot}\tau_o$. Strong compatibility of $\stackrel{\mathtt{i}}{\Rightarrow}$ gives $[\mu_o]{\cdot}Q \stackrel{\mathtt{i}}{\Rightarrow} [\mu\langle\nu/x\rangle]{\cdot}\tau$ and $[M]{\cdot}\tau_o \stackrel{\mathtt{i}}{\Rightarrow} [\mu]{\cdot}\tau\langle\nu/x\rangle$. Finally we conclude by the $\overline{\mathtt{sum}}$ rule:

$$\alpha\langle N/x\rangle = [M\langle N/x\rangle]{\cdot}Q + [M]{\cdot}Q\langle N/x\rangle \stackrel{\mathtt{o*}}{\longrightarrow} [\mu_o]{\cdot}Q + [M]{\cdot}\tau_o$$
$$\stackrel{\mathtt{i}}{\Rightarrow} [\mu\langle\nu/x\rangle, \mu]{\cdot}\tau + [\mu]{\cdot}\tau\langle\nu/x\rangle = \beta\langle\nu/x\rangle.$$

Subcase II.d (Otherwise). The rule $\overline{@}$ is handled similarly to the case $\overline{\mathtt{bag}\ell}$; the cases $\overline{\lambda}$ and $\overline{\mathtt{sum}}$ are easy consequences of the induction hypothesis; the rule $\mathtt{bag1}$ is immediate. □

Lemma 13 (Postponement). *We have* $\stackrel{\mathtt{i}}{\Rightarrow}\stackrel{\mathtt{o}}{\rightarrow} \subseteq \stackrel{\mathtt{o*}}{\longrightarrow}\stackrel{\mathtt{i}}{\Rightarrow}$.

Proof. Let $\alpha \stackrel{\mathtt{i}}{\Rightarrow} \alpha' \stackrel{\mathtt{o}}{\rightarrow} \beta$, we prove there is $\gamma \in \mathbb{N}\langle\Lambda^{(b)}\rangle$ such that $\alpha \stackrel{\mathtt{o*}}{\longrightarrow} \gamma \stackrel{\mathtt{i}}{\Rightarrow} \beta$. Suppose that $\alpha' \stackrel{\mathtt{o}}{\rightarrow} \beta$ is inferred by rule $\mathtt{g}$, all other cases are easy variants and omitted. So, let $\alpha' = (\lambda x.M')P'$ and $\beta = M'\langle\!\langle P'/x\rangle\!\rangle\,\{0/x\}$. Under these hypothesis $\alpha \stackrel{\mathtt{i}}{\Rightarrow} \alpha'$ can be obtained only by means of a $\overline{@}$ rule, therefore $\alpha = (\lambda x.M)P$ with $M \stackrel{\mathtt{i}}{\Rightarrow} M'$ and $P \stackrel{\mathtt{i}}{\Rightarrow} P'$. By Lemma 12 there is a sum $\nu \in \mathbb{N}\langle\Lambda\rangle$ such that

$M\langle\langle P/x\rangle\rangle\{0/x\} \xrightarrow{\mathtt{o}*} \nu \overset{\mathtt{i}}{\Rightarrow} M'\langle\langle P'/x\rangle\rangle\{0/x\}$. Hence $\alpha \xrightarrow{\mathtt{o}} M\langle\langle P/x\rangle\rangle\{0/x\} \xrightarrow{\mathtt{o}*} \nu \overset{\mathtt{i}}{\Rightarrow} M'\langle\langle P'/x\rangle\rangle\{0/x\} = \beta$. □

Theorem 6 (Standardization). *We have* $\xrightarrow{*} = \xrightarrow{\mathtt{o}*}\xrightarrow{\mathtt{i}*}$.

Proof. Fact 1 gives $\xrightarrow{*} = (\xrightarrow{\mathtt{o}} \cup \xrightarrow{\mathtt{i}})^*$, and Lemma 10 $\xrightarrow{\mathtt{o}} \cup \xrightarrow{\mathtt{i}} \subseteq \xrightarrow{\mathtt{o}} \cup \overset{\mathtt{i}}{\Rightarrow}$. Then $\alpha \xrightarrow{*} \beta$ entails $\alpha \xrightarrow{\mathtt{o}*}\overset{\mathtt{i}}{\Rightarrow} \cdots \xrightarrow{\mathtt{o}*}\overset{\mathtt{i}}{\Rightarrow} \beta$. By iterating Lemma 13 we have $\alpha \xrightarrow{\mathtt{o}*}\overset{\mathtt{i}*}{\Rightarrow} \beta$. So Lemma 10 allows us to conclude $\alpha \xrightarrow{\mathtt{o}*}\xrightarrow{\mathtt{i}*} \beta$. □

In λ-calculus we have a notion of *strong* standardization stating that there is a deterministic *history-free* strategy leading to a normal form (resp. head normal form), e.g. left reduction. By history-free, we mean that the redex is chosen by just looking at the term, regardless of the previous steps. In contrast, we argue that resource calculus has no history-free effective strategy assuring a normal form (resp. a head normal form) whenever it exists.

Example 1. Let us consider $\mathbf{I}[\mathbf{I}^!, (x[\mathbf{\Omega}, \mathbf{I}1])^!]$, where $\mathbf{\Omega} = (\lambda x.x[x^!])\lambda x.x[x^!]$ is the typical diverging term. We have $\mathbf{I}[\mathbf{I}^!, (x[\mathbf{\Omega}, \mathbf{I}1])^!] \xrightarrow{\mathtt{o}} \mathbf{I}+x[\mathbf{\Omega}, \mathbf{I}1] \xrightarrow{\mathtt{o}} \mathbf{I}$. In the second term, we have two choices among the two linear arguments of the bag. Choosing the first loops, while the second normalizes. However in general making the right decision should be akin to solving the halting problem.

What could probably be done, though it is outside the scope of this work, is devising a kind of *fair* strategy, in the sense of concurrent programming. By craftily marking the redexes, one could probably make sure that, though sequentially, all parallel subterms get a chance to be reduced, so that if there is a reduction to 0 it would be found.

4.1 An Application

In a forthcoming paper the first author and Ronchi della Rocca characterize different notions of resource calculus solvability by means of the following definition of *may-head* and *must-head normalizability*:

Definition 9 (Head Normal Form). *We define simultaneously the class of terms and that of bags in* head normal form, hnf *for short:*

- $\lambda x.M$ *is a* hnf *iff* M *is a* hnf*;*
- $yP_1 \dots P_n$ *is a* hnf *iff each* P_i *is a* hnf*;*
- $P = [M_1^{(!)}, \dots, M_m^{(!)}]$ *is a* hnf *iff for each* i, $M_i^{(!)} = M_i$ *entails* M_i *is a* hnf.

In case of a sum $\sum_{i=1}^m A_i$ *of expressions, we have two different notions of head normal form:*

- $\sum_{i=1}^m A_i$ *is a* may-head normal form, mhnf *for short, iff there is a* $i \leq m$ *such that* A_i *is a head normal form;*
- $\sum_{i=1}^m A_i$ *is a* must-head normal form, Mhnf *for short, iff* $m \neq 0$ *and for every* $i \leq m$, A_i *is a head normal form.*

An expression A is may-head normalizable *(resp.* must-head normalizable*) if it is reducible to a* mhnf *(resp.* Mhnf*).*

Corollary 1 (Head Normalization). *Whenever α is may-head (resp. must-head) normalizable, there is a* mhnf *(resp.* Mhnf*) β such that $\alpha \xrightarrow{\mathtt{o}*} \beta$.*

Proof. Immediate from Theorem 6 and the fact that whenever $\beta' \xrightarrow{\mathtt{i}*} \beta$ we have β' mhnf (resp. Mhnf) iff β mhnf (resp. Mhnf). □

5 Baby-Step Reduction

This section is devoted to presenting another, more atomic reduction of resource terms.

Definition 10. *The* baby-step reduction $\xrightarrow{\mathtt{b}}$ *(resp.* outer baby-step reduction $\xrightarrow{\mathtt{ob}}$*) is the relation generated by the rules for passing to context (resp. to linear context) of Figure 3 plus the following two:*

$$\frac{}{(\lambda x.M)[N^{(!)}]\cdot P \xrightarrow{\mathtt{b}} (\lambda x.M\langle\!\langle N^{(!)}/x\rangle\!\rangle)P}\ \mathtt{b} \qquad \frac{}{(\lambda x.M)1 \xrightarrow{\mathtt{b}} M\{0/x\}}\ \mathtt{b1}$$

The inner baby-step reduction $\xrightarrow{\mathtt{ib}}$ *is* $\xrightarrow{\mathtt{b}} \setminus \xrightarrow{\mathtt{ob}}$.

Lemma 14. *We have $(\lambda x.\mu)P \xrightarrow{\mathtt{b}*} (\lambda x.\mu\langle\!\langle P/x\rangle\!\rangle)1$. In particular $\rightarrow\, \subseteq\, \xrightarrow{\mathtt{b}*}$. The same holds for the outer and inner versions.*

Proof. We can proceed by induction on P: if $P = 1$ then the reduction chain is empty and we are done. If $P = [L^{(!)}]\cdot Q$ then (supposing $\mu = \sum_i M_i$)

$$\begin{aligned}(\lambda x.\mu)P = \textstyle\sum_i(\lambda x.M_i)[L^{(!)}]\cdot Q &\xrightarrow{\mathtt{b}*} \textstyle\sum_i(\lambda x.M_i\langle\!\langle L^{(!)}/x\rangle\!\rangle)Q \\ &\xrightarrow{\mathtt{b}*} \textstyle\sum_i(\lambda x.M_i\langle\!\langle L^{(!)}/x\rangle\!\rangle\langle\!\langle Q/x\rangle\!\rangle)1 = (\lambda x.\mu\langle\!\langle P/x\rangle\!\rangle)1,\end{aligned}$$

where in the first reduction we used compatibility with sum, while in the second both it and inductive hypothesis. Applying final baby steps to all addends in $(\lambda x.M)P \xrightarrow{*} (\lambda x.M\langle\!\langle P/x\rangle\!\rangle)1$ and closing by (linear) context gives the result on $\rightarrow$ (resp. $\xrightarrow{\mathtt{o}}$). The result for $\xrightarrow{\mathtt{ib}}$ and $\xrightarrow{\mathtt{i}}$ follows. □

Lemma 15. *We have that $\xrightarrow{\mathtt{b}}\, \subseteq\, \equiv_\beta$, where the β-equivalence $\equiv_\beta$ is as usual $(\leftarrow \cup \rightarrow)^*$. The same holds for the outer versions of the two reductions.*

Proof. We check that $\rightarrow\overset{*}{\leftarrow}$ satisfies the rules of $\xrightarrow{\mathtt{b}}$, concluding $\xrightarrow{\mathtt{b}}\, \subseteq\, \rightarrow\overset{*}{\leftarrow}\, \subseteq\, \equiv_\beta$. Notice first of all that $\overset{*}{\leftarrow}$ is compatible as $\xrightarrow{*}$ is (Lemma 5). Then $\rightarrow\overset{*}{\leftarrow}$ passes to context, and we need to check just the two new rules. Of the two `b1` is a special case of `g`, while for the `b` rule we have

$$(\lambda x.M)[L^{(!)}]\cdot P \rightarrow M\langle\!\langle [L^{(!)}]\cdot P/x\rangle\!\rangle\{0/x\} \overset{*}{\leftarrow} (\lambda x.M\langle\!\langle [L^{(!)}]/x\rangle\!\rangle)P,$$

where there is the need of the transitive reflexive closure as a sum may have arisen. Notice that Lemma 5 assures that the result is valid for $\xrightarrow{\mathtt{ob}}$ also. □

In particular by the above lemmas we have that the equational theory of the two reductions is the same.

Theorem 7 (Confluence of baby-steps). *The baby-step reduction and the outer baby-step reduction is confluent.*

Proof. By Lemma 15, confluence of $\rightarrow$ (which as known entails $\equiv_\beta = \xrightarrow{*}\xleftarrow{*}$) and Lemma 14, we have $\xleftarrow{\mathtt{b}*}\xrightarrow{\mathtt{b}*} \subseteq \equiv_\beta = \xrightarrow{*}\xleftarrow{*} \subseteq \xrightarrow{\mathtt{b}*}\xleftarrow{\mathtt{b}*}$. The same passages on $\xrightarrow{\mathtt{ob}}$ give the result for the outer reduction. □

The next question is whether the standardization result as presented by Theorem 6 is valid also for $\xrightarrow{\mathtt{b}}$, but the answer is negative.

Example 2. Take $M = (\lambda d.I)[(I[x^!, y^!])^!]$. It is easily shown that $I[x^!, y^!] \xrightarrow{\mathtt{ob}*} x + y$, which in turn gives rise to the following chain:

$$M \xrightarrow{\mathtt{i}*} (\lambda d.I)[(x+y)^!] = (\lambda d.I)[x^!, y^!] \xrightarrow{\mathtt{ob}} (\lambda d.I)[y^!].$$

However the only outer redex in M gives rise in a single step to $M \xrightarrow{\mathtt{ob}} (\lambda d.I)1$, so that y is lost as soon as we make an outer reduction, which makes $(\lambda d.I)[y^!]$ unreachable.

The catch is that the baby-step reduction is somewhat too atomic: as inner sums may split the elements of a bag, an inner reduction may change outer redexes in way to which only the baby reduction is sensitive to. However, as normal forms of the two reduction coincide, we can still get a weaker result.

Theorem 8. *Whenever $\alpha \xrightarrow{\mathtt{b}*} \beta$ and β is normal (resp. a* mhnf *or a* Mhnf*), then $\alpha \xrightarrow{\mathtt{ob}*}\xrightarrow{\mathtt{ib}*} \beta$.*

Proof. By Lemma 15 and confluence (thus uniqueness of normal form) we get $\alpha \xrightarrow{*} \beta$. By Theorem 6 $\alpha \xrightarrow{\mathtt{o}*}\xrightarrow{\mathtt{i}*} \beta$, which by Lemma 14 entails the result.

The part about head normalization is a direct consequence of Corollary 1 and the above fact. □

References

1. Boudol, G.: The lambda-calculus with multiplicities. INRIA Research Report 2025 (1993)
2. Milner, R.: Functions as processes. Mathematical Structures in Computer Science 2, 119–141 (1992)
3. Ehrhard, T., Regnier, L.: The differential lambda-calculus. Theor. Comput. Sci. 309(1), 1–41 (2003)
4. Tranquilli, P.: Intuitionistic differential nets and lambda calculus. Theor. Comput. Sci. (2008) (to appear)
5. Ehrhard, T., Regnier, L.: Differential interaction nets. Theor. Comput. Sci. 364(2), 166–195 (2006)
6. Girard, J.Y.: Linear logic. Th. Comp. Sc. 50, 1–102 (1987)

7. Takahashi, M.: Parallel reductions in lambda-calculus. Information and Computation 118(1), 120–127 (1995)
8. Ehrhard, T., Regnier, L.: Böhm trees, Krivine's machine and the Taylor expansion of lambda-terms. In: Beckmann, A., Berger, U., Löwe, B., Tucker, J.V. (eds.) CiE 2006. LNCS, vol. 3988, pp. 186–197. Springer, Heidelberg (2006)
9. Ehrhard, T., Regnier, L.: Uniformity and the Taylor expansion of ordinary lambda-terms. Theor. Comput. Sci. 403(2-3), 347–372 (2008)
10. Tranquilli, P.: Nets between determinism and nondeterminism. Ph.D. thesis, Università Roma Tre/Université Paris Diderot (Paris 7) (April 2009)

Classical Natural Deduction for S4 Modal Logic

Daisuke Kimura and Yoshihiko Kakutani

Department of Computer Science, University of Tokyo
7-3-1 Hongo, Tokyo 113-8656, Japan
kimura@lyon.is.s.u-tokyo.ac.jp, kakutani@is.s.u-tokyo.ac.jp

Abstract. This paper proposes a natural deduction system $\mathrm{CND}^{\mathrm{S4}}$ for classical S4 modal logic with necessity and possibility modalities. This new system is an extension of Parigot's Classical Natural Deduction with dual-context to formulate S4 modal logic. The modal $\lambda\mu$-calculus is also introduced as a computational extraction of $\mathrm{CND}^{\mathrm{S4}}$. It is an extension of both the $\lambda\mu$-calculus and the modal λ-calculus. Subject reduction, confluency, and strong normalization of the modal $\lambda\mu$-calculus are shown. Finally, the computational interpretation of the modal $\lambda\mu$-calculus, especially the computational meaning of the modal possibility operator, is discussed.

1 Introduction

Classical Natural Deduction (CND) [16] is a natural deduction system for classical logic. It is introduced to extend the paradigm 'proofs as programs' to classical logic.

Proofs as programs is known as the Curry-Howard correspondence, which is an isomorphism between proofs in logical systems and programs in computational systems. It is studied widely, since it gives computational aspect in logical systems and theoretical foundation of programming languages. The typical example of the correspondence is the one between intuitionistic propositional logic and the simply typed λ-calculus.

Griffin [7] extended the Curry-Howard correspondence to classical logic by discovering the connection between the type of `call/cc` and Peirce's law. The $\lambda\mu$-calculus introduced by Parigot [16] corresponds to CND in the same way that the λ-calculus corresponds to intuitionistic natural deduction. The $\lambda\mu$-calculus has played a central role for studying the Curry-Howard correspondence of classical logic in many approaches such as semantics, abstract machine, functional programming with exception handling, and the computational duality between call-by-value and call-by-name [17,15,2,20,5,8,23,9,11]D.

The Curry-Howard correspondence is also extended to intuitionistic modal logic. Davies and Pfenning [4] showed that the λ-calculus with the S4 modal necessity operator $\Box$ provides a theoretical framework of staged computation by interpreting a formula $\Box A$ as a type of program codes of type A. Staged computation is a computational mechanism that is used for programming techniques such as dynamic code generation and partial evaluation [22]. This mechanism is realized by specifying stages where partial programs should be executed. A partial program that can be used at the current or *any* later stages is treated as a program code at the current stage. Type theoretic approach of staged computation based on intuitionistic modal logic is studied actively [4,3,6,18,13,24].

Z. Hu (Ed.): APLAS 2009, LNCS 5904, pp. 243–258, 2009.

The purpose of this paper is the following two points. First, we aim to extend the paradigm 'proofs as programs' to classical modal proofs. We extend CND to classical S4 modal logic, and construct a term calculus that corresponds to the extended system. Second, we aim to give a computational interpretation of classical modal proofs. In particular, we focus on the computational meaning of the modal possibility operator. The λ-calculi with both the modal necessary and possibility operators were introduced in [1,18]. However, since they were constructed based on the analysis from a logical viewpoint, it is still unclear how the possibility operator is interpreted in staged computation.

Some computational systems for classical modal logic have been proposed. Kakutani [10] introduced the $\lambda\mu$-calculi for classical normal modal logic starting from categorical semantics, and extended the computational duality in classical logic to classical modal logic. Shan [21] gave a term calculus that corresponds to sequent calculus for classical S4 modal logic.

This paper presents an extension of classical natural deduction $\mathrm{CND}^{\mathrm{S4}}$ for classical S4 modal logic. This system is a natural deduction system with multiple conclusions to formulate classical logic, and dual-context to formulate S4 modal logic. $\mathrm{CND}^{\mathrm{S4}}$ has both the modal necessity and possibility operators as primitives. We then introduce the $\lambda\mu^{S4}$-calculus as the extracted computational system from $\mathrm{CND}^{\mathrm{S4}}$. It extends proofs as types of classical logic to classical modal logic. The $\lambda\mu^{S4}$-calculus satisfies subject reduction, strong normalization, and confluency.

As for the formulation of classical S4 modal logic in natural deduction style, the one given by Prawitz [19] is known well. However, normalization in Prawitz's system does not hold. Medeiros pointed out it, and showed normalization by giving a modified system [12]. This paper gives a stronger result than Medeiros's one, since strong normalization and confluency of $\mathrm{CND}^{\mathrm{S4}}$ is obtained from the results of the $\lambda\mu^{S4}$-calculus.

We also discuss computational interpretation of the $\lambda\mu^{S4}$-calculus. This calculus provides both mechanisms of staged computation and exception handling, because it is an extension of both the modal λ-calculus and the $\lambda\mu$-calculus. A computational interpretation of the possibility operator can be obtained via the duality of classical modal logic: $\Diamond A$ is a type of programs that can be used at *some* later stage. We consider an application of the possibility operator by giving a program example of staged computation with exception handling.

This paper is organized as follows. Section 2 introduces the classical natural deduction $\mathrm{CND}^{\mathrm{S4}}$, and shows its provability is equivalent to classical S4 modal logic. Section 3 gives the $\lambda\mu^{S4}$-calculus as the corresponding system of $\mathrm{CND}^{\mathrm{S4}}$. In Section 4, we show subject reduction, strong normalization, and confluency of the $\lambda\mu^{S4}$-calculus. Section 5 gives some discussions on the computational interpretation of $\lambda\mu^{S4}$. Finally, we conclude the paper in Section 6.

2 Classical Modal Propositional Logic

We propose a natural deduction system for classical S4 modal logic (called $\mathrm{CND}^{\mathrm{S4}}$) extending Parigot's Classical Natural Deduction (CND) [16]. CND is a natural deduction system for classical logic, and has sequents with multiple conclusions. Though Parigot gave CND for the second-order classical predicate logic, we consider the system for the $\{\supset, \neg, \Box, \Diamond\}$-fragment of classical S4 modal propositional logic for simplicity.

Definition 1 (Formulas). Formulas (denoted by $A, B, \ldots$) are defined by
$A ::= X \mid A \supset A \mid \neg A \mid \Box A \mid \Diamond A$,
where $X, Y, Z, \ldots$ are atomic formulas.

Let Γ, Δ, Σ, and Θ range over finite multisets of formulas.

The sequents of CND^{S4} have the following form:

$$A_1, \ldots, A_n; B_1, \ldots, B_m \vdash_{\mathrm{ND}} C_1, \ldots, C_p; D_1, \ldots, D_q,$$

where $n, m, p, q \geq 0$. The parts $A_1, \ldots, A_n; B_1, \ldots, B_m$ and $C_1, \ldots, C_p; D_1, \ldots, D_q$ are the antecedent and the succedent of this sequent, respectively. Each of them is separated into two zones by the symbol ;. The classical antecedent and the classical succedent of this sequent are the parts $B_1, \ldots, B_m$ and $C_1, \ldots, C_p$, respectively. They are sometimes called the classical part of the sequent. The modal antecedent and the modal succedent of this sequent are the parts $A_1, \ldots, A_n$ and $D_1, \ldots, D_q$, respectively. They are sometimes called the modal part of the sequent. We implicitly assume $\Box$ at the head of each A_i. We also assume $\Diamond$ at the head of each D_j. The interpretation of the above sequent is given as follows: If all of $\Box A_1, \ldots \Box A_n$ and $B_1, \ldots, B_m$ are true, then some of $C_1, \ldots, C_p$ or $\Diamond D_1, \ldots, \Diamond D_q$ is true.

Definition 2 (Inference rules). Inference rules of CND^{S4} are defined as follows.

$$\frac{}{\Sigma; \Gamma, A \vdash_{\mathrm{ND}} A, \Delta; \Theta}\,(AxC) \qquad \frac{}{\Sigma, A; \Gamma \vdash_{\mathrm{ND}} A, \Delta; \Theta}\,(AxM)$$

$$\frac{\Sigma; \Gamma, A \vdash_{\mathrm{ND}} B, \Delta; \Theta}{\Sigma; \Gamma \vdash_{\mathrm{ND}} A \supset B, \Delta; \Theta}\,(\supset I) \qquad \frac{\Sigma; \Gamma \vdash_{\mathrm{ND}} A \supset B, \Delta; \Theta \quad \Sigma; \Gamma \vdash_{\mathrm{ND}} A, \Delta; \Theta}{\Sigma; \Gamma \vdash_{\mathrm{ND}} B, \Delta; \Theta}\,(\supset E)$$

$$\frac{\Sigma; \Gamma, A \vdash_{\mathrm{ND}} \Delta; \Theta}{\Sigma; \Gamma \vdash_{\mathrm{ND}} \neg A, \Delta; \Theta}\,(\neg I) \qquad \frac{\Sigma; \Gamma \vdash_{\mathrm{ND}} \neg A, \Delta; \Theta \quad \Sigma; \Gamma \vdash_{\mathrm{ND}} A, \Delta; \Theta}{\Sigma; \Gamma \vdash_{\mathrm{ND}} \Delta; \Theta}\,(\neg E)$$

$$\frac{\Sigma; \quad \vdash_{\mathrm{ND}} A \quad ; \Theta}{\Sigma; \Gamma \vdash_{\mathrm{ND}} \Box A, \Delta; \Theta}\,(\Box I) \qquad \frac{\Sigma; \Gamma \vdash_{\mathrm{ND}} \Box A, \Delta; \Theta \quad \Sigma, A; \Gamma \vdash_{\mathrm{ND}} \Delta; \Theta}{\Sigma; \Gamma \vdash_{\mathrm{ND}} \Delta; \Theta}\,(\Box E)$$

$$\frac{\Sigma; \Gamma \vdash_{\mathrm{ND}} \Delta; A, \Theta}{\Sigma; \Gamma \vdash_{\mathrm{ND}} \Diamond A, \Delta; \Theta}\,(\Diamond I) \qquad \frac{\Sigma; \Gamma \vdash_{\mathrm{ND}} \Diamond A, \Delta; \Theta \quad \Sigma; A \vdash_{\mathrm{ND}} \quad ; \Theta}{\Sigma; \Gamma \vdash_{\mathrm{ND}} \Delta; \Theta}\,(\Diamond E) \qquad \frac{\Sigma; \Gamma \vdash_{\mathrm{ND}} A, \Delta; \Theta}{\Sigma; \Gamma \vdash_{\mathrm{ND}} \Delta; A, \Theta}\,(IR)$$

The formulas explicitly mentioned in the rules are called active. The active formula $A \supset B$ of $(\supset E)$, $\neg A$ of $(\neg E)$, $\Box A$ of $(\Box E)$, or $\Diamond A$ of $(\Diamond E)$ is said to be the major premise of each rule.

(AxC) is the axiom rule for the classical part. (AxM) is the axiom rule for the modal part. (IR) moves a formula from the classical succedent to the modal succedent. $(\supset I)$, $(\neg I)$, $(\Box I)$, and $(\Diamond I)$ are introduction rules. $(\supset E)$, $(\neg E)$, $(\Box E)$, and $(\Diamond E)$ are elimination rules.

Remark 1. (AxM) implicitly removes a $\Box$-operator, since each formula at the modal antecedent is implicitly boxed. $(\Box E)$ simply eliminates its major premise $\Box A$ without removing the $\Box$-operator. Both rules are necessary to show $\;;\;\vdash_{\mathrm{ND}} \Box A \supset A;\;$. Dually, (IR) implicitly introduces a $\Diamond$-operator, since each formula at the modal succedent is implicitly diamonded. $(\Diamond I)$ specifies the $\Diamond$-operator that is implicitly introduced by (IR). We need both rules to show $\;;\;\vdash_{\mathrm{ND}} A \supset \Diamond A;\;$.

Remark 2. The separation symbol ; in the sequents of CND^{S4} is necessary for normalization. Let $\mathrm{CND}^{S4'}$ be a natural deduction system obtained by replacing sequents

$\Sigma;\Gamma \vdash_{\mathrm{ND}} \Delta;\Theta$ of $\mathrm{CND}^{\mathrm{S4}}$ by $\Box\Sigma,\Gamma \vdash \Delta,\Diamond\Theta$. Then normalization of $\mathrm{CND}^{\mathrm{S4}\prime}$ does not hold. For example, the following proof is not normalizable.

$$\dfrac{\dfrac{\dfrac{\overline{\Box B \vdash \Box B}}{\Box B \vdash \Box\Box B}(\Box I)}{\vdash \Box B \supset \Box\Box B}(\supset I) \qquad \dfrac{\overline{\Box A \supset \Box B \vdash \Box A \supset \Box B} \quad \overline{\Box A \vdash \Box A}}{\Box A \supset \Box B, \Box A \vdash \Box B}(\supset E)}{\Box A \supset \Box B, \Box A \vdash \Box\Box B}(\supset E)$$

$\mathrm{CND}^{\mathrm{S4}}$ admits weakening and contraction rules.

Lemma 1 (Weakening). *Assume $\Sigma \subseteq \Sigma'$, $\Gamma \subseteq \Gamma'$, $\Delta \subseteq \Delta'$, and $\Theta \subseteq \Theta'$. Then $\Sigma;\Gamma \vdash_{\mathrm{ND}} \Delta;\Theta$ implies $\Sigma';\Gamma' \vdash_{\mathrm{ND}} \Delta';\Theta'$.*

Proof. The claim is shown by induction on the length of proofs.

In the following, if $\Sigma;\Gamma \vdash_{\mathrm{ND}} \Delta;\Theta$ is obtained from $\Sigma';\Gamma' \vdash_{\mathrm{ND}} \Delta';\Theta'$ by applying rules $R_1,\ldots,R_n$ several times, then we write $\dfrac{\Sigma';\Gamma' \vdash_{\mathrm{ND}} \Delta';\Theta'}{\Sigma;\Gamma \vdash_{\mathrm{ND}} \Delta;\Theta} R_1,\ldots,R_n$. We will write R' if an elimination rule R is used with weakening. For example, $(\neg E)'$ is used as follows:

$$\dfrac{\Sigma_1,\Sigma_2;\Gamma_1,\Gamma_2 \vdash_{\mathrm{ND}} \neg A,\Delta_1,\Delta_2;\Theta_1,\Theta_2 \quad \Sigma_2,\Sigma_3;\Gamma_2,\Gamma_3 \vdash_{\mathrm{ND}} A,\Delta_2,\Delta_3;\Theta_2,\Theta_3}{\Sigma_1,\Sigma_2,\Sigma_3;\Gamma_1,\Gamma_2,\Gamma_3 \vdash_{\mathrm{ND}} \Delta_1,\Delta_2,\Delta_3;\Theta_1,\Theta_2,\Theta_3}(\neg E)'.$$

Lemma 2. (1) *$\Sigma,A;\Gamma \vdash_{\mathrm{ND}} \Delta;\Theta$ holds if and only if $\Sigma;\Box A,\Gamma \vdash_{\mathrm{ND}} \Delta;\Theta$ holds.*
(2) *$\Sigma;\Gamma \vdash_{\mathrm{ND}} \Delta;A,\Theta$ holds if and only if $\Sigma;\Gamma \vdash_{\mathrm{ND}} \Delta,\Diamond A;\Theta$ holds.*

Proof. (1) Assume $\Sigma,A;\Gamma \vdash_{\mathrm{ND}} \Delta;\Theta$. Then we have $\Sigma;\Box A,\Gamma \vdash_{\mathrm{ND}} \Delta;\Theta$ by (AxC), and $(\Box E)'$. Conversely, assume $\Sigma;\Box A,\Gamma \vdash_{\mathrm{ND}} \Delta;\Theta$, then we have $\Sigma;\Gamma \vdash_{\mathrm{ND}} \neg\Box A,\Delta;\Theta$ by $(\neg I)$. Here $\Sigma,A;\Gamma \vdash_{\mathrm{ND}} \Box A,\Delta;\Theta$ is shown by (AxM) and $(\Box I)$. Therefore we obtain $\Sigma,A;\Gamma \vdash_{\mathrm{ND}} \Delta;\Theta$ by $(\neg E)'$.

(2) We obtain $\Sigma;\Gamma \vdash_{\mathrm{ND}} \Delta,\Diamond A;\Theta$ from $\Sigma;\Gamma \vdash_{\mathrm{ND}} \Delta;A,\Theta$ by using (IR). Conversely, assume $\Sigma;\Gamma \vdash_{\mathrm{ND}} \Delta,\Diamond A;\Theta$. Then we have $\Sigma;\Gamma \vdash_{\mathrm{ND}} \Delta;A,\Theta$ by (AxC), (IR), and $(\Diamond E)'$.

Lemma 3 (Left contraction). (1) *If $\Sigma,A,A;\Gamma \vdash_{\mathrm{ND}} \Delta;\Theta$, then $\Sigma,A;\Gamma \vdash_{\mathrm{ND}} \Delta;\Theta$ hold.*
(2) *If $\Sigma;\Gamma,A,A \vdash_{\mathrm{ND}} \Delta;\Theta$, then $\Sigma;\Gamma,A \vdash_{\mathrm{ND}} \Delta;\Theta$ hold.*

Proof. (1) and (2) are shown by induction on the length of proofs.

Lemma 4 (Right contraction). (1) *If $\Sigma;\Gamma \vdash_{\mathrm{ND}} \Delta,A,A;\Theta$, then $\Sigma;\Gamma \vdash_{\mathrm{ND}} \Delta,A;\Theta$ hold.*
(2) *If $\Sigma;\Gamma \vdash_{\mathrm{ND}} \Delta;\Theta,A,A$, then $\Sigma;\Gamma \vdash_{\mathrm{ND}} \Delta;\Theta,A$ hold.*

Proof. (1) Suppose we have $\Sigma;\Gamma \vdash_{\mathrm{ND}} \Delta,A,A;\Theta$. Then $\Sigma;\Gamma \vdash_{\mathrm{ND}} \Delta,A;\Theta$ is obtained by:

$$\dfrac{\begin{matrix}\vdots \\ ;\vdash_{\mathrm{ND}} \neg\neg A \supset A;\end{matrix} \qquad \dfrac{\dfrac{\dfrac{\overline{;\neg A \vdash_{\mathrm{ND}} \neg A;} \quad \Sigma;\Gamma \vdash_{\mathrm{ND}} \Delta,A,A;\Theta}{\Sigma;\Gamma,\neg A \vdash_{\mathrm{ND}} \Delta,A;\Theta}(\neg E)' \quad \overline{;\neg A \vdash_{\mathrm{ND}} \neg A;}}{\Sigma;\Gamma,\neg A \vdash_{\mathrm{ND}} \Delta;\Theta}(\neg E)'}{\Sigma;\Gamma \vdash_{\mathrm{ND}} \neg\neg A,\Delta;\Theta}(\neg I)}{\Sigma;\Gamma \vdash_{\mathrm{ND}} \Delta,A;\Theta}(\supset E)'$$

We claim that $;\vdash_{\mathrm{ND}} \neg\neg A \supset A;$ is proved from (AxC) by using $(\neg I)$ and $(\neg E)$. (2) is shown by using (1) and Lemma 2.

We sometimes write weakening and left contraction rules as follows.

$$\frac{\Sigma;\Gamma \vdash_{\mathrm{ND}} \Delta;\Theta}{\Sigma';\Gamma' \vdash_{\mathrm{ND}} \Delta';\Theta'}\,(Wk) \quad \frac{\Sigma;\Gamma,A,A \vdash_{\mathrm{ND}} \Delta;\Theta}{\Sigma;\Gamma,A \vdash_{\mathrm{ND}} \Delta;\Theta}\,(CtrC_L) \quad \frac{\Sigma,A,A;\Gamma \vdash_{\mathrm{ND}} \Delta;\Theta}{\Sigma,A;\Gamma \vdash_{\mathrm{ND}} \Delta;\Theta}\,(CtrM_L)$$

$$\frac{\Sigma;\Gamma \vdash_{\mathrm{ND}} A,A,\Delta;\Theta}{\Sigma;\Gamma \vdash_{\mathrm{ND}} A,\Delta;\Theta}\,(CtrC_R) \quad \frac{\Sigma;\Gamma \vdash_{\mathrm{ND}} \Delta;A,A,\Theta}{\Sigma;\Gamma \vdash_{\mathrm{ND}} \Delta;A,\Theta}\,(CtrM_R)$$

where $\Sigma \subseteq \Sigma'$, $\Gamma \subseteq \Gamma'$, $\Delta \subseteq \Delta'$, and $\Theta \subseteq \Theta'$. $(CtrC_R)$ and $(CtrC_L)$ are the right and left contraction rules for the classical part. $(CtrM_R)$ and $(CtrM_L)$ are the right and left contraction rules for the modal part.

$\mathrm{CND}^{\mathrm{S4}}$ is equivalent to the classical S4 modal logic in the sense of provability. Here we remember the sequent calculus style formulation of classical S4 modal logic.

The sequent calculus have sequents of the form $\Gamma \vdash_{\mathrm{SC}} \Delta$. The antecedent and succedent of a sequent $\Gamma \vdash_{\mathrm{SC}} \Delta$ is defined by Γ and Δ, respectively. The interpretation of a sequent $\Gamma \vdash_{\mathrm{SC}} \Delta$ is given as follows: If all formulas in Γ are true, then some formula in Δ is true.

The inference rules of the sequent calculus for classical modal logic are given as usual. We display only the rules for modal operators:

$$\frac{\Box\Gamma \vdash_{\mathrm{SC}} A,\Diamond\Delta}{\Box\Gamma \vdash_{\mathrm{SC}} \Box A,\Diamond\Delta}\,(\Box R) \quad \frac{\Gamma,A \vdash_{\mathrm{SC}} \Delta}{\Gamma,\Box A \vdash_{\mathrm{SC}} \Delta}\,(\Box L) \quad \frac{\Gamma \vdash_{\mathrm{SC}} A,\Delta}{\Gamma \vdash_{\mathrm{SC}} \Diamond A,\Delta}\,(\Diamond R) \quad \frac{\Box\Gamma,A \vdash_{\mathrm{SC}} \Diamond\Delta}{\Box\Gamma,\Diamond A \vdash_{\mathrm{SC}} \Diamond\Delta}\,(\Diamond L)$$

where $\Box\Gamma$ is $\Box A_1,\ldots,\Box A_n$ if Γ is $A_1,\ldots,A_n$, $\Diamond\Delta$ is $\Diamond B_1,\ldots,\Diamond B_m$ if Δ is $B_1,\ldots,B_m$.

Theorem 1. *$\Sigma;\Gamma \vdash_{\mathrm{ND}} \Delta;\Theta$ is provable if and only if $\Box\Sigma,\Gamma \vdash_{\mathrm{SC}} \Delta,\Diamond\Theta$ is provable.*

Proof. The *only-if*-part is shown by induction on the proof of $\mathrm{CND}^{\mathrm{S4}}$. To show the *if*-part, we first show the following claim (we call this claim (*)): $\Box\Sigma,\Gamma \vdash_{\mathrm{SC}} \Delta,\Diamond\Theta$ implies $;\Box\Sigma,\Gamma \vdash_{\mathrm{ND}} \Delta,\Diamond\Theta;$. If we have this claim, we can show $\Sigma;\Gamma \vdash_{\mathrm{ND}} \Delta;\Theta$ by using Lemma 2. The claim (*) is shown by induction on the proof of the sequent calculus. We consider the cases $(\Box R)$, $(\Box L)$, $(\Diamond R)$, and $(\Diamond L)$.

The case of $(\Box R)$: Assume that $\Box\Sigma,\Gamma \vdash_{\mathrm{SC}} \Box A,\Delta,\Diamond\Theta$ is proved from $\Box\Sigma,\Gamma \vdash_{\mathrm{SC}} A,\Delta,\Diamond\Theta$. By the condition of $(\Box R)$, Γ and Δ should be $\Box\Gamma'$ and $\Diamond\Delta'$ for some Γ' and Δ', respectively. By the induction hypothesis, we have $;\Box\Sigma,\Box\Gamma' \vdash_{\mathrm{ND}} A,\Diamond\Delta',\Diamond\Theta;$. Then we have $\Sigma,\Gamma'; \vdash_{\mathrm{ND}} A;\Delta',\Theta$ by Lemma 2. Thus $\Sigma,\Gamma'; \vdash_{\mathrm{ND}} \Box A;\Delta',\Theta$ is shown by $(\Box I)$. By using Lemma 2 again, we obtain $;\Box\Sigma,\Box\Gamma' \vdash_{\mathrm{ND}} \Box A,\Diamond\Delta',\Diamond\Theta;$. The case of $(\Diamond L)$ is shown similarly. The case of $(\Box L)$ is proved by using the induction hypothesis and Lemma 2. The case of $(\Diamond R)$ is proved by using the induction hypothesis.

We define the normalization procedure of $\mathrm{CND}^{\mathrm{S4}}$. Each reduction step of the procedure removes a formula occurrence (we call cut-formula) that is the consequence of an introduction rule and the major premise of an elimination rule. We distinguish a reduction step between *logical* reduction and *structural* reduction according to the occurrence of its cut-formula. A reduction step is called logical when its cut-formula is the major premise of an elimination rule, and it is introduced by the immediate preceding rule. A reduction step is called structural when its cut-formula is the major premise of an elimination rule, and it is not active in the immediate preceding rule.

The logical reduction and the structural reduction are defined as well as that of CND [16] when its cut-formula is $A \supset B$ or $\neg A$. We give the definition when the cut-formula is $\Box A$ or $\Diamond A$.

Logical $\Box$-reduction: We assume that the cut-formula has the form $\Box A$, and is the major premise of a $(\Box E)$ rule, and is introduced by the immediate preceding $(\Box I)$ rule. Then we have the following proof:

$$\dfrac{\dfrac{\begin{array}{c}\vdots\\ \Sigma;\ \ \vdash_{\mathrm{ND}} A;\Theta\end{array}}{\Sigma;\Gamma\vdash_{\mathrm{ND}}\Box A,\Delta;\Theta}\,(\Box I) \qquad \begin{array}{c}\overline{\Sigma_0,A;\Gamma_0\vdash_{\mathrm{ND}}A,\Delta_0;\Theta_0}\\ \vdots\\ \Sigma,A;\Gamma\vdash_{\mathrm{ND}}\Delta;\Theta\end{array}}{\Sigma;\Gamma\vdash_{\mathrm{ND}}\Delta;\Theta}\,(\Box E)\ .$$

This proof is reduced to the proof:

$$\begin{array}{c}\vdots\\ \dfrac{\Sigma;\ \ \vdash_{\mathrm{ND}} A;\Theta}{\Sigma,\Sigma_0;\Gamma_0\vdash_{\mathrm{ND}}A,\Delta_0;\Theta,\Theta_0}\,(Wk)\\ \vdots\\ \dfrac{\Sigma,\Sigma;\Gamma\vdash_{\mathrm{ND}}\Delta;\Theta,\Theta}{\Sigma;\Gamma\vdash_{\mathrm{ND}}\Delta;\Theta}\,(CtrM_L),(CtrM_R)\end{array}\ .$$

Logical $\Diamond$-reduction: We assume that the cut-formula has the form $\Diamond A$, and is the major premise of a $(\Diamond E)$ rule, and is introduced by the immediate preceding $(\Diamond I)$ rule. Then we have the following proof:

$$\begin{array}{c}\vdots\\ \dfrac{\Sigma_0;\Gamma_0\vdash_{\mathrm{ND}}A,\Delta_0;\Theta_0}{\Sigma_0;\Gamma_0\vdash_{\mathrm{ND}}\Delta_0;A,\Theta_0}\,(IR)\\ \vdots\\ \dfrac{\dfrac{\Sigma;\Gamma\vdash_{\mathrm{ND}}\Delta;A,\Theta}{\Sigma;\Gamma\vdash_{\mathrm{ND}}\Diamond A,\Delta;\Theta}\,(\Diamond I) \qquad \begin{array}{c}\vdots\\ \Sigma;A\vdash_{\mathrm{ND}}\ \ ;\Theta\end{array}}{\Sigma;\Gamma\vdash_{\mathrm{ND}}\Delta;\Theta}\,(\Diamond E)\end{array}\ .$$

This proof is reduced to the proof:

$$\begin{array}{c}\dfrac{\dfrac{\begin{array}{c}\vdots\\ \Sigma;A\vdash_{\mathrm{ND}}\ \ ;\Theta\end{array}}{\Sigma;\ \ \vdash_{\mathrm{ND}}\neg A;\Theta}\,(\neg I) \qquad \begin{array}{c}\vdots\\ \Sigma_0;\Gamma_0\vdash_{\mathrm{ND}}A,\Delta_0;\Theta_0\end{array}}{\Sigma,\Sigma_0;\Gamma_0\vdash_{\mathrm{ND}}\Delta_0;\Theta,\Theta_0}\,(\neg E)'\\ \vdots\\ \dfrac{\Sigma,\Sigma;\Gamma\vdash_{\mathrm{ND}}\Delta;\Theta,\Theta}{\Sigma;\Gamma\vdash_{\mathrm{ND}}\Delta;\Theta}\,(CtrM_L),(CtrM_R)\end{array}\ .$$

Structural $\Box$-reduction: We assume that the cut-formula has the form $\Box A$, and is the major premise of a $(\Box E)$ rule, and is not active in the immediate preceding rule. Then we have the following proof:

$$\begin{array}{c}\vdots\,\pi_0\\ \Sigma_0;\Gamma_0\vdash_{\mathrm{ND}}\Box A,\Delta_0;\Theta_0\\ \vdots\,\pi_1\\ \dfrac{\Sigma;\Gamma\vdash_{\mathrm{ND}}\Box A,\Delta;\Theta \qquad \begin{array}{c}\vdots\\ \Sigma,A;\Gamma\vdash_{\mathrm{ND}}\Delta;\Theta\end{array}}{\Sigma;\Gamma\vdash_{\mathrm{ND}}\Delta;\Theta}\,(\Box E)\end{array}\ ,$$

where $\Box A$ is active in the last rule of π_0, and not active in all rules of π_1. This proof is reduced to the following proof:

$$\begin{array}{c}\dfrac{\begin{array}{c}\vdots\,\pi_0\\ \Sigma_0;\Gamma_0\vdash_{\mathrm{ND}}\Box A,\Delta_0;\Theta_0\end{array} \qquad \begin{array}{c}\vdots\\ \Sigma,A;\Gamma\vdash_{\mathrm{ND}}\Delta;\Theta\end{array}}{\Sigma,\Sigma_0;\Gamma,\Gamma_0\vdash_{\mathrm{ND}}\Delta,\Delta_0;\Theta,\Theta_0}\,(\Box E)'\\ \vdots\,\pi_1\\ \dfrac{\Sigma,\Sigma;\Gamma,\Gamma\vdash_{\mathrm{ND}}\Delta,\Delta;\Theta,\Theta}{\Sigma;\Gamma\vdash_{\mathrm{ND}}\Delta;\Theta}\,(CtrC_L),(CtrC_R),(CtrM_L),(CtrM_R)\end{array}\ .$$

Structural $\Diamond$-reduction: We assume that the cut-formula has the form $\Diamond A$, and is the major premise of a $(\Diamond E)$ rule, and is not active in the immediate preceding rule. Then we have the following proof:

$$\dfrac{\begin{array}{c}\vdots\ \pi_0\\ \Sigma_0;\Gamma_0 \vdash_{\mathrm{ND}} \Diamond A, \Delta_0; \Theta_0\\ \vdots\ \pi_1\\ \Sigma;\Gamma \vdash_{\mathrm{ND}} \Diamond A, \Delta; \Theta\end{array} \qquad \begin{array}{c}\vdots\\ \Sigma; A \vdash_{\mathrm{ND}}\ ; \Theta\end{array}}{\Sigma;\Gamma \vdash_{\mathrm{ND}} \Delta; \Theta}\,(\Diamond E)\ ,$$

where $\Diamond A$ is active in the last rule of π_0, and not active in all rules of π_1. This is reduced to the following proof:

$$\dfrac{\begin{array}{c}\dfrac{\begin{array}{c}\vdots\\ \Sigma_0;\Gamma_0 \vdash_{\mathrm{ND}} \Diamond A, \Delta_0; \Theta_0\end{array} \quad \begin{array}{c}\vdots\\ \Sigma;\ A \vdash_{\mathrm{ND}}\ ; \Theta\end{array}}{\Sigma_0,\Sigma;\Gamma_0,\Gamma \vdash_{\mathrm{ND}} \Delta_0,\Delta; \Theta_0,\Theta}\,(\Diamond E)'\\ \vdots\\ \Sigma,\Sigma;\Gamma,\Gamma \vdash_{\mathrm{ND}} \Delta,\Delta;\Theta,\Theta\end{array}}{\Sigma;\Gamma \vdash_{\mathrm{ND}} \Delta;\Theta}\,(CtrC_L),(CtrC_R),(CtrM_L),(CtrM_R)\ .$$

In the next section, we introduce the $\lambda\mu^{S4}$-calculus that corresponds to $\mathrm{CND}^{\mathrm{S4}}$. The reduction procedure of $\mathrm{CND}^{\mathrm{S4}}$ satisfies confluency and normalizability. They are obtained from confluency (Theorem 4) and strong normalizability (Theorem 2) of the $\lambda\mu^{S4}$-calculus.

3 Modal $\lambda\mu$-calculus

This section gives the definition of the modal $\lambda\mu$-calculus (called $\lambda\mu^{S4}$).

Definition 3 (Types). Let $X, Y, Z \ldots$ range over type variables. A type of the $\lambda\mu^{S4}$-calculus (denoted by $T, U, \ldots$) is either the special type $\bot$ or a normal type (denoted by $A, B, \ldots$) defined as follows:

Types $\quad T ::= A \mid \bot$
Normal types $\quad A ::= X \mid A \supset A \mid \neg A \mid \Box A \mid \Diamond A$

There are four kinds of variables for the $\lambda\mu^{S4}$-calculus, called classical variables, classical covariables, modal variables, and modal covariables. They are respectively corresponding to classical antecedent, classical succedent, modal antecedent, and modal succedent of sequents in $\mathrm{CND}^{\mathrm{S4}}$.

Then we define expressions of the $\lambda\mu^{S4}$-calculus.

Definition 4 (Expressions). Let $x, y, \ldots$ range over classical variables, $a, b, \ldots$ range over classical covariables, $\chi, \upsilon, \ldots$ range over modal variables, and $\alpha, \beta, \ldots$ range over modal covariables. An expression (denoted by $E, F, \ldots$) of the $\lambda\mu^{S4}$-calculus is either a term (denoted by $M, N, \ldots$) or a statement (denoted by $R, S, \ldots$). They are defined as follows.

Expressions $\quad E ::= M \mid R$
Terms $\quad M ::= x \mid \lambda x.M \mid MM \mid \lambda x.R \mid \mu a.R \mid \chi \mid \Box M \mid \Diamond\alpha.R$
Statements $\quad R ::= [a]M \mid M \cdot M \mid \mathtt{let}\ \Box\chi\ \mathtt{be}\ M\ \mathtt{in}\ R \mid \alpha M \mid \mathtt{dia}\langle x.R\rangle(M)$

$\lambda x.M$ binds the classical variable x in M. $\lambda x.R$ and $\mathtt{dia}\langle x.R\rangle(M)$ bind the classical variable x in R. $\mu a.R$ binds the classical covariable a in R. $\mathtt{let}\ \Box\chi\ \mathtt{be}\ M\ \mathtt{in}\ R$ binds the modal variable χ in R. $\Diamond\alpha.R$ binds the modal covariable α in R. A variable is called free in an expression if it is not bound in the expression. The set of free variables in an expression E is denoted by $FV(E)$.

Terms are extensions of unnamed terms of Parigot's $\lambda\mu$-calculus [16]. They are expressions for normal types in the type system. Statements are extensions of named terms of the $\lambda\mu$-calculus. They are expressions for $\bot$ type.

Substitution $E[^M/_x]$ for a classical variable x is defined by the expression obtained from E replacing each free occurrence of x by M. Substitution $E[^M/_\chi]$ for a modal variable χ is defined by the expression obtained from E replacing each free occurrence of χ by M. Substitution $E[^M/_\alpha]$ for a modal covariable α is defined by the result recursively replacing each subexpression of the form αN in E by $M \cdot (N[^M/_\alpha])$. We write $E[^\beta/_\alpha]$ for the expression obtained from E replacing α by β.

An expression with one hole $\{-\}$ that accepts a term is called contexts. $C\{M\}$ is the expression obtained from a context C by putting a term M in the hole. Elimination contexts (denoted by $\mathcal{E}$) are contexts defined as follows:

$\mathcal{E} ::= [a]\{-\} \mid \{-\} \cdot N \mid [a]\{-\}N \mid \texttt{let}\ \Box\chi\ \texttt{be}\ \{-\}\ \texttt{in}\ S \mid \texttt{dia}\langle x.S\rangle(\{-\})$.

Then we define substitution $E[^{\mathcal{E}}/_{[a]\{-\}}]$ for a classical covariable a by the result recursively replacing each subexpression of the form $[a]N$ in E by $\mathcal{E}\{\, M[^{\mathcal{E}}/_{[a]\{-\}}]\,\}$. We sometimes write $E[^b/_a]$ for $E[^{[b]\{-\}}/_{[a]\{-\}}]$.

Definition 5 (Typing judgments and typing rules). A modal typing context (denoted by Σ) is a set $\chi_1 : A_1, \ldots, \chi_n : A_n$ of modal variable declarations. A classical typing context (denoted by Γ) is a set $x_1 : B_1, \ldots, x_m : B_m$ of classical variable declarations. A classical typing cocontext (denoted by Δ) is a set $a_1 : C_1, \ldots, a_p : C_p$ of classical covariable declarations. A modal typing cocontext (denoted by Θ) is a set $\alpha_1 : D_1, \ldots, \alpha_q : D_q$ of modal covariable declarations. We assume that any two variables in a typing context and cocontext are distinct.

A typing judgment (denoted by J) for the $\lambda\mu^{S4}$-calculus takes either the form $\Sigma; \Gamma \vdash M\colon A \mid \Delta; \Theta$, or the form $\Sigma; \Gamma \vdash S : \bot \mid \Delta; \Theta$, We will write $\Sigma; \Gamma \vdash E\colon T \mid \Delta; \Theta$ for denoting the two forms of typing judgments together.

The intuitive meaning of a typing judgment J is given by the sequent J^- of CND^{S4} defined as follows. If J is $\Sigma; \Gamma \vdash M\colon A \mid \Delta; \Theta$, then J^- is defined by $\Sigma^-; \Gamma^- \vdash_{ND} A, \Delta^-; \Theta^-$, where Σ^- is $A_1, \ldots, A_n$ if Σ is $\chi_1\colon A_1, \ldots, \chi_n\colon A_n$, Γ^- is $B_1, \ldots, B_m$ if Γ is $x_1\colon B_1, \ldots, x_m\colon B_m$, Δ^- is $C_1, \ldots, C_p$ if Δ is $a_1\colon C_1, \ldots, a_p\colon C_p$, and Θ^- is $D_1, \ldots, D_q$ if Θ is $\alpha_1\colon D_1, \ldots, \alpha_q\colon D_q$. We also give J^- by $\Sigma^-; \Gamma^- \vdash_{ND} \Delta^-; \Theta^-$ if J is $\Sigma; \Gamma \vdash S : \bot \mid \Delta; \Theta$. The computational interpretation of typing judgments of the $\lambda\mu^{S4}$-calculus will be discussed in Section 5.

Definition 6 (Typing rules). The typing rules for the $\lambda\mu^{S4}$-calculus are defined as follows.

$$\frac{}{\Sigma; \Gamma, x\colon A \vdash x\colon A \mid \Delta; \Theta}\,(AxC) \qquad \frac{}{\Sigma, \chi\colon A; \Gamma \vdash \chi\colon A \mid \Delta; \Theta}\,(AxM)$$

$$\frac{\Sigma; \Gamma, x\colon A \vdash M\colon B \mid \Delta; \Theta}{\Sigma; \Gamma \vdash \lambda x.M\colon A \supset B \mid \Delta; \Theta}\,(\supset I) \qquad \frac{\Sigma; \Gamma \vdash M\colon A \supset B \mid \Delta; \Theta \quad \Sigma; \Gamma \vdash N\colon A \mid \Delta; \Theta}{\Sigma; \Gamma \vdash MN\colon B \mid \Delta; \Theta}\,(\supset E)$$

$$\frac{\Sigma; \Gamma, x\colon A \vdash S : \bot \mid \Delta; \Theta}{\Sigma; \Gamma \vdash \lambda x.S : \neg A \mid \Delta; \Theta}\,(\neg I) \qquad \frac{\Sigma; \Gamma \vdash M\colon \neg A \mid \Delta; \Theta \quad \Sigma; \Gamma \vdash N\colon A \mid \Delta; \Theta}{\Sigma; \Gamma \vdash M \cdot N\colon \bot \mid \Delta; \Theta}\,(\neg E)$$

$$\frac{\Sigma;\ \ \vdash M: A \mid\ ;\Theta}{\Sigma;\Gamma \vdash \Box M: \Box A \mid \Delta;\Theta}\ (\Box I) \qquad \frac{\Sigma;\Gamma \vdash M: \Box A \mid \Delta;\Theta \quad \Sigma,\chi: A;\Gamma \vdash S: \bot \mid \Delta;\Theta}{\Sigma;\Gamma \vdash \mathtt{let}\ \Box\chi\ \mathtt{be}\ M\ \mathtt{in}\ S: \bot \mid \Delta;\Theta}\ (\Box E)$$

$$\frac{\Sigma;\Gamma \vdash S: \bot \mid \Delta;\Theta,\alpha: A}{\Sigma;\Gamma \vdash \Diamond\alpha.S: \Diamond A \mid \Delta;\Theta}\ (\Diamond I) \qquad \frac{\Sigma;\Gamma \vdash M: \Diamond A \mid \Delta;\Theta \quad \Sigma;x: A \vdash S: \bot \mid\ ;\Theta}{\Sigma;\Gamma \vdash \mathtt{dia}\langle x.S\rangle(M): \bot \mid \Delta;\Theta}\ (\Diamond E)$$

$$\frac{\Sigma;\Gamma \vdash M: A \mid \Delta;\Theta}{\Sigma;\Gamma \vdash \alpha M: \bot \mid \Delta;\Theta,\alpha: A}\ (Pass_M)$$

$$\frac{\Sigma;\Gamma \vdash M: A \mid \Delta;\Theta}{\Sigma;\Gamma \vdash [a]M: \bot \mid \Delta,a: A;\Theta}\ (Pass_C) \qquad \frac{\Sigma;\Gamma \vdash S: \bot \mid \Delta,a: A;\Theta}{\Sigma;\Gamma \vdash \mu a.S: A \mid \Delta;\Theta}\ (Act)$$

Note that J is derivable in $\lambda\mu^{S4}$ implies J^- is provable in CND^{S4}. On the other hand, we can extract expressions of $\lambda\mu^{S4}$ from proofs of CND^{S4}. Each inference rule (AxC), (AxM), $(\supset I)$, $(\supset E)$, $(\neg I)$, $(\neg E)$, $(\Box I)$, $(\Box E)$, $(\Diamond I)$, or $(\Diamond E)$ of CND^{S4} is interpreted as the typing rule of $\lambda\mu^{S4}$ with the same name. $(Pass_M)$ simulates (IR).

Definition 7 (Reduction). The one-step reduction relation $\longrightarrow$ is defined as the compatible closure of the following reduction rules.

$(\beta \supset)$ $(\lambda x.M)N \longrightarrow M[{}^N/_x]$
$(\beta\neg)$ $(\lambda x.S)\cdot N \longrightarrow S[{}^N/_x]$
$(\beta\Box)$ $\mathtt{let}\ \Box\chi\ \mathtt{be}\ \Box M\ \mathtt{in}\ S \longrightarrow S[{}^M/_\chi]$
$(\beta\Diamond)$ $\mathtt{dia}\langle x.S\rangle(\Diamond\alpha.R) \longrightarrow R[{}^{\lambda x.S}/_\alpha]$
$(\mu \supset)$ $(\mu a.S)N \longrightarrow \mu b.S[{}^{[b]\{-\}N}/_{[a]\{-\}}]$ $\quad (b \notin FV(S) \cup FV(N))$
$(\mu\neg)$ $(\mu a.S)\cdot N \longrightarrow S[{}^{\{-\}\cdot N}/_{[a]\{-\}}]$
$(\mu\Box)$ $\mathtt{let}\ \Box\chi\ \mathtt{be}\ (\mu a.S)\ \mathtt{in}\ R \longrightarrow S[{}^{\mathtt{let}\ \Box\chi\ \mathtt{be}\ \{-\}\ \mathtt{in}\ R}/_{[a]\{-\}}]$
$(\mu\Diamond)$ $\mathtt{dia}\langle x.R\rangle(\mu a.S) \longrightarrow S[{}^{\mathtt{dia}\langle x.R\rangle(-)}/_{[a]\{-\}}]$
(rn) $[b]\mu a.S \longrightarrow S[{}^{[b]\{-\}}/_{[a]\{-\}}]$
$(\eta\mu)$ $\mu a.[a]M \longrightarrow M$ $\quad (a \notin FV(M))$

We write $\longrightarrow^+$ and $\longrightarrow^*$ for the transitive closure and the reflexive transitive closure of $\longrightarrow$, respectively.

An expression E is called normal if there is no expression F such that $E \longrightarrow F$.

We claim that each reduction rule $(\beta \supset)$, $(\beta\neg)$, $(\beta\Box)$, or $(\beta\Diamond)$ is interpreted as the logical reduction of each connectives in CND^{S4}. Each reduction rule $(\mu \supset)$, $(\mu\neg)$, $(\mu\Box)$, or $(\mu\Diamond)$ is interpreted as the structural reduction of each connectives in CND^{S4}. (rn) and $(\eta\mu)$ are interpreted as identity in CND^{S4}.

4 Subject Reduction, Confluence, and Strong Normalization of the $\lambda\mu^{S4}$-Calculus

In this section, we show subject reduction, strong normalization, and confluence of the $\lambda\mu^{S4}$-calculus.

Lemma 5 (Weakening of $\lambda\mu^{S4}$). *Let $\Sigma \subseteq \Sigma'$, $\Gamma \subseteq \Gamma'$, $\Delta \subseteq \Delta'$, and $\Theta \subseteq \Theta'$. Then if $\Sigma;\Gamma \vdash E: T \mid \Delta;\Theta$ is derivable, then $\Sigma';\Gamma' \vdash E: T \mid \Delta';\Theta'$ holds.*

Proof. This claim is shown by induction on the structure of E.

Lemma 6 (Substitution). (1) *If* $\Sigma;\Gamma,x\colon A \vdash E\colon T \mid \Delta;\Theta$ *and* $\Sigma;\Gamma \vdash M\colon A \mid \Delta;\Theta$ *are derivable, then* $\Sigma;\Gamma \vdash E[^{M}/_{x}]\colon T \mid \Delta;\Theta$ *holds.*

(2) *If* $\Sigma,\chi\colon A;\Gamma \vdash E\colon T \mid \Delta;\Theta$ *and* $\Sigma; \vdash M\colon A \mid\ ;\Theta$ *are derivable, then* $\Sigma;\Gamma \vdash E[^{M}/_{\chi}]\colon T \mid \Delta;\Theta$ *holds.*

(3) *If* $\Sigma;\Gamma \vdash E\colon T \mid \Delta,a\colon A;\Theta$ *and* $\Sigma;\Gamma,x\colon A \vdash \mathcal{E}\{x\}\colon \bot \mid \Delta;\Theta$ *are derivable, then* $\Sigma;\Gamma \vdash E[^{\mathcal{E}}/_{[a]\{-\}}]\colon T \mid \Delta;\Theta$ *holds.*

(4) *If* $\Sigma;\Gamma \vdash E\colon T \mid \Delta;\Theta,\alpha\colon A$ *and* $\Sigma;\Gamma,x\colon A \vdash S\colon \bot \mid \Delta;\Theta$ *are derivable, then* $\Sigma;\Gamma \vdash E[^{\lambda x.S}/_{\alpha}]\colon T \mid \Delta;\Theta$ *holds.*

(5) *If* $\Sigma;\Gamma \vdash E\colon T \mid \Delta;\Theta,\alpha\colon A$ *and* $\Sigma;\Gamma,x\colon A \vdash \beta x\colon \bot \mid \Delta;\Theta$ *are derivable, then* $\Sigma;\Gamma \vdash E[^{\beta}/_{\alpha}]\colon T \mid \Delta;\Theta$ *holds.*

Proof. They are shown by induction on the structure of E.

By using substitution lemma, we can show that contraction rules of CND^{S4} are admissible in $\lambda\mu^{S4}$.

Lemma 7 (Contraction of $\lambda\mu^{S4}$). (1) *If* $\Sigma;\Gamma,x\colon A,y\colon A \vdash E\colon T \mid \Delta;\Theta$ *is derivable, then* $\Sigma;\Gamma,y\colon A \vdash E[^{y}/_{x}]\colon T \mid \Delta;\Theta$ *holds.*

(2) *If* $\Sigma,\chi\colon A,\upsilon\colon A;\Gamma \vdash E\colon T \mid \Delta;\Theta$, *then* $\Sigma,\upsilon\colon A;\Gamma \vdash E[^{\upsilon}/_{\chi}]\colon T \mid \Delta;\Theta$ *holds.*

(3) *If* $\Sigma;\Gamma \vdash E\colon T \mid \Delta,a\colon A,b\colon A;\Theta$, *then* $\Sigma;\Gamma \vdash E[^{b}/_{a}]\colon T \mid \Delta,b\colon A;\Theta$ *holds.*

(4) *If* $\Sigma;\Gamma \vdash E\colon T \mid \Delta;\Theta,\alpha\colon A,\beta\colon A$, *then* $\Sigma;\Gamma \vdash E[^{\beta}/_{\alpha}]\colon T \mid \Delta;\Theta,\beta\colon A$ *holds.*

The types of expressions of $\lambda\mu^{S4}$ are preserved by reduction.

Proposition 1 (Subject Reduction). *If* $\Sigma;\Gamma \vdash E\colon T \mid \Delta;\Theta$ *and* $E \longrightarrow F$, *then* $\Sigma;\Gamma \vdash F\colon T \mid \Delta;\Theta$ *holds.*

Proof. This claim is shown by induction on the structure of one-step reduction with Lemma 6.

We will prove strong normalization of the $\lambda\mu^{S4}$-calculus. An expression is defined to be strongly normalizing if there does not exist any infinite reduction sequence starting from the expression.

Theorem 2 (Strong normalization of $\lambda\mu^{S4}$). *If* $\Sigma;\Gamma \vdash E : T \mid \Delta;\Theta$ *is derivable in* $\lambda\mu^{S4}$, *then E is strongly normalizing.*

We will show this theorem by giving translation from the $\lambda\mu^{S4}$-calculus into the $\lambda\mu$-calculus, and using strong normalization of the $\lambda\mu$-calculus. Strong normalization of the (second-order) $\lambda\mu$-calculus is already shown by Parigot [17].

Parigot's $\lambda\mu$-calculus [16] is given as follows.

Definition 8 (Parigot's $\lambda\mu$-calculus). Types (denoted by $\tau,\sigma,\ldots$) of the $\lambda\mu$-calculus are defined by:

Types $\tau ::= X \mid \tau \supset \tau \mid \bot$.

We will write $\neg\tau$ as an abbreviation of $\tau \supset \bot$.

The $\lambda\mu$-calculus has λ-variables (denoted by $x,y,\ldots,\chi,\upsilon,\ldots$) and μ-variables (denoted by $a,b,\ldots,\alpha,\beta,\ldots$). We use distinguished μ-variables $\xi,\zeta,\ldots$ for type $\bot$. An expression (denoted by e) of the $\lambda\mu$-calculus is either an unnamed term (denoted by $t,u,\ldots$) or a named term (denoted by $n,m,\ldots$) defined by:

Expressions $e ::= t \mid n$

Unnamed terms $t ::= x \mid \lambda x.t \mid tt \mid \mu a.n$,
Named terms $n ::= [a]t$.

A typing judgment of the $\lambda\mu$-calculus is either the form $\Gamma \vdash_{\lambda\mu} t\colon \tau \mid \Delta$ or the form $n\colon \Gamma \vdash_{\lambda\mu} \Delta$, where Γ is a set $x_1 : \tau_1, \ldots, x_n : \tau_n, \chi_1 : \sigma_1, \ldots, \chi_m : \sigma_m$ of λ-variable declarations, Δ is a set $a_1 : \tau'_1, \ldots, a_p : \tau'_p, \alpha_1 : \sigma'_1, \ldots, \alpha_q : \sigma'_q$ of μ-variable declarations. The μ-variable declarations of the type $\bot$ are not mentioned explicitly in typing judgments.

The typing rules of the $\lambda\mu$-calculus are given as follows.

$$\frac{}{\Gamma, x\colon \tau \vdash_{\lambda\mu} x\colon \tau \mid \Delta} \qquad \frac{\Gamma, x\colon \tau \vdash_{\lambda\mu} u\colon \sigma \mid \Delta}{\Gamma \vdash_{\lambda\mu} \lambda x.u\colon \tau \supset \sigma \mid \Delta} \qquad \frac{\Gamma \vdash_{\lambda\mu} t\colon \tau \supset \sigma \mid \Delta \quad \Gamma \vdash_{\lambda\mu} u\colon \tau \mid \Delta}{\Gamma \vdash_{\lambda\mu} tu\colon \sigma \mid \Delta}$$

$$\frac{\Gamma \vdash_{\lambda\mu} u\colon \tau \mid \Delta}{[a]u : \Gamma \vdash_{\lambda\mu} \Delta, a\colon \tau} \qquad \frac{n : \Gamma \vdash_{\lambda\mu} \Delta, a\colon \tau}{\Gamma \vdash_{\lambda\mu} \mu a.n\colon \tau \mid \Delta.}$$

We claim that $[\xi]u\colon \Gamma \vdash_{\lambda\mu} \Delta$ is derived from $\Gamma \vdash_{\lambda\mu} u\colon \bot \mid \Delta$, and $\Gamma \vdash_{\lambda\mu} \mu\xi.n\colon \bot \mid \Delta$ is derived from $n\colon \Gamma \vdash_{\lambda\mu} \Delta$, since the μ-variable declaration $\xi\colon \bot$ is not mentioned explicitly in typing judgments.

One step reduction $\rhd$ of the $\lambda\mu$-calculus is defined as the compatible closure of the following relations.

(Beta) $(\lambda x.u)t \rhd u[t/x]$
(Mu) $(\mu a.n)u \rhd \mu b.n[{}^{[b]\{-\}u}/_{[a]\{-\}}]$
(Rename) $[b]\mu a.n \rhd n[{}^{[b]\{-\}}/_{[a]\{-\}}]$
(Eta) $\mu a.[a]u \rhd u$ (a is not free in u)

$\rhd^+$ and $\rhd^*$ are defined as the transitive closure and the reflexive transitive closure of $\rhd$, respectively.

Theorem 3 (Strong normalization of $\lambda\mu$ (Parigot [17])). *Every typable expression is strongly normalizing in the $\lambda\mu$-calculus.*

Strictly speaking, strong normalization of the $\lambda\mu$-calculus without (Eta)-rule was shown by Parigot. Strong normalization of the system with (Eta)-rule is also shown immediately from Parigot's result.

Here we give a translation $(-)^{\mathrm{dn}}$ from the $\lambda\mu^{S4}$-calculus into the $\lambda\mu$-calculus. It maps each modal operator to double negation.

Definition 9 (Translation $(-)^{\mathrm{dn}}$). Let A be a normal type in the $\lambda\mu^{S4}$-calculus. The type $(A)^{\mathrm{dn}}$ of the $\lambda\mu$-calculus is defined by:

$(X)^{\mathrm{dn}} = X \qquad (A \supset B)^{\mathrm{dn}} = (A)^{\mathrm{dn}} \supset (B)^{\mathrm{dn}} \qquad (\neg A)^{\mathrm{dn}} = \neg(A)^{\mathrm{dn}}$
$(\Box A)^{\mathrm{dn}} = \neg\neg(A)^{\mathrm{dn}} \qquad (\Diamond A)^{\mathrm{dn}} = \neg\neg(A)^{\mathrm{dn}}.$

Let E be an expression of the $\lambda\mu^{S4}$-calculus. The expression $(E)^{\mathrm{dn}}_{\xi}$ of the $\lambda\mu$-calculus is defined by using a μ-variable ξ as follows.

$(x)^{\mathrm{dn}}_{\xi} = x \quad (\lambda x.M)^{\mathrm{dn}}_{\xi} = \lambda x.(M)^{\mathrm{dn}}_{\xi} \quad (MN)^{\mathrm{dn}}_{\xi} = (M)^{\mathrm{dn}}_{\xi}(N)^{\mathrm{dn}}_{\xi} \quad (\mu a.S)^{\mathrm{dn}}_{\xi} = \mu a.(S)^{\mathrm{dn}}_{\xi}$
$(\lambda x.S)^{\mathrm{dn}}_{\xi} = \lambda x.\mu\zeta.(S)^{\mathrm{dn}}_{\xi} \quad (M \cdot N)^{\mathrm{dn}}_{\xi} = [\xi]((M)^{\mathrm{dn}}_{\xi}(N)^{\mathrm{dn}}_{\xi}) \quad ([a]M)^{\mathrm{dn}}_{\xi} = [a](M)^{\mathrm{dn}}_{\xi}$
$(\chi)^{\mathrm{dn}}_{\xi} = \chi \qquad (\alpha M)^{\mathrm{dn}}_{\xi} = [\alpha](\lambda x.x(M)^{\mathrm{dn}}_{\xi})$
$(\Box M)^{\mathrm{dn}}_{\xi} = \lambda x.x(M)^{\mathrm{dn}}_{\xi} \qquad (\mathtt{let}\ \Box\chi\ \mathtt{be}\ M\ \mathtt{in}\ S)^{\mathrm{dn}}_{\xi} = [\xi]((M)^{\mathrm{dn}}_{\xi}(\lambda\chi.\mu\zeta.(S)^{\mathrm{dn}}_{\xi}))$
$(\Diamond\alpha.S)^{\mathrm{dn}}_{\xi} = \mu\alpha.(S)^{\mathrm{dn}}_{\xi} \qquad (\mathtt{dia}\langle x.S\rangle(M))^{\mathrm{dn}}_{\xi} = [\xi]((M)^{\mathrm{dn}}_{\xi}(\lambda x.\mu\zeta.(S)^{\mathrm{dn}}_{\xi}))$,

where ζ and ξ are different μ-variables.

We define $(\Gamma)^{\mathrm{dn}}$ by $x_1\colon (A_1)^{\mathrm{dn}}, \ldots, x_n\colon (A_n)^{\mathrm{dn}}$ if Γ is a classical typing context $x_1 : A_1, \ldots, x_n : A_n$ in $\lambda\mu^{S4}$. We similarly define $(\Sigma)^{\mathrm{dn}}$ of a modal typing context Σ, and $(\Delta)^{\mathrm{dn}}$ of a classical typing cocontext Δ. We also define $\neg\neg(\Theta)^{\mathrm{dn}}$ by

$\alpha_1 : \neg\neg(B_1)^{\mathrm{dn}}, \ldots, \alpha_m : \neg\neg(B_m)^{\mathrm{dn}}$ if a modal cocontext Θ is $\alpha_1 : B_1, \ldots, \alpha_m : B_m$. Then the judgment $(J)^{\mathrm{dn}}_\xi$ of the $\lambda\mu$-calculus for a judgment J of the $\lambda\mu^{S4}$-calculus is given as follows:

$(\Sigma; \Gamma \vdash M : A \mid \Delta; \Theta)^{\mathrm{dn}}_\xi = (\Sigma)^{\mathrm{dn}}, (\Gamma)^{\mathrm{dn}} \vdash_{\lambda\mu} (M)^{\mathrm{dn}}_\xi : (A)^{\mathrm{dn}} \mid (\Delta)^{\mathrm{dn}}, \neg\neg(\Theta)^{\mathrm{dn}}$,
$(\Sigma; \Gamma \vdash S : \bot \mid \Delta; \Theta)^{\mathrm{dn}}_\xi = (S)^{\mathrm{dn}}_\xi : (\Sigma)^{\mathrm{dn}}, (\Gamma)^{\mathrm{dn}} \vdash_{\lambda\mu} (\Delta)^{\mathrm{dn}}, \neg\neg(\Theta)^{\mathrm{dn}}$.

This translation preserves typing.

Proposition 2. *If J is derivable in $\lambda\mu^{S4}$, then $(J)^{\mathrm{dn}}_\xi$ is derivable in $\lambda\mu$.*

Proof. This claim is shown by induction on the derivation of the $\lambda\mu^{S4}$-calculus.

The translation satisfies the following property.

Lemma 8. (1) *$(E)^{\mathrm{dn}}_\xi[{}^{(N)^{\mathrm{dn}}_\xi}/_x] = (E[{}^N/_x])^{\mathrm{dn}}_\xi$ and $(E)^{\mathrm{dn}}_\xi[{}^{(N)^{\mathrm{dn}}_\xi}/_\chi] = (E[{}^N/_\chi])^{\mathrm{dn}}_\xi$ hold.*
(2) *$(E)^{\mathrm{dn}}_\xi[{}^{[\xi]\{-\}(N)^{\mathrm{dn}}_\xi}/_{[\alpha]\{-\}}] \rhd^* (E[{}^N/_\alpha])^{\mathrm{dn}}_\xi$ holds.*

Proof. (1) is shown by induction on the construction of E. (2) is also shown by induction on the construction of E.

Definition 10. Let $\mathcal{E}$ be an elimination context of the $\lambda\mu^{S4}$-calculus. Then $(\mathcal{E})^{\mathrm{dn}}_\xi$ is defined as follows: $([a]\{-\})^{\mathrm{dn}}_\xi = [a]\{-\}$, $([a]\{-\}N)^{\mathrm{dn}}_\xi = [a]\{-\}(N)^{\mathrm{dn}}_\xi$, $(\{-\} \cdot N)^{\mathrm{dn}}_\xi = [\xi]\{-\}(N)^{\mathrm{dn}}_\xi$, $(\texttt{let}\ \Box\chi\ \texttt{be}\ \{-\}\ \texttt{in}\ S)^{\mathrm{dn}}_\xi = [\xi]\{-\}(\lambda\chi.\mu\zeta.(S)^{\mathrm{dn}}_\xi)$, $(\texttt{dia}\langle x.S\rangle(\{-\}))^{\mathrm{dn}}_\xi = [\xi]\{-\}(\lambda x.\mu\zeta.(S)^{\mathrm{dn}}_\xi)$.

Then $(\mathcal{E})^{\mathrm{dn}}_\xi$ satisfies the following properties.

Lemma 9. (1) *$(\mathcal{E}\{M\})^{\mathrm{dn}}_\xi = (\mathcal{E})^{\mathrm{dn}}_\xi\{(M)^{\mathrm{dn}}_\xi\}$ holds.*
(2) *$(E)^{\mathrm{dn}}_\xi[{}^{(\mathcal{E})^{\mathrm{dn}}_\xi}/_{[a]\{-\}}] = (E[{}^{\mathcal{E}}/_{[a]\{-\}}])^{\mathrm{dn}}_\xi$ holds.*
(3) *$(\mathcal{E})^{\mathrm{dn}}_\xi\{\mu a.n\} \rhd^+ n[{}^{(\mathcal{E})^{\mathrm{dn}}_\xi}/_{[a]\{-\}}]$ holds.*

Proof. (1) is shown by the case analysis of $\mathcal{E}$. (2) is shown by induction on E. (3) is shown by the case analysis of $\mathcal{E}$.

The translation $(-)^{\mathrm{dn}}_\xi$ maps each one-step reduction of the $\lambda\mu^{S4}$-calculus to one or more steps reduction of the $\lambda\mu$-calculus.

Proposition 3. *If $E \longrightarrow E'$ in $\lambda\mu^{S4}$, then $(E)^{\mathrm{dn}}_\xi \rhd^+ (E')^{\mathrm{dn}}_\xi$ in $\lambda\mu$.*

Proof. The claim is proved by induction on the construction of $E \longrightarrow E'$ by using Lemmas 8 and 9. We show the cases of $(\beta\Box)$, $(\beta\Diamond)$, $(\mu\Box)$, and $(\mu\Diamond)$-rules. The case of $(\beta\Box)$ is shown as follows: $(\texttt{let}\ \Box\chi\ \texttt{be}\ \Box M\ \texttt{in}\ S)^{\mathrm{dn}}_\xi = [\xi]((\Box M)^{\mathrm{dn}}_\xi(\lambda\chi.\mu\zeta.(S)^{\mathrm{dn}}_\xi)) = [\xi]((\lambda x.x(M)^{\mathrm{dn}}_\xi)(\lambda\chi.\mu\zeta.(S)^{\mathrm{dn}}_\xi)) \rhd [\xi]((\lambda\chi.\mu\zeta.(S)^{\mathrm{dn}}_\xi)(M)^{\mathrm{dn}}_\xi) \rhd [\xi]\mu\zeta.((S)^{\mathrm{dn}}_\xi[{}^{(M)^{\mathrm{dn}}_\xi}/_\chi]) = [\xi]\mu\zeta.(S[{}^M/_\chi])^{\mathrm{dn}}_\xi \rhd (S[{}^M/_\chi])^{\mathrm{dn}}_\xi$. The case of $(\beta\Diamond)$ is shown as follows: $(\texttt{dia}\langle x.R\rangle(\Diamond\alpha.S))^{\mathrm{dn}}_\xi = [\xi]((\Diamond\alpha.S)^{\mathrm{dn}}_\xi(\lambda x.\mu\zeta.(R)^{\mathrm{dn}}_\xi)) = [\xi]((\mu\alpha.(S)^{\mathrm{dn}}_\xi)(\lambda x.R)^{\mathrm{dn}}_\xi)) \rhd [\xi]\mu\zeta.(S)^{\mathrm{dn}}_\xi[{}^{[\zeta]\{-\}(\lambda x.R)^{\mathrm{dn}}_\xi}/_{[\alpha]\{-\}}] \rhd (S)^{\mathrm{dn}}_\xi[{}^{[\xi]\{-\}(\lambda x.R)^{\mathrm{dn}}_\xi}/_{[\alpha]\{-\}}] \rhd^* (S[{}^{\lambda x.R}/_\alpha])^{\mathrm{dn}}_\xi$. The rules $(\mu\Box)$ and $(\mu\Diamond)$ are written together by $\mathcal{E}\{\mu a.S\} \longrightarrow S[{}^{\mathcal{E}}/_{[a]\{-\}}]$, where $\mathcal{E}$ is an elimination contexts. Then these cases are shown using by Lemma 9 as follows: $(\mathcal{E}\{\mu a.S\})^{\mathrm{dn}}_\xi = (\mathcal{E})^{\mathrm{dn}}_\xi\{(\mu a.S)^{\mathrm{dn}}_\xi\} = (\mathcal{E})^{\mathrm{dn}}_\xi\{\mu a.(S)^{\mathrm{dn}}_\xi\} \rhd^+ (S)^{\mathrm{dn}}_\xi[{}^{(\mathcal{E})^{\mathrm{dn}}_\xi}/_{[a]\{-\}}] = (S[{}^{\mathcal{E}}/_{[a]\{-\}}])^{\mathrm{dn}}_\xi$.

We complete the proof of strong normalization of the $\lambda\mu^{S4}$-calculus.

Proof (Theorem 2). Assume that E is typable in $\lambda\mu^{S4}$ and there is an infinite reduction sequence $E \longrightarrow E_1 \longrightarrow \ldots$ starting from E. Then $(E)^{\mathrm{dn}}_{\xi} \rhd^{+} (E_1)^{\mathrm{dn}}_{\xi} \rhd^{+} (E_2)^{\mathrm{dn}}_{\xi} \rhd^{+} \ldots$ is an infinite reduction sequence starting from $(E)^{\mathrm{dn}}_{\xi}$ by Proposition 3. Since $(E)^{\mathrm{dn}}_{\xi}$ is typable in $\lambda\mu$ by proposition 2, it contradicts Theorem 3.

Finally, we will show confluence of the $\lambda\mu^{S4}$-calculus.

Proposition 4 (Local confluence of $\lambda\mu^{S4}$). *If $E \longrightarrow E_1$ and $E \longrightarrow E_2$, then there exists E_3 that satisfies $E_1 \longrightarrow^* E_3$ and $E_2 \longrightarrow^* E_3$ for any expressions E, E_1, and E_2 of $\lambda\mu^{S4}$.*

Proof. This claim is shown by induction on the structure of E.

Confluence of the $\lambda\mu^{S4}$-calculus is immediately shown by using Theorem 2, Proposition 4, and Newman's lemma [14].

Theorem 4 (Confluence of $\lambda\mu^{S4}$). *If $E \longrightarrow^* E_1$ and $E \longrightarrow^* E_2$, then there exists E_3 that satisfies $E_1 \longrightarrow^* E_3$ and $E_2 \longrightarrow^* E_3$ for any expressions E, E_1, and E_2 of $\lambda\mu^{S4}$.*

5 Discussions

(1) Syntax sugars. We define an additional term $\mathtt{let}\ \Box\chi\ \mathtt{be}\ M\ \mathtt{in}\ N$ as an abbreviation of $\mu a.\mathtt{let}\ \Box\chi\ \mathtt{be}\ M\ \mathtt{in}\ [a]N$. This term validates the following rules:

$$\frac{\Sigma,\chi\colon A;\Gamma \vdash N\colon B \mid \Delta;\Theta \quad \Sigma;\Gamma \vdash M\colon \Box A \mid \Delta;\Theta}{\Sigma;\Gamma \vdash \mathtt{let}\ \Box\chi\ \mathtt{be}\ M\ \mathtt{in}\ N\colon B \mid \Delta;\Theta}, \text{ and } \mathtt{let}\ \Box\chi\ \mathtt{be}\ \Box M\ \mathtt{in}\ N \longrightarrow^{+} N[M/\chi].$$

We also define an additional statement $\langle\alpha\rangle M$ by $\mathtt{dia}\langle x.\alpha x\rangle(M)$. It validates the following rules:

$$\frac{\Sigma;\Gamma \vdash M\colon \Diamond A \mid \Delta;\Theta}{\Sigma;\Gamma \vdash \langle\alpha\rangle M\colon \bot \mid \Delta;\Theta,\alpha\colon A}, \text{ and } \langle\beta\rangle\Diamond\alpha.S \longrightarrow^{+} S[{}^{\beta}/_{\alpha}].$$

(2) (η)-rules for $\Box$ and $\Diamond$ types. In this paper, we gave only (β) and (μ)-rules for $\Box$ and $\Diamond$ types, since we started from the normalization procedure of CND^{S4}. We may define (η)-rules for $\Box$ and $\Diamond$-operators by:

$(\eta\Box)$ $\mathtt{let}\ \Box\chi\ \mathtt{be}\ M\ \mathtt{in}\ \Box\chi \longrightarrow M$ (a is not free in M),
$(\eta\Diamond)$ $\Diamond\alpha.\langle\alpha\rangle M \longrightarrow M$ (α is not free in M).

Unfortunately, $(\eta\Box)$ breaks confluency of $\lambda\mu^{S4}$. For example, $[a]\mathtt{let}\ \Box\chi\ \mathtt{be}\ M\ \mathtt{in}\ \Box\chi$ is reduced to $\mathtt{let}\ \Box\chi\ \mathtt{be}\ M\ \mathtt{in}\ [a](\Box\chi)$ by (rn)-rule, and is also reduced to $[a]M$ by $(\eta\Box)$-rule.

(3) Computational interpretation of $\lambda\mu^{S4}$. Finally, we try to give a computational interpretation of the $\lambda\mu^{S4}$-calculus. The $\lambda\mu^{S4}$-calculus is an extension of the modal λ-calculus [4,6] without (η)-rules. Davies and Pfenning [4] showed the modal λ-calculus provides a framework for studying computation in stages. A value of type $\Box A$ is considered as a program which can be used at *any* later stages. Thus they interpreted a type $\Box A$ as a type of program codes of type A. By taking the dual statement, a type $\Diamond A$ will be interpreted as a type of programs that can be used at *some* later stage.

A judgment $\overline{\chi\colon A};\overline{x\colon B} \vdash E\colon T \mid \overline{a\colon C};\overline{\alpha\colon D}$ of $\lambda\mu^{S4}$ will be interpreted as follows: If each modal variable χ is supplied a program code of type A, and each classical variable

x is supplied a value of type B, then evaluation of the expression E will either return a value of type T, or pass a value of type C to some classical variable a, or pass a program of type D that will be used at some later stage to some modal variable α.

Each expression for possibility operator is interpreted as follows. A statement αM passes the value of M to α. A term $\Diamond\alpha.S$ returns a value which is passed to α in S. These interpretations are similar to those of $[a]M$ and $\mu a.S$. The different point is that the returned value of $\Diamond\alpha.S$ is used at some later stage though the returned value of $\mu a.S$ is used at the current stage. A statement $\mathtt{dia}\langle x.R\rangle(M)$ receives the output from M at some later stage, and passes it to the continuation $\lambda x.R$. The continuation $\mathtt{dia}\langle x.R\rangle(-)$ is understood as a package of the continuation $\lambda x.R$, and keeps waiting for input values exceeding stages. We call this a *persistent continuation* as the dual counterpart of persistent code [24].

(4) Staged computation with exception handling. As a possible application of persistent continuations, we give an example of staged computation with exception handling. We will informally assume the call-by-value $\lambda\mu^{S4}$ with a recursion operator `fix`, **if-then-else** expression, and the types `int` (integers) and `list` (lists of integers). By using expressions of the $\lambda\mu$-calculus, exception operators `catch` and `throw` are represented as follows: $\mathtt{catch}\, a.M := \mu a.[a]M$, and $\mathtt{throw}\,(a, M) := \mu b.[a]M$. For example, let us consider the following program with `catch` and `throw` operators.

$$
\begin{aligned}
\mathtt{mlist} &= \lambda N.\lambda L.\mathtt{catch}\, a.(\mathtt{mul}\ N\ L)\\
\mathtt{mul} &= \mathtt{fix}\ \lambda F.\lambda N.\lambda L.\ \mathtt{if}\ N = 0\ \mathtt{then}\ 1\ \mathtt{else}\\
&\qquad\qquad \mathtt{if}\ L = \mathtt{nil}\ \mathtt{then}\ 1\ \mathtt{else}\\
&\qquad\qquad \mathtt{if}\ \mathrm{hd}(L) = 0\ \mathtt{then}\ \mathtt{throw}\,(a, 0)\ \mathtt{else}\ \mathrm{hd}(L) * (F\ (N-1)\ \mathtt{tl}(L)).
\end{aligned}
$$

The function `mlist` of type $\mathtt{int} \supset \mathtt{list} \supset \mathtt{int}$ takes an integer N and a list L as its inputs, and `mul` recursively multiplies the first N elements of L. If `mul` encounters an element 0 during the calculation, then $\mathtt{throw}\,(a, 0)$ throws exception to `catch` operator in `mlist`, and `mlist` immediately returns 0. However, we cannot write a staged program using `catch` and `throw` that generates a program code of $(\mathtt{mlist}\ N)$ when the argument N is statically known, because `catch` and `throw` must be used in the same scope of a $\Box$-operator. For example, the program $\mathtt{catch}\, a.\Box(\mathtt{throw}\,(a, 0))$ is not valid, since the classical covariable a occurs freely in the scope of $\Box$-operator.

On the other hand, the following new operators can be defined in $\lambda\mu^{S4}$:

$$\mathtt{catch}_{\Diamond}\alpha.M := \Diamond\alpha.\langle\alpha\rangle M, \quad \text{and} \quad \mathtt{throw}_{\Diamond}(\alpha, M) := \Diamond\beta.\langle\alpha\rangle M \quad (\beta \text{ is not free in } M).$$

They operate similar to `catch` and `throw` by assuming $(\eta\Diamond)$-rule:

$$
\begin{aligned}
&\mathtt{catch}_{\Diamond}\alpha.V \longrightarrow^{*} V \quad (\alpha \text{ is not free in } V, \text{ and } V \text{ is a value}),\\
&\mathtt{catch}_{\Diamond}\alpha.(\mathtt{throw}_{\Diamond}(\alpha, M)) \longrightarrow^{*} M \quad (\alpha \text{ is not free in } M),\\
&\Diamond\beta.\mathtt{dia}\langle x.R\rangle(\mathtt{throw}_{\Diamond}(\alpha, M)) \longrightarrow^{*} \mathtt{throw}_{\Diamond}(\alpha, M).
\end{aligned}
$$

We claim that $\mathtt{catch}_{\Diamond}$and $\mathtt{throw}_{\Diamond}$can be used if they are *not* in the same scope of a $\Box$-operator. For example, the program $\mathtt{catch}_{\Diamond}\alpha.\Box(\mathtt{throw}_{\Diamond}(\alpha, 0))$ is a valid program, since the modal covariable α can occur freely in the scope of $\Box$-operator. We also define a term $\mathtt{cast}(M)$ by $\Diamond\alpha.\alpha M$, where α is not free in M. The meaning of $\mathtt{cast}(M)$ is that the value of M will be used at some later stage. This term takes out the inside continuation by unpacking a persistent continuation, and passes the value of M to the inside continuation. Thus, $\mathtt{dia}\langle x.R\rangle(\mathtt{cast}(M))$ is reduced to $(\lambda x.R)M$.

We then define the function $\texttt{mlist}_S$ of type $\texttt{int} \supset \Box(\texttt{list} \supset \Diamond\texttt{int})$ as follows.

$$\texttt{mlist}_S(N) = \texttt{let}\ \Box\chi\ \text{be}\ (\texttt{mul}_S N)\ \text{in}\ \Box(\lambda L.\texttt{catch}_\Diamond \alpha.(\chi L)),$$
$$\texttt{mul}_S = \texttt{fix}\ \lambda F.\lambda N.\ \texttt{if}\ N = 0\ \texttt{then}\ \Box(\lambda L.\texttt{cast}(1))\ \texttt{else}\ \texttt{let}\ \Box\chi\ \text{be}\ F(N-1)\ \text{in}\ \Box P(\chi),$$
$$P(\chi) = \lambda L.\texttt{if}\ L = \texttt{nil}\ \texttt{then}\ \texttt{cast}(1)\ \texttt{else}$$
$$\texttt{if}\ \texttt{hd}(L) = 0\ \texttt{then}\ \texttt{throw}_\Diamond(\alpha, \texttt{cast}(0))\ \texttt{else}\ \ \Diamond\beta.\texttt{dia}\langle x.\beta(\texttt{hd}(L) * x)\rangle(\chi\,\texttt{tl}(L)).$$

The term $\texttt{mlist}_S(n)$ generates a program code of type $\Box(\texttt{list} \supset \Diamond\texttt{int})$ that calculates the multiplication of the first n elements of the input list. The term $(\texttt{mul}_S n)$ is reduced to $\Box(P^n(\lambda L.\texttt{cast}(1)))$, where $P^n(M)$ is $P(\ldots P(M)\ldots)$ (n times of P). Thus the term $\texttt{mlist}_S(n)$ is reduced to $\Box(\lambda L.\texttt{catch}_\Diamond \alpha.P^n(\lambda L'.\texttt{cast}(1))L)$. Hence $\texttt{unbox}(\texttt{mlist}_S(4))[2,4,1,3,5]$ is reduced to $\texttt{catch}_\Diamond\alpha.\Diamond\beta.\texttt{dia}\langle\, x.\beta(2 * 4 * 1 * 3 * x)\,\rangle(\texttt{cast}(1))$, and then $\texttt{cast}(24)$ is obtained. where $\texttt{unbox}(M)$ is $\texttt{let}\ \Box\chi\ \texttt{be}\ M\ \texttt{in}\ \chi$. On the other hand, $\texttt{unbox}(\texttt{mlist}_S(4))[2,4,0,3,5]$ is reduced to $\texttt{catch}_\Diamond\alpha.\Diamond\beta.\texttt{dia}\langle\, x.\beta(2{*}4{*}x)\,\rangle(\texttt{throw}_\Diamond(\alpha, \texttt{cast}(0))$, and then it reduced to $\texttt{cast}(0)$ by $\texttt{catch}_\Diamond/\texttt{throw}_\Diamond$mechanism. This simulates the $\texttt{catch}/\texttt{throw}$ mechanism in $\texttt{mlist}$.

6 Conclusion and Future Work

We proposed a new natural deduction system CND^{S4} for classical S4 modal logic. This system was an extension of Parigot's Classical Natural Deduction for classical logic. We then introduced the $\lambda\mu^{S4}$-calculus as a computational extraction of CND^{S4}, and showed subject reduction, confluency, and strong normalization. In the previous section, we discussed computational interpretation of the possibility operator introducing the notion of persistent continuation. As we observed, the possibility operator enabled the necessity operator to provide a theoretical framework for staged computation with exception handling.

Our future work is as follows. (1) The call-by-value $\lambda\mu^{S4}$-calculus: The calculus given in this paper is based on call-by-name. We can also give the call-by-value variant of $\lambda\mu^{S4}$-calculus, which is informally considered in Section 5. CPS based analysis is deeply related to call-by-value systems. It will give us a new approach for studying computational aspect of classical modal logic. (2) Formulation and application of persistent continuations: For the clearer understanding of the possibility operator, persistent continuations should be explored more deeply in the further work. (3) Computational duality in classical modal logic: The $\lambda\mu^{S4}$-calculus is given by adding the necessity and possibility operators to the $\lambda\mu$-calculus in a symmetric way. This means that the duality between call-by-value and call-by-name of classical logic will be naturally extended to classical modal logic. This expected result will give us an approach for studying persistent continuations.

References

1. Bierman, G.M., de Paiva, V.: On an intuitionistic modal logic. Studia Logica 65(3), 383–416 (2000)
2. Curien, P.L., Herbelin, H.: The duality of computation. In: Proceedings of the 5th ACM SIGPLAN International Conference on Functional Programming, ICFP, pp. 233–243 (2000)
3. Davies, R.: A temporal-logic approach to binding-time analysis. In: Proceedings of 11 th Annual IEEE Symposium on Logic in Computer Science, pp. 184–195. IEEE Computer Society Press, Los Alamitos (1996)

4. Davies, R., Pfenning, F.: A modal analysis of staged computation. Journal of the ACM 48(3), 555–604 (2001)
5. de Groote, P.: On the relation between the lambda-mu-calculus and the syntactic theory of sequential control. In: Pfenning, F. (ed.) LPAR 1994. LNCS, vol. 822, pp. 31–43. Springer, Heidelberg (1994)
6. Ghani, N., de Paiva, V., Ritter, E.: Explicit Substitutions for Constructive Necessity. In: Larsen, K.G., Skyum, S., Winskel, G. (eds.) ICALP 1998. LNCS, vol. 1443, pp. 743–754. Springer, Heidelberg (1998)
7. Griffin, T.G.: A formulae-as-types notion of control. In: Proc. of the 1990 Principles of Programming Languages Conference, pp. 47–58. IEEE Computer Society Press, Los Alamitos (1990)
8. Groote, P.D.: An environment machine for the $\lambda\mu$-calculus. Mathematical Structures in Computer Science 8(6), 637–669 (1998)
9. Kakutani, Y.: Duality between Call-by-Name Recursion and Call-by-Value Iteration. In: Bradfield, J.C. (ed.) CSL 2002. LNCS, vol. 2471, pp. 506–521. Springer, Heidelberg (2002)
10. Kakutani, Y.: Call-by-Name and Call-by-Value in Normal Modal Logic. In: Shao, Z. (ed.) APLAS 2007. LNCS, vol. 4807, pp. 399–414. Springer, Heidelberg (2007)
11. Kimura, D.: Duality between Call-by-value Reductions and Call-by-name Reductions. IPSJ Journal 48(4), 1721–1757 (2007)
12. de Paz, M., Medeiros, N.: A new S4 classical modal logic in natural deduction. Journal of Symbolic Logic 71(3), 799–809 (2006)
13. Nanevski, A.: A Modal Calculus for Exception Handling. In: The 3rd intuitionistic modal logics and applications workshop (2005)
14. Newman, M.H.A.: On theories with a combinatorial definition of "equivalence". Annals of Mathematics 43(2), 223–243 (1942)
15. Ong, C.-H.L., Stewart, C.A.: A Curry-Howard foundation for functional computation with control. In: Proc. of the Symposium on Principles of Programming Languages, pp. 215–227 (1997)
16. Parigot, M.: $\lambda\mu$-calculus: an algorithmic interpretation of classical natural deduction. In: Voronkov, A. (ed.) LPAR 1992. LNCS, vol. 624, pp. 190–201. Springer, Heidelberg (1992)
17. Parigot, M.: Strong normalization for second order classical natural deduction. In: Proceedings of Eighth Annual IEEE Symposium on Logic in Computer Science, pp. 39–46 (1993)
18. Pfenning, F., Davies, R.: A judgmental reconstruction of modal logic. Mathematical Structures in Computer Science 11, 511–540 (2001)
19. Prawitz, D.: Natural Deduction: A Proof-Theoretical Study. Almqvist and Wiksell, Stockholm (1965)
20. Selinger, P.: Control Categories and Duality: on the Categorical Semantics of the Lambda-Mu Calculus. Mathematical Structures in Computer Science, 207–260 (2001)
21. Shan, C.-C.: A Computational Interpretation of Classical S4 Modal Logic. In: The 3rd intuitionistic modal logics and applications workshop (2005)
22. Taha, W., Sheard, T.: MetaML and multi-stage programming with explicit annotations. Theoretical Computer Science 248(1-2), 211–242 (2000)
23. Wadler, P.: Call-by-Value is Dual to Call-by-Name – Reloaded. In: Giesl, J. (ed.) RTA 2005. LNCS, vol. 3467, pp. 185–203. Springer, Heidelberg (2005)
24. Yuse, Y., Igarashi, A.: A modal type system for multi-level generating extensions with persistent code. In: Proceedings of the 8th ACM SIGPLAN Symposium on Principles and Practice of Declarative Programming, pp. 201–212 (2006)

Bi-abductive Resource Invariant Synthesis

Cristiano Calcagno[1], Dino Distefano[2], and Viktor Vafeiadis[3]

[1] Imperial College
[2] Queen Mary University of London
[3] Microsoft Research, Cambridge

Abstract. We describe an algorithm for synthesizing resource invariants that are used in the verification of concurrent programs. This synthesis employs bi-abductive inference to identify the footprints of different parts of the program and decide what invariant each lock protects. We demonstrate our algorithm on several small (yet intricate) examples which are out of the reach of other automatic analyses in the literature.

1 Introduction

Resource invariants are a popular thread-modular verification technique for concurrent lock-based programs. The idea is to associate with each lock an assertion, called the resource invariant, that is true whenever no thread has acquired the lock. When a lock is initialized, we must prove that the associated resource invariant holds. When a thread acquires a lock, it can assume that the corresponding resource invariant holds. When it releases the lock, it must ensure that the resource invariant is still true.

In concurrent separation logic (CSL), O'Hearn [8] has adapted the notion of resource invariants by making them record exactly the part of the memory that a given lock protects. His elegant examples show how the ownership of memory cells can be transferred from one thread to another via a resource invariant. CSL provides simple proofs of programs such as the one in Fig. 1, where a memory cell is allocated in one thread and deallocated in another.

The central problem facing any attempt to construct CSL proofs automatically is the synthesis of suitable resource invariants. For instance, consider the two programs in Fig. 2 (taken from [8]) implementing a *one place pointer-transferring buffer*. In the first program, the memory cell `x` is transferred from the first thread to the second one, and can be easily verified once we have guessed the resource invariant $(\mathit{full} \wedge c \mapsto -) \vee (\neg \mathit{full} \wedge \mathsf{emp})$. In the second program, there is no transfer of ownership and the resource invariant is simply emp. To establish a proof for these programs the choice of the resource invariant must mirror the ownership property. O'Hearn does not address the issue of how to come up with the correct resource invariant and states that "ownership is in the eye of the asserter." This is also the approach taken by Smallfoot [2], which required the user to specify the resource invariants.

More recently, Gotsman et al. [6] proposed a very practical, heuristic method for calculating resource invariants. Their method is based on a thread-modular

Z. Hu (Ed.): APLAS 2009, LNCS 5904, pp. 259–274, 2009.

```
put(x) ≝ with buf when (!full) do { c := x; full := true; }
get(y) ≝ with buf when (full) do { y := c; full := false; }
```

Fig. 1. Definitions of put(x) and get(y) operations

```
    resource buf(c)                        resource buf(c)
x = new(); || get(y);               x = new();                   ||
put(x);    || dispose(y);           put(x); dispose(x);          || get(y);
```

Fig. 2. Single element buffers with ownership transfer (left) and without (right)

program analysis to compute resource invariants by a global fixpoint calculation. In order to decide which part of the memory is owned by a thread and which part belongs to a given lock, they use a predetermined reachability heuristic. The problem with this approach is that it relies heavily on an *ad hoc* local heuristic. For instance, in both programs of Fig. 2, at the end of the put(x) critical region, we have the state $\mathit{full} \wedge c = x \wedge c \mapsto -$. To verify the left program, we need to associate the memory cell $c \mapsto -$ to the resource. To verify the right program, the same memory cell must remain owned by the first thread. So, in general, the splitting cannot be decided by a purely local heuristic. Instead, the contexts of all conditional critical regions protecting the same resource need to be considered and therefore global methods are required.

In general, designing a method able to synthesize resource invariants in a *thread-modular* and *automatic* manner and susceptible to the ownership policy of the program is very tricky since ownership is a global property of the system. In this paper, we present an algorithm aiming at achieving this goal. Our method is not based on reachability but rather on the idea of *footprint* — i.e., the region of memory that a command requires in order to run safely. By employing the footprint concept, we obtain a more systematic way for computing resource invariants. We describe an algorithm that uses bi-abduction [3] to calculate what state is actually protected by the resource. We show the effectiveness of our algorithm by applying it to all the involved examples given by O'Hearn [8].

2 Informal Description of the Synthesis Algorithm

Intuitively, our algorithm works by guessing an initial set of resource invariants and by iteratively refining the guess until either this is strong enough to prove the program or the algorithm gives up because it cannot find a better refinement of the current guess. More precisely, our algorithm can be described as follows:

1. For each Conditional Critical Region (CCR) in the system we take the empty heap as the initial approximation of the state protected by the resource.
2. The current guess of the Resource Invariants (RI) is used to compute specifications for all the CCRs. This step might refine the current RIs.
3. An attempt is made to prove each thread (separately) using the current guess of RIs and current specifications of CCRs. If a proof can be built,

the algorithm exits successfully: the current RIs are strong enough to prove memory safety. Otherwise, the current RIs are refined, as described below.

4. The refinement is done by applying bi-abduction [3] on the continuation of the CCR where the previous proof attempt failed. This is done to check whether the program involves ownership transfer.

Note that in step 3, in constructing a proof for the threads, we assume that the user annotates the program with both the association of variable names to resources and preconditions for the threads, but not the resource invariants (or loop invariants). We remark that the association of variables to resources can sometimes be discovered by a tool like Locksmith [9], and it seems likely that bi-abduction might be employed to discover these thread preconditions, just as it was used in [3] to discover procedure preconditions. So in applying our algorithm it is likely that an even greater degree of automation is possible. However, in this paper, we make these assumptions to focus our study on the core algorithmic difficulty of discovering the resource invariants.

3 Basics

3.1 Programming Language

We describe a simple parallel programming language following [8]. Let *Res* be a countable set of resource names. A concurrent program *Prg* in this language consists of an initialization phase where variables may be assigned a value, a single resource declaration, and a single parallel composition of sequential commands

$$\begin{aligned} \mathit{Prg} ::= {} & \mathit{init}; \\ & \texttt{resource}\ r_1(\text{variable list}), \ldots, r_m(\text{variable list}) \\ & C_1 \parallel \cdots \parallel C_n \end{aligned}$$

Sequential commands are defined by the grammar:

$$\begin{aligned} C ::= {} & x := E \mid x := [y] \mid [x] := E \mid x := \texttt{new()} \mid \texttt{dispose}(x) \\ & \mid \texttt{skip} \mid C;C \mid \texttt{if}\ B\ \texttt{then}\ C\ \texttt{else}\ C \mid \texttt{while}\ B\ \texttt{do}\ C\ \texttt{endwhile} \\ & \mid \texttt{with}\ r\ \texttt{when}\ B\ \texttt{do}\ C\ \texttt{endwith} \end{aligned}$$

where $E \in \mathit{PVar} \cup \{\mathsf{nil}\}$ and PVar is a countable set of program variables ranged over by $x, y, z, \ldots$. Sequential commands include standard constructs (assignment, sequential composition, conditional, and iteration), dynamic allocation ($x := \texttt{new()}$), explicit deallocation ($\texttt{dispose}(x)$), and operations for accessing the heap: look-up ($x := [y]$) and mutation ($[x] := E$). Resources are accessed using CCR commands `with` r `when` B `do` C `endwith`, where B is a (heap-independent) boolean condition and C is a command. A CCR is a unit of mutual exclusion; therefore two `with` commands for the same resource cannot be executed simultaneously. In detail, `with` r `when` B `do` C `endwith` can be executed if the condition B is true and no other CCR for r is currently executing. Otherwise its execution is delayed until both conditions are satisfied.

Notation. We introduce some notation used throughout the paper. Given a concurrent program Prg, let $CCR(Prg)$ denote the set of all its conditional critical regions. Let $Res(Prg)$ be the set of resources defined in Prg and let $CCR(r, Prg)$, with $r \in Res(Prg)$, be the subset of $CCR(Prg)$ acting on resource r. For $C = \texttt{with}\, r\, \texttt{when}\, B\, \texttt{do}\, C'\, \texttt{endwith}$, we define $guard(C) \stackrel{def}{=} B$, $body(C) \stackrel{def}{=} C'$ and $res(C) \stackrel{def}{=} r$ the guard, the body and the resource of the CCR C, respectively.

3.2 Storage Model and Symbolic Heaps

We describe the storage model and symbolic heaps: a fragment of separation logic formulae suitable for symbolic execution [1,5]. Let $LVar$ (ranged over by $x', y', z', \ldots$) be a set of logical variables, disjoint from program variables $PVar$, to be used in the assertion language. Let $Locs$ be a countably infinite set of locations, and let $Vals$ be a set of values that includes $Locs$. The storage model is given by:

$$Heaps \stackrel{def}{=} Locs \rightharpoonup_{\mathsf{fin}} Vals \qquad Stacks \stackrel{def}{=} (PVar \cup LVar) \rightarrow Vals$$
$$States \stackrel{def}{=} Stacks \times Heaps$$

Program states are symbolically represented by special separation logic formulae called *symbolic heaps*. They are defined as follows:

$$\begin{array}{lcll} E & ::= & x \mid x' \mid \mathsf{nil} & \textit{Expressions} \\ \Pi & ::= & E{=}E \mid E{\neq}E \mid \mathsf{true} \mid \Pi \wedge \Pi & \textit{Pure formulae} \\ S & ::= & E \mapsto E \mid \mathsf{ls}(E,E) & \textit{Basic spatial predicates} \\ \Sigma & ::= & S \mid \mathsf{true} \mid \mathsf{emp} \mid \Sigma * \Sigma & \textit{Spatial formulae} \\ D & ::= & \exists \boldsymbol{x'}.\, (\Pi \wedge \Sigma) & \textit{Disjuncts} \\ H & ::= & D \mid H \vee H & \textit{Symbolic heaps} \end{array}$$

Expressions are program or logical variables x, x' or nil. Pure formulae are conjunctions of equalities and disequalities between expressions, and describe properties of variables. Spatial formulae specify properties of the heap. The predicate emp holds only in the empty heap where nothing is allocated. The formula $\Sigma_1 * \Sigma_2$ uses the separating conjunction of separation logic and holds in a heap h which can be split into two *disjoint parts* h_1 and h_2 such that Σ_1 holds in h_1 and Σ_2 in h_2. In symbolic heaps some (not necessarily all) logical variables are existentially quantified. The set of all symbolic heaps is denoted by SH. S is a set of basic spatial predicates. In this paper we consider a simple instance of S. However, our algorithm works equally well for other more sophisticated choices of spatial predicates such those described in [4,7]. The *points-to* predicate $x \mapsto y$ denotes a heap with a single allocated cell at address x with content y, and $\mathsf{ls}(x, y)$ denotes a *non-empty* list segment from x to y (not including y).

3.3 Bi-abduction

The notion of *bi-abduction* was recently introduced in [3]. It is the combination of two dual notions that extend the entailment problem: *frame inference* and *abduction*. Frame inference [1] is the problem of determining a formula $\mathfrak{F}$ (called the *frame*) which we need to add to the conclusions of an entailment $H \vdash H' * \mathfrak{F}$ in order to make it valid. In other words, solving a frame inference problem means to find a description of the extra parts of heap described by H and not by H'. Abduction is dual to frame inference. It consists in determining a formula $\mathfrak{A}$ (called the *anti-frame*) describing the pieces of heap missing in the hypothesis and needed to make an entailment $H * \mathfrak{A} \vdash H'$ valid.

Bi-abduction is the combination of frame inference and abduction. It consists in deriving at the same time interdependent frames and anti-frames.

Definition 1 (Bi-Abduction). *Given two heaps H and H' find a frame $\mathfrak{F}$ and an anti-frame $\mathfrak{A}$ such that $H * \mathfrak{A} \vdash H' * \mathfrak{F}$*

Many solutions are possible for $\mathfrak{A}$ and $\mathfrak{F}$. A criterion to judge the quality of solutions as well as a bi-abductive prover were defined in [3]. A modified version of bi-abduction was proposed in [7].

Bi-abduction was introduced as a useful mechanism to construct compositional shape analyses. Such analyses can be seen as the attempt to build proofs for Hoare triples of a program. More precisely, given a program composed by procedures $p_1(\boldsymbol{x_1}), \ldots, p_n(\boldsymbol{x_n})$ the proof search automatically synthesizes preconditions $P_1, \ldots, P_n$ and postcondition $Q_1, \ldots, Q_n$ such that the following are valid Hoare triples:

$$\{P_1\}\, p_1(\boldsymbol{x_1})\, \{Q_1\}, \ldots, \{P_n\}\, p_n(\boldsymbol{x_n})\, \{Q_n\}$$

The triples are constructed by symbolically executing the program and by composing existing triples. The composition (and therefore the construction of the proof) is done in a bottom-up fashion starting from the leaves of the call-graph and then using their triples to build other proofs for procedures which are on a higher-level in the call-graph. To achieve that, the following derived rule for sequential composition [3] is used:

$$\frac{\{P_1\}\, C_1\, \{Q_1\} \qquad \{P_2\}\, C_2\, \{Q_2\}}{\{P_1 * \mathfrak{A}\}\, C_1; C_2\, \{Q_2 * \mathfrak{F}\}}\; Q_1 * \mathfrak{A} \vdash P_2 * \mathfrak{F} \qquad \text{(BA-seq)}$$

In this paper we show that bi-abduction can be useful to achieve compositional proofs of concurrent programs.

Throughout this paper we will write the frame and anti-frame to be determined in the bi-abduction problem in "frak" fonts (e.g., $\mathfrak{A}, \mathfrak{F}, \mathfrak{B} \ldots$) in order to distinguish them from the known parts of the entailment.

4 Comparing Resource Invariants

In this section we study the structure of the solutions to the resource invariant inference problem from a theoretical perspective. We define an order used to compare those solutions, and show that an optimal invariant with respect to that order always exists.

Definition 2 (Safe Resource Invariant). *Given a precondition P which holds before entering a CCR with guard B and body C, we say that I is a* safe resource invariant *starting from P if and only if the triple $\{P * I \wedge B\}\, C\, \{I * \mathsf{true}\}$ holds.*

In other words, I describes resource large enough for C to execute safely, yet I is weak enough that C can re-establish it. For example, $x \mapsto 3$ is too strong if C is $[x] := 4$ (cannot be re-established), and emp does not describe enough resource for C to execute safely. Perhaps surprisingly, these two requirements are compatible with an order relation that admits an optimal solution, which we describe below.

Definition 3. *If I and I' are resource invariants, we define the preorder $I \leq I'$, meaning that I is* better *(or* smaller*) than I', to hold if and only if $I' \models I * \mathsf{true}$.*

When $I \leq I'$ we sometimes say that I' *extends* I. Note that $\leq$ is not antisymmetric as $I \leq I'$ and $I' \leq I$ does not imply $I = I'$. However, it implies $\mathsf{min}(I) = \mathsf{min}(I')$, where min is an operation that removes non-minimal states, defined as follows: $(s, h) \models \mathsf{min}(X) \iff (s, h) \models X$ and $\forall h'.\ s, h' \models X$ implies $h \leq h'$.

Therefore, $\leq$ is antisymmetric modulo the equivalence relation $I \sim I' \iff \mathsf{min}(I) = \mathsf{min}(I')$. For example, $\mathsf{emp} \leq \mathsf{true}$ and $\mathsf{true} \leq \mathsf{emp}$, but $\mathsf{min}(\mathsf{emp}) = \mathsf{min}(\mathsf{true}) = \mathsf{emp}$.

Notice that if I_1 and I_2 are safe resource invariants starting from P, then so is $I_1 \vee I_2$, by direct application of Hoare's disjunction rule. Since $I' \Rightarrow I$ implies $I \leq I'$, it can be readily seen that a (unique modulo $\sim$) minimal resource invariant I_{best} exists, and can be described directly as $I_{\text{best}} = \bigvee\{I \mid I \text{ r.i. for all CCRs}\}$. Hence the best invariant is logically weakest and spatially smallest.

The presentation of I_{best} given above involves an infinite disjunction. This is an ideal that any algorithm for invariant inference should try to approximate, just as one usually does with loop invariants. One such algorithm is given in the next section.

5 The Invariant Synthesis Algorithm

Algorithm 1 computes the set $\mathcal{I}$ of resource invariants for the program *Prg* or returns failure. $\mathcal{I}$ is a function $\mathcal{I} : \mathit{Res} \rightarrow \mathsf{SH}$ associating to each resource r a resource invariant $\mathcal{I}(r)$. The basic idea is to start with the minimal invariant emp and then repeatedly refine it to a bigger one w.r.t. $\leq$ during symbolic execution. The role of (perfect) abduction is to refine it by the *minimum* amount necessary for the symbolic execution to go through. So the informal argument for each refinement from I to I' is of the form "if there exists a safe invariant, it must be $\geq I'$". The initial approximation emp models a situation where resources are neither protected nor transferred; only if the program requires it, is the invariant refined into one which does so. More precisely, the basic idea is implemented as follows. Initially the resource invariant of every resource r is initialized to be

Algorithm 1. InvariantSynthesis(Prg)

1: $\mathcal{I} := \{(r, \bigvee_{C_r \in CCR(r,Prg)}(\mathsf{emp} \wedge guard(C_r))) \mid r \in Res(Prg)\}$;
2: $Failed := \emptyset$;
3: **while** $\mathcal{I} \notin Failed$ **do**
4: $\quad(\mathcal{I}, Specs) :=$ CompSpecs($\mathcal{I}$);
5: $\quad$**if** ProofSearch($Prg, \mathcal{I}, Specs$) fails **then**
6: $\quad\quad Failed := Failed \cup \{\mathcal{I}\}$
7: $\quad\quad C_1; \cdots ; C_j :=$ FailingPath($Prg, \mathcal{I}, Specs$);
8: $\quad\quad \mathcal{I} :=$ RefineOwnership($C_1; \cdots ; C_j, \mathcal{I}$);
9: $\quad$**else**
10: $\quad\quad$**return** $\mathcal{I}$
11: $\quad$**end if**
12: **end while**
13: **return** failure

a disjunction of emp and the guard of its CCRs (Step 1).[1] This gives the first approximation for $\mathcal{I}$. $Specs$ is the set of Hoare triples $\{P\}\,C\,\{Q\}$ defining a specification for all CCRs in the program. $Specs$ is computed by using the function CompSpecs which is applied the current guess of the invariants. CompSpecs is explained in detail in Sec. 5.1, and while it generates specifications it may modify $\mathcal{I}$ giving a first refinement. CompSpecs returns a set of pairs $(\mathcal{I}', Specs)$ or fails. ProofSearch($Prg, \mathcal{I}, Specs$) (see Sec. 5.2) is a procedure that tries to build a separation logic proof of Prg using the specifications $Specs$ and the resource invariants $\mathcal{I}$. The set $Failed$ contains those invariants for which the algorithm failed to build a proof. The loop starting at step 3 attempts to build a proof with the result of CompSpecs. If the proof succeeds, the algorithm terminates with success and returns the computed resource invariants. Otherwise, the algorithm tries to refine the current guess. In that case, the invariant of the failing CCR is refined using the procedure RefineOwnership (see Sec. 5.3). After $\mathcal{I}$ is refined the set of CCR specifications is updated accordingly before attempting a new proof of the program. The algorithm fails in case the refinement process returns an invariant which was tried before with no success. Notice that CompSpecs is a partial function, therefore, the algorithm fails also in case CompSpecs does not return a value.

5.1 Computing Specifications for CCRs

The computation of CCRs' specifications requires an *abstraction function* for symbolic heaps $\alpha : \mathsf{SH} \longrightarrow \mathsf{SH}$. Given the kind of symbolic heaps used in this paper, it is enough to have α defined as in [5], although our algorithm is not

[1] The rationale for adding CCRs' guards to the initial invariant is that, when the algorithm refines $\mathcal{I}(r)$ by examining a CCR C_r, the missing part will be added only to the disjunct corresponding to C_r. This disjunct is determined by $guard(C_r)$. Adding $*$-conjuncts only to one disjunct (rather than to all of them) provides us with a better invariant w.r.t. the defined order $\leq$.

dependent on a specific choice. Moreover, let $[P]^{loc}_Q$ be a function that replaces shared variables (i.e., those listed in the resource declaration) in P using equalities in Q. $[\cdot]^{loc} : \mathsf{SH}\times\mathsf{SH} \longrightarrow \mathsf{SH}$ is defined as:

$$[P]^{loc}_Q = P[x_1/c_1, \cdots, x_n/c_n]$$

where x_i are local variables, c_i are shared variables, and $Q \equiv x_1 = c_1 \wedge \cdots \wedge x_n = c_n \wedge Q'$ and in Q' there are no further equality terms between local and shared variables.[2] Similarly, define $[\cdot]^{sha}$ as the dual function which tries to replace local variables with shared variables.

Computing the Specification of a Single CCR. The computation of a specification for the CCR `with` r `when` B `do` C `endwith` is done by performing a compositional bottom-up analysis ([3] and Sec. 3.3) on the body C. The analysis starts from the following precondition: $B \wedge \mathsf{emp} * \mathcal{I}(r)$.

This is different from [3], where the analysis started with precondition emp. The bottom-up analysis will construct a proof of C by synthesizing P and Q such that the triple $\{B \wedge P * \mathcal{I}(r)\}\, C\, \{Q\}$ holds.[3] Once this triple is computed, a specification for the `with` command is obtained by applying the following new rule (called BA-with):

$$\frac{\{B \wedge (P * \mathcal{I}(r))\}\, C\, \{Q\}}{\{P * [\mathfrak{A}]^{loc}_Q\}\, \texttt{with}\ r\ \texttt{when}\ B\ \texttt{do}\ C\ \texttt{endwith}\, \{\alpha(\exists \mathbf{c}.\mathfrak{F})\}}\ Q * \mathfrak{A} \vdash \mathcal{I}(r) * \mathfrak{F}$$

with additional side conditions:

1. no variable occurring free in $[\mathfrak{A}]^{loc}_Q$ is modified by C,
2. no other process modifies variables free in $P * [\mathfrak{A}]^{loc}_Q$ or $\alpha(\exists \mathbf{c}.\mathfrak{F})$.

Starting from a proof of the CCR's body, this rule uses bi-abduction to derive two symbolic heaps $\mathfrak{A}$ and $\mathfrak{F}$. The anti-frame $\mathfrak{A}$ needs to be added to the precondition P to re-establish r's resource invariant $\mathcal{I}(r)$. The frame $\mathfrak{F}$ corresponds to the postcondition of the `with` statement. Both frame and anti-frame are massaged before using them in the specification to remove terms related to shared variables (which should not appear in pre/postcodintions). In particular in the anti-frame $\mathfrak{A}$, terms containing shared variables are rewritten (when possible) in terms of local variables using known equalities in Q. This is the purpose of the function $[\cdot]^{loc}$. The frame $\mathfrak{F}$ is simplified by replacing uses of shared variables by local variables whenever possible using the existing equalities, and by dropping pure formulae involving shared variables. This is achieved by existentially quantifying shared variables in $\mathfrak{F}$ and by applying the abstraction α.

[2] $[\cdot]^{loc}$ is a well defined function if a fixed order among local variables is chosen.

[3] The reason for not using a simple forward symbolic execution starting from $\mathsf{emp} * \mathcal{I}(r) \wedge B$ to build a proof of C is that, in general, this precondition is not enough for proving C. Hence a precondition $P \neq \mathsf{emp}$ needs to be derived, and this is done by the bottom-up analysis.

Lemma 1. *The* BA-with *rule is sound.*

Example 1. Assume the resource invariant $I \equiv (\neg full \wedge \mathsf{emp}) \vee (full \wedge \mathsf{emp})$. We show the induced specifications for the CCRs in Fig. 1. Using emp as precondition, for `put(x)` we have the triple

$$\{\neg full \wedge \mathsf{emp} * I\}\; c := x; full := true\; \{full \wedge c{=}x \wedge \mathsf{emp}\}$$

From this, the bi-abduction engine is queried to derive $\mathfrak{F}$ and $\mathfrak{A}$ for the entailment $full \wedge c{=}x \wedge \mathsf{emp} * \mathfrak{A} \vdash I * \mathfrak{F}$. The solution is $\mathfrak{A} \equiv \mathsf{emp}$ and $\mathfrak{F} \equiv c{=}x \wedge \mathsf{emp}$. This is further simplified to remove terms with shared variables: $[\mathsf{emp}]^{loc}_{c=x\wedge I} = \mathsf{emp}$ and $\alpha(\exists c.\, c{=}x \wedge \mathsf{emp}) = \mathsf{true} \wedge \mathsf{emp}$. Therefore, by applying the rule BA-with we obtain the specification $\{\mathsf{emp}\}$ `put(x)` $\{\mathsf{emp}\}$.

Similarly for the CCR `get(y)`, using emp as precondition of BA-with we have:

$$\{full \wedge \mathsf{emp} * I\}\; y := c; full := false\; \{\neg full \wedge y = c \wedge \mathsf{emp}\}$$

Now we appeal to bi-abduction for the query $\neg full \wedge y = c \wedge \mathsf{emp} * \mathfrak{A} \vdash I * \mathfrak{F}$. The solution is $\mathfrak{A} \equiv \mathsf{emp}$ and $\mathfrak{F} \equiv y{=}c \wedge \mathsf{emp}$ and hence after the simplification of $[\cdot]^{loc}$ and α and applying BA-with we obtain the specification $\{\mathsf{emp}\}$ `get(y)` $\{\mathsf{emp}\}$.

Example 2. Consider now a different resource invariant $I \equiv (\neg full \wedge \mathsf{emp}) \vee (full \wedge c \mapsto -)$. As in the previous example, we show the induced specifications for the CCRs in Fig. 1, using this invariant instead. For `put(x)` we can derive the triple:

$$\{\neg full \wedge \mathsf{emp} * I\}\; c := x; full := true\; \{c{=}x \wedge full \wedge \mathsf{emp}\}.$$

Then, asking bi-abduction the question $c{=}x \wedge full \wedge \mathsf{emp} * \mathfrak{A} \vdash I * \mathfrak{F}$ yields the solution $\mathfrak{A} \equiv c \mapsto -$ and $\mathfrak{F} \equiv c{=}x \wedge \mathsf{emp}$. By simplifying the anti-frame we obtain $[c \mapsto -]^{loc}_{c=x\wedge full} = x \mapsto -$, whereas for the frame we have $\alpha(\exists c.\, c{=}x \wedge \mathsf{emp}) = \mathsf{true} \wedge \mathsf{emp}$. Therefore, applying BA-with gives $\{x \mapsto -\}$ `put(x)` $\{\mathsf{emp}\}$.

Similarly for `get(y)` we have:

$$\{full \wedge \mathsf{emp} * I\}\; y := c; full := false\; \{\neg full \wedge y{=}c \wedge c \mapsto -\}$$

When posed the query $\neg full \wedge y{=}c \wedge c \mapsto - * \mathfrak{A} \vdash I * \mathfrak{F}$ the bi-abduction engine finds the solutions $\mathfrak{A} \equiv \mathsf{emp}$ and $\mathfrak{F} \equiv y{=}c \wedge c \mapsto -$. $\mathfrak{A}$ is already simplified, whereas $\mathfrak{F}$ is simplified to $\alpha(\exists c.\, y{=}c \wedge c \mapsto -) = y \mapsto -$. Hence BA-with returns the specification $\{\mathsf{emp}\}$ `get(y)` $\{y \mapsto -\}$.

The Function CompSpecs. The computation of specifications for all the CCRs in the program is performed by CompSpecs. Given a set of resource invariants $\mathcal{I}$, this function is defined as:

$$\begin{aligned}
&\mathsf{CompSpecs} : (Res \to \mathsf{SH}) \longrightarrow (Res \to \mathsf{SH}) \times \mathcal{P}(\mathsf{SH} \times C \times \mathsf{SH})\\
&\mathsf{CompSpecs}(\mathcal{I}) \stackrel{def}{=} (\mathcal{I}', \{Spec(\mathcal{I}', C_r) \mid C_r \in CCR(Prg)\})\\
&\qquad\qquad\text{when } (CCR(Prg), \mathcal{I}) \longrightarrow_1^* \longrightarrow_2^* \longrightarrow_3^* (\emptyset, \mathcal{I}')
\end{aligned}$$

Table 1. Transition rules for computing *Specs* and possibly refining $\mathcal{I}$

$$\frac{\mathit{Spec}(\mathcal{I}, C_r) = \mathsf{Fail}\ P}{L, \mathcal{I} \longrightarrow_1 L, \mathcal{I}[r \leftarrow I_r]} \quad \begin{array}{l}\mathcal{I}(r) \leq I_r \text{ and } C_r \in L \\ I_r = \alpha(\mathcal{I}(r) * P_{\mathit{Shared}})\end{array}$$

$$\frac{}{L, \mathcal{I} \longrightarrow_2 L, \mathcal{I}[r \leftarrow \bigvee_{i \in X} D_i]} \quad \begin{array}{l}\mathcal{I}(r) = D_1 \vee \ldots \vee D_n \\ X \subseteq \{i \mid 1 \leq i \leq n\}\end{array}$$

$$\frac{\mathit{Spec}(\mathcal{I}, C_r) = \{P\}\ C_r\ \{Q\}}{L, \mathcal{I} \longrightarrow_3 L \setminus \{C_r\}, \mathcal{I}} \quad C_r \in L$$

This definition uses the transition rules in Table 1 in three distinct phases: invariant refinement ($\longrightarrow_1^*$), pruning of disjuncts ($\longrightarrow_2^*$), and checking of the result ($\longrightarrow_3^*$). Let *Shared*(P) be the set of shared variables occurring in P, and let P_{Shared} be the sub-formula of P containing only shared variables. L contains the CCRs for which specifications have not yet been successfully computed. The rules are applied to L and $\mathcal{I}$ until a specification has been computed for all CCRs. The function $\mathit{Spec}(\mathcal{I}, C_r)$ tries to compute the specification for the CCR C_r w.r.t. $\mathcal{I}$ as described above, i.e., using bottom-up analysis and BA-with. If this succeeds, it returns the inferred triple $\{P\}\ C_r\ \{Q\}$; if, however, the side conditions of the BA-with rule are violated, then it returns Fail P, where P is the inferred precondition of the block, had the side conditions been satisfied. The rule $\longrightarrow_1$ refines the current resource invariant when an attempt to find a spec for the CCR's body using the current invariant fails. The rationale is that if shared state is needed by the critical region this should be provided by the resource invariant and not by the precondition.[4] The rule therefore tries to refine $\mathcal{I}(r)$ by adding the terms with shared variables in P. If the resulting invariant I_r extends the current guess for r, then this extension is used to replace $\mathcal{I}(r)$. Rule $\longrightarrow_2$ can be applied when $\longrightarrow_1$ cannot refine $\mathcal{I}(r)$ any further. The task of $\longrightarrow_2$ is to remove from $\mathcal{I}(r)$ those disjuncts that cannot be re-established by the CCR's body. Finally, rule $\longrightarrow_3$ records the fact that a spec for C_r has been found by removing it from L.

Lemma 2. *If the number of program variables in Prg is finite, then the transition system defined in Table 1 is finite.*

The immediate consequence of this lemma is that CompSpecs can be effectively computed by a fixpoint computation which applies systematically the rules avoiding to re-apply them to previously visited states. Hence we have:

Corollary 1. *The computation of* CompSpecs *terminates.*

Example 3. We now consider a more involved example that shows the computation of the function CompSpecs. Here we use the memory manager described

[4] Recall that precondition computed by bi-abduction corresponds to the footprint of C, therefore it expresses the state needed to run the command.

```
alloc(x) ≝ with mm when (true) do {
             if (f=nil) then x := new();
             else x := f; f:=[x];
           }

dealloc(y) ≝
  with mm when (true) do {
    [y] := f; f:= y;
  }
```

Fig. 3. Definitions of `alloc(x)` and `dealloc(y)`

in [8] and reported in Fig. 3. We start by computing the specification of `alloc(x)` using $I_0 \equiv \mathsf{true} \wedge \mathsf{emp}$. We can prove the triple $\{P_0\}$ `alloc(x)` $\{x \mapsto -\}$ where

$$P_0 \equiv (f{=}\mathsf{nil} \wedge \mathsf{emp}) \vee (f \mapsto -).$$

However, the precondition specifies properties of the shared variable f, so we need to apply rule $\longrightarrow_1$ of Table 1. The invariant is refined by adding P_0 to the current I_0 and then abstraction α:

$$I_1 = \alpha(I_0 * P_0) = (f{=}\mathsf{nil} \wedge \mathsf{emp}) \vee (f \mapsto f')$$

where we have explicitly named the existential variable f' because it will be used in the next iteration. When recomputing the specification of `alloc(x)` using I_1 we obtain the triple $\{P_1\}$ `alloc(x)` $\{x \mapsto -\}$ where

$$P_1 \equiv (f{=}\mathsf{nil} \wedge \mathsf{emp}) \vee (f{\neq}\mathsf{nil} \wedge f'{=}\mathsf{nil} \wedge \mathsf{emp}) \vee (f{\neq}\mathsf{nil} \wedge f' \mapsto -).$$

Again by rule $\longrightarrow_1$ we obtain

$$\begin{aligned} I_2 = \alpha(I_1 * P_1) &= \alpha((f{=}\mathsf{nil} \wedge \mathsf{emp}) \vee (f \mapsto \mathsf{nil}) \vee (f \mapsto f' * f' \mapsto -)) \\ &= (f{=}\mathsf{nil} \wedge \mathsf{emp}) \vee (f \mapsto \mathsf{nil}) \vee \mathsf{ls}(f, f') \end{aligned}$$

A further iteration of $\longrightarrow_1$ produces the same P_1 and

$$I_3 = (f{=}\mathsf{nil} \wedge \mathsf{emp}) \vee (f \mapsto \mathsf{nil}) \vee \mathsf{ls}(f, f') \vee \mathsf{ls}(f, \mathsf{nil})$$

The candidate I_3 is a fixpoint w.r.t. $\longrightarrow_1$ but it still produces the same P_1, therefore rule $\longrightarrow_3$ cannot be applied yet. This is caused by the disjunct $\mathsf{ls}(f, f')$, which is too weak: starting from $\mathsf{ls}(f, f')$ the candidate invariant I_3 cannot be re-established. But now, rule $\longrightarrow_2$ can fire to remove disjunct $\mathsf{ls}(f, f')$ and obtain

$$I_3 \longrightarrow_2 I_4 = (f{=}\mathsf{nil} \wedge \mathsf{emp}) \vee (f \mapsto \mathsf{nil}) \vee \mathsf{ls}(f, \mathsf{nil})$$

Now rule $\longrightarrow_3$ can be applied, so I_4 is a resource invariant for alloc(x). The final specification of `alloc(x)` using I_4 is $\{\mathsf{emp}\}$ `alloc(x)` $\{x \mapsto -\}$.

Finally, I_4 directly allows us to obtain $\{y \mapsto -\}$ `dealloc(y)` $\{\mathsf{emp}\}$ as specification for `dealloc(y)`.

5.2 Proof Search

This phase attempts to build a compositional proof of the program by trying to prove each thread in isolation. The building process is done using the bottom-up analysis which starts from the beginning of the thread and tries to construct a valid Hoare triple by symbolically executing the program as described in Sec. 3.3. Let the concurrent program be

$$Prg = init;\ \texttt{resource}\ r_1(\boldsymbol{x_1}), \ldots, r_m(\boldsymbol{x_m});\ C_1 \parallel \cdots \parallel C_n$$

Given P_{C_i}, a precondition for the thread C_i we can execute a proof search for C_i by ProofSearch. This procedure uses the BA-seq rule to build the proof but requires that at every application of this rule we have $\mathfrak{A} \equiv \mathsf{emp}$. This condition ensures that a proof for the thread C_i can actually be built from the precondition P_{C_i}. In fact, it provides us with a notion of failure for a proof attempt. We say that the proof search for $C_i = C_i'; C_i''$ (from P_{C_i}) *fails* if by an application of BA-seq we obtain the triple $\{P_{C_i} * \mathfrak{A}\}\, C_i'\, \{Q\}$ for some $Q \in \mathsf{SH}$ and $\neg(\mathfrak{A} \equiv \mathsf{emp})$. We are usually interested in the shortest prefix C_i' which makes the proof fail. The synthesis algorithm uses this notion of failure to detect when and where the invariant needs to be refined because of possible ownership transfer.[5]

5.3 Refining Resource Invariants for Ownership Transfer

Algorithm 2 defines the procedure RefineOwnership, called by InvariantSynthesis when the proof search fails. This typically happens because some ownership transfer is needed for the program to be safe, but it is not enabled by the current invariants $\mathcal{I}$. RefineOwnership takes as parameter a sequence of commands containing a CCR for which a proof attempt has failed. Consider the sequence $C_1; \cdots; C_j; C$ where the failure of the proof occurred in C. Let $\rho \subseteq [1, j]$ be the indexes of all the CCRs in the sequence. The algorithm starts from the last CCR, i.e. C_k where $k = \max \rho$, and tries to refine its invariant using function RefOwn. If no refinement is possible (i.e. the invariant remains unchanged), then the algorithm tries to refine the invariant of the previous CCR in the sequence, and so on until no further CCR exists.

We now describe how the function $\mathsf{RefOwn}((\hat{C}; C_r), \hat{C}')$ operates, where $C_r \equiv \texttt{with}\ r\ \texttt{when}\ B\ \texttt{do}\ C''\ \texttt{endwith}$ is the CCR whose invariant will be refined, and the $\hat{C}$ notation is used for sub-sequences of the failing sequence. Let P be the precondition of the current thread, and let $\{P\}\, \hat{C}\, \{Q\}$ the result of the forward analysis just before C_r and $\{B \wedge (Q * \mathcal{I}(r))\}\, C''\, \{Q'' * \mathcal{I}(r)\}$ the results of forward analysis until before exiting the CCR C_r. Let also $\{P'\}\, \hat{C}'\, \{Q'\}$ be the result of spec inference for the continuation $\hat{C}'$. We can then define

$$\begin{aligned}\mathsf{RefOwn}((\hat{C}; C_r), \hat{C}') \stackrel{def}{=} &((B \wedge [\mathfrak{A}]^{sha}_{(Q'' * \mathcal{I}(r))}) \vee (\neg B \wedge \mathsf{emp})) * \mathcal{I}(r)\\ &\text{if } (Q'' * \mathcal{I}(r)) * \mathfrak{A} \vdash (P' * \mathcal{I}(r)) * \mathfrak{F}\end{aligned}$$

[5] Clearly the proof can fail for other reasons than the resource invariant. Other issues for failure can be manifested in the fact that $\neg(\mathfrak{A} \equiv \mathsf{emp})$.

Algorithm 2. RefineOwnership$(C_1; \ldots; C_j; C, \mathcal{I})$

$\rho = \{i \in [1, j] \mid C_i \text{ is a CCR}\}$;
do
    $k := \max \rho$;
    $\rho := \rho \setminus \{k\}$
    $I' :=$ RefOwn$((C_1; \cdots; C_k), (C_{k+1}; \cdots; C_j; C))$
while $\mathcal{I}(res(C_k)) = I' \;\wedge\; \rho \neq \emptyset$;
return $\mathcal{I}[res(C_k) \leftarrow I']$

where recall that $[\cdot]^{sha}$, defined in Sec. 5.1, tries to replace local variables with shared variables.

Intuitively RefOwn takes a trace ending in a CCR C_r and its continuation $\hat{C}'$, and returns a refined resource invariant for r which is updated only for the part related to C_r and which takes into account the heap needed by $\hat{C}'$. The refinement is computed by solving a bi-abduction question involving the symbolic state inside C_r before releasing the invariant, and the precondition of the continuation suitably augmented with the invariant. In addition, only the part of the anti-frame $\mathfrak{A}$ involving shared variables is taken to refine the invariant. In this context notice that a resource invariant should define properties of shared variables of a resource. Therefore, since bi-abduction may express the anti-frame in terms of local variables, in the newly computed invariant we use $[\cdot]^{sha}$ for replacing these local variables by equivalent shared ones.

Soundness and Termination. We now give some results about our invariant generation method.

Theorem 1. *The* InvariantSynthesis *algorithm is sound.*

Corollary 2. *If* InvariantSynthesis(Prg) *returns a set* $\mathcal{I}$ *then* Prg *is race-free.*

Theorem 2. *The* InvariantSynthesis *algorithm terminates provided that the underlying forward analysis does.*

5.4 Full Examples

Example 4. We describe the execution of the synthesis algorithm on the program on the left side of Fig. 2 which performs transfer of ownership. The first approximation of the resource invariant for resource *buf* is $I_0 = I_{put} \vee I_{get}$ where

$$I_{put} = \neg full \wedge \mathsf{emp} \qquad\qquad I_{get} = full \wedge \mathsf{emp} \tag{1}$$

Using I_0 we obtain the first approximation of `put(x)` and `get(y)` specifications (see Example 1 for the detailed derivation of these specs):

$$\{\mathsf{emp}\}\,\texttt{put(x)}\,\{\mathsf{emp}\} \qquad\qquad \{\mathsf{emp}\}\,\texttt{get(y)}\,\{\mathsf{emp}\} \tag{2}$$

We then execute the ProofSearch procedure of both threads using I_0 and emp as preconditions. By BA-seq for the LHS thread we have:

$$\frac{\{\mathsf{emp}\}\, x = \mathtt{new()}\, \{x \mapsto -\} \qquad \{\mathsf{emp}\}\, \mathtt{put(x)}\, \{\mathsf{emp}\}}{\{\mathsf{emp}\}\, x = \mathtt{new();put(x)}\, \{x \mapsto -\}}$$

by taking $\mathfrak{A} \equiv \mathsf{emp}$ and $\mathfrak{F} \equiv x \mapsto -$. Since $\mathfrak{A}$ is emp, no refinement of I is required and this completes the proof of the LHS thread. For the RHS we have:

$$\frac{\{\mathsf{emp}\}\, \mathtt{get(y)}\, \{\mathsf{emp}\} \qquad \{y \mapsto -\}\, \mathtt{dispose}(y)\, \{\mathsf{emp}\}}{\{y \mapsto -\}\, \mathtt{get(y);dispose}(y)\, \{\mathsf{emp}\}} \tag{3}$$

However, we obtain this derivation by the anti-frame $\mathfrak{A} \equiv y \mapsto -$, and by our notion of failure of the proof search introduced in Sec. 5.2 this means that we cannot actually prove the RHS thread. The algorithm starts the refinement of the invariant by inspecting the RHS and using the body of the CCR `get(y)`:[6]

$$\{(c = c' \wedge y = y' \wedge \mathsf{emp}) * (full \wedge I_0)\}\ \mathtt{y=c;full=false}\ \{c = c' \wedge y = c' \wedge \neg full \wedge \mathsf{emp}\}$$

According to the definition of RefOwn we have to solve

$$(c = c' \wedge y = c' \wedge \neg full \wedge \mathsf{emp}) * \mathfrak{A} \vdash (I_0 * y \mapsto -) * \mathfrak{F}$$

Here we have $\mathfrak{A} \equiv y \mapsto -$ and $[\mathfrak{A}]^{sha}_{(c=c' \wedge y=c' \wedge \neg full \wedge \mathsf{emp})} \equiv c \mapsto -$. Following the algorithm, we extend the *full* disjunct of I_0 to obtain a new candidate invariant:

$$I_1 = (\neg full \wedge \mathsf{emp}) \vee (full \wedge c \mapsto -) \tag{4}$$

CompSpecs then updates the specifications for `put(x)` and `get(y)` using the new invariant and the rule BA-with. As shown in Ex. 2 we obtain:

$$\{x \mapsto\}\, \mathtt{put(x)}\, \{\mathsf{emp}\} \qquad\qquad \{\mathsf{emp}\}\, \mathtt{get(y)}\, \{y \mapsto -\} \tag{5}$$

The algorithm then uses the new specs in an attempt to prove LHS and RHS.

$$\frac{\{\mathsf{emp}\}\, x = \mathtt{new()}\, \{x \mapsto -\} \qquad \{x \mapsto -\}\, \mathtt{put(x)}\, \{\mathsf{emp}\}}{\{\mathsf{emp}\}\, x = \mathtt{new();put(x)}\, \{\mathsf{emp}\}}$$

$$\frac{\{\mathsf{emp}\}\, \mathtt{get(y)}\, \{y \mapsto -\} \qquad \{y \mapsto -\}\, \mathtt{dispose}(y)\, \{\mathsf{emp}\}}{\{\mathsf{emp}\}\, \mathtt{get(y);dispose}(y)\, \{\mathsf{emp}\}}$$

This time the proof succeeds, and the algorithm returns I_1 as resource invariant.

Example 5. Here we discuss the execution of the synthesis algorithm on the program on the right of Fig. 2, which does not involve ownership transfer. As in Ex. 3 the algorithm initializes the resource invariant for *buf* to $I_0 = I_{put} \vee I_{get}$, where I_{put} an I_{get} are defined as in (1). Moreover, the initial specs for `put(x)` and `get(y)` are again as in (2). The forward analysis then easily proves the following triples (at each step BA-seq rule gets $\mathfrak{A} \equiv \mathsf{emp}$) :

$$\{\mathsf{emp}\}\, x = \mathtt{new();put(x);dispose}(x)\, \{\mathsf{emp}\} \qquad\qquad \{\mathsf{emp}\}\, \mathtt{get(y)}\, \{\mathsf{emp}\}$$

Hence the algorithm returns I_0 as a suitable resource invariant for this program.

---

[6] As in [3], we use auxiliary variables to record the initial value of program variables.

Example 6. We now discuss a complex program which combines the one-place pointer transferring buffer and the memory manager [8]:

```
alloc(x); || get(y);
put(x);   || dealloc(y);
```

Step 1 of Algorithm 1 initializes the resource invariants to

$$I^0_{buf} = (\neg \mathit{full} \wedge \mathsf{emp}) \vee (\mathit{full} \wedge \mathsf{emp}) \qquad I^0_{mm} = \mathsf{true} \wedge \mathsf{emp}$$

CompSpecs derives specifications for the CCRs, and, as seen in Ex. 3, it refines I^0_{mm} to obtain a resource invariant I^1_{mm} for the CCRs of resource mm. We have

$$\{\mathsf{emp}\}\,\texttt{put(x)}\,\{\mathsf{emp}\} \qquad \{\mathsf{emp}\}\,\texttt{get(y)}\,\{\mathsf{emp}\}$$
$$\{\mathsf{emp}\}\,\texttt{alloc}(x)\,\{x \mapsto -\} \qquad \{y \mapsto -\}\,\texttt{dealloc}(y)\,\{\mathsf{emp}\}$$

$$I^1_{mm} = (f{=}\mathsf{nil} \wedge \mathsf{emp}) \vee (f \mapsto \mathsf{nil}) \vee \mathsf{ls}(f, \mathsf{nil})$$

As in Ex. 1, using such specifications we can derive a proof for the LHS:

$$\frac{\{\mathsf{emp}\}\,\texttt{alloc}(x)\,\{x \mapsto -\} \qquad \{\mathsf{emp}\}\,\texttt{put(x)}\,\{\mathsf{emp}\}}{\{\mathsf{emp}\}\,\texttt{alloc}(x);\texttt{put(x)}\,\{x \mapsto -\}}$$

However, we cannot derive a proof for RHS since we get a non-empty anti-frame:

$$\frac{\{\mathsf{emp}\}\,\texttt{get(y)}\,\{\mathsf{emp}\} \qquad \{y \mapsto -\}\,\texttt{dealloc}(y)\,\{\mathsf{emp}\}}{\{y \mapsto -\}\,\texttt{get(y)};\texttt{dealloc}(y)\,\{\mathsf{emp}\}}$$

Therefore, refinement is required. This is done as in Ex. 4 where we get $I_{buf} \equiv (\neg \mathit{full} \wedge \mathsf{emp}) \vee (\mathit{full} \wedge c \mapsto -)$ and specifications $\{x \mapsto -\}\,\texttt{put(x)}\,\{\mathsf{emp}\}$ and $\{\mathsf{emp}\}\,\texttt{get(y)}\,\{y \mapsto -\}$. Using them, both LHS and RHS are then proved.

6 Related Work

Our method for computing resource invariants uses bi-abduction [3], a technique that was introduced for discovering specifications of sequential programs. For simplicity, we have assumed that each resource declarations is annotated with the set of global variables it protects. Such annotations need not be given always by the user, as they can often be inferred by tools such as Locksmith [9].

The only shape analysis based on concurrent separation logic that attempts to calculate resource invariants is the thread-modular shape analysis by Gotsman et al. [6]. This analysis uses a heuristic to decide how to partition the state into local and shared after every critical region. As a result, it cannot use the same heuristic to verify both programs in Fig. 2.

Note that these small programs can be verified with analyses that are not thread-modular: e.g. by considering all thread interleavings as in Yahav [11], or by keeping track of the correlations between the local states of each pair of threads as in Segalov et al. [10]. The drawback of such analyses is that they do not scale very well to large programs. In contrast, as our algorithm computes resource invariants in a bottom-up fashion, we are hopeful that it will scale to larger programs.

7 Conclusion

In this paper, we have proposed a sound method for automating concurrent separation logic proofs by synthesizing suitable resource invariants. Our method is thread-modular in that it requires isolated inspection of sequential threads instead of the global parallel composition. Its strength relies on the ability to address one of the main open issues in the automation of proofs for concurrent separation logic. This is the ability to discern, in a thread-local way, the cases where the resource invariant needs to describe the transfer of ownership (among threads) from those cases where no transfer should be involved. This inherent complication has been described by O'Hearn by the expression "ownership is in the eye of the asserter". The technique proposed in this paper pushes the state of the art in automatic generation of proofs towards the more ideal situation where "ownership is in the eye of the mechanical method". We believe that this will open up interesting possibilities for achieving more scalable automatic techniques for concurrent programs.

Acknowledgements. We thank P. O'Hearn, N. Rinetzky, and M. Raza for invaluable comments. Calcagno was supported by an EPSRC Advanced Fellowship and Distefano by a Royal Academy of Engineering research fellowship.

References

1. Berdine, J., Calcagno, C., O'Hearn, P.: Symbolic execution with separation logic. In: Yi, K. (ed.) APLAS 2005. LNCS, vol. 3780, pp. 52–68. Springer, Heidelberg (2005)
2. Berdine, J., Calcagno, C., O'Hearn, P.: Smallfoot: Automatic modular assertion checking with separation logic. In: de Boer, F.S., Bonsangue, M.M., Graf, S., de Roever, W.-P. (eds.) FMCO 2005. LNCS, vol. 4111, pp. 115–137. Springer, Heidelberg (2006)
3. Calcagno, C., Distefano, D., O'Hearn, P.W., Yang, H.: Compositional shape analysis by means of bi-abduction. In: POPL. ACM, New York (2009)
4. Chang, B., Rival, X., Necula, G.: Shape analysis with str. invariant checkers. In: Riis Nielson, H., Filé, G. (eds.) SAS 2007. LNCS, vol. 4634, pp. 384–401. Springer, Heidelberg (2007)
5. Distefano, D., O'Hearn, P.W., Yang, H.: A local shape analysis based on separation logic. In: Hermanns, H., Palsberg, J. (eds.) TACAS 2006. LNCS, vol. 3920, pp. 287–302. Springer, Heidelberg (2006)
6. Gotsman, A., Berdine, J., Cook, B., Sagiv, M.: Thread-modular shape analysis. In: PLDI 2007. ACM, New York (2007)
7. Gulavani, B., Chakraborty, S., Ramalingam, G., Nori, A.: Bottom-up shape analysis. In: Palsberg, J., Su, Z. (eds.) SAS 2009. LNCS, vol. 5679. Springer, Heidelberg (2009)
8. O'Hearn, P.W.: Resources, concurrency and local reasoning. Theoretical Computer Science 375(1-3), 271–307 (2007)
9. Pratikakis, P., Foster, J.S., Hicks, M.: Context-sensitive correlation analysis for detecting races. In: PLDI 2006. ACM, New York (2006)
10. Segalov, M., Lev-Ami, T., Manevich, R., Ramalingam, G., Sagiv, M.: Abstract transformers for thread correlation analysis. In: Hu, Z. (ed.) APLAS 2009. LNCS, vol. 5904. Springer, Heidelberg (2009)
11. Yahav, E.: Verifying safety properties of concurrent Java programs using 3-valued logic. In: POPL 2001. ACM, New York (2001)

Certify Once, Trust Anywhere: Modular Certification of Bytecode Programs for Certified Virtual Machine

Yuan Dong, Kai Ren, Shengyuan Wang, and Suqin Zhang

Department of Computer Science and Technology Tsinghua University Beijing China, 100084
dongyuan@tsinghua.edu.cn, gleemanrk@gmail.com,
{wwssyy,zsq-dcs}@tsinghua.edu.cn

Abstract. Bytecodes and virtual machines (VM) are prevailing programming facilities in contemporary software industry due to their ease of portability across various platforms. Thus, it is critical to improve their trustworthiness. This paper addresses the interesting and challenging problem of certifying bytecode programs over certified VMs. Our solutions to this problem include: 1) A logical systems (CBP) for a bytecode machine is built to modularly certify bytecode programs with abstract control stacks and unstructured control flows, 2) and the corresponding stack-based virtual machine is implemented and certified, 3) a simulation relation between bytecode program and VM implementation is developed and proved to achieve the objective that once some safety property of a bytecode program is certified in CBP system, the property will be preserved on any certified VM. We prove the soundness and demonstrate its power by certifying some example programs with the Coq proof assistant. This work not only provides a solid theoretical foundation for reasoning about bytecode programs, but also gains insight into building proof-preserving compilers.

1 Introduction

Bytecode (such as Java bytecode [16] and .NET CIL [8]) and language VM (virtual machine) are the key components of the many current web applications.

Major Challenges. Formal reasoning about bytecode programs is required both for trustworthy web applications and proof-transforming compilers. Java and CIL are already verifiably type safe with the well-defined type system. Clearly, we want to certify more properties such as memory safety and partial correctness. Although some efforts [18, 4, 2] on building logic system for bytecode programs have been made, the task still remains challenging because of the complexity of abstract control stacks and the lack of control flows information. Moreover, all these logic systems do focus on bytecode programs; none of them takes virtual machines into account. Unfortunately, there are lots of bugs in the well tested virtual machine [20]. Thus, even a certified program may get stuck due to the virtual machine faults.

To tackle these challenges, this paper presents a way of building certified virtual machine and an end-to-end certification logic system for bytecode programs. We provide a logic system for modularly verifying bytecode programs, a certified virtual machine for interpreting bytecode programs, and a guarantee that a certified bytecode program

Z. Hu (Ed.): APLAS 2009, LNCS 5904, pp. 275–293, 2009.

```
;Method: factorial   |  -{(p0, g0)}  ;entry point, instruction sequence 1
;with while loop     |  0  pushc 1  ;push imm 1  8  pushc 1   ;push imm 1
int factor(){        |  1  pop r    ;r = 1       9  binop_    ;n-1
  r = 1;             |  2  goto 11  ;to the end  10 pop n     ;save var n
  while(n != 0){     |  -{(p3, g3)}  ;start loop -{(p11, g11)} ;inst seq 3
    r = r*n;         |  3  pushv r  ;push var r  11 pushv n   ;push var n
    n = n-1;         |  4  pushv n  ;push var n  12 pushc 0   ;push imm 0
  }                  |  5  binop*   ;r*n         13 binop#    ;n#0?
}                    |  6  pop r    ;save var r  14 brture 3  ;conditional goto
                     |  7  pushv n  ;push var n  15 ret       ;function ret
```

Fig. 1. Stack-Based Bytecode Program

will run fine on the certified virtual machine. It is very difficult to build a logic system for certifying bytecode programs as well as a corresponding certified virtual machine. The major points are:

- How can we link certified bytecode programs and certified VM together? An open logic framework was designed to integrate [9] the proof of different logic systems for the X86 machine. But, it is very difficult to integrate the separated certified program modules of different logic systems for different machines.
- To certify bytecode programs modularly, program logic for the virtual machine is required to support both runtime stacks and unstructured control flows. We should use similar logic systems for both the assembly program and the bytecode program to make it easy to link the proof together. But, is the idea of logic system for assembly code certification applicable to bytecode programs for a virtual machine?

Our Approach. A bytecode program with source code which involving while loop control structure is shown in Figure 1. The contents in the shadow box can be ignored now, which will be discussed in details later. Here we give an informal overview about how to certify this program in our method.

Firstly, we formalize two machines. We present the formal definition of bytecode language which runs on a stack-based virtual machine named BCM (ByteCode Machine). We use the formal definition of the X86 machine mentioned in SCAP paper [10].

Then, two logic systems for these two machines are provided to verify bytecode programs and the virtual machine implementation separately and modularly. CertVM (Certified VM), an implementation of BCM on the X86 machine is constructed. We use SCAP, a simple but flexible Hoare-style logic (see Feng *et al.*, [10]), to certify CertVM modularly. Furthermore, we present a Hoare-style logic CBP(Certifying Bytecode Programs) system for BCM. This logic follows the invariant-based proof technique. We define a program invariant to encode the memory safety property and the partial correctness which we are interested in.

Finally, the most important thing is to put these two logic systems together to guarantee that certified bytecode programs run on the certified virtual machines without getting stuck. The simulation relation proof shows that CertVM implementation is satisfied with BCM operational semantics. This main theorem proves that for each bytecode program that is verified in the CBP logic, one can find an equivalent X86 program which is in a simulation relation with the execution of the bytecode program by the virtual machine. This equivalent program is verifiable in SCAP.

Our Contributions. In general, the most interesting point made by this paper about the improvement over previous work is that of the certified virtual machine CertVM. We present a Hoare-style logic system to support modular verification of bytecode programs with all kinds of stack-based control abstractions and unstructured control flows. Formalizing the memory model of our CertVM, we give a certified virtual machine with machine simulation relation proof. Building upon previous work on verification, we make the following contributions:

- As far as we know, our work presents the first program logic facility with certified VM for certifying the partial correctness of bytecode programs. Our work is static certification so there is no additional runtime overhead.
- With the "plus simulation" relation, we prove the semantics preservation property of our virtual machine. Furthermore, VM implementation and simulation relation proof can be developed on any physical machines. As an important advantage, once the properties of a bytecode program are certified, they will be preserved on any certified virtual machine. That's the reason of "Certify once, trust anywhere".
- This logic system is, to our best knowledge, the first to extend FPCC(Foundational Proof-Carrying Code) concepts [1] which is useful for machine code certification to mid-level bytecode language. As we know, an interpreter is similar to the code generator of a compiler. So, it is a feasible way to build a logic system for proof and semantics preserving compilation from bytecode to machine code.

This system is fully mechanized. We give the complete soundness proof and a full verification of an example in the Coq proof assistant [7]. The virtual machine CertVM is implemented in X86 assembly language and is certified with SCAP logic system. Furthermore, it is executable in the Bochs simulator [12].

The rest of this paper is organized as follows: we first formalize the bytecode virtual machine BCM, give its operational semantics, and present a Hoare-style logic system CBP for bytecode program certifying(Sec 2). We then give the implementation of CertVM, prove the simulation relation, and put them together to prove the soundness (Sec 3). After that, we show some examples and the implementation with Coq proof assistant tools (Sec 4). Finally we discuss related works and draw a conclusion.

2 CBP Logic for ByteCode Virtual Machine

In this section, we present the definition and the operational semantics of BCM bytecode machine. Then, we give the program logic CBP for certifying bytecode programs.

2.1 Bytecode Machine BCM

BCM Definition. In Figure 2, we show BCM definition. The whole machine configuration is called a "World" ($\mathbb{W}$), and consists of a read-only code heap ($\mathbb{C}$), an updatable

$$
\begin{array}{rrcl}
(\textit{World}) & \mathbb{W} & ::= & (\mathbb{C},\mathbb{S},\mathbb{K}_c,\texttt{pc}) \\
(\textit{CodeHeap}) & \mathbb{C} & ::= & \{\texttt{f} \rightsquigarrow \mathbb{I}\}^* \\
(\textit{State}) & \mathbb{S} & ::= & (\mathbb{H},\mathbb{K}) \\
(\textit{CStack}) & \mathbb{K}_c & ::= & \textsf{nil} \mid \texttt{f} :: \mathbb{K}_c \\
(\textit{ProgCnt}) & \texttt{pc} & ::= & n \ (\textit{nat nums}) \\
(\textit{Memory}) & \mathbb{H} & ::= & \{\texttt{k} \rightsquigarrow \texttt{w}\}^* \\
(\textit{EStack}) & \mathbb{K} & ::= & \textsf{nil} \mid \texttt{w} :: \mathbb{K} \\
(\textit{Labels}) & \texttt{f},\texttt{k} & ::= & n \ (\textit{nat nums}) \\
(\textit{Word}) & \texttt{w} & ::= & i \ (\textit{integers}) \\
(\textit{OprNum}) & \texttt{m} & ::= & \{+\ldots/,-\cdots+\} \\
(\textit{Instr}) & \iota & ::= & \textsf{pushc}\ \texttt{w} \mid \textsf{pushv}\ \texttt{k} \mid \textsf{pop}\ \texttt{k} \mid \textsf{binop}\ \texttt{m} \mid \textsf{unop}\ \texttt{m} \mid \textsf{brtrue}\ \texttt{f} \mid \textsf{call}\ \texttt{f} \\
(\textit{Commd}) & \texttt{c} & ::= & \iota \mid \textsf{ret} \mid \textsf{goto}\ \texttt{f} \\
(\textit{InstrSeq}) & \mathbb{I} & ::= & \iota;\mathbb{I} \mid \textsf{ret} \mid \textsf{goto}\ \texttt{f}
\end{array}
$$

Fig. 2. Definition of BCM Bytecode Machine

$$
\mathbb{C}[\texttt{f}] \triangleq \begin{cases} \texttt{c} & \texttt{c} = \mathbb{C}(\texttt{f}) \text{ and } \texttt{c} = \textsf{goto}\ \texttt{f}', \text{ or } \textsf{ret} \\ \iota;\mathbb{I} & \iota = \mathbb{C}(\texttt{f}) \text{ and } \mathbb{I} = \mathbb{C}[\texttt{f}+1] \end{cases} \qquad (F\{a \rightsquigarrow b\})(x) \triangleq \begin{cases} b & \textit{if } x = a \\ F(x) & \textit{otherwise} \end{cases}.
$$

$$
\texttt{validK}\ n\ \mathbb{K} \triangleq \texttt{top}(\mathbb{K}) + n \leq \texttt{max}(\mathbb{K}) \qquad \texttt{validK}_c\ n\ \mathbb{K}_c \triangleq \texttt{top}(\mathbb{K}_c) + n \leq \texttt{max}(\mathbb{K}_c)
$$

$$
\texttt{validRa}\quad \mathbb{K}_c \triangleq \exists \texttt{f}, \exists \mathbb{K}_c{}'.\mathbb{K}_c = \texttt{f} :: \mathbb{K}_c{}'
$$

Fig. 3. Definition of Representations

state ($\mathbb{S}$), a function call stack ($\mathbb{K}_c$), and a program counter (pc). The code heap is a finite partial mapping from code labels (f) to instruction sequences ($\mathbb{I}$). The state $\mathbb{S}$ contains a memory heap ($\mathbb{H}$) and an evaluation stack ($\mathbb{K}$). The program counter pc points to the current command in $\mathbb{C}$. The instruction sequence $\mathbb{I}$ is a sequence of sequential instructions ending with jump or return commands. $\mathbb{C}[\texttt{f}]$ extracts an instruction sequence starting from f in $\mathbb{C}$, as defined in Figure 3. We use the dot notation to represent a component in a tuple, *e.g.*, $\mathbb{S}.\mathbb{K}$ means the stack in state $\mathbb{S}$. We also use function top() and max() to get the current pointers and the upper bounds of $\mathbb{K}$, $\mathbb{K}_c$. Valid $\mathbb{K}$ or $\mathbb{K}_c$ means that current pointer top() is in domain $[0,\texttt{max}()]$ and points to some value.

The BCM Operational Semantics. In Figure 4, we also define the machine configuration transition operational semantics of each instruction in a formal way. Here $\texttt{Enable}(\texttt{c})\mathbb{K}_c\,\mathbb{S}$ gives the weakest condition for instruction c to execute. The relation $\texttt{NextS}_{(\texttt{c},\texttt{pc},\mathbb{K}_c)}$ shows the transition of states by executing c with program counter pc and call stack $\mathbb{K}_c$. While $\texttt{NextPC}_{(\texttt{c},\mathbb{S},\mathbb{K}_c)}$ shows how pc changes after c is executed with $\mathbb{S}$ and $\mathbb{K}_c$. $\texttt{NextKc}_{(\texttt{c},\texttt{pc},\mathbb{S})}$ gives the $\mathbb{K}_c$ changes after c execution with program counter pc and $\mathbb{S}$. The semantics of most instructions are straightforward. The execution of programs is modeled as a small-step transition from one world to another. $\mathbb{W} \longmapsto \mathbb{W}'$ is made by executing the instruction pointed to by pc.

Specification Language. We use the mechanized *meta-logic* which is implemented in the Coq proof assistant [7] as our specification language. The logic corresponds to a higher-order predicate logic with inductive definitions. To specify a program with code heap $\mathbb{C}$, the programmer must insert specifications s at instruction sequence start points, see Figure 1. As shown in Figure 5, the specification s is a pair (p, g). The assertion p is a predicate over function call stack $\mathbb{K}_c$ and program state $\mathbb{S}$, while guarantee g is a predicate over two program states. We use p to specify the precondition over function call stack, memory heap and stack. And use g to specify the guaranteed behavior from the specified program point to the point when the *current* function returns.

$\texttt{NextS}_{(\mathsf{c},\mathsf{pc},\mathbb{K}_c)}\ \mathbb{S}\ \mathbb{S}'$ where $\mathbb{S} = (\mathbb{H},\mathbb{K})$

if c =	if $\texttt{Enable}_{(\mathsf{c})}\ \mathbb{K}_c\ \mathbb{S}$ =	then $\mathbb{S}'$ =
pushc w	$\texttt{valid}\mathbb{K}\ 0\ \mathbb{K}$	$(\mathbb{H}, \mathtt{w}::\mathbb{K})$
pushv f	$\texttt{valid}\mathbb{K}\ 0\ \mathbb{K}$ and $\mathbb{H}(\mathtt{f}) = \mathtt{w}$	$(\mathbb{H}, \mathtt{w}::\mathbb{K})$
pop f	$\mathbb{K} = \mathtt{w}::\mathbb{K}'$	$(\mathbb{H}\{\mathtt{f}\leadsto\mathtt{w}\}, \mathbb{K}')$
binop *bop*	$\mathbb{K} = \mathtt{w}_1::\mathtt{w}_2::\mathbb{K}', \mathtt{w} = bop(\mathtt{w}_1,\mathtt{w}_2)$	$(\mathbb{H}, \mathtt{w}::\mathbb{K}')$
unop *uop*	$\mathbb{K} = \mathtt{w}_1::\mathbb{K}', \mathtt{w} = uop(\mathtt{w}_1)$	$(\mathbb{H}, \mathtt{w}::\mathbb{K}')$
brtrue f	$\mathbb{K} = \mathtt{w}::\mathbb{K}', \mathtt{w} =$ True or False	$(\mathbb{H}, \mathbb{K}')$
call f	$\texttt{valid}\mathbb{K}_c\ 0\ \mathbb{K}_c$	$(\mathbb{H}, \mathbb{K})$
ret	$\texttt{validRa}\ \ \mathbb{K}_c$	$(\mathbb{H}, \mathbb{K})$
...		$(\mathbb{H}, \mathbb{K})$

$\texttt{NextKc}_{(\mathsf{c},\mathsf{pc},\mathbb{S})}\ \mathbb{K}_c\ \mathbb{K}_c{}'$ where $\mathbb{S} = (\mathbb{H},\mathbb{K})$

if c =	if $\texttt{Enable}_{(\mathsf{c})}\ \mathbb{K}_c\ \mathbb{S}$ =	then $\mathbb{K}_c{}'$ =
call f	$\texttt{valid}\mathbb{K}_c\ 0\ \mathbb{K}_c$	$(\mathsf{pc}+1)::\mathbb{K}_c$
ret	$\texttt{validRa}\ \ \mathbb{K}_c$	$\mathbb{K}_c{}'$
...	...	$\mathbb{K}_c$

$\texttt{NextPC}_{(\mathsf{c},\mathbb{S},\mathbb{K}_c)}\ \mathsf{pc}\ \mathsf{pc}'$ where $\mathbb{S} = (\mathbb{H},\mathbb{K})$

if c =	if $\texttt{Enable}_{(\mathsf{c})}\ \mathbb{K}_c\ \mathbb{S}$ =	then pc$'$ =
brtrue f	$\mathbb{K} = \mathtt{w}::\mathbb{K}', \mathtt{w} =$ True	f
	$\mathbb{K} = \mathtt{w}::\mathbb{K}', \mathtt{w} =$ False	pc + 1
call f	$\texttt{valid}\mathbb{K}_c\ 0\ \mathbb{K}_c$	f
ret	$\texttt{validRa}\ \ \mathbb{K}_c$	f
goto f		f
...	...	pc+1

$$\frac{\mathsf{c} = \mathbb{C}(\mathsf{pc}) \quad \texttt{Enable}_{(\mathsf{c})}\ \mathbb{K}_c\ \mathbb{S} \quad \texttt{NextS}_{(\mathsf{c},\mathsf{pc},\mathbb{K}_c)}\ \mathbb{S}\ \mathbb{S}' \quad \texttt{NextKc}_{(\mathsf{c},\mathsf{pc},\mathbb{S})}\ \mathbb{K}_c\ \mathbb{K}_c{}' \quad \texttt{NextPC}_{(\mathsf{c},\mathbb{S},\mathbb{K}_c)}\ \mathsf{pc}\ \mathsf{pc}'}{(\mathbb{C},\mathbb{S},\mathbb{K}_c,\mathsf{pc}) \longmapsto (\mathbb{C},\mathbb{S}',\mathbb{K}_c{}',\mathsf{pc}')}\ (\mathrm{PC})$$

Fig. 4. Operational semantics of *BCM*

$$
\begin{array}{rrcl}
(Pred) & \mathtt{p} & \in & CStack \rightarrow State \rightarrow Prop \\
(Spec) & \mathtt{s} & ::= & (\mathtt{p},\mathtt{g}) \\
(CdHpSpec) & \Psi & ::= & \{(\mathtt{f}_1,\mathtt{s}_1),\ldots,(\mathtt{f}_n,\mathtt{s}_n)\}
\end{array}
\qquad
\begin{array}{rrcl}
(Guarantee) & \mathtt{g} & \in & State \rightarrow State \rightarrow Prop \\
(MPred) & \mathtt{m} & \in & Memory \rightarrow Prop
\end{array}
$$

Fig. 5. Specification Constructs for *CBP*

As we can see, the $\texttt{Enable}(\mathsf{c})$ defined in Figure 4 is a special p. And the $\texttt{NextS}_{(\mathsf{c},\mathsf{pc})}$ relation is a special form of g which is over the two adjacent states. We use the predicate m to specify the memory heap. Specification Ψ for code heap $\mathbb{C}$ associates code labels f with corresponding s. Note that multiple s may be associated with the same f, just as a function may have multiple specified interfaces.

2.2 The CBP Program Logic

We use the following judgments to define the inference rules:

$$
\begin{array}{ll}
\Psi \vdash \{\mathtt{s}\}\,\mathbb{W} & \text{(well-formed world)} \\
\Psi \vdash \mathbb{C}:\Psi' & \text{(well-formed code heap)} \\
\Psi \vdash \{\mathtt{s}\}\,\mathbb{I} & \text{(well-formed instruction sequence)}
\end{array}
$$

Inference rules of the program logic are shown in Figure 6.

$\boxed{\Psi \vdash \{s\}\mathbb{W}}$ ***(Well-formed World)***

$$\frac{\Psi \vdash \mathbb{C}:\Psi' \quad \Psi \subseteq \Psi' \quad \Psi \vdash \{s\}\texttt{pc} : \mathbb{C}[\texttt{pc}] \quad \{s\}\,\Psi'\,\mathbb{S}}{\Psi \vdash \{s\}(\mathbb{C},\mathbb{S},\texttt{pc})} \quad \text{(WLD)}$$

$\boxed{\Psi \vdash \mathbb{C}:\Psi'}$ ***(Well-formed Code Heap)***

$$\frac{\text{for all } (\texttt{f},s) \in \Psi' : \quad \Psi \vdash \{s\}\texttt{f} : \mathbb{C}[\texttt{f}]}{\Psi \vdash \mathbb{C}:\Psi'} \quad \text{(CDHP)}$$

$$\frac{\Psi_1 \vdash \mathbb{C}_1:\Psi_1' \quad \Psi_2 \vdash \mathbb{C}_2:\Psi_2' \quad \mathbb{C}_1\#\mathbb{C}_2}{\Psi_1 \cup \Psi_2 \vdash \mathbb{C}_1 \cup \mathbb{C}_2 : \Psi_1' \cup \Psi_2'} \quad \text{(LINK)}$$

$\boxed{\Psi \vdash \{s\}\mathbb{I}}$ ***(Well-formed Instr. Sequence)***

$$\frac{\iota \notin \{\mathsf{brtrue}, \mathsf{call}\} \quad \Psi \vdash \{(p'',g'')\}\texttt{pc}+1 : \mathbb{I} \quad p \Rightarrow g_\iota \quad (p \triangleright g_\iota) \Rightarrow p'' \quad (p \circ (g_\iota \circ g'')) \Rightarrow g}{\Psi \vdash \{(p,g)\}\texttt{pc} : \iota;\mathbb{I}} \quad \text{(SEQ)}$$

$$\frac{\begin{array}{c}(\texttt{f}',(p',g')) \in \Psi \qquad \Psi \vdash \{(p'',g'')\}\texttt{pc}+1 : \mathbb{I} \\ (p \triangleright g_{\mathsf{brT}}) \Rightarrow p' \quad (p \circ (g_{\mathsf{brT}} \circ g')) \Rightarrow g \quad (p \triangleright g_{\mathsf{brF}}) \Rightarrow p'' \quad (p \circ (g_{\mathsf{brF}} \circ g'')) \Rightarrow g\end{array}}{\Psi \vdash \{(p,g)\}\texttt{pc} : \mathsf{brtrue}\ \texttt{f}';\mathbb{I}} \quad \text{(BRTURE)}$$

$$\frac{\begin{array}{c}(\texttt{pc}+1,(p'',g'')) \in \Psi \qquad \Psi \vdash \{(p'',g'')\}\texttt{pc}+1 : \mathbb{I} \\ (p \triangleright g_{\mathsf{call}}) \Rightarrow p' \quad (p \triangleright g_{\mathsf{fun}}) \Rightarrow p'' \quad (p \circ (g_{\mathsf{fun}} \circ g'')) \Rightarrow g \quad (\texttt{f}',(p',g')) \in \Psi \quad g_{\mathsf{fun}} = ((g_{\mathsf{call}} \circ g') \circ g_{\mathsf{ret}})\end{array}}{\Psi \vdash \{(p,g)\}\texttt{pc} : \mathsf{call}\ \texttt{lf}';\mathbb{I}} \quad \text{(CALL)}$$

$$\frac{(p \circ g_{\mathsf{ret}}) \Rightarrow g}{\Psi \vdash \{(p,g)\}\texttt{pc} : \mathsf{ret}} \quad \text{(RET)}$$

$$\frac{(\texttt{f}',(p',g')) \in \Psi \quad (p \triangleright g_{\mathsf{goto}}) \Rightarrow p' \quad (p \circ (g_{\mathsf{goto}} \circ g')) \Rightarrow g}{\Psi \vdash \{(p,g)\}\texttt{pc} : \mathsf{goto}\ \texttt{f}'} \quad \text{(GOTO)}$$

Fig. 6. CBP Inference Rules

Program Invariants. The WLD rule formulates the program invariant enforced by our program logic:

- The code heap $\mathbb{C}$ needs to be well-formed following the CDHP rule.
- The imported interface Ψ is a subset of the exported interface Ψ', therefore $\mathbb{C}$ is self-contained and each imported specification has been certified.
- Current pc has a specification s in Ψ, thus the current instruction sequence $\mathbb{C}[\texttt{pc}]$ is well-formed with respect to s.
- Given exported Ψ', the current state $\mathbb{S}$ satisfies the assertion s.

Program Modules. In the CDHP rule, Ψ contains specifications for external code (imported by the local module $\mathbb{C}$), while Ψ' contains specifications for code blocks in the module $\mathbb{C}$ for other modules. Thus, the *CBP* logic supports *separate verification* of program modules. Modules are modeled as small code heaps which contain at least one code block. The specification of a module contains not only specifications of the code blocks in the current module, but also specifications of external code blocks which will be called by this module. The well-formedness of each individual module is established via the CDHP rule. Then, two non-intersecting well-formed modules can be linked together via the LINK rule. The WLD rule requires all modules to be linked into a well-formed global code heap.

$$\mathsf{g}_{\mathsf{brT}} \triangleq \lambda\mathbb{S},\mathbb{S}'.\mathtt{NextS}_{(\mathsf{brture},\_)}\ \mathbb{S}\ \mathbb{S}' \qquad \text{(where } \mathbb{S}.\mathbb{K} = w :: \mathbb{K}', w = \mathsf{True})$$
$$\mathsf{g}_{\mathsf{brF}} \triangleq \lambda\mathbb{S},\mathbb{S}'.\mathtt{NextS}_{(\mathsf{brture},\_)}\ \mathbb{S}\ \mathbb{S}' \qquad \text{(where } \mathbb{S}.\mathbb{K} = w :: \mathbb{K}', w = \mathsf{False})$$
$$\mathsf{g}_{\mathsf{c}} \triangleq \lambda\mathbb{S},\mathbb{S}'.\mathtt{NextS}_{(\mathsf{c},\_)}\ \mathbb{S}\ \mathbb{S}' \qquad \text{(for all other c)}$$

Fig. 7. Local State and Program Point Transitions

$$\mathsf{p} \Rightarrow \mathsf{g} \triangleq \forall\mathbb{S}.\,\mathsf{p}\,\mathbb{S} \rightarrow \exists\mathbb{S}',\mathsf{g}\,\mathbb{S}\,\mathbb{S}' \qquad \mathsf{p} \rhd \mathsf{g} \triangleq \lambda\mathbb{S}.\,\exists\mathbb{S}_0,\mathsf{p}\,\mathbb{S}_0 \wedge \mathsf{g}\,\mathbb{S}_0\,\mathbb{S}$$
$$\mathsf{g} \circ \mathsf{g}' \triangleq \lambda\mathbb{S},\mathbb{S}''.\,\exists\mathbb{S}'.\,\mathsf{g}\,\mathbb{S}\,\mathbb{S}' \wedge \mathsf{g}'\,\mathbb{S}'\,\mathbb{S}'' \qquad \mathsf{p} \Rightarrow \mathsf{p}' \triangleq \forall\mathbb{S}.\,\mathsf{p}\,\mathbb{S} \rightarrow \mathsf{p}'\,\mathbb{S}$$
$$\mathsf{g} \Rightarrow \mathsf{g}' \triangleq \forall\mathbb{S},\mathbb{S}'.\,\mathsf{g}\,\mathbb{S}\,\mathbb{S}' \rightarrow \mathsf{g}'\,\mathbb{S}\,\mathbb{S}' \qquad \mathsf{p} \circ \mathsf{g} \triangleq \lambda\mathbb{S},\mathbb{S}'.\,\mathsf{p}\,\mathbb{S} \wedge \mathsf{g}\,\mathbb{S}\,\mathbb{S}'$$

Fig. 8. Connectors for p and g

Sequential Instructions. Like traditional Hoare-logic [11], our logic also uses the pre- and post-condition as specifications for programs. The SEQ rule is a *schema* for instruction sequences starting with an instruction ι (ι cannot be conditional jump or function call instructions). It says it is safe to execute the instruction sequence $\mathbb{I}$ starting at the code label pc, given the imported interface in Ψ and a precondition (p,g). An intermediate specification $(\mathsf{p}'',\mathsf{g}'')$ with respect to which the remaining instruction sequence is well-formed should be found. It is also used as a post-condition for the current instruction ι. We use g_ι to represent the state transition made by the instruction ι, which is defined in Figure 7 and Figure 4. Since NextS does not depend on the current program counter for these instructions "_" is used to represent arbitrary pc.

The definitions in Figure 8 are used in these rules. The predicate $\mathsf{p} \rhd \mathsf{g}_\iota$ specifies the state resulting from the state transition g_ι, knowing the initial state satisfies p. The composition of two subsequent transitions g and g' is represented as $\mathsf{g} \circ \mathsf{g}'$, and $\mathsf{p} \circ \mathsf{g}$ refines g with the extra knowledge that the initial state satisfies p. The predicate $\mathsf{p} \Rightarrow \mathsf{g}_\iota$ means that the state transition g_ι would not get stuck as long as the starting state satisfies p. The second premise in the SEQ rule means if the current state satisfies p, after state transition g_ι, the new state satisfies p'. The last premise in the SEQ rule requires the composition of g_ι and g'' fulfilling g, knowing the current state satisfies p.

Function Call and Return. Figure 9(b) shows the meaning of the specification (p,g) for the function foo defined in Figure 9(a). Note that g may cover multiple instruction sequences. If a function has multiple return points, g governs all the traces from the current program point to any return point. Figure 9(c) illustrates a function call to bar (point B) from foo at point A (label $\mathtt{pc} = 5$), with the return address $\mathtt{pc}+1$ (point D). The specification of bar is $(\mathsf{p}_B,\mathsf{g}_B)$. Specifications at A and D are $(\mathsf{p}_A,\mathsf{g}_A)$ and $(\mathsf{p}_D,\mathsf{g}_D)$ respectively, where g_A governs the code segment A-E and g_D governs D-E.

To ensure that the program behaves correctly, we must enforce the following conditions with a special guarantee $\mathsf{g}_{\mathsf{fun}} \triangleq \lambda\mathbb{S},\mathbb{S}''.\exists\mathbb{S}',\exists\mathbb{S}^*,\mathsf{g}_{\mathsf{cal}}\,\mathbb{S}\,\mathbb{S}' \wedge \mathsf{g}_B\,\mathbb{S}'\,\mathbb{S}^* \wedge \mathsf{g}_{\mathsf{ret}}\,\mathbb{S}^*\,\mathbb{S}''$.

- the precondition of bar should be satisfied, *i.e.*, $\forall\mathbb{S},\exists\mathbb{S}'.\mathsf{p}_A\,\mathbb{S} \wedge \mathsf{g}_{\mathsf{cal}}\,\mathbb{S}\,\mathbb{S}' \rightarrow \mathsf{p}_B\,\mathbb{S}'$;
- after bar returns, caller foo resumes from D, $\forall\mathbb{S},\mathbb{S}''.\mathsf{p}_A\,\mathbb{S} \rightarrow \mathsf{g}_{\mathsf{fun}}\,\mathbb{S}\,\mathbb{S}'' \rightarrow \mathsf{p}_D\,\mathbb{S}''$;
- if the function bar and the code segment D-E satisfy their specifications, the specification for A-E is satisfied, *i.e.*, $\forall\mathbb{S},\mathbb{S}'',\mathbb{S}'''.\mathsf{p}_A\,\mathbb{S} \rightarrow \mathsf{g}_{\mathsf{fun}}\,\mathbb{S}\,\mathbb{S}'' \rightarrow \mathsf{g}_D\,\mathbb{S}''\,\mathbb{S}''' \rightarrow \mathsf{g}\,\mathbb{S}\,\mathbb{S}'''$.

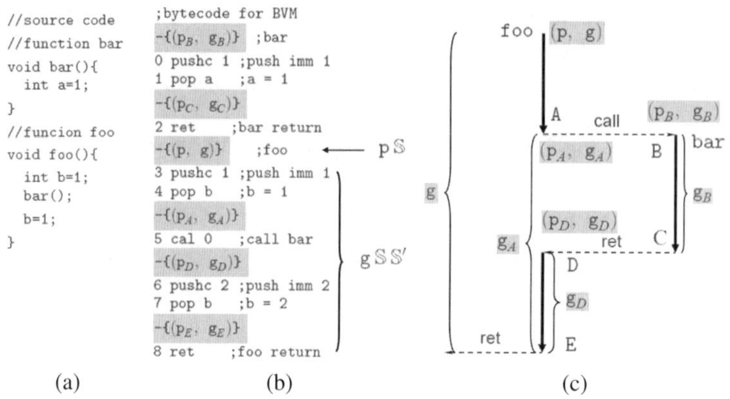

Fig. 9. The Model for Function Call/Return in CBP

The RET rule simply requires that the function has finished its guaranteed transition at this point. In this rule, we do not need to know any information about the return address. So it can be used to modularly certify any callee function separately.

Call Stack Invariant. Generalizing the safety requirement, we recursively define the "well-formed function call stack" as follows:

$$\begin{array}{l}\mathsf{WFST}(\mathtt{g},\mathbb{K}_c,\mathbb{S},\Psi) \triangleq \neg\exists\mathbb{S}'.\ \mathtt{g}\ \mathbb{S}\ \mathbb{S}', \quad \text{where } \mathbb{K}_c = \mathsf{nil}.\\ \mathsf{WFST}(\mathtt{g},\mathbb{K}_c,\mathbb{S},\Psi) \triangleq \forall\mathbb{S}'.\mathtt{g}\ \mathbb{S}\ \mathbb{S}' \rightarrow \mathtt{p}'\ \mathbb{S}' \wedge \mathsf{WFST}(\mathtt{g}',\mathbb{K}_c{}',\mathbb{S}',\Psi),\\ \text{where } \exists\mathtt{f},\exists\mathbb{K}_c{}'.\mathbb{K}_c = \mathtt{f} :: \mathbb{K}_c{}', (\mathtt{p}',\mathtt{g}') = \Psi(\mathtt{f}).\end{array}$$

When the function call stack is empty, we are in the top function which has no return code pointer,*i.e.*, $\neg\exists\mathbb{S}'.\ \mathtt{g}\ \mathbb{S}\ \mathbb{S}'$. Then the stack invariant at every step of program execution is that, at each program point with $(\mathtt{p},\mathtt{g})$, the program state $\mathbb{S}$ must satisfy $\mathtt{p}$ and there exists a well-formed control stack in $\mathbb{S}$. So the stack invariant is:

$$\{(\mathtt{p},\mathtt{g})\}\ \Psi\ \mathbb{S} \triangleq \mathtt{p}\ \mathbb{S} \wedge \mathsf{WFST}(\mathtt{g},\mathbb{K}_c,\mathbb{S},\Psi).$$

Soundness of CBP. The soundness of the program logic is proved following the syntactic approach based on the progress and preservation lemmas. It guarantees that the complete system after linking never gets stuck as long as the initial state satisfies the program invariant defined by the WLD rule. Furthermore, the invariant will be always holding during execution, from which we can derive rich properties of programs.

Lemma 1 (Progress). If $\Psi \vdash \{\mathtt{s}\}\mathbb{W}$, there exists a program $\mathbb{W}'$, such that $\mathbb{W} \longmapsto \mathbb{W}'$.

Lemma 2 (Preservation). If $\Psi \vdash \{\mathtt{s}\}\mathbb{W}$, and $\mathbb{W} \longmapsto \mathbb{W}'$, then there exists $\mathtt{s}'$, $\Psi \vdash \{\mathtt{s}'\}\mathbb{W}'$.

Theorem 1 (CBP Soundness). For all program $\mathbb{W}$, specification Ψ and assertion $\mathtt{s}$. If $\Psi \vdash \{\mathtt{s}\}\mathbb{W}$, then for all natural number n, there exists a program $\mathbb{W}'$ such that $\mathbb{W} \longmapsto^n \mathbb{W}'$.

3 Proof of ByteCode Virtual Machine

In this section, we present how to certify the implementation of a virtual machine CertVM for BC/0. We first give the formal definition of x86 real-mode machine where CertVM runs on. Then we introduce the program logic for this machine. Finally, we show the design, implementation and formal proof of CertVM.

3.1 x86 Machine and SCAP Program Logic

X86 machine is defined in Figure 10. And Figure 11 shows its operational semantics. This is a simplified version which includes only four general purpose registers. We use SCAP [10] logic system to verify the CertVM implementation. The inference rules of SCAP program logic are given in Figure 12. The soundness proof of SCAP is carried out based on the progress and preservation lemmas which are similar to that of CBP.

3.2 The Design of CertVM

CertVM is implemented in real-mode x86 assembly language, and it is executable in the Bochs simulator. The current implementation of CertVM mainly includes the loader and the interpreter. Other advanced features such as garbage collection and just in-time compilation are not included yet.

The memory space of CertVM consists of four major parts: code heap ($\mathbb{C}$), memory heap ($\mathbb{H}$), evaluation stack ($\mathbb{K}$) and function call stack ($\mathbb{K}_c$). All of them are located in x86 machine's memory heap ($\mathbb{H}_\mathtt{X}$) as arrays. In the following analysis, function `base()` and `max()` are used to get the base address and the maximum length of $\mathbb{C}$, $\mathbb{H}$, $\mathbb{K}$ and $\mathbb{K}_c$. And `top()` denotes the top pointer of stack $\mathbb{K}$ and $\mathbb{K}_c$.

A loader is designed to launch the bytecode program. It loads bytecode programs into $\mathbb{C}$, initializes the memory heap $\mathbb{H}$ and the evaluation stacks $\mathbb{K}$ (setting the stack pointer `sp` to zero). For the top level function, the bottom cell of function call stack $\mathbb{K}_c$ is set to -1 (0xFFFF) and the stack pointer `csp` points to the second cell. And CertVM's `pc` is set to the entry point of the loaded bytecode program. After all the initializations, it is ready to execute the bytecode program.

Every bytecode instruction is simulated by a sequence of x86 assembly instructions. The simulation of a bytecode instruction consists of four phases: instruction fetching, decoding, dispatching and interpreting. Figure 13 shows the assembly instruction sequence which simulate bytecode instruction goto as an example. The instruction sequence of bytecode fetching, decoding and dispatching is shared by all BC/0 instructions. Thus the simulation of every bytecode start at the label `fetch`. After fetching

$$
\begin{array}{rrcl@{\qquad}rrcl}
(\mathit{World}) & \mathbb{W} & ::= & (\mathbb{C},\mathbb{S},\mathtt{pc}) & (\mathit{Labels}) & l,\mathtt{f},\mathtt{pc} & ::= & n\ (\mathit{nat\ nums}) \\
(\mathit{CodeHeap}) & \mathbb{C} & ::= & \{\mathtt{f} \leadsto \mathbb{I}\}^* & (\mathit{Flags}) & \mathtt{zf} & ::= & \mathtt{b} \\
(\mathit{State}) & \mathbb{S} & ::= & (\mathbb{H},\mathbb{R},\mathtt{zf}) & (\mathit{Bit}) & \mathtt{b} & ::= & 0 \mid 1 \\
(\mathit{Memory}) & \mathbb{H} & ::= & \{l \leadsto \mathtt{w}\}^* & (\mathit{Word}) & \mathtt{w} & ::= & i\ (\mathit{integers}) \\
(\mathit{RegFile}) & \mathbb{R} & ::= & \{\mathtt{r} \leadsto \mathtt{w}\}^* & (\mathit{WordReg}) & \mathtt{r} & ::= & \mathtt{r}_{AX} \mid \mathtt{r}_{BX} \mid \mathtt{r}_{CX} \mid \mathtt{r}_{DX}
\end{array}
$$

$$
\begin{array}{rrcl}
(\mathit{Instr}) & \iota & ::= & \mathsf{je}\ \mathtt{f} \mid \mathsf{movw}\ \mathtt{w},\mathtt{r} \mid \mathsf{movw}\ \mathtt{r}_s,\mathtt{r}_d \mid \mathsf{movw}\ w(\mathtt{r}_s),\mathtt{r}_d \mid \mathsf{movw}\ \mathtt{r}_s,w(\mathtt{r}_d) \mid \mathsf{addw}\ \mathtt{w},\mathtt{r} \mid \mathsf{subw}\ \mathtt{w},\mathtt{r} \mid \mathsf{cmpw}\ \mathtt{w},\mathtt{r} \\
(\mathit{Commd}) & \mathtt{c} & ::= & \iota \mid \mathsf{jmp}\ \mathtt{f} \mid \mathsf{jmpw}\ \mathtt{r} \\
(\mathit{InstrSeq}) & \mathbb{I} & ::= & \iota;\mathbb{I} \mid \mathsf{jmp}\ \mathtt{f} \mid \mathsf{jmpw}\ \mathtt{r}
\end{array}
$$

Fig. 10. Definition of x86 Machine

$\mathtt{NextS}_{c,pc}\ \mathbb{S}\ \mathbb{S}'$ where $\mathbb{S} = (\mathbb{H}, \mathbb{R}, \mathtt{zf})$

if c =	then $\mathbb{S}'$ =
movw $\mathtt{w}, \mathtt{r}$	$(\mathbb{H}, \mathbb{R}\{\mathtt{r} \rightsquigarrow \mathtt{w}\}, \mathtt{zf})$
movw $\mathtt{r}_s, \mathtt{r}_d$	$(\mathbb{H}, \mathbb{R}\{\mathtt{r}_d \rightsquigarrow \mathbb{R}(\mathtt{r}_s)\}, \mathtt{zf})$
movw $\mathtt{r}_s, w(\mathtt{r}_d)$	$(\mathbb{H}\{l \rightsquigarrow \mathbb{R}(\mathtt{r}_s)\}, \mathbb{R}, \mathtt{zf})$, if $l = \mathbb{R}(\mathtt{r}_d) + w$ and $l \in dom(\mathbb{H})$
movw $w(\mathtt{r}_s), \mathtt{r}_d$	$(\mathbb{H}, \mathbb{R}\{\mathtt{r}_d \rightsquigarrow \mathbb{R}(l)\}, \mathtt{zf})$, if $l = \mathbb{R}(\mathtt{r}_s) + w$ and $l \in dom(\mathbb{H})$
addw $\mathtt{w}, \mathtt{r}$	$(\mathbb{H}, \mathbb{R}\{\mathtt{r} \rightsquigarrow (\mathbb{R}(\mathtt{r}) + \mathtt{w})\}, \mathtt{zf})$
subw $\mathtt{w}, \mathtt{r}$	$(\mathbb{H}, \mathbb{R}\{\mathtt{r} \rightsquigarrow (\mathbb{R}(\mathtt{r}) - \mathtt{w})\}, \mathtt{zf})$
cmpw $\mathtt{w}, \mathtt{r}$	$(\mathbb{H}, \mathbb{R}, \mathtt{b})$, $\mathtt{b} = 0$, if $\mathtt{w} = \mathbb{R}(\mathtt{r})$; $\mathtt{b} = 1$, else
...	$(\mathbb{H}, \mathbb{R}, \mathtt{zf})$

$\mathtt{NextPC}_{(c,\mathbb{S})}\ \mathrm{pc}\ \mathrm{pc}'$ where $\mathbb{S} = (\mathbb{H}, \mathbb{R}, \mathtt{zf})$

if c =	then pc′ =
je $\mathtt{f}$	$\mathtt{f}$ if $\mathtt{zf} = 0$; pc + 1 others
jmp $\mathtt{f}$	$\mathtt{f}$
jmpw $\mathtt{r}$	$\mathtt{f}$ if $\mathtt{f} = \mathbb{R}(\mathtt{r})$
...	pc+1

$$\frac{\mathrm{c} = \mathbb{C}(\mathrm{pc}) \quad \mathtt{NextS}_{(c,pc)}\ \mathbb{S}\ \mathbb{S}' \quad \mathtt{NextPC}_{(c,\mathbb{S})}\ \mathrm{pc}\ \mathrm{pc}'}{(\mathbb{C}, \mathbb{S}, \mathrm{pc}) \longmapsto (\mathbb{C}, \mathbb{S}', \mathrm{pc}')} \quad (\mathrm{PC})$$

Fig. 11. Operational semantics of x86 machine

$\boxed{\Psi \vdash \{s\}\,\mathbb{W}}$ ***(Well-formed World)***

$$\frac{\Psi \vdash \mathbb{C} : \Psi' \quad \Psi \subseteq \Psi' \quad \Psi \vdash \{s\}\mathrm{pc} : \mathbb{C}[\mathrm{pc}] \quad \{s\}\ \Psi'\ \mathbb{S}}{\Psi \vdash \{s\}\,(\mathbb{C}, \mathbb{S}, \mathrm{pc})} \quad (\mathrm{WLD})$$

$\boxed{\Psi \vdash \mathbb{C} : \Psi'}$ ***(Well-formed Code Heap)***

$$\frac{\text{for all } (\mathtt{f}, s) \in \Psi' : \quad \Psi \vdash \{s\}\mathtt{f} : \mathbb{C}[\mathtt{f}]}{\Psi \vdash \mathbb{C} : \Psi'} \quad (\mathrm{CDHP})$$

$$\frac{\Psi_1 \vdash \mathbb{C}_1 : \Psi_1' \quad \Psi_2 \vdash \mathbb{C}_2 : \Psi_2' \quad \mathbb{C}_1 \# \mathbb{C}_2}{\Psi_1 \cup \Psi_2 \vdash \mathbb{C}_1 \cup \mathbb{C}_2 : \Psi_1' \cup \Psi_2'} \quad (\mathrm{LINK})$$

$\boxed{\Psi \vdash \{s\}\,\mathbb{I}}$ ***(Well-formed Instr. Sequence)***

$$\frac{\iota \notin \{\mathrm{je}\} \quad \Psi \vdash \{(p'', g'')\}\mathrm{pc}{+}1 : \mathbb{I} \quad p \Rightarrow g_\iota \quad (p \triangleright g_\iota) \Rightarrow p'' \quad (p \circ (g_\iota \circ g'')) \Rightarrow g}{\Psi \vdash \{(p, g)\}\mathrm{pc} : \iota; \mathbb{I}} \quad (\mathrm{SEQ})$$

$$\frac{\begin{array}{c}(\mathtt{f}', (p', g')) \in \Psi \qquad \Psi \vdash \{(p'', g'')\}\mathrm{pc}{+}1 : \mathbb{I} \\ (p \triangleright g_{\mathrm{jeT}}) \Rightarrow p' \quad (p \circ (g_{\mathrm{jeT}} \circ g')) \Rightarrow g \quad (p \triangleright g_{\mathrm{jeF}}) \Rightarrow p'' \quad (p \circ (g_{\mathrm{jeF}} \circ g'')) \Rightarrow g\end{array}}{\Psi \vdash \{(p, g)\}\mathrm{pc} : \mathrm{je}\ \mathtt{f}'; \mathbb{I}} \quad (\mathrm{JE})$$

$$\frac{(\mathtt{f}', (p', g')) \in \Psi \quad (p \triangleright g_{\mathrm{jmp}}) \Rightarrow p' \quad (p \circ (g_{\mathrm{jmp}} \circ g')) \Rightarrow g}{\Psi \vdash \{(p, g)\}\mathrm{pc} : \mathrm{jmp}\ \mathtt{f}'} \quad (\mathrm{JMP})$$

$$\frac{(\mathbb{R}(\mathtt{r}), (p', g')) \in \Psi \quad (p \triangleright g_{\mathrm{jmpw}}) \Rightarrow p' \quad (p \circ (g_{\mathrm{jmpw}} \circ g')) \Rightarrow g}{\Psi \vdash \{(p, g)\}\mathrm{pc} : \mathrm{jmpw}\ \mathtt{r}} \quad (\mathrm{JMPW})$$

Fig. 12. SCAP Inference Rules for x86 Machine

```
#Source code of CertVM                        | 12  addw %ax, %bx     # 2 word long
-{(p_fetch, g_fetch)}     #entry point        | 13  movw (%bx), %ax #get entry point
1  fetch:                 #bytecode fetch     | 14  jmpw *%ax         #jump to code entry
2    movw (pc), %ax       #bytecode pc        | -{(p_goto, g_goto)}   #instr. sequence 2
3    cmpw $0xFFFF,%ax     #compare ra         | 15 goto:
4    je    fetch          #loop forever       | 16  movw (pc), %ax    # code point
5  decode:                                    | 17  movw $code, %bx   # code base
6    movw $code, %bx      #code base          | 18  addw %ax, %bx     # current base
7    addw %ax, %bx        #current code       | 19  movw 2(%bx),%cx   # fetch i.a
8    movw (%bx), %ax      #fetch i.f          | 20  addw %cx, %cx     # 4 bytes instr.
9  dispatch:                                  | 21  addw %cx, %cx     #
10   movw $table, %bx     #dispatch table     | 22  movw %cx, (pc)    # target address
11   addw %ax, %bx        #offset of code     | 23  jmp  fetch
```

Fig. 13. Fragment of CertVM Implementation

and decoding a bytecode, CertVM will jump to the unique entry point for each bytecode. For bytecode goto, the entry point is the label "goto" of line 15 in Figure 13. The entry points for all BC/0 instructions are stored in a bytecode instruction dispatching table. Data structure "table" of line 9 in Figure 13 is the dispatching table of CertVM. It should be preserved during virtual machine execution.

3.3 Proof of the Correctness of CertVM

Simulation Relation. To execute bytecode programs correctly, the x86 simulation program should maintain an invariant for the interpretation of every bytecode instruction. This invariant, called "simulation relation", is defined as a relation between the bytecode machine world $\mathbb{W} = (\mathbb{C}, (\mathbb{H}, \mathbb{K}), \mathbb{K}_c, \mathtt{pc})$ and x86 machine world $\mathbb{W}_\mathtt{X} = (\mathbb{C}_\mathtt{X}, (\mathbb{H}_\mathtt{X}, \mathbb{R}, \mathtt{zf}), \mathtt{pc}_\mathtt{X})$. This relation should be maintained when the simulation program executes to the fetching phase. This relation is shown in Figure 14, which indicates:

- the code heap of x86 world should be the code of CertVM,
- current program counter of x86 world points to `fetch`,
- the bytecode machine world $\mathbb{W}_\mathtt{X}$ is mapped to x86 machine memory heap $\mathbb{H}_\mathtt{X}$, following the memory relation α,
- there is no constrain for register file and flag.

We define certified virtual machine $\mathsf{WFVM}(\mathbb{W}, \mathbb{W}_\mathtt{X})$ for all bytecode program $\mathbb{W}$ and X86 program $\mathbb{W}_\mathtt{X}$ as a virtual machine with this simulation relation:

Definition 1 (Well-Formed VM). For all bytecode program $\mathbb{W}, \mathbb{W}'$ and x86 program $\mathbb{W}_\mathtt{X}$, if $\mathbb{W} \sim \mathbb{W}_\mathtt{X}$ and $\mathbb{W} \longmapsto \mathbb{W}'$, there exists a x86 program $\mathbb{W}'_\mathtt{X}$ such that $\mathbb{W}' \sim \mathbb{W}'_\mathtt{X}$ and $\mathbb{W}_\mathtt{X} \longmapsto^+ \mathbb{W}'_\mathtt{X}$.

$$\frac{\mathbb{W}_\mathtt{X}.\mathbb{C}_\mathtt{X} = \mathbb{C}_{\mathsf{VM}} \quad \mathbb{W}_\mathtt{X}.\mathtt{pc}_\mathtt{X} = \mathtt{fetch} \quad \alpha(\mathbb{W}, \mathbb{W}_\mathtt{X}.\mathbb{H}_\mathtt{X})}{\mathbb{W} \sim \mathbb{W}_\mathtt{X}}$$

Fig. 14. Simulation Relation

$$\frac{\begin{array}{c}\mathbb{H}_{\mathtt{x}} = \mathbb{H}_{\mathtt{xc}} \uplus \mathbb{H}_{\mathtt{xh}} \uplus \mathbb{H}_{\mathtt{xk}} \uplus \mathbb{H}_{\mathtt{xkc}} \uplus \mathbb{H}_{\mathtt{xp}} \uplus \mathbb{H}_{\mathtt{xo}} \\ \mathbb{H}_{\mathtt{xc}}(\mathtt{f} \times 4) = \mathbb{C}(\mathtt{f}),\ \forall \mathtt{f} \in [0, \mathtt{max}(\mathbb{C})] \quad \mathbb{H}_{\mathtt{xh}}(l \times 2) = \mathbb{H}(l),\ \forall l \in [0, \mathtt{max}(\mathbb{H})] \\ \mathbb{H}_{\mathtt{xk}}(l \times 2) = \mathbb{K}(l),\ \forall l \in [0, \mathtt{max}(\mathbb{K})] \quad \mathbb{H}_{\mathtt{xkc}}(l \times 2) = \mathbb{K}_c(l),\ \forall l \in [0, \mathtt{max}(\mathbb{K}_c)] \\ \mathbb{H}_{\mathtt{xp}}(0) = \mathtt{pc} \quad \mathbb{H}_{\mathtt{xp}}(2) = \mathtt{top}(\mathbb{K}) \quad \mathbb{H}_{\mathtt{xp}}(4) = \mathtt{top}(\mathbb{K}_c)\end{array}}{\alpha(\mathbb{W},\ \mathbb{W}_{\mathtt{x}}.\mathbb{H}_{\mathtt{x}})}$$

Fig. 15. The Memory Map Relation

We use "Plus" simulation relation to describe the bytecode interpretation of VM. This relation shows that CertVM implementation is satisfied with BCM operational semantics. Once we carry out the simulation relation proof, we get a certified virtual machine.

The Memory Relation. As mentioned before, the code heap, memory heap, evaluation stack and function call stack of bytecode machine are all stored as arrays in x86 machine memory heap. These arrays are denoted as $\mathbb{H}_{\mathtt{xc}}, \mathbb{H}_{\mathtt{xh}}, \mathbb{H}_{\mathtt{xk}}$ and $\mathbb{H}_{\mathtt{xkc}}$ respectively. In addition, $\mathbb{H}_{\mathtt{xp}}$ denotes the memory chunk that stores the value of $\mathtt{pc}, \mathtt{sp}$ and $\mathtt{csp}$, and $\mathbb{H}_{\mathtt{xo}}$ denotes the free memory space.

The exact configuration of this memory heap partition is defined as follows:

$$\begin{array}{ll}\mathbb{H}_{\mathtt{xc}} & \triangleq \mathbb{H}_{\mathtt{x}}[\mathtt{base}(\mathbb{H}_{\mathtt{xc}}), (\mathtt{base}(\mathbb{H}_{\mathtt{xc}}) + \mathtt{max}(\mathbb{C}) \times 4)] \\ \mathbb{H}_{\mathtt{xh}} & \triangleq \mathbb{H}_{\mathtt{x}}[\mathtt{base}(\mathbb{H}_{\mathtt{xh}}), (\mathtt{base}(\mathbb{H}_{\mathtt{xh}}) + \mathtt{max}(\mathbb{H}) \times 2)] \\ \mathbb{H}_{\mathtt{xk}} & \triangleq \mathbb{H}_{\mathtt{x}}[\mathtt{base}(\mathbb{H}_{\mathtt{xk}}), (\mathtt{base}(\mathbb{H}_{\mathtt{xk}}) + \mathtt{max}(\mathbb{K}) \times 2)] \\ \mathbb{H}_{\mathtt{xkc}} & \triangleq \mathbb{H}_{\mathtt{x}}[\mathtt{base}(\mathbb{H}_{\mathtt{xkc}}), (\mathtt{base}(\mathbb{H}_{\mathtt{xkc}}) + \mathtt{max}(\mathbb{K}_c) \times 2)] \\ \mathbb{H}_{\mathtt{xp}} & \triangleq \mathbb{H}_{\mathtt{x}}[\mathtt{base}(\mathbb{H}_{\mathtt{xp}}), (\mathtt{base}(\mathbb{H}_{\mathtt{xkc}}) + 6)]\end{array}$$

Note that every bytecode instruction is 4 bytes long, and so it occupies $\mathtt{max}(\mathbb{C}) \times 4$ cells in $\mathbb{H}_{\mathtt{x}}$. And every item of $\mathbb{K}$ and $\mathbb{K}_c$ is only 2 bytes long. Therefore, the map relation between x86 machine memory heap and bytecode world is defined in Figure 15.

Proof by Simulation. From CertVM implementation, we know that the entry point of every bytecode is label `fetch`. To prove its correctness, we only have to show "simulation relation" is achieved when CertVM jumps to `fetch`, and the bytecode world defined in this relation has its successive state. Thus, we use the specification language of SCAP to describe this simulation relation.

Suppose the specification at `fetch` is $(p_{\mathtt{C}}, g_{\mathtt{C}})$:

$$\begin{array}{ll}p_{\mathtt{C}} & \triangleq \lambda \mathbb{S}_{\mathtt{x}}, \exists \mathbb{W}.\alpha(\mathbb{W}, \mathbb{S}_{\mathtt{x}}.\mathbb{H}_{\mathtt{x}}) \wedge \mathit{Enable}(c, \mathbb{S}, \mathbb{K}_c) \text{ where } \mathbb{W} = (\mathbb{C}, \mathbb{S}, \mathbb{K}_c, \mathtt{pc}) \wedge c = \mathbb{C}(pc) \\ g_{\mathtt{C}} & \triangleq \lambda \mathbb{S}'_{\mathtt{x}}, \exists \mathbb{W}, \mathbb{W}'.\mathbb{W} \rightarrow \mathbb{W}' \wedge \alpha(\mathbb{W}, \mathbb{S}_{\mathtt{x}}.\mathbb{H}_{\mathtt{x}}) \wedge \alpha(\mathbb{W}', \mathbb{S}'_{\mathtt{x}}.\mathbb{H}_{\mathtt{x}})\end{array}$$

$p_{\mathtt{C}}$ means that before executing `fetch`, the x86 machine world should maintain the simulation relation with a bytecode world that can transit to its next step. And $g_{\mathtt{C}}$ ensures that after interpreting a bytecode instruction, the simulation relation is still held. Thus, we only need to use the inference rules of SCAP to prove that:

$$\Psi_{\mathtt{xc}} \vdash \{[\![(p_{\mathtt{C}},\ g_{\mathtt{C}})]\!]\}\, \mathtt{fetch}:\ \mathbb{C}_{\mathtt{VM}}[\mathtt{fetch}].$$

where $\Psi_{\mathtt{xc}} = \{(\mathtt{fetch}, [\![(p_{\mathtt{C}}, g_{\mathtt{C}})]\!]), (\mathtt{f}, [\![(p_{\mathtt{C}}, g_{\mathtt{C}})]\!])\}$, `f` is the entry point in dispatch table for bytecode `c`. By the well-formedness of code heap module $\mathbb{C}_{\mathtt{VM}}[\mathtt{fetch}]$, we can conclude that the CertVM is a well-formed virtual machine.

Theorem 2 (Soundness Theorem). For all bytecode program $\mathbb{W}$ and x86 program $\mathbb{W}_X$, if $\Psi \vdash \{s\}\mathbb{W}$ and $\mathsf{WFVM}(\mathbb{W}, \mathbb{W}_X)$, there exists specification Ψ_X and assertion s_X such that $\Psi_X \vdash \{s_X\}\mathbb{W}_X$.

Well-formed bytecode program guarantees that every instruction can be executed, while the CBP inference rules guarantee that the properties are still held in the new program state. With WFVM, we know that for every bytecode execution step, there is a well-formed x86 code heap. The SCAP logic guarantees that all well-formed x86 code heaps be linked into one single well-formed global one.

4 Example and Implementation

A factorial function implemented with while loop and non-local variables and its caller are shown in this section to demonstrate the particular features of our logic, and to show how to write specification and how to prove bytecode programs with CBP. Actually, the only work a programmer needs to do is to prove bytecode programs with CBP. Then this logic system guarantees that a well-formed bytecode program will runs on CertVM without getting stuck provided the x86 machine works.

4.1 Modular Certification: Factorial Function

Get Instruction Sequences. Factorial function source code and the bytecode program with its specifications for BCM are shown in Figure 1 (Section 1). Finding the instruction sequence is the first step to certify a program. From the definition in Figure 2, we know that an instruction sequence is a set of instructions ending with unconditional jump jmp or function return ret. Thus, it can be seen that there are three instruction sequences in while loop program. The instructions with labels 0~2 form the first instruction block. And the second one is the instructions with label from 3 to 10. And the last one is the block of remain instructions.

Write Specification for Instruction Sequences. Then the programmer needs to give code heap specification Ψ, which is a finite mapping from code labels $\mathtt{f}$ to code specifications $\mathtt{s}$ which is a pair (p, g). CBP specifications for code heap are embedded in the code, enclosed by -{} in shadow box. Specifications of this example are given in Figure 16. To simplify our presentation, we write the predicate p in the form of a proposition with free variables referring to components of the state $\mathbb{S}$.

Following the inference rules, the code specifications should be given for these points: the head of a instruction sequence, the target labels of function call instruction call and

$$
\begin{array}{ll}
\mathsf{p}_{pre} \triangleq (\mathtt{valid}\mathbb{K}\ 2\ \mathbb{K}) \wedge (\mathtt{valid}\mathbb{K}_c\ 0\ \mathbb{K}_c) \wedge (\mathtt{validRa}\quad \mathbb{K}_c) & \\
\mathsf{p}_0 \triangleq \mathsf{p}_{pre} \wedge ((r \rightsquigarrow \_) * (\exists i >= 0,\ n \mapsto i)), & \mathsf{g}_0 \triangleq \mathsf{p}_0 \rightarrow (\mathbb{H}'(\mathsf{r}) = \mathbb{H}(\mathsf{n})!) \\
\mathsf{p}_3 \triangleq \mathsf{p}_{pre} \wedge ((\mathbb{H}(r) >= 1) \wedge (\mathbb{H}(n) >= 0)), & \mathsf{g}_3 \triangleq \mathsf{p}_3 \rightarrow (\mathbb{H}'(\mathsf{r}) = \mathbb{H}(\mathsf{r}) * \mathbb{H}(\mathsf{n})!) \\
\mathsf{p}_{11} \triangleq \mathsf{p}_3, & \mathsf{g}_{11} \triangleq \mathsf{g}_3
\end{array}
$$

Fig. 16. Specifications: While Loop Example

jump instructions (including goto and brture), and the function call return address which is just after call instruction call.

The specification of the this procedure is given as (p_0, g_0). From p_0, we know that the values of variables r and n stored in memory heap are inside the proper scope. The guarantee g_0 specifies the behavior of the function: the non-local variables r and n fulfill $(\mathbb{H}'(r) = \mathbb{H}(n)!)$.

(p_3, g_3) is the assertion for while loop body. The pre-condition p_3 means that the values of variables r and n are still inside the proper scope. The guarantee g_3 says that the result which is stored in memory heap must fulfill the loop fixpoint. The specification (p_{11}, g_{11}) at the begin point of this while loop is equal to (p_3, g_3).

Certify and Link Them Together. To check the well-formedness of an instruction sequence beginning with ι, a programmer should apply the appropriate inference rules and find intermediate assertions such as (p', g'), which serves both as the post-condition for ι and the pre-condition for the remaining instruction sequence.

After that, a programmer is also required to establish the well-formedness of each individual module via the CDHP rule. Two non-intersecting well-formed code heaps can then be linked together via the LINK rule. The WLD rule requires that all code heaps be linked into one single well-formed global one.

Support Modular Certification. All the code specifications Ψ used in CBP rules are the *local* specifications for the current module. Thus, CBP supports modular reasoning about function call/return in the sense that caller and callee can be in different modules and be certified separately. When specifying the callee procedure, we do not need any knowledge about the return address in its pre-condition. The RET rule for the instruction "ret" does not have any constraints on the return address.

4.2 Modular Certification: Caller of Factorial Function

Source code and bytecode program with specification of the caller for the while loop factorial example are shown in Figure 17.

This function just initializes the variables n, and then calls function factor. The specification at the entry point is (p_{16}, g_{16}). The pre-condition p_{16} simply says that the memory cells for variables n and r are there for this function to run. The guarantee g_{16}

```
//function caller   | -{(p16, g16)}    ;spec for caller
void caller(){      | 16 pushc 3       ;push imm 3
  int n=3;          | 17 pop n         ;n = 3
  call factor;      | 18 call 0        ;call factor()
}                   | -{(p19, g19)}    ;spec for return point
                    | 19 ret           ;caller return
```

$$p'_{pre} \triangleq (\mathtt{valid}\mathbb{K}\ 2\ \mathbb{K}) \wedge (\mathtt{valid}\mathbb{K}_c\ 1\ \mathbb{K}_c) \wedge (\mathtt{validRa}\ \ \mathbb{K}_c)$$

$$p_{16} \triangleq p'_{pre} \wedge ((r \rightsquigarrow \_) * (n \rightsquigarrow \_)), \qquad g_{16} \triangleq p_{16} \rightarrow (\mathbb{H}'(r) = 3!)$$

$$p_{19} \triangleq p'_{pre} \wedge ((r \mapsto 3!) * n \mapsto 0)), \qquad g_{19} \triangleq p_{19} \rightarrow (\mathbb{H}'(r) = 3!)$$

$$p_0 \triangleq ?, \qquad g_0 \triangleq ?$$

Fig. 17. Caller of Factorial Function

specifies the behavior of the caller procedure: the result r in memory heap is the factorial of 3. The specification of the return point is (p_{19}, g_{19}). p_{19} means that the memory cells for variables n and r are still there. The guarantee g_{19} is just the same as g_{16}.

From CAL inference rule, we know that the specification of the callee's entry point should be added. The specification (p_0, g_0) in Figure 16 can be used. Furthermore, the specification of function entry point defines its interface. A Caller can invoke any callees which share the same interface.

4.3 Implementation with Coq

Our logic system presented in this paper has been applied to bytecode programs for our verified stack-based virtual machine. We have formalized BCM, its operational semantics, and the program logic CBP. We have also formalized a X86 machine, its operational semantics, and the SCAP program logic for it in the Coq proof assistant. With SCAP logic, we proved the simulation relations of our virtual machine CertVM.

The syntax of our machine (both the bytecode machine and x86 machine), is encoded in Coq using inductive definitions. Operational semantics of the machine and all the inference rules of program logic are defined as inductive relations. The soundness of the framework itself is formalized and certified in Coq following the syntactic approach.

These examples are usually implemented directly in bytecode and are hard to certify using the existing approaches. Manually optimized bytecode or code generated by optimizing compilers can also be certified using our systems. The proof is also formalized and implemented in Coq and is machine-checkable.

The Coq implementation has taken several months per person, out of which a significant amount of efforts have been put on the implementation of basic facilities, including lemmas and tactics for partial mappings and Separation Logic assertions. These common facilities are independent of the task of certifying examples. The implementation of CBP logic system includes around 3200 lines of Coq encoding of BCM and its operational semantics, 1000 lines encoding of CBP rules and the soundness proof. We have written more than 15 thousand lines of Coq tactics to certify CertVM with SCAP logic. We also have written about 1500 lines of Coq tactics to certify practical bytecode examples, including the while-loop and function call/return.

Compared the experiences in CBP with that in SCAP, we found that the code size ratios of bytecode programs to proofs and assembly code to proofs looks almost the same.

Component Name	Number of lines
Basic Utility Definitions & Lemmas	2,367
BCM Machine & Operational Semantics	3,285
CBP Rules & Soundness	1,032
X86 Machine & SCAP logic	2,710
CertVM Memory Layout & Proof	15,429
Bytecode Examples Source Code Spec. & Proof	1,469
Total	26,292

Fig. 18. The Verified Package in Coq

While bytecode is a fairly compact format compared to native code. Most JVM instructions use only 1 or 2 bytes. Moreover, they are sophisticated instructions that cannot be translated into a single native processor instruction as a rule. In fact, our CertVM expand code size by the factor of 15, while most Java compilers expand code size by a factor of 5 to 10 [23]. With our logic, we only write proof for bytecode programs rather than write proof for the corresponding assembly code directly. So the workload will be greatly reduced by a factor of 5 to 10. That will be a significant improvement for fully certified subroutines with machine checkable proofs.

Extensions and Future Work. The support of object-oriented features such as objects, references, methods, and inheritance are important and useful. Extension of the program logic to support exception handling is straightforward and interesting work. Following the similar idea of function call/return, reasoning about exceptions is not much different from reasoning about functions. Our logic system does not support concurrency yet. It is actually an easy work to extend the machine to support concurrency. But it is difficult to define a simple logic system to modularly certify concurrent bytecode programs. We will try it in the near future.

On the certified virtual machine, there are also some interesting extensions. Verification of the useful features such as memory management, just in-time compilation, garbage collectors will lead to some exciting challenges.

5 Related Works and Conclusion

Logic for Bytecode and Virtual Machine. Quigley [18] has demonstrated that it is possible to define a Hoare-style logic for bytecode programs to prove the program containing loops. A program logic [2] which combines Hoare triples for methods with instruction specifications is presented for a Java-like bytecode language by Bannwart and Müller. Their logic supports lots of object-oriented features such as objects, references, methods, and inheritance. Benton [4] proposed a typed, compositional logic for a stack-based abstract machine to verify bytecode programs which are written in an imperative subset of .NET CIL.

But, all these work only considered logic system for bytecode programs. None of them took the virtual machine into account. Linking certified bytecode programs with certified VM is very difficult. An open logic framework was designed to integrate [9] the proof of different logic systems for the X86 machine only. In this paper, we integrate the separated proof modules of different logic systems for different machine by simulation relation proof. To our best knowledge, our logic system is the first facility to link certified virtual machine with modularly certified bytecode programs.

Reasoning about Control Stacks. Reasoning about control stacks is extremely difficult for low-level code programs. STAL and its variations [22] can only treat return code pointers as first-class code pointers and stacks as "closures". Tan and Appel [21] use the implicit finite unions structure to study the low-level language. As a result, they arrived at continuation-style Hoare logic explainable by indexed model, with a rather convoluted interpretation of Hoare triples involving explicit fixpoint approximations. Saabas and Uustalu [19] introduced a compositional natural semantics and Hoare logic based on the implicit finite unions structure for a simple low-level language with expressions. Ni and Shao's work [17] combines the syntactic approach used in type systems with logic systems to support code pointer specification. Following the producer/consumer model, Feng *etc.* [10] proposed SCAP to modularly certify assembly code with stack-based control abstractions. Benton's typed, compositional logic for bytecode programs uses a higher-level abstract machine with separate data stack and control stack.

We build a Hoare-style logic system to certify bytecode programs which run on verified virtual machine. As the examples shown, program with complex control stack operations can be certified within our logic. Our BCM is a higher-level machine with a dedicated function call stack. It looks like Benton's abstract machine. While our logic system CBP is established following SCAP's producer/consumer stack model. This idea brings much convenience to the integration of SCAP and CBP proof.

Certified Compiler and Interpreter. Large efforts have been made on building reliable compiler and interpreter with formal methods. Leagure *etc.* built a type preserving Java compiler [13] and Chen *etc.* developed a type preserving optimizing compiler for MSIL [5]. Chlipala presented a certified compiler from the simply-typed lambda calculus to assembly language [6]. C0 compiler [14], a compiler from C subset language C0 to the DLX machine language, is formally specified and proved in Isabelle/HOL. The realistic and verified CompCert compiler [15], is developed and verified in Coq. But all these work only focus on semantics preserving without well-formed properties of source programs. Barthe *etc.*'s certificate translation provides a means to transfer the benefits of source code verification to code consumers using PCC architectures [3].

With the formalization and the certification of the simulation relation, our work gives a logic system to link the verified bytecode programs with the verified execution environment. Based on FPCC architectures, our method guarantees that a certified bytecode program runs on certified virtual machine will never get stuck as long as hardware works. It's an end-to-end solution and can be considered as one of the proof and semantics preserving compilers.

Conclusion. This paper presents a logic system to verify the bytecode programs on JVM. The main feature of the approach is that its verification not only takes the bytecode programs, but also the VM into account. The paper also discusses some results on using Coq to verify several small examples. To certify a bytecode program, a programmer's task is only required to find the specification and establish the well-formedness of individual bytecode module. This logic system guarantees that a certified bytecode program will run on the certified VM without getting stuck unless hardware faults occur. Our work provides a logic system for reasoning about bytecode programs for stack-based virtual machine and makes an advance toward building a proof-transforming compilation environment.

Acknowledgments

The authors thank anonymous referees for suggestions and comments on an earlier version of this paper. We also thank Prof. Zhong Shao of Yale, Dr. Xinyu Feng of TTI-Chicago, Dr. Gang Tan of Lehigh University, and Dr. Juan Chen of Microsoft for useful discussions about FPCC. This work is supported in part by National Natural

Science Foundation of China (No. 90818019 and 90816006), Hi-Tech Research and Development Program of China (No. 2008AA01Z102 and 2009AA011902). Any opinions, findings, and contributions contained in this document are those of the authors and do not reflect the views of these agencies.

References

[1] Appel, A.W.: Foundational proof-carrying code. In: Proc. 16th IEEE Symposium on Logic in Computer Science, pp. 247–258. IEEE Computer Society, Los Alamitos (2001)
[2] Bannwart, F., Müller, P.: A program logic for bytecode. In: Proceedings of Bytecode?5. Electronic Notes in Theoretical Computer Science, pp. 255–273. Elsevier, Amsterdam (2005)
[3] Barthe, G., Grégoire, B., Kunz, C., Rezk, T.: Certificate translation for optimizing compilers. ACM Transactions on Programming Languages and Systems 31(5), 18:1–18:45 (2009)
[4] Benton, N.: A typed, compositional logic for a stack-based abstract machine. In: Yi, K. (ed.) APLAS 2005. LNCS, vol. 3780, pp. 364–380. Springer, Heidelberg (2005)
[5] Chen, J., Hawblitzel, C., Perry, F., Emmi, M., Condit, J., Coetzee, D., Pratikaki, P.: Type-preserving compilation for large-scale optimizing object-oriented compilers. In: Prog. Lang. Design and Impl (PLDI 2008), pp. 183–192. ACM, New York (2008)
[6] Chlipala, A.: A certified type-preserving compiler from lambda calculus to assembly language. In: Prog. Lang. Design and Impl (PLDI 2007), pp. 54–65. ACM, New York (2007)
[7] Coq Development Team. The Coq proof assistant reference manual. Version 8.2 (2008)
[8] ECMA. Standard ECMA-335 Common Language Infrastructure (2006)
[9] Feng, X., Ni, Z., Shao, Z., Guo, Y.: An open framework for foundational proof-carrying code. In: Proc. 2007 Workshop on Types in Lang. Design and Impl., pp. 67–78 (2007)
[10] Feng, X., Shao, Z., Vaynberg, A., Xiang, S., Ni, Z.: Modular verification of assembly code with stack-based control abstractions. In: Prog. Lang. Design and Impl (PLDI 2006), pp. 401–414. ACM Press, New York (2006)
[11] Hoare, C.A.R.: An axiomatic basis for computer programming. Communications of the ACM 26(1), 53–56 (1969)
[12] Lawton, K., Denney, B., Guarneri, N.D., Ruppert, V., Bothamy, C.: Bochs user manual (2008), `http://bochs.sourceforge.net/`
[13] League, C., Shao, Z., Trifonov, V.: Precision in practice: A type-preserving java compiler. In: Hedin, G. (ed.) CC 2003. LNCS, vol. 2622, pp. 106–120. Springer, Heidelberg (2003)
[14] Leinenbach, D., Paul, W., Petrova, E.: Towards the formal verification of a c0 compiler: Code generation and implementation correctnes. In: SEFM 2005: Proceedings of the Third IEEE International Conference on Software Engineering and Formal Methods, Washington, DC, USA, pp. 2–12. IEEE Computer Society, Los Alamitos (2005)
[15] Leroy, X.: A formally verified compiler back-end. Draft (2008), `http://pauillac.inria.fr/~leroy/publi/compcert-backend.pdf`
[16] Lindholm, T., Yellin, F.: The java virtual machine specification, 2nd edn. (1999)
[17] Ni, Z., Shao, Z.: Certified assembly programming with embedded code pointers. In: POPL 2006, pp. 320–333 (2006)
[18] Quigley, C.L.: A programming logic for java bytecode programs. In: Proc. of 16th Int. Conf. on Theorem Proving in Higher-Order Logics, pp. 41–54. Springer, Heidelberg (2003)
[19] Saabas, A., Uustalu, T.: Compositional type systems for stack-based low-level languages. In: Proc. of 12th Computing, Australasian Theory Symp., Australian, pp. 27–39 (2006)
[20] Sun Microsystem. Top25 bugs (2009), `http://bugs.sun.com/bugdatabase/top25_bugs.do/`

[21] Tan, G., Appel, A.W.: A compositional logic for control flow. In: Emerson, E.A., Namjoshi, K.S. (eds.) VMCAI 2006. LNCS, vol. 3855, pp. 80–94. Springer, Heidelberg (2006)
[22] Vanderwaart, J.C., Crary, K.: A typed interface for garbage collection. In: Types in Lang. Design and Impl (TLDI 2003), pp. 109–122 (2003)
[23] Weiss, M., de Ferrire, F., Delsart, B., Fabre, C., Hirsch, F., Johnson, E.A., Joloboff, V., Roy, F., Siebert, F., Spengler, X.: Turboj, a java bytecode-to-native compiler. In: Müller, F., Bestavros, A. (eds.) LCTES 1998. LNCS, vol. 1474, pp. 119–130. Springer, Heidelberg (1998)

Asymptotic Resource Usage Bounds

Elvira Albert[1], Diego Alonso[1], Puri Arenas[1], Samir Genaim[1], and German Puebla[2]

[1] DSIC, Complutense University of Madrid, E-28040 Madrid, Spain
[2] CLIP, Technical University of Madrid, E-28660 Boadilla del Monte, Madrid, Spain

Abstract. When describing the resource usage of a program, it is usual to talk in *asymptotic* terms, such as the well-known "big O" notation, whereby we focus on the behaviour of the program for large input data and make a rough approximation by considering as equivalent programs whose resource usage grows at the same rate. Motivated by the existence of *non-asymptotic* resource usage analyzers, in this paper, we develop a novel transformation from a non-asymptotic cost function (which can be produced by multiple resource analyzers) into its asymptotic form. Our transformation aims at producing tight asymptotic forms which do not contain *redundant* subexpressions (i.e., expressions asymptotically subsumed by others). Interestingly, we integrate our transformation at the heart of a cost analyzer to generate asymptotic *upper bounds* without having to first compute their non-asymptotic counterparts. Our experimental results show that, while non-asymptotic cost functions become very complex, their asymptotic forms are much more compact and manageable. This is essential to improve scalability and to enable the application of cost analysis in resource-aware verification/certification.

1 Introduction

A fundamental characteristics of a program is the amount of resources that its execution will require, i.e., its *resource usage.* Typical examples of resources include execution time, memory watermark, amount of data transmitted over the net, etc. *Resource usage analysis* [15,14,8,2,9] aims at automatically estimating the resource usage of programs. Static resource analyzers often produce *cost bound functions*, which have as input the size of the input arguments and return bounds on the resource usage (or *cost*) of running the program on such input.

A well-known mechanism for keeping the size of cost functions manageable and, thus, facilitate human manipulation and comparison of cost functions is *asymptotic analysis*, whereby we focus on the behaviour of functions for large input data and make a rough approximation by considering as equivalent functions which grow at the same rate w.r.t. the size of the input date. The asymptotic point of view is basic in computer science, where the question is typically how to describe the resource implication of scaling-up the size of a computational problem, beyond the "toy" level. For instance, the big O notation is used to define *asymptotic upper bounds*, i.e, given two functions f and g which map natural numbers to real numbers, one writes $f \in O(g)$ to express the fact that there is a natural constant $m \geq 1$

Z. Hu (Ed.): APLAS 2009, LNCS 5904, pp. 294–310, 2009.

and a real constant $c > 0$ s.t. for any $n \geq m$ we have that $f(n) \leq c * g(n)$. Other types of (asymptotic) computational complexity estimates are lower bounds ("Big Omega" notation) and asymptotically tight estimates, when the asymptotic upper and lower bounds coincide (written using "Big Theta"). The aim of *asymptotic resource usage analysis* is to obtain a cost function f_a which is *syntactically simple* s.t. $f_n \in O(f_a)$ (correctness) and ideally also that $f_a \in \Theta(f_n)$ (accuracy), where f_n is the non-asymptotic cost function.

The scopes of non-asymptotic and asymptotic analysis are complementary. Non-asymptotic bounds are required for the estimation of precise execution time (like in WCET) or to predict accurate memory requirements [4]. The motivations for inferring asymptotic bounds are twofold: (1) They are essential during program development, when the programmer tries to reason about the efficiency of a program, especially when comparing alternative implementations for a given functionality. (2) Non-asymptotic bounds can become unmanageably large expressions, imposing huge memory requirements. We will show that asymptotic bounds are syntactically much simpler, can be produced at a smaller cost, and, interestingly, in cases where their non-asymptotic forms cannot be computed.

The main techniques presented in this paper are applicable to obtain asymptotic versions of the cost functions produced by any cost analysis, including lower, upper and average cost analyses. Besides, we will also study how to perform a tighter integration with an upper bound solver which follows the classical approach to static cost analysis by Wegbreit [15]. In this approach, the analysis is parametric w.r.t. a *cost model*, which is just a description of the resources whose usage we should measure, e.g., time, memory, calls to a specific function, etc. and analysis consists of two phases. (1) First, given a program and a cost model, the analysis produces *cost relations* (CRs for short), i.e., a system of recursive equations which capture the resource usage of the program for the given cost model in terms of the sizes of its input data. (2) In a second step, *closed-form*, i.e., non-recursive, upper bounds are inferred for the CRs. How the first phase is performed is heavily determined by the programming language under study and nowadays there exist analyses for a relatively wide range of languages (see, e.g., [2,8,14] and their references). Importantly, such first phase remains the same for both asymptotic and non-asymptotic analyses and thus we will not describe it. The second phase is language-independent, i.e., once the CRs are produced, the same techniques can be used to transform them to closed-form upper bounds, regardless of the programming language used in the first phase. The important point is that this second phase can be modified in order to produce asymptotic upper bounds directly. Our main contributions can be summarized as follows:

1. We adapt the notion of *asymptotic complexity* to cover the analysis of realistic programs whose limiting behaviour is determined by the limiting behaviour of its loops.
2. We present a novel transformation from *non-asymptotic cost functions* into asymptotic form. After some syntactic simplifications, our transformation detects and eliminates subterms which are *asymptotically subsumed* by others while preserving the complexity order.

3. In order to achieve motivation (2), we need to integrate the above transformation within the process of obtaining the cost functions. We present a tight integration into (the second phase of) a resource usage analyzer to generate directly asymptotic upper bounds without having to first compute their non-asymptotic counterparts.
4. We report on a prototype implementation within the COSTA system [3] which shows that we are able to achieve motivations (1) and (2) in practice.

2 Background: Non-asymptotic Upper Bounds

In this section, we recall some preliminary definitions and briefly describe the method of [1] for converting *cost relations* (CRs) into upper bounds in *closed-form*, i.e., without recurrences.

2.1 Cost Relations

Let us introduce some notation. The sets of natural, integer, real, non-zero natural and non-negative real values are denoted respectively by $\mathbb{N}$, $\mathbb{Z}$, $\mathbb{R}$, $\mathbb{N}^+$ and $\mathbb{R}^+$. We write x, y, and z, to denote variables which range over $\mathbb{Z}$. A *linear expression* has the form $v_0 + v_1x_1 + \ldots + v_nx_n$, where $v_i \in \mathbb{Z}$, $0 \leq i \leq n$. Similarly, a *linear constraint* (over $\mathbb{Z}$) has the form $l_1 \leq l_2$, where l_1 and l_2 are linear expressions. For simplicity we write $l_1 = l_2$ instead of $l_1 \leq l_2 \wedge l_2 \leq l_1$, and $l_1 < l_2$ instead of $l_1 + 1 \leq l_2$. The notation $\bar{t}$ stands for a sequence of entities $t_1, \ldots, t_n$, for some $n{>}0$. We write φ, ϕ or ψ, to denote sets of linear constraints which should be interpreted as the conjunction of each element in the set and $\varphi_1 \models \varphi_2$ to indicate that the linear constraint φ_1 implies the linear constraint φ_2. Now, the basic building blocks of cost relations are the so-called *cost expressions* e which can be generated using this grammar:

$$e ::= r \mid \mathsf{nat}(l) \mid e + e \mid e * e \mid e^r \mid \log(\mathsf{nat}(l)) \mid n^{\mathsf{nat}(l)} \mid \max(S)$$

where $r \in \mathbb{R}^+$, $n \in \mathbb{N}^+$, l is a linear expression, S is a non empty set of cost expressions, $\mathsf{nat} : \mathbb{Z} \rightarrow \mathbb{N}$ is defined as $\mathsf{nat}(v){=}\max(\{v, 0\})$, and the base of the log is 2 (since any other base can be rewritten to 2). Observe that linear expressions are always wrapped by nat as we explain below.

Example 1. Consider the simple Java method m shown in Fig. 1, which invokes the auxiliary method g, where x is a linked list of boolean values implemented

```
static void m(List x, int i, int n){
  while (i<n){
    if (x.data) {g(i,n); i++;}
    else {g(0,i); n=n-1;}
    x=x.next;
}}
```

(1) $\langle C_m(i,n) = 3$
$\quad , \varphi_1 = \{i \geq n\}\rangle$
(2) $\langle C_m(i,n) = 15 + C_g(i,n) + C_m(i',n)$
$\quad , \varphi_2 = \{i < n, i' = i+1\}\rangle$
(3) $\langle C_m(i,n) = 17 + C_g(0,i) + C_m(i,n')$
$\quad , \varphi_3 = \{i < n, , n' = n-1\}\rangle$

Fig. 1. Java method and CR

in the standard way. For this method, the COSTA analyzer outputs the cost expression $C_m^+=6+\mathsf{nat}(n-i)*\max(\{21+5*\mathsf{nat}(n-1), 19+5*\mathsf{nat}(n-i)\})$ as an upper bound on the number of *bytecode* instructions that m executes. Each Java instruction is compiled to possibly several bytecode instructions, but this is not relevant to this work. We are assuming that an upper bound on the number of executed instructions in g is $C_g^+(a,b)=4+5*\mathsf{nat}(b-a)$. Observe that the use of nat is required in order to avoid incorrectly evaluating upper bounds to negative values. When $i \geq n$, the cost associated to the recursive cases has to be nulled out, this effect is achieved with $\mathsf{nat}(n-i)$ since it will evaluate to 0. □

W.l.o.g., we formalize our mechanism by assuming that all recursions are *direct* (i.e., all cycles are of length one). Direct recursion can be automatically achieved by applying *Partial Evaluation* [11] (see [1] for the technical details).

Definition 1 (Cost Relation). *A cost relation system $\mathcal{S}$ is a set of equations of the form $\langle C(\bar{x}) = e + \sum_{i=1}^{k} D_i(\bar{y}_i), \varphi\rangle$ with $k \geq 0$, where C and D_i are cost relation symbols, all variables $\bar{x}$ and $\bar{y}_i$ are distinct variables; e is a cost expression; and φ is a set of linear constraints over $\bar{x} \cup vars(e) \bigcup_{i=1}^{k} \bar{y}_i$.*

Example 2. The *cost relation* (CR for short) associated to method m is shown in Fig. 1 (right). The relations C_m and C_g capture, respectively, the costs of the methods m and g. Intuitively, in CRs, variables represent the sizes of the corresponding data structures in the program and in the case of integer variables they represent their integer value. Eq. 1 is a base case and captures the case where the loop body is not executed. It can be observed that we have two recursive equations (Eq. 2 and Eq. 3) which capture the respective costs of the then and else branches within the while loop. As the list x has been abstracted to its length, the values of x.data are not visible in the CR and the two equations have the same (incomplete) guard, which results in a non-deterministic CR. Also, variables which do not affect the cost (e.g., x) do not appear in the CR. How to automatically obtain a CR from a program is the subject of the first phase of cost analysis as described in Sec. 1. More details can be found in [2,8,14,15]. □

2.2 Non-asymptotic Upper-Bounds

We now describe the approach of [1] to infer the upper bound of Ex. 1 from the equations in Ex. 2. It starts by computing upper bounds for CRs which do not depend on any other CRs, referred to as *standalone cost relations*, and continues by replacing the computed upper bounds on the equations which call such relations. For instance, after computing the upper bound for g shown in Ex. 1, the cost relation in Ex. 2 becomes standalone:

$$(1)\ \langle C_m(i,n) = 3 \quad , \varphi_1 = \{i \geq n\}\rangle$$
$$(2)\ \langle C_m(i,n) = 15 + \mathsf{nat}(n-i) + C_m(i',n) \quad , \varphi_2 = \{i < n, i' = i+1\}\rangle$$
$$(3)\ \langle C_m(i,n) = 17 + \mathsf{nat}(i) + C_m(i,n') \quad , \varphi_3 = \{i < n, n' = n-1\}\rangle$$

Given a standalone CR made up of nb base cases of the form $\langle C(\bar{x}){=}base_j, \varphi_j\rangle$, $1{\leq}j{\leq}nb$ and nr recursive equations of the form, $\langle C(\bar{x}){=}rec_j{+}\sum_{i=1}^{k_j} C(\bar{y}_i), \varphi_j\rangle$, $1{\leq}j{\leq}nr$, an upper bound can be computed as:

$$(*) \quad C(\bar{x})^{+} = \mathsf{l_b} * worst(\{base_1, \ldots, base_{nb}\}) + \mathsf{l_r} * worst(\{rec_1, \ldots, rec_{nr}\})$$

where $\mathsf{l_b}$ and $\mathsf{l_r}$ are, respectively, upper bounds of the number of visits to the base cases and recursive equations and $worst(\{Set\})$ denotes the worst-case (the maximum) value that the expressions in Set can take. Below, we describe the method in [1] to approximate the above upper bound.

Bounds on the Number of Application of Equations. The first dimension of the problem is to bound the maximum number of times an equation can be applied. This can be done by examining the structure of the CR (i.e., the number of explicit recursive calls in the equations), together with how the values of the arguments change when calling recursively (i.e., the linear constraints).

We first explain the problem for equations that have at most one recursive call in their bodies. In the above CR, when calling C_m recursively in (2), the first argument i of C_m increases by 1 and in (3) the second argument n decreases by 1. Now suppose that we define a function $f(a,b) = b - a$. Then, we can observe that $\varphi_2 \models f(i,n) > f(i',n) \wedge f(i,n) \geq 0$ and $\varphi_3 \models f(i,n) > f(i,n') \wedge f(i,n) \geq 0$, i.e, for both equations we can guarantee that they will not be applied more than $\mathsf{nat}(f(i_0,n_0)) = \mathsf{nat}(n_0 - i_0)$ times, where i_0 and n_0 are the initial values for the two variables. Functions such as f are usually called *ranking functions* [13]. Given a cost relation $C(\bar{x})$, we denote by $f_C(\bar{x})$ a ranking function for all loops in C. Now, consider that we add an equation that contains two recursive calls:

$$(4)\ \langle C_m(i,n) = C_m(i,n') + C_m(i,n') \ \ , \ \varphi_4 = \{i < n, n' = n-1\}\rangle$$

then the recursive equations would be applied in the worst-case $\mathsf{l_r} = 2^{\mathsf{nat}(n-i)} - 1$ times, which in this paper, we simplify to $\mathsf{l_r} = 2^{\mathsf{nat}(n-i)}$ to avoid having negative constants that do not add any technical problem to asymptotic analysis. This is because each call generates 2 recursive calls, and in each call the argument n decreases at least by 1. In addition, unlike the above examples, the base-case equation would be applied in the worst-case an exponential number of times. In general, a CR may include several base-case and recursive equations whose guards, as shown in the example, are not necessarily mutually exclusive, which means that at each evaluation step there are several equations that can be applied. Thus, the worst-case of applications is determined by the fourth equation, which has two recursive calls, while the worst cost of each application will be determined by the first equation, which contributes the largest direct cost. In summary, the bounds on the number of application of equations are computed as follows:

$$\mathsf{l_r} = \begin{cases} \mathsf{nr}^{\mathsf{nat}(f_C(\bar{x}))} & \text{if } \mathsf{nr} > 1 \\ \mathsf{nat}(f_C(\bar{x})) & \text{otherwise} \end{cases} \qquad \mathsf{l_b} = \begin{cases} \mathsf{nr}^{\mathsf{nat}(f_C(\bar{x}))} & \text{if } \mathsf{nr} > 1 \\ 1 & \text{otherwise} \end{cases}$$

where nr is the maximum number of recursive calls which appear in a single equation. A fundamental point to note is that the (linear) combination of variables which approximates the number of iterations of loops is wrapped by nat. This will influence our definition of asymptotic complexity. In logarithmic cases, we can further refine the ranking function and obtain a tighter upper bound. If each recursive equation satisfies $\varphi_j \models f_C(\bar{x}) \geq k * f_C(\bar{y}_i)$, $1 \leq i \leq nr$, where $k>1$ is a constant, then we can infer that $\mathsf{l_r}$ is bounded by $\lceil \log_k(\mathsf{nat}(f_C(\bar{x}))+1) \rceil$, as each time the value of the ranking function decreases by k. For instance, if we replace φ_2 by $\varphi_2'=\{i<n, i'=i*2\}$ and φ_3 by $\varphi_3'=\{i<n, n'=n/2\}$ (and remove equation 4) then the method of [1] would infer that $\mathsf{l_r}$ is bound by $\lceil \log_k(\mathsf{nat}(n-i)+1) \rceil$.

Bounds on the Worst Cost of Equations. As it can be observed in the above example, in each application the corresponding equation might contribute a non-constant number of cost units. Therefore, it is not trivial to compute the worst-case (the maximum) value of all of them. In order to infer the maximum value of such expressions automatically, [1] proposes to first infer *invariants* (linear relations) between the equation's variables and the initial values. For example, the cost relation $C_m(i,n)$ admits as invariant for the recursive equations the formula $\mathcal{I}$ defined as $\mathcal{I}((i_0,n_0),(i,n)) \equiv i \geq i_0 \wedge n \leq n_0 \wedge i < n$, which captures that the values of i (resp. n) are greater (resp. smaller) or equal than the initial value and that i is smaller than n at all iterations. Once we have the invariant, we can *maximize* the expressions w.r.t. these values and take the maximal:

$$worst(\{rec_1,\ldots,rec_{nr}\}) = \max(maximize(\mathcal{I},\{rec_1,\ldots,rec_{nr}\}))$$

The operator *maximize* receives an invariant $\mathcal{I}$ and a set of expressions to be maximized and computes the maximal value of each expression independently and returns the corresponding set of maximized expressions in terms of the initial values (see [1] for the technical details). For instance, in the original CR (without Eq. (4)), we compute $worst(\{rec_1, rec_2\}) = \max(maximize(\mathcal{I}, \{\mathsf{nat}(n-i), \mathsf{nat}(i)\}))$ which results in $worst(\{rec_1, rec_2\}) = \max(\{\mathsf{nat}(n_0 - i_0), \mathsf{nat}(n_0 - 1)\})$. The same procedure can be applied to the expressions in the base cases. However, it is unnecessary in our example, because the base case is a constant and therefore requires no maximization. Altogether, by applying Equation (*) to the standalone CR above we obtain the upper bounds shown in Ex. 1.

Inter-Procedural. In the above examples, all CRs are standalone and do not call any other equations. In the general case, a cost relation can contain k calls to external relations and n recursive calls: $\langle C(\bar{x}) = e + \sum_{i=1}^{k} D_i(\bar{y}_i) + \sum_{j=1}^{n} C(\bar{z}_j), \varphi \rangle$ with $k \geq 0$. After computing the upper bounds $D_i^+(\bar{y}_i)$ for the standalone CRs, we replace the computed upper bounds on the equations which call such relations, i.e., $\langle C(\bar{x}) = e + \sum_{i=1}^{k} D_i^+(\bar{y}_i) + \sum_{j=1}^{n} C(\bar{z}_j), \varphi \rangle$.

3 Asymptotic Notation for Cost Expressions

We now present extended versions of the standard definition of the asymptotic notations *big O* and *big Theta*, which handle functions with multiple input arguments, i.e., functions of the form $\mathbb{N}^n \mapsto \mathbb{R}^+$.

Definition 2 (big O, big Theta). *Given two functions $f, g : \mathbb{N}^n \mapsto \mathbb{R}^+$, we say that $f \in O(g)$ iff there is a real constant $c > 0$ and a natural constant $m \geq 1$ such that, for any $\bar{v} \in \mathbb{N}^n$ such that $v_i \geq m$, it holds that $f(\bar{v}) \leq c * g(\bar{v})$. Similarly, $f \in \Theta(g)$ iff there are real constants $c_1 > 0$ and $c_2 > 0$ and a natural constant $m \geq 1$ such that, for any $\bar{v} \in \mathbb{N}^n$ such that $v_i \geq m$, it holds that $c_1 * g(\bar{v}) \leq f(\bar{v}) \leq c_2 * g(\bar{v})$.*

The big O refers to asymptotic upper bounds and the big Θ to asymptotically tight estimates, when the asymptotic upper and lower bounds coincide. The asymptotic notations above assume that the value of the function increases with the values of the input such that the function, unless it has a constant asymptotic order, takes the value ∞ when the input is ∞. This assumption does not necessarily hold when CRs are obtained from realistic programs. For instance, consider the loop in Fig. 1. Clearly, the execution cost of the program increases by increasing the number of iterations of the loop, i.e., $n-i$, the ranking function. Therefore, in order to observe the limiting behavior of the program we should study the case when $\mathsf{nat}(n-i)$ goes to ∞, i.e., when, for example, n goes to ∞ and i stays constant, but not when both n and i go to ∞. In order to capture this asymptotic behaviour, we introduce the notion of nat-free cost expression, where we transform a cost expression into another one by replacing each nat-expression with a variable. This guarantees that we can make a consistent usage of the definition of asymptotic notation since, as intended, after some threshold m, larger values of the input variables result in larger values of the function.

Definition 3 (nat-free cost expressions). *Given a set of cost expression $E = \{e_1, \ldots, e_n\}$, the* nat*-free representation of E, is the set $\tilde{E} = \{\tilde{e}_1, \ldots, \tilde{e}_n\}$ which is obtained from E in four steps:*

1. *Each* nat*-expression $\mathsf{nat}(a_1x_1 + \cdots + a_nx_n + c) \in E$ which appears as an exponent is replaced by $\mathsf{nat}(a_1x_1 + \cdots + a_nx_n)$;*
2. *The rest of* nat*-expressions $\mathsf{nat}(a_1x_1 + \cdots + a_nx_n + c) \in E$ are replaced by $\mathsf{nat}(\frac{a_1}{b}x_1 + \cdots + \frac{a_n}{b}x_n)$, where b is the* greatest common divisor *(gcd) of $|a_1|, \ldots, |a_n|$, and $|\cdot|$ stands for the absolute value;*
3. *We introduce a fresh (upper-case) variable per syntactically different nat-expression.*
4. *We replace each* nat*-expression by its corresponding variable.*

Cases 1 and 2 above have to be handled separately because if $\mathsf{nat}(a_1x_1 + \cdots + a_nx_n + c)$ is an exponent, we can remove the c, but we cannot change the values of any a_i. E.g., $2^{\mathsf{nat}(2x+1)} \notin O(2^{\mathsf{nat}(x)})$. This is because $4^x \notin O(2^x)$. Hence, we cannot simplify $2^{\mathsf{nat}(2x)}$ to $2^{\mathsf{nat}(x)}$. In the case that $\mathsf{nat}(a_1x_1 + \cdots + a_nx_n + c)$ does not appear as an exponent, we can remove c and normalize all a_i by dividing them by the *gcd* of their absolute values. This allows reducing the number of variables which are needed for representing the nat-expressions. It is done by using just one variable for all nat expressions whose linear expressions are *parallel* and grow in the same direction. Note that removing the independent term plus dividing all constants by the gcd of their absolute values provides a canonical representation for linear expressions. They satisfy this property iff their canonical representation is the same. This allows transforming both $\mathsf{nat}(2x{+}3)$ and $\mathsf{nat}(3x{+}5)$ to $\mathsf{nat}(x)$, and $\mathsf{nat}(2x{+}4y)$ and $\mathsf{nat}(3x{+}6y)$ to $\mathsf{nat}(x{+}2y)$.

Example 3. Given the following cost function:

$$5{+}7{*}\mathsf{nat}(3x+1){*}\max(\{100{*}\mathsf{nat}(x)^2{*}\mathsf{nat}(y)^4, 11{*}3^{\mathsf{nat}(y-1)}{*}\mathsf{nat}(x+5)^2\}){+}$$
$$2{*}\log(\mathsf{nat}(x+2)){*}2^{\mathsf{nat}(y-3)}{*}\log(\mathsf{nat}(y+4)){*}\mathsf{nat}(2x{-}2y)$$

Its nat-free representation is:

$$5{+}7*A{*}\max(\{100*A^2{*}B^4, 11*3^B{*}A^2\}){+}2{*}\log(A){*}2^B*\log(B){*}C$$

where A corresponds to $\mathsf{nat}(x)$, B to $\mathsf{nat}(y)$ and C to $\mathsf{nat}(x{-}y)$. □

Definition 4. *Given two cost expressions e_1, e_2 and its nat-free correspondence $\tilde{e}_1, \tilde{e}_2$, we say that $e_1{\in}O(e_2)$ (resp. $e_1{\in}\Theta(e_2)$) if $\tilde{e}_1{\in}O(\tilde{e}_2)$ (resp. $\tilde{e}_1{\in}\Theta(\tilde{e}_2)$).*

The above definition lifts Def. 2 to the case of cost expressions. Basically, it states that in order to decide the asymptotic relations between two cost expressions, we should check the asymptotic relation of their corresponding nat-free expressions. Note that by obtaining their nat-free expressions simultaneously we guarantee that the same variables are syntactically used for the same linear expressions.

In some cases, a cost expression might come with a set of constraints which specifies a class of input values for which the given cost expression is a valid bound. We refer to such set as *context constraint*. For example, the cost expression of Ex. 3 might have $\varphi{=}\{x{\geq}y, x{\geq}0, y{\geq}0\}$ as context constraint, which specifies that it is valid only for non-negative values which satisfy $x{\geq}y$. The context constraint can be provided by the user as an input to cost analysis, or collected from the program during the analysis.

The information in the context constraint φ associated to the cost expression can sometimes be used to check whether some nat-expressions are guaranteed to be asymptotically larger than others. For example, if the context constraint states that $x \geq y$, then when both $\mathsf{nat}(x)$ and $\mathsf{nat}(y)$ grow to the infinite we have that $\mathsf{nat}(x)$ asymptotically subsumes $\mathsf{nat}(y)$, this information might be useful in order to obtain more precise asymptotic bounds. In what follows, given two nat-expressions (represented by their corresponding nat-variables A and B), we say that $\varphi{\models}A \succeq B$ if A asymptotically subsumes B when both go to ∞.

4 Asymptotic Orders of Cost Expressions

As it is well-known, by using Θ we can partition the set of all functions defined over the same domain into *asymptotic orders*. Each of these orders has an infinite number of members. Therefore, to accomplish the motivations in Sect. 1 it is required to use one of the elements with simpler syntactic form. Finding a good representative of an asymptotic order becomes a complex problem when we deal with functions made up of non-linear expressions, exponentials, polynomials, and logarithms, possibly involving several variables and associated constraints. For example, given the cost expression of Ex. 3, we want to automatically infer the asymptotic order "$3^{\mathsf{nat}(y)} * \mathsf{nat}(x)^3$".

Apart from simple optimizations which remove constants and normalize expressions by removing parenthesis, it is essential to remove *redundancies*, i.e., subexpressions which are asymptotically subsumed by others, for the final expression to be as small as possible. This requires effectively comparing subexpressions of different lengths and possible containing multiple complexity orders. In this section, we present the basic definitions and a mechanism for transforming non-asymptotic cost expressions into non-redundant expressions while preserving the asymptotic order. Note that this mechanism can be used to transform the output of any cost analyzer into an non-redundant, asymptotically equivalent one. To the best of our knowledge, this is the first attempt to do this process in a fully automatic way. Given a cost expression e, the transformations are applied on its $\tilde{e}$ representation, and only afterwards we substitute back the nat-expressions, in order to obtain an asymptotic order of e, as defined in Def. 4.

4.1 Syntactic Simplifications on Cost Expressions

First, we perform some syntactic simplifications to enable the subsequent steps of the transformation. Given a nat-free cost expression $\tilde{e}$, we describe how to simplify it and obtain another nat-free cost expression $\tilde{e}'$ such that $\tilde{e} \in \Theta(\tilde{e}')$. In what follows, we assume that $\tilde{e}$ is not simply a constant or an arithmetic expression that evaluates to a constant, since otherwise we simply have $\tilde{e} \in O(1)$. The first step is to transform $\tilde{e}$ by removing constants and max expressions, as described in the following definition.

Definition 5. *Given a* nat*-free cost expression $\tilde{e}$, we denote by $\tau(\tilde{e})$ the cost expression that results from $\tilde{e}$ by: (1) removing all constants; and (2) replacing each subexpression $max(\{\tilde{e}_1, \ldots, \tilde{e}_m\})$ by $(\tilde{e}_1 + \ldots + \tilde{e}_m)$.*

Example 4. Applying the above transformation on the nat-free cost expression of Ex. 3 results in: $\tau(\tilde{e}) = A*(A^2*B^4 + 3^B*A^2) + \log(A)*2^B*\log(B)*C$. □

Lemma 1. $\tilde{e} \in \Theta(\tau(\tilde{e}))$

Once the τ transformation has been applied, we aim at a further simplification which safely removes sub-expressions which are asymptotically subsumed by other sub-expressions. In order to do so, we first transform a given cost expression into a *normal form* (i.e., a sum of products) as described in the following definition, where we use *basic* nat*-free cost expression* to refer to expressions of the form 2^{r*A}, A^r, or $\log(A)$, where r is a real number. Observe that, w.l.o.g., we assume that exponentials are always in base 2. This is because an expression n^A where $n > 2$ can be rewritten as $2^{\log(n)*A}$.

Definition 6 (normalized nat-free cost expression). *A normalized* nat*-free cost expression is of the form $\Sigma_{i=1}^{n} \Pi_{j=1}^{m_i} b_{ij}$ such that each b_{ij} is a basic* nat*-free cost expression.*

Since $b_1 * b_2$ and $b_2 * b_1$ are equal, it is convenient to view a product as the multiset of its elements (i.e., basic nat-free cost expressions). We use the letter M to denote such multi-set. Also, since M_1+M_2 and M_2+M_1 are equal, it is convenient to view the sum as the multi-set of its elements, i.e., products (represented as multi-sets). Therefore, a normalized cost expression is a multi-set of multi-sets of basic cost expressions. In order to normalize a nat-free cost expression $\tau(\tilde{e})$ we will repeatedly apply the distributive property of multiplication over addition in order to get rid of all parenthesis in the expression.

Example 5. The normalized expression for $\tau(\tilde{e})$ of Ex. 4 is $A^3*B^4+2^{\log(3)*B}*A^3+\log(A)*2^B*\log(B)*C$ and its multi-set representation is $\{\{A^3,B^4\},\{2^{\log(3)*B},A^3\},\{\log(A),2^B,\log(B),C\}\}$ □

4.2 Asymptotic Subsumption

Given a normalized nat-free cost expression $\tilde{e}=\{M_1,\ldots,M_n\}$ and a context constraint φ, we want to remove from $\tilde{e}$ any product M_i which is *asymptotically subsumed* by another product M_j, i.e., if $M_j \in \Theta(M_j+M_i)$. Note that this is guaranteed by $M_i \in O(M_j)$. The remaining of this section defines a decision procedure for deciding if $M_i \in O(M_j)$. First, we define several *asymptotic subsumption templates* for which it is easy to verify that a single basic nat-free cost expression b subsumes a complete product. In the following definition, we use the auxiliary functions pow and deg of basic nat-free cost expressions which are defined as: $\mathsf{pow}(2^{r*A})=r$, $\mathsf{pow}(A^r)=0$, $\mathsf{pow}(\log(A))=0$, $\mathsf{deg}(A^r)=r$, $\mathsf{deg}(2^{r*A})=\infty$, and $\mathsf{deg}(\log(A))=0$. In a first step, we focus on basic nat-free cost expression b with one variable and define when it asymptotically subsumes a set of basic nat-free cost expressions (i.e., a product). The product might involve several variables but they must be subsumed by the variable in b.

Lemma 2 (asymptotic subsumption). *Let b be a basic* nat*-free cost expression, $M=\{b_1,\cdots,b_m\}$ a product, φ a context constraint, $vars(b)=\{A\}$ and $vars(b_i)=\{A_i\}$. We say that M is asymptotically subsumed by b, i.e., $\varphi \models M \in O(b)$ if for all $1 \le i \le m$ it holds that $\varphi \models A \succeq A_i$ and one of the following holds:*

1. *if $b=2^{r*A}$, then*
   (a) $r > \Sigma_{i=1}^{m}\mathsf{pow}(b_i)$; or
   (b) $r \ge \Sigma_{i=1}^{m}\mathsf{pow}(b_i)$ and every b_i is of the form $2^{r_i*A_i}$;
2. *if $b=A^r$, then*
   (a) there is no b_i of the form $\log(A_i)$, then $r \ge \Sigma_{i=1}^{m}\mathsf{deg}(b_i)$; or
   (b) there is at least one b_i of the form $\log(A_i)$, and $r \ge 1+\Sigma_{i=1}^{m}\mathsf{deg}(b_i)$
3. *if $b=\log(A)$, then $m=1$ and $b_1=\log(A_1)$*

Let us intuitively explain the lemma. For exponentials, in point 1a, we capture cases such as $3^A=2^{\log(3)*A}$ asymptotically subsumes $2^A*A^2*\ldots*\log(A)$ where in "..." we might have any number of polynomial or logarithmic expressions. In 1b, we ensure that 3^A does not embed $3^A*A^2*\log(A)$, i.e., if the power is the same, then we cannot have additional expressions. For polynomials, 2a captures that the largest degree is the upper bound. Note that an exponential would introduce an ∞ degree. In 2b, we express that there can be many logarithms and still the maximal polynomial is the upper bound, e.g., A^2 subsumes $A * \log(A) * \log(A) * \ldots * \log(A)$. In 3, a logarithm only subsumes another logarithm.

Example 6. Let $b = A^3$, $M = \{\log(A), \log(B), C\}$, where A, B and C corresponds to $\mathsf{nat}(x)$, $\mathsf{nat}(y)$ and $\mathsf{nat}(x-y)$ respectively. Let us assume that the context constraint is $\varphi = \{x \geq y, x \geq 0, y \geq 0\}$. M is asymptotically subsumed by b since $\varphi \models (A \succeq B) \wedge (A \succeq C)$, and condition 2b in Lemma 2 holds. □

The basic idea now is that, when we want to check the subsumption relation on two expression M_1 and M_2 we look for a partition of M_2 such that we can prove the subsumption relation of each element in the partition by a different basic nat-free cost expression in M_1. Note that M_1 can contain additional basic nat-free cost expressions which are not needed for subsuming M_2.

Lemma 3. *Let M_1 and M_2 be two products, and φ a context constraint. If there exists a partition of M_2 into k sets $P_1, \ldots, P_k$, and k distinct basic* nat*-free cost expressions $b_1, \ldots, b_k \in M_1$ such that $P_i \in O(b_i)$, then $M_2 \in O(M_1)$.*

Example 7. Let $M_1 = \{2^{\log(3)*B}, A^3\}$ and $M_2 = \{\log(A), 2^B, \log(B), C\}$, with the context constraint φ as defined in Ex. 6. If we take $b_1 = 2^{\log(3)*A}$, $b_2 = A^3$, and partition M_2 into $P_1 = \{2^B\}$, $P_2 = \{\log(A), \log(B), C\}$ then we have that $P_1 \in O(b_1)$ and $P_2 \in O(b_2)$. Therefore, by Lemma 3, $M_2 \in O(M_1)$. Also, for $M_2' = \{A^3, B^4\}$ we can partition it into $P_1' = \{B^4\}$ and $P_2' = \{A^3\}$ such that $P_1' \in O(b_1)$ and $P_2' \in O(b_2)$ and therefore we also have that $M_2' \in O(M_1)$. □

Definition 7 (asymp). *Given a cost expression e, the overall transformation* asymp *takes e and returns the cost expression that results from removing all subsumed products from the normalized expression of $\tau(\tilde{e})$, and then replace each* nat*-variable by the corresponding* nat*-expression.*

Example 8. Consider the normalized cost expression of Ex. 5. The first and third products can be removed, since they are subsumed by the second one, as explained in Ex. 7. Then $\mathtt{asymp}(e)$ would be $2^{\log(3)*\mathsf{nat}(y)} * \mathsf{nat}(x)^3 = 3^{\mathsf{nat}(y)} * \mathsf{nat}(x)^3$, and it holds that $e \in \Theta(\mathtt{asymp}(e))$. □

In the following theorem, we ensure that after eliminating the asymptotically subsumed products, we preserve the asymptotic order.

Theorem 1 (soundness). *Given a cost expression e and a context constraint φ, then $\varphi \models e \in \Theta(\mathtt{asymp}(e))$.*

4.3 Implementation in COSTA

We have implemented our transformation and it can be used as a back-end of existing non-asymptotic cost analyzers for average, lower and upper bounds (e.g., [9,2,12,5,7]), and regardless of whether it is based on the approach to cost analysis of [15] or any other. We plan to distribute it as free software soon.

Currently, it can be tried out through a web interface available from the COSTA web site: `http://costa.ls.fi.upm.es`. COSTA is an abstract interpretation-based COSt and Termination Analyzer for Java bytecode which receives as input a bytecode program and (a choice of) a resource of interest, and tries to obtain an upper bound of the resource consumption of the program.

In our first experiment, we use our implementation to obtain asymptotic forms of the upper bounds on the memory consumption obtained by [4] for the JOlden suite [10]. This benchmark suite was first used by [6] in the context of memory usage verification and is becoming a standard to evaluate memory usage analysis [5,4]. None of the previous approaches computes asymptotic bounds. We are able to obtain accurate asymptotic forms for all benchmarks in the suite and the transformation time is negligible (less than 0.1 milliseconds in all cases). As a simple example, for the benchmark `em3d`, the non-asymptotic upper bound is $8*\mathsf{nat}(d-1)*\mathsf{nat}(b)+8*\mathsf{nat}(d)+8*\mathsf{nat}(b)+56*\mathsf{nat}(d-1)+16*\mathsf{nat}(c)+73$ and we transform it to $\mathsf{nat}(d)*\mathsf{nat}(b)+\mathsf{nat}(c)$. The remaining examples can be tried online in the above `url`.

5 Generation of Asymptotic Upper Bounds

In this section we study how to perform a tighter integration of the asymptotic transformation presented Sec. 4 within resource usage analyses which follow the classical approach to static cost analysis by Wegbreit [15]. To do this, we reformulate the process of inferring upper bounds sketched in Sect. 2.2 to work directly with asymptotic functions at all possible (intermediate) stages. The motivation for doing so is to reduce the huge amount of memory required for constructing non-asymptotic bounds and, in the limit, to be able to infer asymptotic bounds in cases where their non-asymptotic forms cannot be computed.

Asymptotic CRS. The first step in this process is to transform cost relations into asymptotic form before proceeding to infer upper bounds for them. As before, we start by considering standalone cost relations. Given an equation of the form $\langle C(\bar{x})=e+\sum_{i=1}^{k} C(\bar{y}_i), \varphi\rangle$ with $k \geq 0$, its associated *asymptotic* equation is $\langle C_A(\bar{x})=\mathsf{asymp}(e)+\sum_{i=1}^{k} C_A(\bar{y}_i), \varphi\rangle$. Given a cost relation C, its asymptotic cost relation C_A is obtained by applying the above transformation to all its equations. Applying the transformation at this level is interesting in order to simplify both the process of computing the worst case cost of the recursive equations and the base cases when computing Eq. $(*)$ as defined in Sect. 2.2.

Example 9. Consider the following CR:

$$\begin{array}{l}\langle C(a,b) = \underline{\mathsf{nat}(a+1)^2} \ , \ \{a\geq 0, b\geq 0\}\rangle \\ \langle C(a,b) = \underline{\mathsf{nat}(a-b)+\log(\mathsf{nat}(a-b))}+C(a',b') \ , \ \{a\geq 0, b\geq 0, a'=a-2, b'=b+1\}\rangle \\ \langle C(a,b) = \underline{2^{\mathsf{nat}(a+b)}+\mathsf{nat}(a)*\log(\mathsf{nat}(a))}+C(a',b') \ , \ \{a\geq 0, b\geq 0, a'=a+1, b'=b-1\}\rangle\end{array}$$

By replacing the underlined expressions by their corresponding `asymp` expressions as explained in Theorem 1, we obtain the asymptotic relation:

$\langle C_A(a,b) = \mathsf{nat}(a)^2 \ , \ \{a{\geq}0, b{\geq}0\}\rangle$
$\langle C_A(a,b) = \mathsf{nat}(a{-}b){+}C_A(a',b') \ , \ \{a{\geq}0, b{\geq}0, a'{=}a{-}2, b'{=}b{+}1\}\rangle$
$\langle C_A(a,b) = 2^{\mathsf{nat}(a+b)}{+}C_A(a',b') \ , \ \{a{\geq}0, b{\geq}0, a'{=}a{+}1, b'{=}b{-}1\}\rangle$

In addition to reducing their sizes, the process of maximizing the nat expressions is more efficient since there are fewer nat expressions in the asymptotic CR. □

An important point to note is that, while we can remove all constants from e, it is essential that we keep the constants in the size relations φ to ensure soundness. This is because they are used to infer the ranking functions and to compute the invariants, and removing such constants might introduce imprecision and more important soundness problems as we explain in the following examples.

Example 10. The above relation admits a ranking function $f(a,b){=}\mathsf{nat}(2a + 3b{+}1)$ which is used to bound the number of applications of the recursive equations. Clearly, if we remove the constants in the size relations, e.g., transform $a'{=}a{-}2$ into $a'{=}a$, the resulting relation is non-terminating and we cannot find a ranking function. Besides, removing constants from constraints which are not necessarily related to the ranking function also might result in incorrect invariants. For example, changing $n'{=}n{+}1$ to $n'{=}n$ in the following equation:

$$\langle C(m,n) = \mathsf{nat}(n) + C(m',n') \ , \ \{m{>}0, m'{<}m, n'{=}n{+}1\}\rangle$$

would result in an invariant which states that the value of n is always equal to the initial value n_0, which in turn leads to the upper-bound $\mathsf{nat}(m_0){*}\mathsf{nat}(n_0)$ which is clearly incorrect. A possible correct upper-bound is $\mathsf{nat}(m_0){*}\mathsf{nat}(n_0 + m_0)$ which captures that the value of $\mathsf{nat}(n)$ increases up to $\mathsf{nat}(n_0{+}m_0)$. □

Asymptotic Upper Bounds. Once the standalone CR is put into asymptotic form, we proceed to infer an upper bound for it as in the case of non-asymptotic CRs and then we apply the transformation to the result. Let $C_A(\bar{x})$ be an asymptotic cost relation. Let $C_A^+(\bar{x})$ be its upper bound computed as defined in Eq. $(*)$. Its asymptotic upper bound is $C_{asymp}^+(\bar{x}) = \mathtt{asymp}(C_A^+(\bar{x}))$. Observe that we are computing $C_A^+(\bar{x})$ in a non-asymptotic fashion, i.e., we do not apply asymp to each $\mathsf{l_b}$, $\mathsf{l_r}$, *worst* in $(*)$, but only to the result of combining all elements. We could apply asymp to the individual elements and then to the result of their combination again. In practice, it almost makes no difference as this operation is really inexpensive.

Example 11. Consider the second CR of Ex. 9. The analyzer infers the invariant $\mathcal{I} = \{0{\leq}a{\leq}a_0, 0{\leq}b{\leq}b_0, a{\geq}0, b{\geq}0\}$, from which we maximize $\mathsf{nat}(a)^2$ to $\mathsf{nat}(a_0)^2$, $\mathsf{nat}(a{-}b)$ to $\mathsf{nat}(a_0)$ (since the maximal value occurs when b becomes 0), and $2^{\mathsf{nat}(a+b)}$ to $2^{\mathsf{nat}(a_0+b_0)}$. The number of applications of the recursive equations is $\mathsf{nat}(2a_0{+}3b_0{+}1)$ (see Ex. 10). By applying Eq. $(*)$, we obtain the upper bound: $C_A^+(a,b) = \mathsf{nat}(2a{+}3b{+}1) * \max(\{\mathsf{nat}(a), 2^{\mathsf{nat}(a+b)}\}) + \mathsf{nat}(a)^2$. Applying asymp to the above upper bound results in: $C_{asymp}^+(a,b) = 2^{\mathsf{nat}(a+b)} * \mathsf{nat}(2a + 3b)$. □

Inter-procedural. The practical impact of integrating the asymptotic transformation within the solving method comes when we consider relations with calls to external relations and compose their asymptotic results. This is because, when the number of calls and equations grow, the fact that we manipulate more compact asymptotic expressions is fundamental to enable the scalability of the system. Consider a cost relation with k calls to external relations and n recursive calls: $\langle C(\bar{x}){=}e{+}\sum_{i=1}^{k} D_i(\bar{y}_i){+}\sum_{j=1}^{n} C(\bar{z}_j), \varphi\rangle$ with $k \geq 0$. Let $D^+_{i_{asymp}}(\bar{y}_i)$ be the asymptotic upper bound for $D_i(\bar{y}_i)$. $C^+_{asymp}(\bar{x})$ is the asymptotic upper bound of the standalone relation $\langle C(\bar{x}){=}e{+}\sum_{i=1}^{k} D^+_{i_{asymp}}(\bar{y}_i){+}\sum_{j=1}^{n} C(\bar{z}_j), \varphi\rangle$.

Theorem 2 (soundness). $C^+(\bar{x}) \in O(C^+_{asymp}(\bar{x}))$.

Note that the soundness theorem, unlike Th. 1, guarantees only that the asymptotic expression is O and not Θ. Let us show an example.

Example 12. Consider $ub{=}\mathsf{nat}(a{-}b{+}1){*}2^{\mathsf{nat}(c)}{+}5$ and $\mathtt{asymp}(ub){=}\mathsf{nat}(a{-}b){*}2^{\mathsf{nat}(c)}$. Plugging ub in a context where $b{=}a{+}1$ results in 5 (since then $\mathsf{nat}(a{-}b{+}1)$ $=0$). Plugging $\mathtt{asymp}(ub)$ in the same context results in $2^{\mathsf{nat}(c)}$ which is clearly less precise. □

Intuitively, the source of the loss of precision is that, when we compute the asymptotic upper bound, we are looking at the cost in the limiting behavior only and we might miss a particular point in which such cost becomes zero. In our experience, this does not happen often and it could be easily checked before plugging in the asymptotic result, replacing the upper bound by zero.

5.1 Experimental Results on Scalability

In this section, we aim at studying how the size of cost expressions (non-asymptotic vs. asymptotic) increases when larger CRs are used, i.e., the scalability of our approach. To do so, we have used the benchmarks of [1] shown in Table 1. These benchmarks are interesting because they cover the different complexity order classes, as it can be seen, the benchmarks range from constant to exponential complexity, including polynomial and divide and conquer. The source code of such programs is also available at the COSTA web site.

As in [1], in order to assess the scalability of the approach, we have connected together the CRs for the different benchmarks by introducing a call from each CR to the one appearing immediately above it in the table. Such call is always introduced in a recursive equation. Column **#Eq** shows the number of equations in the corresponding benchmarks. Reading this column top-down, we can see that when we analyze BST we have 31 equations. Then, for Fibonacci, the number of equations is 39, i.e., its 8 equations plus the 31 which have been previously accumulated. Progressively, each benchmark adds its own number of equations to the one above. Thus, in the last row we have a CR with all the equations connected, i.e., we compute an upper bound of a CR with at least 20 nested loops and 385 equations.

Columns $\mathbf{T}_{ub}$ and $\mathbf{T}_{aub}$ show, respectively, the times of composing the non-asymptotic and asymptotic bounds, after discarding the time common part for both, i.e., computing the ranking functions and the invariants. It can be observed

Table 1. Scalability of asymptotic cost expressions

Bench.	$\mathbf{T}_{ub}$	$\mathbf{T}_{aub}$	$\mathbf{Size}_{ub}$	$\mathbf{Size}_{aub}$	**#Eq**	$\frac{\mathbf{Size}_{ub}}{\mathbf{\#Eq}}$	$\frac{\mathbf{Size}_{aub}}{\mathbf{\#Eq}}$	$\frac{\mathbf{Size}_{ub}}{\mathbf{Size}_{aub}}$
BST	0	0	23	4	31	0.74	0.13	5.75
Fibonacci	0	0	47	9	39	1.21	0.23	5.22
Hanoi	0	0	67	14	48	1.39	0.29	4.78
MatMult	0	0	152	38	67	2.27	0.56	4.00
Delete	0	4	320	65	100	3.20	0.65	4.92
FactSum	4	4	717	95	117	6.12	0.81	7.54
SelectOrd	0	4	1447	155	136	10.63	1.14	9.33
ListInter	4	16	3804	257	173	21.98	1.48	14.80
EvenDigits	4	20	7631	400	191	39.95	2.09	19.07
Cons	12	32	15268	585	214	71.34	2.73	26.09
Power	24	40	24265	588	223	108.81	2.63	41.26
MergeList	96	60	48536	828	245	198.10	3.37	58.61
ListRev	140	76	48545	829	254	191.12	3.26	58.55
Incr	×	112	×	1126	282	×	3.99	×
Concat	×	164	×	1538	296	×	5.19	×
ArrayRev	×	232	×	2127	305	×	6.97	×
Factorial	×	284	×	2130	314	×	6.78	×
DivByTwo	×	328	×	2135	323	×	6.60	×
Polynomial	×	436	×	2971	346	×	8.58	×
MergeSort	×	440	×	3234	385	×	8.40	×

that the times are negligible from BST to EvenDigits, which are the simplest benchmarks and also have few equations. The interesting point is that when cost expressions start to be considerably large, $\mathbf{T}_{ub}$ grows significantly, while $\mathbf{T}_{aub}$ remains small. This is explained by the sizes of the expressions they handle, as we describe below. For the columns that contain "×", COSTA has not been able to compute a non-asymptotic upper bound because the underlying Prolog process has run out of memory.

Columns $\mathbf{Size}_{ub}$ and $\mathbf{Size}_{aub}$ show, respectively, the sizes of the computed non-asymptotic and asymptotic upper bounds. This is done by regarding the upper bound expression as a tree and counting its number of nodes, i.e., each operator and each operand is counted as one. As for the time, the sizes are quite small for the simplest benchmarks, and they start to increase from SelectOrd. Note that for these examples, the size of the non-asymptotic upper bounds is significantly larger than the asymptotic. Columns $\frac{\mathbf{Size}_{ub}}{\mathbf{\#Eq}}$ and $\frac{\mathbf{Size}_{aub}}{\mathbf{\#Eq}}$ show, resp., the size of the non-asymptotic and asymptotic bounds per equation. The important point is that while this ratio seems to grow exponentially for non-asymptotic upper bounds, $\frac{\mathbf{Size}_{aub}}{\mathbf{\#Eq}}$ grows much more slowly. We believe that this demonstrates that our approach is scalable, even if the implementation is still preliminary.

6 Conclusions and Future Work

We have presented a general asymptotic resource usage analysis which can be combined with existing non-asymptotic analyzers by simply adding our transformation as a back-end or, interestingly, integrated into the mechanism for obtaining upper bounds of recurrence relations. This task has been traditionally done manually in the context of complexity analysis. When it comes to apply it to an automatic analyzer for a real-life language, there is a need to develop the techniques to infer asymptotic bounds in a precise and effective way. To the best of our knowledge, our work is the first one which presents a generic and fully automatic approach. In future work, we plan to adapt our general framework to infer asymptotic lower-bounds on the cost and also to integrate our work into a proof-carrying code infrastructure.

Acknowledgments. This work was funded in part by the Information Society Technologies program of the European Commission, Future and Emerging Technologies under the IST-231620 *HATS* project, by the MEC under the TIN-2008-05624 *DOVES* and HI2008-0153 (Acción Integrada) projects, by the UCM-BSCH-GR58/08-910502 (GPD-UCM) , and the CAM under the S-0505/TIC/0407 *PROMESAS* project.

References

1. Albert, E., Arenas, P., Genaim, S., Puebla, G.: Automatic Inference of Upper Bounds for Recurrence Relations in Cost Analysis. In: Alpuente, M., Vidal, G. (eds.) SAS 2008. LNCS, vol. 5079, pp. 221–237. Springer, Heidelberg (2008)
2. Albert, E., Arenas, P., Genaim, S., Puebla, G., Zanardini, D.: Cost Analysis of Java Bytecode. In: De Nicola, R. (ed.) ESOP 2007. LNCS, vol. 4421, pp. 157–172. Springer, Heidelberg (2007)
3. Albert, E., Arenas, P., Genaim, S., Puebla, G., Zanardini, D.: COSTA: Design and Implementation of a Cost and Termination Analyzer for Java Bytecode. In: de Boer, F.S., Bonsangue, M.M., Graf, S., de Roever, W.-P. (eds.) FMCO 2007. LNCS, vol. 5382, pp. 113–132. Springer, Heidelberg (2008)
4. Albert, E., Genaim, S., Gómez-Zamalloa, M.: Live Heap Space Analysis for Languages with Garbage Collection. In: ISMM. ACM Press, New York (2009)
5. Braberman, V., Fernández, F., Garbervetsky, D., Yovine, S.: Parametric Prediction of Heap Memory Requirements. In: ISMM. ACM Press, New York (2008)
6. Chin, W.-N., Nguyen, H.H., Qin, S., Rinard, M.C.: Memory Usage Verification for OO Programs. In: Hankin, C., Siveroni, I. (eds.) SAS 2005. LNCS, vol. 3672, pp. 70–86. Springer, Heidelberg (2005)
7. Chin, W.-N., Nguyen, H.H., Popeea, C., Qin, S.: Analysing Memory Resource Bounds for Low-Level Programs. In: ISMM. ACM Press, New York (2008)
8. Debray, S.K., Lin, N.W.: Cost analysis of logic programs. TOPLAS 15(5) (1993)
9. Gulwani, S., Mehra, K.K., Chilimbi, T.M.: Speed: precise and efficient static estimation of program computational complexity. In: POPL, pp. 127–139. ACM, New York (2009)
10. JOlden Suite Collection, `http://www-ali.cs.umass.edu/DaCapo/benchmarks.html`

11. Jones, N.D., Gomard, C.K., Sestoft, P.: Partial Evaluation and Automatic Program Generation. Prentice Hall, New York (1993)
12. Navas, J., Méndez-Lojo, M., Hermenegildo, M.: User-Definable Resource Usage Bounds Analysis for Java Bytecode. In: BYTECODE. Elsevier, Amsterdam (2009)
13. Podelski, A., Rybalchenko, A.: A complete method for the synthesis of linear ranking functions. In: Steffen, B., Levi, G. (eds.) VMCAI 2004. LNCS, vol. 2937, pp. 239–251. Springer, Heidelberg (2004)
14. Sands, D.: Complexity Analysis for a Lazy Higher-Order Language. In: Jones, N.D. (ed.) ESOP 1990. LNCS, vol. 432, pp. 361–376. Springer, Heidelberg (1990)
15. Wegbreit, B.: Mechanical Program Analysis. Comm. of the ACM 18(9) (1975)

The Higher-Order, Call-by-Value Applied Pi-Calculus*

Nobuyuki Sato and Eijiro Sumii

Tohoku University
{nsato,sumii}@kb.ecei.tohoku.ac.jp

Abstract. We define a higher-order process calculus with algebraic operations such as encryption and decryption, and develop a bisimulation proof method for behavioral equivalence in this calculus. Such development has been notoriously difficult because of the subtle interactions among generative names, processes as data, and the algebraic operations. We handle them by carefully defining the calculus and adopting Sumii et al.'s environmental bisimulation, and thereby give (to our knowledge) the first "useful" proof method in this setting. We demonstrate the utility of our method through examples involving both higher-order processes and asymmetric cryptography.

1 Introduction

Higher-order communication and encryption. The combination of cryptographic operations and higher-order, concurrent programs is ubiquitous in modern computer systems. For instance, software distribution systems (such as Windows Update) usually employ some digital signature scheme to verify the authenticity of the downloaded programs before installing them. For another example, Web-based e-mail user agents (such as Gmail) often distribute complex code (typically in HTML and JavaScript) interpreted at the client side, where the code itself is transferred through a secure channel, as well as the messages sent and received by the code. Guaranteeing the security of such systems is even more important than in first-order programs, because of the higher chance of "accidentally" executing arbitrary, malicious code.

Process calculi such as CCS and π-calculus have been useful for the verification of concurrent systems in general. In particular, spi-calculus [2] and applied π-calculus [1] are equipped with cryptographic operations such as encryption and decryption, and can be used for formal reasoning about cryptographic protocols. On the other hand, higher-order π-calculus [7] allows communication of processes themselves, and is able to model systems that transfer programs.

To our knowledge, however, there has been little research[1] on process calculus with *both* higher-order communication and cryptographic operations, probably because their combination is highly non-trivial. For instance, consider a process $P = \overline{c}\langle Q\rangle$ that sends another process $Q = \overline{c}\langle \mathit{encrypt}(m, k)\rangle$ to a public communication channel c. The process Q itself, when executed, sends message m encrypted under a secret key k. Now, is it possible for an observer on c to obtain m by intercepting the communications? One

* Detailed proofs are available online [12].

[1] An exception is a type system for higher-order spi-calculus [6], but it does not consider general algebra, decomposition, behavioral equivalence, nor bisimulations.

Z. Hu (Ed.): APLAS 2009, LNCS 5904, pp. 311–326, 2009.

might say no, because k is secret. Another might disagree, because the observer can analyze the program text of Q and extract k from it. Yet another one might argue that such an analysis is impossible, because m is encrypted *before* Q is published on the network. But what if $Q = c(x).\overline{c}\langle encrypt(x, k)\rangle$ instead? How about $Q = c(x).\overline{c}$ $\langle encrypt(m, k)\rangle$ when m is independent of x?

The above gedankenexperiment leads us to our first observation that, unlike in applied π-calculus, the *values* of function applications must be explicitly distinguished from the function applications themselves in this setting. Thus, let us write $\hat{f}(V_1, \ldots, V_l)$ for the values of function applications $f(V_1, \ldots, V_l)$. In the last example, for instance, k (and m) can be extracted if $Q = c(x).\overline{c}\langle encrypt(m, k)\rangle$, but they cannot if $Q = c(x).\overline{c}$ $\langle \widehat{encrypt}(m, k)\rangle$.

Accordingly, we need to provide a construct to decompose the syntax of communicated terms (but not values) including communicated processes (but not *running* processes), so that an observer can analyze them. For this purpose we introduce operations of the form $match\ M\ as\ x\ in\ R$, which decompose the syntax (not value) of M and bind x to the tuple of the decomposed elements. The point is that, if M is already a value, like $\widehat{encrypt}(m, k)$, then it cannot be decomposed any further.

To make our theory realistic, we require that first-order terms are evaluated before they are sent to the network. Our calculus is thus "call-by-value." As usual, however, call-by-name computation can easily be encoded by means of thunks (which are straightforward to implement as processes).

Behavioural equivalence and bisimulations. The distinction between already computed values and yet-to-be-computed terms is crucial but not sufficient for our development. Specifically, we need a method for proving properties of processes. Traditionally, *behavioral equivalence* and *bisimulations* have been known to be useful for specifying and proving many interesting properties of concurrent systems, including security properties such as secrecy and authenticity.

However, traditional bisimulation proof methods for π-calculi are not of help here. Context bisimulation [7] is not useful by itself as a practical proof technique, because of the universal quantification over all receiver (and sender) contexts. Normal bisimulation [7] essentially encodes higher-order processes into the first order by passing pointers only, and therefore would not be sound under the presence of decomposition operation like ours.[2] Environment-sensitive bisimulations in spi-calculus (see [5] for example) are not applicable in our higher-order language, because the environment itself would include processes.

For these reasons, we adapt more recent work on *environmental bisimulation* [9, 14, 15] and extend it to account for the decomposition operation as well as the algebraic operations (which generalize various cryptographic operations, as in applied π-calculus). Although environmental bisimulations have previously been applied to λ-calculus with

[2] In general, fully abstract (i.e., equivalence-preserving) encoding of our calculus into another would be extremely non-trivial. This includes an "obvious" translation from higher-order processes into the first order, where one communicates first-order terms *representing* the syntax of processes and runs a process to *interpret* them. To prove it correct, one must anyway define a higher-order calculus and then prove the translation to be fully abstract, which is more indirect *and* requires more work than the present approach.

encryption [14] and to higher-order π-calculus [9], our extension is far from trivial: to formalize decomposition, we need to introduce quotations (as in Lisp) for terms as well as for processes, which requires careful definition of several kinds of contexts and context closure operations. Specification of the algebra also requires careful generalization of the conditions on terms in previous environmental bisimulations.

Our contributions in the present paper are thus twofold: the definition of the calculus itself, and the environmental bisimulation proof method for this calculus.

Overview of the environmental bisimulation. Our environmental bisimulation $\mathcal{X}$ is a set of triples of the form $(\mathcal{E}, P, Q)$, where P and Q are the tested processes and $\mathcal{E}$ is the environment, i.e., a binary relation on terms, representing the observer's knowledge. The membership $(\mathcal{E}, P, Q) \in \mathcal{X}$, which is often written $P\mathcal{X}_{\mathcal{E}}Q$ for readability, means that processes P and Q are bisimilar under environment $\mathcal{E}$. There are several conditions on $\mathcal{X}$, each corresponding to a change of the state of the observer and the processes. For instance, as in traditional (weak) bisimulations, if either P or Q makes an internal transition, then the other should make 0 or more internal transitions, and the resulting processes should also be bisimilar (under the same environment $\mathcal{E}$, because the observer's state has not changed). For output actions, if P sends a value V and becomes P', then Q should also send some value W and become Q', with the requirement that P' and Q' are bisimilar under the environment $\mathcal{E} \cup \{(V, W)\}$, which is extended with the values the observer has learned.

For input, we must consider any pair of values that can be synthesized by the attacker from its knowledge $\mathcal{E}$. We use $(\hat{\mathcal{E}})^*$ for the set of such value pairs, where $\hat{\mathcal{E}}$ is the set of pairs of values that can be obtained from $\mathcal{E}$ by first-order computation, and $(\hat{\mathcal{E}})^*$ is the context closure of $\hat{\mathcal{E}}$. Roughly, we define:

$$\begin{aligned}\hat{\mathcal{E}} &= \{\, (eval(D[\tilde{V}]),\ eval(D[\tilde{W}])) \mid \tilde{V}\mathcal{E}\tilde{W},\ \mathsf{fn}(D) = \emptyset,\ D \text{ is first-order} \,\}\\ \mathcal{E}^* &= \{\, (C[\tilde{V}],\ C[\tilde{W}]) \mid \tilde{V}\mathcal{E}\tilde{W},\ \mathsf{fn}(C) = \emptyset \,\}\end{aligned}$$

(Here, $\tilde{V}$ denotes a sequence $V_1, \ldots, V_l$, and $\tilde{V}\mathcal{E}\tilde{W}$ denotes $V_i\mathcal{E}W_i$ for all i. We use similar notations for various kinds of meta-variables throughout the paper.) Recall that, unlike in previous environmental bisimulations with "built-in" conditions for some particular algebra (e.g., [14]), we need to consider general algebras. $\hat{\mathcal{E}}$ accounts for the synthesis of knowledge within such algebras.

For instance, let $decrypt(encrypt(x, y), y) = x$. If the ciphertexts $(encrypt(V, k),$ $encrypt(W, k))$ and the key pair (k, k) belong to $\mathcal{E}$, then the plaintexts (V, W) belong to $\hat{\mathcal{E}}$. This is because the first-order observer context $D = decrypt([]_1, []_2)$ can compute them by putting the ciphertexts into its first hole $[]_1$ and the key to $[]_2$, like:

$$\begin{aligned}D[encrypt(V, k), k] &= decrypt(encrypt(V, k), k) = V\\ D[encrypt(W, k), k] &= decrypt(encrypt(W, k), k) = W\end{aligned}$$

Thus, the bisimulation condition for input would be: for any $V(\hat{\mathcal{E}})^*W$, if P receives V and becomes P', then Q receives W and becomes Q', with P' and Q' bisimilar again under environment $\mathcal{E}$.

Furthermore, the observer can spawn arbitrary new processes from its knowledge $\mathcal{E}$. Thus, we also require $P|P'\mathcal{X}_{\mathcal{E}}Q|Q'$ for any $P\mathcal{X}_{\mathcal{E}}Q$ and $P'\hat{\mathcal{E}}Q'$. This may seem to be a heavy condition because of the universal quantification over processes P' and Q', drawn from $\hat{\mathcal{E}}$. However, we in fact work out an up-to context technique, where the requirement is weakened to $P|P'\mathcal{X}_{\mathcal{E}}^{(*)}Q|Q'$ for a certain form of context closure $\mathcal{X}_{\mathcal{E}}^{(*)}$ for $\mathcal{X}$. This essentially removes the universal quantification and significantly lightens the burden of a bisimulation proof in higher-order process calculus.[3] (Another subtle but important trick here is that, unlike for input, $\hat{\mathcal{E}}$ suffices in place of $(\hat{\mathcal{E}})^*$. Informally, this is because processes in $(\hat{\mathcal{E}})^*$ can only make the same observations as those in $\hat{\mathcal{E}}$.)

Finally, for decomposition of processes and terms, we require $P\mathcal{X}_{\mathcal{E}\cup\{(M',N')\}}Q$ for any $P\mathcal{X}_{\mathcal{E}}Q$ and $M\hat{\mathcal{E}}N$, where M' and N' are the result of decomposing M and N, respectively. (Obviously, this $\hat{\mathcal{E}}$ does not have to be $(\hat{\mathcal{E}})^*$, because there is no point in synthesizing a term and then decomposing it.) Again, this condition may seem heavy because, by repeatedly applying it, we need to transitively include all the subterms of M and N. As in the previous case, however, most of them can be removed by the up-to context technique.

Overview of the paper. The rest of this paper is structured as follows. Section 2 formally presents the syntax and labeled transition semantics of our calculus, which is (formally) parametrized by the semantics of terms. Sections 3 and 4 define the environmental bisimulation and the up-to context technique. Section 5 proves their soundness and completeness with respect to reduction-closed barbed equivalence. Section 6 gives examples and Section 7 concludes.

Throughout the paper, readers are assumed to be familiar with standard technical developments in the π-calculus [11] and be comfortable with basic mathematical notions such as inductive (and coninductive) definitions of sets (and relations).

2 The Calculus

2.1 Syntax

As in applied π-calculus [1], our language consists of terms and processes. Terms represent channel names and communicated data. Processes represent running programs. The set of terms is defined as follows:

$$
\begin{array}{rcll}
M & ::= & x \quad \text{(variable)} \mid a \quad \text{(name)} \mid f \quad \text{(function)} \\
& \mid & `P \quad \text{(quoted process)} \mid `M \quad \text{(quoted term)} \\
& \mid & M(M_1,\ldots,M_l) & \text{(uncomputed application)} \\
& \mid & \hat{f}(V_1,\ldots,V_l) & \text{(computed application)}
\end{array}
$$

Meta-variables M, N range over terms, a, b, c, d, k, n over names, x, y over variables and f, g over functions. Term $M(M_1,\ldots,M_l)$ represents function application that is yet to be computed. Conversely, $\hat{f}(V_1,\ldots,V_l)$ represents function application that is already computed, where function f of arity l has been applied to values $V_1,\ldots,V_l$. Note that function symbols f are first-class but different from names (or variables) and therefore cannot be bound. Term $`P$ represents the syntax of processes, which allows

[3] This was previously not possible and therefore is yet another technical contribution of the present work. See footnote 4 in the next section for details.

us to communicate terms containing processes (i.e, higher-order terms). Although it has been written just P in previous work (e.g., [7, 9]) and in the introduction, we here put the quotation mark to clarify the distinction between communicated and running processes.[4] Term $`M$ represents the syntax of terms themselves. It is necessary for the decomposition operation explained below.

Simultaneously, we define a subset of terms as values, i.e., results of computation:

$$V ::= a \mid f \mid `P \mid `M \mid \hat{f}(V_1, \ldots, V_l)$$

Meta-variables V, W range over values. We write **Quo** for the set of values of the form $`P$ or $`M$.

The set of processes is defined by:

$$\begin{array}{rlllll} P & ::= & 0 & \text{(nil)} & \mid & run(M) \quad \text{(execution)} \\ & \mid & M(x).P & \text{(input)} & \mid & \overline{M}\langle N\rangle.P \quad \text{(output)} \\ & \mid & !P & \text{(replication)} & \mid & \nu a.P \quad \text{(restriction)} \\ & \mid & (P|Q) & & & \text{(parallel composition)} \\ & \mid & \multicolumn{3}{l}{if\ M = N\ then\ P\ else\ Q} & \text{(conditional)} \\ & \mid & \multicolumn{3}{l}{match\ M\ as\ x\ in\ P} & \text{(decomposition)} \end{array}$$

P, Q, R range over processes. Their informal semantics is as follows. Process 0 does nothing. Process $run(M)$ executes quoted processes (i.e., $`P$). Parallel composition $P|Q$ represents concurrent execution of P and Q. Replication $!P$ executes as many copies of P as necessary in parallel. Restriction $\nu a.P$ creates a new name a and then becomes P. Conditional $if\ M = N\ then\ P\ else\ Q$ compares the values of M and N (up to α-equivalence, because they may contain processes), and executes either P or Q accordingly. Input $M(x).P$ receives a value and output $\overline{M}\langle N\rangle.P$ sends the value of N on channel M, before becoming P. Process $match\ M\ as\ x\ in\ P$ decomposes the value of M (which should be either $`P$ or $`N$), binds x to the decomposed elements, and executes P. Formal semantics of processes will be given in the next subsection.

As usual, we identify processes (and terms containing processes) up to α-conversion. We write $\mathsf{fn}(M)$ and $\mathsf{fn}(P)$ for the set of free names that appear in M and P, respectively. We often omit trailing 0.

Contexts and context closure. Because we have terms, values and processes in our language, we correspondingly define term contexts, value contexts and process contexts. They have multiple holes (indexed by positive integers 1, 2, ...) for values.

$$\begin{aligned} C_t &::= x \mid C_v \mid C_t(C_t, \ldots, C_t) \\ C_v &::= [\,]_i \mid a \mid f \mid `C_p \mid `C_t \mid \hat{f}(C_v, \ldots, C_v) \\ C_p &::= 0 \mid run(C_t) \mid C_t(x).C_p \mid \overline{C_t}\langle C_t\rangle.C_p \mid !C_p \mid \nu a.C_p \mid (C_p|C_p) \mid \\ &\qquad if\ C_t = C_t\ then\ C_p\ else\ C_p \mid match\ C_t\ as\ x\ in\ C_p \end{aligned}$$

---

[4] This distinction permits a more convenient up-to context technique (clause 6 in Definition 3) when the observer spawns new processes synthesized from its knowledge, because (unlike in traditional higher-order π-calculus [7]) the execution of a process now requires an internal transition step $run(`P) \xrightarrow{\tau} P$. This was not the case in previous work [9] on environmental bisimulation for higher-order π-calculus (with a limited version of up-to context [8, Definition E.1]), which often forced one to construct a significantly larger $\mathcal{X}$ than necessary in their bisimulation proof.

We write C for any of the contexts above, and $\mathsf{bn}(C)$ for the set of names bound in C. As usual, contexts (unlike processes) are *not* identified by α-conversion in general, e.g., $\nu m.\overline{a}\langle[]_1\rangle.0 \neq \nu n.\overline{a}\langle[]_1\rangle.0$ so $\mathsf{bn}(\nu m.\overline{a}\langle[]_1\rangle.0) = \{m\} \neq \{n\} = \mathsf{bn}(\nu n.\overline{a}\langle[]_1\rangle.0)$.

Since we are interested in behavioural equivalence of processes under contexts, we define context closure operations as follows. Let $\mathcal{E}$ be a (binary) relation on closed values. (As is often the case in π-calculi [11], "closed" in this paper means the lack of free *variables* only. Free *names* are still possible.) Relation $\mathcal{E}^*$ on closed terms is:

$$\{ (C_t[\tilde{V}], C_t[\tilde{W}]) \mid \tilde{V}\mathcal{E}\tilde{W},\ \mathsf{bn}(C_t) \cap \mathsf{fn}(\tilde{V}, \tilde{W}) = \mathsf{fn}(C_t) = \emptyset \}$$

We sometimes (ab)use $\mathcal{E}^*$ as a relation on closed processes, in which case it denotes:

$$\{ (C_p[\tilde{V}], C_p[\tilde{W}]) \mid \tilde{V}\mathcal{E}\tilde{W},\ \mathsf{bn}(C_p) \cap \mathsf{fn}(\tilde{V}, \tilde{W}) = \mathsf{fn}(C_p) = \emptyset \}$$

In the definitions above, $\mathsf{fn}(C_t)$ and $\mathsf{fn}(C_p)$ are required to be empty so that context cannot "guess" secret names just by chance. These conditions could be $\mathsf{fn}(C_t) \cap \mathsf{fn}(\tilde{V}, \tilde{W}) = \emptyset$ and $\mathsf{fn}(C_p) \cap \mathsf{fn}(\tilde{V}, \tilde{W}) = \emptyset$, instead of $\mathsf{fn}(C_t) = \emptyset$ and $\mathsf{fn}(C_p) = \emptyset$, but we preferred the latter for the sake of simplicity. This choice does *not* restrict observations made by contexts: one can put arbitrary free names into the holes of the contexts by including them in $\mathcal{E}$ whenever necessary. Note also that contexts can create as many fresh names as needed for observations, because $\mathsf{bn}(C_t)$ and $\mathsf{bn}(C_p)$ are *not* required to be empty, though they should again be distinct from other free names as usual.

As already stated, our calculus is parametrized by the semantics of terms. To formalize our assumptions on these semantics, we define *first-order* contexts, i.e., contexts with no quotation (and no names).

$$D_t ::= D_v \mid D_t(D_t, \ldots, D_t) \qquad D_v ::= []_i \mid f \mid \hat{f}(D_v, \ldots, D_v)$$

By using first-order contexts, we define another kind of context closure $\hat{\mathcal{E}}$ as follows. Let $\mathcal{E}$ be a relation on closed values. Then, relation $\hat{\mathcal{E}}$ is defined to be:

$$\{ (eval(D_t[\tilde{V}]), eval(D_t[\tilde{W}])) \mid \tilde{V}\mathcal{E}\tilde{W} \}$$

The function $eval$ will be defined in the next subsection. Intuitively, $\hat{\mathcal{E}}$ is the set of (pairs of) values that can be computed from $\mathcal{E}$ only at the first order, i.e., without using quotation or processes. Note that $\mathsf{bn}(D_t) = \mathsf{fn}(D_t) = \emptyset$ by definition.

2.2 Semantics

Semantics of terms. We require that the meaning of terms is formally defined by a rewriting system [3] (cf. [4, Section 5], though their formulation is slighly different from ours) on closed terms, and that the system is confluent and strongly normalizing for ground terms. An example representing asymmetric cryptography is given in Section 6. Readers are referred to a standard textbook [3] for basic definitions in term rewriting.

In the system, we also assume tuples (and projection operations for them) and constant (i.e., nullary function) symbols `name`, `fun`, ... (and equality tests on them) to represent the syntax of processes. Recall that (function and) constant symbols are different from names.

The partial function $eval$ returns the value of a given term. It is undefined if the normal form of the term does not belong to the set of values defined in the previous subsection. For example, $eval(\#_1(a, b)) = a$ and $eval(\#_2(c))$ is undefined.

Finally, we require that $M(\hat{\mathcal{E}})^* N$ implies $eval(M)(\hat{\mathcal{E}})^* eval(N)$. This requirement is critical (and sufficient) throughout our developments. It means that the *values* of (pairs of) terms synthesized from $\hat{\mathcal{E}}$ can be synthesized from $\hat{\mathcal{E}}$ itself. That is, $eval$ does not introduce any new names or higher-order values. Recall that $\hat{\mathcal{E}}$ is a closure (and evaluation) under nameless and first-order contexts only.

Semantics of processes. We define the semantics of processes by a labeled transition system. The labels have three forms: τ, $a(V)$, and $\nu\tilde{c}.\overline{a}\langle V\rangle$, representing the silent action, an input action, and an output action, respectively. Metavariable α ranges over labels. $\mathsf{bn}(\alpha)$ is defined as $\mathsf{bn}(\nu\tilde{c}.\overline{a}\langle V\rangle) = \{\tilde{c}\}$ and $\mathsf{bn}(\tau) = \mathsf{bn}(a(V)) = \emptyset$. The transitions are defined by the rules below, with symmetric rules (Par-R) and (Tau-R) omitted. We write $\Rightarrow$ for the reflexive and transitive closure of $\xrightarrow{\tau}$.

$$\frac{eval(M) = a}{M(x).P \xrightarrow{a(V)} \{^V/_x\}P}\ \text{(In)} \qquad \frac{eval(M) = a}{\overline{M}\langle N\rangle.P \xrightarrow{\overline{a}\langle eval(N)\rangle} P}\ \text{(Out)}$$

$$\frac{P \xrightarrow{\alpha} P' \quad \mathsf{bn}(\alpha) \cap \mathsf{fn}(Q) = \emptyset}{P|Q \xrightarrow{\alpha} P'|Q}\ \text{(Par-L)}$$

$$\frac{P \xrightarrow{\nu\tilde{b}.\overline{a}\langle V\rangle} P' \quad Q \xrightarrow{a(V)} Q' \quad \{\tilde{b}\} \cap \mathsf{fn}(Q) = \emptyset}{P|Q \xrightarrow{\tau} \nu\tilde{b}.(P'|Q')}\ \text{(Tau-L)}$$

$$\frac{P|!P \xrightarrow{\alpha} Q}{!P \xrightarrow{\alpha} Q}\ \text{(Rep)} \qquad \frac{P \xrightarrow{\alpha} P' \quad a \notin \mathsf{bn}(\alpha) \cup \mathsf{fn}(\alpha)}{\nu a.P \xrightarrow{\alpha} \nu a.P'}\ \text{(Scope)}$$

$$\frac{P \xrightarrow{\nu\tilde{b}.\overline{a}\langle V\rangle} P' \quad c \neq a \quad c \in \mathsf{fn}(V) \setminus \{\tilde{b}\}}{\nu c.P \xrightarrow{\nu\tilde{b},c.\overline{a}\langle V\rangle} P'}\ \text{(Open)} \qquad \frac{eval(M) = \text{`}P}{run(M) \xrightarrow{\tau} P}\ \text{(Run)}$$

$$\frac{eval(M) = eval(N)}{\mathit{if}\ M = N\ \mathit{then}\ P\ \mathit{else}\ Q \xrightarrow{\tau} P}\ \text{(IfTrue)} \qquad \frac{eval(M) \neq eval(N)}{\mathit{if}\ M = N\ \mathit{then}\ P\ \mathit{else}\ Q \xrightarrow{\tau} Q}\ \text{(IfFalse)}$$

$$\frac{eval(M) = V \quad V \in \mathbf{Quo} \quad n \notin \mathsf{fn}(V, P)}{\mathit{match}\ M\ \mathit{as}\ x\ \mathit{in}\ P \xrightarrow{\tau} \nu n.\{^{reify_n(V)}/_x\}P}\ \text{(Match)}$$

Most of the rules are straightforward adaptation of standard labelled transition in the π-calculus [11]. As usual in untyped small-step operational semantics, transition gets stuck if the assumptions are not satisfied, e.g., if $eval(M)$ is not a name in rules (In) and (Out). In rule (Match), the operator $reify_n$ takes a quoted process or a quoted term and decomposes it into a tuple. (The name n is used for substituting a bound name or a bound variable, if there is any, in the reified process.) Formally, it is defined as:

$$\begin{array}{llll}
reify_n(\text{`}0) & = (\widehat{\mathtt{zero}}) & reify_n(\text{`}run(M)) & = (\widehat{\mathtt{exe}}, \text{`}M) \\
reify_n(\text{`}(M(x).P)) & = (\widehat{\mathtt{in}}, \text{`}M, n, \text{`}\{^n/_x\}P) & reify_n(\text{`}(\overline{M_1}\langle M_2\rangle.P)) & = (\widehat{\mathtt{out}}, \text{`}M_1, \text{`}M_2, \text{`}P) \\
reify_n(\text{`}!P) & = (\widehat{\mathtt{rep}}, \text{`}P) & reify_n(\text{`}\nu c.P) & = (\widehat{\mathtt{new}}, n, \text{`}\{^n/_c\}P) \\
reify_n(\text{`}(P_1|P_2)) & = (\widehat{\mathtt{par}}, \text{`}P_1, \text{`}P_2) & &
\end{array}$$

$$reify_n(\text{`}\mathit{if}\ M_1 = M_2\ \mathit{then}\ P_1\ \mathit{else}\ P_2) = (\widehat{\mathtt{cond}}, \text{`}M_1, \text{`}M_2, \text{`}P_1, \text{`}P_2)$$
$$reify_n(\text{`}\mathit{match}\ M\ \mathit{as}\ x\ \mathit{in}\ P) = (\widehat{\mathtt{mtch}}, \text{`}M, n, \text{`}\{^n/_x\}P)$$

$$\begin{array}{llll}
reify_n(\text{`}a) & = (\widehat{\mathtt{name}}, a) & reify_n(\text{`}f) & = (\widehat{\mathtt{fun}}, f) \\
reify_n(\text{``}P) & = (\widehat{\mathtt{pquo}}, \text{`}P) & reify_n(\text{``}M) & = (\widehat{\mathtt{tquo}}, \text{`}M)
\end{array}$$
$$reify_n(\text{`}(M(M_1, \ldots, M_l))) = (\widehat{\mathtt{uapp}}, \text{`}M, \text{`}M_1, \ldots, \text{`}M_l)$$
$$reify_n(\text{`}\hat{f}(V_1, \ldots, V_l)) = (\widehat{\mathtt{capp}}, \hat{f}(V_1, \ldots, V_l))$$

Structural equivalence. Define evaluation contexts by $C ::= [] \mid (C|P) \mid (P|C) \mid \nu c.C$. Structural equivalence $\equiv$ is the smallest equivalence relation on processes that is closed under evaluation contexts, with:

$$\begin{array}{llll} P \equiv P|0 & P_1|(P_2|P_3) \equiv (P_1|P_2)|P_3 & P_1|P_2 \equiv P_2|P_1 & !P \equiv P|!P \\ \nu a.0 \equiv 0 & \nu a.\nu b.P \equiv \nu b.\nu a.P & \multicolumn{2}{l}{P_1|(\nu a.P_2) \equiv \nu a.(P_1|P_2) \ (\textit{if } a \notin \mathsf{fn}(P_1))} \end{array}$$

The next lemma is useful for proving the soundness of some up-to techniques.

Lemma 1 (reduction respects structural equivalence)

1. *$P \equiv Q$ and $P \xrightarrow{\alpha} P'$ imply $Q \xrightarrow{\alpha} Q'$ and $P' \equiv Q'$*
2. *$P \equiv Q$ and $Q \xrightarrow{\alpha} Q'$ imply $P \xrightarrow{\alpha} P'$ and $P' \equiv Q'$.*

Proof. By induction on the derivation of $P \equiv Q$.

3 Environmental Bisimulation

As outlined in the introduction, an environmental relation is a set of elements of the form $(\mathcal{E}, P, Q)$, where P, Q are closed processes and $\mathcal{E}$ is a binary relation on closed values. Intuitively, P and Q are the tested processes and $\mathcal{E}$ is the environment, i.e., the knowledge of the observer. We write $P\mathcal{X}_{\mathcal{E}}Q$ for $(\mathcal{E}, P, Q) \in \mathcal{X}$.

Definition 1 (environmental bisimulation). *Environmental relation $\mathcal{X}$ is an environmental bisimulation if $P\mathcal{X}_{\mathcal{E}}Q$ implies:*

1. *$P \xrightarrow{\tau} P'$ implies $Q \Rightarrow Q'$ and $P'\mathcal{X}_{\mathcal{E}}Q'$*
2. *$P \xrightarrow{a(V)} P'$ with $a\hat{\mathcal{E}}b$ and $V(\hat{\mathcal{E}})^*W$ implies $Q \Rightarrow\xrightarrow{b(W)}\Rightarrow Q'$ and $P'\mathcal{X}_{\mathcal{E}}Q'$*
3. *$P \xrightarrow{\nu\tilde{c}.\overline{a}\langle V\rangle} P'$ with $a\hat{\mathcal{E}}b$ and $\tilde{c} \notin \mathsf{fn}(\#_1(\mathcal{E}))$ implies $\exists\tilde{d} \notin \mathsf{fn}(\#_2(\mathcal{E}))$. $Q \Rightarrow \xrightarrow{\nu\tilde{d}.\overline{b}\langle W\rangle}\Rightarrow Q'$ and $P'\mathcal{X}_{\mathcal{E}\cup\{(V,W)\}}Q'$*
4. *the converse of (1-3) on Q*
5. *$V_1\hat{\mathcal{E}}W_1$ and $V_2\hat{\mathcal{E}}W_2$ imply $V_1 = V_2 \iff W_1 = W_2$*
6. *$`(P')\hat{\mathcal{E}}`(Q')$ implies $P|P'\mathcal{X}_{\mathcal{E}}Q|Q'$*
7. *$P\mathcal{X}_{\mathcal{E}\cup\{(a,b)\}}Q$ for any $a \notin \mathsf{fn}(P, \#_1(\mathcal{E}))$ and $b \notin \mathsf{fn}(Q, \#_2(\mathcal{E}))$*
8. *$V\hat{\mathcal{E}}W$ implies:*
   (a) *$V = a$ implies $W = b$ (i.e., if V is a name, then W is also a name)*
   (b) *$V = f$ implies $W = f$*
   (c) *$V = \hat{f}(V_1, \ldots, V_l)$ implies $W = \hat{g}(W_1, \ldots, W_m)$*
   (d) *$V \in$ **Quo** implies $\exists b \notin \mathsf{fn}(\mathcal{E}, P, Q)$. $P\mathcal{X}_{\mathcal{E}\cup\{(reify_b(V), reify_b(W))\}}Q$*
9. *the converse of 8 on W*

Modulo symmetry, Definition 1 has 7 clauses. Clause 1 is the usual one for τ-transitions. Clause 2 is the input case. The channel names a and b are related by the observer's knowledge $\hat{\mathcal{E}}$. The input values V and W are synthesized from $\hat{\mathcal{E}}$, as discussed in the introduction. Clause 3 is the output case. Again, a and b are related by $\hat{\mathcal{E}}$. The environment is extended with the output values, again as discussed in the introduction. Clause 5 accounts for conditional contexts *if* $[]_1 = []_2$ *then* P *else* Q. Clause 6 allows the observer to run processes from the environment at any time. Clause 7 allows creation of fresh names by the observer. Clause 8 accounts for decomposition, with 8a–8c for contexts of the form $match\,`[]_1\ as\ x\ in\ P$ (which analyze the shape of the related values) and 8d for $match\ []_1\ as\ x\ in\ P$.

Environmental bisimilarity $\sim$ is the union of all environmental bisimulations, which exists because the union of all environmental bisimulations is an environmental bisimulation (all the conditions above are monotone on $\mathcal{X}$). Therefore, $P \sim_{\mathcal{E}} Q$ if $P\mathcal{X}_{\mathcal{E}}Q$ for some environmental bisimulation $\mathcal{X}$. The most important case is when $\mathcal{E} = \{(a,a) \mid a \in \mathsf{fn}(P,Q)\}$. We write $P \simeq Q$ for $P \sim_{\mathcal{E}} Q$ in this case. It asserts the equivalence between two processes when the observer knows all of their free names.

4 Up-to Context Technique

Up-to techniques are enhancements of the bisimulation proof method (see, e.g., [10]). "Bisimulations up-to" have weaker conditions than the original bisimulation clauses, and are therefore easier to use, but yet are included in the bisimilarity (provided that they are sound). We here present one of the most useful up-to techniques for our bisimulation.

We first define context closure for environmental bisimulations.

Definition 2. *For an environmental relation $\mathcal{X}$, we write $P\mathcal{X}_{\mathcal{E}}^{(*)}Q$ if $P \equiv \nu\tilde{c}.(P_0|P_1)$ and $Q \equiv \nu\tilde{d}.(Q_0|Q_1)$ where $P_0\mathcal{X}_{\mathcal{E}'}Q_0$ and $P_1(\hat{\mathcal{E}}')^*Q_1$, and if*

$$\hat{\mathcal{E}} \subseteq \{\, (V,W) \mid V(\hat{\mathcal{E}}')^*W,\ \mathsf{fn}(V) \cap \{\tilde{c}\} = \mathsf{fn}(W) \cap \{\tilde{d}\} = \emptyset \,\}.$$

Intuitively, it is an extension of context closure for terms, where the observer's processes P_1, Q_1 are running in parallel with the tested processes P_0, Q_0, and fresh names $\tilde{c}$, $\tilde{d}$ have been generated but not exported yet.

Now we define the up-to technique. Essentially, this definition is obtained by replacing $\mathcal{X}$ with $\mathcal{X}^{(*)}$ in each clause of Definition 1.

Definition 3 (environmental bisimulation up-to context). *Environmental relation $\mathcal{X}$ is an environmental bisimulation up-to context[5] if $P\mathcal{X}_{\mathcal{E}}Q$ implies:*

1. $P \xrightarrow{\tau} P'$ *implies* $Q \Rightarrow Q'$ *and* $P'\mathcal{X}_{\mathcal{E}}^{(*)}Q'$
2. $P \xrightarrow{a(V)} P'$ *with* $a\hat{\mathcal{E}}b$ *and* $V(\hat{\mathcal{E}})^*W$ *implies* $Q \Rightarrow\xrightarrow{b(W)}\Rightarrow Q'$ *and* $P'\mathcal{X}_{\mathcal{E}}^{(*)}Q'$
3. $P \xrightarrow{\nu\tilde{c}.\overline{a}\langle V\rangle} P'$ *with* $a\hat{\mathcal{E}}b$ *and* $\tilde{c} \notin \mathsf{fn}(\#_1(\mathcal{E}))$ *implies* $\exists\tilde{d} \notin \mathsf{fn}(\#_2(\mathcal{E}))$. $Q \Rightarrow\xrightarrow{\nu\tilde{d}.\overline{b}\langle W\rangle}\Rightarrow Q'$ *and* $P'\mathcal{X}_{\mathcal{E}\cup\{(V,W)\}}^{(*)}Q'$
4. *the converse of (1-3) on* Q
5. $V_1\hat{\mathcal{E}}W_1$ *and* $V_2\hat{\mathcal{E}}W_2$ *imply* $V_1 = V_2 \iff W_1 = W_2$
6. $`(P')\hat{\mathcal{E}}`(Q')$ *implies* $P|P'\mathcal{X}_{\mathcal{E}}^{(*)}Q|Q'$
7. $P\mathcal{X}_{\mathcal{E}\cup\{(a,b)\}}Q$ *for any* $a \notin \mathsf{fn}(P,\#_1(\mathcal{E}))$ *and* $b \notin \mathsf{fn}(Q,\#_2(\mathcal{E}))$
8. $V\hat{\mathcal{E}}W$ *implies:*

[5] In fact, this is also up-to environment and up-to structural equivalence because of the use of $\subseteq$ and $\equiv$ in Definition 2.

(a) $V = a$ *implies* $W = b$ *(i.e., if* V *is a name, then* W *is also a name)*
(b) $V = f$ *implies* $W = f$
(c) $V = \hat{f}(V_1, \ldots, V_l)$ *implies* $W = \hat{g}(W_1, \ldots, W_m)$
(d) $V \in$ **Quo** *implies* $\exists b \notin \mathsf{fn}(\mathcal{E}, P, Q).\ P\mathcal{X}^{(*)}_{\mathcal{E}\cup\{(reify_b(V), reify_b(W))\}}Q$

9. *the converse of 8 on* W

Environmental bisimulations up-to context require weaker conditions than environmental bisimulations. (Thus an environmental bisimulation is always an environmental bisimulation up-to context.) Specifically, in clauses 1 to 3, the processes after transitions are required to be bisimilar only "up to context," i.e., modulo context closure. Similarly, in clauses 6 and 8d, the resulting processes are required to be bisimilar only modulo the context. Note that clause 6 is not a tautology because it allows to extract (and execute) the quoted processes P' and Q', while the context closure $\mathcal{X}^{(*)}_{\mathcal{E}}$ does not (see Definition 2).

Soundness of the up-to technique is guaranteed by the fact that an environmental relation satisfying all the conditions above is a subset of $\sim$.

Theorem 1 (soundness of environmental bisimulation up-to context). *Let* $\mathcal{Y}$ *be the environmental bisimilarity up-to context. Then* $\mathcal{X} = \{(\mathcal{E}, P, Q) \mid P\mathcal{Y}^{(*)}_{\mathcal{E}}Q\}$ *is an environmental bisimulation.*

Proof. By checking each clause of environmental bisimulation against $\mathcal{X}$. The non-trivial cases are clauses 1, 2 and 3, which follow from the lemmas below (and their symmetric versions).

Lemma 2 (input transition). *Let* $P_1\mathcal{E}^*Q_1$ *and* $a\mathcal{E}b$*. Suppose that* $\hat{\mathcal{E}}$ *respects equality of names on the left hand side, i.e., for any* a*, there exists some* b *such that, for any* W_1*,* $a\hat{\mathcal{E}}W_1$ *implies* $W_1 = b$*. If* $P_1 \xrightarrow{a(V)} P_1'$*, then for any* W*, there exists some* Q_1' *such that* $Q_1 \xrightarrow{b(W)} Q_1'$ *with* $P_1'(\mathcal{E} \cup \{(V, W)\})^*Q_1'$*.*

Proof. By induction on the derivation of $P_1 \xrightarrow{a(V)} P_1'$.

Lemma 3 (output transition). *Let* $P_1\mathcal{E}^*Q_1$ *and* $a\mathcal{E}b$*. Suppose* $\hat{\mathcal{E}}$ *respects equality of names on the left hand side (see above for definition). If* $P_1 \xrightarrow{\nu\tilde{c}.\overline{a}\langle V\rangle} P_1'$ *with* $\tilde{c} \notin \mathsf{fn}(\#_1(\mathcal{E}))$*, then there exist some* Q_1'*,* W *and* $\tilde{d}$ *with* $V\widehat{(\mathcal{E} \cup \{(\tilde{c}, \tilde{d})\})^*}W$ *such that* $Q_1 \xrightarrow{\nu\tilde{d}.\overline{b}\langle W\rangle} Q_1'$ *with* $\tilde{d} \notin \mathsf{fn}(\#_2(\mathcal{E}))$ *and* $P_1'(\mathcal{E} \cup \{(\tilde{c}, \tilde{d})\})^*Q_1'$*.*

Proof. By induction on the derivation of $P_1 \xrightarrow{\nu\tilde{c}.\overline{a}\langle V\rangle} P_1'$.

Note that, in the two lemmas above, no other assumption is necessary for $\mathcal{E}$.

Lemma 4 (τ transition). *Suppose* $P_1(\hat{\mathcal{E}})^*Q_1$ *and* $P_0\mathcal{Y}_{\mathcal{E}}Q_0$ *for an environmental bisimulation* $\mathcal{Y}$ *up-to context. If* $P_1 \xrightarrow{\tau} P_1'$*, then there exists some* Q_1' *such that* $Q_1 \xrightarrow{\tau} Q_1'$ *with* $P_0|P_1'\mathcal{Y}^{(*)}_{\mathcal{E}}Q_0|Q_1'$*.*

Proof. By induction on the derivation of $P_1 \xrightarrow{\tau} P_1'$, using Lemma 2 and 3.

Full details of the above proofs are available online [12].

While the up-to technique is useful for a bisimulation proof in general, we also use Theorem 1 to prove the soundness of the environmental bisimulation itself in the next section.

5 Soundness and Completeness of Environmental Bisimilarity

We first define our criterion of observational equivalence, i.e., reduction-closed barbed equivalence. In this definition, meta-variable μ ranges over names and co-names ($\bar{a}$ etc.), $P \downarrow_a$ and $P \downarrow_{\bar{a}}$ mean that P can make an input and output transition on a, and $P \Downarrow_\mu$ is an abbreviation of $P \Rightarrow\downarrow_\mu$.

Definition 4 (reduction-closed barbed equivalence). *Reduction-closed barbed equivalence is the largest binary relation $\approx$ on closed processes such that $P \approx Q$ implies:*

1. *$P \xrightarrow{\tau} P'$ implies $Q \Rightarrow Q'$ and $P' \approx Q'$*
2. *$P \downarrow_\mu$ implies $Q \Downarrow_\mu$*
3. *the converse of 1 and 2 on Q*
4. *$P|R \approx Q|R$ for all processes R*

Theorem 2 (soundness and completeness of environmental bisimulation). *If $P \simeq Q$, then $P \approx Q$ and vice versa.*

Proof. For soundness (the forward implication), we check each clause in Definition 4 against $\simeq$. The non-trivial case is clause 4. Suppose $P \simeq Q$, i.e., $P \sim_{\mathcal{E}} Q$ for $\mathcal{E} = \{(a,a) \mid a \in \mathsf{fn}(P,Q)\}$. Let $\mathcal{E}' = \{(b,b) \mid b \in \mathsf{fn}(R)\}$. By clause 7 of environmental bisimulation, $P \sim_{\mathcal{E}\cup\mathcal{E}'} Q$. Since $R(\mathcal{E} \cup \mathcal{E}')^* R$, we have $P|R \sim^{(*)}_{\mathcal{E}\cup\mathcal{E}'} Q|R$ by Definition 2. Since $\sim$ is an environmental bisimulation up-to context, $P|R \sim_{\mathcal{E}\cup\mathcal{E}'} Q|R$ by Theorem 1. Hence $P|R \simeq Q|R$. For completeness (the backward implication), we take an environmental relation $\mathcal{X}$ that subsumes reduction-closed barbed equivalence, and prove it to be an environmental bisimulation. Again, see the online material [12] for details.

Note that reduction-closed barbed *congruence* is uninteresting in our calculus, since it almost coincides with α-equivalence (modulo possible differences between computed applications) because of quotation and decomposition, i.e., contexts like $match\ `[]_1\ as\ x$ $in\ P$. (It is not interesting either to consider only contexts with no decomposition, because such contexts are *too* restricted, missing the whole point of our work.) In addition, it is anyway easy to (state and) prove the congruence of P and Q just by considering the equivalence of $\overline{a}\langle`P\rangle$ and $\overline{a}\langle`Q\rangle$ instead, because an evaluation context can receive $`P$ or $`Q$ from a and use them in arbitrary manners.

6 Examples

In the examples below, we use the following rewriting rules for terms, representing asymmetric cryptography.

$$pk(V) \to \widehat{pk}(V) \qquad sk(V) \to \widehat{sk}(V)$$
$$f(V, \widehat{pk}(W)) \to \widehat{f}(V, \widehat{pk}(W)) \qquad f^{-1}(V, \widehat{sk}(W)) \to \widehat{f^{-1}}(V, \widehat{sk}(W))$$
$$f^{-1}(\widehat{f}(V, \widehat{pk}(W)), \widehat{sk}(W)) \to V \qquad f(\widehat{f^{-1}}(V, \widehat{sk}(W)), \widehat{pk}(W)) \to V$$

Functions pk and sk compute public and secret keys, respectively, from its argument. Functions f and f^{-1} denote encryption (or verification) and decryption (or signing). See e.g. [13] for more information on public-key encryption and digital signature.

The point of the examples is to show how to model and reason about higher-order communication systems involving (public-key) encryption by using our approach. It may also be possible to implement first-order variants of the systems, but they do not devalue our examples (just as the existence of first-order programs such as `mail(1)` does not devalue higher-order systems such as Gmail).

6.1 Software Distribution with Digital Signature

The following system P consists of a server and clients. The server distributes a program R, which is then executed by the clients. For comparison, another system Q is defined where the clients "somehow" know R in the first place.

$$\begin{array}{ll} P = \nu k.(\mathit{Server}_k | \mathit{Client}_k) & Q = \nu k.(\mathit{Server}_k | \mathit{Client}'_k) \\ \mathit{Client}_k = !a(x).\mathit{run}(f(x, pk(k))) & \mathit{Client}'_k = !a(x).\nu c.(\overline{c}\langle f(x, pk(k))\rangle | c(y).R) \\ \mathit{Server}_k = !\overline{a}\langle pk(k)\rangle | !\overline{a}\langle f^{-1}(`R, sk(k))\rangle & \end{array}$$

We assume $k, c \notin \mathsf{fn}(R)$. Client_k receives a quoted process R signed under the secret key $\widehat{sk}(k)$, and then verifies and executes it. By contrast, Client'_k receives the same process but discards it, and then executes R. Equivalence of the two systems P and Q means that the clients can only execute R, not any Trojan horses. To prove this, we give an environmental relation $\mathcal{X}$ such that $P\mathcal{X}^{(*)}_{\mathcal{E}}Q$ for $\mathcal{E} = \{(b, b) \mid b \in \mathsf{fn}(P, Q)\}$.

Proposition 1. *The $\mathcal{X}$ below is an environmental bisimulation up-to context.*

$$\begin{array}{rl} \mathcal{X} = \{(\mathcal{E}_0, P_0, Q_0) \mid & P_0 = \mathit{Server}_{k'} | \mathit{Client}_{k'} | P_1 | \dots | P_l, \\ & Q_0 = \mathit{Server}_{k''} | \mathit{Client}'_{k''} | Q_1 | \dots | Q_l, \\ & l \geq 0, \\ & P_i = \mathit{run}(f(V_i, pk(k'))) \text{ for } i \geq 1, \\ & Q_i = \nu c.(\overline{c}\langle f(W_i, pk(k''))\rangle | c(y).R) \text{ with } c \notin \mathsf{fn}(W_i), \text{ for } i \geq 1, \\ & \tilde{V}(\hat{\mathcal{E}}_0)^* \tilde{W}, \\ & \mathcal{E}_0 = \mathcal{E}_1 \cup \mathcal{E}_2, \\ & \mathcal{E}_1 = \{(\widehat{pk}(k'), \widehat{pk}(k'')), (\widehat{f^{-1}}(`R, \widehat{sk}(k')), \widehat{f^{-1}}(`R, \widehat{sk}(k'')))\}, \\ & \mathcal{E}_2 \supseteq \{(b, b) \mid b \in \mathsf{fn}(R, a)\}, \\ & \mathcal{E}_2 \text{ is a finite bijection on names}, \\ & k' \notin \mathsf{fn}(\#_1(\mathcal{E}_2)) \text{ and } k'' \notin \mathsf{fn}(\#_2(\mathcal{E}_2))\} \end{array}$$

Proof. By checking the conditions of environmental bisimulation up-to context, which follow from the construction of $\mathcal{X}$. Note, in particular, that we do *not* have to put (any number of) R in parallel with P_0 and Q_0, thanks to the up-to context technique.

First, observe that $P\mathcal{X}^{(*)}_{\mathcal{E}}Q$ by the definition of $\mathcal{X}$ (with $l = 0$) and by Definition 2 (context closure for environmental bisimulations). Hence $P \simeq Q$ by Theorem 1 (soundness of environmental bisimulation up-to context) if $\mathcal{X}$ is an environmental bisimulation up-to context.

To check $\mathcal{X}$ against the conditions of environmental bisimulation up-to context (Definition 3), consider first the transitions from P_0 (Conditions 1, 2 and 3).

The output of $pk(k')$ to a by $Server_{k'}$ on the left hand side can be matched by that of $pk(k'')$ to a by $Server_{k''}$ on the right hand side. In these transitions, neither the knowledge increases, nor the processes change (up-to structural equivalence). Ditto for the output of $f^{-1}(`R, sk(k'))$ and $f^{-1}(`R, sk(k''))$.

The input of V_i from a by $Client_{k'}$ spawns a new P_i, which can be matched by that of W_i from a by $Client'_{k''}$, spawning a new Q_i. Ditto for the internal communication from $Server_{k'}$ to $Client_{k'}$ (and from $Server_{k''}$ to $Client'_{k''}$) over a.

The internal transition by the process execution $run(f(V_i, pk(k')))$ in P_i succeeds only if the verification succeeds, i.e., only if V_i is of the form $\widehat{f^{-1}}(`R', \widehat{sk}(k'))$ for some $R'$. Since $k' \notin \mathsf{fn}(\#_1(\mathcal{E}_2))$, this is possible only if $V_i = \widehat{f^{-1}}(`R, \widehat{sk}(k'))$, in which case $W_i = \widehat{f^{-1}}(`R, \widehat{sk}(k''))$. Then R is spawned both on the left hand side and on the right, which is cancelled out by up-to context.

The transitions from Q_0 (Condition 4) are similar. New processes spawned by the context (Condition 6) are also cancelled out by up-to context. This is straightforward because there are no quoted processes other than R in $\hat{\mathcal{E}}_0$. Conditions 5, 8 and 9 follow by straightforward induction on the first-order context D_t in the definition of $\hat{\mathcal{E}}_0$ (see Section 2.1). Finally, fresh names generated by the context (Condition 7) are immediately subsumed by the sub-environment $\mathcal{E}_2$.

We therefore have $P \approx Q$ from the soundness of environmental bisimulation (up-to context).

6.2 Secure Mail User Agent

Consider a client-server system where the user downloads (from the server) an e-mail user agent (MUA) to send an encrypted message.

$$
\begin{array}{ll}
P = \nu k_1.(Server_{k_1} | Client_{p,k_1}) & Q = \nu k_1.(Server_{k_1} | Client_{q,k_1}) \\
Client_{x,k_1} = \nu r.\overline{d}\langle f(r, pk(k_1))\rangle.r(y).run(\#_1(y)) | \overline{\#_2(y)}\langle x\rangle & \\
Server_{k_1} = !\overline{c}\langle pk(k_1)\rangle \mid !d(x).\nu k_2.\nu m.\overline{f^{-1}(x, sk(k_1))}\langle \widehat{Pack}_{m,k_2}\rangle & \\
\widehat{Pack}_{m,k_2} = (`MUA_{m,k_2}, m) & MUA_{m,k_2} = m(y).\overline{c}\langle f(y, \widehat{pk}(k_2))\rangle
\end{array}
$$

In this example, c and d are public channels. The client first sends a request $f(r, pk(k_1))$ to download the MUA, and waits for a reply on channel r. The server then sends the MUA back to the client, with a fresh channel m for accepting the message y, and a fresh secret key k_2 for encrypting y. (We are using the private channel r only for the sake of simplicity. It could be implemented over a public network just as in the previous example.) Finally, the client sends its message x through m. Secrecy of the message x can be formalized by a standard non-interference property, i.e., that the system is equivalent regardless of the value of x. We here use two fresh, public names p and q for the values of x.

Again, to prove this equivalence, we give an environmental relation $\mathcal{X}$ s.t. $P\mathcal{X}_{\mathcal{E}}^{(*)}Q$ for $\mathcal{E} = \{(b, b) \mid b \in \mathsf{fn}(P, Q)\}$.

Proposition 2. *The $\mathcal{X}$ in Figure 1 is an environmental bisimulation up-to context.*

$$
\begin{aligned}
\mathcal{X} &= \mathcal{X}_1 \cup \mathcal{X}_2 \cup \mathcal{X}_3 \\
\mathcal{X}_1 &= \{(\mathcal{E}_0, \{{}^{k_1', \tilde{V}}/_{k_1, \tilde{z}}\}P_1, \{{}^{q}/_{p}\}\{{}^{k_1'', \tilde{W}}/_{k_1, \tilde{z}}\}P_1) \mid \\
&\quad P_1 = Server_{k_1} | R_{k_1} | Client_{p,k_1}, \\
&\quad R_{k_1} = \nu k_2.\nu m.\overline{f^{-1}(z_1, sk(k_1))}\langle \widehat{Pack}_{m,k_2}\rangle | \ldots | \nu k_2.\nu m.\overline{f^{-1}(z_l, sk(k_1))}\langle \widehat{Pack}_{m,k_2}\rangle, \\
&\quad l \geq 0, \\
&\quad \tilde{V}(\hat{\mathcal{E}}_0)^* \tilde{W}, \\
&\quad \mathcal{E}_0 = \mathcal{E}_1 \cup \mathcal{E}_2, \\
&\quad \mathcal{E}_1 = \{\ (\widehat{pk}(k_1'), \widehat{pk}(k_1''))\ \}, \\
&\quad \mathcal{E}_2 \supseteq \{(d,d), (c,c), (p,p), (q,q)\}, \\
&\quad \mathcal{E}_2 \text{ is a finite bijection on names}, \\
&\quad k_1' \notin \mathsf{fn}(\#_1(\mathcal{E}_2)) \text{ and } k_1'' \notin \mathsf{fn}(\#_2(\mathcal{E}_2))\} \\
\mathcal{X}_2 &= \{(\mathcal{E}_0, \{{}^{k_1', \tilde{V}, r'}/_{k_1, \tilde{z}, r}\}P_2, \{{}^{q}/_{p}\}\{{}^{k_1'', \tilde{W}, r''}/_{k_1, \tilde{z}, r}\}P_2), \\
&\quad (\mathcal{E}_0, \{{}^{k_1', \tilde{V}, r'}/_{k_1, \tilde{z}, r}\}P_3, \{{}^{q}/_{p}\}\{{}^{k_1'', \tilde{W}, r''}/_{k_1, \tilde{z}, r}\}P_3), \\
&\quad (\mathcal{E}_0, \{{}^{k_1', \tilde{V}, r'}/_{k_1, \tilde{z}, r}\}P_4, \{{}^{q}/_{p}\}\{{}^{k_1'', \tilde{W}, r''}/_{k_1, \tilde{z}, r}\}P_4), \\
&\quad (\mathcal{E}_0, \{{}^{k_1', \tilde{V}, r'}/_{k_1, \tilde{z}, r}\}P_5, \{{}^{q}/_{p}\}\{{}^{k_1'', \tilde{W}, r''}/_{k_1, \tilde{z}, r}\}P_5) \mid \\
&\quad P_2 = Server_{k_1} | R_{k_1} | r(y).(run(\#_1(y)) | \overline{\#_2(y)}\langle p\rangle), \\
&\quad P_3 = Server_{k_1} | R_{k_1} | \nu k_2.\nu m.(run(\#_1(\widehat{Pack}_{m,k_2})) | \overline{\#_2(\widehat{Pack}_{m,k_2})}\langle p\rangle), \\
&\quad P_4 = Server_{k_1} | R_{k_1} | \nu k_2.\nu m.(MUA_{m,k_2} | \overline{\#_2(\widehat{Pack}_{m,k_2})}\langle p\rangle), \\
&\quad P_5 = Server_{k_1} | R_{k_1} | \nu k_2.\overline{c}\langle f(p, \widehat{pk}(k_2))\rangle, \\
&\quad R_{k_1} = \nu k_2.\nu m.\overline{f^{-1}(z_1, sk(k_1))}\langle \widehat{Pack}_{m,k_2}\rangle | \ldots | \nu k_2.\nu m.\overline{f^{-1}(z_l, sk(k_1))}\langle \widehat{Pack}_{m,k_2}\rangle, \\
&\quad l \geq 0, \\
&\quad \tilde{V}(\hat{\mathcal{E}}_0)^* \tilde{W}, \\
&\quad \mathcal{E}_0 = \mathcal{E}_1 \cup \mathcal{E}_2, \\
&\quad \mathcal{E}_1 = \{\ (\widehat{pk}(k_1'), \widehat{pk}(k_1'')), \\
&\qquad\quad (\widehat{f}(r', \widehat{pk}(k_1')), \widehat{f}(r'', \widehat{pk}(k_1'')))\ \}, \\
&\quad \mathcal{E}_2 \supseteq \{(d,d), (c,c), (p,p), (q,q)\}, \\
&\quad \mathcal{E}_2 \text{ is a finite bijection on names}, \\
&\quad k_1', r' \notin \mathsf{fn}(\#_1(\mathcal{E}_2)) \text{ and } k_1'', r'' \notin \mathsf{fn}(\#_2(\mathcal{E}_2))\} \\
\mathcal{X}_3 &= \{(\mathcal{E}_0, \{{}^{k_1', \tilde{V}, r'}/_{k_1, \tilde{z}, r}\}P_6, \{{}^{q}/_{p}\}\{{}^{k_1'', \tilde{W}, r''}/_{k_1, \tilde{z}, r}\}P_6) \mid \\
&\quad P_6 = Server_{k_1} | R_{k_1}, \\
&\quad R_{k_1} = \nu k_2.\nu m.\overline{f^{-1}(z_1, sk(k_1))}\langle \widehat{Pack}_{m,k_2}\rangle | \ldots | \nu k_2.\nu m.\overline{f^{-1}(z_l, sk(k_1))}\langle \widehat{Pack}_{m,k_2}\rangle, \\
&\quad l \geq 0, \\
&\quad \tilde{V}(\hat{\mathcal{E}}_0)^* \tilde{W}, \\
&\quad \mathcal{E}_0 = \mathcal{E}_1 \cup \mathcal{E}_2, \\
&\quad \mathcal{E}_1 = \{\ (\widehat{pk}(k_1'), \widehat{pk}(k_1'')), \\
&\qquad\quad (\widehat{f}(r', \widehat{pk}(k_1')), \widehat{f}(r'', \widehat{pk}(k_1''))), \\
&\qquad\quad (\widehat{f}(p, \widehat{pk}(k_2')), \widehat{f}(q, \widehat{pk}(k_2'')))\ \}, \\
&\quad \mathcal{E}_2 \supseteq \{(d,d), (c,c), (p,p), (q,q)\}, \\
&\quad \mathcal{E}_2 \text{ is a finite bijection on names}, \\
&\quad k_1', r', k_2' \notin \mathsf{fn}(\#_1(\mathcal{E}_2)) \text{ and } k_1'', r'', k_2'' \notin \mathsf{fn}(\#_2(\mathcal{E}_2))\}
\end{aligned}
$$

Fig. 1. Environmental relation for the secure mail user agent

Proof. By checking each condition of environmental bisimulation up-to context. Again, this is easy thanks to the construction of $\mathcal{X}$ and to the up-to context technique.

As in the case of Proposition 1, we have $P\mathcal{X}_{\mathcal{E}}^{(*)}Q$ (by taking $l = 0$ in $\mathcal{X}_1$) and therefore $P \simeq Q$, provided that $\mathcal{X}$ is an environmental bisimulation up-to context.

Let us first consider the transitions from $\{{}^{k_1', \tilde{V}}/_{k_1, \tilde{z}}\}P_1$ in $\mathcal{X}_1$. The output of $pk(k_1')$ to c by $Server_{k_1'}$ on the left hand side is matched by that of $pk(k_1'')$ to c by $Server_{k_1''}$ on the right, with no increase of knowledge and no change of processes (up-to structural equivalence). The input of V_i from d by $Server_{k_1'}$ is matched by that of W_i from d by $Server_{k_1''}$, just incrementing the number l of processes in $R_{k_1'}$ and $R_{k_1''}$, respectively.

The possible output of $\widehat{Pack}_{m',k_2'}$ (with m' and k_2' fresh) by $R_{k_1'}$ is matched by that of $\widehat{Pack}_{m'',k_2''}$ (with m'' and k_2'' fresh) by $R_{k_1''}$. This increase of knowledge can then be cancelled out by up-to context with (m', m'') and (k_2', k_2'') added in $\mathcal{E}_2$.

The output of $f(r', pk(k_1'))$ (with r' fresh) to d by $Client_{p,k_1'}$ is matched by that of $f(r'', pk(k_1''))$ (with r'' fresh) to d by $Client_{q,k_1''}$. The results are included in $\mathcal{X}_2$.

Consider the transitions from $\{^{k_1',\tilde{V},r'}/_{k_1,\tilde{z},r}\}P_2$ in $\mathcal{X}_2$. The input and output by $Server_{k_1'}$ and $R_{k_1'}$ are the same as in the case of $\mathcal{X}_1$ (see above). The internal communication between $\nu k_2.\nu m.\overline{f^{-1}(V_i, sk(k_1'))}\langle\widehat{Pack}_{m,k_2}\rangle$ (in $R_{k_1'}$, with $V_i = \widehat{f}(r', \widehat{pk}(k_1'))$) and $r'(y).(run(\#_1(y))|\overline{\#_2(y)}\langle p\rangle)$ is matched by that between $\nu k_2.\nu m.\overline{f^{-1}(W_i, sk(k_1''))}\langle\widehat{Pack}_{m,k_2}\rangle$ (in $R_{k_1''}$, with $W_i = \widehat{f}(r'', \widehat{pk}(k_1''))$) and $r''(y).(run(\#_1(y))|\overline{\#_2(y)}\langle q\rangle)$. The processes then become $\{^{k_1',\tilde{V},r'}/_{k_1,\tilde{z},r}\}P_3$ and $\{^q/_p\}\{^{k_1'',\tilde{W},r''}/_{k_1,\tilde{z},r}\}P_3$, respectively.

These processes make an internal transition by process execution $run(\#_1(\widehat{Pack}_{m,k_2}))$, becoming $\{^{k_1',\tilde{V},r'}/_{k_1,\tilde{z},r}\}P_4$ and $\{^q/_p\}\{^{k_1'',\tilde{W},r''}/_{k_1,\tilde{z},r}\}P_4$. They then make an internal communication over m and become $\{^{k_1',\tilde{V},r'}/_{k_1,\tilde{z},r}\}P_5$ and $\{^q/_p\}\{^{k_1'',\tilde{W},r''}/_{k_1,\tilde{z},r}\}P_5$, which send $\widehat{f}(p, \widehat{pk}(k_2'))$ and $\widehat{f}(q, \widehat{pk}(k_2''))$ (with k_2' and k_2'' fresh) to c. The results are included in $\mathcal{X}_3$. The other transitions are the same as in the case of $\{^{k_1',\tilde{V},r'}/_{k_1,\tilde{z},r}\}P_2$ (see above).

The transitions from $\{^{k_1',\tilde{V},r'}/_{k_1,\tilde{z},r}\}P_6$ in $\mathcal{X}_3$ are subsumed by the previous cases. Transitions from the right hand side are symmetric. Conditions on the environments follow again by straightforward induction on the first-order context D_t in the definition of $\hat{\mathcal{E}}_0$ (Section 2.1). Again as in the case of Proposition 1, processes spawned by the context are cancelled out by up-to context and fresh names generated by the context are subsumed by $\mathcal{E}_2$.

To repeat, the point of these examples is to illustrate our reasoning method for higher-order cryptographic processes ("Gmail"), even if it is possible to define first-order systems ("`mail(1)`") with a similar functionality.

7 Conclusion

We defined a higher-order process calculus parametrized by general algebra (which, for example, includes asymmetric cryptography), and developed a bisimulation proof method for proving behavioral equivalence in this language. We gave examples involving the security of higher-order systems with public-key encryption and digital signing.

As is the case with any bisimulation technique (or any "proof method" in general), it is always possible in hindsight to prove the same results as ours without explicitly using bisimulations, just by inlining (thereby duplicating) their soundness proof everywhere. In our case, doing so amounts to a brute-force proof based on the definition of reduction-closed barbed equivalence only. We emphasize that it is way too heavy to repeat such a proof in *every* instance of equivalence, so it pays to extract the proof pattern as a separate technique like ours. As in the present work, such development gives an essential insight—based on environments—for the (otherwise sightless) proof.

Acknowledgements. We thank the members of Kobayashi Laboratory in Tohoku University for their comments and helps. This work was partially supported by KAKENHI 18680003 and 20240001.

References

[1] Abadi, M., Fournet, C.: Mobile values, new names, and secure communication. In: Proceedings of the 28th ACM SIGPLAN-SIGACT Symposium on Principles of Programming Languages, pp. 104–115 (2001)

[2] Abadi, M., Gordon, A.D.: A calculus for cryptographic protocols: The spi calculus. Information and Computation 148(1), 1–70 (1999); Preliminary version appeared in Proceedings of the 4th ACM Conference on Computer and Communications Security, pp. 36–47 (1997)

[3] Baader, F., Nipkow, T.: Term Rewriting and All That. Cambridge University Press, Cambridge (1999)

[4] Blanchet, B., Abadi, M., Fournet, C.: Automated verification of selected equivalences for security protocols. In: 20th Annual IEEE Symposium on Logic in Computer Science, pp. 331–340 (2005)

[5] Borgström, J., Nestmann, U.: On bisimulations for the spi calculus. In: Kirchner, H., Ringeissen, C. (eds.) AMAST 2002. LNCS, vol. 2422, pp. 287–303. Springer, Heidelberg (2002)

[6] Maffeis, S., Abadi, M., Fournet, C., Gordon, A.D.: Code-carrying authorization. In: Jajodia, S., Lopez, J. (eds.) ESORICS 2008. LNCS, vol. 5283, pp. 563–579. Springer, Heidelberg (2008)

[7] Sangiorgi, D.: Expressing Mobility in Process Algebras: First-Order and Higher-Order Paradigm. PhD thesis, University of Edinburgh (1992)

[8] Sangiorgi, D., Kobayashi, N., Sumii, E.: Appendices to "environmental bisimulations for higher-order languages", `http://www.cs.unibo.it/~sangio/DOC_public/appLICS07.pdf`

[9] Sangiorgi, D., Kobayashi, N., Sumii, E.: Environmental bisimulations for higher-order languages. In: Twenty-Second Annual IEEE Symposium on Logic in Computer Science, pp. 293–302 (2007)

[10] Sangiorgi, D., Milner, R.: The problem of "weak bisimulation up to". In: Cleaveland, W.R. (ed.) CONCUR 1992. LNCS, vol. 630, pp. 32–46. Springer, Heidelberg (1992)

[11] Sangiorgi, D., Walker, D.: The Pi Calculus – A Theory of Mobile Processes. Cambridge University Press, Cambridge (2001)

[12] Sato, N., Sumii, E.: Proofs for "the higher-order, call-by-value applied pi-calculus", `http://www.kb.ecei.tohoku.ac.jp/~nsato/hoapp.pdf`

[13] Schneier, B.: Applied Cryptography. John Wiley & Sons, Inc., Chichester (1996)

[14] Sumii, E., Pierce, B.C.: A bisimulation for dynamic sealing. Theoretical Computer Science 375(1-3), 169–192 (2004); Extended abstract appeared in Proceedings of the 31st ACM SIGPLAN-SIGACT Symposium on Principles of Programming Languages, pp. 161–172 (2004)

[15] Sumii, E., Pierce, B.C.: A bisimulation for type abstraction and recursion. Journal of the ACM 54(5-26), 1–43 (2007); Extended abstract appeared in Proceedings of the 32nd ACM SIGPLAN-SIGACT Symposium on Principles of Programming Languages, pp. 63–74 (2005)

Branching Bisimilarity between Finite-State Systems and BPA or Normed BPP Is Polynomial-Time Decidable*

Hongfei Fu

BASICS**, Department of Computer Science
Laboratory for Intelligent Computing and Intelligent Systems
Shanghai Jiaotong University, Shanghai 200240, China
hongfeifu1984@gmail.com

Abstract. In this paper we present polynomial time algorithms deciding branching bisimilarity between finite-state systems and several classes of infinite-state systems: BPA and normed BPP. The algorithm for BPA improves a previous one given by Kučera and Mayr, while the one for normed BPP demonstrates the polynomial-time decidability of the problem, which is unknown previously. The proof style follows an early work of Kučera and Mayr, where similar results for weak bisimilarity are established.

1 Introduction

Verification of infinite structures has been studied intensively during the past two decades [1]. A subarea is the decidability and complexity issues on bisimulation-like equivalence checking. This paper investigates the problem of checking *branching bisimulation equivalence* between infinite-state processes and finite-state ones.

The motivation of this study is that the intended behavior is often easier to specify (by a finite-state system), but a 'real' implementation may contain components which are infinite-state (e.g. counters, buffers). The aim of formal verification is to check whether the finite-state specification and the infinite-state implementation are semantically equivalent (i.e., bisimilar).

The infinite-state processes we consider here are BPA (*Basic Process Algebra*) and BPP (*Basic Parallel Processes*), two subclasses in the PRS-hierarchy [2]. BPA models pure sequential programs, while BPP models pure parallel programs. A BPA process can also be regarded as a pushdown automata which contains only one state, while a BPP process can be viewed as a labeled Petri net which is communication-free. A process is *normed* if it can terminate successfully from any reachable state. The normed subclass of BPA (BPP) is denoted by nBPA (nBPP or normed BPP).

* The work is supported by The National 973 Project (2003CB317005), The National Nature Science Foundation of China (60873034, 60703033).

** Laboratory for Basic Studies in Computing Science (http://basics.sjtu.edu.cn). The extended version of this paper which contains more details is available at: http://basics.sjtu.edu.cn/~hongfei/

Z. Hu (Ed.): APLAS 2009, LNCS 5904, pp. 327–342, 2009.

Many results have been established for bisimilarity checking, especially on models in the PRS-hierarchy, for which a recent survey is given by J. Srba [3]. Most of these concern *strong bisimilarity*. In 1987, J.C.M. Baeten, J.A. Bergstra and J.W. Klop [4] discovered that strong bisimilarity is decidable for processes generating context-free languages, namely nBPA, for which the language equivalence is already undecidable [5]. Later, S. Christensen *et al* extended the decidability result to BPA [6] and BPP [7]. J. Srba gave **PSPACE**-hard complexity lower bounds in the case of BPA [8] and BPP [9]. For BPP, P. Jančar further proved that the problem is **PSPACE**-complete [10]. In the normed case, i.e. for nBPA and nBPP, polynomial algorithms are presented by Y. Hirshfeld, M. Jerrum and F. Moller [11,12]. Checking *weak bisimilarity* is somehow more difficult. Even in the case of nBPA or nBPP, the decidability is still open.

Since bisimilarity checking seems very hard for two infinite-state processes, many literatures consider the problem between an infinite-state process and a finite-state one, especially in the weak case. In [13], P. Jančar *et al* established a general result that many bisimulation-like equivalences (including strong and weak) are decidable between PAD and finite-state processes. PAD is a process class that strictly subsumes BPA and BPP. Their result is based on a general reduction from the bisimulation problem to the model checking problem for the logic EF, which is decidable on PAD [14]. Following this approach, strong bisimilarity with finite-state processes is decidable even for *weakly extended* PRS [15]. However, the approach adopted by P. Jančar *et al* cannot lead to efficient algorithms. The first efficient algorithm in the weak case is due to A. Kučera and R. Mayr [16], who presented polynomial algorithms deciding weak bisimilarity between BPA (nBPP) and finite-state processes.

An alternative notion of weak bisimulation, called *branching bisimulation* [17], receives special attention. Intuitively, in the 'branching' case, silent actions which change the internal states is differed from which do not change. Baeten [18] gives many examples on branching bisimulation and compare the difference between branching and weak bisimilarity. As for the verification on infinite structures, an early result is by H. Hüttel [19] who proved that branching bisimilarity is decidable for weakly normed BPA. Recently, Kučera and Mayr [20] presented a coarse algorithm that decides branching bisimilarity between pushdown processes and finite-state ones. A consequence of their algorithm is that branching bisimilarity between BPA and finite-state processes is polynomial time decidable. Besides the two remarkable results, little is known.

In this paper we present polynomial algorithms deciding branching bisimilarity between BPA (nBPP) and finite-state systems. The algorithm for BPA improves the previous one by Kučera and Mayr [20] significantly, while the one for nBPP demonstrates the polynomial-time decidability of the problem, which is unknown previously. Our work makes up for the lack of study on the verification for branching bisimulation over infinite structures.

We follow the scheme developed by Kučera and Mayr [16] for weak bisimilarity, which goes with the general notion of *bisimulation base*. This notion is first introduced by D.Caucal [21] and is used in many efficient algorithms [6,7,16].

The scheme in [16] is divided into two stages. The first stage is to establish the finite representability of bisimilarity. The core of this stage is to find a finite relation, called *bisimulation base*, from which each pair of bisimilar processes can be effectively generated. The second stage is to develop an algorithm that computes the bisimulation base. To this end, the *refinement* technique is used. It starts from a relation large enough to contain the base, and then iteratively performs the refinement step by computing the *expansion*. If no further refinement is possible, then the base is obtained. Throughout the refinement procedure, a *symbolic method* is adopted to help compute the expansion in polynomial time.

In our algorithms, the first stage of the scheme is directly applied. Our main efforts fall in the second stage, where substantial difference between weak and branching bisimulation lies. We elaborate the phase of expanding. This elaboration will not only cope with the specific feature of branching bisimulation, but technically benefit the refinement procedure as well. Under such efforts, we obtain upper bounds which are both lower than the counterparts in [16].

The paper is organized as follows. Section 2 introduces some preliminaries. Section 3 and Sect. 4 demonstrate the algorithms for BPA and normed BPP, respectively. Section 5 concludes the paper.

2 Preliminaries

A *labeled transition system* (LTS) is a tuple $(\mathcal{S}, \mathscr{A}, \rightarrow)$, where $\mathcal{S}$ is a set of *states*, $\mathscr{A}$ is a set of *actions* and $\rightarrow \subseteq \mathcal{S} \times \mathscr{A} \times \mathcal{S}$ is a set of *transitions*. The action label $\mathscr{A}$ is ranged over by $a, b, c, \ldots$, except for a special action τ which represents the *silent action*. $(p, a, q) \in \rightarrow$ is conventionally written $p \xrightarrow{a} q$, and this notation is extended to all elements of $\mathscr{A}^*$ in the standard way. We say that q is *reachable* from p if $p \xrightarrow{w} q$ for some $w \in \mathscr{A}^*$. $\stackrel{\tau}{\Rightarrow}$ indicates the transitive closure of $\xrightarrow{\tau}$, while $\Rightarrow$ indicates the reflexive transitive closure of $\xrightarrow{\tau}$.

Let $(\mathcal{S}, \mathscr{A}, \rightarrow)$ be the underlying LTS. A binary relation $\mathcal{R}$ over $\mathcal{S}$ is a *branching bisimulation* iff whenever $(p, q) \in \mathcal{R}$ then for each $a \in \mathscr{A}$:

- if $p \xrightarrow{a} p'$ then either $q \Rightarrow q' \xrightarrow{a} q''$ for some q' and q'' such that $(p, q') \in \mathcal{R}$ and $(p', q'') \in \mathcal{R}$, or $a = \tau$ and $(p', q) \in \mathcal{R}$
- if $q \xrightarrow{a} q'$ then either $p \Rightarrow p' \xrightarrow{a} p''$ for some p' and p'' such that $(p', q) \in \mathcal{R}$ and $(p'', q') \in \mathcal{R}$, or $a = \tau$ and $(p, q') \in \mathcal{R}$

branching bisimilarity $\approx_{\mathrm{br}}$ is the largest branching bisimulation. Two states p, q are *branching bisimilar*, if $p \approx_{\mathrm{br}} q$. $\approx_{\mathrm{br}}$ is an equivalence relation.

Finite-state, BPA and BPP systems are subclasses of *process rewrite systems* [2], a formal model of processes. Let $Const = \{X, Y, Z \ldots\}$ be a set of *process constants* and $Act = \{a, b, c \ldots\} \cup \{\tau\}$ be a set of actions. The class of *process expressions* $\mathcal{E}$ is generated by the grammar: $E ::= \varepsilon \mid X \mid E \| E \mid E.E$, where $X \in Const$ and ε is a special constant that denotes the empty expression. Intuitively, '.' and '$\|$' stand for sequential composition and parallel composition, respectively. We do not distinguish expressions up to the congruence induced by the following laws: '.' is associative, '$\|$' is associative and commutative, and ε is the unit for '.' and '$\|$'.

A process rewrite system is specified by a finite set of *rules* Δ of which each rule has the form $E \xrightarrow{a} F$, where $E, F \in \mathcal{E}$ and $a \in Act$. The sets of process constants and actions appeared in Δ are denoted $Const(\Delta)$ and $Act(\Delta)$, respectively. Each process rewrite system Δ defines an LTS, where states are process expressions over $Const(\Delta)$, $Act(\Delta)$ is the set of actions, and transitions are determined by Δ and the following inference rules: (note that '$\|$' is commutative)

$$\frac{(E \xrightarrow{a} F) \in \Delta}{E \xrightarrow{a} F} \qquad \frac{E \xrightarrow{a} E'}{E.F \xrightarrow{a} E'.F} \qquad \frac{E \xrightarrow{a} E'}{E\|F \xrightarrow{a} E'\|F}$$

Sequential and *parallel* expressions are process expressions without the '$\|$' and the '.' operator, respectively. Finite-state, BPA and BPP systems are obtained by putting certain restrictions on the form of the rules. Finite-state, BPA and BPP allow only a single constant at the left-hand side of a rule, and a single constant, sequential expression and parallel expression at the right-hand side, respectively. The set of states of the LTS generated by a finite-state, BPA or BPP system Δ is confined to $Const(\Delta)$, all sequential expressions over $Const(\Delta)$, and all parallel expressions over $Const(\Delta)$, respectively. The number of process constants contained in E is denoted by $|E|$ ($|\varepsilon| = 0$).

An expression E under a BPA or BPP system Δ is *normed* if $E \xrightarrow{w} \varepsilon$ for some $w \in Act(\Delta)^*$. Note that E is normed iff all constants in E are normed. A BPA or BPP system Δ is *normed* if every constant of $Const(\Delta)$ is normed.

In the following, the BPA or BPP system considered is denoted by Δ, and the finite-state system is denoted by Γ. Δ and Γ is usually considered as a single system by taking their disjoint union. $Const(\Delta)$ is ranged over by $X, Y, Z \ldots$, and $Const(\Gamma)$ is ranged over by $f, g, h \ldots$. The size of Δ and Γ are denoted by n and m, respectively.

An extra convention is useful to us:

- For $f, g \in Const(\Gamma)$, $f \neq g$ implies $f \not\approx_{\text{br}} g$;
- There is no $f \in Const(\Gamma)$ such that $f \stackrel{\tau}{\Rightarrow} f$.

The two requirements can be met by the following procedure on Γ: first compute the $\approx_{\text{br}}$ over Γ using the algorithm in [22], then combine the equivalent states induced by $\approx_{\text{br}}$ (i.e. the quotient construction), and finally delete all self-loops labeled with τ, i.e., transitions of the form $f \xrightarrow{\tau} f$. This procedure is called *contraction* in this paper. With this convention, the definition of a branching bisimulation $\mathcal{R}$ between Δ and Γ can be simplified as follows: whenever $(E, f) \in \mathcal{R}$,

- if $E \xrightarrow{a} E'$ then either there is some $f \xrightarrow{a} f'$ such that $(E', f') \in \mathcal{R}$, or $a = \tau$ and $(E', f) \in \mathcal{R}$;
- if $f \xrightarrow{a} f'$ then there is some $E \Rightarrow E' \xrightarrow{a} E''$ such that $(E', f) \in \mathcal{R}$ and $(E'', f') \in \mathcal{R}$.

See [23] for more information on contraction.

3 BPA Processes

In this section we present an efficient algorithm deciding branching bisimilarity between BPA system Δ and finite-state system Γ. Our algorithm improves a previous one given in [20], which is rather coarse in general.

The set $Const(\Delta)$ falls into two disjoint subsets of *normed* and *unnormed* constants. The set of all normed constants is denoted by $Normed(\Delta)$, which can be computed in advance in $\mathcal{O}(n^2)$ time. Elements of $Const(\Delta)^*$ are ranged over by $\alpha, \beta, \ldots$. In our demonstration, we will also use processes of the form αf; they are regarded as BPA processes with the underlying system $\Delta \cup \Gamma$.

First of all we establish a notion of bisimulation base between Δ and Γ. We follow the scheme in [16] and much of the development is similar.

Definition 1. *Let $\mathcal{G}_\Gamma$ be the set:*

$$\mathcal{G}_\Gamma = \{(f,f) | f \in Const(\Gamma)\} \cup \{(\varepsilon, f) | f \in Const(\Gamma), \varepsilon \approx_{\text{br}} f\}$$

A relation K is well-formed *iff $\mathcal{G}_\Gamma \subseteq K$ and K is a subset of the relation $\mathcal{G}$ defined by:*

$$\mathcal{G} = ((Normed(\Delta) \cdot Const(\Gamma)) \times Const(\Gamma)) \cup (Const(\Delta) \times Const(\Gamma)) \cup \mathcal{G}_\Gamma$$

The bisimulation base, *denoted $\mathcal{B}$, is a well-formed relation defined as follows:*

$$\mathcal{B} = \{(Yf, g) | Yf \approx_{\text{br}} g, Y \in Normed(\Delta)\} \cup \{(Y, g) | Y \approx_{\text{br}} g\} \cup \mathcal{G}_\Gamma$$

Any well-formed relation is of size $\mathcal{O}(nm^2)$. $\mathcal{G}$ is the greatest well-formed relation.

As branching bisimilarity is a left congruence w.r.t. sequential composition, we can generate from $\mathcal{B}$ new branching bisimilar pairs by substitution. This generation procedure can be defined for any well-formed relation as follows:

Definition 2. *Let K be a well-formed relation. The* closure *of K, denoted $Cl(K)$, is the least relation M which satisfies the following conditions:*

1. *$K \subseteq M$,*
2. *if $(Yf, g) \in K$ and $(\alpha, f) \in M$, then $(Y\alpha, g) \in M$,*
3. *if $(Yf, g) \in K$ and $(\alpha h, f) \in M$, then $(Y\alpha h, g) \in M$,*
4. *if $(\alpha, g) \in M$ and α is unnormed, then $(\alpha\beta, g), (\alpha\beta h, g) \in M$ for every $\beta \in Const(\Delta)^*$ and $h \in Const(\Gamma)$.*

Note that $Cl(K)$ contains elements of just two forms: (α, g) and $(\alpha f, g)$. Clearly $Cl(K) = \bigcup_{i=0}^{\infty} Cl(K)^i$ where $Cl(K)^0 = K$ and $Cl(K)^{i+1}$ consists of $Cl(K)^i$ and the pairs which can be immediately derived from $Cl(K)^i$ by the rule 2-4 of Definition 2.

The following theorem shows that although the closure of a well-formed relation can be infinite, its structure is in some sense regular.

Theorem 1. *Let K be a well-formed relation. For each $g \in Const(\Gamma)$ there is a finite automaton $\mathcal{A}_g^K$ of size $\mathcal{O}(nm^2)$ constructible in $\mathcal{O}(nm^2)$ time such that $L(\mathcal{A}_g^K) = \{\alpha | (\alpha, g) \in Cl(K)\} \cup \{\alpha f | (\alpha f, g) \in Cl(K)\}$*

From the construction of $\mathcal{A}_g^K$, we can obtain that: for various g, the automaton $\mathcal{A}_g^K$ is only differed by the initial state which is determined by g (see also [16, Sect. 6]). (Here the redundant part of the automaton is kept.) This initial state is recorded as $\tilde{g}$. Below we will use $\mathcal{A}^K$ to denote the automaton attached to K with initial state unspecified.

Following Theorem 1, the membership problem of checking if $(\alpha, g) \in Cl(K)$ or $(\alpha f, g) \in Cl(K)$ is decidable in $\mathcal{O}((|\alpha|+1)nm^2)$ time.

Another property of $Cl(K)$ is as follows.

Lemma 1. *Let* $(\alpha f, g) \in Cl(K)$. *If* $(\beta h, f) \in Cl(K)$, *then also* $(\alpha\beta h, g) \in Cl(K)$. *Similarly, if* $(\beta, f) \in Cl(K)$, *then also* $(\alpha\beta, g) \in Cl(K)$.

The importance of the bisimulation base is clarified by the following theorem.

Theorem 2. *For all* α, f, g *we have* $\alpha \approx_{\rm br} g$ *iff* $(\alpha, g) \in Cl(\mathcal{B})$, *and* $\alpha f \approx_{\rm br} g$ *iff* $(\alpha f, g) \in Cl(\mathcal{B})$.

Remark 1. All results above in this section have counterparts in [16]. The (only) difference is as follows. Since we have the convention that Γ is contracted in advance, the form of Definition 1, Definition 2 is confined; The proof of Theorem 2 can be obtained by modifying the semantics of weak bisimulation with the one of branching bisimulation in the proof of [16, Theorem 8].

By Theorem 1 and Theorem 2, once $\mathcal{B}$ is computed, it can be used to decide branching bisimilarity between Δ and Γ in polynomial time.

Now we illustrate the computation of the bisimulation base. The computation involves a notion of *expansion* and an approximation procedure. The expansion serves as a one-step refinement on well-formed relations. With this notion, the approximation procedure is as follows: we start from $\mathcal{G}$ as the initial approximation of $\mathcal{B}$, and then iteratively compute the expansion on $\mathcal{G}$. In each refinement step, some pairs could be deleted from the current approximation. Whenever there is no pair to delete during a refinement step, then the current approximation is exactly $\mathcal{B}$.

Let K be a well-formed relation. Like [16, Definition 9], it seems that we may define that a pair, say (X, g), expands in K by the following conditions:

- for each $X \xrightarrow{a} \alpha$, either there is some $g \xrightarrow{a} g'$ such that $(\alpha, g') \in Cl(K)$, or $a = \tau$ and $(\alpha, g) \in Cl(K)$
- for each $g \xrightarrow{a} g'$, there is some $X \Rightarrow \alpha' \xrightarrow{a} \alpha$ such that $(\alpha', g) \in Cl(K)$ and $(\alpha, g') \in Cl(K)$

However the second condition involves two-level correlations: α' matching g and α matching g'. This leads to extra complexity for verification. To avoid this, we adopt an indirect approach. The general idea is that for each $g \xrightarrow{a} h \in \Gamma$, we introduce a regular language $L^K_{[g,a,h]}$ which accepts all expressions that can immediately (without extra τ-steps) match the transition $g \xrightarrow{a} h$. With this idea, the second condition above can be rewritten as follows:

– for each $g \xrightarrow{a} g'$, there is some α' such that $X \Rightarrow \alpha'$ and $\alpha' \in L^K_{[g,a,g']}$

The actual situation is a little bit different, as will be illustrated below.

Definition 3. *Let K be a well-formed relation. For each $g \xrightarrow{a} h \in \Gamma$, we say that a pair $(X,g),(Xf,g) \in K$ satisfies the condition $\phi^K_{[g,a,h]}$, if:*

- *For (X,g): X is unnormed and there is some $X \xrightarrow{a} \alpha$ such that $(\alpha,h) \in Cl(K)$*
- *For (Xf,g): there is some $X \xrightarrow{a} \alpha$ such that $(\alpha f,h) \in Cl(K)$*

Then, the (regular) language $L^K_{[g,a,h]}$ is defined as the union of the regular languages below:

- *$\{X\} \cdot L(\mathcal{A}^K_f)$, for (Xf,g) satisfies $\phi^K_{[g,a,h]}$*
- *$\{X\} \cdot Const(\Delta)^* + \{X\} \cdot Const(\Delta)^* \cdot Const(\Gamma)$, for (X,g) satisfies $\phi^K_{[g,a,h]}$*

The regular language $L^K_{[g,a,h]}$ tries to accept all processes E of the form α or αf satisfying: $(E,g) \in Cl(K)$, and there is some $E \xrightarrow{a} F$ such that $(F,h) \in Cl(K)$. This point is formulated in the next two lemmas.

Lemma 2. *Let K be a well-formed relation and $g \xrightarrow{a} h \in \Gamma$. If $\alpha \in L^K_{[g,a,h]}$, then $(\alpha,g) \in Cl(K)$ and there is some $\alpha \xrightarrow{a} \beta$ such that $(\beta,h) \in Cl(K)$. If $\alpha f \in L^K_{[g,a,h]}$, then $(\alpha f,g) \in Cl(K)$ and there is some $\alpha \xrightarrow{a} \beta$ such that $(\beta f,h) \in Cl(K)$.*

Lemma 3. *Let K be a well-formed relation such that $\mathcal{B} \subseteq K$ and $g \xrightarrow{a} h \in \Gamma$. If $\alpha \approx_{\rm br} g$ and there is $\alpha \xrightarrow{a} \beta$ such that $\beta \approx_{\rm br} h$, then $\alpha \in L^K_{[g,a,h]}$. If $\alpha f \approx_{\rm br} g$ and there is $\alpha \xrightarrow{a} \beta$ such that $\beta f \approx_{\rm br} h$, then $\alpha f \in L^K_{[g,a,h]}$.*

Note that we use the relation $\approx_{\rm br}$ in the premiss of Lemma 3. It cannot be replaced by $Cl(K)$, for which a counterexample is given in [23, Example 1]. However Lemma 3 will be strong enough for $L^K_{[g,a,h]}$ to 'represent' the set of processes that can immediately match the transition $g \xrightarrow{a} h$ w.r.t $Cl(K)$.

Another two properties of the language $L^K_{[g,a,h]}$ are as follows.

Lemma 4. *Let K be a well-formed relation, $g \xrightarrow{a} h \in \Gamma$ and $t \in Const(\Gamma)$. If $\alpha f \in L^K_{[g,a,h]}$ and $(\beta,f) \in Cl(K)$, then $\alpha\beta \in L^K_{[g,a,h]}$. If $\alpha f \in L^K_{[g,a,h]}$ and $(\beta t,f) \in Cl(K)$, then $\alpha\beta t \in L^K_{[g,a,h]}$.*

Lemma 5. *Let K be a well-formed relation. If $\alpha \in L^K_{[g,a,h]}$ and α is unnormed, then $\alpha\beta \in L^K_{[g,a,h]}$ and $\alpha\beta f \in L^K_{[g,a,h]}$ for any $\beta \in Const(\Delta)^*$ and $f \in Const(\Gamma)$.*

The proofs for Lemma 2-5 are put in [23] (Lemma 3-6) for lack of space.

Remark 2. Let K be a well-formed relation. To construct a finite automaton that accepts $L^K_{[g,a,h]}$, we need only to add small ingredients into $\mathcal{A}^K$. Thus, only *one* copy of $\mathcal{A}^K$ is needed. This fact comes from the simple definition in Definition 3, and will benefit the approximation procedure later on.

Now we define the notion of *expansion* following the idea mentioned before. It specifies the conditions on which a given pair is *not* deleted from the current approximation of $\mathcal{B}$.

Definition 4. *Let K be a well-formed relation. A pair in K* expands K *iff*

- *the pair is of the form (Y, g) satisfying: whenever $Y \xrightarrow{a} \alpha$, there is some $g \xrightarrow{a} g'$ such that $(\alpha, g') \in Cl(K)$, or $a = \tau$ and $(\alpha, g) \in Cl(K)$; and whenever $g \xrightarrow{a} g'$, there is some $Y \Rightarrow \alpha$ such that $\alpha \in L^K_{[g,a,g']}$.*
- *the pair is of the form (Yf, g) satisfying: whenever $Yf \xrightarrow{a} \alpha f$, there is some $g \xrightarrow{a} g'$ such that $(\alpha f, g') \in Cl(K)$, or $a = \tau$ and $(\alpha f, g) \in Cl(K)$; and either whenever $g \xrightarrow{a} g'$ there is some $Y \Rightarrow \alpha$ such that $\alpha f \in L^K_{[g,a,g']}$, or $Y \Rightarrow \varepsilon$ and $f = g$.*
- *the pair is of the form (f, f) or (ε, f).*

The set $Exp(K)$ is defined as all pairs in K that expand K.

Remark 3. The second part of the condition for a pair of the form (Yf, g) is a stronger setting of branching bisimulation. It stresses that to match the transition $g \xrightarrow{a} g'$, f should not be involved. This takes advantage of the fact that, given $Yf \approx_{\mathrm{br}} g$ and $g \xrightarrow{a} g'$, if there is $Yf \Rightarrow f \Rightarrow f' \xrightarrow{a} f''$ such that $g \approx_{\mathrm{br}} f'$ and $g' \approx_{\mathrm{br}} f''$, then by the stuttering lemma [17], we have $f \approx_{\mathrm{br}} g$ thus $f = g$ by the contraction.

Similar to [16, Lemma 10], the notion of expansion is in some sense compatible with branching bisimulation. This is specified in the following lemma.

Lemma 6. *Let K be a well-formed relation such that $Exp(K) = K$. Then $Cl(K)$ is a branching bisimulation.*

Proof. We prove alternately that every pair (α, g), $(\alpha f, g)$ of $Cl(K)^i$ with $\alpha \neq \varepsilon$ satisfies the following conditions :

- For (α, g): whenever $\alpha \xrightarrow{a} \beta$, there is some $g \xrightarrow{a} g'$ such that $(\beta, g') \in Cl(K)$, or $a = \tau$ and $(\beta, g) \in Cl(K)$; and whenever $g \xrightarrow{a} g'$, there is some $\alpha \Rightarrow \beta$ such that $\beta \in L^K_{[g,a,g']}$.
- For $(\alpha f, g)$: whenever $\alpha f \xrightarrow{a} \beta f$, there is some $g \xrightarrow{a} g'$ such that $(\beta f, g') \in Cl(K)$, or $a = \tau$ and $(\beta f, g) \in Cl(K)$; and either whenever $g \xrightarrow{a} g'$ there is some $\alpha \Rightarrow \beta$ such that $\beta f \in L^K_{[g,a,g']}$, or $f = g$ and $\alpha \Rightarrow \varepsilon$.

Pairs of the form (f, f) and (ε, f) in $Cl(K)$ are already branching bisimilar, thus are not concerned here. By Lemma 2, these conditions guarantee that $Cl(K)$ is a branching bisimulation. The proof is by induction on i of $Cl(K)^i$, and we will only consider pairs of the form $(\alpha f, g)$ (the other is similar).

Base step: $i = 0$. Then $(\alpha f, g) \in K$ and the pair satisfies the conditions directly by the fact that $K = Exp(K)$.

Induction step: Let $(\alpha f, g) \in Cl(K)^{i+1}$. There are two possibilities:

1. $\alpha = Y\beta$, and there is some h such that $(Yh, g) \in K$, $(\beta f, h) \in Cl(K)^i$.
   Consider the pair $(Yh, g) \in K$. On one hand, suppose that $Y \xrightarrow{a} \gamma$. Since $K = Exp(K)$, either there is some $g \xrightarrow{a} g'$ such that $(\gamma h, g') \in Cl(K)$, or $a = \tau$ and $(\gamma h, g) \in Cl(K)$. By Lemma 1, we have either $(\gamma\beta f, g') \in Cl(K)$ or $(\gamma\beta f, g) \in Cl(K)$ as desired.

   On the other hand, we have two cases: either, whenever $g \xrightarrow{a} g'$ there is some $Y \Rightarrow \gamma$ such that $\gamma h \in L^K_{[g,a,g']}$, or, $h = g$ and $Y \Rightarrow \varepsilon$. In the former case, we have $\gamma\beta f \in L^K_{[g,a,g']}$ by Lemma 4 as desired. In the latter case, consider the pair $(\beta f, g)$. By inductive assumption, either $f = g$ and $\beta \Rightarrow \varepsilon$, or, whenever $g \xrightarrow{a} g'$, there is some $\beta \Rightarrow \gamma$ such that $\gamma f \in L^K_{[g,a,g']}$. In the first situation, we have $\alpha \Rightarrow \varepsilon$ and we are done; and in the second situation, the result follows immediately by the fact that $\alpha f \Rightarrow \gamma f$.
2. $\alpha = \beta\gamma$, $(\beta, g) \in Cl(K)^i$ and β is unnormed.
   On one hand, whenever $\beta \xrightarrow{a} \beta'$, by inductive assumption, either there is some $g \xrightarrow{a} g'$ such that $(\beta', g') \in Cl(K)$, or $a = \tau$ and $(\beta', g) \in Cl(K)$. By the fourth rule of Definition 2, we have either $(\beta'\gamma f, g') \in Cl(K)$ or $(\beta'\gamma f, g) \in Cl(K)$ as desired.

   On the other hand, we have by inductive assumption: whenever $g \xrightarrow{a} g'$, there is some $\beta \Rightarrow \beta'$ such that $\beta' \in L^K_{[g,a,g']}$ (note that $\beta \not\Rightarrow \varepsilon$ and β' is unnormed). By Lemma 5, we have $\beta'\gamma f \in L^K_{[g,a,g']}$ as desired. □

With the notion of expansion established, $\mathcal{B}$ can be approximated in the following way: $\mathcal{B}^0 = \mathcal{G}$, $\mathcal{B}^{i+1} = Exp(\mathcal{B}^i)$.

Theorem 3. *There is a natural number j, bounded by $\mathcal{O}(nm^2)$, such that $\mathcal{B}^j = \mathcal{B}^{j+1}$. Moreover, $\mathcal{B}^j = \mathcal{B}$.*

Proof. It may be tedious but not difficult to observe that Exp (viewed as a function on the complete lattice of well-formed relations) is monotone. Thus the greatest fixed point exists and can be reached after $\mathcal{O}(nm^2)$ steps, since the size of $\mathcal{G}$ is $\mathcal{O}(nm^2)$. The task remained is to show that $\mathcal{B}^j = \mathcal{B}$.

$\mathcal{B}^j \subseteq \mathcal{B}$: Directly by Lemma 6 and the fact that $\mathcal{B}^j \subseteq Cl(\mathcal{B}^j)$.

$\mathcal{B} \subseteq \mathcal{B}^j$: We need only to show that if $\mathcal{B} \subseteq K$, then $\mathcal{B} \subseteq Exp(K)$. Equivalently we show that $\mathcal{B} = Exp(\mathcal{B})$ since Exp is monotone. We only consider pairs of the form (Yf, g), the other is similar. Let $(Yf, g) \in \mathcal{B}$. The first part of the condition for the pair (Yf, g) in Definition 4 is satisfied directly by the contraction and Theorem 2. As for the second part, we assume that $Y \not\Rightarrow \varepsilon$ or $f \neq g$ (otherwise we are done). Then whenever $g \xrightarrow{a} h$, there is some $Y \Rightarrow \alpha \xrightarrow{a} \beta$ such that $\alpha f \approx_{\rm br} g$ and $\beta f \approx_{\rm br} h$ (recall the contraction and Remark 3). By Lemma 3, we have $\alpha f \in L^{\mathcal{B}}_{[g,a,h]}$ as desired. □

Theorem 3 demonstrates the eligibility of the expansion. The task remained is to show that the approximation procedure can be carried out in polynomial time. In [16, Theorem 12], a 'symbolic technique' is used to represent infinite subsets in the BPA state space. We reproduce it here in the following theorem.

Theorem 4. *For all $X \in Const(\Delta)$, there is a finite automaton D_X of size $\mathcal{O}(n)$ and constructible in $\mathcal{O}(n^2)$ time such that $L(D_X) = \{\alpha | X \Rightarrow \alpha\}$.*

Proof. The proof is a simplified version of the one for [16, Theorem 12]. See [23, Theorem 4] for details. □

The crucial part of the computation is presented in the following theorem. Some extra notations are adopted. Let A be a finite automaton. The set of states, the transition relation and the set of final states of A is denoted $Q(A)$, $\delta(A)$ and $F(A)$, respectively. Further the finite automaton obtained by letting p be the initial state in A is denoted $A\langle p \rangle$.

Theorem 5. *Let K be a well-formed relation. The set $Exp(K)$ can be computed in $\mathcal{O}(n^3m^3)$ time.*

Proof. We need some preparations. For each $X \in Const(\Delta)$ and $f \in Const(\Gamma)$, we construct $D_X{\cdot}f$ which is the obvious concatenate automaton that accepts the regular language $L(D_X){\cdot}\{f\}$. We construct another finite automaton ρ as follows: $\delta(\rho)$ is initially empty, and then for each $Y \xrightarrow{a} \alpha \in \Delta$, two extended transitions $(Y_a^\alpha, \alpha, q_\rho)$ and (Y, α, q_ρ) are added to $\delta(\rho)$. Here Y_a^α, Y and q_ρ are states of $Q(\rho)$ (which we do not state explicitly), and the extended transitions can be decomposed to obtain the underlying standard transitions. Set $F(\rho) = \{q_\rho\}$ and the initial state of ρ is not concerned. This ends the construction for ρ. Further for each $f \in Const(\Gamma)$, we construct the automaton $\rho{\cdot}f$ in the same way as $D_X{\cdot}f$, where the initial state is ignored as well. Note that ρ and each $\rho{\cdot}f$, $D_X{\cdot}f$ is of size $\mathcal{O}(n)$, and is constructible in $\mathcal{O}(n^2)$ time. After these constructions, we compute two subsets of $Q(D_X{\cdot}f)$ for each $D_X{\cdot}f$, namely $Q'(D_X{\cdot}f)$ and $Q''(D_X{\cdot}f)$. $Q'(D_X{\cdot}f)$ contains all the states that accept a non-empty language as a initial state. $Q''(D_X{\cdot}f)$ is the set of states which are reachable from the initial state of $D_X{\cdot}f$ by only (possibly zero) ε transitions. Similar computation is also carried out on each automaton D_X. All these takes $\mathcal{O}(n^2m)$ time.

For each $X \in Const(\Delta)$, and $f \in Const(\Gamma)$, we construct λ_X (resp. $\lambda_{(X,f)}$) to be the product automaton between D_X (resp. $D_X{\cdot}f$) and $\mathcal{A}^K$, and we construct μ (resp. μ_f) to be the product automaton between ρ (resp. $\rho{\cdot}f$) and $\mathcal{A}^K$. We stipulate that $\mathcal{A}^K$ is on the right of these products. Note that each automaton constructed above in this passage is of size $\mathcal{O}(n^2m^2)$ and constructible in $\mathcal{O}(n^2m^2)$ time. Further, for each automaton A constructed above in this passage, we compute a boolean marking $M\{A\}$ on $Q(A)$ such that for each $p \in Q(A)$, $M\{A\}[p] = true$ iff $L(A\langle p \rangle)$ is non-empty. This takes $\mathcal{O}(n^2m^2)$ time for one such A, and $\mathcal{O}(n^3m^3)$ time for all such A.

From Remark 2, the automaton $\mathcal{A}^K$ can serve as a common component: we need only to adjust the initial state if necessary. As we shall see, the automata ρ and $\rho{\cdot}f$ will also be treated as certain common components in this proof.

We need to decide $\phi^K_{[g,a,h]}$ for each $g \xrightarrow{a} h \in \Gamma$. However it is already computed. By the construction of μ and Theorem 1, (Y, g) satisfies $\phi^K_{[g,a,h]}$ if and only if $(Y, g) \in K$, Y is unnormed and $M\{\mu\}[(Y, \tilde{h})] = true$ (note that $(Y, \tilde{h}) \in Q(\mu)$).

Similarly, (Yf, g) satisfies $\phi^K_{[g,a,h]}$ if and only if $(Yf, g) \in K$ and $M\{\mu_f\}[(Y, \tilde{h})] = true$.

Now we compute $Exp(K)$. Consider pairs of the form (Yf, g). First we find all $Y \in Const(\Delta)$, $f \in Const(\Gamma)$ and $g \xrightarrow{a} h \in \Gamma$ such that $(L(D_Y)\cdot\{f\}) \cap L^K_{[g,a,h]} \neq \emptyset$. To this end, for each $g \xrightarrow{a} h \in \Gamma$ and each $D_Y \cdot f$ we do the following: for each transition $(p, Z, q) \in \delta(D_Y \cdot f)$ such that $p \in Q''(D_Y \cdot f)$, $q \in Q'(D_Y \cdot f)$ and $Z \in Const(\Delta)$, we check

- whether (Z, g) satisfies $\phi^K_{[g,a,h]}$ (already computed);
- whether there is some $r \in Const(\Gamma)$ such that (Zr, g) satisfies $\phi^K_{[g,a,h]}$ and $M\{\lambda_{(Y,f)}\}[(q, \tilde{r})] = true$.

If either one is true, we assert that $(L(D_Y) \cdot \{f\}) \cap L^K_{[g,a,h]} \neq \emptyset$. This assertion is guaranteed by Definition 3, Remark 2 and the product construction. The time complexity is $\mathcal{O}(nm)$, since $D_Y \cdot f$ is of size $\mathcal{O}(n)$ and each checking above takes $\mathcal{O}(m)$ time. Thus the total time complexity here is $\mathcal{O}(n^2m^3)$. Then, we check the conditions in Definition 4 for a pair $(Yf, g) \in K$. On one hand, we check: whenever $Yf \xrightarrow{a} \alpha f$, either $a = \tau$ and $M\{\mu_f\}[(Y^\alpha_a, \tilde{g})] = true$, or there is some $g \xrightarrow{a} h$ such that $M\{\mu_f\}[(Y^\alpha_a, \tilde{h})] = true$ (note that $(Y^\alpha_a, \tilde{g}), (Y^\alpha_a, \tilde{h}) \in Q(\mu_f)$). By the construction of μ_f and Theorem 1, one can see that this really checks the first part of the condition for the pair (Yf, g) in Definition 4. The checking requires $\mathcal{O}(nm)$ queries of $M\{\mu_f\}$, thus takes $\mathcal{O}(nm)$ time. On the other hand, we need to check: either $f = g$ and $Y \Rightarrow \varepsilon$, or whenever $g \xrightarrow{a} h$ there is some $Y \Rightarrow \alpha$ such that $\alpha f \in L^K_{[g,a,h]}$. The former takes $\mathcal{O}(n^2)$ time. For the latter, we check by the 'symbolic' method: if $(L(D_Y) \cdot \{f\}) \cap L^K_{[g,a,h]} \neq \emptyset$ for all $g \xrightarrow{a} h \in \Gamma$, which are already computed. Since there are $\mathcal{O}(nm^2)$ pairs of such form, the total time complexity is loosely $\mathcal{O}(n^3m^3)$. Thus the overall time complexity for this case is $\mathcal{O}(n^3m^3)$.

Pairs of the form (Y, g) in K are handled in nearly the same way as for the previous case. First we find all $Y \in Const(\Delta)$ and $g \xrightarrow{a} h \in \Gamma$ such that $L(D_Y) \cap L^K_{[g,a,h]}$ is non-empty. Then we perform the checking based on this computation. The only difference is that we do not bother the special case in Remark 3, and the appearance of 'f' in the previous case is ignored. The overall time complexity here will be lower. At this point we conclude that $Exp(K)$ can be computed in $\mathcal{O}(n^3m^3)$ time. □

Then to compute $\mathcal{B}$, we need to perform the computation of the expansion $\mathcal{O}(nm^2)$ times (Theorem 3). Thus we have the following theorem:

Theorem 6. *The bisimulation base $\mathcal{B}$ can be computed in $\mathcal{O}(n^4m^5)$ time.*

Based on Theorem 6, we obtain an efficient algorithm deciding branching bisimilarity between BPA and finite-state processes. The algorithm largely refines the previous one given in [20].

4 Normed BPP Processes

In this section we show that branching bisimilarity can be decided in polynomial time between normed BPP system Δ and finite-state system Γ. The basic structure is similar to the one for BPA. Following [16], the bisimulation base is established. Our main efforts lie in the computation of the base. We will only state the main results for lack of space. The details can be found in [23].

We introduce some additional notations. The set of all parallel expressions over $Const(\Delta)$ is denoted by $Const(\Delta)^{\otimes}$. Elements of $Const(\Delta)^{\otimes}$ are ranged over by α, β, γ, and elements of $Const(\Delta)^*$ are ranged over by ζ, η, θ and ξ.

We assume w.l.o.g that (†): for every $f, g \in Const(\Gamma)$ with g reachable from f, there is h reachable from g such that $\varepsilon \approx_{\text{br}} h$. States of $Const(\Gamma)$ which do not meet (†) can be safely removed, since they will not be branching bisimilar with any nBPP processes. It can be obtained that the contraction, which is performed on Γ in advance, preserves (†).

We pre-compute the relation $\{(f\|g, h) \mid f\|g \approx_{\text{br}} h\}$. This can be achieved by performing the algorithm described in [22] on $\Gamma \cup (\Gamma\|\Gamma)$, where $\Gamma\|\Gamma$ contains exactly all processes of the form $f\|g$ with $f, g \in Const(\Gamma)$. It takes $\mathcal{O}(m^4)$ time since the size of $\Gamma \cup (\Gamma\|\Gamma)$ is $\mathcal{O}(m^2)$.

We reproduce the notion of *linear representation* in [16] here. For each $\alpha \in Const(\Delta)^{\otimes}$, the set $Lin(\alpha)$ is defined as follows:

$$Lin(X_1\|\ldots\|X_k) = \{X_{\pi(1)}\ldots X_{\pi(k)} | \pi \text{ is a permutation of the set } \{1, 2, \ldots k\}\}$$

For example, $Lin(X\|Y\|Z) = \{XYZ, XZY, YXZ, YZX, ZXY, ZYX\}$. We assume that each $Lin(\alpha)$ contains some unique element called *canonical form* of $Lin(\alpha)$, denoted $\overline{\alpha}$. The canonical form can be chosen arbitrarily, e.g., one can fix a linear order on $Const(\Delta)$ and let $\overline{\alpha}$ be the sorted order of α. For each $\zeta \in Const(\Delta)^*$, We use $[\zeta]$ to indicate the $\alpha \in Const(\Delta)^{\otimes}$ such that $\zeta \in Lin(\alpha)$.

Definition 5. *Let $\mathcal{G}_\Gamma$ be the set $\{(\varepsilon, f) | f \in Const(\Gamma), \varepsilon \approx_{\text{br}} f\}$. A relation K is* well-formed *iff $\mathcal{G}_\Gamma \subseteq K$ and K is a subset of $\mathcal{G}$ defined by:*

$$\mathcal{G} = (Const(\Delta) \times Const(\Gamma)) \cup \mathcal{G}_\Gamma$$

The bisimulation base *for Δ and Γ, denoted $\mathcal{B}$, is defined as follows:*

$$\mathcal{B} = \{(X, f) | X \approx_{\text{br}} f\} \cup \mathcal{G}_\Gamma$$

Definition 6. *Let K be a well-formed relation. The* closure *of K, denoted $Cl(K)$, is the least relation M satisfying:*

1. *$K \subseteq M$*
2. *if $(X, g) \in K, (\beta, h) \in M$, and $f \approx_{\text{br}} g\|h$, then $(X\|\beta, f) \in M$*

Theorem 7. *Let $\alpha \in Const(\Delta)^{\otimes}$, $f \in Const(\Gamma)$. We have that $\alpha \approx_{\text{br}} f$ iff $(\alpha, f) \in Cl(\mathcal{B})$.*

The following theorem is an enhanced version of [16, Theorem 24]. It shows that the closure of any well-formed relation is in some sense regular.

Theorem 8. *Let K be a well-formed relation. For each $h \in Const(\Gamma)$, there is a finite automaton $\mathcal{A}_h^K$ with $\mathcal{O}(m)$ states, of size $\mathcal{O}(nm^2)$ constructible in $\mathcal{O}(nm^2)$ time and without ε transitions such that the following two conditions hold:*

- *if $\mathcal{A}_h^K$ accepts some elements of $Lin(\alpha)$, then $(\alpha, h) \in Cl(K)$;*
- *if $(\alpha, h) \in Cl(K)$, then $\mathcal{A}_h^K$ accepts all elements of $Lin(\alpha)$.*

In the proof of Theorem 8, one can see that: for various h, the automaton $\mathcal{A}_h^K$ is only differed by the initial state (which is *exactly* h). We use $\mathcal{A}^K$ to indicate the automaton attached to K with initial state unspecified.

Remark 4. A small error is detected in [16, Theorem 24]. The time complexity should be $\mathcal{O}(nm^2)$ instead of $\mathcal{O}(nm)$ for the appearance of rules of the form $s \to Xf$ in the construction of G_g. Then the overall complexity for nBPP in [16] should be $\mathcal{O}(n^{12}m^{11})$, instead of $\mathcal{O}(n^{12}m^9)$.

The following theorem establishes the symbolic representation of the set of states reachable from a given $X \in Const(\Delta)$ through '$\Rightarrow$'.

Theorem 9. *For all $X \in Const(\Delta)$ there is a context-free grammar G_X in 3-GNF (Greibach normal form, i.e., with at most 2 variables at the right hand side of every production) of size $\mathcal{O}(n^4)$, constructible in time $\mathcal{O}(n^4)$ such that the following three conditions hold:*

1. *if G_X generates one element of $Lin(\alpha)$, then $X \Rightarrow \alpha$;*
2. *if $X \Rightarrow \alpha$, then G_X generates at least one element of $Lin(\alpha)$;*
3. *if $\zeta \in L(G_X) \cap Lin(\alpha)$ and $\zeta = \eta Y \theta$ for some $Y \in Const(\Delta)$ and $\eta, \theta \in Const(\Delta)^*$, then there is some $\xi \in Lin([\eta] \| [\theta])$ such that $Y\xi \in L(G_X)$.*

The third condition of Theorem 9 is special. Informally it says that if $X \Rightarrow \alpha$, then in $L(G_X)$ each constant of α has a chance to appear at the beginning.

Then we establish the notion of expansion. The general idea is the same as in Sect. 3. However its form is more complicated by the commutativity of '$\|$'.

Definition 7. *Let K be a well-formed relation. For each $g \xrightarrow{a} h \in \Gamma$, we say that a tuple $(X, r, s) \in Const(\Delta) \times Const(\Gamma) \times Const(\Gamma)$ satisfies the condition $\phi^K_{[g,a,h]}$, if:*

- *$(X, r) \in K$ and $r \| s \approx_{\mathrm{br}} g$*
- *there is $r \xrightarrow{a} t \in \Gamma$ and $X \xrightarrow{a} \alpha \in \Delta$ such that $t \| s \approx_{\mathrm{br}} h$ and $\overline{\alpha} \in L(\mathcal{A}_t^K)$*

We say that (X, s) satisfies $\phi^K_{[g,a,h]}$ if there is some $r \in Const(\Gamma)$ such that (X, r, s) satisfies $\phi^K_{[g,a,h]}$. Then the regular language $L^K_{[g,a,h]}$ is defined as the union of all $\{X\} \cdot L(\mathcal{A}_s^K)$ such that (X, s) satisfies $\phi^K_{[g,a,h]}$.

Remark 5. Again for any well-formed K, a finite automaton that accepts $L^K_{[g,a,h]}$ is constructible from only one copy of $\mathcal{A}^K$, provided that $\phi^K_{[g,a,h]}$ has been computed. The point is that all such automata shares the major part, i.e., $\mathcal{A}^K$.

The relation between $L^K_{[g,a,h]}$ and the set of processes that can immediately match the transition $g \xrightarrow{a} h$ w.r.t $Cl(K)$ is formulated in the following two lemmas.

Lemma 7. *Let K be a well-formed relation. If $L^K_{[g,a,h]}$ contains some elements of $Lin(\alpha)$, then $(\alpha, g) \in Cl(K)$ and there is some $\alpha \xrightarrow{a} \beta$ such that $(\beta, h) \in Cl(K)$.*

Lemma 8. *Let K be a well-formed relation such that $\mathcal{B} \subseteq K$ and $g \xrightarrow{a} h \in \Gamma$. If $\alpha \approx_{\mathrm{br}} g$, $\alpha = X \| \gamma$ and there is $X \xrightarrow{a} \alpha' \in \Delta$ such that $\alpha' \| \gamma \approx_{\mathrm{br}} h$, then $L^K_{[g,a,h]}$ contains all elements of $\{X\} \cdot Lin(\gamma)$.*

Lemma 8 is weak, since it does not guarantee that all elements of $Lin(\alpha)$ fall in $L^K_{[g,a,h]}$. This is mainly because in Definition 7, the commutativity of '$\|$' is ignored. However this deficiency is in some sense made up by the third condition of Theorem 9, as we shall see in the proof of Theorem 10.

Definition 8. *Let K be a well-formed relation. We say that a pair $(X, f) \in K$* expands *K iff*

- *whenever $X \xrightarrow{a} \alpha$, either there is some $f \xrightarrow{a} f'$ such that $\overline{\alpha} \in L(\mathcal{A}^K_{f'})$, or $a = \tau$ and $\overline{\alpha} \in L(\mathcal{A}^K_f)$*
- *whenever $f \Rightarrow g \xrightarrow{a} h$, $L(G_X) \cap L^K_{[g,a,h]}$ is non-empty*

Moreover, all pairs of the form (ε, g) in K expand *K. The set $Exp(K)$ is defined as all pairs of K that expand K.*

Lemma 9. *Let K be a well-formed relation such that $K = Exp(K)$. Then $Cl(K)$ is a branching bisimulation.*

The approximation of $\mathcal{B}$ is the same as in Sect. 3.

Theorem 10. *There is a $j \in \mathbb{N}$ bounded by $\mathcal{O}(nm)$ such that $\mathcal{B}^j = \mathcal{B}^{j+1}$ and $B^j = \mathcal{B}$.*

Proof. The existence of such j that $\mathcal{B}^j = \mathcal{B}^{j+1}$ can be argued in the same way as in Theorem 3. We only show that $B^j = \mathcal{B}$.

$\mathcal{B}^j \subseteq \mathcal{B}$: Directly by Lemma 9 and the fact that $\mathcal{B}^j \subseteq Cl(\mathcal{B}^j)$.

$\mathcal{B} \subseteq \mathcal{B}^j$: Equivalently we show that $\mathcal{B} = Exp(\mathcal{B})$ since Exp is monotone. Let $(X, f) \in \mathcal{B}$, we argue that the pair satisfies the conditions in Definition 8. Whenever $X \xrightarrow{a} \alpha$, either $a = \tau$ and $\alpha \approx_{\mathrm{br}} f$ or there is some $f \xrightarrow{a} f'$ such that $\alpha \approx_{\mathrm{br}} f'$. By Theorem 7, we have $(\alpha, f) \in Cl(\mathcal{B})$ in the former case and $(\alpha, f') \in Cl(\mathcal{B})$ in the latter case. Then by Theorem 8, $\overline{\alpha} \in L(\mathcal{A}^{\mathcal{B}}_f)$ in the former case and $\overline{\alpha} \in L(\mathcal{A}^{\mathcal{B}}_{f'})$ in the latter case. Hence the first condition of Definition 8 is satisfied. Now we consider the second condition of Definition 8. Whenever $f \Rightarrow g \xrightarrow{a} h$, there is some $X \Rightarrow \alpha \xrightarrow{a} \beta$ such that $\alpha \approx_{\mathrm{br}} g$ and $\beta \approx_{\mathrm{br}} h$ (by the contraction). Let $\alpha = Z \| \gamma$, $\beta = \alpha' \| \gamma$ and $Z \xrightarrow{a} \alpha' \in \Delta$. By Theorem 9, there is some $\xi \in Lin(\gamma)$ such that $Z\xi \in L(G_X)$. And by Lemma 8, we have $Z\xi \in L^{\mathcal{B}}_{[g,a,h]}$. Thus we have $L(G_X) \cap L^{\mathcal{B}}_{[g,a,h]}$ is non-empty. Hence the second condition of Definition 8 is satisfied. □

Theorem 11. *Let K be a well-formed relation. The set $Exp(K)$ can be computed in $\mathcal{O}(n^{11}m^8)$ time.*

Proof. The proof follows the methodology of the one for [16, Theorem 28], and uses the fact stated in Remark 5. See [23, Theorem 11] for details. □

Then to compute $\mathcal{B}$, we need to perform the computation of the expansion within $\mathcal{O}(nm)$ times (Theorem 10). Thus we have the following theorem.

Theorem 12. *The bisimulation base $\mathcal{B}$ can be computed in $\mathcal{O}(n^{12}m^9)$ time.*

The main theorem of this section is as follows.

Theorem 13. *Branching bisimilarity between normed BPP and finite-state systems is decidable in polynomial time.*

Proof. Let $\alpha \in Const(\Delta)^{\otimes}$ and $f \in Const(\Gamma)$. To decide whether $\alpha \approx_{\mathrm{br}} f$, we first compute $\mathcal{B}$ in $\mathcal{O}(n^{12}m^9)$ time. Then we need only to check whether $\overline{\alpha} \in L(\mathcal{A}_g^{\mathcal{B}})$ by Theorem 7 and Theorem 8. □

5 Conclusion

We have presented polynomial time algorithms deciding branching bisimilarity between BPA/nBPP and finite-state processes. The algorithm for BPA refines the previous one in [20]. The one for nBPP shows the polynomial-time decidability of the verification problem, which is not known previously. The techniques developed in this paper (e.g. the expansion) are effective for branching bisimulation. We believe that they can be applied to other bisimulations with two-level correlations, e.g., η-bisimulation [17].

Since branching bisimulation often serves as an alternative for weak bisimulation, it is interesting to compare the complexity of verification problems between the two bisimulations. In this paper, the running time for computing the bisimulation base is $\mathcal{O}(n^4m^5)$ for BPA and $\mathcal{O}(n^{12}m^9)$ for normed BPP. They are both lower than the ones in [16], where the complexity is $\mathcal{O}(n^5m^7)$ for BPA and $\mathcal{O}(n^{12}m^{11})$ for nBPP (by Remark 4). It is possible to apply some of our techniques back to [16] (e.g., common components in Remark 2 and Remark 5), but the complexity will still be a little bit higher. Thus we have established a case on infinite structure where branching bisimulation takes less time to decide than weak bisimulation, for which similar comparison has already been made on finite-state systems [22].

Acknowledgements. I thank Mr. Chaodong He for valuable help on the writing of this article. I also thank anonymous referees for useful advices.

References

1. Burkart, O., Caucal, D., Moller, F., Steffen, B.: Verification on infinite structures. In: Bergsta, J., Ponse, A., Smolka, S. (eds.) Handbook of Process Algebra, pp. 545–623. Elsevier Science, Amsterdam (2001)

2. Mayr, R.: Process rewrite systems. Inf. Comput. 156, 264–286 (2000)
3. Srba, J.: Roadmap of infinite results. Bulletin of the EATCS 78, 163–175 (2002)
4. Baeten, J.C.M., Bergstra, J.A., Klop, J.W.: Decidability of bisimulation equivalence for processes generating context-free languages. J. ACM 40, 653–682 (1993)
5. Hopcroft, J., Ullman, J.: Introduction to Automata Theory, Languages, and Computations. Addison-Wesley, Reading (1979)
6. Christensen, S., Hüttel, H., Stirling, C.: Bisimulation equivalence is decidable for all context-free processes. Inf. Comput. 121, 143–148 (1995)
7. Christensen, S., Hirshfeld, Y., Moller, F.: Bisimulation equivalence is decidable for basic parallel processes. In: Best, E. (ed.) CONCUR 1993. LNCS, vol. 715, pp. 143–157. Springer, Heidelberg (1993)
8. Srba, J.: Strong bisimilarity and regularity of basic process algebra is PSPACE-hard. In: Widmayer, P., Triguero, F., Morales, R., Hennessy, M., Eidenbenz, S., Conejo, R. (eds.) ICALP 2002. LNCS, vol. 2380, pp. 716–727. Springer, Heidelberg (2002)
9. Srba, J.: Strong bisimilarity and regularity of basic parallel processes is PSPACE-hard. In: Alt, H., Ferreira, A. (eds.) STACS 2002. LNCS, vol. 2285, pp. 535–546. Springer, Heidelberg (2002)
10. Jančar, P.: Strong bisimilarity on basic parallel processes is pspace-complete. In: LICS, p. 218 (2003)
11. Hirshfeld, Y., Jerrum, M., Moller, F.: A polynomial algorithm for deciding bisimilarity of normed context-free processes. Theor. Comput. Sci. 158, 143–159 (1996)
12. Hirshfeld, Y., Jerrum, M., Moller, F.: A polynomial-time algorithm for deciding bisimulation equivalence of normed basic parallel processes. Mathematical Structures in Computer Science 6, 251–259 (1996)
13. Jančar, P., Kučera, A., Mayr, R.: Deciding bisimulation-like equivalences with finite-state processes. Theor. Comput. Sci. 258, 409–433 (2001)
14. Mayr, R.: Decidability of model checking with the temporal logic ef. Theor. Comput. Sci. 256, 31–62 (2001)
15. Kretínský, M., Rehák, V., Strejcek, J.: Reachability of hennessy-milner properties for weakly extended PRS. In: Sarukkai, S., Sen, S. (eds.) FSTTCS 2005. LNCS, vol. 3821, pp. 213–224. Springer, Heidelberg (2005)
16. Kucera, A., Mayr, R.: Weak bisimilarity between finite-state systems and bpa or normed bpp is decidable in polynomial time. Theor. Comput. Sci. 270, 677–700 (2002)
17. van Glabbeek, R.J., Weijland, W.P.: Branching time and abstraction in bisimulation semantics. J. ACM 43, 555–600 (1996)
18. Baeten, J., Weijland, W.: Process Algebra. Cambridge (1990)
19. Hüttel, H.: Silence is golden: Branching bisimilarity is decidable for context-free processes. In: Larsen, K.G., Skou, A. (eds.) CAV 1991. LNCS, vol. 575, pp. 2–12. Springer, Heidelberg (1992)
20. Kucera, A., Mayr, R.: A generic framework for checking semantic equivalences between pushdown automata and finite-state automata. In: IFIP TCS, pp. 395–408 (2004)
21. Caucal, D.: Graphes canoniques de graphes algébriques. ITA 24, 339–352 (1990)
22. Groote, J.F., Vaandrager, F.W.: An efficient algorithm for branching bisimulation and stuttering equivalence. In: Paterson, M. (ed.) ICALP 1990. LNCS, vol. 443, pp. 626–638. Springer, Heidelberg (1990)
23. Fu, H.: Branching bisimilarity between finite-state systems and bpa or normed bpp is polynomial-time decidable, http://basics.sjtu.edu.cn/~hongfei/

Refining Abstract Interpretation-Based Static Analyses with Hints

Vincent Laviron[1] and Francesco Logozzo[2]

[1] École Normale Supérieure, 45, rue d'Ulm, Paris, France
Vincent.Laviron@ens.fr
[2] Microsoft Research, Redmond, WA, USA
logozzo@microsoft.com

Abstract. We focus our attention on the loss of precision induced by abstract domain *operations*. We introduce a new technique, *hints*, which allows us to systematically refine the operations defined over elements of an abstract domain. We formally define hints in the abstract interpretation theory, we prove their soundness, and we characterize two families of hints: syntactic and semantic. We give some examples of hints, and we provide our experience with hints in `Clousot`, our abstract interpretation-based static analyzer for `.Net`.

1 Introduction

The three main elements of an abstract interpretation are: (i) the abstract elements (*"which properties am I interested in?"*); (ii) the abstract transfer functions (*"which is the abstract semantics of basic statements?"*); and (iii) the abstract operations (*"how do I combine the abstract elements?"*).

The loss of precision induced by the abstract elements is exemplified by Fig. 1(a). The assertion cannot be proved using only convex numerical abstract domains such as Intervals [4], Pentagons [18], Octagons [23] or even Polyhedra [8]. The reason for that is that the most precise property at the join point $\mathtt{x} == -1 \vee \mathtt{x} == 1$ cannot be exactly represented in any of those domains. For instance Intervals (Intv) approximate it with $-1 \leq \mathtt{x} \leq 1$, so that the fact that $\mathtt{x} \neq 0$ is lost. Many techniques have been proposed to overcome this problem. They essentially rely on the refinement of the *elements* of the abstract domain. Solutions include trace partitioning [16,20,9], domain completion [5], powerset construction [1,19], and abstract domain extension [25]. Abstract transfer functions may introduce an orthogonal loss of precision. For instance, in Fig. 1(b) the expression initializer for `z` is in a quadratic form. Thus no linear numerical abstract domain can precisely capture the relation between `x`, `y` and `z`. Standard domain refinements are of no help. A rough transfer function can simply abstract away `z`. A more precise one can approximate `z` with an interval. However, a compositional evaluation of the expressions which mimics the concrete one is not precise enough to discharge the assertion $-2 \leq \mathtt{z}$. Several authors suggested methods to infer optimal transfer functions in particular settings as, *e.g.*, constraint matrices [24], shape analysis [26] or constant propagation [3].

Z. Hu (Ed.): APLAS 2009, LNCS 5904, pp. 343–358, 2009.

```
void AbsEl(int x) void Transfer(int x, y) void DomOp()
{ if(...)  x  =-1;{ assume 2 <= x <= 3;   { int x = 0, y = 0;
  else     x  = 1;  assume -1 <= y <= 1;    while (...)
                                            { if (...) { x++; y += 100; }
  assert   x != 0;  int z = (x + y) * y;      else if (...)
}                                              if (x >= 4) { x++; y++; }
                    assert -2 <= z;           }
                  }                        (*) assert x <= y;
                                               assert y <= 100 * x;
                                           }
        (a)                (b)                        (c)
```

Fig. 1. Examples of orthogonal losses of precision in abstract interpretations: (a) a convex domain cannot represent $\mathtt{x} \neq 0$; (b) a compositional transfer function does not infer the tightest lower bound for z; and (c) the standard domain operations on Polyhedra are not precise enough to infer the loop invariant $\mathtt{x} \leq \mathtt{y}$

Surprisingly enough, the refinement of the *operations* over abstract elements has been widely ignored in the literature (with the exceptions of [14,1,11,12] which however focused their attention just on the widening operator).

Example. Let us consider the code snippet in Fig. 1(c). In order to prove the assertions valid, the static analysis should infer the loop invariant $\mathtt{x} \leq \mathtt{y} \leq 100 \cdot \mathtt{x}$. Different abstract domains infer different invariants. The Octagon abstract domain (Oct) is a *weakly relational* domain which captures properties in the form of $\pm\mathtt{x} \pm \mathtt{y} \leq k$. It infers the loop invariant: $0 \leq \mathtt{x} \wedge 0 \leq \mathtt{y} \wedge \mathtt{x} \leq \mathtt{y}$. The Polyhedra abstract domain (Poly) is a *fully relational* domain. It can infer and represent arbitrary linear inequalities: Abstract elements are in the form $\sum_i a_i \cdot \mathtt{x}_i \leq k$. As a consequence one expects Poly to always be more precise than Oct. However, when applied to the example, Poly infers the loop invariant: $0 \leq \mathtt{x} \wedge 0 \leq \mathtt{y} \wedge \mathtt{y} \leq 100 \cdot \mathtt{x}$: Even if Poly can *exactly* represent the constraint $\mathtt{x} \leq \mathtt{y}$, it fails inferring it! This is quite surprising. The reason for that should be found in the widening operators over the two domains. The (standard) widening over Octagons explicitly seeks an upper bound for the difference $\mathtt{x} - \mathtt{y}$ (in the example 0). The (standard) widening over Polyhedra preserves the inequalities that are stable over two loop iterations. In the example, the constraint $\mathtt{x} \leq \mathtt{y}$, even if implied by the abstract states to be widened, is never materialized. Therefore, the state after widening does not contain it either. Intuitively, in order to obtain the most precise loop invariant for DomOp, one needs to refine the widening operator for Poly to be at least as precise as the one for Oct. One way to refine the widening is by remarking that the predicate $\mathtt{x} \leq \mathtt{y}$ appears as a condition of some assertion, and then trying to explicitly materialize it. Another possible refinement is by seeking upper bounds for the expression $\mathtt{x} - \mathtt{y}$. The first is an example of *syntactic hint*. The latter is an example of *semantic hint*. Those observations can be extended and generalized to other abstract domain operators.

The case for hints. The main goal for a static analysis designer is the precision/speed trade-off. To achieve it, the common practice is to drop some of the expressive power of the analysis while maximizing the inference power. In `Clousot`, our static analyzer for `.Net`, we needed additional flexibility. `Clousot` is mainly used to validate code contracts expressed by users in form of pre-conditions, post-conditions and object invariant. First, we observed that usual weakly-relational abstract domains are not precise enough to be used in a modular checker: for instance, it is often the case that the argument to establish an "easy" precondition (*e.g.*, $\mathtt{x} \leq \mathtt{y}$) at the call site involves a complex reasoning between several linear inequalities which require expensive abstract domains as Poly. Second, we needed `Clousot` to be adaptable, in that it can either run in an interactive environment (faster, but with more noise) or on a build machine overnight (slower, but much more precise). As a consequence, we took a different direction in the design of the abstract domains in `Clousot`: we retained the *expressive* power while we gave up some of the *inference* (*e.g.*, Pentagons [18] and Subpolyhedra [17]). Hints, introduced in this paper, are an orthogonal to the abstract domain, and they allow us to incrementaly increase the precision of the analysis by refining the transfer functions.

Contribution. We introduce hints, a new technique which allows us to systematically refine static analyses. The main ideas of hints are: (i) to have a separate module to figure out which constraints or families of constraints are of interest for the analysis; and (ii) to use such a module to refine the *operations* of the abstract domain. The main difference with related works on automatic refinement of static analyses is that hints refine the *operations* over abstract elements and *not* the elements themselves nor the transition relations. The main advantages of hints are that: (i) they enable an easy refinement of static analyses; (ii) they enable a fine-tuning of the cost/performance ratio; (iii) they make the analysis more robust with respect to implementation-related precision bugs. Hints are useful when the abstract operations are not complete w.r.t. the concrete ones, which is often the case in practice.

We formalize hints using the abstract interpretation theory, and we prove them correct w.r.t. a generic abstract interpreter. We characterize syntactic (user-defined, thresholds) and semantic hints (saturation, die-hard, computed, reductive). We show how they generalize existing techniques as, *e.g.*, widening with thresholds [2]. We applied hints to SubPolyhedra (SubPoly), a new, very efficient numerical abstract domain to propagate arbitrary linear inequalities. SubPoly has the same expressive power as Poly, but drops some of the inference to achieve scalability. Hints allow SubPoly to recover precision without giving up performances. Hints are implemented in `Clousot`, our static analyzer for .NET available at [21].

2 Abstract Interpretation Frameworks

Abstract interpretation is a general theory of approximations which formalizes the intuition that the semantics of a program is more or less precise depending on the observation level. In particular, the static analysis of a program is a semantics precise enough to capture the properties of interest and coarse enough to be computable. The *concrete* and *abstract* semantics of a program are defined as fixpoints respectively over a concrete and an abstract domain. The concrete and the abstract domains are related by a soundness relation, which induces the soundness of the abstract semantics [6].

Static approximation: Abstract Domain. In the Galois connections approach to abstract interpretation [4], the concrete domain and the abstract domain are assumed to be two *complete* lattices, respectively $\langle \mathsf{C}, \sqsubseteq, \sqcup \rangle$ and $\langle \mathsf{A}, \bar{\sqsubseteq}, \bar{\sqcup} \rangle$. The soundness relation is expressed by a pair of monotonic functions $\langle \alpha, \gamma \rangle$, such that $\forall \mathsf{e} \in \mathsf{C}. \forall \bar{\mathsf{e}} \in \mathsf{A}.\ \alpha(\mathsf{e}) \bar{\sqsubseteq} \bar{\mathsf{e}} \iff \mathsf{e} \sqsubseteq \gamma(\bar{\mathsf{e}})$. In such a setting, the abstract join operator $\bar{\sqcup}$ is optimal in that: $\forall \mathsf{e}_1, \mathsf{e}_2 \in \mathsf{C}.\ \alpha(\sqcup(\mathsf{e}_1, \mathsf{e}_2)) = \bar{\sqcup}(\alpha(\mathsf{e}_1), \alpha(\mathsf{e}_2))$ [5]. In practice, most analyses do not require the existence of the *best* approximation for concrete elements, a sound approximation suffices. For instance, there is no best polyhedron approximating the set of concrete points $B = \{(\mathrm{x}, \mathrm{y}) \in \mathbb{R}^2 \mid \mathrm{x}^2 + \mathrm{y}^2 \leq 1\}$. However, any polyhedron including B is a sound abstraction. In the relaxed form of abstract interpretation [6], the abstract domain is not required to be complete under $\bar{\sqcup}$. It is simply a *pre-order* $\langle \mathsf{A}, \preceq, \curlyvee, \curlywedge \rangle$. The soundness relation is expressed by a monotonic concretization function $\gamma \in [\mathsf{A} \to \mathsf{C}]$, *i.e.*, no abstraction function is required. The abstract union $\curlyvee$ gathers together the information flowing from incoming edges. It is not required to be the *least* upper bound (which may not exist at all): $\forall \bar{\mathsf{e}}_0, \bar{\mathsf{e}}_1 \in \mathsf{A}.\ \bar{\mathsf{e}}_0 \preceq \bar{\mathsf{e}}_0 \curlyvee \bar{\mathsf{e}}_1 \wedge \bar{\mathsf{e}}_1 \preceq \bar{\mathsf{e}}_0 \curlyvee \bar{\mathsf{e}}_1$. It is a sound, but not *optimal*, approximation of the concrete join: $\forall \bar{\mathsf{e}}_0, \bar{\mathsf{e}}_1 \in \mathsf{A}.\ \sqcup (\gamma(\bar{\mathsf{e}}_0), \gamma(\bar{\mathsf{e}}_1)) \sqsubseteq \gamma(\curlyvee(\bar{\mathsf{e}}_0, \bar{\mathsf{e}}_1))$. The abstract intersection returns a common lower bound for the operands, which approximates the concrete meet: $\forall \bar{\mathsf{e}}_0, \bar{\mathsf{e}}_1 \in \mathsf{A}.\ \gamma(\bar{\mathsf{e}}_0) \sqcap \gamma(\bar{\mathsf{e}}_1) \sqsubseteq \gamma(\bar{\mathsf{e}}_0 \curlywedge \bar{\mathsf{e}}_1)$.

Hereafter we assume: (i) the concrete domain to be the complete lattice $\langle \mathcal{P}(\Sigma), \subseteq, \cup, \cap \rangle$ where Σ is a set of concrete program states mapping variables to values; (ii) the abstract domain to be a pre-order $\langle \mathsf{A}, \preceq, \curlyvee, \curlywedge \rangle$, therefore putting ourselves in the setting of the relaxed form of abstract interpretation.

Dynamic approximation: Widening/Narrowing. In general A is of infinite height, so that the fixpoint computation may not terminate. A widening operator $\triangledown$ should then be defined to ensure the convergence of the iteration to a *post*-fixpoint. Formally $\triangledown$ satisfies: (i) $\forall \bar{\mathsf{e}}_0, \bar{\mathsf{e}}_1 \in \mathsf{A}.\ \bar{\mathsf{e}}_0, \bar{\mathsf{e}}_1 \preceq \triangledown(\bar{\mathsf{e}}_0, \bar{\mathsf{e}}_1)$; and (ii) for each (possibily infinite) sequence of abstract elements $\bar{\mathsf{e}}_0, \bar{\mathsf{e}}_1 \dots \bar{\mathsf{e}}_k$ the sequence defined by $\bar{\mathsf{e}}_0^\triangledown = \bar{\mathsf{e}}_0, \bar{\mathsf{e}}_1^\triangledown = \triangledown(\bar{\mathsf{e}}_0^\triangledown, \bar{\mathsf{e}}_1) \dots \bar{\mathsf{e}}_k^\triangledown = \triangledown(\bar{\mathsf{e}}_{k-1}^\triangledown, \bar{\mathsf{e}}_k)$ is ultimately stationary. It is worth noting that a widening operator is not commutative. The loss of precision introduced by the widening can be partially recovered using a narrowing operator. A narrowing $\vartriangle$ operator satisfies: (i) $\forall \bar{\mathsf{e}}_0, \bar{\mathsf{e}}_1 \in \mathsf{A}.\ \curlywedge (\bar{\mathsf{e}}_0, \bar{\mathsf{e}}_1) \preceq \vartriangle (\bar{\mathsf{e}}_0, \bar{\mathsf{e}}_1) \preceq \bar{\mathsf{e}}_0, \bar{\mathsf{e}}_1$; and (ii) for each (possibily infinite) sequence of abstract elements $\bar{\mathsf{e}}_0, \bar{\mathsf{e}}_1 \dots \bar{\mathsf{e}}_k$ the sequence defined by $\bar{\mathsf{e}}_0^\vartriangle = \bar{\mathsf{e}}_0, \bar{\mathsf{e}}_1^\vartriangle = \vartriangle (\bar{\mathsf{e}}_0^\vartriangle, \bar{\mathsf{e}}_1) \dots \bar{\mathsf{e}}_k^\vartriangle = \vartriangle (\bar{\mathsf{e}}_{k-1}^\vartriangle, \bar{\mathsf{e}}_k)$ is ultimately stationary.

Transfer functions. It is common practice for the implementation of an abstract domain A to provide some primitive transfer functions. The assignment abstract transfer function, $\mathsf{A.assign}$, is an over-approximation of the states reached after the concrete assignment ($\mathbb{E}[\![\mathsf{E}]\!](\sigma)$ denotes the evaluation of the expression E in the state σ) : $\forall \mathtt{x}, \mathtt{E}. \forall \bar{e} \in \mathsf{A}.\ \{\sigma[\mathtt{x} \mapsto v] \mid \sigma \in \gamma(\bar{e}), \mathbb{E}[\![\mathtt{E}]\!](\sigma) = v\} \subseteq \gamma(\mathsf{A.assign}(\bar{e}, \mathtt{x}, \mathtt{E}))$. The test abstract transfer function, A.test, filters the input states ($\mathbb{B}[\![\mathtt{B}]\!](\sigma)$ denotes the evaluation of the Boolean expression B in the state σ): $\forall \mathtt{B}. \forall \bar{e} \in \mathsf{A}.\ \{\sigma \in \gamma(\bar{e}) \mid \mathbb{B}[\![\mathtt{B}]\!](\sigma) = \mathit{true}\} \subseteq \gamma(\mathsf{A.test}(\bar{e}, \mathtt{B}))$. The abstract checking A.check verifies if an assertion A holds in an abstract state $\bar{e}$. It has four possible outcomes: *true* (A holds in all the concrete states $\gamma(\bar{e})$); *false* (!A holds in all the concrete states $\gamma(\bar{e})$); *bottom* (the assertion is unreached); *top* (the validity of A cannot be decided in $\gamma(\bar{e})$).

3 Concrete and Abstract Semantics for a While language

We illustrate hints on a simple abstract interpreter for a while language. The concrete, reachable states semantics $[\![\cdot]\!] \in [\mathtt{Stm} \times \mathcal{P}(\Sigma) \to \mathcal{P}(\Sigma)]$ is in Fig. 3. The abstract semantics $\bar{s}[\![\cdot]\!] \in [\mathtt{Stm} \times \mathsf{A} \to \mathsf{A}]$ is in Fig. 2. It is parametrized by the abstract domain $\langle \mathsf{A}, \preceq, \curlyvee, \curlywedge \rangle$ and a set of primitives assign, test, and check. The `skip` statement has no effect on the abstract state. The effects of the assignment, the assumption and the assertion are handled by the corresponding primitives of the abstract domain. Please note that for the purposes of the analysis the effects of `assume` and `assert` coincide: The assertions will be checked in a second phase, after the analysis has inferred the program invariants for all the program points. The abstract semantics of sequence is function composition. The abstract semantics of conditional: (i) pushes the guard and its negation onto the two branches; and (ii) gathers the effects using the abstract union. The abstract semantics of `while` is given in terms of fix, which computes the loop invariant as the limit of the fixpoint iterations with widening. Given a function $F \in [\mathsf{A} \to \mathsf{A}]$, $\mathsf{fix}(F)$ is the limit of the iteration sequence: $I^0 = \bot; I^{n+1} = \text{ if } F(I^n) \preceq I^n \text{ then } I^n \text{ else } I^n \triangledown F(I^n)$. The post-state for `while` is then obtained by intersecting the loop invariant with the negation of the guard. It is easy to show that for any program P, $\forall \mathsf{e} \in \mathcal{P}(\Sigma). \forall \bar{e} \in \mathsf{A}.\ \mathsf{e} \subseteq \gamma(\bar{e}) \Longrightarrow [\![\mathtt{P}]\!](\mathsf{e}) \subseteq \gamma(\bar{s}[\![\mathtt{P}]\!](\bar{e}))$.

$$\begin{aligned}
\bar{s}[\![\mathtt{skip;}]\!](\bar{e}) &= \bar{e} \qquad\qquad \bar{s}[\![\mathtt{x = E;}]\!](\bar{e}) = \mathsf{A.assign}(\bar{e}, \mathtt{x}, \mathtt{E})\\
\bar{s}[\![\mathtt{assume\ B;}]\!](\bar{e}) &= \bar{s}[\![\mathtt{assert\ B;}]\!](\bar{e}) = \mathsf{A.test}(\mathtt{B}, \bar{e})\\
\bar{s}[\![\mathtt{C_1\ C_2}]\!](\bar{e}) &= \bar{s}[\![\mathtt{C_2}]\!](\bar{s}[\![\mathtt{C_1}]\!](\bar{e}))\\
\bar{s}[\![\mathtt{if(B)\ \{C_1\}else\ \{C_2\};}]\!](\bar{e}) &= \bar{s}[\![\mathtt{C_1}]\!](\mathsf{A.test}(\mathtt{B}, \bar{e})) \curlyvee \bar{s}[\![\mathtt{C_2}]\!](\mathsf{A.test}(!\mathtt{B}, \bar{e}))\\
\bar{s}[\![\mathtt{while(B)\ \{C\};}]\!](\bar{e}) &= \text{let } \bar{\mathsf{I}} = \mathsf{fix}\lambda X.\ \bar{e} \curlyvee \bar{s}[\![\mathtt{C}]\!](\mathsf{A.test}(\mathtt{B}, X))\\
&\quad\ \text{in } \mathsf{A.test}(!\mathtt{B}, \bar{\mathsf{I}})
\end{aligned}$$

Fig. 2. The abstract semantics for the while-language

$$\begin{aligned}
[\![\mathtt{skip;}]\!](\mathsf{e}) &= \mathsf{e} \qquad\qquad [\![\mathtt{x = E;}]\!](\mathsf{e}) = \{\sigma[\mathtt{x} \mapsto v] \mid \sigma \in \mathsf{e}, \mathbb{E}[\![\mathtt{E}]\!](\sigma) = v\}\\
[\![\mathtt{assume\ B;}]\!](\mathsf{e}) &= [\![\mathtt{assert\ B;}]\!](\mathsf{e}) = \{\sigma \in \mathsf{e} \mid \mathbb{B}[\![\mathtt{B}]\!](\sigma) = \mathit{true}\}\\
[\![\mathtt{C_1\ C_2}]\!](\mathsf{e}) &= [\![\mathtt{C_2}]\!]([\![\mathtt{C_1}]\!](\mathsf{e}))\\
[\![\mathtt{if(B)\ \{C_1\}else\ \{C_2\};}]\!](\mathsf{e}) &= [\![\mathtt{C_1}]\!](\{\sigma \in \mathsf{e} \mid \mathbb{B}[\![\mathtt{B}]\!](\sigma) = \mathit{true}\}) \cup [\![\mathtt{C_2}]\!](\{\sigma \in \mathsf{e} \mid !\mathbb{B}[\![\mathtt{B}]\!](\sigma) = \mathit{true}\})\\
[\![\mathtt{while(B)\ \{C\};}]\!](\bar{e}) &= \text{let } \mathsf{I} = \textstyle\bigcup_i [\![\mathtt{C}]\!]^i(\{\sigma \in \mathsf{I} \mid \mathbb{B}[\![\mathtt{B}]\!](\sigma) = \mathit{true}\})\\
&\quad\ \text{in } \{\sigma \in \mathsf{I} \mid !\mathbb{B}[\![\mathtt{B}]\!](\sigma) = \mathit{true}\}.
\end{aligned}$$

Fig. 3. The reachable states semantics for the while-language

4 Hints

Hints are precision improving operators which can be used to systematically refine and improve the precision of domain operations in abstract interpretation. Domain operations are either *basic* domain operations (*e.g.*, $\curlyvee$ or $\curlywedge$) or their compositions (*e.g.*, $\lambda(\bar{e}_0, \bar{e}_1, \bar{e}_2).\ (\bar{e}_0 \curlywedge \bar{e}_1) \curlyvee (\bar{e}_0 \curlywedge \bar{e}_2)$).

Definition 1 (Hint, $\mathbb{h}$). *Let $\diamond \in [\mathsf{C}^n \to \mathsf{C}]$ be a concrete domain operation defined over a concrete domain $\langle \mathsf{C}, \sqsubseteq, \sqcup, \sqcap \rangle$. Let $\bar{\diamond} \in [\mathsf{A}^n \to \mathsf{A}]$ be the abstract counterpart for $\diamond$ defined over the abstract domain $\langle \mathsf{A}, \preceq, \curlyvee, \curlywedge \rangle$. A hint $\mathbb{h}_{\bar{\diamond}} \in [\mathsf{A}^n \to \mathsf{A}]$ is such that:*

$$\mathbb{h}_{\bar{\diamond}}(\bar{e}_0 \dots \bar{e}_{n-1}) \preceq \bar{\diamond}(\bar{e}_0 \dots \bar{e}_{n-1}) \qquad \textit{(Refinement)}$$
$$\diamond(\gamma(\bar{e}_0) \dots \gamma(\bar{e}_{n-1})) \sqsubseteq \gamma(\mathbb{h}_{\bar{\diamond}}(\bar{e}_0 \dots \bar{e}_{n-1})) \qquad \textit{(Soundness)}.$$

The first condition states that $\mathbb{h}_{\bar{\diamond}}$ is a more precise operations than $\bar{\diamond}$. The second condition requires $\mathbb{h}_{\bar{\diamond}}$ to be a sound approximation of $\diamond$. An important property of hints is that they can be designed separately and the combined to obtain a more precise hint. Therefore, if $\mathbb{h}^1_{\bar{\diamond}}$ and $\mathbb{h}^2_{\bar{\diamond}}$ are hints, then $\mathbb{h}^{\curlywedge}_{\bar{\diamond}}(\bar{e}_0 \dots \bar{e}_{n-1}) = \mathbb{h}^1_{\bar{\diamond}}(\bar{e}_0 \dots \bar{e}_{n-1}) \curlywedge \mathbb{h}^2_{\bar{\diamond}}(\bar{e}_0 \dots \bar{e}_{n-1})$ is a hint, too. Hints improve the precision of static analyses without introducing unsoundness and preserving termination:

Theorem 1 (Refinement of the abstract semantics). *Let $\mathbb{h}_{\triangledown}$ and $\mathbb{h}_{\curlyvee}$ be two hints refining respectively the widening and the abstract union, and let $\mathbb{h}_{\triangledown}$ be a widening operator. Let $\bar{s}^*[\![\cdot]\!]$ be the abstract semantics obtained from $\bar{s}[\![\cdot]\!]$ by replacing $\triangledown$ with $\mathbb{h}_{\triangledown}$ and $\curlyvee$ with $\mathbb{h}_{\curlyvee}$. Let P be a program. Then, $\forall \mathsf{e} \in \mathcal{P}(\Sigma). \forall \bar{e} \in \mathsf{A}$.*

$$\bar{s}^*[\![\mathsf{P}]\!](\bar{e}) \preceq \bar{s}[\![\mathsf{P}]\!](\bar{e}) \qquad \textit{(Refinement)}$$
$$\mathsf{e} \subseteq \gamma(\bar{e}) \Longrightarrow [\![\mathsf{P}]\!](\mathsf{e}) \subseteq \gamma(\bar{s}^*[\![\mathsf{P}]\!](\bar{e})) \qquad \textit{(Soundness)}.$$

5 Syntactic Hints

Syntactic hints use some part of the program text to refine the operations of the abstract domain. They exploit user annotations to preserve as much information as possible in gathering operations (user-provided hints), and systematically improve the widening heuristics to find tighter loop invariants (thresholds hints).

They are the easiest, and probably cheapest form of hints. First, we collect all the predicates appearing as assertions or as guards. Then, the gathering operations are refined by explicitly checking for each collected predicate `B`, if it holds for *all* the operands. If this is the case, `B` is added to the result. The predicate seeker $\mathsf{pred} \in [\mathtt{Stm} \to \mathcal{P}(\mathtt{BExp})]$ extracts from the program text the predicates appearing in conditional and loop guards. User provided hints do not affect the termination of the widening as we can only add finitely many new predicates:

Lemma 1 (User-provided hints). *Let $\diamond \in \{\curlyvee, \triangledown\}$, and let P be a program. Then: (i) $\mathbb{h}^{\mathsf{pred}}_{\diamond}$ defined below is a hint; and (ii) $\mathbb{h}^{\mathsf{pred}}_{\triangledown}$ is a widening operator.*

$$\mathbb{h}^{\mathsf{pred}}_{\diamond}(\bar{\mathsf{e}}_0, \bar{\mathsf{e}}_1) = \text{let } S = \{\mathsf{B} \in \mathsf{pred}(\mathsf{P}) \mid \mathsf{A.check}(\mathsf{B}, \bar{\mathsf{e}}_0) = \mathit{true} \wedge \mathsf{A.check}(\mathsf{B}, \bar{\mathsf{e}}_1) = \mathit{true}\}$$
$$\text{in } \mathsf{A.test}(\textstyle\bigwedge_{\mathsf{B} \in S} \mathsf{B}, \diamond(\bar{\mathsf{e}}_0, \bar{\mathsf{e}}_1)).$$

In example of Fig. 1(b), $\mathsf{pred}(\mathtt{DomOp}) = \{\mathtt{x} \leq \mathtt{y}, 4 \leq \mathtt{x}, \mathtt{y} \leq 100 \cdot \mathtt{x}\}$. The refined domain operations keep the predicate $\mathtt{x} \leq \mathtt{y}$, which is stable among loop iterations, and hence is a loop invariant.

We found user-provided hints very useful in `Clousot`, our abstract interpretation based static analyzer for `.Net`. `Clousot` analyzes methods in isolation, and supports assume/guarantee reasoning ("contracts") via executable annotations. Precision in propagating and checking program annotations is crucial to provide a satisfactory user experience. User-provided hints help to reach this goal as the analyzer makes sure that at each joint point no user annotation is lost, if it is implied by the incoming abstract states. They make the analyzer more robust w.r.t. incompleteness of $\curlyvee$ or a buggy implementation which may cause $\curlyvee$ to return a more abstract element than the one predicted by the theory. The downside is that user-provided hints are syntactically based: For instance, if in Fig. 1(c) we replace the assertion at $(*)$ with `if 10 <= x then assert 5 <= y`, then $\mathsf{pred}(\mathtt{DomOp}) = \{10 \leq \mathtt{x}, 5 \leq \mathtt{y}\}$, so that $\mathbb{h}^{\mathsf{pred}}_{\nabla_{\mathsf{Poly}}}$ cannot figure out that $\mathtt{x} \leq \mathtt{y}$, and hence the analyzer cannot prove that the assertion is valid. Semantic hints (Sect. 6.3) will fix it.

5.1 Thresholds Hints

Widening with threshold has been introduced in [2] to improve the precision of standard widenings over non-relational or weakly relational domains. Roughly, the idea of a widening with thresholds is to stage the extrapolation process, so that before projecting a bound to the infinity, values from a set T are considered as candidate bounds. The set T can be either provided by the user or it can be extracted from the program text. The widening with thresholds is just another form of hint. Let $\bar{\mathsf{e}}_0$ and $\bar{\mathsf{e}}_1$ be abstract states belonging to some numerical abstract domain. Without loss of generality we can assume that the basic facts in $\bar{\mathsf{e}}_0, \bar{\mathsf{e}}_1$ are in the form $\mathtt{p} \leq k$, where $\mathtt{p}$ is some polynomial. For instance $\mathtt{x} \in [-2, 4]$ is equivalent to $\{-\mathtt{x} \leq 2, \mathtt{x} \leq 4\}$. The standard widening preserves the linear forms with stable upper bounds: $\nabla(\bar{\mathsf{e}}_0, \bar{\mathsf{e}}_1) = \{\mathtt{p} \leq k \mid \mathtt{p} \leq k_0 \in \bar{\mathsf{e}}_0, \mathtt{p} \leq k_1 \in \bar{\mathsf{e}}_1, k = \text{if } k_1 > k_0 \text{ then } +\infty \text{ else } k_0\}$. Given a finite set of values $\mathtt{T}$, threshold hints refine the standard widening by:

$$\mathbb{h}^{T}_{\nabla}(\bar{\mathsf{e}}_0, \bar{\mathsf{e}}_1) = \{\mathtt{p} \leq k \mid \mathtt{p} \leq k_0 \in \bar{\mathsf{e}}_0, \mathtt{p} \leq k_1 \in \bar{\mathsf{e}}_1,$$
$$k = \text{if } k_1 > k_0 \text{ then } \min\{t \in T \cup \{+\infty\} \mid k_1 \leq t\} \text{ else } k_0\}.$$

Lemma 2. $\mathbb{h}^{T}_{\nabla}$ *is: (i) a hint; and (ii) a widening.*

Example 1 (Widening with thresholds). Let us consider the code snippets in Fig. 4 to be analyzed with Intervals. In the both cases, the (post-)fixpoint is

```
void LessThan() {
  int x = 0;
  while (x < 1000)
    x++;
}
```
(a) Narrowing

```
void NotEq() {
  int x = 0;
  while (x != 1000)
    x++;
}
```
(b) Thresholds

Fig. 4. Two programs to be analyzed with Intervals. The iterations with widening infer the loop invariant $\mathtt{x} \in [0, +\infty]$. In the first case, the narrowing step refines the loop invariant to $\mathtt{x} \in [0, 1000]$. In the second case, the narrowing fails to refine it.

reached after the first iteration $\triangledown([0,0],[1,1]) = [0,+\infty]$. In the first case, the invariant can be improved by a narrowing step to $\vartriangle([0,+\infty],[-\infty,1000]) = [0,1000]$ (see [4] for a definition of narrowing of Intv). In the second case, the narrowing is of no help as $\vartriangle([0,+\infty],\curlyvee([-\infty,1000],[1002,+\infty])) = [0,+\infty]$. A widening with Thresholds $T = \{1000\}$ helps discovering the tightest loop invariant for both examples in one step as $\mathbb{h}^{T}_{\triangledown}([0,0],[1,1]) = [0,1000]$. □

Please note that user-provided hints are of no help in the previous example, as $\mathsf{pred}(\mathtt{NotEq}) = \{\mathtt{x} \neq 1000\}$ does not hold for all the operands of the widening.

The set T of thresholds is a parameter of the analyzer, which can either be provided by the user, preset to some common values (*e.g.*, $T = \{-1,0,1\}$), or extracted from the program text. In `Clousot`, we use a function $\mathsf{const} \in [\mathtt{Stm} \to \mathcal{P}(\mathtt{int})]$ which extracts the constants appearing in the guards. We found the hint $\mathbb{h}^{\mathsf{const}}_{\triangledown}$ very satisfactory: (i) it helps inferring precise *numerical* loop invariants without requiring the extra iteration steps required for applying the narrowing; and (ii) it improves the precision of the analysis of code involving disequalities, *e.g.*, Fig. 4(b). A drawback is that the set T may grow too large, slowing down the convergence of the fixpoint iterations. In `Clousot`, we infer thresholds on a per-method basis, which helps maintaining the cardinality of T quite small.

6 Semantic Hints

Semantic hints provide a more refined yet more expensive form of operator refinement. For instance, they exploit information in the abstract states to materialize constraints that were implied by the operands (saturation hints, die-hard hints and template hints) or they iterate the application of operators to get a more precise abstract state (reductive hints).

6.1 Saturation Hints

A common way to design abstract interpreters is to build the abstract domain as a composition of basic abstract domains, which interact through a well-defined interface [7,15]. Formally, given two abstract domains $\mathsf{A}_0, \mathsf{A}_1$, the Cartesian product $\mathsf{A}^{\times} = \mathsf{A}_0 \times \mathsf{A}_1$ is still an abstract domain, whose operations are defined as the point-wise extension of those over A_0 and A_1. Let $\bar{\diamond}_i \in [\mathsf{A}_i^n \to \mathsf{A}_i]$, $i \in \{0,1\}$, then $\bar{\diamond}^{\times}((\bar{e}_0^0, \bar{e}_1^0)\ldots(\bar{e}_0^{n-1}, \bar{e}_1^{n-1})) = (\bar{\diamond}_0(\bar{e}_0^0 \ldots \bar{e}_0^{n-1}), \bar{\diamond}_1(\bar{e}_1^0 \ldots \bar{e}_1^{n-1}))$. The Cartesian product enables the modular design (and refinement) of static analyses. However, a naive design which does not consider the flow of information between the abstract elements may lead to imprecise analyses, as illustrated by the following example.

Example 2 (Cartesian join). Let us consider the abstract domain $\mathsf{Z} = \mathsf{Intv} \times \mathsf{LT}$, where $\mathsf{LT} = [\mathtt{Var} \to \mathcal{P}(\mathtt{Var})]$ is an abstract domain capturing the *"less than"* relation between *variables*. For instance, $\mathtt{x} < \mathtt{y} \wedge \mathtt{x} < \mathtt{z}$ is represented in LT by $[\mathtt{x} \mapsto \{\mathtt{y}, \mathtt{z}\}]$. The domain operations are defined as one may expect [18]. Let $\bar{\mathsf{z}}_0 = ([\mathtt{x} \mapsto [-\infty, 0], \mathtt{y} \mapsto [1, +\infty]], [\cdot])$ and $\bar{\mathsf{z}}_1 = ([\cdot], [\mathtt{x} \mapsto \{\mathtt{y}\}])$ be two elements of Z ($[\cdot]$ denotes the empty map). Then the Cartesian join loses all the information: $\curlyvee^{\times}(\bar{\mathsf{z}}_0, \bar{\mathsf{z}}_1) = ([\cdot], [\cdot])$. □

A common solution is: (i) saturate the operands; and (ii) apply the operation pairwise. The saturation materializes all the constraints implicitly expressed by the product abstract state. Let $\rho \in [\mathsf{A}^{\times} \to \mathsf{A}^{\times}]$ be a saturation (*a.k.a.* closure) procedure. Then the next lemma provides a systematic way to refine an operator $\bar{\diamond}^{\times}$.

Lemma 3. *The operator* $\mathbb{h}^{\rho}_{\bar{\diamond}^{\times}}$ *below is a hint.*

$$\mathbb{h}^{\rho}_{\bar{\diamond}^{\times}}((\bar{e}_0^0, \bar{e}_1^0)\ldots(\bar{e}_0^{n-1}, \bar{e}_1^{n-1})) = \text{ let } \bar{r}^i = \rho(\bar{e}_0^i, \bar{e}_1^i) \text{ for } i \in 0 \ldots n-1 \text{ in } \bar{\diamond}^{\times}(\bar{r}^0 \ldots \bar{r}^{n-1}).$$

Example 3 (Cartesian join, continued). The saturation of $\bar{\mathsf{z}}_0$ materializes the constraint $\mathtt{x} < \mathtt{y}$: $\bar{\mathsf{r}}_0 = ([\mathtt{x} \mapsto [-\infty, 0], \mathtt{y} \mapsto [1, +\infty], [\mathtt{x} \mapsto \{\mathtt{y}\}])$, and it leaves $\bar{\mathsf{z}}_1$ unchanged. The constraint $\mathtt{x} < \mathtt{y}$ is now present in both the operands, and it is retained by the pairwise join. □

It is worth noting that in general $\mathbb{h}^{\rho}_{\nabla}$ does not guarantee the convergence of the iterations, as the saturation procedure may re-introduce constraints which were abstracted away from the widening (*e.g.*, Fig. 10 of [23]).

Saturation hints can provide very precise operations for Cartesian abstract interpretations: They allow the analysis to get additional precision by combining the information present in different abstract domains. The main drawbacks of saturation hints are that: (i) the iteration convergence is not ensured, so that extra care should be put in the design of the widening; (ii) the systematic application of saturation may cause a dramatic slow-down of the analysis. In our experience with the combination of domains implemented in `Clousot`, we found that the slow-down introduced by saturation hints was too high to be practical. Die-hard hints, introduced in the next section, are a better solution to achieve precision without giving up scalability.

6.2 Die-Hard Hints

These hints are based on the observation that often the constraints that one wants to keep at a gathering point often appears explicitly in one of the operands. For instance in Ex. 2 the constraint $\mathtt{x} < \mathtt{y}$ is explicit in $\bar{\mathsf{z}}_1$, and implicit in $\bar{\mathsf{z}}_0$ (as $\mathtt{x} \leq 0 \wedge 1 \leq \mathtt{y} \Longrightarrow \mathtt{x} < \mathtt{y}$). Therefore $\mathtt{x} < \mathtt{y}$ holds for all the operands of the join so it is sound to add it to its result. Die-hard hints generalize and formalize it. They work in three steps: (i) apply the gathering operation, call the result $\bar{\mathsf{r}}$; (ii) collect the constraints C that are explicit in one of the operands, but are neither present nor implied by $\bar{\mathsf{r}}$; and (iii) add to $\bar{\mathsf{r}}$ all the constraints in C which are implied by *all* the operands. Formally:

$$\begin{aligned}\mathbb{h}^d_{(\bar{\diamond},I)}(\bar{\mathsf{e}}_0,\bar{\mathsf{e}}_1) = \text{let } &\bar{\mathsf{r}} = \bar{\diamond}(\bar{\mathsf{e}}_0,\bar{\mathsf{e}}_1), C = \cup_{i\in I}\{\kappa \in \bar{\mathsf{e}}_i \mid \mathsf{A.check}(\kappa,\bar{\mathsf{r}}) = top\}\\ \text{let } &S = \{\kappa \in C \mid \mathsf{A.check}(\kappa,\bar{\mathsf{e}}_0) = \mathsf{A.check}(\kappa,\bar{\mathsf{e}}_1) = true\}\\ \text{in } &\mathsf{A.test}\left(\wedge_{\kappa\in S}\kappa,\bar{\mathsf{r}}\right).\end{aligned}$$

In defining the die-hard hint for $\triangledown$, one should pay attention to avoid loops which re-introduce a constraint that as been dropped by the widening. One way to do it is to have an asymmetric hint, which restricts C only to the first operand (*e.g.*, the candidate invariant):

Lemma 4. $\mathbb{h}^d_{(\curlyvee,\{0,1\})}$ *and* $\mathbb{h}^d_{(\triangledown,\{0\})}$ *are hints and* $\mathbb{h}^d_{(\triangledown,\{0\})}$ *is a widening.*

6.3 Computed Hints

Hints can be inferred from the abstract states themselves. By looking at some properties of the elements involved in the operation, one can try to guess useful hints.

Lemma 5 (Computed hints). *Let* $\bar{\mathsf{e}}_0, \bar{\mathsf{e}}_1 \in \mathsf{A}$, $\Xi \in [\mathsf{A}\times\mathsf{A} \to \mathsf{A}]$ *a function which returns a set of likely bounds of* $\bar{\mathsf{e}}_0 \curlyvee \bar{\mathsf{e}}_1$. *Then* $\mathbb{h}^{\Xi}_{\curlyvee}$ *below is a hint.*

$$\begin{aligned}\mathbb{h}^{\Xi}_{\curlyvee}(\bar{\mathsf{e}}_0,\bar{\mathsf{e}}_1) = \text{let } &S = \{\mathsf{B} \in \Xi(\bar{\mathsf{e}}_0,\bar{\mathsf{e}}_1) \mid \mathsf{A.check}(\mathsf{B},\bar{\mathsf{e}}_0) = true \wedge \mathsf{A.check}(\mathsf{B},\bar{\mathsf{e}}_1) = true\}\\ \text{in } &\mathsf{A.test}(\textstyle\bigwedge_{\mathsf{B}\in S}\mathsf{B}, \bar{\mathsf{e}}_0 \curlyvee \bar{\mathsf{e}}_1).\end{aligned}$$

Computed hints are useful when the abstract join $\curlyvee$ is not optimal. Otherwise, $\mathbb{h}^{\Xi}_{\curlyvee}$ is no more precise than $\bar{\sqcup}$. For instance, in a Galois connections-based abstract interpretation, $\bar{\sqcup}$ is optimal, in that it returns the most precise abstract element approximating the concrete union. As a consequence, no further information can be extracted from the operands. It is worth noting that in general $\mathbb{h}^{\Xi}_{\triangledown}$ is not a widening. However, one can extend the arguments of the previous section to define an asymmetric hint $\mathbb{h}^{\Xi}_{\triangledown}$.

Template hints. Let $\mathsf{A.range} \in [\mathsf{Exp}\times\mathsf{A} \to \mathsf{Intv}]$ be a function that returns the range for an expression in some abstract state, *e.g.*, it satisfies: $\forall \mathsf{E}.\ \forall \bar{\mathsf{e}} \in \mathsf{A}.\ \mathsf{A.range}(\mathsf{E},\bar{\mathsf{e}}) = [l,u] \Longrightarrow \forall\sigma \in \gamma(\bar{\mathsf{e}}).\ l \leq \mathbb{E}[\![\mathsf{E}]\!](\sigma) \leq u$. If $\mathsf{A.range}(\mathsf{E},\bar{\mathsf{e}}_i) = [l_i,u_i]$ for $i \in \{0,1\}$, then $\gamma(\sqcup_{\mathsf{Intv}}([l_0,u_0],[l_1,u_1]))$ is an upper bound for E in $\cup(\gamma(\bar{\mathsf{e}}_0),\gamma(\bar{\mathsf{e}}_1))$. As a consequence given a set P of polynomial forms, one can design the guessing function Ξ^P:

$$\Xi^P(\bar{\mathsf{e}}_0,\bar{\mathsf{e}}_1) = \{l \leq \mathsf{p} \leq u \mid \mathsf{p} \in P \wedge [l,u] = \sqcup_{\mathsf{Intv}}(\mathsf{A.range}(\mathsf{p},\bar{\mathsf{e}}_0), \mathsf{A.range}(\mathsf{p},\bar{\mathsf{e}}_1))\}.$$

The main difference between $\mathbb{h}^{\Xi^P}_{\curlyvee}$ and syntactic hints is that the bounds for the polynomials in P are *semantic*, as they are inferred from the abstract states and not from the program text. For instance, computed hints infer the right invariant in the counter-example of Sect. 1 with the set of templates $Oct \equiv \{\mathtt{x}_0 - \mathtt{x}_1 \mid \mathtt{x}_0, \mathtt{x}_1 \text{ are program variables}\}$. In general, template hints with Oct refine Poly so to make it as precise as Oct.

2D-Convex Hull hints. New linear inequalities can be discovered at join points using the convex hull algorithm. For instance, the standard join on Poly is defined in that way [8]. However the convex hull algorithm requires an expensive conversion from a tableau of linear constraints to a set of vertexes and generators, which causes the analysis time to blow up. A possible solution is to consider a planar convex hull, which computes possible linear relations between *pairs* of variables by: (i) projecting the abstract states on all the two-dimensional planes; and (ii) computing the planar convex hull on those planes. Planar convex hull, combined with a smart representation of the abstract elements allows us to automatically discover complex invariants without giving up performances. Let us consider the code in Fig. 5 from [8]. At a price of exponential complexity, Poly can infer the correct loop invariant, and prove the assertion correct. SubPoly refined with 2D-Convex hull hints can prove the assertion, yet keeping a worst-case polynomial complexity [17].

```
void Foo() {
  int i = 2, j = 0;
  while (...)
    if (...) { i = i + 4; }
    else     { i = i + 2; j++; }
  assert  2 <= i - 2 * j; }
```

Fig. 5. Example requiring the use of 2D-convex hull hints

6.4 Reductive Hints

Intuitively, one way to improve the precision of a unary operator is to iterate its application [13]. However, an unconditional iteration may be source of unsoundness. For instance, let $- \in [\mathsf{Intv} \to \mathsf{Intv}]$ be the operator which applies the unary minus to an interval. In general, $\forall n \in \mathbb{N}.\ \bar{\mathsf{e}} = -^{2n}(\bar{\mathsf{e}}) \neq -^{2n+1}(\bar{\mathsf{e}})$. We say that a function f is *reductive* if $\forall x. f(x) \sqsubseteq x$; and *closing* if it is reductive and $\forall x. f(f(x)) = f(x)$.

Lemma 6 (Reductive hints). *Let* $\diamond \in [\mathsf{C} \to \mathsf{C}]$ *be a unary operator and* $\bar{\diamond} \in [\mathsf{A} \to \mathsf{A}]$ *its abstract counterpart. Let* $\diamond$ *be closing,* $\bar{\diamond}$ *be reductive, and* $n \geq 0$*. Then* $\mathbb{h}_{\bar{\diamond}}(\bar{\mathsf{e}}) = \bar{\diamond}^n(\bar{\mathsf{e}})$ *is a hint.*

The main application of reductive hints is to improve the precision in handling the guards in non-relational abstract domains. Given a Boolean guard B and an abstract domain A, $\psi \equiv \lambda\bar{\mathsf{e}}.\ \mathsf{A.test}(\mathtt{B}, \bar{\mathsf{e}})$ is an abstract operator which satisfies the hypotheses of Lemma 6. Abstract compilation can be used to express ψ in terms of domain operations, their compositions and state update. Lemma 6 justifies the use of local fixpoint iterations to refine the result of the analysis. For instance, in the abstract domain $[\mathtt{Var} \to \{\mathsf{true}, \mathsf{false}, \top, \bot\}]$ the abstract compilation of the predicate $\mathtt{b1} == \mathtt{b2} \wedge \mathtt{b2} == \mathtt{b3}$ is $\psi \equiv \lambda \mathsf{b}.(\mathsf{b}[\mathtt{b1}, \mathtt{b2} \mapsto \mathsf{b}(\mathtt{b1}) \wedge \mathsf{b}(\mathtt{b2})])\dot{\wedge}(\mathsf{b}[\mathtt{b2}, \mathtt{b3} \mapsto \mathsf{b}(\mathtt{b2}) \wedge \mathsf{b}(\mathtt{b3})]$, where $\dot{\wedge}$ denotes the pointwise extension of $\wedge$. In an initial abstract state $\mathsf{b}_0 = [\mathtt{b1}, \mathtt{b2} \mapsto \top; \mathtt{b3} \mapsto \mathsf{true}]$, $\psi(\mathsf{b}_0) = [\mathtt{b1} \mapsto \top; \mathtt{b2}, \mathtt{b3} \mapsto \mathsf{true}]$ is refined by $\psi^2(\mathsf{b}_0) = [\mathtt{b1}, \mathtt{b2}, \mathtt{b3} \mapsto \mathsf{true}] = \psi^n(\mathsf{b}_0)$, $n \geq 2$.

```
public BitArray(byte[] bytes) {
  Contract.Requires(bytes != null);

  this.m_array = new int[(bytes.Length + 3) / 4];
  this.m_length = bytes.Length * 8;
  int index = 0, j = 0;
  for (; (bytes.Length - j) >= 4; j+=4)
    this.m_array[index++] = (((bytes[j] & 0xff) | ((bytes[j + 1] & 0xff) << 8))
      | ((bytes[j + 2] & 0xff) << 0x10)) | ((bytes[j + 3] & 0xff) << 0x18);

  switch ((bytes.Length - j)) {
    case 1 : goto Label_00DB;
    case 2 : break;
    case 3 : this.m_array[index] = (bytes[j + 2] & 0xff) << 0x10; break;
    default: goto Label_00FC;
  }
  this.m_array[index] |= (bytes[j + 1] & 0xff) << 8;
Label_00DB:
    this.m_array[index] |= bytes[j] & 0xff;
Label_00FC:
    this.version = 0;
}
```

Fig. 6. Example of code from `mscorlib.dll`. Out of the 23 total array bound checks, `Clousot` with $\langle \mathsf{Pnt}, \mathbb{h}^d_{\curlyvee,\triangledown} \rangle$ validates 13, `Clousot` with $\langle \mathsf{SubPoly}, \emptyset \rangle$ validates 6 more, and `Clousot` with $\langle \mathsf{SubPoly}, \mathbb{h}^d_{\curlyvee} \rangle$ validates the remaining 4.

7 Experience

We implemented hints in `Clousot`, our abstract interpretation-based static analyzer for `.Net`. `Clousot` has been designed and it is used as the static checker for the CodeContracts project [21]. CodeContracts provide a language-agnostic approach to the definition of object invariants, method preconditions and postconditions. Contracts are specified by static methods of the `Contracts` class, *e.g.*, `Contracts.Requires(x! = null);` specifies that the parameter `x` should be not null. More details on the specification language can be found in the documentation on the CodeContracts website[21]. The `Contracts` class will be shipped in the version 4.0 of the `.Net` framework [22] (at the moment of writing, in the public beta 1 phase). `Clousot` is shipped on the DevLabs [21] website, and it is available for free downloading for Academic use at `http://research.microsoft.com/en-us/projects/contracts/`.

`Clousot` analyzes each method `m` in isolation. It assumes the precondition of `m`, it progates it through the body, it computes loop invariants, and it uses the inferred invariants to validate: (i) the method postcondition; (ii) the preconditions of the methods invoked by `m`; (iii) the user provided assertions; and (iv) the absence of runtime errors (*e.g.*, null pointers, array out-of-bounds, divisions by zero, negation of MinInt ...) and of buffer overruns [10]. When a method has no annotations, `Clousot` simply assumes the worst case scenario (*e.g.*, the parameters can assume any value compatible with their type). Orthogonally, `Clousot` can infer pre-conditions and post-conditions to help reduce the annotation burden. `Clousot` analyzes `m` incrementally. The user specifies a sequence of pairs of domains and set of hints $\langle \mathsf{A}_0, H_0 \rangle \ldots \langle \mathsf{A}_n, H_n \rangle$. `Clousot` instantiates the abstract semantics of `m` with the abstract domain A_i refined with the hints in H_i. If it cannot discharge all the proof obligations, `Clousot` tries to discharge the remaining proof obligations using the abstract domain A_{i+1} refined with the hints H_{i+1}. We designed new numerical abstract domains, ranging from imprecise yet very fast (Pnt, [18]) to very precise but more expensive (SubPoly, [17]). In the incremental setting of `Clousot`, hints allow a very fine tuning of the precision/cost ratio. For instance, the same abstract domain can be refined with several hints: the more the hints, the more precise the analysis, but also the more expensive it is.

We report the experimental results of refining the abstract operations of the two extremes of the precision spectrum of `Clousot`'s numerical abstract domains: Pnt and SubPoly. Pnt is a weakly relational domain which captures properties in the form of $\mathtt{x} \in [a, b] \wedge \mathtt{x} < \mathtt{y}$. SubPoly is a strongly relational domain which is as expressive as Poly, but drops some of the inference power to achieve scalability: Hints are cardinal to recover precision yet mantaining performace. We run the experiments on a Core2 Duo E6850@3.00 Ghz PC, with 4 GB of RAM, running Windows 7. We analyzed four of the main libraries of the current release of the .`Net` framework (v.3.5), available in every Windows distribution. The `mscorlib.dll` library is the core of the .`Net` framework: it contains the definitions for the `Object`, `Int32` ... types, but also common data structures such as `List`, `Dictionary`, and many other usefull classes (for reflection, security ...). The `System.dll` library is a higher layer on `mscorlib.dll`. `System.Web.dll` and `System.Design.dll` contain classes that simplify the access to the Web and the creation of user interfaces. In order to provide an uniform and repeatable test bench: (i) we considered shipped assemblies (hence with no annotations: The annotation processing is undergoing internally at Microsoft); (ii) we turned off the inference capabilities of `Clousot`; and (iii) we used `Clousot` *only* to check array creations and accesses (lower and upper bounds): the shipped assemblies do not contain annotations, so there are no contracts to check. The framework libraries contains tenths of thousands of array accesses, some of them are quite easy (*e.g.*, the sequential access of an array in a `for` loop) but others require inferring more complex relations between the array lengths and the indexes. For instance, Fig. 6 shows the constructor of the `BitArray` type (we picked it randomly from `Clousot`'s log). The Pnt and SubPoly abstract domains alone can be used to prove most of the array accesses correct, however, all the proof obligations can be discharged only using die-hard hints. One may object that the same result can be obtained using existing domains such as Oct or Poly. However, Oct is unable to capture the constraint $4 \cdot \mathtt{m\_array.Length} - \mathtt{bytes.Length} == 3$, which is necessary to prove that $\mathtt{index} < \mathtt{m\_array.Length}$, and Poly suffers of a huge scalability problem, which shows up even in small code snippets like the one in Fig. 6.

Figure 7 compares die-hard hints and saturation hints when used to refine the join and widening of Pnt. The figure reports the analyzed assemblies, the total number of analyzed methods, the total number of proof obligations checked (*i.e.*, array creations, lower bounds, and upper bounds), the number of proof

Assembly	Methods	P.O. Checked	Pnt Valid	Pnt Time	$\mathsf{Pnt} + \mathbb{h}^{d}_{\curlyvee,\nabla}$ Valid	$\mathsf{Pnt} + \mathbb{h}^{d}_{\curlyvee,\nabla}$ Time	Slow-down	$\mathsf{Pnt} + \mathbb{h}^{\rho}_{\{\sqcup,\nabla\}^{\times}}$ Valid	$\mathsf{Pnt} + \mathbb{h}^{\rho}_{\{\sqcup,\nabla\}^{\times}}$ Time	Slow-down
mscorlib		17 286	14 059	3:03(0)	14 293	3:10(0)	1.0x	14 220	10:33(4)	3.3x
System	15 497	12 037	9 979	2:28(0)	10 321	2:36(0)	1.0x	10 143	9:43(2)	3.7x
System.Web	23 655	14 304	12 952	2:49(0)	13 034	2:55(0)	1.0x	13 048	8:30(0)	2.9x
System.Design	12 922	10 577	9 562	2:18(0)	10 135	2:21(0)	1.0x	9 947	7:39(5)	3.2x

Fig. 7. The experimental results of refining Pnt with die-hard hints and saturation hints. Pnt with die-hard hints validates 1 231 more proof obligations. Pnt with saturation hints are 3x slower, hit 11 timeouts (2 min), and validate 425 less accesses than $\mathbb{h}^{d}$.

obligations validated and the analysis time for the pair-wise gathering operations and two refinements of the Pnt operations. The values in brackets denote the number of methods for which the analysis timed out. Time out was set to 2 minutes. Die-hard hints allow `Clousot` to validate 1 231 accesses more than the pair-wise joins at no extra cost. On the other hand, saturation hints induce an average 3x slow-down of the analysis, which causes the analysis to time out for 11 methods, and hence to validate 425 less accesses. We manually inspected the analysis logs. We found that $\langle \mathsf{Pnt}, \mathbb{h}^{d}_{\curlyvee,\nabla} \rangle$ missed only few validations w.r.t. $\langle \mathsf{Pnt}, \mathbb{h}^{\rho}_{\{\curlyvee,\nabla\}^{\times}} \rangle$. As a consequence, the use of a saturation procedure with Pnt seems to be disadvantageous: the cost is too high, and the precision can be recovered by more precise abstract domains anyway. Furthermore, we checked some of the proof obligations reported as unproven or unreachable from `Clousot`. Most of the unproven conditions are caused by the lack of contracts (mainly postconditions and object invariants). However, some of the unproven conditions turned out to be real bugs, and the unreachable ones, after fixing some bug of the analyzer, were effectively dead-code.

Figure 8 focuses on the analysis of `mscorlib` using SubPoly refined with hints. SubPoly is a very expressive abstract domain (as expressive as Poly), whose inference precision can be fine tuned thanks to hints. The first column in the table shows the results of the analysis with no hints. This is roughly equivalent to precisely propagating arbitrary linear equalities and intervals, with limited inference and no propagation of information between linear equalities and intervals. User-provided hints and die-hard hints add more inference power, at the price of a still acceptable slow-down. Computed hints (with Octagons and 2D-Convex hull) further slow-down of the analysis, causing the analysis of various methods to time out. We manually inspected the analysis logs to investigate the differences. Ignoring the methods that timed-out, with respect to $\mathsf{SubPoly}^{*}$, $\langle \mathsf{SubPoly}^{*}, \mathbb{h}^{\Xi^{Oct}}_{\curlyvee} \rangle$ and $\langle \mathsf{SubPoly}^{*}, \mathbb{h}^{\Xi^{2DCH}}_{\curlyvee} \rangle$ report respectively 125 and 124 less false positives. Out of those, only 13 overlap.

One may wonder if computed hints are needed at all. We observed that, when considering annotated code (unfortunately, just a small fraction of the overall codebase at the moment of writing), one needs to refine the operations of the abstract domains with hints in order to get a very low (and hence acceptable) false alarms ratio (around 0.5%) . In fact, even if (relatively) rare, assertions

SubPoly		SubPoly*		Slow	SubPoly* + $\mathbb{h}_{\curlyvee}^{\Xi^{Oct}}$		Slow	SubPoly* + $\mathbb{h}_{\curlyvee}^{\Xi^{2DCH}}$		Slow
Valid	Time	Valid	Time	down	Valid	Time	down	Valid	Time	down
14 230	4:29(0)	14 432	20:22(0)	4.5x	13 948	81:24(20)	18.2x	14 396	36:33(7)	8.1x

Fig. 8. The experimental results analyzing `mscorlib` with SubPoly and different semantic hints. SubPoly* denotes SubPoly refined with $\mathbb{h}_{\diamond}^{\mathsf{pred}}$ and $\mathbb{h}_{\curlyvee,\nabla}^{d}$. Computed hints significantly slow-down the analysis, but they are needed to reach a very low false alarm ratio.

as in Fig. 1(b) and Fig. 5 are present in real code. Thanks to the incremental structure of `Clousot`, we do not need to run SubPoly with *all* the hints on *all* the analyzed methods, but we can focus the highest precision only on the few methods which require it.

8 Conclusions

We introduced hints, a technique to systematically refine abstract domain *operations*. Hints allow us improving the precision of abstract operation whenever those are not complete, *e.g.*, when the underlying abstract domain is not a complete lattice (the common case in practice). We formalized hints in a relaxed abstract interpretation setting, we proved their soundness, and we distinguished between syntactic and semantics hints. We showed how some existing techniques to improve the precision of static analyses, such as widening with thresholds and reductive iterations are just instances of hints. We applied hints to the numerical abstract domains defined in our abstract interpretation-based analyzer, showing how they enable a powerful tuning of the precision/cost ratio. However, hints are not restricted to numerical domains, and they can be easily generalized to other kind of domains (for instance, for heap analysis) Future work will consider combining hints with other forms of refinement, as domain refinement, counter example-based refinement, and inference of optimal transfer functions.

References

1. Bagnara, R., Hill, P.M., Zaffanella, E.: Widening operators for powerset domains. In: Steffen, B., Levi, G. (eds.) VMCAI 2004. LNCS, vol. 2937, pp. 135–148. Springer, Heidelberg (2004)
2. Blanchet, B., Cousot, P., Cousot, R., Feret, J., Mauborgne, L., Miné, A., Monniaux, D., Rival, X.: A static analyzer for large safety-critical software. In: PLDI 2003. ACM Press, New York (2003)
3. Colby, C., Lee, P.: Trace-based program analysis. In: POPL 1996. ACM Press, New York (1996)
4. Cousot, P., Cousot, R.: Abstract interpretation: a unified lattice model for static analysis of programs by construction or approximation of fixpoints. In: POPL 1977 (1977)
5. Cousot, P., Cousot, R.: Abstract interpretation and application to logic programs. Journal of Logic Programming 13(2-3), 103–179 (1992)
6. Cousot, P., Cousot, R.: Abstract interpretation frameworks. Journal of Logic and Computation 2(4) (August 1992)

7. Cousot, P., Cousot, R., Feret, J., Mauborgne, L., Miné, A., Monniaux, D., Rival, X.: Combination of abstractions in the ASTRÉE static analyzer. In: Okada, M., Satoh, I. (eds.) ASIAN 2006. LNCS, vol. 4435, pp. 272–300. Springer, Heidelberg (2008)
8. Cousot, P., Halbwachs, N.: Automatic discovery of linear restraints among variables of a program. In: POPL 1978 (1978)
9. Das, M., Lerner, S., Seigle, M.: Esp: Path-sensitive program verification in polynomial time. In: PLDI 2002, pp. 57–68 (2002)
10. Ferrara, P., Logozzo, F., Fähndrich, M.A.: Safer unsafe code in.Net. In: OOPSLA 2008 (2008)
11. Gonnord, L., Halbwachs, N.: Combining widening and acceleration in linear relation analysis. In: Yi, K. (ed.) SAS 2006. LNCS, vol. 4134, pp. 144–160. Springer, Heidelberg (2006)
12. Gopan, D., Reps, T.W.: Lookahead widening. In: Ball, T., Jones, R.B. (eds.) CAV 2006. LNCS, vol. 4144, pp. 452–466. Springer, Heidelberg (2006)
13. Granger, P.: Improving the results of static analyses programs by local decreasing iteration. In: Shyamasundar, R.K. (ed.) FSTTCS 1992. LNCS, vol. 652. Springer, Heidelberg (1992)
14. Gulavani, B.S., Chakraborty, S., Nori, A.V., Rajamani, S.K.: Automatically refining abstract interpretations. In: Ramakrishnan, C.R., Rehof, J. (eds.) TACAS 2008. LNCS, vol. 4963, pp. 443–458. Springer, Heidelberg (2008)
15. Gulwani, S., McCloskey, B., Tiwari, A.: Lifting abstract interpreters to quantified logical domains. In: POPL 2008. ACM Press, New York (2008)
16. Handjieva, M., Tzolovski, S.: Refining static analyses by trace-based partitioning using control flow. In: Levi, G. (ed.) SAS 1998. LNCS, vol. 1503, pp. 200–214. Springer, Heidelberg (1998)
17. Laviron, V., Logozzo, F.: Subpolyhedra: a (more) scalable approach to infer linear inequalities. In: Jones, N.D., Müller-Olm, M. (eds.) VMCAI 2009. LNCS, vol. 5403, pp. 229–244. Springer, Heidelberg (2009)
18. Logozzo, F., Fähndrich, M.A.: Pentagons: A weakly relational abstract domain for the efficient validation of array accesses. In: SAC 2008 (2008)
19. Manevich, R., Field, J., Henzinger, T.A., Ramalingam, G., Sagiv, M.: Abstract counterexample-based refinement for powerset domains. In: Reps, T., Sagiv, M., Bauer, J. (eds.) Wilhelm Festschrift. LNCS, vol. 4444, pp. 273–292. Springer, Heidelberg (2006)
20. Mauborgne, L., Rival, X.: Trace partitioning in abstract interpretation based static analyzers. In: Sagiv, M. (ed.) ESOP 2005. LNCS, vol. 3444, pp. 5–20. Springer, Heidelberg (2005)
21. Microsoft. Codecontracts tools, `http://msdn.microsoft.com/en-us/devlabs/dd491992.aspx`
22. Microsoft. Contracts namespace, `http://msdn.microsoft.com/en-us/library/system.diagnostics.contracts(VS.100).aspx`
23. Miné, A.: The octagon abstract domain. In: WCRE 2001 (2001)
24. Monniaux, D.: Automatic modular abstractions for linear constraints. In: POPL 2009 (2009)
25. Péron, M., Halbwachs, N.: An abstract domain extending difference-bound matrices with disequality constraints. In: Cook, B., Podelski, A. (eds.) VMCAI 2007. LNCS, vol. 4349, pp. 268–282. Springer, Heidelberg (2007)
26. Yorsh, G., Reps, T.W., Sagiv, S.: Symbolically computing most-precise abstract operations for shape analysis. In: Jensen, K., Podelski, A. (eds.) TACAS 2004. LNCS, vol. 2988, pp. 530–545. Springer, Heidelberg (2004)

Author Index